W9-AXD-922

Contributions to Statistics

V. Fedorov/W.G. Müller/I.N. Vuchkov (Eds.)
Model-Oriented Data Analysis,
XII/248 pages, 1992

J. Antoch (Ed.)
Computational Aspects of Model Choice,
VII/285 pages, 1993

W.G. Müller/H.P. Wynn/A.A. Zhigljavsky (Eds.)
Model-Oriented Data Analysis,
XIII/287 pages, 1993

P. Mandl/M. Hušková (Eds.)
Asymptotic Statistics,
X/474 pages, 1994

P. Dirschedl/R. Ostermann (Eds.)
Computational Statistics,
VII/553 pages, 1994

C.P. Kitsos/W.G. Müller (Eds.)
MODA4 – Advances in Model-Oriented Data Analysis,
XIV/297 pages, 1995

H. Schmidli
Reduced Rank Regression,
X/179 pages, 1995

W. Härdle/M.G. Schimek (Eds.)
Statistical Theory and Computational Aspects of Smoothing,
VIII/265 pages, 1996

S. Klinke
Data Structures for Computational Statistics,
VIII/284 pages, 1997

A.C. Atkinson/L. Pronzato/H.P. Wynn (Eds.)
MODA 5 – Advances in Model-Oriented Data
Analysis and Experimental Design
XIV/300 pages, 1998

M. Moryson
Testing for Random Walk
Coefficients in Regression
and State Space Models
XV/317 pages, 1998

Silvia Biffignandi (Ed.)

Micro- and Macrodata of Firms

Statistical Analysis and International Comparison

With 109 Figures
and 220 Tables

HD
56.25
.M53
1999

Physica-Verlag

A Springer-Verlag Company

Series Editors
Werner A. Müller
Martina Bihn

Editor
Prof. Dr. Silvia Biffignandi
University of Bergamo
Department of Mathematics and Statistics
Piazza Rosate n. 2
I-24100 Bergamo
Italy

ISBN 3-7908-1143-2 Physica-Verlag Heidelberg New York

Cataloging-in-Publication Data applied for
Die Deutsche Bibliothek – CIP-Einheitsaufnahme
Micro- and macrodata of firms: statistical analysis and international comparison; with 220
tables / Silvia Biffignandi (ed.). – Heidelberg: Physica-Verl., 1999
  (Contributions to statistics)
  ISBN 3-7908-1143-2

This work is subject to copyright. All rights are reserved, whether the whole or part of the
material is concerned, specifically the rights of translation, reprinting, reuse of illustrations,
recitation, broadcasting, reproduction on microfilm or in any other way, and storage in data
banks. Duplication of this publication or parts thereof is permitted only under the provisions
of the German Copyright Law of September 9, 1965, in its current version, and permission
for use must always be obtained from Physica-Verlag. Violations are liable for prosecution
under the German Copyright Law.

© Physica-Verlag Heidelberg 1999
Printed in Germany

The use of general descriptive names, registered names, trademarks, etc. in this publication
does not imply, even in the absence of a specific statement, that such names are exempt
from the relevant protective laws and regulations and therefore free for general use.

Softcover design: Erich Kirchner, Heidelberg

SPIN 10685179   88/2202-5 4 3 2 1 0 – Printed on acid-free paper

CAED '97

FOREWORD

The issues regarding productivity efficiency and competitiveness are a common trouble in most industrial countries. As a matter of fact, globalization emphasizes the importance of economic efficiency and competitiveness, thereby diminishing the effectiveness of industrial support policies based only on the national identity of an industry. As regards businesses, in the integrated EU internal market the prospect of an economic and monetary union and globalization all require that the firms consistently improve their competitiveness.

For this reason, both international markets, economic organizations and firms are drawing the attention to the need of international comparison of economic aggregates, especially of business data. As a matter of fact, understanding the sources of differences in economic performance and the causes of differences (regulation, economic factor, technology....) is a crucial matter for decisions both at a single firm level and at political economy level. For instance, a subject of growing interest for scenario analysis is represented by the different policies of investment chosen by the countries, this subject is not taken into account by traditional macroeconomic analysis. Looking at macroaggregates and at productivity, some considerations are to be put into consideration. As regards macroaggregates, they are the result of heterogeneous economic behaviours; microdata analysis shows significant differences in business behaviour with reference to many dimensions. The representative agent assumption underlying the macroaggregates analysis in a context of heterogeneous technology seems less adequate than into the past. As regards productivity, it is a dynamic process, t.i.: a) its evolution is realized through reallocation processes; b) efficiency is not only based on capital and labour, but on more intangible factors as technology, managerial skills.

This volume, which mainly contains papers presented at the conference on Analysis of Economic (micro)Data 1997 (CAED97), is intended to show the main research areas which are being developed in order to compare economic situation internationally or at least to go in the direction of international comparability of business data.

Starting from the above considerations the conference on Analysis of Economic (micro)Data 1997 (CAED97), held in Bergamo from December the 15th to the 17th, intended to focus on the availability of comparable data and to the statistical analysis of them. The CAED97 has been organized   by the Department of Mathematics, Statistics of the University of Bergamo and the ISTAT (National Italian Institute) with the Eurostat sponsorship and the Italian Statistical Society scientific patronage (SIS)[1]. The 9 Members of the International Committee[2] and the local organizers[3], by promoting this conference, aimed to present the state of art and to give an impulse for future research on methods and applications for international comparison of business data. This aim was fairly well achieved; the conference had more than 40 papers, about more than 80 participants. The conference has shown that there is a strong interest in the topic and that a lot of work has to be done to improve the research in many directions especially :

- need for better data integration
- need for data collection and reporting at lower levels of aggregation
- need for greater geographic detail
- need for application and theoretical development of more advanced statistical methods.

During the conference a parallel session on "Eurostat Brainstorming and Open Discussion on Longitudinal Enterprise Studies at the European Level" has been organized with the participation of Marie Paule Benassi (on the "General Introduction to the Topic"), Eric De Brabanter ("The Current State of the Exercise of the Longitudinal Studies on Small and Medium Size Enterprises in EU Member States"), Edward Ojo and Pierre Lavallée on "Mergers and Demergers and Demography of Enterprises"; organizer Edward Ojo and promoter François de Geuser.

Part A of this volume (papers of R. McGuckin and Sang V. Nguyen, F. Boccara, V. Thollon Pommerol, A. Carone) focuses on the group enterprises. The statistical analysis of groups and of their economic performance is relevant mainly in the international context; it is however shown that the group enterprises assume a crucial role for the local economy, too. At European level

---

[1] The Scientific Committee, the Organizers (the Department of Mathematics and Statistics of the University of Bergamo and the ISTAT, National Statistical Institute) and the editor of this volume are grateful to Eurostat for the financial sponsorship. We wish to thank the Italian Statistical Society for scientific patronage and the University of Bergamo which has been a highly appreciable venue for the conference.
[2] Pierre Blanchard,(Université de Paris, France), Raoul Depoutot (EUROSTAT, Luxembourg), Tor Eriksson (University of Arhus, Denmark), Robert H. McGuckin (conference Board, USA), Kazuyuki Motohashi (Economic Analysis and Statistics Division, France), Seppo Laaksonen (Statistics Finland, Finland), Joachim Wagner (University of Lüneburg, Germany), Silvia Biffignandi (University of Bergamo, Italy), Enrico Giovannini (Istat, Italy).
[3] The local organizing committee included staff of the Department of Mathematics, Statistics, Informatics and Applications, University of Bergamo (Italy): Silvia Biffignandi, Christine Butti and Barbara Vedovello.

the UE Regulation Number 696/93 defines among various units of analysis the enterprise group as a possible unit of analysis. At the moment, the degree of statistical information on enterprise groups, and consequently its analysis, differs from country to country. Thus, some papers are more oriented to the problem of identifying and describing groups, others are more devoted to the analysis of their economic role and performance.

Part B - especially the papers of R. Depoutot et al. and R. Jarmin and K. Motohashi - looks at international comparison of the aggregates and quality.

Starting from the consideration that, in spite of increasing globalization in the world economy, enterprises operate under highly specific national conditions, the remaining papers (Part C) mainly refer to specific national or country limited comparison. In fact, differences in legal institutions, regulations, private business practices and key cost parameters continue to characterize each business environment. These differences appear significant enough to influence the competitive behaviour, profitability and performance of firms operating in different locations and spur the growing policy interest in national competitiveness. To meet this challenge and swiftly revive employment and productivity, Europe must systematically and resolutely address those components that weaken its growth potential. To this end the European Committee suggested a wide ranging adoption of benchmarking, i.e. a comparative analysis of competitiveness in economic and social matters in order to assess performances linked to key section and factors affecting economic development.

The empirical analyses presented in this volume focus mainly on productivity and efficiency factors, on technology, on territorial analyses, on labour. At the end of the volume are presented papers handling applications to specific topics such as tourism and agricultural firms.

The volume and the conference show that international comparison is an important matter for understanding global economy, but in any case studies which refer to specific countries play an important role to develop data and economic hypotheses that should be tested at international level, in other words to identify:

- public policy information needs
- the conceptual framework to guide data collection activities and to provide a base for the analysis of the data
- improved data collection
- new models of analysis of the available data.

I hope that the ideas set out in this book represent starting points and encouragements for improving this research area which is a new one, involving the need of advanced theoretical studies as well as of empirical analyses and presenting relevant implications both from the political economic and from the firms benchmarking and decision analysis point of view. Probably the next

CAED98 conference (to be held in Netherland, spring 1999) will be able to represent a more refined and further steps toward a more defined set of data and a more precise methodological and logical framework for international comparison.

The editor, through careful reading of the papers, has brought them to the same format and removed some printing errors. In any case, no substantial modification has been applied to the papers, for whose content only the authors are responsible.

Silvia Biffignandi
The Editor

Bergamo, September 1998

The effort of the organization of the conference and the scientific knowledge acquired in such an experience are part of the research project CNR 97.00963.ct10.

Barbara Vedovello has typed the final draft of the papers and the camera-ready manuscript of the volume.

TABLE OF CONTENTS

page

page

EXPLORING THE ROLE OF ACQUISITION IN THE PERFORMANCE OF FIRMS: IS THE "FIRM" THE RIGHT UNIT OF ANALYSIS?

Robert H. McGuckin[1] and Sang V. Nguyen[2]

[1] *The Conference Board*
[2] *U.S. Bureau of the Census*

1 Introduction

Recent empirical studies -- Lichtenberg and Siegel (1992), Long and Ravenscraft (1993), McGuckin and Nguyen (1995) and McGuckin, Nguyen, and Reznek (1996) -- provide strong evidence that plants undergoing an ownership change improve performance. Baldwin and Gorecki (1991) also find improved performance following plant ownership changes using Canadian data. None of these studies deals explicitly with acquiring firms: Rather, they examine the performance of plants before and after they were transferred from one firm to another.

The positive picture that these plant-level studies provide for mergers contrasts with the well-documented findings that the gains to shareholders of acquiring firms in mergers and acquisitions are, at best, typically very small.[1] There are a variety of explanations for why mergers and acquisitions might not improve the measured profits of acquiring firms. For example, acquiring firms might

---

[1] While there are exceptions, the typical finance study concludes that the overall gains from merger are positive. But with few exceptions they also find most, if not all, of the gains accrue to the selling firms' shareholders and not to those of the acquiring firm. On average, shareholders of acquired firms in mergers and tender offers gained 20 and 32 percent, respectively. However, the gains for acquiring firms' shareholders were either small or not statistically significantly different from zero (Jensen and Ruback, 1983; Smith, 1986; and Jarrell, et al., 1988). Recently, Kaplan (1989) studied 48 management buyouts and found an increase in operating returns after buyouts. Smith (1990) used a similar dataset with different methodologies and found similar results. Matsusaka (1993) and Klein(1994) found that a subset of acquisitions achieved significant returns. But, they also find that on average, returns to acquirers are near zero. Industrial organization studies (e.g., Ravenscraft and Scherer 1987), by and large, also find little in the way of gains to acquirers. Moreover, industrial organization studies of mergers in the 1950s, 1960s, and early 1970s generally found negative effects on efficiency from mergers (see Mueller, 1993).

systematically overpay. But the recent plant-level studies suggest that ownership changes generate real efficiencies.[2] Here we begin the process of extending these plant-level studies to the level of the firm by focusing on an important issue in studying the impact of acquisitions on acquiring firms' performance. That is, what is the appropriate unit of analysis? More specifically, is the "firm" productivity or "plant" the right unit of analysis for productivity analysis?

We suggest that the plant rather than the firm is the appropriate unit of analysis because firm data are too aggregative to capture composition effects of acquisitions on the performance of firms. Because acquisition is part of a strategy to realign the resources and operations of the firm -- a strategy that may encompass acquisition, divestiture, and internal growth -- the composition effects associated with the nature and timing of the transactions may be important in assessing the gains or losses to particular transactions. In particular, the mix of plants of an acquiring firm before and after acquisition can differ substantially. Before acquisition, the firm owns a set of plants, some will be closed, some will be sold and others will be retained by the firm. After acquisition, the structure of the firm may look much different than before: It now includes acquired plants, and plants that are newly built, in addition to its surviving own plants. Thus, simply looking at the productivity performance of the whole firm before and after acquisition may not be appropriate.

To examine this issue, we construct a panel of 18,141 food manufacturing firms for the period 1977-87. These include 722 acquiring firms (i.e., acquiring at least one food manufacturing plant) and 17,409 non-acquiring firms that owned at least one food manufacturing plant in 1977. These data were taken from the Census Bureau's Longitudinal Research Database (LRD) and cover the entire population of the U.S. food manufacturing industry (SIC 20). We choose this industry because it exhibits a substantial number of acquisitions that involve a significant portion of total industry shipments during the period under study. The data set is comprehensive, covering firms and plants of all sizes, and provides a large, tractable set of firms and plants for empirical work.

Using these data, we first estimate the effect of acquisitions on acquiring firms' productivity growth at the firm level. We then apply the same analysis to plant-level data. To explore this issue further, we decompose the productivity change of multi-unit firms to examine the contribution of acquired plants to acquiring firms' productivity change. Several findings emerge from this analysis.

First, our firm-level regression results show that acquisitions have a positive effect on acquiring firms' productivity growth when single-unit firms are included in the regressions. However, when applying the model to multi-unit firms only, we find an insignificant effect of acquisitions on acquiring firms' productivity growth.

---

[2] In work underway that extends the plant-level estimates in McGuckin and Nguyen (1995) to all manufacturing and to the merger wave of the 1960s and early 1970s, we also are finding improvements in plant productivity performance.

Second, regression estimates based on plant-level data uniformly show, consistent with other studies at the plant level, that acquired plants' productivity growth is higher than that of non-acquired plants for both single and multi-unit firms. Moreover, there is strong evidence that the plants owned by acquiring firms prior to acquisition also improved their productivity growth rate.

Third, analysis of the components of productivity growth demonstrates that acquisitions have a significant, positive effect on acquiring firms' productivity, but this effect is hidden in firm-level regression analyses using samples dominated by large multi-unit firms. Overall, these results strongly suggest that changes in the structure of the firm can obscure the gains to acquisitions.

Finally, our concluding comments attempt to put these results in the context of industrial organization and finance studies. As noted earlier, these studies typically find, using financial measures of firm performance, that gains to the acquiring firms are not high. While we cannot, in this paper, draw a tight analytic link between our results and these firm-level studies, we think that composition effects are likely to be important for these studies as well.

The paper is organized into four sections. Section II describes our data source, sample design, description of the data, and performance measurement. Section III presents our regression analysis at both the firm and plant levels. Section IV discusses our procedure of decomposing firms' productivity growth and reports the results. Section V discusses our principal findings and concludes the paper.

2 Empirical Strategy and Performance Measurement

2.1 Sample Design and Coverage

Our data are for the food manufacturing industry (SIC 20) over the period 1977-87 and are taken from the LRD[3]. The sample includes all food manufacturing firms that survived over the ten-year period or entered through a diversification acquisition and retained some portion of the properties they purchased. The sample was developed as follows.

We first identified each food manufacturing plant operating in 1977 using the Census Bureau's Standard Industrial Classification (SIC) codes. Because 1977 is a Census year, the entire population of food manufacturing plants and firms is available. We first identified plants that had ownership change during the periods 1977-82 and 1982-87.[4] After identifying all plants that experienced

---

[3] For a detailed description of the LRD, see McGuckin and Pascoe (1988).

[4] A complete description of the procedures used to identify ownership changes in the LRD is available in an appendix to McGuckin, Nguyen, and Reznek (1996).

ownership change in these periods, we use each plants' 1977, 1982 and 1987 Census firm identification number (ID) to identify sellers (acquired firms), buyers (acquiring firms, i.e., firms that acquired at least one food manufacturing plant during the period), and firms that did not have any plant experiencing ownership change. Finally, we group all plants under common ownership in the beginning year (1977) of our study period into two categories (1) surviving own plants (plants owned by the firm in 1977 and surviving through 1987), and (2) closed plants (existed in 1977 but closed by 1987). Using a similar classification for 1987 gives three categories for acquiring firms: (1) surviving own plants, (2) acquired plants, and (3) new plants. Non-acquiring firms include only categories (1) and (3). These categories allow us to examine shifts in the composition of the firm over time.

We identify ownership changes occurring during the periods 1977-82 and 1982-87. Each period encompasses two Censuses of Manufactures so that we are confident of correctly identifying all ownership changes. In non-census years, information is available only for a sample of plants. The full period 1977-87 includes the beginning and ending years of the latest merger movement, which extended until 1986 or 1987. Our primary focus is on ownership changes between 1977 and 1982. This allows us to evaluate performance five to nine years after an ownership change transaction. This provides plenty of time for the acquiring firm to integrate acquisitions into the firm, or to dispose of them. Using 1977-87 as the measurement interval for our performance measures also avoids the influence of the 1982 recession.

For the period 1977-82, we identified 733 firms that sold at least one food manufacturing plant. These 733 firms sold totally 2,111 plants (including 1,573 food plants and 538 non-food plants) to 732 acquiring firms. The acquired food plants amounted to 38,764 million dollars in value of shipments in 1977, which accounted for 20.8 percent of total value of shipments of the entire food manufacturing industry (SIC 20). After acquisition, 984 acquired plants (46.6 percent) remained with the acquiring firms, 618 plants (29.3 percent) were closed, and 409 (19.4 percent) plants were resold to other firms. In addition to the 2,111 plants identified above as obtained from food producing firms, the 732 acquiring firms acquired 460 non-food plants from non-food producing firms. Of these 460 plants, they retained 139 plants (30.2 percent), sold 154 plants (33.5 percent), and closed 167 plants (36.3 percent).

Not all of the acquiring firms survived until 1987. Of the 732 acquiring firms, 425 firms survived (58.1 percent) and 307 firms were closed (41.7 percent). However, most of the closed firms were either single-unit firms or the manufacturing portions of non-manufacturing firms. Only 24.5 percent (87 out of 355) multi-unit firms were closed by 1987.

These surviving acquirers also purchased 1,719 plants (672 food plants and 1,047 non-food plants) between 1982 and 1987. Most of these plants were acquired by 268 surviving multi-unit food manufacturing acquiring firms: They purchased 1,562 (of the 1,719) plants including 637 food plants and 925 non-food plants. The non-food acquiring firms in our sample purchased only 157 plants during the period.

The 732 acquiring firms consisted of 93 SU firms, 284 new MU firms, and 355 MU firms. Of the 284 new MU firms, 134 entered manufacturing by acquiring only one manufacturing food plant. Each of the remaining 150 non-manufacturing firms acquired at least two or more plants. The 355 MU manufacturing firms that operated in the food industry in 1977 had the biggest role in the 1977-82 acquisition movement. Together, they acquired 1,455 of the 2,111 transferred plants (68.9 percent), and accounted for 37,435 of the 38,764 millions of dollars of total value of shipments acquired over the period (98 percent). Of the remaining 656 plants, 93 plants were acquired by 93 SU firms, 134 plants were acquired by 132 non-manufacturing firms, and 431 plants were sold to 150 other non-manufacturing MU firms.

For the non-acquiring group, we identified 17,409 firms that had at least one food manufacturing plant in 1977. Of the 17,409 firms, 15,062 were SU firms, 1,185 were non-manufacturing firms having one food manufacturing plant, and 1,157 were MU manufacturing firms. These 1,157 firms owned 7,701 manufacturing plants (both food and non-food plants) in 1977.

Thus, our data cover the entire 1977 population of food manufacturing firms in the U.S. This population consists of 18,141 firms, of which 17,763 firms operated primarily in the food industry. The 18,141 firms owned 30,086 plants in 1977, of which 23,980 plants were owned by food firms and 6,106 plants were owned by non-food firms.

2.2 Performance Measurement

The best-known measure of efficiency performance is productivity, measured as the ratio of firm output to its inputs. We use value of shipments rather than value-added as our output measure because data on value-added are not always available, particularly for small plants. In practice, productivity results using either measure are highly correlated. For example, the results in McGuckin and Nguyen (1995), which also used food industry data over this period, were unaffected by the choice of value added or value of shipments. (See also Baily, Campbell, and Hulten, 1992; and Baily, Bartelsman, and Haltiwanger, 1994).

Productivity can be either measured for each single input such as labor (the well-known labor productivity) or measured for all inputs, total factor productivity (TFP). Theoretically, TFP is the appropriate measure of productivity because it takes into account all inputs. In practice, labor productivity is often used because data on inputs, such as capital, that are required for the measurement of TFP are not available. Because of data limitations, we base our analysis on labor productivity.[5]

Plant labor productivity, LP, is measured as value of shipments in 1987 dollars divided by the number of hours worked.[6] We use the 4-digit industry price deflator taken from the NBER database to deflate values of shipment in our calculation of labor productivity.

While single-unit firms are classified in a single industry, multi-unit firms often have plants operating in various industries. For multi-unit firms, we calculate the productivity for each plant separately, then obtain the firm productivity as a weighted sum of plant productivities. Thus, we measure the labor productivity (LP) of the firm by

$$LP_i^F = \sum_j^n w_{ij} LP_{ij},$$ [1]

where LP_i^F is LP of firm i, the weight w_{ij} is the ratio of plant j's hours worked to the total hours worked of firm i. Labor weights provide exact aggregation of labor productivities at the plant to the firm level. An alternative weighting scheme is to use shipments rather than labor. If a plant is increasing output through downsizing its labor force, its labor weight will fall. As a result, the establishment will receive less weight at the end of the period because of the way it achieved it's productivity growth if labor rather than value of shipment is the weighting factor.[7]

2.3 Characteristics of Acquiring Firms

In Table 1, the 732 acquiring firms consist of 93 single-unit firms, 284 multi-unit non-manufacturing[8] firms, and 355 multi-unit manufacturing firms. Of the 284 multi-unit firms with non-manufacturing activities, 134 entered manufacturing

---

[5] In our earlier work (McGuckin and Nguyen, 1995), we estimated TFP for a number of large plants for which the required data were available. We then compared the TFP results to the LP results, and found that both measure led to the same conclusions regarding plant performance.

[6] Data on production worker hours are available in the LRD. However, hours worked are not available for non-production workers. We estimated total plant production worker equivalent hours as $H = (SW/WW) * PH$, where SW is total plant salaries and wages, WW is wages paid to production workers, and PH is plant production worker hours. This measure of H (total hours worked) assumes that relative wages are proportional to marginal productivity.

[7] As a practical matter, choice of labor or shipments weights does not affect the results of our analysis.

[8] We identified these firms as non-manufacturing because they had a multi-unit identification, but did not have any manufacturing plants before acquisition.

by acquiring one manufacturing plant. Each of the remaining 150 non-manufacturing firms acquired at least two manufacturing plants (431 in total).

Multi-unit manufacturing firms accounted for most of the acquisition activity. These firms acquired 1,455 of 2,113 transferred plants (69 percent), that accounted for 35,571 million dollars in 1977 value of shipments acquired or 92 percent of total acquired shipments. Multi-unit manufacturing firms also were most important among the non-acquirers. The 1,157 non-acquiring multi-unit firms owned 7,701 manufacturing plants (both food and non-food plants) in 1977 shipments. These firms accounted for 129,446 million dollars in value of shipments or 79 percent of non-acquirer's total shipments in 1977.

The average size of acquiring firms in all categories is much larger than that of non-acquiring firms. The average sizes of acquiring single-unit firms, multi-unit non-manufacturing firms, and multi-unit manufacturing firms are 158, 131 and 3,389 employees, while those of non-acquiring firms are 19, 70 and 1,083, respectively.

Table 1 shows that measured levels of productivity are generally lower for single than multi-unit firms.[9] In addition, the productivity of acquiring firms is uniformly higher than that of non-acquiring firms. For example, the average labor productivity of multi-unit acquiring firms is 118.2, while that of non-acquiring multi-unit manufacturing firms is only 89.42.

In summary, the data show that, in contrast to non-acquiring firms, acquiring firms are bigger and more productive. In addition, while not reported, the data also suggest that survival rates are higher for acquiring firms.[10]

3 The Effects of the Unit of Analysis on Estimates of the Impacts of Acquisitions on Acquiring Firms

In this section, we undertake a two step examination of the impact of acquisitions on the labor productivity of the firm. Our procedure is to run regressions of productivity performance at the firm level and then to perform similar analysis at the plant level.

The model specifications follow McGuckin and Nguyen (1995): We regress growth rates of LP on the firm's initial (1977) LP, size (log TE_{77}), and a dummy

---

[9] We think part of this is real and part of it derives from unmeasured central office and related auxiliary operations that are more prevalent among multi-unit firms. Productivity for small single-unit firms, both acquiring and non-acquiring, is below that of the larger multi-unit firms because of measurement errors associated with services from central offices, as well as the positive relationship between size and productivity.

[10] Probit regressions (not reported here) show significant, positive relationships between both size and initial productivity, and the probability of being an acquiring firm. Moreover, the relationships are non-linear.

variable identifying whether a firm is an acquiring firm. We also include other dummy variables to capture the effects of industry and the types of firm, (i.e., single versus multi-unit firms) and allow for interactions between some key variables.

The plant-level specifications allow us to examine the performance of acquired plants, plants previously owned by acquiring firms, and non-acquiring multi-unit firms. This provides a direct comparison to the firm-level results and some indication of the source of any differences.

Because single-unit firms are essentially the same as plants and the results for this group of firms are similar to those found in the plant-level studies cited earlier, we focus our discussion on estimates of our model for multi-unit manufacturing firms. If there are significant composition effects they should be observed in the multi-unit portion of the sample.

3.1 Firm-Level Results

Table 2 reports the firm-level regression results. In the table, LP_{77} and TE_{77} denote labor productivity and total employment in 1977, respectively. The remaining variables are (0,1) dummy variables which are defined as follows: FULLACQ = 1 if the firm acquired a complete firm; PARTACQ = 1 if the firm acquired a part of another firm; FOOD = 1 if the firm primarily produced food products; and finally, MULTI = 1 if the firm is a multi-unit firm.

Columns (1) and (2) of Table 2 present the coefficient estimates based on data for 814 surviving manufacturing multi-unit firms only (266 acquiring and 547 non-acquiring firms).[11] The coefficient for ACQ7882 in Column (1) is statistically insignificant, suggesting that acquisitions did not have a significant effect on productivity growth. This conclusion holds also when we classify acquiring firms into two categories: complete acquisition and partial acquisition (Column 2). The coefficients for both FULLACQ and PARTACQ are statistically insignificant.[12]

---

[11]Non-manufacturing firms in the sample are those that did not have any manufacturing plants before acquisition, but had acquired one or more food manufacturing plants between 1978 and 1982 and kept them through 1987. Multi-unit non-manufacturing firms are not included in the multi-unit regressions so we can work with one comparable sample throughout the paper: We do not observe them prior to acquisition. Nonetheless, exclusion or inclusion of this small group of firms has no effect on the results presented.

[12]We do not report all controls in the tables. The coefficients for the MULTI variable are statistically insignificant in all equations. The insignificance of the MULTI variable is somewhat surprising. Because the size of multi-unit firms is larger than that of single-unit firms, the effect of MULTI is probably captured by the size variable (log TE77).

Finally, Columns (3) and (4) present the results from including the entire data set of 6,452 surviving firms (including single-unit firms and manufacturing plants or groups of plants owned by non-manufacturing firms) in the regressions. We find that the coefficient for the ACQ7782 (Column 3) is positive and significant at the one percent level. The coefficient for FULLACQ (Column 4) is also positive and significant. Moreover, the effects appear economically significant. The coefficient on ACQ7882 in Column (3) indicates that acquirers have a 22.2 percent higher productivity growth than non-acquiring firms.

Thus, once single-unit manufacturing firms and manufacturing portions owned by non-manufacturing firms are added to the sample, acquisitions show a positive and statistically significant effect on acquiring firms' productivity growth. This is a consequence of the dominance of small, single-unit firms in the full sample. It is important to note that this kind of sample structure is not typical of most merger studies that are dominated by the large multi-unit companies that make up most samples based on publicly traded firms.

3.2 Plant-Level Results

Table 3 reports the regression results based on plant-level data. While the specifications of the empirical models are nearly identical, the plant-level analysis exploits a far richer set of information. The variables in the table are defined as follows: ACQ7882 is a $(0,1)$ dummy variable equal to 1 if the plant is acquired during 1977-82. Acquired plants are also be classified into plants acquired through a complete acquisition (FULLACQ = 1; else FULLACQ = 0), and (2) plants acquired through a partial acquisition (PARTACQ = 1; else PARTACQ = 0). OWNPLT$_{AF}$ equals 1 if the plant was owned by the acquiring firm in 1977. We incorporate this variable in the plant level regression to distinguish the existing plants of acquiring firms from those of non-acquiring firms. In particular, if acquisitions are motivated by synergies, then one would expect that existing plants of acquiring firms will outperform those of non-acquiring firms in the post acquisition period. Other variables are defined as before. The omitted category is plants owned by non-acquiring firms.

Columns (1) through (4) of Table 3 contain the coefficients estimated using data for the 5,428 plants owned by the 814 firms that constituted the sample for the firm-level analysis in Table 1. The coefficient for ACQ7882 is positive, but it is insignificant in Column (1). However, once we separately control for plants owned by acquiring firms, the coefficient for ACQ7882 (Column 2) is significant at the one percent level. The coefficients for FULLACQ and PARTACQ are both positive, but only the coefficient for PARTACQ is statistically significant.

Columns (5) through (8) of Table 3 show the regression estimates based on the full sample of 12,995 surviving plants owned by the 6,452 surviving firms in our data set. All the coefficients for ACQ7882, FULLACQ, and PARTACQ are statistically significant. We also find that the coefficient for PARTACQ is as large and significant as that for FULLACQ. Thus, we find no evidence indicating that plants acquired through divestitures decreased their productivity in the post-acquisition period.

The coefficients for the interaction terms (e.g., $ACQ7882*logTE_{77}$) are always negative, implying that plants' productivity growth is non-linearly associated with size. For example, using the estimates in Column (8) and using (log) employment at the sample mean (mean $log\ TE_{77} = 3.8$ for surviving plants) we find that the productivity of plants acquired through complete acquisition during 1978-82 (FULLACQ) grew faster than that of plants owned by non-acquirers by 12.87 percent (i.e., $.348-.059(3.8) = .128$). However, this advantage of acquired plants diminishes as plant size increases. To be exact, when $log\ (TE_{77}) = 6.00$ (i.e., $.348/.059 = 6.00$) productivity of the acquired plants and that of plants owned by non-acquirers grew at the same rate. Beyond this size (i.e., $ln(TE_{77}) = 6.00$) productivity of plants owned by non-acquirers grew faster than that of acquired plants. We note, however, that because the 95th percentile value of $log\ (TE_{77})$ equals 6.00, only the top five percent of plants owned by non-acquirers had productivity growth that is higher than that of plants acquired through complete acquisitions during 1978-82.

3.3 Comparison of Firm and Plant Results

Our regression results suggest that acquisitions are generally associated with increases in productivity growth. Plant-level results show that both acquired plants and acquiring firms' existing plants increased their productivity 5-9 years after acquisitions. However, for large multi-unit firms, regression results based on firm-level data fail to show significant gains from acquisitions to acquiring firms. This supports the proposition that regression estimates based on aggregated multi-unit firm data are obscured by composition changes.

The differences in results obtained from the plant-level and firm-level regressions are illustrative. But, the reconciliation of the results must be undertaken with care because the fundamental comparisons reflected in the estimating equations are different. In the plant-level regressions, plants with ownership change are compared to those that did not change owners. In these regressions, the comparisons are between acquired plants' operating experience under the old and new ownership. In the firm-level regressions, in contrast, the acquired plants comprise only a (sometimes small) portion of the acquiring firm, and their performance is averaged with plants that were previously owned, and newly opened by the acquiring firm. The plant-level regressions provide a methodology that allows these different components of the firm to be examined separately. This is extremely important. Indeed, until we controlled separately for the productivity growth of the plants owned by acquiring firms, the effect of ownership change on productivity growth (Table 3, Column 1), while positive, was statistically insignificant, even in the plant- regressions. This result derives from the fact that the plants of acquiring firms that were owned prior to their acquisition programs were, on average, the most productive plants in the sample.

4 A Decomposition of Firm Productivity Growth

In order to evaluate the contribution of ownership change to firm productivity, we construct a decomposition of firm productivity growth into three components: 1) external (buying and selling), 2) internal (existing plants), and 3) new exit and greenfield entry.

4.1 Method of Decomposition

In the beginning year of any period over which we desire to measure productivity change, a firm is composed of three types of plants; (1) plants that are kept (k) to the end of the period, (2) plants that are sold (s) before the end of the period, and (3) plants that are closed before the end of the period. At the end of the period, the firm is also composed of three groups of plants; (1) plants that were originally owned and kept (k), (2) plants acquired from other firms and kept (a), and (3) newly built plants (n).

Using these categories the productivity of firm i, LP_i^F, in the beginning year (b) is written as

$$LP_{ib}^{F} = w_{ikb}LP_{ikb} + w_{icb}LP_{icb} + w_{isb}LP_{isb}, \qquad [2]$$

and the firm's LP in the ending year (e) is

$$LP_{ie}^{F} = w_{ike}LP_{ike} + w_{ine}LP_{ine} + w_{iae}LP_{iae}, \qquad [3]$$

where w_{ijb} (j = k, c, s) and w_{ije} (j = k, n, a) are the shares of category j in the total hours worked in firm i in the beginning and ending years, respectively. LP_{ijb} and LP_{ije} are the weighted average labor productivity of category j in firm i in the beginning and ending years. The firm's productivity change is

$$LP_i^F = LP_{ie}^{F} - LP_{ib}^{F}. \qquad [4]$$

Substituting (2) and (3) into (4) and adding and subtracting terms yields

$$LP_i^F = [W_{ike}LP_{ike} - W_{ikb}LP_{ikb} + W_{ike}LP_{ikb} - W_{ike}LP_{ikb}] \tag{5}$$

$$+ [W_{ine}LP_{ine} - W_{icb}LP_{icb} + W_{ine}LP_{icb} - W_{ine}LP_{icb}]$$

$$+ [W_{ine}LP_{ine} - W_{isb}LP_{isb} + W_{iae}LP_{isb} - W_{iae}LP_{isb}]$$

and simplifying and rearranging gives us

$$LP_i^F = [W_{ike} (LP_{ike} - LP_{ikb}) + LP_{ikb} (W_{ike} - W_{ikb})] \tag{6}$$

$$+ [W_{ine} (LP_{ine} - LP_{icb}) + LP_{icb} (W_{ine} - W_{icb})]$$

$$+ [W_{iae} (LP_{iae} - LP_{isb}) + LP_{isb} (W_{iae} - W_{isb})] .$$

Equation (6) provides a decomposition of the firm's productivity change into three sources: (1) existing plants -- the first bracketed term of the equation, (2) new plants and exiting plants -- the second bracketed term, and (3) acquired plants -- the third bracketed term. Each of the bracketed terms consists of two parts, a productivity effect and a share effect. The first part is the contribution of the productivity change in the relevant component to the firm's productivity growth. This term measures the contribution of the component assuming the share of the component in the firm's activities remains fixed at its initial level. The second part measures the components' contribution to the firm's productivity growth arising from change in the output share of the firm allocated to plants in the relevant component. The share effect measures the contribution to productivity growth assuming that the productivity of the plants in the component remained fixed at their initial level, while the output shares adjust to the observed levels at the end of the period. We note that, as with the change in productivity of the individual components, the change in output shares can be positive or negative. Further, these changes can be in opposite directions. For example, the productivity of a component can increase while its weight (share) declines. Thus, a component with increasing productivity could make a negative contribution to the firm's productivity growth if its share weight declines enough to offset its productivity growth.

This decomposition provides a framework for assessing the contributions of external and internal changes in the firm's structure to a firm's productivity growth. Moreover, the decomposition is equally valid for firms growing purely through internal means and those using acquisition and divestiture. For convenience, we treat divestitures by non-acquiring firms as closings. This means that firms using strictly internal growth will have zero values for the external growth category.

4.2 Decomposition Results

The results of the application of this decomposition of productivity change for the multi-unit firms in our sample are reported in Table 4. The table shows the 1977 and 1987 weighted and unweighted average LPs for both acquiring and non-acquiring firms, changes in their LPs and the decomposition of these changes over the period 1978-87. Examining first the simple (unweighted) average LPs, we find that acquiring firms are more productive than non-acquiring firms in both 1977 and 1987. This is true for the entire period and for each subperiod reported in Table 4. For example, during 1977-87, labor productivity of acquiring firms (1977-87) grew by 18 percent (from $119 to $140 per hour worked), while that of non-acquiring firms grew by 21 percent from $85 to $102. For firms acquiring plants during the latter part of the period 1983-87, 1977 average LP was somewhat smaller at $110. But, by 1987, the average LP of these firms increased to $132, a nearly identical increase of 22 percent. The output weighted productivity changes for both acquiring and non-acquiring firms were higher than the unweighted averages, but they give a very similar productivity growth picture for all periods. For example, on a weighted basis, firms acquiring plants during 1978-82 gained 17 percent in labor productivity, whereas non-acquirers gained 21 percent. The comparative unweighted figures were 18 and 21 percent, respectively.

These overall productivity growth figures are consistent with the earlier regression analysis, showing a small difference, if any, between the performance of acquiring and non-acquiring multi-unit firms before and after acquisitions. This would lead one to conclude that acquisitions bring virtually no gains to acquiring firms. However, the results of the decomposition tell a different story, one more comparable to the plant-level regressions.

Table 4 shows that acquisitions -- the external component (acquired/sold)-- had a large, positive contribution to the productivity growth of acquiring firms. The productivity change of continuously operating plants was positive and somewhat larger than that attributable to entry and exit. But, the change in output shares of both previously owned plants and entry/exit (built/closed)are large and negative. Thus, the net contribution that these groups of plants make to the productivity change of acquiring firms is negative. In short, their positive productivity gains are negated by declining shares of the output produced by the firm at the start of the period -- acquiring firms closed more and bigger plants than they built and became less concentrated in high productivity activities.

As with acquiring firms, non-acquirers obtained productivity gain from the replacement of closed plants with newly-built plants. However, this gain is offset by a decline in the share of this component in the total firm. The major factor that helped non-acquirers increase their productivity is the expansion and improvement of their continuously operating plants.

In one sense, these results seem obvious: The acquisitions of new properties reduce the proportion of the firm involved in its pre-acquisition activities. It is, of course, possible that a firm could expand its existing activities by enough to offset the diluting effects of the new ones on its shares. But these results make it clear that portfolio adjustments that alter the composition of the activities undertaken by large, multi-unit firms can obscure the positive effects of acquisitions on productivity growth.

The results of decomposition of productivity change indicate that acquisitions made a large contribution to firm productivity growth. Indeed, these results show that while the productivity of the external component (acquired plants) of multi-unit acquiring firms improved substantially after acquisitions, the share of the internal components (continuous existing plants) declined. This results in a labor productivity change for large multi-unit acquiring firms that is similar to that for non-acquiring firms. Thus, assessing the impact of acquisitions on the structure and performance of firms requires a careful look at individual components of the firms, particularly for large multi-unit firms.

4.3 Discussion and Implications for Financial Studies

The changes in composition observed for these acquiring firms are very large. They raise many questions, the most important of which is what are the reasons for the observed changes in the structure of the firm? In particular, why are the acquiring firms changing the composition of their activities in such a way as to increase the proportion of the firm in relatively low productivity activities?

As could be anticipated from the plant-level regressions, the productivity levels of plants owned by acquiring firms prior to acquisition and kept until 1987 had higher productivity than plants acquired over the period.[13] This productivity advantage was observed in both 1977 and 1987. Thus, acquiring firms tend to acquire (and improve) lower productivity plants than those they already own and keep as well as those that they build. This means that the proportion of the acquiring firm's activities accounted for by its most (in an absolute sense) productive plants is declining, even though the output of such plants is increasing.

Acquisition of well performing plants can provide footholds into growing markets (demand pull objectives) and/or exploit synergies between the acquiring firm's existing activities. Acquisitions are also motivated by the opportunities offered by fixing up poorly performing plants through the elimination of managerial inefficiencies. We know from earlier work (McGuckin and Nguyen, 1995) that most (in terms of number) of ownership changes involve motives in the former categories since they involve purchase of high productivity plants and

---

[13]They also were more productive than the plants of non-acquiring firms.

their improvement. A key aspect of future work in this area must be more detailed and refined analysis of those factors driving changes in the firm's portfolio of activities. Empirical studies that isolate demand pull, synergy, and other explanations for merger decisions are an important direction for future work.

Most generally, the motive for an acquisition should be that it will improve the firm's bottom line. But, as we indicated in the introduction, most empirical studies using financial returns have failed to find positive gains to firms involved in acquisition activity. This failure is disquieting, particularly in light of the long history and continuing high levels of merger activity in the economy.

While we cannot resolve the issue here, we think our results are relevant to a resolution of the empirical puzzle.[14] The evidence developed here suggests that most acquisitions are small, representing minor proportions of the acquiring firm. If an acquisition is small relative to the pre-acquisition size of the firm, measurement errors will make it difficult to identify the effects of the merger in the combined firm. This is a problem for most merger studies because they tend to rely on samples made up of large public corporations. Whether the study is based on the stock market return or accounting profit measures, small acquisitions are unlikely to have large enough impacts to show up in the data. (See Klein 1994, McGuckin, Warren-Boulton, and Waldstein 1992, and Matsusaka 1993).

In principle, this difficulty could be reduced by looking at a sample of firms with large acquisitions or firms with multiple acquisitions that could be grouped so that the impact of the "acquisition program" is large enough to overcome the noise. But, for large acquisitions or a group of small acquisitions that are cumulatively big enough to make a significant change in the firm, the portfolio changes seriously complicate empirical studies. In such situations, the composition effects become relevant and may obscure a positive empirical relationship between firm profits and merger activity.

For studies based on accounting profits, the composition changes complicate the already difficult problems involved in determining the correct asset values for the firm undertaking even the simplest merger. Simply keeping track of the business units owned by the firm, their products and assets, is difficult at best when the firm is changing structurally. This adds major obstacles to the already difficult task of determining appropriate values for the firm's capital. The Herculean efforts of Ravenscraft and Scherer (1987) in developing appropriate asset and equity values for deflating profit flows emphasize this point dramatically. And despite these efforts, their profit measures have been subject to various criticisms.

---

[14]We note that productivity is a measure of efficiency, not profits. While profits are positively related to productivity, the patterns of demand in conjunction with efficiency determine the distribution of profits of the firm.

Studies based on market models are also plagued by measurement problems. In McGuckin, Warren-Boulton, and Waldstein (1992), the problems in developing a proper portfolio for the "market" return are described in detail for eight mergers evaluated by the antitrust authorities. They conclude that the construction of an appropriate portfolio is typically very difficult because of the wide range of activities undertaken by large firms. They also find that the absence of a proper portfolio obscures the effects of the merger.

5 Concluding Remarks

Our empirical results can be summarized into the following three findings: First, our regression results based on both plant- and firm-level data for the entire population of surviving food manufacturing firms over the period 1977-87 show that acquisitions had a significant, positive effect on firms' productivity growth. Second, the regression results based on multi-unit firm-level data show no significant differences in productivity growth between acquiring and non-acquiring firms. Finally, our productivity decomposition results show that while the external component (acquired plants) had a significant, positive contribution to productivity growth of multi-unit acquiring firms, the productivity contribution of their internal component (existing own plants) was negative due to the decline in the output share of this component. Overall, the productivity change of acquiring firms is no greater and no worse than that for non-acquiring firms. (The level is higher for acquirers).

The first finding is consistent with the results obtained by recent studies using plant-level data. It is also consistent with major merger theories, including managerial-discipline and synergy theories. All these theories predict that acquired plants should improve their performance in the post-acquisition period.

The second finding suggests that internal and external growth can be viewed as substitutable methods for firms to grow.[15] As shown in Table 4, the differences in performance that we observe have more to do with the composition of the activities undertaken by the firm, than with the firm's overall performance. Acquirers show a decline in the output share of their existing plants. In contrast, non-acquirers are characterized by increasing concentration in their existing plants. Part of this is algebraic, of course: Purchase of new plants will, other things equal, reduce the share of total activity in existing plants. But it is important to note that acquirers increase the productivity of the plants they purchase over pre-merger levels and both acquirers and non-acquirers shut down unproductive plants and build more productive plants. All in all, both groups of surviving firms are undertaking active programs of change.

---

[15]The fact that external and internal growth are substitutes does not imply that all firms are equally able to undertake growth by each method.

The third finding shows that while acquisitions make important, positive contributions to the productivity growth of multi-unit acquiring firms, these positive contributions are obscured by the decline in the contribution of continuously operating plants. The important factor in this decline is the declining share of these continuously operating plants in the firm's activities. This decline negated the large productivity contribution of acquired plants. As a result, it appears that acquisitions had no significant effect on firms' productivity growth.

In light of these results, it is not surprising that most previous studies find little in the way of gains to acquiring firms. Multi-unit firms are typically the large public companies used in most empirical work on mergers and acquisitions. Moreover, the composition effects examined here for only the manufacturing portions of the firm are likely to be exacerbated when all the diverse operations of acquiring firms are taken into account. Thus, our empirical results suggest that the difference between the results of studies based on firm-level data and those of plant-level studies can be found in composition effects. In turn, assessing the impact of acquisitions on the structure and performance of firms requires a careful look at the individual components (i.e., plants) of the firms, particularly for large multi-unit firms. Therefore, plants rather than firms appear to be the more appropriate unit of analysis.

R.H. McGuckin, S.V. Nguyen

Table 1 Acquiring and non-acquiring food producing firms, 1977

	Number of Firms			Total Shipments (000,000)	Total Employment	Average Employment	1977 Labor Productivity (In 1987 dollars)
	Food[a]	Non-Food	Total				
ACQUIRING FIRMS (1978-82)							
1. Single-Unit Firms	62	31	93	1,381	14,694	158	73.94
2. Non-Manufacturing (bought 1 food plant)	109	25	134	1,798	17,554	131	75.06
3. Non-Manufacturing (bought more than 1 food plant)	103	47	150	9,623	75,600	504	86.73
4. Multi-Unit Manufacturing Firms	236	119	355	172,164	1,203,095	3,389	118.82
TOTAL	510	222	732	184,967	1,278,695	1,747	97.75
NON-ACQUIRING FIRMS[b] (1978-82)							
1. Single-Unit	15,067	-----	15,067	26,124	286,273	19	67.20
2. Non-Manufacturing (with 1 food plant)	1,185	-----	1,185	8,361	82,950	70	73.67
3,4. Multi-Unit Firms[c]	1,001	156	1,157	129,466	1,253,031	1,083	89.42
TOTAL	17,253	156	17,409	163,931	1,622,254	93	69.08

[a] Firms are allocated to food or non-food industries based on the largest category of shipments.

[b] These firms had no acquisitions in the 1978-82 period, but may have had acquisitions in the 1983-87 period.

[c] Includes multi-unit firms with non-manufacturing operations.

Table 2 Regression of surviving firms[1] productivity growth
(t-ratios in parentheses) *Dependent Variable*: Log (LP^F_{87}/LP^F_{77})

	Manufacturing Firms with Multi-Unit Operations		All Firms	
	(1)	(2)	(3)	(4)
Intercept	3.233**	3.221**	2.584**	2.584**
	(8.89)	(8.83)	(26.13)	(26.10)
Log (LP^F_{77})	-.749**	-.747**	-.649**	-.649**
	(8.59)	(8.51)	(28.16)	(7.82)
Log (TE_{77})	-.324**	-.322**	-.220**	-.220**
	(5.06)	(4.98)	(7.85)	(7.82)
ACQ7882	.021	-----	.222*	-----
	(.14)		(2.04)	
FULLACQ	-----	-.025	-----	.344**
		(.14)		(2.45)
PARTACQ	-----	.095	-----	.067
		(.45)		(.40)
ACQ7882 * Log (TE_{77})	.0004	-----	-.038*	-----
	(.02)		(2.15)	
FULLACQ * Log (TE_{77})	-----	.007	-----	-.053**
		(.27)		(2.42)
PARTACQ * Log (TE_{77})	-----	-.011	-----	-.019
		(.34)		(.70)
Log(LP^F_{77})* Log (TE_{77})	.078**	-----	.064**	.064**
	(5.11)		(9.42)	(9.38)
FOOD	.082+	.082+	.109*	.094+
	(1.73)	(1.68)	(2.13)	(1.77)
R^2	.1846	.1828	.2144	.2144
n	814	814	6,452	6,452

LP^F = firm labor productivity (defined as deflated value of shipment divided by worked hours).
+   denotes "significant" at the ten percent level.
*   denotes "significant" at the five percent level.
**   denotes "significant" at the one percent level.

Table 3 Regression of surviving plants[1] productivity growth (t-ratios in parentheses) *Dependent Variable:* Log (LP87/LP77)

	Plants of Firms with Multi-Unit Manufacturing Operations				All Manufacturing Plants			
	(1)	(2)	(3)	(4)	(1)	(2)	(3)	(4)
Intercept	1.904** (13.95)	1.941** (14.26)	1.895** (13.86)	1.933** (14.18)	2.221** (29.18)	2.273** (29.93)	2.220** (29.15)	2.272** (29.40)
Log(LP77)	-.401** (13.21)	-.441** (14.36)	-.399** (13.13)	-.439** (14.27)	-.570** (32.13)	-.591** (33.24)	-.564** (32.08)	-.590** (33.19)
Log(TE77)	-.173** (6.08)	-.182** (6.40)	-.171** (5.99)	-.180** (6.32)	-.257** (14.46)	-.254** (14.40)	-.256** (14.40)	-.254** (14.34)
ACQ7882	.081 (.94)	.215** (2.38)			.295** (3.90)	.393** (5.18)		
FULLACQ			-.015 (.13)	.119 (1.04)			.249** (2.38)	.348** (3.32)
PARTACQ			.209+ (1.64)	.345** (2.66)			.329** (3.08)	.425** (3.98)
OWNPLT_AF		.347** (5.43)		.347** (5.42)		.564** (10.15)		.564** (10.15)
ACQ7882*Log(TE77)	-.011 (.61)	-.027 (1.48)			-.058** (3.72)	-.072** (4.60)		
FULLACQ*Log(TE77)			.008 (.34)	-.009 (.37)			-.045* (2.03)	-.059* (2.64)
PARTACQ*Log(TE77)			-.035 (1.38)	-.051* (2.01)			-.067** (3.13)	-.080** (3.78)
OWNPLT_AF*Log(TE77)		-.046** (3.56)		-.046** (3.56)		-.093** (8.47)		-.093** (8.47)
Log(LP77)*Log(TE77)	.038** (5.88)	.044** (6.71)	.038** (5.78)	.043** (6.61)	.067** (15.94)	.069** (16.57)	.066** (15.87)	.069** (16.50)
MULTI					.217** (13.76)	.158** (9.53)	.217** (13.73)	.158** (9.50)
FOOD	.110** (6.63)	.124** (7.53)	.110** (6.66)	.125* (7.56)	.117** (8.31)	.117** (8.40)	.116** (8.21)	.116** (8.29)
R²	.1149	.1254	.1049	.1254	.1636	.1712	.1635	.1711
n	5,428	5,428	5,428	5,428	12,995	12,995	12,995	12,995

[a] LP = firm labor productivity (defined as deflated value of shipment divided by worked hours).

+ denotes "significant" at the ten percent level.

* denotes "significant" at the five percent level.   ** denotes "significant" at the 1 percent level.

Table 4 Evolution of the firm: the components of productivity change, 1977-87[a] (In 1987 dollars, Extreme Values Excluded)

Observation Year/Period	n	Internal (Continuously Operating)		External (Acquired/Sold)		Internal (Built/Closed)		Total Firm		
		Productivity Change	Share Change	Productivity Change	Share Change	Productivity Change	Share Change	Productivity Change	1977 LP	1987 LP
				Acquirers						
1977-82 (unweighted)	265	13.66	-27.06	33.52	3.22	11.12	-12.37	22.09	122.34	144.43
1977-82 (weighted)[b]	265	25.82	-47.26	42.67	14.89	9.26	-12.47	32.92	179.91	212.63
1982-87 (unweighted)	118	12.81	-10.42	25.16	-.06	5.54	-11.59	21.44	110.58	132.03
1982-87 (weighted)[b]	118	16.36	-8.20	7.27	-.39	14.32	-9.76	19.59	165.21	184.81
1978-87 (unweighted)	383	13.51	-21.20	29.85	2.03	9.43	-12.17	21.44	118.76	140.20
1978-87 (weighted)[b]	383	23.00	-31.62	29.77	10.17	10.96	-12.12	30.17	173.55	203.72
				Non-Acquirers						
(Unweighted)	539	14.04	3.14	-----	-----	10.95	-10.32	17.80	84.56	102.36
(Weighted)	539	19.42	14.02	-----	-----	15.99	-23.66	25.76	121.56	147.32

a Productivity is defined as deflated value of shipment divided by worked hours.
b Weighted productivity is calculated using total firm employment weights.

REFERENCES

Baily, M.N., Bartelsman, E.J., and Haltiwanger, J. (1994), *"Downsizing and Productivity Growth: Myth or Reality?"* CES Discussion Paper Series, U.S. Bureau of the Census, Washington, D.C.

Baily, M.N., Campbell, D. and Hulten, C. (1992), *"The Distribution of Productivity in Manufacturing Plants"*, Brookings Papers: Microeconomics, 1992, The Brookings Institution, Washington, D.C.

Baldwin, J. and Gorecki, P. (1991), *"Productivity Growth and the Competitive Process: The Role of Firm and Plant Turnover"*, Blackwell, B., Entry and Market Contestability: An International Comparison, pp. 244-56.

Jarrel, G.A., Bricley, J.A., and Netter, J.M. (1988), *"The Market for Corporate Control: The Empirical Evidence Since 1980"*, Journal of Economic Perspectives, 2, pp. 49-68.

Jensen, M.C. and Ruback, R.S. (1983), *"The Market for Corporate Control: The Scientific Evidence"*, Journal of Financial Economics, 11, pp. 5-50.

Kaplan, S. (1989), *"The Effect of Management Buyouts on Operating Performance and Value"*, Journal of Financial Economics, 24, pp. 217-54.

Klein, P.G. (1994), *"Did the Conglomerates Add Values?"*, working paper, Department of Economics, University of California, Berkeley, California.

Lichtenberg, F.R. (1992), *Corporate Takeovers and Productivity*, The MIT Press, Cambridge, Massachusetts.

Lichtenberg, F.R. and Siegel, D. (1992a), *"Productivity and Changes in Ownership of Manufacturing Plants"*, Lichtenberg, F.R., Corporate Takeovers and Productivity, The MIT Press, Cambridge, Massachusetts, pp. 25-43.

Lichtenberg, F.R. and Siegel, D. (1992b), *"Leveraged Buyouts"*, Lichtenberg, F.R., Corporate Takeovers and Productivity, The MIT Press, Cambridge, Massachusetts.

Long, W.F. and Ravenscraft, D.J. (1993) *"The Financial Performance of Whole Company LBOs"*, CES Discussion Paper Series, U.S. Bureau of the Census, Washington, D.C.

Matsusaka, J.G. (1993a), *"Takeover Motives During the Conglomerate Merger Wave"*, Rand Journal of Economics, 24, 3.

McGuckin, R.H. and Pascoe, G. (1988), *"The Longitudinal Research Database: Status and Research Possibilities"*, Survey of Current Business, 68, 11, pp. 30-37.

MCGuckin, R.H. and Nguyen, S.V. (1995), *"On Productivity and Plant Ownership Change: New Evidence from the LRD"*, RAND Journal of Economics, 26, 2, pp. 257-76.

McGuckin, R.H., Nguyen, S.V. and Reznek, A.P. (1995), *"The Impact of Ownership Change on Employment, Wages, and Labor Productivity in U.S. Manufacturing 1977-87"*, CES Discussion Paper Series, U.S. Bureau of the Census, Washington, D.C., Forthcoming in Labor Statistics Measurement Issues.

McGuckin, R.H., Warren-Bolton, F. and Walstein P. (1992), *"The Use of Stock Market Returns in Antitrust Analysis of Mergers"*, Review of Industrial Organization, 7, pp.1-11.

Mueller, D.C. (1993), *"Mergers: Theory and Evidence"*, mimeo.

Ravenscraft, D.J. and Scherer, F.M. (1987), *Mergers, Sell-Offs, and Economic Efficiency*, The Brookings Institution, Washington, D.C.

Smith, A. (1990), *"Corporate Ownership Structure and Performance: The Case of Management Buyouts"*, Journal of Financial Economics, 27, pp. 143-64.

Smith, C.W., JR. (1986), *"Investing Banking and the Capital Acquisition Process"*, Journal of Financial Economics, 15, pp. 3-29.

THE ROLE OF FRENCH AND FOREIGN ENTERPRISE GROUPS IN THE FRENCH PRODUCTIVE SYSTEM INTERNATIONALIZATION[1]

Frédéric Boccara

INSEE (Institut National de la Statistique et des Etudes Economiques)

1 Introduction

1.1 The approach

Foreign trade is essentially realized by enterprises. They play this way an important role to link countries and develop them. The results of their activity can, indeed, be transferred within a same company or, in the case of foreign trade, within a same group, between its various locations. This could be done towards other countries than the country where the results transferred were produced. That is an essential possibility allowed to multinationals. Indeed, those latter constitute in France important decision centers (Chabanas, Vergeaud, 1997) which contribute thus, in their particular way, to develop international transfers systems between countries.

We draw here some parts of a picture of these international transfers systems and suggest some hypothesis to analyze them.

The transfers through international trade are part of countries dynamics, by developing differently units of firms located in different countries, but also by differently developing populations, infrastructure, productive and informational networks of countries, thanks to distributed wages, financing of public and social spending and the relations with the other firms (P. Boccara, 1985, Storper, Salais, 1997).

The way the foreign trade side of those transfers systems is structured in connection with French territory an its changes is what we focus on this paper.

---

[1] INSEE, Direction des Statistiques d'Entreprises. The author expresses here his own views. That version benefited of commentaries by Paul Boccara on a previous one. Another, less detailed study on the same subject has been published in Insee et alii (1997).

1.2 Definitions, sources and indicators used

Foreign trade is measured here by trade of merchandises, excluding military goods, recorded by French Customs between France (without overseas possessions) and the rest of the world (including French overseas possessions). That is to say, in particular, in the sense of a physical move of a merchandise[2]. There could thus be a discrepancy between this indicator and the amount of monetary values which circulate. For example, payments can be delayed relatively to the date at which products cross the frontier and change of ownership, this is done through international loans or various financial conditions. Furthermore, international subcontracting can induce flows of goods, recorded by Customs, but without payments. Lastly, we also depend on the transfer prices practices. It can touch goods exchanged between two affiliates of a same enterprise group (cf. Lall 1973, for an economical analysis, Richard, Simons, Bailly, 1987, for a financial analysis framework at the group level, and Le Bas 1994, for practices). More generally speaking, we have to keep in mind that a splitting of flows between the «autonomous» ones and the other which would only be their «counterparts» (revenues, ...) has a very restricted and relative meaning (see for example Krugman, Obstfeld, 1991).

The relationship of a company to a group is measured by its financial links with other companies. That is to say the voting rights in shareholders' general assembly, (or sometimes the ownership share of capital) as given by the LIFI survey (cf. a methodological presentation in Chabanas, Thollon-Pommerol, 1991). This survey gives a «statistical» approach of enterprise groups. In particular, *the inclusion of a company within an enterprise group is defined by its (full) control (direct or indirect)* by another *company,* and not a physical person. The *head of the enterprise group* is a company not controlled by another and controlling at least another company, as LIFI can identify it without, generally, information about links between different foreign companies, except their name or their trademark. As a consequence, that is the country where the head of the enterprise group company is localized which defines the *nationality of the enterprise group.* Practically, we restrict us to French companies of each group. The head and its (fully) controlled companies taken together constitute the *hard-core,* its French enterprises are here classified as the «fully controlled enterprises». The other companies which have financial links but no one being a link of full control (direct or indirect) complete the *sphere of influence* of enterprise groups, they are classified here as «other enterprises linked to a group».

We do not survey other particular economic variables than the financial links at the group level. We use variables collected in other business surveys and match

---

[2] For Germany, we always consider the German Federal Republic. That is in 1983, the German Democratic Republic is a separate country, in 1993, territories from the past GDR are included within the GFR.

them with the LIFI information. At the group level, only certain *variables can be added* without double counting as value added, employment, gross operating surplus (but not *current* profits, which includes financial gains and losses). In this study, since we restrict us to the French companies of each group, we can add exports or imports without double counting, regardless they are inside or outside the group.

2 Higher oppositions between global trade balances

2.1 French enterprise groups on the center of the French balance upturn

This part treats globally different enterprises populations, split in sub-populations according to their kind of control-status. We evaluate globally the external trade flows and balance of each sub-population, before to treat of more *individual* characteristics of units.

Table 1 Foreign Trade of French Enterprises according to their control status as of 1993 (all goods)   *current billions of francs*

	1983[1]				1993			
	Exports	Imports	Balance	Exp/Imp (*100)	Exports	Imports	Balance	Exp/Imp (*100)
All enterprises in France	**694.6**	**799.3**	**-104.7**	**87**	**1177.4**	**1150.7**	**26.8**	**102**
of which								
Enterprises of a French group	295.9	255.7	40.2	*116*	581.7	339.6	242.1	*171*
Enterprises of a foreign group	132.2	229.8	-97.6	*58*	266.0	339.8	-73.8	*78*
Other enterprises linked to a group[2]	40.6	30.1	10.5	*135*	53.6	45.2	8.5	*119*
Independent Enterprises	225.9	283.7	-57.8	*80*	276.1	426.1	-150.0	*65*

(1) Enterprise Group perimeter of 1993 in 1983.
(2) Sphere of influence, excluding hard-core.
Field: merchandises, all countries, excluding military goods.
Source: Customs, Insee (LIFI survey).

After being negative from 1983 to 1991, the French external trade balance (all goods) upturned to be positive in 1993. That year, the amount of the balance of *manufactured* is comparable to that of 1983, after being negative from 1988 to 1991. On the contrary, the rest of the balance steadily improved, thanks to more exports of agricultural products and energy and to less imports of energy products (value and volume).

The upturn of the French trade balance of French enterprise groups, as a whole, stands as central in the global upturn of the total French trade balance (table 1 and graph. 1). The balances according to the control status are highly contrasted. Indeed, French enterprise groups (or more exactly their French part) reach in 1993 a high global surplus, while affiliates of foreign groups, located in France, show a global deficit and French independent enterprises a heavier one. For manufactured, the picture is more or less the same (table 2 and graph. 2).

Table 2 Foreign Trade of French Enterprises according to their control status as of 1993 (manufactured)   *current billions of francs*

	1983[1]				1993			
	Exports	Imports	Balance	*Exp/Imp (*100)*	Exports	Imports	Balance	*Exp/Imp (*100)*
All enterprises in France	**602.5**	**557.8**	**44.7**	*108*	**1047.4**	**983.1**	**64.3**	*107*
of which								
Enterprises of a French group	274.0	136.3	137.7	*201*	530.2	267.6	262.6	*198*
Enterprises of a foreign group	109.3	146.9	-37.6	*74*	247.6	292.8	-45.2	*85*
Other enterprises linked to a group [2]	35.0	25.4	9.6	*138*	45.1	39.2	5.9	*115*
Independent Enterprises	184.2	249.2	-65.0	*74*	224.6	383.5	-158.9	*59*

(1) Enterprise Group perimeter of 1993 in 1983.
(2) Sphere of influence, excluding hard-core.
Field: merchandises, all countries, excluding military goods.
Source: Customs, Insee (LIFI survey).

The oppositions between categories of enterprises seem to be higher in 1993, according to their relation to French territory, even if we obtain a qualitatively similar image than in 1983.

The breakdown of the *evolution shows opposite movements* behind a similar global balance for manufactured. While the French enterprise groups excess improved, the foreign groups deficit increased and the deficit of French independent enterprises approximately doubled in current value. For the other products, the deficits lightened, except for independent enterprises. But the lightening for foreign groups comes from same movements of both flows (less exports and less imports), since that for French groups comes from a doubling of exports and a strong decrease of imports.

Graph 1 All products Trade Balances of French Enterprises 1983 and 1993
in current billions of francs

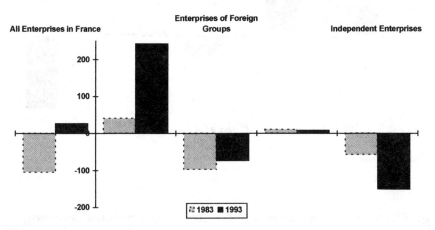

1993 enterprise groups perimeter

Those changes point the different kinds of links to French territory, opposing French and foreign groups. They also stress that different kinds of French «firms» (French groups / independent companies) could have different amount of leeway *vis à vis* their national territory to adapt themselves to changing conditions.

The export-import ratio, which is more significant for a medium term comparison, leads us to similar qualitative results. But the strong improvement of French groups surplus corresponds to a mere stability of their global export-import ratio, since the slight increase of foreign groups deficit corresponds to an improvement in their export-import global ratio.

One part of the deficit here charged to independent enterprises may be a deficit of enterprises controlled by a foreign group because the source used for measuring the control status has some imperfections to grasp foreign affiliates located in France. Especially when they are of a small size and/or the only one of their group located in France. The use of administrative sources should reduce that uncertainty in future works.

Graph 2 Manufactured Trade Balances of French Enterprises 1983 and 1993
in current billions of francs

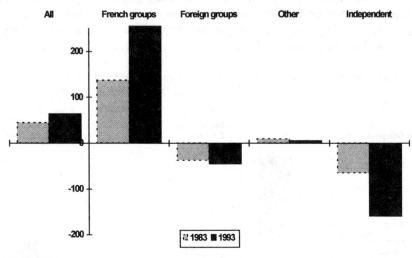

1993 enterprise groups perimeter

2.2 The same kind of oppositions at the "firm" (group or company) level

Such contrasts seem to be meaningful also at a more individual level. Each year, the contrasts are deepened by some very large units (large exporters or large importers), but in each control-status category, a majority of enterprises (companies) belong to a group having a trade balance with the same sign than the total of the category (table 3), excepted for the category of the enterprises without full control, but financially linked to others.

Since several management decision take their meaning within the enterprise group framework, we can speak of a "firm" level, made of the enterprise group level[3], for full controlled companies, and the company level for the others (independent or not fully controlled). That "firm" level appears more meaningful for enterprise groups than the company level: a lot of enterprises controlled by a French group reach a deficit whereas it takes place within a global surplus of its enterprise group (table 4) and similarly for Foreign groups, but with reversed signs.

---

[3] Restricted as registered in French territory.

Table 3 Weight of companies according to their controlling firm foreign trade balance sign

"firm"	Kind of "firm"							
	"enterprise Group"				"No controlled companies"			
	French enterprise Group		Foreign enterprise Group		Independent		Sphere of influence of groups	
aggregated Balance of "firm"	>= 0		< 0		< 0		>= 0	
	1983	1993	1983	1993	1983	1993	1983	1993
% companies	57.8	63.9	57.2	54.0	62.8	52.6	41.9	48.6
% workforce	58.3	64.5	54.9	50.5	54.1	54.0	49.2	49.2
% VA	52.8	59.5	65.0	60.8	58.0	55.2	37.3	49.0

Reading: 63.9 % of companies controlled by a French Group are in a Group having a Foreign Trade surplus.

Table 4 Company versus "Firm" Trade Balance Sign (1993)

	French Enterprise Groups					
Enterprise Group Balance	>= 0			< 0		
Company Balance	>= 0	< 0	no FT*	>= 0	< 0	no FT*
Number of companies	3,913	1,887	14,478	876	2,829	7,769
% of companies	19%	9%	72%	7%	25%	68%
% of employees	69%	15%	15%	16%	70%	14%
	Foreign Enterprise Groups					
Enterprise Group Balance	>= 0			< 0		
Company Balance	>= 0	< 0	no FT*	>= 0	< 0	no FT*
Number of companies	775	318	1,716	348	1,090	1,857
% of companies	28%	11%	61%	11%	33%	56%
% of employees	84%	13%	3%	17%	78%	5%

* FT = Foreign Trade of merchandises (customs definition)

Table 5 Gini coefficients

Variable	Gini's coefficient *(in %)*
Exports (goods)	99.3
Imports (goods)	98.9
Workforce	85.6
Value Added	99.0
Purchases	91.0
Sales	90.1

(all companies, included the non exporters and non importers)

Graph 3 Gini Curves

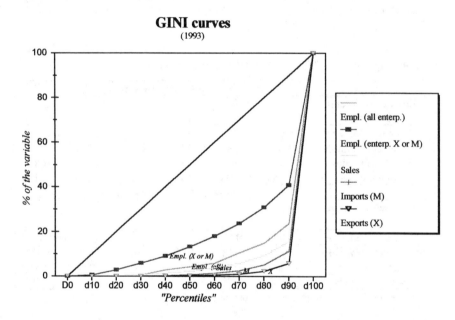

The Gini curve, in terms of companies involved, shows higher companies' concentration for foreign trade than for value added, total sales or employees (graph 3 and table 5). The workforce of the exporters or importers companies are also larger, as Gini curve shows it.

2.3 Exports generating imports: some indications

Several elements are given by Quélennec, Mathieu (1997) for manufactured *sector* (excluding other sectors, even those involved in trade of manufactured *products*). Our data show a significant number of companies realizing both flows (a half of exporters and a half of importers) and, above all, the external trade in merchandises of those exporters-importers is more than 90% of each flow (table 6). That is likely to reveal a significant share of imports devoted to subsequent exports, eventually after a productive operation. In average, merchandise imports of importers-exporters amount to one half of their total purchases (goods and services).

Table 6 Pure exporters (X), pure importers (M) and exporters-importers (X and M)

1993	Number of companies	% of total X	% of total M	X/Sales (in %)	M/Purch. (in %)	VA/Sales (in %)
No X and No M	517 823					35.3
Pure X	52 779	6.0		8.0		28.7
Pure M	50 148		6.6		33.3	24.8
X and M	55 179	94.0	93.4	15.6	49.9	32.4
Total	675 929			9.1	30.1	31.8

2.4 An increased share of groups in French foreign trade

In 1993, *French and foreign groups more participate in French foreign trade* of manufactured than in 1983, especially for exports (graph. 4). Groups realize together 75% of exports of manufactured (12 points more than in 1983) and 57% of the imports (7 points more than in 1983). We are not able to split it between «extra» and «intra» enterprise groups foreign trade for the two years. But those figures show, nevertheless, that a larger share of macro-economic flows is thus subject to a logic *potentially* different from that of a mere and ''classical'' competition on a same market between two firms of two different countries. That can contribute to explain apparent changes in global relations, as macro-econometric relations between aggregates concerning French foreign trade[4].

Moreover, we know by other studies French foreign trade between affiliates, but only in 1993. It amounts to almost a half of exports and imports of multinationals located in France, if we take together manufacturing affiliates

---

[4] For similar reasoning, see EPA (1994-95) quoted by OECD (1996), and see p.25-32 of OECD (1996), French edition.

(Guerrier, Hannoun, 1995) and wholesale affiliates (Le Bris, 1996). This share was probably weaker in 1983. Nevertheless, if we apply the proportion of 1993 to 1983 amounts, we obtain an increase of the shares of trade between affiliates: from 32% to 37% for exports and from 25% to 29% for imports. These calculations probably underestimate the phenomenon: the beginning year is overestimated because we take the 1993 groups perimeter for the two years and keep the same proportion of intra-firm trade.

Graph 4 Shares of Enterprise Groups in Trade of Manufactured

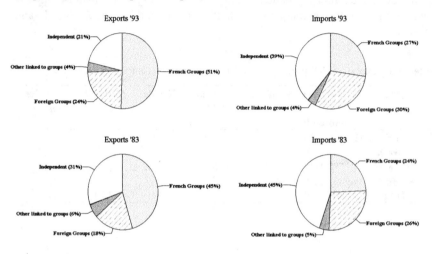

2.5 Trade balance of enterprise groups/ independent: an ambiguous opposition...

The opposition between the positive contribution of enterprise groups to the upturn of global foreign trade balance and the negative one of the independent enterprises may correspond to a specific behavior of independent enterprise as well as a negative feedback on them of the reduction of the French enterprise groups «external constraint». For example, in which extent the French groups purchases of 1983 realized through direct imports have been turned to purchases to independent enterprises in 1993, generating a comparable but «indirect» import content ? We should make analysis in terms of *intra-national competition as well as international one*. Nevertheless, French groups were capable to find and/or to benefit of degrees of freedom that independent enterprises, as a whole, were not capable to find or did not have.

Tables 1 and 2 give information on the whole amounts but not allowed us to further analysis in terms of individual firms behavior or strategies. In addition, for an individual approach, we should also take into consideration a double move: that of the foreign trade of individual units and that of the perimeter of groups between 1983 and 1993. The strategies of enterprise groups integrate indeed the takeovers and disposals possibilities they have, modifying their perimeter. These changes seems to be significant in other fields, as employment, as recent studies showed (Corbel, Fréchou, 1994, F. Boccara, 1997). Unfortunately, for data availability reasons, we here only use the 1993 perimeter. As a consequence, here the changes of composition of each category of enterprises is restricted to creations/disappearances of enterprises.

2.6 ... which affects also small enterprises

Staying at a semi aggregated level, we find also the control-by-a-group/independent opposition within the small and medium sized enterprises population. The SMEs, defined as the companies of a workforce less than 500, have an important weight in foreign trade of manufactured (table 7). This weight is almost the same in 1983 and in 1993 (taking each time the perimeter of the year 1993). The SMEs indeed realize 55% of the exports, but also more than 60% of the imports. So globally, in 1993, they generate a deficit of more than 120 billions francs, concentrated in the less-than-200-employees enterprises. Again, a breakdown of this deficit shows a surplus for SMEs controlled by a French groups (shared between less-than-200-employees enterprises and more-than-200), a deficit of SMEs controlled by a foreign group and a deficit of independent SMEs (table 8).

Table 7 Weight of Foreign Trade by enterprise size, 1993

Company Size as of 1993	Exports *% of the total*	Imports *% of the total*	Trade Balance *billions francs*
less than 200 employees	32 %	48 %	-136,7
200 to 500 employees	13 %	13 %	+9,5
500 employees and more	55 %	39 %	+191,4
Total	*100 %*	*100 %*	*+64,2*

Field: manufactured products , excl. military goods.
3 Customs, Insee (LIFI survey).

The deficit of SMEs controlled by a foreign group is to be understood as that of the foreign affiliates in general, which are mainly of a medium size, rather than that of a certain size-class of enterprises. Furthermore, beyond than 200 employees enterprises, the share of independent enterprises in foreign trade is very weak (3% of the total of exports and imports).

Table 8 1993 Foreign Trade Balances, according to Enterprise Size and Control Status

in current billions of francs

Enterprises Size in Control Status
1993

	French Enterprise Groups[1]	Foreign Enterprise Groups[1]	Independent Enterprises[1]	*(incl. other enterprises linked to groups[2])*
less than 200 employees	+ 35,3	- 19,7	- 156,2	- 136,7
200 to 500 employees	+ 24,6	- 15,9	- 2,5	+ 9,5
500 employees and more	+ 202,7	- 9,6	- 0,1	+ 191,4
Total	*+ 262,4*	*- 45,3*	*- 158,9*	*+ 64,2*

[1] 1993 perimeter

[2] Sphere of influence of groups, excluding hard-core.

Field: manufactured products , excl. military goods.

Source: Customs, Insee (LIFI survey).

3 Value added transfers: sector of activity and national base

3.1 Transfers of value added between countries

French and foreign groups have globally very different relations to French territory. The French groups surplus means that, this way, they globally transfer value added from other countries to France. Conversely, the foreign groups deficit indicates, in 1993 and in 1983, that this way they transfer value added from France to other countries (cf. box 1). The broadening of the total French surplus the years after 1993 leads us to assume that this configuration has roughly maintained, despite the specificity of the 1993 surplus emergence (exports and imports both decreased).

Box 1 Interpretation of External Trade Balances in Value Added Terms

Values exchanged through French external trade are a component of the production of the value added of the enterprises located in France, thus of the overall value added of the national French territory[*].

Imports M are a component of external purchases of firms, that is their intermediate consumption in merchandises and services IC, while exports X are a component of their turnover measured by sales S[**]. The value added VA of a given firm can be related to its trade balance Δ, as follows:

$$\text{Value Added} = VA = S - IC = (S_{France} + X) - (IC_{purchased\ in\ France} + M)$$
$$= VA_{\text{«on French Market»}} + (X-M)_{merchandises} + (X-M)_{services}$$
$$= VA_{\text{«on French Market»}} + \Delta_{merch} + \Delta_{services}$$

We can also analyze the contribution of trade balance to value added: Δ_{merch}/VA (or simply Δ/VA).

The trade balance (Δ_{merch}) can itself be broken down according to the countries with which it is realized. If it is negative with a given region or country, we can say that the enterprise, or the group, transfers value added in favor of that region or country, because this deficit decreases the value added. If it is positive, we can say that the enterprise, or the group, transfers value added in favor of France.

When, moreover, the enterprise is controlled by a group, – a multinational or not – this value added can be «globalized» between the companies of the group.

Foreign trade does not cover the whole contribution of international activities of an enterprise to its resources. We have to add trade in services, which is another component of the value added, as well as factor revenues. But thus, it has to be compared with a «global» value added, which would include financial incomes at the firm level (interests, dividends, etc.).

---

[*] If transfer pricing may introduce a bias relatively to effective activity on a given location, it nevertheless corresponds to a reality, which is that of the payments.

[**] Exchanges without payments, in particular those generated by international sub-contracting, can introduce a bias in the ratio Δ_{merch}/VA, for they are recorded by Customs since they do not have a counterpart in a sold value added.

The value added transfer by French enterprise groups, in favor of France, may be accompanied by an investment of those incomes partly inside and partly outside of France. Trade balances give us information only on the «primary distribution» of enterprise income and not on the «use of income» operations. The balance of payments would allowed us to specify the sign of these transfers by kinds of enterprises. Taken globally, the French balance of payments shows a net negative transfer of financial incomes towards other countries, in 1993 (almost 42 billions), broader than in 1983 (see Banque de France, 1993). Precisely, the 1983-93 period corresponds to an increase of French enterprise groups internationalization, of their international *financial* activities, even of a certain extroversion.

Balances of foreign trade, of financial incomes, of technological payments (fees, royalties, technical cooperation...) and of capital flows correspond to the connection between the locations of decision centers and of the different activities of firms (production, trade, research, logistics, financing...). Indeed, in 1993, commercial affiliates play a central role in the manufactured exchanges of foreign groups located in France. They realize 35% of foreign groups manufactured imports, against 20% in the case of French groups. As a consequence, the *non* manufacturing enterprises generate (directly) a high manufactured deficit (more than 85 billions in 1993), since the manufacturing affiliates have globally a surplus.

This can be related to employment and value added contribution, for, those different activities need different volumes of employment and capital: for manufacturing companies, the median workforce level is higher than for commercial ones, since services ones are in a intermediate place (table 9). For French groups, these differences are less marked than for foreign groups, and their services affiliates generate more employment than those of foreign groups. For independent, although the levels are sharply lower, the differences remain high.

Table 9 Company workforce level, according to the activity and the control status

	French enterprise groups		Foreign Enterprise groups		Independent Enterprises	
	1983	1993	1983	1993	1983	1993
Manufacturing	102	100	215	180	16	17
Trade	42	42	42	46	6	6
Services	78	65	84	49	9	8

Reading note: medians

As far as the size is concerned, the Δ/VA ratio seems to better take its meaning and its coherence at the "firm" level[5] than at the company level (graph 5).

---

[5] Restricted to France, i.e. as measured from the French territory.

Graph 5 (X-M)/VA, in % : "Firm" size versus Company size: year 1993

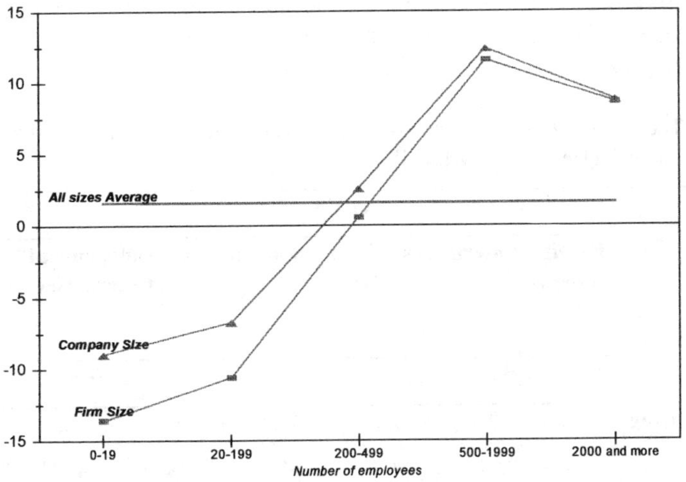

3.2 The opposition between commercial and manufacturing affiliates

The different kinds of affiliates, according to their main activity (manufacturing/trade) also show opposed contributions of foreign trade balance to value added. The breakdown by flows, related to sales and to purchases, shows also contrasted levels for each flows ratio. The opposite evolutions of contributions correspond to more internationalization of each activities, but with different equilibria between them (table 10).

Table 10 Global ratios, manufactured products, *in % of total products.*

	1983			1993		
	X/Sales	M/Purch.	Δ/VA	X/Sales	M/Purch.	Δ/VA
	average *med*	average *med*	average *med*	average *med*	average *med*	average *med*
Manufacturing	18% *(3.6)*	16% *(5.7)*	22% *(-ε)*	22% *(3.6)*	18% *(3.6)*	+29% *(3.6)*
Trade & others	3% *(1.1)*	9% *(3.7)*	-8% *(2.2)*	3% *(1.1)*	11% *(1.1)*	-5% *(1.1)*

Reading: Average : each ratio divides the both totals for each category ; Med = median of the company level ratios.
(Sales = Total TurnOver, Purch.= Total Purchases, VA = Value Added, Δ=Foreign Trade Balance in manufactured products, X = Exports, M = Imports).

The oppositions are also highly contrasted in terms of activity crossed by kind of enterprise group. But it is also the case inside each category. The opposition between commercial and manufacturing affiliates is rather complete, even for French enterprise groups and for Independent companies (table 11).

Table 11 The contribution of Trade Balance to Value Added, breakdown by kind of control and activity (1993, manufactured)

	Δ / VA					
	Foreign Enterprises Groups		French Enterprises Groups		Independent Enterprises	
	Average	Med	Average	Med	Average	Med
Manufacturing	17.0%	+5.3 %	49.0%	+2.3 %	8.0%	+0.7 %
Trade	-197.0%	-51.4 %	-4.0%	-3.6 %	-46.0%	-13.1 %
Others	0.3%	-0.1 %	0.3%	0.0 %	-1.0%	-0.1 %
Total	-11.2%		+11.7%		-12.5%	

Reading: Average : each ratio divides the both totals for each category ; Med = median of the company level ratios.
(VA = Value Added, Δ=Foreign Trade Balance in manufactured products).

The geographical scission of different activities within a same enterprise group is radically accelerated and transformed by the beginnings of a technological revolution, which can be dubbed *informational revolution* (P. Boccara, 1991). The replacement of the human hand by machine-tools (*industrial revolution*) is prolonged and surpassed by the beginnings of the replacement of certain human mind functions (the most standardized) by new machines (informational-machines). This is a completely different kind of replacement and partly in opposition with that of the different phases of the industrial revolution. New possibilities of dissociating and associating information and persons or information and machines are developing. In the same time, the sharable nature of informational «products» and of their costs pushes to transform management of firms, relations between firms and the role of socio-economic institutions[6] (P. Boccara, 1991, Barraux, 1997).

The enterprise groups and the internationalization developments are deeply related to the beginnings of that informational revolution, in a long wave context where enterprises seek to recover their profitability (Insee, 1974). This development take use of new kinds of linkages between manufacturing, services

---

[6] As public research system, formation and education system, organisms of mutual services for SMEs, etc..

and trade. In feedback, the financial control of the activities within large sets of enterprises orientates that couplings.

In 1993, the divergences between manufacturing affiliates and others are more marked than ten years before (graph 6). That stresses the increasing importance of activities dissociations, as trade constitute one of them. The export/import ratio of manufacturing affiliates of foreign groups is 16 points higher than that of 1983, while that of other foreign groups affiliates (trade, services, transports...) is 11 points below. There is also a tremendous decrease for French groups (-35 points).

Graph 6 Evolution of Export/Import ratios, according to the activity of the companies and their control status

Manufacturing   **Trade + Services**

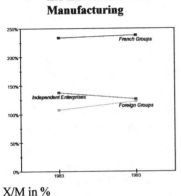

X/M in %

Dealing about the increasing role of services activities in all firms needs to keep in mind that external trade in merchandise is only a part of the balance of payments. In fact, *"external"* intermediate consumption of services should be treated symmetrically. The value added ratios (VA/Sales) gives us some directions for further analysis. It shows a "systematic" difference between French and Foreign enterprise groups, globally taken, even when the trade contribution to VA is positive (table 12). Not surprisingly, it is likely to confirm a stronger link of French groups to France. But it is also consistent with services payments (royalties, fees, etc.[7]) creating the difference: the lower Foreign group contribution to French value added would come from both their merchandise trade extroversion, with the high deficit we have identified, and from a higher dependency to overseas services and payments.

---

[7] "Explicit" or, possibly, through transfer pricing.

Table 12 Value Added to Sales ratio

	Δ "firm" < 0	Δ "firm" >= 0
French enterprise groups	39 %	34 %
Foreign enterprise groups	28 %	30 %
Independent	20 %	24 %
Other enterp. linked to a group	23 %	24 %
Total	31 %	31 %

Reading note: average ratios: total Value added of the category divide by total Sales of the category: "firm" is the French part of the group for enterprise groups, the company for other categories..

3.3 The notion of national base in question

The high differences of relationships with French territory that French and foreign enterprise groups seems to develop lead to wonder about the kind of the internationalization process and its meaning.

The systematic deficit of, taken globally, each kind of foreign group with its origin-country is in contradiction with a vision where the large multinationals would not have particular relationships with their country of origin (Reich, 1991). The notion of a «national base» which would persist, in a certain way, through the so-called globalization movement seems to have some relevancy. But it is true that it is a too limited and too partial concept to describe the underlying phenomena. That notion should be revisited and enriched. We should at least distinguish the different combinations of principal locations of a multinational: the main country of production, that (or those) where it employs the most of its employees, the country favored for profits inflows, the country of financing (in particular that of the controlling capital), the country where its R&D is mainly developed, etc. And we should articulate them with the main products of the group as a whole. That is to say we need to *define profiles of combinations between informational base, production base and financial base.* The financial base being a favored mean to appropriate informational resources (those of a competitor as well as to keep the own ones out of a takeover) in a perspective of a high rivalry between groups and bases.

Furthermore, we have *to take into consideration the role of States.* Firstly, the States play an important role in *financing foreign trade* of enterprise groups, through a system of specialized institutions[8]. Secondly, States continue to support

---

[8] For instance, in France, discounts on loans costs, various warrants on big contracts, loans by the Treasury to other States, made by COFACE (*Compagnie Française d'Assurance*

them by various other forms of *public financing in general[9]*. In France, a lot of large internationalized-enterprise-groups get substantial capital transfers and other public financing. They also were able to temporary endure lower rates of profits, in connection with 1982-83 nationalizations, before later privatizations or new mixes with private sector.

Thirdly, and it is the present novelty, the *informational base* of groups is particularly connected with States policies by: *(i) public spendings in research*, formation and education system, links between public agencies and large multinationals (concerning, in France, the nuclear sector, the aircraft, telecoms, military industry, etc.), *(ii)* networks of so called *economic intelligence* where public institutions and large groups act together, *(iii)* and the *exchange rate of the country* where is located the financial base of the group, which is an essential target variable of the economic policy and, for a large part, which conditions «*international financial withdrawings*» (P. Boccara, 1993).

The evaluation of certain informational resources under the form of financial assets, representing what O. E. Williamson (1985) calls «*specific assets*», makes those withdrawings costly. In fact, they can exceed the effective spendings initially purchased to constitute these informational resources. Those international withdrawings can notably be done through international takeovers, or inside oligopolistic sharing structures between several multinationals. As a consequence, a «*national State base*» would be a more appropriate expression. This meets, in a certain way, some criticisms of the unilateral aspect of Reich's views, insisting on the relationships between States and multinationals in most of the countries, as G. Lafay (1996), E. Cohen (1996) or, in a more implicit way, Storper, Salais (1997).

This meets also, coming from the symmetric concern, Ruigrok and Van Tulder (1995) which criticizes an excessive emphasis put on mere nationality of firms. They propose something as to cross *nationality* with the notion of «*industrial system*» or «*industrial complex*» of the firm. Studying the case of some big German and French Multinational Enterprises (MNEs), Sally (1995) shows not such a "straight" and unilateral view of home-base role as Robert Reich seems to argue. One of its arguments is precisely that "*value added is still asymmetrically concentrated*". The second one lies on "*the government role*" through subsidies towards domestic MNEs. In fact Sally calls for opening the national-base

---

pour le Commerce Extérieur), BFCE (*Banque Française du Commerce Extérieur*) and French Treasury, amounted to 17 billions of francs in 1982 (cf. Milewski, 1989, p. 107-113). This represent, for example, almost one half of the French enterprise groups foreign trade surplus in 1983. This system is nowadays deeply being transformed and, partially mutualized between large French and German groups: in particular, the former warrant public company (COFACE) acquired 50,1 % of the stockholders of AKV; one of the main German warrant company.

[9] Allowing what has been dubbed a *devalorization of the capital*, in this case through a *lower valorization* (less profitability) of the public part of the capital (cf. Paul Boccara, 1973 and 1978-79).

concept, given the fact that, in our words, informational technologies can change the deal. The conclusion stresses the necessity to further analyzes which would cross nationality and function (activity) distinctions.

4 Geographical polarizations: continuities and shifts

4.1 Overall outlook

The configuration of global French balances according to the regions of the world (table 13) has the same following pattern in 1993 and in 1983: French foreign groups realize a surplus with all the regions of the world whereas foreign groups and independent enterprises have a deficit with the North, taken globally, and a surplus with the South[10]. Internal oppositions exists nevertheless between independent enterprises and foreign groups but *inside* each large region: the manufactured balance with Latin America and Asia (excl. Japan) is positive for French affiliates of foreign groups, whereas it is negative for independent enterprises. Within western Europe, the affiliates of foreign groups record their main manufactured deficit with Germany and not, contrary to independent, with the rest of the continent taken globally (table 15).

---

[10] The South is more or less "the rest of the world" in our tables.

Table 13 Trade manufactured balances *in current billions of francs,* 1983-93 according to kind of control and geographical regions: 1993 group perimeter

	French Enterprise Groups		Foreign Enterprise Groups		Independent Enterprises		TOTAL (incl. other enterprises linked to a group[1])	
	1983	1993	1983	1993	1983	1993	1983	1993
Western Europe	59,2	153,7	-39,3	-43,8	-75,6	-114,0	-54,9	1,0
USA	10,0	17,6	-10,2	-12,3	-9,9	-18,2	-12,6	-13,6
	8,4	26,1	-3,6	-10,5	-13,5	-40,5	-8,5	-27,4
Country/Region								
Rest of the world	60,2	65,0	15,4	21,3	34,0	13,8	120,7	104,1
Total	137,8	262,4	-37,6	-45,3	-65,0	-158,9	44,7	64,2

[1] Sphere of influence of groups, excluding hard-core.
Field: all countries, manufactured products , excl. military goods.
Source: Customs, Insee (LIFI survey).

French groups relatively retired from Africa and Near and Middle East. In parallel they improved their surpluses with western Europe, USA and Asia (table 16). That geographical shifting was significantly helped by different public institutions devoted to foreign trade financing (COFACE, DREE, Trésor). In the same time, the increase of their disposable profit facilitated their investment abroad, in a context of a rather weak domestic internal demand.

French independent enterprises endured a deterioration of their manufactured balance with the regions of their deficits (western Europe, USA, Asia) as well as with most of the regions of their surpluses (Africa, Near and Middle East). Indeed, the purchasing power of these regions frankly declined whereas they are more or less in the continuity of French internal markets, as regions toward independent enterprises can expand without a so important logistic investments than for further markets.

French affiliates of foreign groups have a broader deficit in 1993, but relatively contained. Weak internal French demand and higher exchange rate of French Franc probably contributed to limit that broadening. Those affiliates intensified their exchanges with Asia, as those of French groups (graph. 7). They also develop their exchanges with western Europe and USA, but in an average proportion.

Table 14 Weights of manufactured trade flows *in %,* 1983-93 according to kind of control and geographical regions: 1993 group perimeter

Country/Region	French Enterprise Groups		Foreign Enterprise Groups		Independent enterprises		TOTAL (incl. other enterprises linked to groups[1])	
	1983	1993	1983	1993	1983	1993	1983	1993
Western Europe	58	64	74	74	67	69	65	68
USA	10	10	9	9	6	6	8	8
Asia	6	9	5	8	7	12	6	10
Rest of the World	27	17	12	9	20	13	21	14
Total	100	100	100	100	100	100	100	100

[1] Sphere of influence of groups, excluding hard-core.
Weight of flows in % : (Exports + Imports of the category of enterprises with the zone) / (Total Exports + Imports of the enterprises category).
Field: all countries, manufactured products , excl. military goods.
Source: Customs, Insee (LIFI survey).

Most of the affiliates of foreign enterprise groups located in France are controlled by heads located in the three main developed countries (USA, Japan, Germany) or in the rest of the «North» Europe (incl. Italy). So, they realize the essential part of their deficits with their origin country (graphs. 9 and 10).

Behind an apparent balancing of foreign trade, the comparison of 1993 and 1983 situations emphasizes the same kind of increase of oppositions than between global balances enterprise categories. That is in support of the hypothesis of more rivalry between enterprises according to their *national State base.*

Graph 7 Trade balances 1983 and 1993 according to kind of control of the enterprises (manufactured)

in current billions of francs.

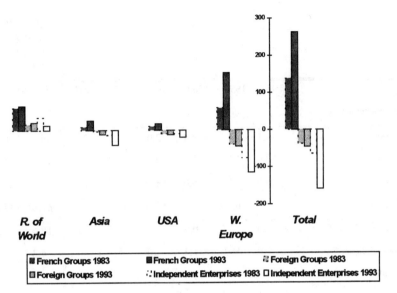

Manufactured

4.2 Western Europe: higher surplus with higher intra-Europe oppositions

More than two third of the French external trade takes place with *western European countries*. The signs pattern of the balances of different categories is the same as for the all-countries balances. Between 1993 and 1983 the polarization on western Europe reinforced, especially for French enterprise groups. But for the later, if western Europe is the region which mainly contributes to their surplus, their flows with western Europe represent a lower part of their exchanges than for the other categories of enterprises.

Table 15 Trade Manufactured Balances *in current billions of francs*, 1983-93 by kind of enterprise control, geographical regions details 1993 group perimeter.

Country/Region	French Enterprise Groups 1983	French Enterprise Groups 1993	Foreign Enterprise Groups 1983	Foreign Enterprise Groups 1993	Independent Enterprises 1983	Independent Enterprises 1993	TOTAL (incl. Other enterprises linked to a group[1]) 1983	TOTAL 1993
Germany	9,1	41,1	-28,4	-32,0	-17,3	-20,4	-36,2	-8,2
USA	10,0	17,6	-10,2	-12,3	-9,9	-18,2	-12,6	-13,6
Japan	0,5	7,2	-5,0	-13,4	-7,7	-14,5	-12,8	-21,8
sub-Total	*19,6*	*65,9*	*-43,6*	*-57,7*	*-34,9*	*-53,1*	*-61,6*	*-43,6*
West Europe excl. Germany	50,0	112,6	-10,9	-11,9	-58,4	-93,6	-18,6	9,2
Asia excl. Japan	7,9	18,9	1,4	3,0	-5,8	-26,1	4,3	-5,6
Rest of the World (Latin Am., DOM, Africa, Near and Mid East, Est. Eur, etc.)	60,2	65,0	15,4	21,3	34,0	13,8	120,7	104,1
Total	137,8	262,5	-37,6	-45,3	-65,0	-158,9	44,7	64,2

[1] Sphere of influence of groups, excluding hard-core.
Field: all countries, manufactured products , excl. military goods.
Source: Customs, Insee (LIFI survey).

The internal configuration of the signs of balances did not much changed. The upturn of the total French-western Europe balance from a deficit to a light surplus come from the change of relative importance of balances of different enterprises categories. We observe as a spillover of 1983 South compensations external to Europe (surpluses with Africa, Near and Middle East) towards South countries internal to western Europe in 1993.

The flows of foreign groups and independent enterprises are relatively more oriented towards western Europe than those of French enterprise groups. The polarization on Western Europe increased for each set of enterprise. Three factors can explain the differences between the categories, *(i)* the proximity of Western Europe market for independent enterprises, *(ii)* the role of commercial platform and *(iii)* the role of *Western European productive relay* played by French territory for foreign groups.

With Germany, 20% of French foreign trade, the deficit persists in 1993 even markedly lightened. The increase of French groups surplus was broader than the deepening of foreign groups and independent enterprises deficits. But the foreign groups deficit with Germany is largely the first deficit. Thus, what appears in aggregates as a balancing of trade relations between France and Germany may correspond to higher oppositions between categories of enterprises. Moreover, the financial side of the exchanges should be taken into consideration, for, the past France-Germany deficits induced accumulated financial claims of German enterprises on French economy.

The coming of noticeable surpluses with the South of Western Europe (Spain and Portugal), between 1983 and 1993, corresponds conversely to a joint amelioration for both French and foreign enterprise groups, while the deficit of independents slightly widened. With UK, the improvement of the traditional surplus follows the same pattern, but the short term demand evolution in the both countries are used to play a rather significant role in this balance. The high surplus with Switzerland is stable.

After Germany, the main deficits of French affiliates of foreign groups are observed with Belgium-Luxembourg and Italy, even if the flows may be higher with other locations. For Belgium, we can see here a mark of the crossroads role played by Belgium in world economic relations, between Western Europe and USA, and inside Western Europe, partly inherited from its colonial past. With Italy, the deficit with independent enterprises is the highest one. It is possible that it is the particular sectors involved (as clothing) which imply that industrial relations are more based on other kinds of relationship than financial control of capital.

France appears also, for foreign multinationals, as a springboard to export to (South) countries pertaining to its region of influence.

The joined surpluses of French enterprise groups and of foreign groups, with Africa and French possessions overseas (DOM) confirm the hypothesis of reaching market of a French influence from a French location, for foreign enterprise groups. Precisely, those two regions are the rare ones with which all the categories record a significant global surplus.

5 Nationality of multinationals

5.1 Foreign multinationals realize transfers to their country of origin

A breakdown of the Foreign multinational balances according to the origin of groups allows us to see the role of the origin-country as a national base. It also gives us some clues about the particular place of France in their globalization process (commercial relay-base, complementarity, competition, final destination, etc.). Globalization does not seem to affect France according to a binary opposition domestic/foreign but according to crossed opposition and complementarity : France as national State base/multiple foreign base/geographical region.

Graph 8 Balances of French Affiliates of Foreign Multinationals (1993) according to their nationality: manufactured products

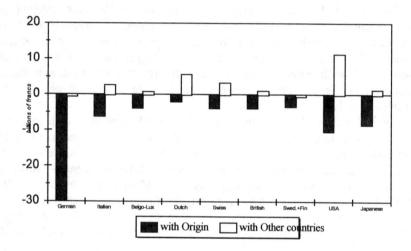

The national base of origin of foreign multinationals plays a central role to attract their external trade. All categories of foreign groups participating to French external trade and significantly present in France, globally transfer value added to their country of origin (graph 8).

Table 16 1993 geographical balances according to the nationality of enterprise groups

billions of francs

Country, Region partnership of exchanges with France	Enterprise Groups Nationality									Total balance of those groups	of which : balance with other countries than the origin
	German	Italian	Belgo-luxembg	Dutch	Swiss	British	Swedish -Finnish	US-American	Japanese		
Germany	**-29,4**	0,5	0,6	-0,5	-2,8	-0,2	0,1	-1,3	1,0	**-32,0**	-2,6
Italy	0,3	**-5,7**	-0,3	-2,5	ε	0,4	0,1	4,4	-0,2	**-3,5**	+2,2
Belgium+Lux[1]	-1,4	0,1	**-3,6**	-1,7	0,4	0,6	-0,5	-1,5	0,2	**-7,4**	-3,8
Netherlands	ε	0,3	ε	**-1,5**	-0,3	1,1	-0,3	0,4	1,3	**1,0**	+2,5
Switzerland	0,2	0,2	0,2	0,5	**-3,6**	0,1	0,2	1,3	0,1	**-0,8**	+2,8
United Kingdom	0,8	0,4	-0,2	0,9	0,4	**-3,8**	0,3	1,0	-0,3	**-0,5**	+3,3
Sweden+Finland	-0,8	0,1	-0,1	-1,1	-0,1	-0,2	**-3,2**	2,1	0,1	**-3,2**	ε
USA	-0,3	-0,3	0,1	-2,1	1,4	-0,6	-0,2	**-9,9**	-0,1	**-12,0**	-2,1
Japan	-1,2	-0,1	-0,4	-0,5	0,3	-1,6	-0,1	-1,5	**-8,3**	**-13,4**	-5,1
Spain	-0,8	0,6	ε	0,8	0,4	ε	0,2	0,5	0,1	1,8	
NME[2] + Turkey	0,5	0,3	0,3	1,5	0,7	0,3	0,2	2,2	ε	-6,0	
Africa	1,0	0,3	0,1	3,5	1,3	1,3	0,2	2,7	0,1	10,5	
4 dragons of Asia	ε	-0,1	0,1	1,0	0,6	-0,3	0,1	0,8	-0,4	1,8	
Latin America	0,2	-0,2	-0,1	2,4	0,4	0,1	0,1	ε	ε	2,9	
Balance with those countries & regions	**-30,9**	**-3,6**	**-3,3**	0,7	-0,9	-2,8	-2,8	1,2	**-6,4**		
Total French Balance of multinationals	-29,9	-3,1	-2,8	4,1	-0,3	-2,8	-3,3	1,4	-7,0		
- of which, with other countries than that of origin	**-0,5**	**+2,6**	**+0,8**	**+5,6**	**+3,3**	**+1,0**	**-ε**	**+11,3**	**+1,3**		
Weight of flows of these affiliates (Exports + Imports) in total France	4,3%	1,3%	0,9%	4,0%	2,5%	1,9%	0,8%	9,5%	1,0%	26,2%	

ε = less than 50 millions of francs.
[1] Belgium-Lux = Belgo-Luxembourg Economic Union.
[2] NME = Near and Middle East.
Field: manufactured products, excl. military goods.
Source: Customs, Insee (LIFI survey).

5.2 The three main nationalities

For one given foreign country C, we define "*bilateral advantage*" of its MNEs[11] (C-MNEs) as the French *deficit* of the C-MNEs' French affiliates with the country C – their own origin country. We define "*multilateral advantage*" of the country C as the French *deficit* of the non-C-MNEs' French affiliates with the country C ; and "*advantage on other countries*" as the French *surplus* of the C-MNEs' French affiliates with non C countries (graph 9).

---

[11] MultiNational Enterprises

Graph 9 Economic Advantages of Main Countries and their Enterprise Groups on France

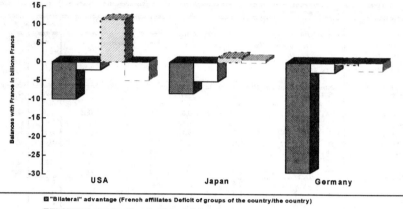

Field: manufactured products, excl. military goods. For patents, technol. payments and cooperation : all products. Other countries = all countries.

Source: Customs, Insee (LIFI survey), Bank of France (Balance of payments).

French affiliates of German, American and Japanese multinationals show a high bilateral deficit with their origin. It indicates that, globally, they are likely to sell in France production from their own national base (table 16, graph 8). They also record a surplus from France on *intermediate* countries and on South. It indicates that France plays a *production base* role or the role of a *commercial platform* to reach these countries (graph 10). Moreover, groups of other nationalities, located in France, widen the French deficit *vis à vis* those three countries. Those balances indicates a form of bilateral advantage of the three locations on the French location, and a multilateral advantage on other foreign groups (graphs 9 and 11).

The bilateral advantage of Germany is the highest, the deficit of French affiliates of German groups is three times higher than that of American or Japanese ones with their respective origin (graphs 9 and 10). In this bilateral deficit one should include a large amount of the 'technical help and cooperation' line of the balance of payments (-2,2 billions, in 1993). For, it essentially includes counterpart of Airbus sales, to the German part, which is directly and strongly connected with manufactured trade. The multilateral advantage is little, compared to the bilateral one, but it is significant (graphs 9 and 11). In particular, US and Swiss multinationals appear rather dependent of Germany in their trade from France. The trade of affiliates from Germany with other countries is rather balanced, with a deficit with Western Europe, USA and Japan, and a surplus with the rest of the world.

For the Japan, the bilateral advantage is the main one, but less markedly than for the German multinationals and with flows of exchanges 4 times weaker. The informational advance of Japan and its extroversion is visible on the remarkable multilateral advantage that it exerts on affiliates of other origins. This can be split in two equal parts: an advantage on affiliates of the two other dominant bases (USA and Germany) and an advantage on affiliates of other countries (graph 9).

The US case is more complex. It mixes bilateral advantage, advantage on other countries and multilateral advantage. In 1993, the deficit of US affiliates *vis à vis* their origin is inferior to their surplus on other countries, thus US affiliates apparently contribute positively to *manufactured* French balance (table 16 and graph 10). But their trade in other products, especially oil, reverse that. Moreover, that manufactured trade takes place in parallel with payments of royalties and various fees by US affiliates to their parent company. Taking into consideration those payments, including a large amount connected with manufactured, would reverse the balance of US affiliates in France (graph 9). Lastly, the trade with USA of other (non American) affiliates contribute to the French-USA deficit for an amount comparable to the German case (graphs 9 and 11).

The worldwide role of the dollar, the economic size of USA, the specificity and the age of foreign affiliates in France and in Western Europe, made of a lot of productive plants, are likely to explain the importance of US affiliates flows in French external trade. They represent 10% of the total flows of manufactured (exports plus imports), whereas the other foreign multinationals represent 13% all together. Their share largely exceeds that of German affiliates (almost 4% of the flows) although those later directly generate a higher deficit for French manufactured external trade, especially with more exclusively commercial plants, for instance in cars.

Graph 10 Balance of Foreign multinational by Nationality balance with *origin / other countries*

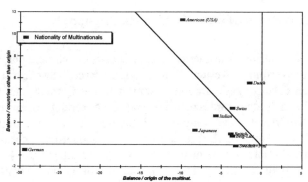

Vertical axis: balance with other countries than the country of origin of the multinational
Field: manufactured products, excl. military good.

Graph 11 Balance of Foreign multinational by Partner-Country balance of multinationals originating from the *partner-country / other countries*

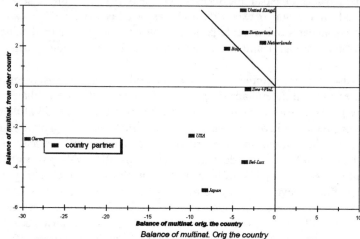

Horizontal axis: balance of French affiliates originating from the country
Vertical axis: balance of affiliates originating from other countries
Field: manufactured products, excl. military goods
Reading of graphs 10 and 11:
French affiliates of Italian multinationals has a 5.7 billions of francs deficit in manufactured with Italy and a surplus of 2,6 billions with other countries (graph 10). Graph 11 shows that the contribution of French affiliates of Foreign multinationals to total balance between France and Italy is broken down of a 5,7 billions deficit of affiliates originating from Italy and a 2,2 billions surplus for French affiliates originating from other countries.

5.3 The extroversion of other foreign multinationals

Most of the other affiliates of foreign multinationals which take place in French foreign trade are from a Western Europe origin. Except Swedish and Finnish groups, which balance configuration is similar to the German one, the foreign groups of the non dominant countries present a certain extroversion: their affiliates realize from France a surplus with the other countries than that of their origin (graph 10). For several, that surplus on other countries exceeds the deficit with their origin (Dutch) or is near to it (Swiss). For others, the surplus is not enough to overbalance the deficit with the origin (Italian, British, Belgo-Luxembourg). Moreover, nationalities of foreign groups can be distinguished according to the balance of other affiliates with their origin (graph 11).

Affiliates from British and Belgo-Luxembourg multinationals appear less extroverted than others, according to their total balance with other countries. But indeed the balances of these affiliates are contrasted according to *each* partner-country, even if taken globally their exchanges appear less unbalanced.

The Belgo-Luxembourg Economic Union is the only one country, apart the three main - USA, Japan, Germany - to present a multilateral advantage: the affiliates of other origins reach a deficit *vis à vis* this country. That is likely to relate with the assembly and commercial platform role in Western Europe of this location for affiliates from the three main countries.

6 Conclusion

Comparison of French global trade balances of different enterprises categories, their Value Added and employment contributions, stands up opposite situations according to their control status. Furthermore, we have opposite shifts and, indeed, the disparities between enterprises seem to be more accentuated in 1993 than in 1983 according to their kind of connection with French territory (French enterprise groups/foreign enterprise groups) and to their degree of freedom *vis à vis* their national territory (independent French enterprises/French enterprise groups). These changes are in favor of hypothesizing higher rivalries and splits *within* French productive system.

The trade relations of foreign groups with their country of origin suggest that if a globalization process is on, the so-called «national base» still plays a central role in merchandise flows, and therefore in value added transfers, because those transfers are mainly in favor of the country of origin. But the notion of national base has to be revisited. Firstly we have to include the role of States with certain of their essential functions (concerning exchange rate, financing, education-training and information).

Moreover, the significant contrast between commercial and manufacturing plants leads us to take into consideration the different geographical structures of the various components of this base (financial, informational, productive, commercial...). The crossing of the contrasts between the company's employment levels and trade balances have to be questioned in this sense, as should also be the different contributions to value added according to the nationalities of the enterprise groups and activity sectors. This should mainly be related with the raise of « informational revolution » and of international inter-linkages.

In connection, according to the nationality of the various enterprise groups, the value added transfers between France and other countries by the USA multinationals do not follow the same pattern as those by the Japanese or those by the German ones, who challenge the US-groups worldwide-leadership. The enterprise groups from «intermediate» countries, comparable to France, have other different patterns.

At this stage, globalization process seems far to be uniform and linear. On the contrary, it appears composed of «external» oppositions (between countries) and of «internal» ones (between types of the units of the French productive system). In answer to economic policy incentives and to the overall globalization, it seems that the different kinds of units reacted by reinforcing their past opposite trends. But the overall effects on growth –weak growth–, on resources development and on inside distortions within French enterprises system is to be evaluated, including financial operation, and questions on the limits to that kind of globalization.

REFERENCES

Banque de France (1993),"*La balance des paiements et la position extérieure de la France*", rapport annuel, Ministère de l'économie et des finances et Banque de France, + separated table for year 1982 to 1993,.

Barraux Jacques (1997), *Entreprises et performance globale. Outils, évaluation, pilotage*, Commissariat Général du Plan-Economica, Paris.

Boccara Frédéric (1997), *"Facts and Myths in employment and SME growth: the role of enterprise groups (1984-1992)"*, Documents de Travail de la Direction des Statistiques d'Entreprises, n° 9711, Insee.

Boccara Paul (1973*), Études sur le Capitalisme Monopoliste d'État : sa crise et son issue*, Editions Sociales.

Boccara Paul (1978-79), *"Travaux statistiques sur le système productif français et théorie des facteurs de la crise"*, Issues, n° 1, p. 5-82 and n° 2, p. 67-142.

Boccara Paul (1985), *Intervenir dans les gestions avec de nouveaux critères*, Messidor/ Editions Sociales.

Boccara Paul (1991), *"Révolution informationnelle et débuts possibles d'un nouveau type de régulation dans un système mixte ouvert*", speech to 6th French-Japanese meeting of economy, October 1991, published in Mondes en développement n° 79/80, Bruxelles, tome 20, 1992, p.125-132.

Boccara Paul (1993), *"Débuts de la révolution informationnelle, marché et partages. Rapport ''capital/produit''*, Guerre économique et défis d'une nouvelle régulation", Issues n°45, p. 140-157.

Chabanas Nicole, Thollon-Pommerol Vincent (1991), *"Place des groupes dans l'économie française"*, note méthodologique, p. 217-249, Insee résultats, n° 138-139, May.

Chabanas Nicole, Vergeaud Eric (1997), *"Le nombre de groupes d'entreprises a explosé en 15 ans"*, Insee Première, n°553, November.

Cohen Elie (1996), *La tentation hexagonale*, Fayard.

Corbel Patrick, Fréchou Hélène (1994*), "Les restructurations industrielles de 1979 à 1981"*, Insee Première, n°318, May, Insee,.

EPA (Economic Planning Agency) (1994-95), *Economic Survey of Japan*, Tokyo.

Hanoun Michel, Guerrier Gilbert (1995), *"Les échanges internes aux groupes industriels"*, Le 4 pages, n° 49, June, Sessi, Ministère de l'Industrie.

Insee (1974), *Fresque Historique du système productif*, Collections de l'Insee, n° 141, série E, n° 27.

Insee, Cepii, Douane, Dree, DP, Banque de France (1997), *"Le commerce extérieur industriel de la France, 1980-1996"*, Synthèses, n° 12-13, Insee.

Krugman Paul R., Obstfeld Maurice (1991), *International Economics: Theory and Policy*, Harper Collins Publishers Inc.

Lafay Gérard (1996), *Comprendre la mondialisation*, Economica.

Lall Sanjaya (1973), *"Transfer pricing by multinational manufacturing firms"*, Oxford Bulletin of Economics and Statistics, vol. 35, n° 3, August, p. 173-195.

Le Bas Michel (1994), *"Répartition des frais généraux dans sept groupes industriels français : une étude de la pratique"*, Revue Française de Comptabilité, n° 252, p.51-58.

Le Bris Florence (1996), *"Mondialisation industrielle : le rôle des filiales de commerce de gros des pays étrangers"*, Insee Première, n° 485, September, Insee.

Milewski Françoise (1989), *Le commerce extérieur de la France*, La Découverte.

Oecd (1996), *Economic Outlook*, OECD, Paris, December.

Parent Marie-Christine (1995), *"Stratégie d'implantation régionale, nationale ou internationale : quelle influence sur le développement des entreprises françaises"*, Economie et Statistique, n° 290, October, Insee, p 3-15.

Quélennec Michel, Mathieu Edouard (1997), *"Industrial Establishments Abroad and Exports"*, DSTI Document, n° DSTI/EAS/IND/SWP(97)18, OECD October Session on Globalisation, OECD.

Reich Robert (1991), *The Work of Nations: Preparing Ourselves for 21st Century*, Alfred A. Knopf, Inc. New-York.

Richard Jacques, Simons Pascal, Bailly Jean-Michel (1987), *Comptabilité et analyse financière des groupes*, Economica.

Ruigrok Winfried, Van Tulder Rob (1995), *The Logic of International Restructuring*, Routledge, London.

Sally Razeen (1995), *States and Firms - Multinational Enterprises in Institutional Competition*, Routledge, London and New-York.

Storper Michael, Salais Robert (1997), *Worlds of Production: The Action Framework of the Economy*, Harvard University Press, French edition in 1993, Cambridge Mass.

Thollon-Pommerol Vincent (1990), *"Les groupes et la déformation du système productif"*, Economie et Statistique, n° 229, p. 21-28, Insee.

Thollon-Pommerol Vincent (1996), *"Données de cadrage sur les groupes"*, Speech to the Sixth congress of National Accounting, Paris, 24-25-26 January, Insee, Paris 1.

Vernon Raymond (1971), *Sovereignty at Bay*, Basic Books.

Williamson Oliver E. (1985), *The Economic Institutions of Capitalism*, The Free Press, MacMillan, New-York.

ENTERPRISE GROUP: THE FRENCH METHODOLOGY AND RESULTS

Vincent Thollon-Pommerol

INSEE

This study is divided in three parts. The first one presents the main concepts, especially those about the statistical units, and the data used in the study. In the second, I will present the main statistical results about the enterprise groups during the years 1980-1995. In the last one, I will expose a methodology about continuity of enterprise group and comment the first results.

1 Concepts and origins of data

1.1 Concepts

The statistical units used in the study and, generally, in the French statistics proceed from the European regulation. The two used here are the enterprise and the enterprise group.

The enterprise is considered as identical to the legal unit (incorporate or unincorporate). This is not according to the regulation. In some cases, the regulation lays down that several legal units must be consolidated to form the enterprise.

The enterprise group is a set of enterprises controlled by the «head of group». The head is a legal unit and must remain uncontrolled by any other one. But she must control at least one other legal unit. So, the case where several legal units are owned by the same shareholders is excluded. The uncontrolled enterprises are excluded too; they do not form an enterprise group by themselves. In general, control results from holding, directly or indirectly, the majority of voting rights. In some cases, consolidated accounts show control in spite of minority of voting rights. The concept of statistical enterprise group is close at hand of the concept of «accounting group» defined by the regulation about consolidated accounts. The European regulation about statistical units quote clearly the accounting regulation to define the statistical group. The main difference (between statistical an accounting group) is that, in case of succession of consolidation, only the highest level is taken into account..

In practice, it is hardly difficult for statisticians to collect all the necessary inquiries. In France, we collect reliable data only about the subset of French enterprises. So, we compute statistics about «truncated group». In the study, we will speak of «group» instead of «truncated group».

1.2 Data used

The data required for computing areas of group are gathered by a statistical survey. The surveyed enterprises, in general, hold a large amount of shares of others companies. The threshold was 4 millions of Francs in 1979, for the first survey. It is 8 millions of Francs since 1981. Since 1985, all enterprises over 500 employees are surveyed, whatever amount of shares they hold. So, about 400 enterprise groups appeared in 1985 for this reason. Moreover, to ensure quality, all the head of group are surveyed the next year.

Economic data about enterprises are collected both by the profit tax formality (income statement and balance sheet) and an annual survey (income statement and fuller information, especially about industries). The administrative data are checked by the statisticians. For the largest enterprises (about 100000), the common data are harmonized. For the others, only administrative data are used in this study.

Data about group are obtained by using data of the enterprises of their area. So, the data are reliable only for «additive» data like employment, value added, gross operating surplus, fixed assets. Others are only «proxy» (turnover, liabilities).

2 Results about enterprise groups

2.1 Number of groups

The main information is that the number of groups increased from 1980 to 1995. The growth is very quick since 1991 (fig. 1).

Figure 1 The bursting out of the number of groups

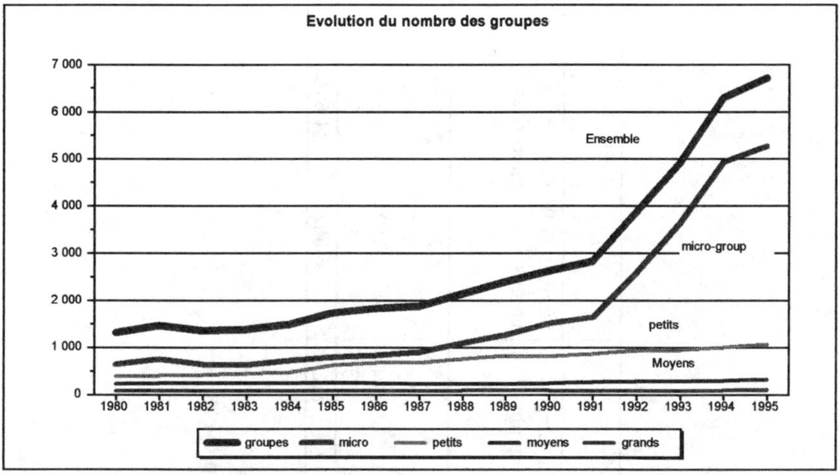

Evolution du nombre des groupes

Origin : «liaisons financières» survey, INSEE

The main part of this growth comes from the smallest group (less than 500 employees). But the number of groups from 500 to 2000 employees was twice in 1995 than in 1980. The growth is 70 for the groups from 2000 to 10000 employees. On contrary, the number of groups over 10000 employees remains at the same level.

In 1995, the 6700 groups controlled less than 3% of the French enterprises. But they employed half of the wage-earners (6,1 millions), producing 60% of value added and own 75% of fixed assets. The largest ones, over 10000 employees, own half of fixed assets, produce half of gross operating surplus and employ a quarter of the workers of the French enterprises.

During the same years, the number of controlled enterprises increased in the same proportion. This growth is partly due to the number of groups. But the other part comes from the average number of controlled enterprises (table 1).

Table 1 Number of groups by size class

	1980			1989			1995 (preliminary results)		
	number of groups	number of enterprises	average number of enterprises	number of groups	number of enterprises	average number of enterprises	number of groups	number of enterprises	average number of enterprises
Micro-groups*	627	1 966	3,1	1 230	4 524	3,6	5 279	20 019	3,8
Small groups*	383	1 791	4,7	820	4 488	5,5	1 027	7 816	7,6
Medium groups*	223	2 443	11,0	241	3 461	14,4	292	6 351	21,8
Large groups*	73	2 987	40,9	92	6 949	75,5	84	10 500	125,0
Total	**1306**	**9 187**	**7,0**	**2 383**	**19 422**	**8,2****	**6 682**	**44 686**	**7,1****

Origin : «liaisons financières» survey, INSEE

*Micro-group : less than 500 employees - Small group : from 500 to 1 999 employees
Medium group : from 2 000 to 9 999 employees - large group : over 10 000

2.2The enterprises of the groups

The main consequence is that the share of employment inside the groups increased for all the size classes (fig. 2).

Figure 2 The number of employees in France increases with the size of the enterprise and over years

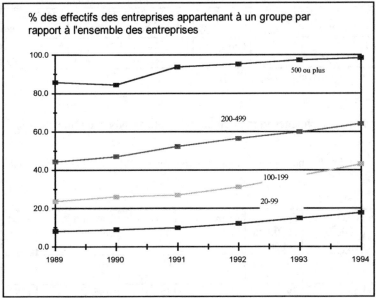

Origin : «liaisons financières» survey, INSEE

The table 2 gives additional results by analyzing the change of the number of enterprises by size of the enterprise and size of the group from 1981 to 1995. We compute also the data about the uncontrolled enterprises. Italic numbers are those of 1981; the others are of 1995.

Table 2 : Number of enterprises inside the areas of the groups in 1981 and 1995

Groups Enterprises	Over 10000 employees	2000 to 10000	500 to 2000	Less than 500	Uncontrolled enterprises	Part of the uncontrolled
20-99	2135 650	1433 624	2024 440	5205 609	57134 59039	84% 96%
100-199	739 281	533 246	731 204	1251 207	4044 5405	55% 85%
200-500	693 370	534 276	673 262	771 190	1304 2733	33% 71%
Over 500	788 610	514 443	660 321	0 0	130 828	6% 38%

Origin : «liaisons financières» survey, INSEE

The table 3 shows the changes in the number of employees for the same classes.

Table 3 Change in the number of employees between 1981 and 1995 (thousands employees)

Groups Enterprises	Over 10000 employees	From 2000 to 10000	From 500 to 2000	Less than 500	Uncontrolled enterprises	Total
From 20 to 99 employees	70	39	75	209	-183	210
From 100 to 199	64	39	75	145	-196	127
From 200 to 499	98	82	129	169	-380	98
Over 500	344	-131	285	0	-1372	-874
Total	576	29	564	523	-2131	-439

Origin : «liaisons financières» survey, INSEE

The table «shows» :
a) -the enterprises over 500 employees loosed 874000 employees
    -the enterprises from 20 to 500 employees won 435000
b) -groups and uncontrolled enterprises over 500 employees loosed 203000 employees
    -groups and uncontrolled enterprises from 20 to 500 loosed 236000 employees.

One knows, since the study of Davis and Haltiwanger that these figures do not mean that some class size created or destroyed more jobs than others. For France, from 1981 to 1995, the conclusions would depend on the used statistical unit.

On contrary, it is right to say that less workers work in a large enterprise (over 500 employees) in 1995 than in 1981 and that less workers have a job in a large group or a large uncontrolled enterprise (over 500 employees), but the decrease is smaller for enterprise groups than for enterprises.

2.3 Foreign groups in France and French groups in foreign countries

Among the 6160 private groups in 1994, the head group of 1400 was a foreign enterprise. They were only 600 in 1981. These 1400 heads groups control 6444 enterprises. They produce 14% of the value added of the groups and employ more than one million of workers.

In 1995, the most important countries are Netherlands, UK, USA, Germany and Switzerland. They concentrate 80% of the enterprises and employment under foreign control. The US groups (300000 employees) are more important than the Netherlands one's (200000 employees). Many holdings are located in Netherlands because of the fiscal policy.

The feint public or private groups increased their influence on the foreign countries. They have 6900 direct foreign subsidiaries in 1995 but only 3900 in 1981. The census of foreign investments conducted by the «Direction des Relations économiques extérieures» show that French enterprise groups control about 16000 foreign enterprises, employing about 2,4 millions workers

Largest is the group, largest is the number of foreign subsidiary. On an average, in the largest groups (over 10000 employees), one of five subsidiary is a foreign one. For the smallest, the figure is one of ten. Only one smallest group for four control a foreign enterprise. The top ten countries concentrate two of three employees. The top five (USA, UK, Germany, Spanish, Belgium) is half of the whole.

3 Continuity of enterprise group

3.1 Basic concept

Many statistics and studies need that the rules of continuity of the statistical units be clearly defined and applied. For instance, to compute relevant statistics instead of tables 2 and 3, one must have the trajectories of the enterprises groups and know the demographic events, like birth by splitting an existing enterprise, death by control. So, preliminary studies were conducted in France in 1988.

The initial idea, identify the continuity of the group from the continuity of the controlled enterprise was quickly left. The grouping organization allow to recombine the plants inside new enterprises: in a group, the enterprises change but not the group. The rules of continuity of French enterprises were not suitable. Fortunately, some years ago, the same question was solved for the local unit. To sum up, the results distinguished large and small local units. For the last, the goodwill was used. Continuity of the goodwill involved continuity of the local unit. For the others, the continuity was connected with the jobs.

The common ideas seem to be the link between the continuity of the unit and the supply to the customers. So, we tried to judge of the group's continuity by the continuity of the products and activities.

A first study was drawn up on the years 1981 to 1987. The group was continuous if or the activities employing half of the total employment of the group, or the activities employing three quarters remain identically during two years. The results seemed enough conclusive so that the method has been introduced in the software of the application in 1993.

3.2 Empirical results

The table 4 shows the results for the experimental study (over the years 1981-1987) and the preliminary results on the years 1993-1994 of the new software. The figures distinguish the continuous and discontinuous groups, the new groups in «n» (birth) and the groups of «n-1» not founded in «n» (death).

Table 4 Number of continuous and discontinuous groups

	Continuous	Discontinuous	«Birth»	«Death»
1981-1982	1032	67	186	271
1982-1983	1005	61	234	219
1983-1984	1028	58	281	214
1984-1985	945	56	682	366
1985-1986	1362	108	249	213
1986-1987	1394	77	297	248
1993-1994	3697	528	2057	525

Origin : «Liaisons financières» survey, INSEE

Over the years 1981-1987, the rate of discontinuity is not high (about 6% a year) The (apparent) rate of birth and death are higher. To compare these results with those of 1993-1994 is not obvious. The total number of groups is very different, because of the increase of the number of micro-groups (less than 500 employees). In particular, one sees that the rate of births in 1994 is widely over the rate of the years 1986-1987 (57% vs. 20%). In the same way, the rate of discontinuity is higher in the recent than in the past years (12,5% vs. 6%). on the contrary, the rate of deaths remain equal (16,2% vs. 14,4%).

A plausible hypothesis to explain the rate of discontinuity in the recent years is to link this rate with the rate of birth of the previous year and assume that it needs two surveys to check the right area of a group. For instance, one can see that in 1986 the rate of discontinuity is higher than these of the near years. Simultaneously, the rate of births in 1985 is higher because all the large enterprises were surveyed for the first time. The results by size classes (tab. 5) corroborate the hypothesis. If the area of the group is not perfect, the consequences on the discontinuity are the same than if the group modified its activities.

Table 5 Breakdown of the number of groups by size class

	Continuous	Discontinuous	«Birth»	«Death»
Total	3697	528	2057	525
Less than 500 employees	2572	451	1885	584
From 500 to 2000	803	55	147	104
From 2000 to 10000	249	19	22	10
Over 10000	73	3	3	3

Origin : «Liaisons financières» survey, INSEE

The rate of discontinuity decreases from 15% for the micro-groups to 3,5% for the largest. the rate is about 6,5% for the small and medium groups..

4 Final remarks

The statistical appliance about the enterprise groups is running since 1979. It allows the statisticians to follow the development of this organization of business. Studies use this unit successfully. Using administrative data may increase quality about foreign implantation (from France to foreign countries and foreign countries to France).

Continuity of enterprise group needs some more experiments. If the basic idea (linking continuity of group and continuity of his activities) seems relevant, it is not possible to compute the indicator only with an automatic algorithm, but necessary to check the results by a clerk. For the largest groups, discontinuity has a very low probability. It seems also possible to assume the continuity of a recent group, because it seems difficult to secure the area of the group the first year.

REFERENCES

"Les entreprises petites et moyennes: croissance et atouts", Économie et Statistique, n° 271-272, numéro spécial, INSEE, 1994.

Boccara F.,*"Mythes et réalités sur l'emploi et la croissance des PME* : le rôle des groupes (1984-1992)"*, Document de travail, E9702, INSEE, 1997.

Hecquet V. et Lainé F.,*"Inscription territoriale des groupes et identité des systèmes productifs locaux"*, Document de travail, E9705/H9701, INSEE, 1997.

INSEE, *Observer et représenter un monde de plus en plus complexe - Un défi pour la statistique d'entreprises* , coll. "INSEE Méthodes", n° 54, juin 1996.

INSEE, *Place des groupes dans l'économie française*, coll. "INSEE Résultats", n°138-139, série "Système productif", n° 41-42, 1991.

INSEE, *Répertoire des entreprises contrôlées majoritairement par l'État au 31/12/1995*, coll. "INSEE Résultats", n°517, série "Système productif", n° 124, 1997.

La présence des entreprises françaises dans le monde, DREE-Résultats, février 1995.

Thollon-Pommerol V.,*"Les groupes et la déformation du système statistique"*, , Economie et Statistique, n° 229, INSEE, 1990.

INTEGRATION OF INFORMATION IN ENTERPRISE GROUPS

Andrea Carone

ISTAT, Istituto Nazionale di Statistica

In the economic research, both theoretical and applied, the role of 'enterprise group' as such is recently being appreciated; the group is intended as a set of enterprises joined together, in the exercise of their production activities, by the reference to the same top management of decision and control, i.e. the subject where entrepreneurial activities can be intended as centralised.

As a matter of fact, relational structures of control between enterprises determine economic subjects that go beyond the juridical borders of legal units; such entities take shape when the productive resources of more enterprises are grouped under the management of the same entrepreneurial subject, physical person or public body; apart this, enterprises are independent units or part of a group of units.

Enterprises tend to form groups for several motivations: to create an internal financial system in order to exercise control with limited resources (hierarchical structure), fiscal reasons, visibility on the market, diversification and flexibility, limitation of responsibilities, incentives to management, publicity, co-operation with external subjects, distribution of management, incentives to management, raising of resources.

It is well-known that enterprises tend more easily to be part of a group when they are large; precisely, the proportion of group enterprises grows with the size of the enterprise (from one-forth to two-thirds going from: 50-99 employees to: over one thousand).

A. Carone

Figure 1 Proportion of group enterprises by employment size-class, all sectors (Source: Istat)

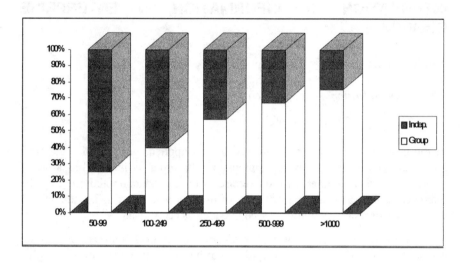

Even small enterprises (in terms of employment) are important for group structures; holdings and other important units, in which some services activities of the group are centralised, usually are small enterprises.

The (hierarchic) group of enterprises can be defined, for statistical purposes, as a set of juridically independent enterprises that are subject to the –direct or indirect– control of a unique 'vertex', the physical or public body that is at the summit of the hierarchic structure of control; the 'holdings' are enterprises at the top of the hierarchy of control and are directly controlled by the vertex (that is not an enterprise). The indirect control is exercised through chains of controlled units.

The organisational pattern of the group evolves the model of multi-divisional large enterprise; the organised set of enterprises is assimilable to an unique economic actor. Even if constituted by a multitude of subjects, often juridically independent, the enterprise group appears as the reference economic agent, the analysis unit, that is derivable by the observation entities (juridical enterprises); in fact such plurality of enterprises forms a whole, with coherent and unitary behaviour (economic enterprise), that is relevant as such. The legal units could therefore be consolidated into groups, to be considered as the economic agents, and the analysis of the structure of the productive system would reveal much higher concentration.

Interest for surveying group structures raised, at Istat, during the co-operation with Eurostat at the production of data for the analysis of globalisation, as well as in view of setting-up a business register (ASIA) that shall also comprehend information about the relationships between its units, especially in terms of ownership and control.

Exhaustive and systematic group data are not yet available but, apart some surveys carried out by Istat and other organisations, there are some administrative sources, namely UIC (foreign currency exchange authority) and CONSOB (body that ensures the transparency of the operations of societies in the stock market), useful to build-up and maintain a statistical archive of enterprise groups; Central Bank covers banking sector; in order to control operations of societies linked to the stock market, CONSOB keeps a database with very detailed information, about relations and structures of ownership and control, for the population of enterprises 'close to the stock market'. As to control external trade, UIC records a set of data about transactions with foreign counterparts that could feed an information system on enterprise groups, especially for that concerns multi-national groups and relations with foreign countries. Other sources (antitrust authority, balance sheets, databanks..) are under analysis in view of their utilisation for a database from integrated inputs.

A collaboration with Eurostat (FATS project, Foreign Affiliates Trade Statistics) showed the feasibility of the integration -within data available at Istat and with other external sources- of data on enterprise groups as to obtain acceptable levels of information: a first dataset (domain: enterprises with more than 50 persons employed in the services trade sectors), for which only in 14% of the cases the information concerning inclusion into groups and -if so- the localisation of the vertex was initially available, has been integrated by data from Istat surveys and from UIC raising the percentage of coverage to 73% (data from CONSOB were not yet available); unfortunately at the moment it was not possible to include any kind of information for about 10% of the resident units.

Table 1a shows the initial distribution of the concerned enterprises by the location of their vertex (that controls them):

Table 1.a Number of enterprises by location of ultimate control-vertex-group head, Italy 1994: enterprises with 50+ persons employed

Sector\Control	N.A.	ITALY	EU	EXTRA-EU	TOTAL
Trade & horeca	**1635**	**224.5**	**28**	**9.5**	**1897**
Vehicles and fuel trade	111	16.0	3	0.0	130
Wholesale	777	96.0	18	6.0	897
Retail & horeca	747	112.5	7	3.5	870
Transport & Communications	**625**	**63.0**	**2**	**4.0**	**694**
Hearth transport	217	17.0	0	0.0	234
Water transport	52	8.0	0	0.0	60
Air transport	338	35.0	2	4.0	379
Communications	18	3.0	0	0.0	21
Real estate & other services	**914**	**151.0**	**16**	**10.0**	**1091**
Real estate & renting	15	3.0	2	0.0	20
Information services and R&D	182	35.0	8	2.0	227
Other	717	113.0	6	8.0	844
TOTAL	**3174**	**438.5**	**46**	**23.5**	**3682**

source: ISTAT, 'n.a.'=not available

Note: decimals are due to the treatment of the joint venture.

After the process of integration of information about enterprise groups with other sources(data resulting from the business register updating surveys, from the R&D surveys and UIC data) we obtained a remarkable reduction of the weigh of the column containing enterprises for which control is not allocated('N.A.'); even is not yet satisfying, the results suggest this is a promising direction(Table 1b):

Table 1.b Number of enterprises by location of ultimate control-vertex-group head, Italy 1994: enterprises with 50+ persons employed

Sector\Control	N.A.	ITA	EU	EXTRA-EU	TOTAL
Trade & horeca	**513**	**1137.5**	**148**	**98.5**	**1897**
Vehicles and fuel trade	25	80.0	18	7.0	130
Wholesale	152	558.0	106	81.0	897
Retail & horeca	336	499.5	24	10.5	870
Transport & Communications	**205**	**465.0**	**15**	**9.0**	**694**
Hearth transport	82	152.0	0	0.0	234
Water transport	8	50.0	2	0.0	60
Air transport	109	248.0	13	9.0	379
Communications	6	15.0	0	0.0	21
Real estate & other services	**273**	**762.0**	**31**	**25.0**	**1091**
Real estate & renting	7	8.0	3	2.0	20
Information services and R&D	43	164.0	13	7.0	227
Other	223	590.0	15	16.0	844
TOTAL	**991**	**2364.5**	**194**	**132.5**	**3682**

source: ISTAT

Note: decimals are due to the treatment of the joint venture.

Interest for this kind of tables arises for evaluating the so-called 'establishment trade' that is the evaluation of the commercial presence of a country A in another, say B, by means of affiliates, that are enterprises in B of a group whose control is located out of that country B, in country A; from the point of view of a given country, 'inward' and 'outward' establishment trade can be distinguished: the former relates to the activities of national resident enterprises that are controlled by foreign subjects, the latter relates to the activities of foreign units that are controlled by national agents. This happens through the multinational groups, comprehending enterprises resident in different countries, not only for which it is relevant to distinguish commercial flows between affiliates, mainly related to the internationalisation of the production economy, by other flows. The globalisation of the production organisation modifies the delimitation of the 'national' enterprises system, depending on how 'nationality' (residence or control) is meant.

The phenomena of the groups becomes very important when considering the services sectors, for which production and consumption are usually only possible 'in loco'; in such cases the main way (often the only one) to reach an external market is to establish a 'commercial presence' (as it is called in the GATS agreements) where necessary through foreign affiliates. These considerations become important, when considering e.g. economic policies towards enterprises, as the decisors could be placed out of the national territory; part of this de-localisation of enterprises control is of course apparent because legal units formally place their holding enterprises (even if still 'national') in fiscal off-shore islands.

Some economic variables were requested by Eurostat in order to produce figures for the evaluation of establishment trade at UE15 level; these data became necessary for monitoring the GATS agreement and, apart EUROSTAT, are also requested by UN international bodies as WTO, IMF, UNCTAD. For this reason, an ad-hoc group has been set-up and jointly supervised by OECD and EUROSTAT involving these organisations and the single countries with the aim of drawing directives for the statistical collections of such kind of data.

We report some of the tables have been produced to give the idea of the information that is obtainable through the technique of linkages (data have been linked to the results of the SCI survey, enterprises economic accounts data, and to data stored in the SIRIO-NAI business register); inward establishment trade data are compiled by allocating the whole values of the variables of an enterprise to the location where its control is situated (excepting joint ventures, see below). The choice to attribute the entire values, i.e. the measurements of activity, to the location of control is in line with the concept of control, intended as the control of all (or nearly) the relevant activities of the enterprise.

Dimensional variables as the number of local units, turnover and employment, are derivable from the business register for the units concerned in the previous table:

Table 2 Number of local units by location of ultimate control-vertex-group head, Italy 1994: enterprises with 50+ persons employed

Sector\Control	N.A.	ITALY	EU	EXTRA-EU	TOTAL
Trade & horeca	**2095**	**4804**	**701**	**375**	**7975**
Vehicles and fuel trade	88	305	68	25	486
Wholesale	523	1930	372	293	3118
Retail & horeca	1484	2569	261	57	4371
Transport & Communications	**637**	**1779**	**153**	**336**	**2905**
Hearth transport	309	835	0	0	1144
Water transport	.	94	.	0	128
Air transport	.	788	.	336	1555
Communications	16	62	0	0	78
Real estate & other services	**614**	**2034**	**108**	**60**	**2816**
Real estate & renting	15	74	.	.	126
Information services and R&D	136	598	.	.	793
Other	463	1362	34	38	1897
TOTAL	**3346**	**8617**	**962**	**771**	**13696**

source: ISTAT, '.'=confidential data

Geographical information about these local units is available from the business register; a territorial analysis of the foreign commercial presence would therefore be possible.

When considering the distribution of employment figures, one could see that, even if considering only available data (which weigh is quite low in some sectors) nearly one third of the workers in sector 'Wholesale' are employed in units controlled by foreign subjects; it could be important when, e.g., considering economic politicies.

Table 3 Number of persons employed by location of ultimate control-vertex-group head, Italy 1994: enterprises with 50+ persons employed

Sector\Control	N.A.	ITALY	EU	EXTRA-EU	TOTAL
Trade & horeca	**147984**	**149048.5**	**35935**	**22685.5**	**355653**
Vehicles and fuel trade	2309	6513.0	4072	1118.0	14012
Wholesale	14268	63486.0	15505	15632.0	108891
Retail & horeca	131407	79049.5	16358	5935.5	232750
Transport & Communications	**312594**	**365513.0**	**5140**	**11282.0**	**694529**
Hearth transport	195482	67534.0	0	0.0	263016
Water transport	.	15359.0	.	0.0	18362
Air transport	.	70037.0	.	11282.0	101840
Communications	98728	212583.0	0	0.0	311311
Real estate & other services	**48920**	**129284.0**	**7913**	**4893.0**	**191010**
Real estate & renting	834	956.0	.	.	2675
Information services and R&D	5373	30512.0	.	.	41842
Other	42713	97816.0	2647	3317.0	146493
TOTAL	**509498**	**643845.5**	**48988**	**38860.5**	**1241192**

source: ISTAT,'.'=confidential data

Note: decimals are due to the treatment of the joint venture.

As mentioned, these 'foreign' subjects could even be Italian themselves, placed in fiscal offshore islands; data about turnover are even more remarkable:

Table 4 Turnover ('000000 £), Italy 1994: enterprises with 50+ persons employed

Sector\Control	N.A.	ITALY	EU	EXTRA-EU	TOTAL
Trade & horeca	49712130	114732538	43596753	26891930	234933351
Vehicles and fuel trade	1930609	3934181	13516578	5427174	24808542
Wholesale	11623272	89176612	25687688	20036611	146524183
Retail & horeca	36158249	21621745	4392487	1428145	63600626
Transport & Communications	43130270	36205940	2361812	4628641	86326663
Hearth transport	9482861	2527228	0	0	12010089
Water transport	.	4212349	.	0	5548144
Air transport	.	18009073	.	4628641	28005784
Communications	29305356	11457290	0	0	40762646
Real estate & other services	4004726	16266165	2015588	1411637	23698116
Real estate & renting	201722	227118	.	.	788054
Information services and R&D	894429	5562187	.	.	7928919
Other	2908575	10476860	692234	903474	14981143
TOTAL	96847126	167204643	47974153	32932208	344958130

source: ISTAT,,'.'=confidential data

It can be noticed that (covering only available data) nearly 60% of the turnover in sector NACE 50 (vehicles and fuel trade) is due to non national EU-controlled enterprises, while 23% is to be related to subjects external to EU; totally 83% of the turnover of medium-large enterprises in Italy is generated by foreign-controlled enterprises.

Considering investments figures, still covering only available data, nearly 50% of the investments in sector NACE 50 (vehicles and fuel trade) is due to foreign EU-controlled enterprises, while 20% is to be related to subjects external to EU; totally, 70% of (such a strategic variable as) investments in this sector is generated by foreign-controlled enterprises.

Even if the overall weigh of the first column is still too large, for few services sectors (as vehicles and wholesale, for which the weigh of control not allocated is 10-15%) it is already clear the heavy commercial presence of other countries in Italy.

Table 5 Investments ('000000 £), Italy 1994: enterprises with 50+ persons employed

Sector\Control	N.A.	ITALY	EU	EXTRA-EU	TOTAL
Trade & horeca	**908619**	**1446369**	**374950**	**316231**	**3046169**
Vehicles and fuel trade	14840	40900	65162	26576	147478
Wholesale	119810	762749	218553	248766	1349878
Retail & horeca	773969	642720	91235	40889	1548813
Transport & Communications	**13062287**	**2716077**	**58290**	**341709**	**16178363**
Hearth transport	4330507	484948	0	0	4815455
Water transport	.	374839	.	0	415490
Air transport	.	1782845	.	341709	2603984
Communications	8269989	73445	0	0	8343434
Real estate & other services	**211749**	**568116**	**250510**	**44563**	**1074938**
Real estate & renting	116246	119333	.	.	452906
Information services and R&D	33801	305298	.	.	399227
Other	61702	143485	6352	11266	222805
TOTAL	**14182655**	**4730562**	**683750**	**702503**	**20299470**

source: ISTAT,'.'=confidential data

It can be noticed that there are decimal values for variables that usually show integer figures (e.g. persons employed, number of enterprises); this comes out by the treatment of joint ventures that has been agreed at the FATS task force meetings in Luxembourg; when there is a joint venture (the capital of an enterprise is equally owned by two subjects) which investors reside in different countries, there is the problem of allocation of that enterprise's figures; the solution has been found is to split the values and allocate 50% of them to the areas concerned[1]. This is just an example of the methodological points arising in the debate about the groups statistics.

As to show data that could be obtained through linkage techniques, some figures could be produced in order to focus, e.g., different variables on single sectors:

---

[1] Statistics on ownership of enterprises can also be considered; in this case, the attribution to the country where a given percentage of direct ownership is located could equal this percentage.

Table 6 Italy 1994: Wholesale sector, enterprises with 50+ persons employed

Sector: "Wholesale"	TOTAL	N.A.	ITALY	EU	EXTRA-EU
Enterprises	897	152	558	106	81
Employment	108891	14268	63486	15505	15632
Employees	107586	14009	62648	15382	15547
Turnover	146524183	11623272	89176612	25687688	20036611
Investments	1349878	119810	762749	218553	248766
Local units	3118	523	1930	372	293
Value added	12412723	1372656	6183306	2299725	2557036
Labour cost	7258322	846106	3743253	1262315	1406648
...					

source: ISTAT

After this positive experience, Istat is evaluating to build-up an archive, systematically updated, that comprehends this kind of information; this choice is in line with the current orientation of Istat strategy for business statistics, that is to relate all the information about enterprises processed in the institute to the harmonised business register, established in conformity to UE regulations; an experiment for setting-up an archive of enterprise groups in Italy is therefore undergoing at Istat; such information is with the business register ASIA.

A working group on enterprise groups, globalisation and related issues is being established at Istat; the first aim is to set-up a theorical coherent system to be at the base of data production strategies and to work with already available data in order to focus crucial points and problems, the goal is to establish a statistical system enabled to produce consistent figures about enterprise groups; at this stage, we are looking for flexible definitions in order to be able to say if an enterprise is part of a group and, if so, the location of its control. It follows the monitoring of the system of relations between enterprises in view of consolidating the single groups.

Even the only information about being or not part of a group already appears to be a strong classification factor: the distributions (sectoral, dimensional) of the units differ when considering the two sub-populations of enterprises (independent vs grouped); further, in the same sector and dimensional size-class, the basic economic parameters (turnover or value added per head) appear to behave differently.

In conclusion, if in a coherent conceptual frame, it seems possible to build-up and maintain an information system on enterprise groups by the integration of statistical data and signals from administrative sources; all the advantages of an available business register could then be exploited.

REFERENCES

Barca F. (1994) *"Imprese in cerca di padrone. Proprietà e controllo nel capitalismo italiano"*, Bari, Laterza.

Barca F. (1995*) "Informare o disinformare: la teoria dell'impresa di Milgrom e Roberts"*, (estratto) Jovene editore, Napoli.

Barca F., Bianco M., Cannari, Cesari, Gola, Manitta, Salvo, Signorini (1994) *"Assetti proprietari e mercato delle imprese, vol.I: Proprietà, modelli di controllo e riallocazione nelle imprese industriali italiane"*, Bologna, Il Mulino.

Barca F., Bianco M., Brioschi F., Buzzacchi L., Casavola P., Filippa L., Pagnini M. (1994) *"Assetti proprietari e mercato delle imprese, vol.II: gruppo, proprietà e conttrollo nelle imprese italiane medio-grandi"*, Bologna, Il Mulino.

Barca F., Casavola, Perassi (1994) *"Controllo e gruppo: natura economica e tutela giuridica"*, in Banca d'Italia, Il mercato della proprietà e del controllo delle imprese: aspetti teorici e istituzionali.

Bianco M. (1994) *"Il controllo nella 'public company'*, in Banca d'Italia, Il mercato della proprietà e del controllo delle imprese: aspetti teorici e istituzionali."

Bianco M., Signorini (1994) *"Evoluzione degli assetti di controllo: gli investitori istituzionali"*, Banca d'Italia, dattiloscritto.

Bleek E. (1991): *'The way to win in cross-border alliances'*, Harvard business review,11/1991.

Boccara F. (1997) *"Facts and myths in employment and SME growth, the role of enterprises groups (1984-1992)"* Documento di lavoro E9702 INSEE, France.

Boccara F. (1998) *"The role of French and foreign enterprise groups in the French Productive system internationalisation"*, Documento di lavoro INSEE, France.

Brioschi, F. (1990) *"Il capitalismo collusivo"*, in 'Micromega', n.3.

Brioschi F., Buzzacchi L., Colombo G.(1990) *"Gruppi di imprese e mercato finanziario"*, Roma, La Nuova Italia Scientifica.

Buzzacchi L., Colombo G. (1994), *"Gruppi di imprese e proprietà"*, in Politica economica a. X, n° 2, agosto 1994.

Centrale dei Bilanci (1992) *"Economia e finanza delle imprese italiane"*, Milano, Il Sole 24 Ore.

Codice Civile (art.2359 sulle società controllate e collegate, art.2435 bis sul consolidamento di bilancio).

Cominotti R., Mariotti S. (1996) *"Italia Multinazionale 1996"*, ricerca del CNEL, VI Rapporto R&P al Consiglio Nazionale dell'Economia e del Lavoro, F.Angeli.

Committeri M. (1991) *"La posizione relativa dell'Italia nell'attività mondiale d'investimento diretto"*, Banca d'Italia, n.5, dattiloscritto.

Eurostat (1995) *"Manuale di raccomandazioni per i registri di imprese"*, quaderni 1-18, D3, Luxembourg.

Eurostat (1996) *"European System of Accounts"* ESA 1995, Luxembourg.

Eurostat (1997) *'Globalisation reflection group: documents'*, Eurostat 1997.

Eurostat (1997) *"Legal text relating to the European business statistical system"*, Luxembourg.

Eurostat (1997): *'FATS data collection guidelines'*, v.1.1 Eurostat 1997.

Gazzetta Ufficiale delle Comunità Europee (IV e VII direttive CEE, def. di 'gruppo di imprese' G.U. del 30/3/1993, acquisizione del controllo G.U. 31/12/1994, Concentrazione).

Goto, A. (1982) *"Business Groups in a market economy"*, in 'European economic review.

Grossman S., Hart O. (1986) *"The costs and benefits of ownership: A theory of vertical and lateral integration"*, in 'Journal of Political Economy', vol.94, n.4.

Hannoun M., Guerrier G. (1993) *"Les èchanges intragroupes dans la mondialisation industrielle"* Sessi 1993.

Hart, Moore, J. (1990) *"Property rigths and the nature of the firm"*, in 'Journal of Political Economy', vol.98, n.6.

Il Sole 24 Ore - *Mondo Economico.*

Macchiati, A. (1989*) "Le holding come intermediario finanziario. Contributo per un'analisi"*, in 'Finanza, imprese e mercati', n.1.

Marchetti P. (1992), *"Note sulla relazione di controllo nella legislazione speciale"*, Rivista delle società, 1992.

Millgrom P., Roberts, J (1992) *"Economics, Organisation and Management"*, Prentice Hall, Englewood Cliffs, NJ, Prenctice Hall.

Salvemini M.T., Bruno S., Succi R. (1995) *"Analisi del possesso integrato nei gruppi di imprese mediante grafi"* in 'l'Industria' / n.s. a. XVI, ottobre-dicembre 1995.

Tollon-Pommerol V. (1990) *"Les groupes et la dèformation du système productif"*, Economie et statistique, n°229, p.21-28 INSEE.

Tollon-Pommerol V. (1996) *"Donnès de cadrage sur les groupes"*, Communication au Sixìeme cooloque de comptabilitè nationale, Paris, 24-26 January, INSEE Paris.

Trento S. (1994) *"Il gruppo di imprese come modello di controllo nei paesi ritardatari"*, in Banca d'Italia, Il mercato della proprietà e del controllo delle imprese: aspetti teorici e istituzionali.

UN (1994) *"GATS, the general agreement on trade in services and related instruments"*

UN-UNCTAD (1996) *"World Investment Report 1996: Investment, Trade and International Policy Arrangements"* New York and Geneve, 1996.

Williamson,O.E. (1975) *"Markets and hierarchies: analysis and antitrust implications"*, Free Press, New York.

MYTHS AND REALITIES ABOUT EMPLOYMENT AND SMES IN FRANCE: THE ROLE OF ENTERPRISE GROUPS (1984-1992)[1]

Frédéric Boccara

Insee (Institut National de la Statistique et des Etudes Economiques), France.

1 Introduction

The 1980s were marked by an increase in the share of SME staff in the total workforce of the productive sector. For France, this can be seen from simple descriptive tables taken from the various statistical yearbooks, which lead us to surmise that the "turning point" came in the mid-1980s, coinciding with the mid-cycle economic upturn (around 1986). This is borne out by a number of studies bearing on data from France[2], as well as from other countries[3].

Many of these studies go beyond simply acknowledging this fact. The first wave of studies, such as Birch (1979 and 1987), coming before the criticisms formulated by Davis and Haltiwanger (1990), reach the conclusion that small units are more dynamic. They emphasize the powerhouse role of these smaller units during the 1980s, compared with larger units, echoing the "Small Is Beautiful" of a purportedly post-industrial society (Schumacher, 1973, and up to a point, Piore and Sabel, 1984). In this vein, the OECD entitled one of its studies, published in *Employment Perspectives*: "Jobs in large and small enterprises: where do they come from?" (OECD, 1985). According to the organization, national studies *"confirm the pivotal role of small local units and enterprises in job creation"*.

This conclusion implies that large units did not make a significant contribution to job creation. However, if what we mean by large units is large

---

[1] This paper is in continuity with the Insee *working paper* n° E9711 (english version).

[2] Parent-Berthier (1994), Parent (1995), Savoye, Péréa (1993), Lagarde-Maurin-Torelli (1994).

[3] For a survey of analyses from some time ago, see OECD (1985). For more recent analyses, see for instance Davis and Haltiwanger (1990) or Dunne, Roberts, Samuelson (1989) on American data, Baldwin, Picot (1995), Picot-Dupuy (1996) on Canadian data, Geoffrey-Robson (1994) or Storey, Johnson (1986) on British data, etc. Loveman and Sengenberger (1991) provide an international comparison.

enterprise groups, not just large local units or large enterprises (companies), there is a risk of misinterpretation. Development of small units has a different meaning when it takes place inside or outside enterprise groups. There is a need, therefore, to pinpoint the role of enterprise groups in the changing size of enterprises, or at least some aspects of this role. For there is no reason to believe that inside a enterprise group, there are watertight boundaries between SMEs and large companies in terms of jobs, wealth created or available or used resources.

Furthermore, since we are striving to understand the *dynamics* of employment, we cannot limit ourselves to a comparative study of isolated years. If we are to reach a conclusion on dynamics, we must use tools for longitudinal analysis of individual data. Our analysis should encompass the whole of the period concerned, across types of enterprises, even including, unlike the studies on "panel data[4]", enterprises which appear or disappear. We must also, so far as we can, look into the trajectories of enterprises.

2 The data

Finally, we must cover as much ground as possible. Generally speaking, it is not enough to pinpoint "gross" job creations, which would appear to be concentrated in SMEs. We must also factor in jobs lost or cut in larger companies late in their trajectory, which may thus contribute to swelling the population of SMEs, when the workforce drops under the threshold of 500 employees. Furthermore, if we confine our analysis to the balance of changes affecting jobs in the various categories of enterprises, with some creating jobs, and others cutting them back, this will not enable us to see the whole picture, since the constraints of some types of enterprises are carried over to other types, ultimately affecting the overall outcome.

To address these questions, the combination of the Longitudinal Analysis Database (LAD) compiled at the Business Statistics Synthesis Unit of INSEE (see M.-C. Parent, 1995b) and of data on enterprise groups taken from the LIFI survey (Thollon-Pommerol, Chabanas 1991) seems like an appropriate tool. This combination encompasses 3.5 million enterprises taken from the category of BIC (Industrial and Commercial Earnings) for the period 1984-1992, and is made up primarily, besides the defining parameters of each enterprise, of figures for workforce size, net assets, turnover, value added, production, intermediate consumption, wages, employer payroll costs, and gross operating surplus, as they appear in SUSE. This figure of 3.5 million enterprises, or some 1.9 million enterprises each given year, should be contrasted with the 2.3 million non-agricultural enterprises inventoried in Sirène. The figure stands for a workforce

---

[4] Balanced samples.

of about 13 million, out of a total of approximately 13.5 million in 1992. The database therefore comes close to being representative in macroeconomic terms.

Indeed, similar longitudinal analysis databases have been developed in a number of national statistical institutes, as have studies based on them (see MacGuckin, 1996, for a discussion of the need for longitudinal analysis, and some of their theoretical and practical implications). Among the countries developing LADs are the United States (MacGuckin and Pascoe, 1988), Japan (Motohashi, 1996), Australia (Pattinson, 1996), Canada (Baldwin, Dupuy, Penner, 1992), the United Kingdom[5] (Robson, Gallagher, 1994), as well as the Netherlands (Hamenesh et al., 1996), Norway (Klette and Mathiassen, 1996), Finland (Hietanemi, 1996), Israel (Gronan and Regev, 1996), and others.

3 Methodological note: the data

3.1 Field and enterprise definition

The data are those of the LAD (Longitudinal Analysis Database) on the business field (NAP73 activity codes U02 to U10), ranging from the farm and food industry to business services, but excluding real-estate, financial and insurance activities, as well as agriculture, and compiled from SUSE (see M.-C. Parent, 1995b). This sector-based field is also known as the Industry, Commerce and Services (ICS) field.

The enterprises are followed over the time by their individual number (SIREN), attributed in business register Sirène to each legal unit. So our definition of enterprise continuity is here, more or less, based on that of the legal units as companies (in certain cases one enterprise of the register may be constituted of several legal units).

3.2 Measuring the enterprise group control

The data are matched with those of the financial links (LIFI) survey, to check whether enterprises belong to an enterprise group, and to obtain the SIREN code of the enterprise group head (for a presentation of this survey, see V. Thollon-Pommerol-N. Chabanas, 1991). Since 1988 data are not available, any figure

---

[5] The case of the United Kingdom is somewhat different, insofar as it is a private source (Dun & Bradstreet) which provides the matrix to build a LAD after matching with certain administrative sources (VAT declarations). Because of this, the quality of the data from the point of view of economic analyses of employment in SMEs is difficult to assess (see Robson, Gallagher, 1994 and Robson, Gallagher, 1992).

provided for that year is simply the product of linear extrapolation between 1987 and 1989. The inclusion of a company within a group perimeter is based on the direct or indirect control of the majority of the votes in the ordinary shareholders assembly by another company (or sometimes, the share of capital). No distinction is made here between enterprises (companies) fully controlled and the broader contours of an enterprise group (see Thollon-Pommerol, Chabanas, 1991).

The year 1986 apparently poses a problem in terms of identifying the heads of enterprise groups, because of the absence of micro-enterprise groups, amongst other reasons. As a result, the trends for that year and for 1987 are not always significant.

3.3 Definition of SMEs

Large enterprises (LEs) for a given year have an average workforce of 500 or more.

Small and mid-sized enterprises (SMEs) for a given year have a yearly average workforce of 20 to 499.

Very small enterprises (VSEs) for a given year have an average workforce of 19 or less. This field, however, is considered to be less well covered by the Financial Links survey than other size-classes.

3.4 Measuring the workforce

Employment is measured according to the "leading average workforce" ("effectif directeur moyen", or Effm) variable of the SUSE system. This is the response which the surveyed enterprise sees as closest to the average yearly full-time equivalent workforce, discounting personnel on loan or doing temporary work, and generally excluding non wage-earning personnel (for more details, see the Suse III "guide d'utilisation des fichiers").

3.5 Which populations are we studying?

Having defined what an SME is for a given year, we must clarify which enterprises will be monitored for the period concerned. Three types of fields of SMEs are used here, which correspond to three different approaches:

- studying the SMEs of the year for each year, which implies including those enterprises which were SMEs for one year at least over the period, and thus enterprises which have moved between size-classes, or which have appeared/disappeared;
- studying the SMEs of a given year—those of the starting year in particular—and tracing them throughout the period;
- studying the trajectories followed: in this context, given the multiplicity of conceivable cases when multiplied by the number of years of the period, we shall focus on the starting and ending situations of the enterprise, rather than on its trajectory.

For the sake of comparison, therefore, we need to identify the sub-field made up of enterprises which were SMEs for a given year. The complement, for that year, is made up of enterprises which have been SMEs, and of those which will be (both creations/disappearances and size-classes changes).

4 The SMEs cannot be defined by their size characteristics a given year

The SMEs cannot be defined by their size characteristics a given year when a longitudinal analysis is conducted.

For example, if we take the workforce size as of 1984 to define the population, the change in workforce between 1984 and 1992 appears as a tremendous loss of 1.3 million jobs (i.e. a 28 % drop). If we take only the survivors, the picture is completely different: an increase of 91,000 jobs (*i.e.* + 2.9 %), and if we take amongst them those which have their workforce still between 20 and 500 employees, as of 1992, the picture become more marked: +212,918 jobs (+ 10 %).

Table 1 SMEs of 1984

Definitions based on '84 characteristics (legal units of workforce between 20 & 500, in 1984)	$\Delta 84,92$ Workforce$_{92}$- Workforce$_{84}$
Total	-1,273,969
of which still existent in '92	+ 91,091
of which workforce still between 20 & 500 in '92	+212,918

If we take the size of workforce between 20 and 500 employees as of 1989, the picture is that of a boom in employment of + 535,900 jobs between 1984 and 1992.

Table 2 SMEs of 1992

Definitions based on '92 characteristics (legal units of workforce between 20 & 500, in 1992)	$\Delta 84,92$ Workforce$_{92}$-Workforce$_{84}$
Total	+1,694,128
of which already existent in '84	+280,949
of which workforce was between 20 & 500 in '84	+212,918

If conversely, we take the end of the period, we would obtain an increase of about 1.7 million between 1984 and 1992, i.e. + 56 %. But, from this amount, 1.4 million come from enterprise appeared[6] in the time interval. Excluding these creations leads us to a change of 9.3 %, for total employment of the remaining enterprises.

Table 3 Comparisons of changes in employment according to the definition of SMEs

Definitions of SMEs *(according to the company workforce)*	Apparent Change in employment
Between 20 & 500 *at the beginning* of the period	- 28.4 %
Between 20 & 500 at the beginning *and still alive* at the end	+ 2.9 %
Between 20 & 500 at the beginning *and* at the end (still alive in 1992)	+ 8.4 %
Between 20 & 500 *a mid year* (1989)	+ 15.3 %
Between 20 & 500 *at the end* of the period	+ 56.0 %
Between 20 & 500 at the end *and already alive* at the beginning	+ 17.5 %

The way which seems to be reasonable, for measuring employment dynamics longitudinally, is to take into account *together* '84 between 20 and 500 enterprises which are still in these limits in '92, *and* new enterprises appeared during the period, *and* disappeared enterprises. We have also no reason to exclude the enterprises of less than 20 employees, which *grew up* beyond that threshold, as well as those which *decreased down* beyond the 500 employees threshold.

This leads us to define *as the relevant field the "envelop" of SMEs during the 1984-92 period.* That means the enterprises which workforce has been between 20 and 500 at least one year during the period under analysis. This

---

[6] As legal unit

population can be considered as representative of enterprises *likely* to become SMEs at some point during their existence.

Thus we echo the concerns expressed by Baldwin, Dupuy and Picot (1994)[7], who suggest taking account not only the initial size of enterprises over the period of interest to define the scope of the field of SMEs, but also the average size over the period, or the average size over one or two years before the period. The average size of enterprises over a pluri-annual period can also be taken into account by focusing on the population of enterprises which were SMEs for at least one year of the period of interest. Indeed, the "average size" criterion is justified primarily by the fact that enterprises move around between size-classes. One could, of course, calculate each enterprise's average size for the whole period. Although this would be a perfectly workable method, it is not the one we have chosen. The reasons for this are partly technical—the size of the files to work with is a serious impediment. But there are also more substantive reasons. While an "average size" criterion may seem quite appropriate for enterprises which are far enough away from the size thresholds, and where changes in the workforce occur slowly, it is inoperative in the case of abrupt variations due to restructuring. Furthermore, the choice of a time interval to calculate such an average size seems arbitrary, and may lead to unacceptable distortion of changes over time within the period.

4.1 Trajectories of enterprises according to size, 1984-1992

To assess the magnitude of the various transfers between populations, as thresholds are passed, we have drawn up tables which relate the initial situation of enterprises to their "final" situation, by comparing the numbers employed at the start and end of the period.

The two years (1984 and 1992) delimiting the period of study fell roughly at the two ends of a middle-term economic cycle[8]. Thus, by bringing together the comparative analysis of the workforce employed in enterprises those two years and the "trajectories" followed by these enterprises — in this case, the starting and ending points of the trajectories — we can obtain information on the factors of SMEs development which is not too dependent on the most transitory component of the short-term economic situation.

---

[7] Who refer to Davis, Haltiwanger (1996).

[8] This is almost true, but for a one-year difference. 1993 would in fact have been better, see Boccara, Bouthevillain, Coeuré, Eyssartier (1997).

4.2 1984 situation-1992 status, SMEs at least one year

A comparison between the new situation as of 1992 and the situation in 1984 of all enterprises in the so-called Industry Commerce Services (ICS) field reveals a population subject to all manner of profound, underlying changes. In quantitative terms, the dominant forms of changes are enterprises appearing or disappearing, and upward/downward movements between size-classes as thresholds are passed, in terms of both jobs concerned and numbers of enterprises[9]. This finding has already been established in a number of studies both in France (notably Berthier, Parent, 1994) and in other countries (Davis, Haltiwanger, 1990, Baldwin, Picot, 1995, Kleijwe, Nieuwenhuijsen, 1996).

4.3 Changes in workforce size, 1984-1992

Table 4 Changes in workforce size, 1984-1992

		Status as of 1992				Total
	Type of enterprise	Disappeared	Very small	SMEs	Large	
	Non-existent	0	+ 58,383	+1,413,179	+ 94,601	+1,568,163
Situation	Very small	-61,692	-3,702	+306,166	+ 10,249	+251,021
in 1984	SMEs	-1,365,060	-370,607	+ 212,918	+248,780	-1,273,969
	Large	-169,481	- 100,022	- 238,135	-11,750	- 519,388
Total	SMEs at least one year between 1984 and 1992	-1,596,233	-415,948	+ 1,694,128	+ 343,880	+ 25,827

Field: enterprises which belonged to the population of Industry Commerce Services SMEs one year of the period

Reading notes: Rows: the workforce employed by those of the 1984 SMEs, which had become very small as of 1992, was 370,607 positions smaller than it had been in 1984

Columns: the workforce employed by those of the 1992 SMEs, which had been large in 1984, was 238,135 positions smaller than it had been in 1984.

In table 4, the SME row and column deserve particular attention. Some of the cells pertaining to large enterprises are not significant, insofar as they encompass a very small number of enterprises (see table 9 in the Appendix). They mainly

---

[9] As we have noted in the box which defines size-classes, the statistical focus on the population of enterprises with a workforce of less than 20 is less sharp than it is for other populations. Any data pertaining to such enterprises should therefore be handled with care.

reflect restructuring within enterprise groups rather than actual changes affecting the size of units in the productive system. There is clearly a great deal of job-creating energy among those of the 1984 SMEs which were also SMEs in 1992, and which could be described as "quasi-perennial"[10]. But its effect on overall changes in employment in the population studied is virtually canceled out by that of enterprises which moved between size-classes (regardless the disappeared companies). Indeed, the workforce of the latter group lost 143,569 jobs (table 5) showing the dominance of downsizings upon upsizings. The grouping in table 5 shows that the greatest job losses occurred among the large enterprises of 1984, which consequently became SMEs or VSEs, or simply disappeared.

It is hardly appropriate to conclude that the SMEs played a pivotal part in a given year, insofar as the disappearances of 1984 SMEs led to more than a million job losses (-1,365,060). The figure for job growth in new enterprises created since 1984, on the other hand, is admittedly somewhat larger (+1,413,179). But these are cumulative figures for different "generations" of enterprises, and it is still unclear what the attrition rate will be among the most recently created enterprises, which were still alive in 1992[11]. Despite their high "gross" flows of companies creations and disappearances, the "net" demographic effect is also rather weak (-28,707).

We must consider the effect as applying which can be considered to apply globally to all enterprises in the target population. Thus, *in the field of enterprises which are liable to be SMEs at some point during the period, the total volume of employment turns out to be highly stable* (+25,827 wage-earners after 8 years). This stability is all the more striking, given that the order of magnitude of job creations and disappearances as a result of enterprises being set up or disappearing—company demographics—is in the million (1,596,233 and 1,568,163 respectively). Similarly, variations in the workforce of enterprises moving between size-classes amount to several hundreds thousands of jobs.

In other words, all the enterprises which might be one year a candidate to issues devoted to so-called "SMEs" (policy measures, economic analysis, banking help, etc.) show a rather weak change in their total employment. The change is to compare on a basis of 5,475,000 for the field at the beginning of the period. It implies a 0.2 % contribution to the change of employment all the business ICS sector (excluding finance).

---

[10]"*quasi*-perennial" rather than perennial, given that, although their workforce were in [20;500[intervall in both 1984 and 1992, it is unclear whether it continued to be in this intervall throughout the period.

[11]According to Bonneau, Francoz (1994), the five-year survival rate for newly-created enterprises, regardless of initial size, was approximately 50% for the generation of 1987. This rate, according to the authors, is comparable to that of the generations of 1985 and 1982. Survival rates improve for enterprises with a larger initial size.

Table 5 Balance of changes in the workforce according to the type of movement between size-classes

Kind of Movement	Change in the Workforce (1984-1992)	
	SMEs' envelop (enterprises with workforce between 20 and 500 during at least one year of the period)	All enterprises
Creations	+ 1,568,163	+ 3,982,070
Upward movement	+ 565,195	+ 632,114
Same size-class in '84 and '92	+ 197,466	+ 23,129
Downward movement	- 708,764	- 827,263
Disappearances	- 1,596,233	- 3,656,264
subtotals:		
Total changes of size-class	- 143,569	- 195,149
Demographic balance	- 28,070	+ 325,806
Total	**+ 25,827**	**+ 153,786**

All enterprises in Industry Commerce Services field (excl. finance, real estate, etc.)

The dominance of downsizing leads to some "optical effect", because the workforce of several large downsized enterprises swell the ranks of the SMEs'population after their downsizing, despite the fact that they lose jobs. And, furthermore, if their workforce increases after that downsizing, it might be viewed as proving dynamism of "SMEs".

This weak change of the total volume of employment in the enterprises pertaining to the SMEs' envelop takes place while the overall change in the workforce of the total field (*i.e.* without size criterion) was approximately 150,000 jobs (or roughly 1.5% of the total number of jobs in 1984), job cuts and creations attributable to company demographics also reached into the million. Needless to say, these figures compare "net" and "gross" job flows, so it is hardly surprising to find different orders of magnitude. However, the *balance* of demographics effect taken alone ("net" effect) is still about twice as high as the overall change. Furthermore, the contribution of company demographics to changes in employment over the period was positive largely thanks to '84 VSEs (+543,473), and quite secondarily thanks to '84 SMEs (+48,119). Finally, we could note that such figures shed no light on the durability of jobs in new enterprises, which many studies have shown to be highly fragile, particularly in VSEs.

Graph 1 Sum up of changes in the workforce

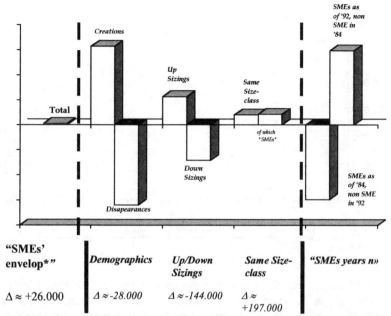

"SMEs' envelop*"	**Demographics**	**Up/Down Sizings**	**Same Size-class**	"SMEs years n»
Δ ≈ +26.000	Δ ≈ -28.000	Δ ≈ -144.000	Δ ≈ +197.000	

* enterprises with Workforce between 20 & 500 one year at least, during the 1984-92 period.

4.4 The evolution profile

A focus to year-to-year evolution of the different categories leads to almost the same picture as the one we drawn by restricting us to the mere comparison of 1992 and 1984 workforce levels.

Graph 2 Workforce changes (wage earner employment)

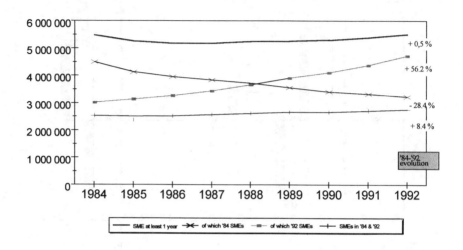

Weak variations for the whole population (envelop of 1984-92 SMEs) are confirmed (graph 2), even weaker than for the whole employment (wage earners)[12] of the same activity sectors (graph 4). Behind these weak changes, we come back to the strong opposite changes of the different sub-populations, as defined by their size-class measured at the beginning or at the end of the period. These oppositions last during the whole period. In particular, the downsizing/upsizing contribution seems to be steadily of the main negative influence (graph 3).

---

[12]Households survey source (*Enquête emploi*).

Graph 3 Workforce changes (wage earner employment)

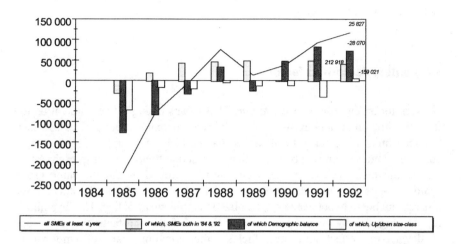

In conclusion of this part, *the dynamism of the, so called, SMEs seems not to be very well established in medium term because of (i) their strong fragility and (ii) the role of downsizing in the whole business sector.* The only category which shows a dynamical evolution, in terms of jobs creation, is the one of the 20 < < 500 employees, as of 1984, *which are still alive in 1992,* and which *stayed inside this size class limits* ("quasi-perennial SMEs"). But this latter assertion could be considered partly as a tautology. Except if we can identify some distinguished factors that those companies have in common.

Graph 4 Workforce changes (index = 100)

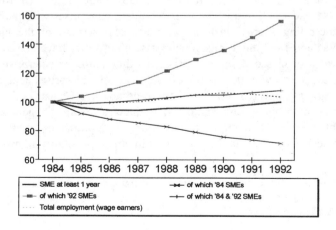

Thus, one economic question that arises from this description is to ask about economic factors of this quasi-perennial-SMEs past dynamism and about the factors of down/up sizings.

5 An enterprise group factor

We seek for an *enterprise group factor*. That means taking into consideration the financial links that may exist between different companies (enterprises). In fact, financial links allow several companies (named head of group) to control sets of other companies. That will be our indicator to define the perimeter of each group. The employment changes in each company controlled within the same group could *"take its meaning only at the group level"* (Parent, 1995a). In other words, it is reasonable to hypothesize a "globalized" employment policy. This hypothesis is also suggested by the concomitance of the two following facts: the magnitude of downsizing effect and, nevertheless, the growing share of employment controlled by the enterprise groups (Chabanas, Vergeaud, 1997).

Indeed, if we split the envelop of 1984-92 SMEs population according to the control-status of each company, as of 1984 and of 1992, we obtain a very contrasted picture of employment changes.

5.1 Overall framework: from the 1984 enterprise groups to the 1992 enterprise groups

Table 7 shows that enterprises which belonged to an enterprise group in 1984 lost almost 500,000 jobs (-492,145) between 1984 and 1992, whereas those which were independent in 1984 added more than 500,000 (+517,972). However, we cannot conclude from this that enterprise groups compressed their workforce between 1984 and 1992, in contrast to independent enterprises with purportedly greater job-creating energy. Instead, we must take account of the fact that, between 1984 and 1992, the limits of enterprise groups may have moved around as they created or closed down enterprises, as they absorbed enterprises, or as they spun them off into the world of independent enterprises and as new enterprises groups appeared (especially micro-groups, see Chabanas, Vergeaud, 1997). These absorptions and spinoffs ("exchanges" with the population of independent enterprises) are clearly just as crucial as appearances/disappearances (demographics). That is one of the main "evolutionist"[13] possibility allowed by the

---

[13]An « evolutionist » (refering to darwinism) or rather, in fact, a « transformist » possibility (refering to Lamarck and the stress he lays on creation of new organs or on « internal » transformations).

group structure. Thus, if we categorize enterprises according to whether or not they were controlled by an enterprise group in the ending rather than the starting year (1984), the changes are inverted: enterprises belonging to enterprise groups in 1992 gained almost 300,000 jobs over the period, whereas independent enterprises lost 270,000.

Table 6 From the 1984 enterprise groups to the 1992 enterprise groups
1992 workforce minus 1984 workforce in the enterprises they controlled

	Overall	1984 non-groups	1984 groups	1992 non-groups	1992 groups
1992 workforce - 1984 workforce	SMEs at least one year	independent enterprises in 1984	enterprises belonging to enterprise groups in 1984	independent enterprises in 1992	enterprises belonging to enterprise groups in 1992
	(a)	(b)=(a)-(c)	**(c)**	(d)=(a)-(e)	**(e)**
Same size-class in '84 and '92	**197,466**	213,119	**-15,653**	158,349	**39,117**
Total size-class changes	**-143,569**	44,181	**-187,750**	-44,725	**-98,844**
Demographic Balance	**-28,070**	260,672	**-288,742**	-387,163	**359,093**
Total	**25,827**	**517,972**	**-492,145**	**-273,539**	**299,366**

* the figures for the distribution between enterprise groups and non-enterprise groups of enterprises appearing or disappearing are not interpretable, because we would need to take into account the control of the SME the year of the event.
Field: SMEs at least one year
Reading notes: Comparing 1992 and 1984 workforce sizes shows that enterprises which belonged to an enterprise group in 1984 lost 492,145 jobs. The same comparison for enterprises which belonged to an enterprise group in 1992 shows that they added 299,366 jobs.

5.2 Three populations of enterprises: internal to enterprise groups, independent, and exchanged

Table 8 details the changes in the workforce of enterprises likely to be SMEs according to whether or not they belonged to an enterprise group at the beginning or end of the period.

Since we are focusing on enterprise groups as a whole, it seems appropriate to distinguish between enterprises which remained inside the perimeter of enterprise groups, enterprises which remained outside of it, and enterprises which "moved" in and out of it in the course of the period. Table 8 comes close to making this distinction, but only in terms of control by an enterprise group at the start or end of the period, rather than throughout it.

In sum, the strongest workforce growth (+75,000) occurred among enterprises which moved in and out of the limits of the population of enterprise groups (or "exchanged" enterprises), in contrast to those which remained within enterprise groups (-100,000). Enterprises independent in both 1984 and 1992 also experienced dynamic growth (+50,000), albeit somewhat less vigorous than in the first group. We must, of course, take account of the existence of different "generations" among the independents, meaning that a number of them are liable to come under the control of an enterprise group later in their existence, beyond our time-frame.

More specifically, for enterprises liable to be SMEs which remained within enterprise groups, the main factor contributing to the shrinking workforce was size-class changes within enterprise groups. There is a marked drop in the workforce of enterprises in this category which changed size-classes. They have a negative impact on the overall change in employment for the field as a whole (-2.9% as against +.5% in total for the field). The balance of the workforce for enterprises changing size-class ("upward" or "downward" movement) within enterprise groups is even higher than the overall figure across enterprises. The "quasi-perennial" SMEs which remained within enterprise groups as of 1992 experienced a very slight contraction in their workforce, in sharp contrast to the dynamism of all "quasi-perennials". The picture which emerges is thus a dominant "restructuring" trend, with job cuts for enterprises likely to be SMEs which *remain* within enterprise groups, meaning also that "enterprise" units within "enterprise group" units shrink, whereas the enterprise groups themselves may expand[14].

---

[14]A fact already noted in Thollon-Pommerol (1990).

Graph 5 Recapitulation 1984-1992: Changes of workforce according moves of companies in and out of groups

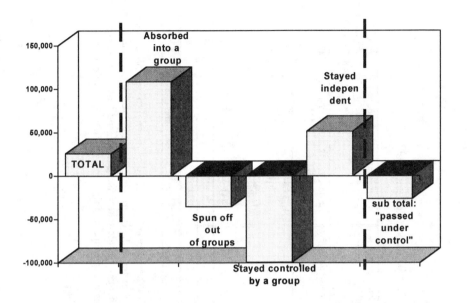

$\Delta = 25,827$ $\Delta=108,596$ $\Delta=-35,080$ $\Delta=-99,324$ $\Delta=51,635$ $\Delta=-25,908$

ICS enterprises with, at least one year, less than 500 employees and more than 20.

Table 7 Changes in the workforce, 1984-1992 SMEs at least one year between 1984 and 1992

Effm92 - Effm84	Overall		of which enterprises inside enterprise groups**		of which enterprises inside non-enterprise groups		of which enterprises exchanged between enterprise groups and non-enterprise groups	
	ΔEffm84.92	Contribution (%) ***	ΔEffm84.92	Contribution (%) ***	ΔEffm84.92	Contribution (%) ***	ΔEffm84.92	Contribution (%) ***
*Creations**	1,568,163	+28.6	413,322*	+7.5	1,154,841	+21.1	*	
Upward movement	565,195	+10.3	123,214	+2.3	268,710	+4.9	173,271	+3.2
Same size-class in '84 and '92	197,466	+3.6	-9,106	-0.2	164,896	+3.0	41,676	+0.8
Downward movement	-708,764	-12.9	-282,431	-5.2	-284,902	-5.2	-141,431	-2.6
*Disappearances**	-1,596,233	-29.2	-344,323*	-6.3	-1,251,910	-22.9	*	
Total size-class changes	-143,569	-2.6	-159,217	-2.9	-16,192	-0.3	31,840	+0.6
*Demographic balance**	-28,070	-0.5	68,999*	+1.3	-97,069*	-1.8	*	
Total	25,827	+0.5	-99,324	-1.8	51,635	+0.9	+73,516	+1.3

Field: enterprises which were SMEs one year at least

* The demographics of enterprises controlled by a group in either 1984 or 1992 have been categorized as internal to enterprise groups, insofar as it is difficult to ascertain the position of the enterprise with respect to the perimeter of the enterprise group in the year of the demographic event.

**belonged to an enterprise group in both 1984 and 1992. The sum of changes "inside enterprise groups" and "inside non-enterprise groups", therefore, does not equal total changes. The last column, which encompasses changes in enterprises moving in and out of enterprise group control must also be added to it.

*** Contributions are calculated relative to the field of SMEs one year at least.

As for the influence of enterprise groups on company demographics, it is difficult to measure to what extent do SMEs appear or disappear when they are outside enterprise groups the year these events occur. In particular, in the calculations presented here, we do not take account of the position of enterprises with respect to the perimeter of enterprise groups in the year of the event, but only in 1984 and 1992.

A second component of the influence of enterprise groups on employment dynamics is exchanges with the rest of the productive system. Indeed, this is a novel type of operation made possible by the enterprise group structure compared to a single company structure. Table 8 looks at these exchanges from the point of view of controlling shares acquired in enterprises. In this table, exchanged enterprises are considered as a population of interest in its own right, even before it is divided into enterprises "spun off" out of the enterprise groups and enterprises "absorbed" from the rest of the productive system (as analyzed in table 8). Perennial enterprises in this population are the only ones, of all those moving into the perimeter of enterprise groups, which achieve significant overall workforce growth (roughly +75,000 wage-earners). In fact, this is the category of enterprises which experiences the most sustained growth in absolute terms, including demographics, and thus contributes most markedly to job growth across the field. Thus, the category of enterprises exchanged between enterprise groups and the productive system appears to be crucial if we are to identify the processes at work in the productive system in terms of job creation.

Merely moving into an enterprise group at some stage of its existence, therefore, is enough to trigger changes in the behavior of an enterprise. Although the relationship between movement in and out of the perimeter of an enterprise group and the changes observed in the workforce is difficult to analyze in terms of causality, we can suggest two hypotheses. The figure of 75,000 jobs created may be a sign that a large proportion of enterprises which are not controlled by an enterprise group, at some point in their existence, may need to gain access to certain resources—in terms of financing, patents and other informational resources, access to markets, specific human resources, etc.—which depend on the capital in control of enterprise groups, and which cannot be accessed otherwise than by moving into the perimeter of the enterprise groups. On the other hand, if we look at the category of enterprises which *at some time or another* were controlled by an enterprise group, their contribution to employment was negative—some 25,000 jobs lost between 1984 and 1992 (total for "internal", "absorbed" and "spun off" categories).

To what degree does this negative contribution mean that the overall costs of this "external growth" of the enterprise group-controlled SME workforce outweigh the synergies it makes possible? For the "quasi-SMEs" field as a whole there was a very slight increase in employment, whereas "quasi-SMEs" which came under enterprise group control at some point in their existence experienced a net drop. It remains to be seen how much this has to do with management constraints during this period regarding the sharing of value added[15]. If we are to achieve a fuller understanding of the contribution of enterprise groups to the overall changes in the field of study, we need to look at the problem from a complementary point of view as well: changes in the wealth generated by the various populations of enterprises.

Graph 6 Workforce changes: SMEs at least one year

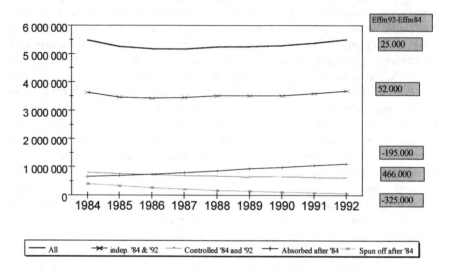

The evolution profile of annual employment for these categories confirms the results given by the mere comparison between the ending and the beginning years (graph 7).

5.3 Micro-enterprise groups

Those of the enterprise groups with a total workforce of less than 500 (i.e., micro-enterprise groups), would deserve separate study, because they actually belong to the same size-class as SMEs. Table 9 shows that movements *inside* this type of enterprise group have only limited effects on overall employment. Workforce changes "internal" to micro-enterprise groups (that is, to enterprises included in the perimeter of micro-enterprise groups both in 1984 and in 1992) represented only 2% of the drop observed for changes "internal" to enterprise groups with a workforce of more than 500. The drop for micro-enterprise groups is small in

---

[15]See CSERC (1996), pp. 9 and 38-39.

relation to their share of the workforce—a substantial 16% of the workforce of enterprise groups with a workforce of more than 500 in 1989, belonging to the ICS field. The balance of job creation/loss as a result of enterprises changing size-classes within micro-enterprise groups is minute. It is far below the balance of overall change, whereas it is roughly the same size as overall change for enterprises which remained within other enterprise groups.[16]

Nevertheless, a breakdown of exchanged enterprises between enterprise groups with a workforce of more than 500 and micro-enterprise groups reveals a sharp drop in the workforce of enterprises "rejected" (as we termed it) towards micro-enterprise groups (-45 311). This strongly suggests a connection between the development of micro-enterprise groups and the dismemberment of larger enterprise groups (hiving off ...).

---

[16] Needless to say, by definition, there can be no transition into—or out of—the category of large enterprises (with more than 500 wage-earners) *within* micro-enterprise groups. This can only happen with VSEs.

Table 8 Workforce changes according to movement in and out of enterprise groups

1992 workforce − 1984 workforce	Overall All enterprises	Overall total internal to enterprise groups ***	"absorptions" into enterprise groups Total 84 non-enterprise group towards 92 enterprise group	"absorptions" non-enterprise group towards enterprise group > 500	"absorptions" non-enterprise group towards micro-enterprise group	"spinoffs" out of enterprise groups Total 84 enterprise group towards 92 non-enterprise group	"spinoffs" enterprise group > 500 towards non-enterprise group	"spinoffs" micro-enterprise group towards non-enterprise group
	(a)	(b)	(c)=(d)+(e)	(d)	(e)	(f)=(g)+(h)	(g)	(h)
*Creations**	**1,568,163**	28,506	379,764	285,468	94,296	5,052	3,647	1,405
Upward movement	**565,195**	123,214	168,840	151,161	17,679	4,431	2,575	1,856
Same size-class in '84 and '92	**197,466**	-9,106	48,223	35,196	13,027	-6,547	-4,640	-1,907
Downward movement	**-708,764**	-282,431	-108,467	-46,359	-62,108	-32,964	-29,499	-3,465
*Disappearances**	**-1,596 233**	-27,154	-22,023	-9,528	-12,495	-295,146	-264,037	-31,109
Total size-class changes	-143,569	-159,217	+60,373	104,802	-44,429	-28,533	-26,924	-1,609
Demographic balance*	-28,070	1,352	357,741	275,940	81,801	-290,094	-260,390	-29,704
Total	**25,827**	**-166,971**	**466,337**	**415,938**	**50,399**	**-325,174**	**-291,954**	**-33,220**
Demographics ascribed internally to enterprise groups		*68,999*	*0*	*0*	*0*	*0*	*0*	*0*
Total with ascribed demographics		**-99,324**	**108,596**	**139,998**	**-31,402**	**-35,080**	**-31,564**	**-3,515**

* enterprises which belonged to an enterprise group in both 1984 and 1992.

** the figure for distribution of creations and disappearances between enterprise groups and non-enterprise groups are not interpretable, because we would need to take account of control of the SMEs in the year of the event.

Field: enterprises which were SMEs one year at least

5.4 Summary

Table 7 showed that it was employment in enterprise groups which benefited from job creation in enterprises likely to be SMEs between 1984 and 1992. In other words, *while the workforce of enterprises which were independent in 1992 lost 270,000 jobs between 1984 and 1992, that of enterprises controlled by an enterprise group in 1992 gained 300,000.* The role of company demographics is difficult to establish, insofar as the figures in table 8 do not take into account whether the enterprise belonged to a group or not in the year of the event itself (creation or disappearance), but in 1984 and 1992[17]. According to this table, in enterprises likely to be SMEs which were controlled by an enterprise group in 1992 job growth did not feed on the energy of enterprises which remained inside enterprise groups in 1984 and 1992. Indeed, the latter lost more than 150,000 jobs (-166,971). The figure for losses "internal" to enterprise groups is somewhat smaller, but still negative, if we add in the effect of the demographics of enterprises controlled by an enterprise group in 1984 or 1992 (-99,324), whatever the date of creation/disappearance. Perennial independent enterprises "absorbed" by enterprise groups with a workforce of more than 500, on the other hand, added almost 140,000 jobs (139,998), whereas the "rejected" ones lost 32,000, an imbalance of 170,000 jobs in favor of enterprise groups. Enterprises coming under the control of micro-enterprise groups, on the other hand, lost workforce overall.

6 The meaning of the «enterprise group factor»

6.1 The importance of exchanges between enterprise groups and non-enterprise groups

We have seen (table 8) that *job growth in enterprises which remained SMEs as of 1992 did not occur in enterprises initially controlled by enterprise groups, micro or not. But table 9 shows that the latter took ex post control over a large proportion of the jobs created in enterprises which stayed in the same size-class from 1984 to 1992 (48,223 out of 197,400, or roughly one in four).* Micro-enterprise groups contributed somewhat to this trend (with some 13 000 jobs), but

---

[17]If we consider that demographics result largely from restructuring within enterprise groups, creations and disappearances of enterprises can be ascribed entirely to the enterprise groups, internally, for all the enterprises which belonged to their perimeter in 1984 or 1992. This is the underlying hypothesis for the "ascribed demographics" line, and the corresponding total. The resulting approximation is probably too high in terms of numbers of enterprises. On the other hand, the effect of the approximation in terms of changes in the workforce has not been calculated.

it is hard to see, at this point in the analytical process, the extent to which an SME which has subsequently entered the perimeter of a micro-enterprise group will tend to take control of other enterprises, or be taken control of by another, pre-existing SME, or to split up and restructure into an enterprise group, or to become part of a set of enterprises which federate and set up as a micro-enterprise group.

The picture which emerges, through demographics as well as through "absorptions" and "spinoffs", is thus the ebb and flow of enterprises in and out of the perimeter of enterprise groups, a phenomenon which stands out particularly in the category of enterprises likely to be SMEs. We drew attention earlier (table 8) to the category of enterprises "exchanged" between enterprise groups and non-enterprise groups, which appears again here. To what extent does the behavior of enterprises of this type, which can vary in size, highlight the importance of specific relationships between enterprises, which do not necessarily imply capital ownership and the more traditional enterprise group structure? For, taken as a whole, this population is part of the "halo" of enterprises which forms around enterprise groups, bound by a whole gradation of relationships ranging all the way to total integration, since it includes fully-controlled enterprises of long standing as well as enterprises which have become independent, but which may have maintained certain joint operations within enterprise groups. In a sense, the enterprises in this population can be seen as forming an integral part of a *de facto* network of more-or-less specific inter-enterprise relations, which may extend across international boundaries[18]. This is a remarkable phenomenon, and perhaps a new one, in terms of magnitude at least. But at the same time, the contrast between the evolution of "absorbed" and "rejected" enterprises shows that fitting into an enterprise group *stricto sensu* is a crucial turning point compared with fitting into a more informal network.

---

[18]This aspect of things is usually emphasised on an international scale, but is equally relevant for enterprises from the same national territory, see for instance Bonturi, Fukasaku (1993) and Airudi (1994). The first stresses the fact that transfer prices, as an instrument for transferring the shared resources of the enterprise group, have been made irrelevant by the "*constitution of networks of companies not bound by shareholding*" with some enterprises "*acting both as intermediaries and organisers in global production and marketing networks*", and which "*usually head up small and mid-sized transformation enterprises in various branches*". The second emphasises "*the opening up of financial markets and the interconnection of information networks [which are alleged to have] changed profoundly the structures of markets and the forms of competition*", "*agreement networks (licensing and cross licensing, joint ventures, OEMs, complex agreements...) [enabling] a higher form of competition.*"

6.2 The overall feedback on human resources

Thus, dividing these exchanged enterprises into "absorbed" and "rejected" ones provides a preliminary view of the articulation between more or less formal networks and the more traditional enterprise group structure. This pattern appears to be shaped by the development of enterprise groups, and to be leaving its own imprint, in turn, on the morphology of enterprise groups. The fact is that, first of all, enterprise groups do not have a neutral effect on exchanged enterprises: employment is lost among the rejected ones, and gained among the absorbed ones, in the case of enterprise groups with a workforce of more than 500, but there are presumably many other effects as well. Indeed, this underlines the importance of human resources, an element which enterprise groups appear to have little compunction about driving drastically downwards (for enterprises remaining within them). Second, the net effect on overall employment (absorptions + rejections + internals) is slightly negative (-25,808), and virtually nil for enterprises moving in and out of the perimeter of enterprise groups with a workforce of more than 500 (-8,668). These two initial observations do not support the commonly expressed notion (Reich, 1991)[19] that the development of networks will make it possible to move beyond destructive competition, thanks to a cooperation profitable to all. In fact, control and business profitability in a financial setting are certainly not neutral here, and cannot be generalized away with the notion of a network. This factual objection meets some of principles made by Piore and Sabel (1984) about the likely depressive effect of the takeovers threat on cooperative networking development and, thus, on the overall growth and human resources development.

The networked form of organization, then, stands opposed to organization in an enterprise group *stricto sensu*, just as much as it is its continuation. As a result, third, what we have to analyze is a *complex relationship between enterprise groups, and non-enterprise groups*. How do the exchanged enterprises affect the enterprise groups themselves when they move in and out of them? It seems likely that they provide them with a number of resources, particularly, as shown by table 9, playing a major part in job growth in enterprise groups for this size-class. They can also more or less durably extend or change the makeup of the enterprise group in terms of job types or activity types.

---

[19]"*The large firm is no longer a 'large' corporation, nor is it simply a set of smaller enterprises. It is a network of enterprises. Its centre provides the strategic wherewithal and connects the parts between them. But the latter often retain enough autonomy to form profitable connections with other networks. There is no clear division between 'inside' and 'outside' the firm, there are only variable distances from its strategic centre*" and "*the distinguished leaders [of the networked enterprises] have little power over anything*", because of the growing "*dissemination of ownership or control*", Reich, 1991, pp. 86 and 87 of the French edition.

6.3 Which resources are «shared» and how ?

Conversely, we must analyze how the enterprises themselves change as they move into the perimeter of enterprise groups. The enterprise-group-form enables certain types of cooperation between units. But this cooperation takes place within a limited entity with variable contours and, moreover, the enterprise-group-form enables transfers and appropriations of financial and informational resources (so called "specific" assets, patents, etc.). The enterprise-group-form also enables some costs to be carried over to the rest of the productive system (e.g., rejection of deficit-ridden subsidiaries) or to minority shareholders (e.g., using transfer prices advantageous to the parent company). The question is how much overall financial control, as opposed to specific information-sharing agreements or full-scale cooperation, stands in the way of larger scale human and information resource development, because of the management constraints financial control (actual or potential) implies for enterprise groups ? Thus, when Darréon and Faiçal (1993)[20] speak of a *"third way"* between absorption and direct competition, they caution that *"this third way can promote development only if both parties reach a level of cooperation likely to bring about strategic resource transfers between the partners, and notably towards SMEs"*. This is another way of highlighting the issue, which focuses exclusively on identified partners already participating in the network, and not on all potential partners[21].

Four potential approaches to these issues could be (i) to analyze the sector-based breakdown of the enterprises exchanged, in particular the respective shares of services, industry and commerce-distribution[22], (ii) to analyze the articulation between productivity, overall economic profitability, and the financial return on shareholders' equity, (iii) to analyze changes in the structure of employment in these various enterprises (inside and outside enterprise groups), (iv) a breakdown by resources shared with the enterprise group (patents, financing, market access resources, particularly international ones, etc.).

Finally, it is worth noting the losses in employment in enterprises "absorbed" by micro-enterprise groups. Enterprises which slipped under the workforce

---

[20]Quoted by Duchéneaut (1995).

[21]Filippi, Pierre and Torre (1996), reviewing existing studies of the notion of networks in economics, emphasise resource creation inside networks, and thanks to them. Commenting the studies of Hakansson and Johanson (1988), as well as Callon, Laredo and Rabeharisoa (1991), they aptly point out that the *"distinction between activities and players is fundatmental"* because the interests of the network members differ, *"and thus include conflicts and cooperations"* which are expressed between players, with for instance the degree of openness of the network, and according to the types of activities concerned (processing or trading), *"in view of controlling another player"*.

[22]The future developments considered in the conclusion of Combier, Mas, Philippe (1996) illustrate one approach to this aspect of things.

threshold of 500 contributed so much to this drop that one cannot help wondering about the respective roles in the rise of the micro-enterprise group of enterprises hiving off enterprise groups, and of, say, pre-existing, independent SMEs forming into a micro-enterprise group, or of larger SMEs reorganizing. This hiving off, in terms of capital structure, does admittedly mean leaving the perimeter of an enterprise, but the new enterprises, in many cases, maintain very close connections with their enterprises of origin (subcontracting, order books, patents, industrial processes, etc.). Some of the micro-enterprise groups could thus be considered as another type of component of the halo described above.

All in all, then, employment in the enterprises of the field concerned which came under enterprise group control in 1984 *or* 1992 remained roughly stable over the period, but the share of enterprise groups in the workforce of SMEs was markedly higher in 1992 than it had been in 1984.

6.4 Economic policy considerations

Various studies have begun to use the terms "gross" and "net" job flows, in USA (Leonard, 1987, Davis, Haltiwanger, 1990), in France (Berthier, Parent, 1994, Lagarde, Maurin, Torelli, 1994) or in other countries. These studies aim to move beyond simply analyzing employment data, often from either a highly "aggregated" viewpoint, or a "households" viewpoint, by introducing a new dimension—enterprises. They also attempt to suggest ways of analyzing overall job flows, rather than simply the evolution of one or several aggregates for populations of enterprises or employees. What is meant by a "gross" flow—a contentious notion—can vary quite widely, but these studies invariably have something to do with the trajectories of enterprises, and the relationship between trajectories and the evolution of a population. In this sense, the present study contributes to the analysis, by enriching the distinction between gross and net flows with the distinction between enterprise groups and non-enterprise groups.

We should call attention to the relativity of job creation in SMEs and to the crucial contribution of enterprise groups, particularly when they take control of dynamic enterprises and reject those which are not energetic enough to the population of independents. At some point, these rejected SMEs may have been energetic enough, and the enterprise groups may have enjoyed the corresponding benefits, in terms of both revenue and resources, including competencies and patents. This leads us to wonder about measures of economic policy which aim to " support SMEs", and how they are evaluated. Who are the ultimate recipients? What are the *in fine* effects on employment, if they are combined with massive losses? In sum, underlying these questions, we find a number of issues pertaining to the assessment of economic policy, which have prompted a search for new ways of devising government, tax, financial and banking incentives.

- ✎ the role of (existing) enterprise groups in creating/destroying jobs in the productive system, all the way down to SMEs, with a new dimension added to the articulation between gross/net job flows;
- ✎ the relevance of the SME level for public employment and incentives policy, with job transfers possibly coupled together with financial transfers, taking place between enterprises within the same enterprise group[23].
- ✎ the extent to which the capital in control of enterprise groups makes use of what might be termed "enterprise group leverage ", in an extension of the notion of leverage[24], and how this impacts the profitability of capital. For the enterprise group configuration enables those who control the capital not to advance as much owners' equity as they would in a single, similar-sized independent enterprise. For the same overall profitability, this could mean allocating profits to minority capital holders at a lower ratio, while increasing that of the owners' equity in control of the corporation[25]. Structuring an enterprise into an enterprise group can make this possible. The use of such mechanisms can of course lead to other problems (stability of minority shareholdings, etc.)[26];
- ✎ looking more closely into the possible differentiation of employment policies between enterprises in the same enterprise group, within a continuing overall management framework, with tighter financial constraints, to seek ways of using labor more intensively (drawing on the special nature of "industrial relations" in SMEs, the external and internal flexibility these enterprises often show, and the possibility of forcing them to accept reduced sales prices,...)[27];

---

[23]A recent European Commission recommendation (96/280/CE, Journal Officiel n° L 107/4, 30.4.96) "adjusts the fire", and takes this dimension into account. It adds the following new criteria to the definition of an SME, which determines eligibility for a variety of entitlements: not belonging to an enterprise group, and other criteria which relate to the size of the enterprise itself (a ceiling on turnover or on balance sheet assets).

[24]See Insee (1980) pp. 122-123.

[25]On the denominator side, the capital is reduced by cascading forms of control which make possible a distinction between the rate of control (which remains a majority rate) and the share of interest or ownership (which may be less than 50%). On the numerator side, the minority shareholders may accept a stable share of profits, but one which is smaller than that of the controlling capital. Those who control the enterprise can also use several mechanisms to "push" a larger share of profits up to the head of the enterprise group than it holds in the downstream enterprises, including, for instance, the use of transfer prices, or of miscellaneous fees and royalties.

[26]Although he does not take the enterprise group dimension into account, Paranque (1994) points out a remarkable specificity of SMEs (regardless of type) in this respect: higher overall economic profitability combined with lower financial returns on owners' equity.

[27]We can refer in France to the Dares roundtable on "employment and industrial relations in SMEs" which was held in October 1994 (see Dares, 1995), and to the CEE (Center

– ✎ on the other hand, we must also measure just how coherently capacity is used in terms of resources (particularly R&D, training, qualifications[28] and education) which are not only financial, but also human[29], and have more or less far-ranging effects on employment and wealth creation. Such coherent utilization can be sought after by enterprises using what some studies have called the beginnings of an *informational revolution*[30]—combining small size, on the one hand, for direct production, workplace relations, and work organization, with a larger scale, on the other hand, for financial mobilization of all kinds of resources[31].

A recent international comparison of the phenomenon (Loveman, Sengenberger, 1991), while providing little in the way of statistical documentation of the "enterprise group" dimension, asks whether *"small enterprises might in a sense become part of 'large' organizations"*. Indeed, the analysis concludes with a reflection on *"new institutional tools"*, in a context where one could also emphasize the pressure of the financial environment of the enterprise (creditors, financial markets, various kinds of shareholders, etc.), which has led many studies to focus on corporate governance.

---

for Employment Studies) research which has focussed on these issues in connection with new technologies (see for instance Gorgeu, Mathieu, 1995), cf. also CSERC, 1996.

[28]P. Templé and S. Lhuillery (1994) partly document the R&D side of SME resource utilization. Amongst other things, they point out that *"enterprises belonging to the same enterprise group form a natural network"*. They emphasise that, according to the enterprises' own declarations in response to a 1991 SESSI survey of industry, *"27% of innovative SMEs* [in the sense of the survey] *take advantage of the technological knowledge of* [the enterprise group network] *they belong to"*.

[29]B. Duchéneaut (1995), amongst others, provides a relatively systematic and comprehensive presentation of this set of resources (notably from p. 192 onwards).

[30]An overall technological revolution, comparable to the industrial revolution. With variations from one author to the next, for the firm dynamics point of view, see Paul David (1994), D. Foray (1995), J. de Bandt and P. Petit (1994) for the articulation between firms and the economy as a whole, see C. Freeman (1994), J. de Bandt (1994), P. Boccara (1991).

[31]On the specific issue of the relationship between organisations and technological change, see Dares, Insee, Liaisons sociales (1996) pp.79–96 "L'organisation du travail dans les PME", as well as Greenan (1995), and Rizzoni (1994), although they do not raise the issue of resources (financial or not), and Audretsch (1995) or Linhart (1994), whose approach is not quantitative, but more general, including workforce management issues. Readers could also refer to Delapierre (1991), who tries to analyse the relations between current technological change (*"a new technological paradigm"*), links between enterprises (*"innovative character of cooperative agreements which aim for cooperation, rather than simply resulting in it"*), *"networked"* company structure, and *"forms of competition"*.

6.5 Economic meanings of «size»

To be sure, it is important to distinguish the reduced scale of units, for direct production activities or direct professional relations (enterprises and local units), from the increased size of the larger entities—such as enterprise groups—which mobilize financial resources, entities within which strategic decisions derive their meaning from the goal of capitalizing on financial resources. At the enterprise group level, the existence of financial links between the enterprises allows for rough validation of the financial dimension by superimposing the financial structure with the financial results of the activities of each component of the enterprise group. But the new importance of informational activities, and above all the (technical and financial) ease with which they dematerialize, leads us to ask similar questions about informational activities (software development, process and patent engineering, competence-building, scientific activities in general, such as those of corporate or even academic research laboratories, education and training, etc.): *what is the appropriate level to make informational activities correspond with the results of these activities?*

6.6 Enterprise group as a particular kind of network

Insofar as informational activities are better-suited to sharing than to appropriation, they take place on a global level. Science, for instance, is an activity which calls for the broadest information-sharing possible, even internationally. But this leads us far beyond the financial boundaries of a given enterprise, not only to other enterprises, other enterprise groups, or between enterprise groups and networks, but even outside the conventional sphere of economics, for instance into the university system, public research laboratories, etc. In this sense, for such activities, the distinction between enterprises is increasingly ill-defined. This even applies to the distinction between the productive system and the rest of society. *This "global" level appears thus as a third level, which extends beyond that of a direct production and work unit (enterprise), or of a financial entity (enterprise group),* albeit an extremely large multinational one. However, the financial benefits derived from informational activities in the form of economic outcomes[32] or financial assets are generated inside entities with defined or definable boundaries.

For instance, a new process may not have been engineered—and thus not financed either—by the financial entity which harvests the profits by putting it to work (sales of merchandise obtained thanks to this new process, etc.).

---

[32]Not only with all manner of fees and licenses, but also through sales of goods which include them.

Development of the patent system seeks to provide for some aspects of the problem. But it seems to be encountering serious difficulties as the products concerned are increasingly based on information covered by potential patents, given that the nature of information is to be sharable[33]. In view of this, *we must ask whether there is a tension, or even an opposition, on this third, global level, between the need for the broadest cooperation possible and a degree of competition, or, in other words, between the huge potential for information-sharing and the financial appropriation of earnings and resources within specific, large entities[34].*

This tension could also be what underlies the "changes in the financial perimeter" of groups over time we have observed here, with the ebb and flow of SMEs in and out of enterprise group control. But how does this tension affect human resource development, an informational resource if there ever was one, and thus a factor of development for these crucial activities[35]?

More generally, the identity and limits of the business world are thus called into question.

---

[33]Marcellin-Taupenas (1994) looks at the example of software in part of a special report on "Technology: the new frontier", called "The limits of patentability". Software is mostly protected by intellectual property rights—which make possible a form of sharing similar to that of the scientific world—rather than by patents. But the pressing demand for patentability is based on the fact that with patenting "*it is easier to make profits from R&D efforts*".

[34]See for instance Foray and Mowery (1990), who emphasise the search for a new functional distribution between inside and outside, starting from the case of R&D. And, on flexible resource monopolisation, Cohendet, Héraud, Zuscovitch (1990). See also Salais (1994), who distinguishes in his conclusion between first, the essential mobility of "*personal competences*", and their fundamental "*universality*", and second, "*advances of funds and resources*", the efficiency of which is assessed within a relatively well-delimited structure, thanks to the identifiability of the products sold. See, finally, Picory (1994), who begins with the "*traditional distinction*" between SMEs and large enterprises, and enquires into the reasons why internal and external strategies find it equally difficult to organise the relationship between "*the identity of the firm*" and "*territorial aggregates*".

[35]In a similar vein, D. Bachet (1995) suggests not viewing territory simply as "*an available resource*", but instead, with a focus on the process of resource *creation*, by considering territory "*as a construct or outcome to be developed*" thanks to "*high-intensity cooperative links between the various socio-economic players*", using "*their potential (...) to mutualise risks, competences and projects*" to "*clear the air of territorial competition*".

6.7 Sharing and appropriation

Analyzing the shifting of the size of production units (towards *"lean production"*) Piore and Sabel (1984) claim that, thanks to the development of networked enterprises with flexible boundaries, *"competition and cooperation serve complementary purposes"*. Meaning that these inter-firm relationships make it possible to go beyond the opposition between competition and cooperation. But in fact they insist further on that, even in this context, competition may go against *"renewing the resources (...) necessary for the continued viability of the whole [productive] system"*. They specifically mention training expenses, and the issue of human resources surfaces once again. They also emphasize the problems the firms have to face takeovers and buyouts, so that the question of appropriation inside enterprise groups is effectively mentioned again as well.

Similarly, G. Naulleau (1993), in a lengthy report of the *Annales des Mines* on international joint-ventures (IJVs), points out that this pattern *"appears to call into question the components of the long-accepted analytical view. [Indeed], for competition, for the market and for the firm as an elementary particle we should now substitute cooperation, the network and the modular enterprise"*. But in the same study, he shows first of all, a high degree of *"instability"* among IJVs, which he sees as being *"part of the very nature of this form of enterprise"*. In support of this thesis, he quotes, amongst others, from a survey of a sample of large IJVs (Bleek and Ernst, 1991), according to which: *"in 75% of cases, when IJVs come to an end, this leads to one of the partners buying back the enterprise as a subsidiary"*. Furthermore, he emphasizes the *"asymmetry between partners"(...), between formal financial control* [of the IJV alone] *and control of strategic resources (...) acquired by a partner who may thus become a competitor overnight"*. He suggests certain limits, made tighter by competition, to the financial treatment of these "strategic resources" (largely informational resources, in fact), even though the enterprises involved in IJVs are usually larger than SMEs as defined here, and IJV configurations have a relatively well-balanced capital structure.

We should also look at the effects on overall growth, and at the "resilience" of the French economic system. As things stand, we see from the profile evolution that the population of SMEs was hit particularly hard by economic difficulties, earlier than the rest of the productive system, as early, in fact, as the late 1980s[36]. To what extent did these difficulties have feedback effects on others enterprises and overall growth? In this case, can we limit ourselves to holding up changes in different categories (enterprise groups/non-enterprise groups, large/small, etc.)?

---

[36]On Canadian data, Julien and Carriere (1994) point to signs that SMEs are *"running out of steam"*, but they do not appear to introduce an enterprise group dimension—not explicitly at least. Gertler, Gilchrist (1994), on American data, seem to confirm the difficulties encountered by SMEs in the turnaround of the early 1990s, although it is not the central focus of their article.

This leads to the question of how patterns of interdependent growth encompassing different components of the productive system can be formalized[37]. In fact, a recent analysis of economic developments in 1994 (Mordant, Thollon-Pommerol, 1996), stressed that the economic upturn hardly affected SMEs—that year—, particularly the ones outside enterprise groups.

7 Conclusion

Two conclusions should not have to be drawn from this study. The first would be to say that enterprise groups are the main threat for independent "SMEs", as the wolf for poor lambs. And to put on the agenda the preservation of a completely atomized economy. It would not be in line with our statistical results. Because enterprise groups showed that, statistically, enterprises "absorbed" has developed a lot, in terms of employment. But the opposite conclusion would be equally disconnected with the statistical elements of the study. It would be to view enterprise groups as white knights saving little firms, and playing the role of the "good" decentralized selector within business system. But, the figures show global significant negative contribution of groups to employment change, if we take into consideration both the "spun off" and the "stayed" companies.

So the conclusion would be the following hypothesis: there is something supplied by groups to independent enterprises, but the price of this "something" seems to be to high for the economy, when this is supplied through (and within) enterprise groups. The question is thus, what is this "something" supplied by groups, when and how ? More in line with our statistical analysis, we would prefer to ask how criteria based on the financial valuation logic (profitability, shareholder value, ...) are fitted to informational and human resource logic and, thus, to "global performance" target. This question is becoming a key one as so far as employment and human/informational resources development turn to be not only *results* of the performance but also *crucial factors* of it. That should ask for needs of new and large sharing-kind institutions, going beyond groups.

As far as research agenda is concerned, the statistical component of the analysis presented here does not provide a breakdown of activities into major branches (industry, commerce, services). As it happens, however, the position of the branch of activity in the "value chain" affects the degree of control enterprises have over that value. Furthermore, activities have been shifting towards services overall (see for instance Rouquette, 1996), and new bridges are forming between services and industry. A recent study by V. Hecquet and D. Roualdès (1995) showed that *"acquisitions and sales, as well as creation and closure of local*

---

[37]These issues are the focus, for instance, of Baldwin (1996) or Jensen and MacGuckin (1996), But they also lead us back to the body of literature on the effects of takeovers (see, eg, Lichtenberg, 1992, or Hubbard and Palia, 1995).

units" by perennial enterprises (rather than enterprise groups) follow quite different patterns in industry, commerce and services[38]. As a continuation, it would be illuminating to fit the development of relations between enterprise groups and non-enterprise groups, as it emerges from the present study, into a sector-based analysis of changes. The second direction would be to analyze the content of both employment and financial payments. It needs building employer-employee-financial accounts files which is one of the main nowadays challenge for business statistics.

Indeed, this would clarify and substantiate the hypotheses formulated here of a search for more ill-defined, but nevertheless real and effective, boundaries between enterprises, and between enterprises and their environment.

8 Appendix

Table 9 Number of companies concerned

	Type of enterprise	Status as of 1992				Total
		Disappeared	Very small	SMEs	Large	
	Non-existent	12,312	5,689	**26,520**	111	44,632
Situation in 1984	**Very small**	5,768	7,079	**12,513**	13	25,373
	SMEs	**24,246**	**11,028**	**38,648**	422	**74,344**
	Large	154	78	**336**	70	638
Total	**20< <500 at least one year between 1984 and 1992**	42,480	23,874	**78,017**	616	144,987

Field: enterprises which belonged to the population of Industry Commerce Services SMEs one year of the period

Reading notes: Rows: the workforce employed by those of the 1984 SMEs, which had become very small as of 1992, was 370,607 positions smaller than it had been in 1984. Columns: the workforce employed by those of the 1992 SMEs, which had been large in 1984, was 238,135 positions smaller than it had been in 1984.

The tables presented here use the so-called *non-interpolated* ("gross") version of the Longitudinal Analysis Database (LAD). This means the LAD has not been

---

[38]See also CSERC (1996) from p. 10.

adjusted for possible false disappearances, beyond the work carried out upstream by the producers of the sources used to construct the LAD.

The fact is that the interpolated LAD reintroduces some "false absences", i.e., presumptive false disappearances of enterprises ("gap" enterprises: gone in year n, but there in years n-1 and n+1). It also ascribes enterprises created in year n, but giving their accounts only in year n+1, to year n. But such adjustments cannot be made for the final year (1992, in this case), since the relevant information only becomes available the following year. In particular, Parent (1995b, p. 20), says that the interpolated LAD is closer to macroeconomic sources (quarterly national accounts) than the gross LAD, in terms of both levels and profiles, *except for the year 1992*, with a relatively stable bias for all the other years. In 1992, however, the interpolated LAD yields a deformed slowdown, which leads to changes over 1984-1992 which conflict with the macroeconomic source (indicating a drop instead of a slight rise). As for the gross LAD, its 1984-1992 evolution seems to fit the macroeconomic source better, despite a sharp discrepancy in levels and a deformed profile for the period. According to Parent (1995b), the additional bias of 1992 in the interpolated LAD is due primarily to newly set up enterprises which had not yet given their accounts in 1992. A rough estimate for the number of enterprises missing as a result of this would be 100,000. The 1984-1992 evolution the LAD will yield, once it has been interpolated with the data from 1993, will enable us to correct much of this bias.

We have, nevertheless, made tables from the *interpolated* LAD. These show that the results differ mainly with respect to large enterprises. As for SMEs, the tables obtained are essentially identical to the ones for non-interpolated data, even when you take account of the field used in the present study, of SMEs at least one year, which could thus have been large enterprises at some point in the period, *except for the total balances*. The other difference is in the order of magnitude of the two component parts of the demographic balance. In the interpolated LAD, the demographic balance for SMEs is negative, whereas it is positive in the gross LAD. It is only natural that interpolation of corrections for false disappearances should alter the demographics, and disappearances in particular. Nevertheless, with the data from 1993, this balance may turn out to be quite different, given that a large number of 1992 creations will be introduced. The sensitivity of this balance led us to be prudent in our comments on it, dwelling not so much on its sign as on its small size compared with the two flows from which it derives.

In the published version of this study, the new interpolated LAD, integrating 1993, will be used. The figures liable to change most markedly in the *interpolated* table are the following (at least):
- upward revision of jobs created in the period 1984-1992 (with repercussions on relevant tables),
- upward revision of creations of independent enterprises,
- and therefore, of demographic balances.

Nevertheless, the orders of magnitude should not change so much as to invalidate the broad framework of the current conclusions.

Finally, with respect to the table for all sizes, taken from the gross LAD, the demographics of large enterprises which were never SMEs will be affected by the correction of the discontinuity experienced by *La Poste* and *France Telecom* as a result of the changed status of the P&T. This change is accounted for, in the gross LAD, in the form of a disappearance, followed by two reappearances, whereas in the interpolated LAD, it is corrected, to ensure continuity. This latter point, however, does not affect the SME and "quasi-SME" segments of the field of study.

Table 10 This table is drawn up from the *interpolated LAD:* Changes in workforce size, 1984-1992 (SMEs one year at least)

		Status as of 1992				
		Disappeared	Very small	SMEs	Large	Total
Situation in 1984	Non-existent	0	46,649	1,263,846	89,712	1,400,207
	Very small	-58,287	-3,754	384,691	21,205	343,855
	SMEs	-1,342,213	-438,292	231,347	251,339	-1,297,819
	Large	-156,727	-119,153	-245,418	-11,705	-533,003
	Total	-1,557,227	-514,550	1,634,466	350,551	- 86,760

Field: enterprises which belonged to the population of Industry Commerce Services SMEs one year of the period

Number of enterprises in gross/interpolated LAD   (SMEs at least one year)

	interpolated LAD	non-interpolated (=gross) LAD	Balance (=interpolated - gross)
1984	108,926	100,355	+8,571
1992	107,619	102,507	+5,112
1984 and/or 1992	145,016	132,675	+12,341

REFERENCES

Airaudi Serge (1994), *"Le destin de la globalisation"*, Revue française de gestion, n° 100, September-October.

Audretsch David (1994), *"Small Business in Industrial Economics - The New Learning"*, Revue d'Economie Industrielle, n° 67, special issue"PME-PMI et économie industrielle", pp. 21-39.

Audretsch David (1995), *Innovation and Industry Evolution*, MIT Press, Cambridge, Massachusetts, 205 pp.

Bachet Daniel (1995), *"Entreprises et territoires - Des dynamiques à repenser"*, in Le Mensuel de l'ANACT (Agence Nationale pour l'Amélioration des Conditions de Travail), September-October, n° 209, pp. 9-10.

Baldwin John (1996), *"Were Small Producers the Engines of Growth in the Canadian Manufacturing Sector in the 1980s ?"*, The International Helsinki Conference on Comparative Analysis of Enterprise Data, Finnish Statistical Institute, Helsinki, 17-19 June, 29 pp.

Baldwin John, Dupuy Richard, Penner William (1992), *"Élaboration de données-panel longitudinales à partir de registres des entreprises : observations du Canada"*, Documents de Recherche, Direction des études analytiques, n° 49, Statistique Canada.

Baldwin John, Dupuy Richard, Picot Garett (1994), *"La part des nouveaux emplois créés au Canada par les petites entreprises est-elle disproportionnée ? Réévaluation des faits"*, Documents de Recherche, Direction des études analytiques, n° 71, novembre, Statistique Canada.

Baldwin John, Picot Garett (1995), *"Employment Generation by Small Producers in the Canadian Manufacturing Sector"*, Small Business Economics, n° 7, p. 317-331, Kluwer Academic Publisher.

Berthier Catherine, Parent Marie-Christine (1994), *"Créations, disparitions et restructurations d'entreprises : les effets sur l'emploi des PME"*, Economie et Statistique, n° 271-272, pp.13-23, Insee.

Birch David L. (1979), *The Job Creation Process*, Program on Neighborhood and Regional Change, MIT.

Birch David L. (1987), *Job Creation in America: How our Smallest Companies Put the Most People to Work*, New-York, Free Press.

Bleek, Ernst (1991), *"The Way to Win in Cross-Border Alliances"*, Harvard Business Review, November, pp.127-135.

Boccara Frédéric, Bouthevillain Karine, Coeuré Benoît, Eyssartier Didier (1996), *"Comment positionner les économies dans le cycle ?"*, Economie Internationale, n° 69, 1st quarter, La Documentation Française, Paris, pp 55-76.

Boccara Paul (1991), *"Révolution informationnelle et débuts possibles d'un nouveau type de régulation dans un système mixte ouvert"*, speech to the Sixth Franco-Japanese Symposium on Economics, October 1991, published in Mondes en développement n° 79/80, tome 20, 1992, pp. 125-132.

Bonneau Jacques (1994), *"La création d'entreprises, source de renouvellement du tissu des PME"*, Economie et Statistique, n° 271-272, pp. 25-36, Insee.

Bonneau Jacques, Francoz Dominique (1994), *"Le devenir des entreprises créées en 1987"*, Insee Première, n° 312, April, Insee-ANCE, 4 pp.

Bonneau Jacques, Francoz Dominique (1995), *"Le profil du créateur influence la survie de l'entreprise"*, Insee Première, n° 372, April, Insee-ANCE, 4 pp.

Bonturi Marcos, Fukasaku Kiichiro (1993), *"Analyse empirique de la mondialisation et des échanges intra-entreprise"*, Revue Economique de l'OCDE, n° 20, spring.

Brown Charles, Hamilton James, Medoff James (1990), *Employers Large and Small*, Harvard University Press, Cambridge, Massachusetts, 109 pp.

Callon M., Laredo P., Rabeharisoa V. (1991), *"Des instruments pour la gestion et l'évaluation des programmes technologiques : le cas de l'AFME"*, in De Bandt Jacques et Foray Dominique éditeurs, Évaluation économique de la recherche et du changement technique, Éditions du CNRS, Paris.

Chabanas Nicole, Thollon-Pommerol Vincent (1991), *"Place des groupes dans l'économie française"*, methodological notes, pp. 217-249, Insee résultats, n° 138-139, May, 264 pp.

Chabanas Nicole, Vergeaud Eric (1997), *"Le nombre de groupes d'entreprises a explosé en 15 ans"*, Insee première, n° 553, November, 4 pp.

Cohendet Patrick, Héraud Jean-Alain, Zuscovitch Ehud (1990), *"Apprentissage technologique, réseaux économiques et appropriabilité des innovations"*, pp. 63-78, in Technologie et richesse des nations, OECD symposium, Foray Dominique et Freeman Christopher éditeurs, Economica, 1992, 517 pp.

Combier Jérôme, Mas Cyrille, Philippe Jérôme (1996), *"Structure verticale et performance de la distribution : théorie et application à des données françaises"*, *mimeo*, Insee, Division Commerce, 46 pp.

Corbel Patrick, Fréchou Hélène (1994*), "Les restructurations industrielles de 1979 à 1981"*, Insee Première, n° 318, May, Insee, 4 pp.

Coriat Benjamin (1991), *Penser à l'envers. Travail et organisation dans l'entreprise japonaise*, Christian Bourgois, Paris, 186 pp.

Cserc (Conseil supérieur de l'emploi des revenus et des coûts) (1996), *"Inégalités d'emploi et de revenus : les années 90"*, deuxième rapport annuel du CSERC, La Documentation Française, 110 pp.

Dares (1995), *"L'emploi et les relations sociales dans les PME"*, Symposium of 11 October 1994, minutes by Bruno Baranger, in Travail et Emploi, n° 63, 2/95, La Documentation Française, pp. 89-99.

Dares, Insee, Liaisons Sociales (1996), *"Les PME et leurs salariés"*, Les Dossiers Thématiques, n° 4, éditions Liaisons, 172 pp.

Darréon Jean-Louis, Faïçal Serge (1993), *"Les enjeux des partenariats stratégiques entre grandes entreprises et PME"*, Revue Française de Gestion, n° 95, September-octobre.

David Paul (1994), *"Les standards des technologies de l'information, les normes de communication et l'État : un problème de biens publics"*, pp.249-278, in Analyse économique des conventions, sous la direction de André Orléan, PUF, 403 pp.

Davis Steven J., Haltiwanger John (1990), *"Gross Job Creation and Destruction: Microeconomic Evidence and Macroeconomic Implications"*, Macroeconomics Annual, NBER, Cambridge Massachusetts, pp. 123-186.

Davis Steven .J., Haltiwanger John et Schuh Scott (1996), *"Small Business and Job Creation: Dissecting the Myth and Reassessing the Facts"*, Small Business Economics, n° 8 (4), août, université de Chicago et NBER, p. 297-315.

De Bandt Jacques (1994), *"De l'économie des biens à l'économie des services : la production de richesse dans et par les services"* pp. 309-338, quatrième partie "Perspectives" de Relations de service, marchés de services, sous la direction de Jacques De Bandt et Jean Gadrey, CNRS éditions, collection recherche et entreprise.

De Bandt Jacques, Petit Pascal (1994), *"Compétitivité : la place des rapports industries/services"*, in Entreprise France - Made in France /2, Le Livre de Poche-Commissariat Général au Plan, LGF, pp. 153-191.

Delapierre Michel (1991), *"Les accords inter-entreprises, partage ou partenariat ? Les stratégies des groupes européens de traitement de l'information"* in Revue d'Economie Industrielle, n° 55, 1st trimester, pp.135-161.

Delattre Michel (1982), *"Les PME face aux grandes entreprises"* in Economie et Statistique, n° 148, October, pp.3-19.

Duchéneaut Bertrand (1995), *Enquête sur les PME françaises. Identités, Contexte, Chiffres*, éd. CEPME et Maxima, Paris, distribution PUF, 577 pp.

Dunne Timothy, Roberts Mark J., Samuelson Larry (1989), *"Plant Turnover and Gross Employment Flows in the US Manufacturing Sector"*, Journal of Labor Economics, Vol. 7, n° 1, January, pp. 48-71.

Dupuy Richard, Picot Garnett, (1996), *"Créations d'emplois selon la taille des entreprises : concentration et persistance des gains et pertes d'emplois dans les entreprises canadiennes"*, Documents de Recherche, Direction des études analytiques, n° 93, April, Statistique Canada.

Economie et Statistique (1988), *numéro spécial sur les créations d'entreprises* n° 215, November.

Eurostat (1994), *"Enterprises Demography"* in Enterprises in Europe. Third report, October, Eurostat.

Filippi Maryline, Pierre Emmanuel, Torre André (1996), *"Quelles approches économiques pour la notion de réseau ? Contenu théorique et dimensions opérationnelles"*, Revue d'Économie Industrielle, n° 77, 3rd trimester, pp. 87-98.

Foray Dominique (1995), *"Innovation, connaissance et information : un rapide tour d'horizon"*, Séminaire Economie de l'information, Commissariat Général au Plan, 20 pp.

Foray Dominique, Mowery David C. (1990), *"L'intégration de la R&D industrielle : nouvelles perspectives d'analyse"*, Revue Economique, Vol. 41, n° 3, pp. 501-530.

Francoz Dominique (1995), *"Estimation des cessations d'entreprises : méthode et résultats"*, IVèmes Journées de Méthodologie Statistique, 18 and 19 October, Insee, 9 pp.

Francoz Dominique (1996), *"Les cessations d'entreprises depuis 1989"*, Insee Première, n° 463, June, Insee, 4 pp.

Freeman Christopher (1994), *"Changement technologique et économie mondiale"*, Futuribles, n° 186, April, pp. 25-48.

Geroski P. A., Schwalbach Joachim (1991), *Entry and Market Contestability. An International Comparison*, Blackwell, Oxford UK & Cambridge Massachusetts, 304 pp.

Gertler Mark, Gilchrist Simon (1994), *"Monetary Policy, Business Cycles, and the Behavior of Small Manufacturing Enterprises"*, Quarterly Journal of Economics, Vol. CIX, n° 2, pp. 309-340, May.

Gorgeu Armelle, Mathieu René (1995), *"Nouvelles usines : nouvelle gestion des emplois?"*, La Lettre du Centre d'Etudes de l'Emploi, n° 36, February, pp. 1-10.

Greenan Nathalie (1995), *"Technologie, changement organisationnel, qualifications et emploi : une étude empirique sur l'industrie manufacturière"*, Documents de travail de la Direction des Etudes et Synthèses Economiques, n° G 9504, November, Insee, 40 pp.

Gronan Reuben, Regev Haim, (1996) *"Job Turnover in Israel's Manufacturing Sector 1970-1994"*, paper presented at The International Helsinki Conference on Comparative Analysis of Enterprise Data, Finnish Statistical Institute, Helsinki, 17-19 June, Helsinki, 20 pp.

Hakansson H., Johanson J. (1990), *"Formal and Informal Cooperation Strategies in International Industrial Networks"*, in Contractor F. et Lorange P., Editors, Cooperative Strategies in International Business, Lexington Book.

Hamermesh Daniel S., Hassink Wolter H. J., Van Ours Jan C. (1996), *"Job Turnover and Labor Turnover: a Taxinomy of Employement Dynamics"*, Annales d'économie et de statistique, n° 41/42, pp.21-40.

Handy Charles (1994), *The Empty Raincoat - Making Sense of the Future*, Hutchinson, Londres, 280 pp.

Hecquet Vincent, Roualdes Danielle (1995*), "Les mouvements de l'emploi au sein des entreprises"*, Insee première, n° 412, October, Insee, 4 p.

Hietaniemi Leena (1996), *"Finnish Manufacturing and Construction Enterprises and their Employees 1987-93: Enterprise Demography and Job Flows Analysis"*, speech delivered at The International Helsinki Conference on Comparative Analysis of Enterprise Data, Finnish Statistical Institute, Helsinki, 17-19 June, 9 pp.

Hubbard R. Glenn, Palia Darius (1995), *"Benefits of Control, Managerial Ownership and the Stock Returns of Acquiring Enterprises"*, The Rand Journal of Economics, Winter 1995, Vol 26, n° 4, pp. 782-792.

Insee (1980), collective work (Bouilly, Citoleux, Dollé, Encaoua, Franck, Hannoun, Héon, Thollon-Pommerol, de Vannoise) , " *les groupes de sociétés dans le système productif français"*, Les collections de l'Insee, n° E71, Insee, 192 pp.

Insee (1992), *La France des entreprises*, L'entreprise et Insee éditeurs, 244 pp.

Jensen J. Bradford, Mac Guckin Robert H. (1996), *"Enterprise Performance and Evolution: Empirical Regularities in the Microdata"*, in The Evolution of Firms and Industries - International Perspectives, proceedings of *CAED '96*, Seppo Laaksonen (ed.), Statistics Finland, Helsinki, pp 24-49.

Julien Pierre-André, Carrière Jean-Bernard (1994), *"L'efficacité des PME et les nouvelles technologies"*, Revue d'Economie Industrielle, n° 67, numéro spécial "PME-PMI et économie industrielle", pp. 120-134.

Kleijweg Aad, Nieuwenhuijsme Henry (1996), *"Job Creation by Size-Class: Measurement and Empirical Evaluation"*, CBS Study, CERES-26, Voorburg, December, 26 pp..

Klette Tor Jacob, Mathiassen Astrid (1996), *"Job destruction and Plant Turnover in Norwegian Manufacturing"*, Annales d'économie et de statistique, n° 41/42, pp. 91-125.

Lagarde Sylvie, Maurin Eric, Torelli Constance (1994), *"Créations et suppressions d'emplois en France, une étude de la période 1984-92"*, Economie et Prévision, n° 112-113, 1994/2-3, pp. 67-88.

Lichtenberg Franck R. (1992), *Corporate Takeovers and Productivity*, The MIT Press, Cambridge, Massachusetts, 153 pp.

Linhart Danièle (1994), *La modernisation des entreprises*, éditions La Découverte, 124 pp.

Loveman Gary, Sengenberger Werner (1991), *"The Re-emergence of Small-Scale Production: an International Comparison"*, Small Business Economics, 3, pp. 1-37.

Mac Guckin Robert H. (1995), *"Local unit Microdata for Economic Research and Policy Analysis: Looking Beyond the Aggregates"*, Journal of Business and Economic Statistics, January, Vol. 13, n° 1, pp. 121-126.

Mac Guckin Robert H., Pascoe George A., Jr. (1988), *"The Longitudinal Database: Status and Research Possibilities"*, Survey of Current Business, November, pp. 30-37.

Marcellin-Taupenas Sabine (1994), *"La brevetabilité des logiciels"*, Annales des Mines, série "Réalités Industrielles", July-August, éditions Eska, pp. 89-92.

Meghir Costas, Ryan Annette, Van Reener John (1996), *"Job Creation, Technological Innovation and Adjustment Costs: Evidence form a Panel of British Enterprises"*, Annales d'économie et de statistique, n° 41/42, pp.255-274.

Motohashi Kazuyuki (1996), *"Japanese Experience of Longitudinal Dataset Analysis and International Perspectives"*, in The Evolution of Firms and Industries - International Perspectives, proceedings of *CAED'96*, Seppo Laaksonen (ed.), Statistics Finland, Helsinki, pp. 50-64.

Mustaniemi Tuija (1996), *"Enterprise Demography as a Method of Studying Real Enterprise's Births: an Application to Enterprise's Births in Manufacturing and Retail Trade"*, in The Evolution of Firms and Industries - International Perspectives, proceedings of CAED'96, Seppo Laaksonen (ed.), Statistics Finland, Helsinki, pp. 207-233.

Nauleau Gérard (1993), *"La Joint-Venture Internationale - Forme complexe et labile d'entreprise"*, Gérer et Comprendre, série trimestrielle des Annales des Mines, mars, éditions Eska, n °30, p. 4-16.

OECD (1985), *"The Employment in the Small and Medium sized Enterprises: Where the Jobs come from ?"*, Employment Outlook, September, chapter IV.

Paranque Bernard (1994), *"Fonds propres, rentabilité et efficacité chez les PMI. Méthodes d'analyse et appréciation des situations financières"*, Revue d'Economie Industrielle, n° 67, numéro spécial "PME-PMI et économie industrielle", p. 175-190.

Parent Marie-Christine (1995a), *"Les PME françaises. Evolutions d'emploi 1985-1992"*, Documents de travail de la Direction des Statistiques d'Entreprises, n° E 9504, June, Insee, 14 p.

Parent Marie-Christine (1995b*), "Une Base longitudinale de données d'entreprises : problèmes et résultats"*, IVèmes Journées de Méthodologie Statistique, 18-19 October, Insee, 29 p.

Pattinson W., Tozer C. (1996), *"Australian Business Longitudinal Survey"*, paper presented at The International Helsinki Conference on Comparative Analysis of Enterprise Data, Finnish Statistical Institute, Helsinki, 17-19 June, 12 pp.

Picory Christian (1994*), "PME, incertitude et organisation industrielle : une mise en perspective"*, Revue d'Economie Industrielle, n° 67, special issue "PME-PMI et économie industrielle", pp. 40-58.

Piore Michael J., Sabel Charles F. (1984), *The Second Industrial Divide*, Basic Books.

Reich Robert (1991), *The Work of Nations*, Alfred A. Knopf, Inc. New-York.

Rizzoni Alina (1994), *"Technology and Organization in Small Enterprises: an Interpretative Framework"*, Revue d'Economie Industrielle, n° 67, special issue "PME-PMI et économie industrielle", pp. 135-155.

Robson Geoffrey B., Gallagher Colin C. (1992), *"An Evaluation of the Dun & Bradstreet Database for Job Generation Research"*, Research Report, Management Division, University of Newcastle upon Tyne, March.

Robson Geoffrey B., Gallagher Colin C. (1994), *"Change in the Size Distribution of UK Enterprises"*, Small Business Economics, Vol. 6 n° 4, August, pp. 299-312, Kluwer Academic Publishers.

Rouquette Céline (1996), *"L'essor des services depuis les années soixante"* Insee Première, n° 498, December, Insee, 4 pp.

Savoye Bertrand, Perea Eva (1993*), "La poussée des PMI en Europe et l'exception allemande"*, Insee Première, n° 246, February, Insee-Eurostat, 4 pp.

Schumacher Fritz-E. (1973), *Small is Beautiful*, Blong and Briggs, Londres, 1973.

Storey David J., Jonhson Stephen (1986), *"Job Generation in Britain: A Review of Recent Studies"*, International Small Business Journal, 4 (4), pp. 29-47.

Templé Philippe, Lhuillery Stéphane (1994), *"L'organisation de la recherche et développement des PME-PMI"*, Economie et Statistique, n° 271-272, Insee, pp. 77-85.

Thollon-Pommerol Vincent (1990), *"Les groupes et la déformation du système productif"*, Economie et Statistique, n° 229, pp. 21-28, Insee.

Thollon-Pommerol Vincent (1996), *"Données de cadrage sur les groupes"*, Communication au Sixième colloque de comptabilité nationale, Paris, January 24-26th, Insee, Paris 1 University, 13 p.

Viennet Henri (1990), *"Survivre : premier souci des jeunes entreprises"*, Insee Première, n° 110, November, Insee, 4 pp.

INTERNATIONAL COMPARABILITY AND QUALITY OF STATISTICS

Raoul Depoutot[1] and Philippe Arondel[2]

1Eurostat
2Planistat Europe

1 Quality of statistics

Although it has been a lasting concern for statistical offices for years, the topic of quality has received explicit attention only relatively recently. Even if some forerunners tackled this problem since the end of the 70s or beginning of the 80s *(USBC, UN, Statistics Canada)*, it was necessary to wait until 95 to see more and more organisations involved in an explicit quality policy *(SMPQ Conference, Bristol, 1995)*. In order to understand better the diversity of approaches, it is convenient to use the ISO 8402 definition of quality, that is in practice the one used explicitly or implicitly by statistical organisations (SOs hereafter). This norm states that: *"Quality is the totality of features and characteristics of a product or service that bear on its ability to satisfy stated or implied needs"*. What is crucial is then *users' satisfaction,* and the diversity of users may explain different behaviours of SOs.
For a good summary on this question, see Elvers and Rosén (1997).

Eurostat has worked on the definition of quality in statistics for several years, and since 1994 it has developed its own approach to the quality measurement. It has in particular benefited from the experience of many organisations (see Eurostat, 1996) and from the explicit support of several national statistical offices of the European Union, in particular Statistics Sweden[1].

1.1 Quality for countries

Most SOs agree on the essential components of quality, that can be presented as:

---

[1] This of course does not imply that Statistics Sweden necessarily supports the choice made by Eurostat in its approach to quality definition and quality reporting.

- *relevance of contents*: the statistical concept is relevant if it is adequate to measure the concept (economic, sociologic, demographic...) in which the users are interested.
- *timeliness*: Most users want up-to-date figures, which are published frequently and on time at pre-established dates.
- *accuracy*: Accuracy is defined as the closeness between the estimated value and the (unknown) true population value.
- *accessibility and availability of statistical information*: Statistical data have most value when they are easily accessible by users, are available in the forms users desire and are adequately documented.
- *consistency*: Statistics are coherent in that statistics pertaining to elementary concepts can be combined reliably in more complex ways. The messages that statistics convey to users will then clearly relate to each other, or at least will not contradict each other. In particular, statistics should be consistent through time, and allow international comparisons.

A good example of that approach is *Statistics Sweden's* quality declaration (Statistics Sweden, 1994).

1.3 Quality for international organisations

International organisations are generally not involved in data collection activities and have little influence on the process. They focus their efforts on comparability and coherence of the produced statistics. Therefore, they devote much energy on the adoption of common norms (concepts and classifications). For instance in Eurostat, in business statistics, there are now agreed definitions on:

- the statistical units,
- the population of reference,
- the classification of activities and of products,
- the characteristics to observe,
- the statistics to produce.

However, as presented by Defays (1995), this does not guarantee totally the comparability.

And coherence of the statistics is still a challenge.

In order to underline the above concern, Eurostat has agreed on a definition of quality of statistics where seven components appear:

1. relevance of the concepts
2. accuracy of the statistics
3. timeliness
4. clarity and accessibility
5. comparability
6. coherence
7. completeness of the statistical system

Compared to the analysis of quality at the national level, comparability insists on the links between statistics from different Member States, when coherence and completeness insist on the links between different statistics of the same statistical system.

In this decomposition, the "relevance of concepts" covers the correspondence between the question raised by the users (in the economic demographic, social domain) with the reference statistical norms adopted at the EU level. This applies as well to any international organisation.

Comparability then covers discrepancies between the national definitions and the EU norms[2] and discrepancies due to the measurement process.

What does accuracy measure?

The distance easiest to measure is the distance between the unknown true value and the estimates based on national concepts. Of course, we would prefer to measure directly the distance between the true value corresponding to the European concept and the estimate. But this is quite impossible in practice since the European concepts are very abstract concepts and especially on a regular basis.

We should note as well that this remark is true as well for the European aggregates, which are simply derived from the national estimates.

Therefore, we have to introduce new terms, the national and European estimates adjusted for lack of comparability.

The precision at national level is the distance between the European concept applied at national level (ECN) and the national measurement corresponding to the European concept ($NMEC$).

The $NMEC$ can not be observed directly and is divided into two observable components:
- the national measurement corresponding to the national concept ($NMNC$)
- the national measurement of lack of comparability ($NMLC$).

Then NMEC= NMNC+ NMLC.

At European level, the precision is given by the distance between ECN for the European Union and the European measurement corresponding to the European concept ($EMEC$).

The $EMEC$ has to be estimated by

$$\sum_{i \in EU} NMEC(i) = \sum_{i \in EU} NMNC(i) + NMLC(i)$$

See the graphs in annex 4 for an illustration.

What about coherence?

The pragmatic approach requires starting with the evaluation of coherence of national statistics based on national concepts. From an international point of

---

[2] Comparability with statistics outside of the EU is also a concern, particularly with major economic partners (USA, Japan).

view, the aim is to get statistics adjusted for lack of comparability that are coherent.

Therefore, the evaluation of coherence has to follow the adjustment for lack of comparability (Note that this is the same for comparability through time, which is required for coherence of statistics of different frequencies).

Note about coherence:

Coherence applies to concepts and measurements as well.

It is difficult to analyse or use for analysis published estimates with different random values (i.e. two series incoherent on the random point of view).

For example: if one series XA is annual and there exists a monthly series XM^i for exactly the same concept, we have

$$XA = E(XA) + u \qquad XM^i = E(XM^i) + u^i$$

$$Var\ u = \Gamma_A^2 \qquad Var\ u^i = \Gamma_M^2 (\text{indep. of } i)$$

If they are conceptually coherent and statistically unbiased:

$$E(XA) = \sum_{i=1}^{12} E(XM^i)$$

However, the accuracy of XA and $XM = \sum_{i=1}^{12} XM^i$ are different and it should be preferable to use series adjusted for random incoherence.

An annual adjusted series (XL) may be built by a linear combination of XA and XM.

Then we are looking for λ, μ such that

$$XL = \lambda\ XA + \mu\ XM \qquad \text{unbiased and minimum variance}$$

It is straightforward to see (Annex 2) that λ and μ can be chosen so has to improve XA and XM.

Therefore, in the absence of budget shortages, all statistics should be "improved", if the bias due to the concepts is known. In particular, infra-annual statistics should be benchmarked on annual or multi-annual statistics (which may be adjusted for lack of random coherence).

Accuracy and comparability:

All comparisons between countries should take into account these aspects: the randomness of the national estimates and their possible bias with respect to the national concept and the adjustment for lack of comparability. Of course, the essential difficulty is to measure this lack of comparability.

Remark: Every analysis of quality into components is arbitrary. Other proposals can be found in Eurostat (1996a). For an in-depth analysis of the logic behind this decomposition and some problems attached to it, see Elvers and Lindstroem (1996). The one above takes particularly into account the work organisation in the EU statistical system. All projects are developed domain by domain and take naturally into account relevance, accuracy, timeliness, comparability. Coherence depends largely from the units in charge of horizontal co-ordination in Eurostat and in the NSOs. Accessibility and Clarity is under the responsibility of each SO, and completeness is under the responsibility of the high level Committee of General Directors of Eurostat and NSOs.

2 International comparability

2.1 The "uniform" approach

The simplest approach, from the theoretical point of view, consists in attempting to define exactly the same concepts, the same measurement process (sampling and non-sampling), and to re-build so some sort of fictive unique reference population as if it were more or less the same country. For an example, see Kish (1994). However, in depth attempt to do that - or even less - is in fact relatively unrealistic. See Defays (1995) for a critic review of many difficulties encountered when doing so from the point of view of the measurement process except the sampling phase. Furthermore, this approach is not politically acceptable, and is implemented only in a limited number of cases.

As shown above in 1.2, in order to guarantee a certain level of comparability, not only the correction for lack of comparability has to be taken into account, but also the randomness of national estimates.

Focusing only on non-sampling errors, to reach the objective of comparability, it is shown in annex 1 that the accuracy of national statistics should be the same for all Member States, leading to proportionally a bigger effort in the smallest Member States. This should mean proportionally higher expenses for their statistical office and higher average sampling rate for their enterprises, especially in sectors where the concentration is low (in some services for instance).

2.2 The "meta-data" approach

Collecting all meta-data on the statistical production process has been attempted by several International organisations - among which Eurostat - as a possible solution on the road to comparability. It appeared however that this is an extraordinarily long task, never achieved due to constant changes in the different national methodologies, and of very little use in practice for many users. This leads to the development of warning signals in the tables of results indicating non-comparability, but with no quantification of this non-comparability. For an example, see Eurostat (1997).

2.3 The "subsidiarity" approach

The subsidiarity approach consists in relying on the National Statistical Offices to produce the statistics along production[3] techniques chosen at the national level, and reporting on all dimensions of the quality - among which comparability. The essential tool for that is a quality report, where the NSOs have to give information on the first six components of quality. For a description of a standard quality report, see Eurostat (1996b).

Facing the difficulty to get a precise measure of all aspects of quality, for important statistics at the EU level, one solution to go round the problem has been the harmonisation of statistics. Two types of harmonisation can be considered:
* harmonisation of the statistics: common classifications, common statistical units, common characteristics are defined at the EU level. Member States are free to choose the survey process.
  Then, this reduces clearly the lack of comparability in a drastic way, but keeps some errors in the implementation process (if the same rules are implemented with different legal, cultural, administrative systems, some minor discrepancies remain).
* harmonisation of the methods: both the concepts and the measurement processes are harmonised. This means that the errors attached to the implementation of the concepts are comparable in the different countries (it is then reasonable to assume some approximate proportionality of the bias due to remaining implementation errors to the size of the country). Even if they are unknown, we have reliable estimates of the ratios between countries.

---

[3] The production activity encompasses all phases between development of concepts and the analyses of results: sampling design, data collection, measurement, processing (editing and imputation), provision of statistical estimates.

For a thorough analysis of the harmonisation and relation with quality, see Eurostat (1998).

3 Modelling approach

3.1 The method

There are however in practice many limits to harmonisation:

- Many international organisations are not in a political position to go beyond the definition of many agreed concepts and cannot make their Member States enforce these agreements.
- More and more often, Member States of the EU are reluctant to go beyond a certain level of harmonisation, and mainly in the most critical domains.
- The harmonisation process is very long and the users are sometimes getting impatient.

In case of partial harmonisation, the different errors found in a quality report should help assessing the remaining lack of harmonisation. However, it might be difficult to quantify some of these, using traditional statistical sampling techniques, as for instance the non-comparability bias. Modelling some aspects is certainly a cheap solution.

Therefore, International Organisations should produce more estimates, based on techniques outside of sampling surveys, preferably in the field of econometrics. This is a sensitive proposal for political reasons:

- Countries tend to consider that the information on their own country is part of their sovereignty;
- the existence of two sets of statistics (the national ones and the internationally harmonised ones) could be a possible source of tensions. In absence of adequate communication about these harmonised statistics, some users would be confused, others would consider that both statistical organisations are competitors, others would choose in both sets the most favourable information... A possible solution would be to express adjusted statistics only in relative terms in the EU total.

Other Member States raise a more ethical issue: public statisticians should not express opinions but only impartial information. In technical terms, the only accepted methods are then those of the traditional sampling survey statistics, i.e. excluding model-based methods. Any use of a model is then assimilated to a judgement and therefore highly subjective. Even the wording may differ:

"estimator" in survey sampling and "estimator" in econometrics are sometimes different words in their language[4].).

Which model for the adjustment of business statistics for comparability?

Let us consider that we face a situation where a set of countries has agreed on: common statistical units' definitions, common classifications and common characteristics. Supposing that these definitions are those of the EU, and that they are fully implemented, is it sufficient for the comparability of the produced statistics?

More precisely, statistics are comparable if one user facing the statistics and the usual meta-information (name of the characteristic, type of aggregate, possibly short comment) on several countries can derive from these the message that is embedded in the set of individual data and the proposed angle of observation.

Taking an example, if we propose to the users the following table in a publication

	Value-added	Employment	Value-added/employment
Country A	100	40	2,5
Country B	120	40	3

They are lead naturally to the conclusion that employment productivity is 20% higher in country B than in country A, and so that the organisation of enterprises in country B is considerably more efficient that in country A.

If the statistics are relevant, they should be described and analysed with the concepts of the users, in our case macro economists, micro-economists or in general analysts of business activities.

Therefore, the concepts of the theory of the firm that underlie the analysis of users have to be used, as their developments:
1. The employment concept has to integrate the length of work ("full-time equivalent" in our jargon) and the qualification of the work force.
2. The type of activity is important, and multi-activity cannot be reduced to the idea of a main activity. Different companies in the same industry can have a very different profile, depending on how much they invest in R&D and innovation, if they are vertically very integrated or solely assemble transformed goods and components produced by others.
3. The structure of capital goods is well known to be very influent on the organisation and structure of the enterprise;

---

[4] In German, this is respectively "Hochrechnung" and "Schätzung", the second being close to "guess".

4. The businesses have different behaviour if they are integrated in a group of enterprises (company) or not. Any isolation of a part of a company as an enterprise is very delicate.
5. This above aspect has more consequences on national aggregates if the considered company is multi-national, and the analysis is conducted at the national level.
6. Businesses are very dependent from their market or even from the providers of "input": this link is sometimes not reflected in the concepts used by statisticians since the "imports" and "exports" can be realised by intermediary sectors like wholesale trade.
7. Externalisation of some activities can change the profile of the enterprises as shown in their accounts (this is particularly the case for sub-contracting). Some sectors can have a more or less importance (services like catering, wholesale) depending on the extent of externalisation by the manufacturing sector.
8. The legal framework has a clear impact on the evaluation of taxes, salaries and social contributions, costs of training.
9. Financial resources and past history of the firms have an important role in the analysis.
10. Enterprises are not necessarily in the same phase of the business cycle. Differences between countries can be observed in this respect, and could be taken into account for special purposes. For an example of model allowing that, see Bienvenue (1997).

It should be noted that many of these limitations are not specific to the international comparisons, but apply to comparisons between regions, industries of a single country or even to comparisons through time. For instance, the fast development of the service industries during the last 30 years in the EU is partly explained by the externalisation of activities realised by the manufacturing sector.

Facing this long list of limitations, one may be tempted to envisage a collection of statistics based on more adapted statistical units, classifications, and concepts. But the constant concern for the burden on enterprises and the limitation of NSOs budget prevent us from doing so. *The alternative is then to re-formulate our description of the businesses and thanks to an adapted modelling use econometric methods to assess non-directly observed concepts.*

How could we proceed?

It is necessary to:
- develop a list of reference econometric models, adapted to the different characteristics that have to be adjusted for lack of comparability, in relation with economists.
- create a database for *textual information*, well structured, containing translated information collected from published information sources like media, companies accounts, monographs by business researchers. Interface this database with modern tools for textual data analysis or semantic research.

- add to the raw statistics "statistics adjusted for lack of comparability", in a way similar to what is done for seasonal adjustment. Make the modelling hypotheses of process known to users and allow the use of alternate models on request of the users. Especially, adjust for the limitations of comparability listed 1 to 10 above.
- intensify the use of administrative data and merge more systematically files of individual data coming from different surveys in order to provide the necessary information for model estimations. (Example: files from social security or labour force survey would be necessary to adjust for length of work, number of work hours and for qualifications).
- preserve the multi-dimensionality of the information by insisting more on the scattering of individual data around the first-order summaries like mean or median. Use ACOVA models with national dummies, quantiles, and graphical methods or data analysis techniques as principal components or factors analysis in order to make users aware of these overlaps of national distributions.

Table 1 Proposal for a standard table for international comparisons

Productivity of labour for sector   .of ISIC/ NACE   Year

	Countries					European Union or International Organisations
	1	2	....	14	15	
Unadjusted comparison % EU						
Adjusted for:						
1 employment structure work length qualification						
2 secondary activity differences						
3 structure of capital goods						
4 affiliation to a national group						
5 affiliation to a foreign group						
6 differences of markets						
7 externalisation of some activities						
8 differences in social compensation						
9 financial resources						
10 differences in business cycle						
Total adjustment						

3.2 An expansion of the method for tackling the non-comparability of the concept of workforce in business statistics

Let us consider now the example of the adjustment for differences in the length of the work and composition of the work force for the comparison of the productivity of labour.

For each country i, we can estimate the production function of the firms f^i defined by:

$$VA^i = f^i\left(Nbh, QW_1, QW_2, \ldots QW_k, Ast_1, Ast_p, R\&D, \ldots\right) \qquad [1]$$

where VA denotes the value-added, Nbh denotes the total of number of worked hours, $QW_1, QW_2, \ldots QW_k$ denote the number of employees with qualification 1 to k, Ast_1, Ast_p denote the assets of type 1 to p, $R\&D$ denotes R&D stock, etc. as defined at the EU level.

Using the individual data coming from different surveys[5] and administrative data, we can get directly the values of exogenous characteristics of $[1]$ on merged individuals in one to one correspondence. On this subset, we can as well estimate functions relating the national summary characteristics collected in some surveys[6] and the most detailed information on which the comparability model can be built.

Therefore, $Nbh, QW_1, QW_2, \ldots QW_k, Ast_1, Ast_p, R\&D, \ldots$ can be either measured or estimated for all enterprises of the sample.

In a similar way, the employment of firm j, denoted can be E^j defined as.

$$E^j = g^i\left(Nbh^j, QW_1^j, \ldots, QW_k^j\right)$$

The functions f^i and g^i can be estimated from the data.

3.2.1 The full adjustment for comparability

Supposing that we know the joint distribution of $Nbh, QW_1, \ldots QW_k$ in country A and in the EU, that we denote these respectively P^A and P^{EU}, then the average productivity of labour for country A is

---

[5] May be limited because of negative co-ordination of samples between surveys.

[6] In business surveys for instance, only total employment is asked. In social surveys, much information on the qualification, length of work and other characteristics is collected

$$LP^A = \frac{\int_A f^A(x)\, dP^A(x)}{\int_A g^A(x)\, dP^A(x)}$$

and the adjusted Labour Productivity is defined by

$$ALP^{A/EU} = \frac{\int_{EU} f^A(x)\, dP^{EU}(x)}{\int_{EU} g^{EU}(x)\, dP^{EU}(x)}$$

where g^{EU} denotes the estimation of the function g at the EU level, that is some sense represents the "average" meaning of the employment concept. It should be noted that this econometric estimation has to take into account the sampling weights of the units, in a coherent way between Member States (the weights are all equal to one in the exhaustive strata, whatever the country).

If a representative sample s^{EU} of EU enterprises j is available, corresponding to the inclusion probabilities Π_j, the above $ALP^{A/EU}$ can be estimated by:

$$EALP^{A/EU} = \frac{\sum_{j \in s^{EU}} f^A(Nbh^j, QW_1^j, ...QW_k^j)/\Pi_j}{\sum_{j \in s^{EU}} g^{EU}(Nbh^j, QW_1^j, ...QW_k^j)/\Pi_j}$$

3.2.2 A simplified adjustment for comparability

If country A has not access to individual data of other countries, it can produce a simplified adjustment by using a calibration technique to re-weight the units in the sample in order to reflect the EU structure. This calibration can be done either on the joint distribution of the explanatory variables $Nbh, QW_1, ...QW_k$ - and then it is the classical a posteriori re-weighting - or on the marginal distributions. Considering that the joint distribution is likely to be more difficult to estimate we can envisage the case where only the marginals are available.

Using the sampling weights Πj of all enterprises j of the sample s^A in country A, we can estimate the joint distribution λ^A of $Nbh, QW_1, ..., QW_k$ in country A.

We can do the same at the EU level and we get a distribution function μ^{EU}. Using for instance the method described in Deville & Särndal (1992), after having chosen a distance function $d\left(\lambda^A, \mu^{EU}\right)$, on the marginal distributions, we can get the Π_j^{*A} that minimises $d\left(\lambda^A, \mu^{EU}\right)$.

Similarly, instead of estimating the g function at the EU level, one can approximate it by a weighted sum of the national functions:

$$g_*^{EU} = \sum_{i=1}^{15} \omega_i g^i$$

Using the g_*^{EU} function above, we can defined the approximately adjusted employment by

$$E_*^j = g_*^{EU}(Nbh^j, QW_1^j, ..., QW_k^j) = \sum_{i=1}^{15} \omega_i g^i(Nbh^j, QW_1^j, ..., QW_k^j)$$

Using these Π_j^{*A}, we can re-estimate the aggregates $\sum_{j \in s(A)} VA^j$ and $\sum_{j \in s(A)} E_*^j$, and define the adjusted ratio by:

$$EALP_s^A = \frac{\sum_{j \in s(A)} VA^j / \Pi_j^{*A}}{\sum_{j \in s(A)} E_*^j / \Pi_j^{*A}}$$

using the following notations,

$$LP_s^A = \frac{\sum_{j \in s(A)} VA^j}{\sum_{j \in s(A)} E^j} \qquad ELP_s^A = \frac{\sum_{j \in s(A)} VA^j / \Pi_j}{\sum_{j \in s(A)} E^j / \Pi_j}$$

we have $ELP_s^A = EALP_s^A \bullet ESCLP_s^A$ with

$$ESCLP_s^A = \frac{\sum\limits_{j\in s(A)} VA^j/\Pi_j}{\sum\limits_{j\in s(A)} VA^j/\Pi_j^*} \bullet \left[\frac{\sum\limits_{j\in s(A)} E^j/\Pi_j}{\sum\limits_{j\in s(A)} E^j/\Pi_j^{*A}} \frac{\sum\limits_{j\in s(A)} E^j/\Pi_j^{*A}}{\sum\limits_{j\in s(A)} E_*^j/\Pi_j^{*A}} \right]^{-1} =$$

$$= ESVA_s^A / ESCE_s^A$$

where *LP* (res. *SCLP, SVA, SCE*) stands for labour productivity (res. structure and concept effects of labour productivity, structure effect of value-added and structure and concept effects of employment), *ALP* for adjusted for comparability labour productivity and the prefix letter *E* stands for estimator.

3.2.3 Decomposing the adjustment for comparability

The "adjustment for comparability" above integrates an *adjustment for differences in structures*. One could envisage to compare two countries A and B, without reference to the international reference structure, but consider the structure-effect of A vis-à-vis B. The trouble would then be that a country A could have a better productivity than country B in the structure of country B, but a smaller in the structure of country A. The new relation "adjusted for comparability" would not be an order relation, and would then not be very useful in practice.

In the case of labour productivity, it would not make sense to ignore the structure effect.

In some other cases however, this adjustment could be ignored. For instance, if one wants to compare aggregated totals -not ratios- it would be adapted to *adjust only for divergence of concepts*. For instance, if one wants to compare the level of sales or of profit of a given sector between countries - say for instance electronic sector - it would be enough to adjust for differences in the notion of main activity. First, one would first estimate in a similar way as above a f^A function to estimate the sales or turnover of the enterprise in a comparable electronic sector using the breakdown of sales by product. Second, one would aggregate the corresponding individual estimates using the original weights of units, in order to get the adjusted totals. The adjustment would then be limited to an adjustment of the concept. For an example of model on main activity that could be used for comparability adjustment, see Mordant (1997).

The other extreme case is when only structure adjustment is considered. It can be the case for some statistics for which the concepts are nearly totally identical in all countries. This could be the case for unit value indices derived from the

Combined Nomenclature of the Customs in the EU that is fully harmonised. Comparing the evolution of export - or import prices - of different Member States requires adjusting for differences in the structure of imports or of exports. For an example, see Depoutot (1993).

Remark:We did not consider here the influence of other production factors on the marginal productivity of labour that has an influence on the average productivity. Clearly, a full adjustment for productivity should consider all factors *(R&D, Ast...)*.

3.3 The centralised organisation

As seen above, comparability adjustment requires having access to individual data. It is impossible to envisage more classification characteristics and deeper breakdown in order to get comparable cells. Only a joint analysis of influential factors with a suitable model can tackle this problem. This is the solution recommended already by Laaksonen (1996).

It is then necessary to be in a position to run econometric models, at least separately on each country's data. In case of collinearity of the exogenous variables or if some difficulty arises in the model estimation, a joint estimation of the national models would be helpful (supposing for instance that the functions describing the behaviour are the same up to a national factor).

Some similarities of sectors across boarders could as well be tested if the econometric models were run on a single datafile (using the traditional tests like Fisher, Wald, Likelihood ratio).

In addition, international organisations are most interested in the comparability. Therefore, they are natural candidates to perform these adjustments, provided they benefit from legal provisions giving them access to individual data.

3.4 The "decentralised" organisation

In the case of the EU, if we consider a computer network of 15 national data sets containing individual data, on which we want to apply econometric methods, without being in a position to transfer any individual data from one data set to the other or to the centre (representing Eurostat), but in which:

- one node of the network or the centre can exchange aggregated data with other nodes;
- one can apply through a network procedure the usual econometric methods or optimisation methods on each national data set;

- the explanatory characteristics allowed by the system are mathematical functions of the explanatory characteristics in the data set - no exogenous characteristic (like a dummy variable for a given observation) can be introduced in the system.

It is shown below that some standard econometrics procedures could be run on such a decentralised system, providing the same results as if the usual econometric procedures were run an a classical single data file.

Proof: Let us consider the usual model of stacked regressions which corresponds to such work in the EC.

We denote y_{tj}^i (res. X_{tj}^i) the dependent variable (res. the regressors) corresponding to country i (superscript) time t and enterprise j (subscripts).

The typical panel data regression model for the EC can be written:

$$y_{tj}^i = X_{tj}^i b^i + u_{tj}^i$$

b^i is the $(k,1)$ vector of parameters $^t b^i = (b_1^i, ..., b_k^i)$ and $X_{tj}^i = (^1 x_{tj}^i, ..., ^k x_{tj}^i)$ the regressors, u_{tj}^i is the random error.

In the usual matrix notation

$$y^i = X^i b^i + u^i \quad \text{for each Member State } i \text{ (model called } M^i\text{)}$$

and

$$y = Xb + u \quad \text{for the whole EC (model called } M\text{)}$$

where y (res. X, b, u) are obtained by stacking the different matrices y^i (res. X^i, b^i, u^i).

It is obvious that under the classical hypothesis of independence of u_{tj}^l and u_{tj}^i if l is different from i, the OLS estimator of the stacked regressions is equal to the stacked OLS estimators.

One of the basic topics in econometrics is either to estimate the parameters b under some (linear ?) constraints between the countries and to test this hypothesis (classical Chow or Fisher test). For instance, the most frequent use of the model could be to estimate the regressions under the constraint that the parameters are the same for all the countries, or to test for the value of a "national" dummy characteristic. In this case, the standard formula of regression under constraint - which is valid only for linear constraint - can no more be used, since we should use explicitly individual data coming from different Member States in the same matrix.

So, the only way would be to use classical optimisation procedures:

Let us call $L(b)$ the function that has to be minimised under European constraint; here it is only the sum of squares of residuals, that is

$$L(b) = {}^{t}(y - Xb)(y - Xb)$$ where t denotes as usual the transposition operator for matrices.

And let us call at the Member State level

$$L^{i}(b^{i}) = {}^{t}(y^{i} - X^{i}b^{i})(y^{i} - X^{i}b^{i})$$

The constraints - linear or not - are called $C(b)=0$.

Clearly, $L(b) = \sum_{i=1,..,15} L^{i}(b^{i})$ [2]

The solution is then to use stepwise methods for the optimisation, for instance Newton's with or without relaxation factor.

Algorithm:

1. *At national level,* each national regression is estimated without taking into account the constraints involving parameters from other Member States.
2. At Eurostat level, the parameters involved in one or several constraints are then given an initial value $b(0)$ for instance by using a (weighted) mean of the non-constrained estimations at the national level.
3. *At national level* using this preceding value $b(n)$, the first order or second order derivatives of the L^{i} with respect to each parameter is then calculated.
4. At Eurostat level, Using [2] above, we get the derivatives of $L(b)$ [7]. We can then use the traditional Newton-Raphson's algorithm (second order derivatives) or the Berndt-Hall-Hall-Hausman's algorithm (first order derivatives), with or without relaxation parameter in order to obtain a new value $b(n+1)$.

If $b(n+1)-b(n)$ does not satisfy the requested precision, then go to step 3.

Since function $L(b)$ is convex, the series of the estimators $b(n)$ converge numerically to the global optimum value.

Since the usual Chow/ Fisher test requires only to know the sum of squared residuals, it is straightforward to use it with such an organisation.

---

[7] More precisely, either it is possible to incorporate explicitly the constraints in the formula of L(b), and the parameter vector should now be called for instance d, with dimension (d) < dimension of b, or we should replace L by the traditional Lagrange function.

The traditional method of analysis of variance is a special case of the general framework above[8].

Even some robust methods can be used in this context:

- outliers (that is "influential data" in the sense defined by Belsley, Kuh, Welsh (1980) can be detected in each Member State after the last iteration;
- the values of the influence associated to these outliers can be compared;
- the most influent outliers can be ignored for a second estimation at the EC level, which is then "robustified".

It is straightforward too, that the likelihood methods (MLE) can be applied in the same way. So, more sophisticated models like Tobit, Probit, Logit, disequilibrium models - all models with latent variables - can be used, as long as the log-likelihood of Y can be written as the sum of the log-likelihood of the y^j. The analysis of time correlation of residuals can then be used too.

Orders statistics (median, percentiles) can be derived in a similar stepwise manner. For instance, the median can be calculated as follows (Lagrange algorithm is applied to the implicit distribution function of the given characteristic):

Algorithm:

1. Eurostat sends to Member States a weighted mean of the national medians as initialisation value.
2. At national level, SOs estimate the number of enterprises above this value for the considered characteristic.
3. *At Eurostat level, calculate the difference between the European proportion of enterprises above this value and 50%. If the absolute value of this difference is more than the requested precision then calculate a new value* using an increase (or decrease) of x% of this preceding value -depending of the difference of the former proportion and 50%, and go to step 2.

As a conclusion, it is necessary to emphasise the security of such a system, which can avoid any disclosure of confidential information, since all results are aggregated information and since all physical accesses to the files and every outgoing information can be checked by built-in programs. This is probably a possible solution to make official statistics more accessible to users requiring sophisticated use of the individual data, without any risk for the confidentiality of the data, this latter being essential in the EU context.

The compatibility of some data analysis methods, such as principal components analysis and factor analysis, with this kind of organisation can be established in a similar way (see Annex 3).

It has still to be proved that methods in which the likelihood cannot be separated (like GLM with correlation of the residuals between countries) can be adapted to this organisation of the individual data.

---

[8] Usual statistics (means) are of course a subset of the results above with only one regressor and with the adequate variance-covariance matrix.

3.5 Robustness and sensitivity analysis

3.5.1 Robustness

Careful modelling requires an analysis of influential observations. The procedures mentioned above raise difficulties in this respect:

- the centralised procedure is currently only possible in Eurostat, where explicit identification is not allowed. Therefore, all additional knowledge on individual information cannot help in deciding if outliers are errors or not, if they observe a special treatment or not (like mergers). Such detailed checks have to be made through contacts with NSOs, what can be long and costly.
- the decentralised approach is more adapted to the sensitivity analysis but requires heavy procedures for the estimation of models with common parameters among the countries. It would as well require a network of partners working in co-operation with the International Organisation (Eurostat) on the topic of comparability. Although it is a fruitful approach, working in such a structure is a challenge as for the work organisation.

3.5.2 Sensitivity analysis

As underlined by Chatfield (1995), the model choice has consequences for the analysis. Data-based selection of models is dangerous, and alternative models should be considered when producing results. Similarly, imposing models as close as possible between countries sharing a similar business culture or legal framework would be fruitful. This suggests an efficient organisation in order to estimate easily several models, and the de-centralised organisation might be a handicap in this respect.

4 Future development

4.1 Users, cost and optimisation

There is a contradiction between *quality* and *equity* at the European level for business statistics.

For Member States relying on questionnaire surveys for the data collection[9], it seems likely to consider that budgetary constraints will lead to similar sampling rates in the different countries, whatever their size. This is an equitable solution for the Statistical Offices and for the enterprises, which may then face similar sampling rates in the different countries[10]. However, it is useful to envisage methods to insure that statistics will be comparable between Member States.[11] As seen in Annex 1, similar quality for comparisons requires far higher mean sampling rates in smaller Member States[12].

Which compromise could we propose for the smaller sectors/ countries?

1st possibility) to envisage only a multi-annual comparability in these countries/ sectors: the sample size would be increased every α-d year, in a co-ordinated way between Member States. For the other years, the sample would be concentrated on the bigger enterprises, where the sample is (totally or nearly) exhaustive.

2d possibility) to envisage a comparability of statistics for the different characteristics on a rotating basis: for the non-exhaustive strata, the list of characteristics would rotate in a co-ordinated way between Member States. Some central characteristics could be maintained every year as for instance turnover and employment.

3d possibility) to realise the comparability studies on averages of multi-year periods (2 to 5) in order to improve the coefficient of variation.

Small area estimation for countries in which one domain has little influence on the EU total

Equity would lead to use the same sampling rate for a given sector and size class, in order not to impose [13] a greater fulfilling burden on businesses in some countries. However, the return would be poor at the national level for small national domains, since the usual "expansion estimators" [14] would not give sufficiently precise estimators.

In practice, EU statisticians face the above problem when deciding upon a common level of breakdown for various classifications, for instance activity classes and size-class. The historical sampling rate allows biggest countries to publish reliable estimates at a detailed level (for instance 4-digit level of NACE,

---

[9] As opposed to Member States relying on administrative data, in which the costs for NSI and statistical burden on enterprises are quite different.

[10] Except if a given Member State wants to increase the sampling rate for its own national purpose.

[11] This may be a requirement since the corresponding statistics are to be used for the evaluation of the GNP contribution of Member States (4th own resource of the EU).

[12] The same statement is valid for sectors of mid-size or big Member States which represent only a small share of the EU total (ex: tourism, fishing, wine-growing...).

[13] There is a real constraint only when a regulation requires a given accuracy level of the estimates, which is not the case currently

[14] Or Horwitz-Thompson estimators

3 digits level x 8 to 10 size-classes) when it is clearly impossible for others. For more details, see Depoutot (1997).

Aggregated estimates could be produced reliably at the EU level, whereas small-area estimates would be established for the national level. These would be in particular based on the models used for comparability adjustment and would represent an important return for the comparability effort.

4.2 Confidentiality and security

Many aspects of international comparisons involve exchange of individual information, in order to assess micro-econometric models.

If the data is centralised, this pre-supposes that the necessary legal environment allows the access to individual data. Up to now, explicit identification is denied to international organisations. This requires an efficient network organisation to check the robustness of the estimated models and might reduce the possibility to improve central models beyond a certain point.

If the data is de-centralised, the necessary network has to be very secure vis-à-vis intruders. This is a challenge since remote processing gives automatically a possibility to enter the confidential data environment from the outside.

On a similar way, the co-operation with economists raises the question of access to individual data. For some international organisations like Eurostat, limited legal provisions make it possible. For others, it is clearly impossible. This is a practical obstacle to the improvement of international comparability.

4.3 Econometrics and statistics

Our proposal consists in shifting what cannot be measured directly due to high cost to an indirect measure through econometric assessment. This raises two issues:

1. The subjectivity of the chosen model.
   One way to limit the subjectivity is to authorise estimation of alternative models, as mentioned above, on request of users. Another, as proposed by Chatfield, is to assess different models and to give the results for each of them.
2. The integration of the design uncertainty.
   As for the inclusion of design uncertainty, an example is given in Bienvenue, Depoutot and Radjabou (1997).

5 Conclusion

We have shown that there are theoretical ways to adjust statistics for non-comparability, when this non-comparability is due to the divergence of national concepts, and when modelling the common international norm is possible. Some applied work is necessary to check the feasibility of the method and the size of adjustments.

In order to complete the evaluation of comparability, some adjustments for observation bias have to be done (this includes sampling and non-sampling bias).

Last but not least, the randomness of estimates has to be included in the comparisons.

Annex 1: National/ Sectoral consequences of the comparability requirement

Let us define:

x: the characteristic considered
X_i the estimator of the total of x for Member State i for a given domain
X the estimator of the total for the Union for that domain
VAR (respectively E, CV) the variance (res. expectation, coefficient of variation) operator
It is straightforward to prove that [15] a natural estimator $CV^*(X)$ of $CV(X)$ is

$$CV^*(X) = \frac{\sum_i X_i^2 CV(X_i)}{\sum_i X_i} \qquad [3]$$

So, for the precision at the EC level, the bigger states (with big values of X_i) should have the smaller CVs.

To compare X between Member States i and j, it is often meaningful to compare ratios (turnover by inhabitant for instance).

Using a Taylor expansion of X_i/X_j, we get the following approximation:

$X_i/X_j \cong E(X_i)/E(X_j) [1+X_i/E(X_i) - X_j/E(X_j)]$

---

[15] Because:

$$CV(X) = \frac{\left[Var\left(\sum X_i\right)\right]^{1/2}}{E\left(\sum X_i\right)} = \frac{\left[\sum Var(X_i)\right]^{1/2}}{\sum E(X_i)} = \frac{\left[\sum E(X_i)^2 CV(X_i)^2\right]^{1/2}}{\sum E(X_i)}$$

$$VAR(X_i/X_j) \cong [E(X_i)/E(X_j)]^2 [VAR(X_i)/E(X_i)^2 + VAR(X_j)/E(X_j)^2]$$

taking into account the independence of estimators coming from two different countries.

Hence, $CV(X_i/X_j) \cong [CV(X_i)^2 + CV(X_j)^2]^{1/2}$

If we want the same precision for all comparisons, it is appropriate to require that $CV(X_i)$ is independent of i.

If such a solution were possible, we would get a CV at the EC level smaller than the required level of the CV at the country level (only use the formula [3] above).

However, it is well known that in a given stratum of a two-stage stratified simple random sample, the coefficient of variation of the estimator of the total of a characteristic is nearly independent of the size of the population[16], and it is proportional to the inverse of the square root of the sample size [17]. So, if this assumption could hold for all the strata, the size of the sample would be the same in the different Member States (MS hereafter), assuming that the distribution of the characteristic x is the same. This is clearly not the case for the exhaustive strata and the strata were the sampling rates are relatively high, even in the "biggest" MS.

That's why it would be overstated to conclude that the sampling rate has to be proportional to the inverse of the size of the country to get the same CV. Some calculations using real data are needed to assess the extent of the difficulty.

Another concern is the *comparison of results over time*. It is important to make sure that the growth rates of the estimations are reliable. The same general requirement prevails for the estimates either at the community level or at the MS level. The coefficient of variation of the growth rate at the EC level can be approximated as the same combination of the CVs of the growth rates at the MS level as in formula [3], simply by noticing that the increase is nearly equal to the difference $[X(t)-X(t-1)] / E\{X(t-1)\}$. So the weights are the same.

The comparison of the increase rates requires of course the CVs to be similar.

The considerations concerning the size of the sample are more complicated, since the estimation of the variance of the growth rate requires calculating the covariance between the estimates related to different years. Therefore, it is necessary to know if the sample is renewed each year, and how. But the message is the same: the burden is relatively heavier for smaller MS than for bigger ones.

---

[16] If the sampling rate of the simple random sample is small.

[17] For instance in the case of a Bernoulli sample

Annex 2: Improvement of estimators for the sake of coherence

$$\begin{pmatrix} XA \\ XM \end{pmatrix} = \begin{pmatrix} E(XA) \\ E(XM) \end{pmatrix} + \begin{pmatrix} u_A \\ \sum u^i \end{pmatrix} = E(XA) \begin{pmatrix} 1 \\ 1 \end{pmatrix} + \begin{pmatrix} u_A \\ \sum u^i \end{pmatrix}$$

Using Gauss-Markov, the best linear estimator of $E(XA)$ is

$$XL = \left[(1 \quad 1) \, \Omega^{-1} \begin{pmatrix} 1 \\ 1 \end{pmatrix} \right]^{-1} (1 \quad 1) \, \Omega^{-1} \begin{pmatrix} XA \\ XM \end{pmatrix}$$

$$= \left[(1 \quad 1) \begin{pmatrix} \sigma_{XM}^2 & -\sigma_{XA,XM} \\ -\sigma_{XA,XM} & \sigma_A^2 \end{pmatrix} \frac{1}{\sigma_A^2 \sigma_{XM}^2 - \sigma^2{}_{XA,XM}} \begin{pmatrix} 1 \\ 1 \end{pmatrix} \right]^{-1} (1 \quad 1) \, \Omega^{-1} \begin{pmatrix} XA \\ XM \end{pmatrix}$$

$$VarXL = \left[(1 \quad 1) \, \Omega^{-1} \begin{pmatrix} 1 \\ 1 \end{pmatrix} \right]^{-1} = \frac{\sigma_A^2 \sigma_{XM}^2 - \sigma^2{}_{XA,XM}}{\sigma_A^2 + \sigma_{XM}^2 - 2\sigma_{XA,XM}} =$$

$$= \sigma_A^2 \underbrace{\left(\frac{\sigma_{XM}^2 - \dfrac{\sigma_{XA,XM}^2}{\sigma_A^2}}{\sigma_A^2 + \sigma_{XM}^2 - 2\sigma_{XA,XM}} \right)}_{<1}$$

Remark:

When $\sigma_A^2 / \sigma_M^2 \to 0$ we find the usual practice : $XL \to XA$ and the monthly series should be benchmarked on the annual one.

Annex 3: Decentralised Data Analysis

Principal component analysis (PCA)

Let us consider K quantitative variables measured on N_c individuals in each Member States c.

Each Member State c has the table of individual information $X^c = \left[x_{ij}^c \right]_{i=1,..,N_c \, ; \, j=1,...,K}$ and can send to the International Organisation the non-confidential information:

• Nc The (weighted) number of individuals,

- $X_j^c = \sum_{i=1}^{N_c} x_{ij}^c$ The total for each variable j on the (weighted) population,

- $$
'X^c X^c = \begin{bmatrix}
\sum_i \left(x_{i1}^c\right)^2 & \cdots & \sum_i x_{i1}^c x_{ij}^c & \cdots & \sum_i x_{i1}^c x_{iK}^c \\
\vdots & & \cdot & & \vdots \\
\sum_i x_{ij}^c x_{i1}^c & \cdots & \sum_i \left(x_{ij}^c\right)^2 & \cdots & \sum_i x_{ij}^c x_{iK}^c \\
\vdots & & \cdot & & \vdots \\
\sum_i x_{iK}^c x_{i1}^c & \cdots & \sum_i x_{iK}^c x_{ij}^c & \cdots & \sum_i \left(x_{iK}^c\right)^2
\end{bmatrix}
$$

Using this information, International Organisation can do the analysis by calculating:
- the number of individuals in the whole population:

$$N = \sum_{c=1}^{15} N_c$$

- the average of variable *j* over the whole population:

$$\overline{X}_j = \frac{1}{N} \sum_c X_j^c ,$$

- the empirical variance of variable *j* over the whole population

$$\sigma_j^2 = \frac{1}{N} \sum_{c=1}^{15} \sum_i \left(x_{ij}^c\right)^2 - \overline{X}_j^2$$

- the normalised matrix to diagonalise is given by: $V = \left[v_{lj}\right]_{l=1,..,K\,;\,j=1,..,K}$

and $v_{lj} = \dfrac{1}{\sigma_l \sigma_j} \sum_{c=1}^{15} \left[\sum_{i=1}^{N_c} x_{il}^c x_{ij}^c - \overline{X}_l X_j^c - X_l^c \overline{X}_j + N_c \overline{X}_l \overline{X}_j \right]$

- In matrix notation:

$$V = \gamma\,'\gamma \otimes \sum_{c=1}^{15} \left['X^c\, X^c - \overline{X}\, 'X_\bullet^c - X_\bullet^c\, '\overline{X} + N_c \overline{X}\, '\overline{X} \right]$$

with $\overline{X} = \begin{bmatrix} \overline{X}_1 \\ \vdots \\ \overline{X}_K \end{bmatrix}$, $X_\bullet^c = \begin{bmatrix} X_1^c \\ \vdots \\ X_K^c \end{bmatrix}$, $\gamma = \begin{bmatrix} 1/\sigma_1 \\ \vdots \\ 1/\sigma_K \end{bmatrix}$

- Then the diagonalisation of V gives the eigenvalues $(\lambda_1, \cdots, \lambda_\alpha)$ and eigenvectors $(U_1, \cdots, U_\alpha)$

- The co-ordinates of each variables j on the principal axes:

$$G_\alpha(j) = u_{\alpha j}\sqrt{\frac{\lambda_\alpha}{N}}$$

- The co-ordinates of Member States as average of individuals on the principal axes:

$$F_\alpha(c) = \sum_{j=1}^{K} X_j^c u_{\alpha j}$$

Factor analysis and multiple correspondence analysis

These analyses are based on contingency or Burt tables.

Contingency tables represent the frequency of the population crossing two characteristics and Burt tables give the frequency of the population by crossing more than 2 characteristics.

Generally, these tables, which do not contain individual data, are not confidential. Member States can send them to International Organisations, which do the analysis by aggregating them.

In the event of very detailed tables, certain cells may be confidential. For example, by crossing size and activity class at the detailed level, users may identify some big enterprises. Therefore, it is impossible to do a factor analysis directly using the same decentralisation methods as for the principal component analysis if the centre is not granted access to confidential information.

For example let's take a factor analysis:

Considering 2 variables of I and J modalities measured on N_c individuals in each Member States c.

Each Member State c has the contingency table $T^c = \left[k_{ij}^c\right]_{i=1,..,I\,;\,j=1,..,J}$ which

may contain confidential data

At the European level the matrix to diagonalise is given by S:

where $s_{jj'} = \sum_i \dfrac{\sum_c k_{ij}^c \sum_{c'} k_{ij'}^{c'}}{k_{i\bullet}\sqrt{k_{\bullet j}k_{\bullet j'}}}$ and

$$k_{i\bullet} = \sum_c \sum_{j=1}^{J} k_{ij}^c, \qquad k_{\bullet j} = \sum_c \sum_{i=1}^{I} k_{ij}^c$$

Since several k_{ij}^c can not be obtained, the S matrix can not be calculated.

A partial solution consists in aggregating modalities of the contingency table in the same way for each Member State in order to transmit this tables. Then, the aggregation of these national contingency tables at International organisation level allows to proceed to the factor analysis.

An other solution consists in obtaining contingency tables from countries having tables without confidential data (in general, the big countries), do the factor analysis, and then send to the other countries the first factors in order to project their data as supplementary variables.

Annex 4

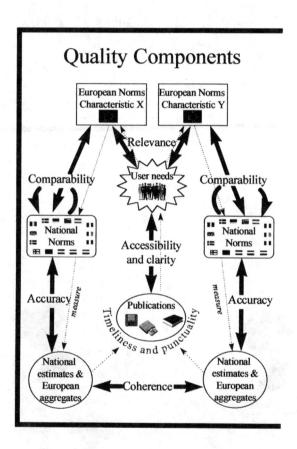

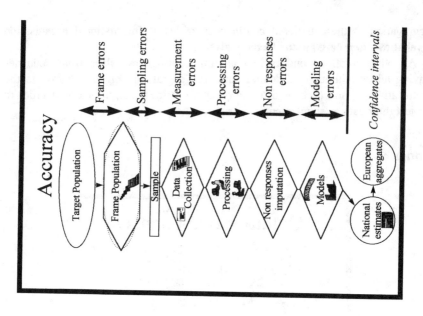

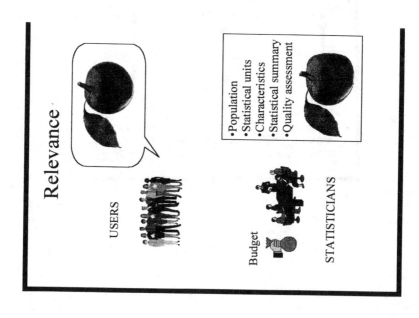

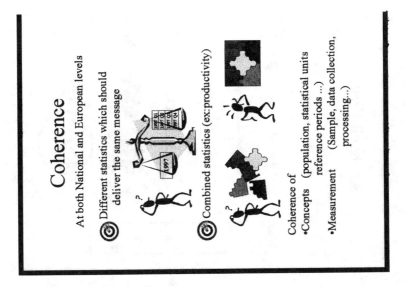

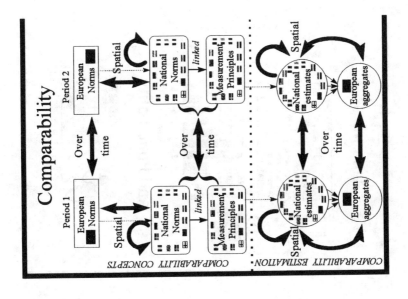

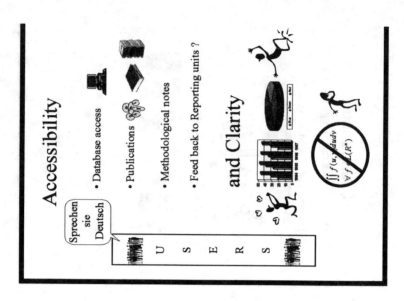

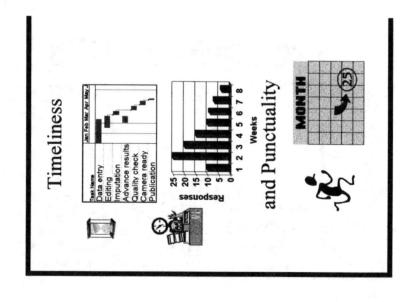

REFERENCES

Belsley D.A., Kuh E., Welsch R.E. (1980), *'Regression Diagnostics: Identifying Influential Data and Sources of Collinearity'*, New York: John Wiley & Sons.

Berndt E.K., Hall B.H., Hall L.R.E.and Hausman J.A. (1974), *'Estimation and Inference in Non Linear Structural Models'*, Annals of Economic and Social Measurement, 3, 653-666.

Bienvenue J.Y., Depoutot R, Radjabou M. (1997), *'Sample dependence: theoretical aspects and illustration'*, Eurostat, presented to CAED 97.

Bienvenue J.Y. (1997), *'Dynamic labour demand model for heterogeneous panels'*, Eurostat, presented to CAED 97.

Champsaur P.(1996), *'Harmonisation internationale et comparabilité statistique'*, Conference on 'Consequences of Globalisation on Statistics Canada's programs'.

Chatfield C. (1995), *'Model uncertainty, Data Mining and Statistical Inference'*, J.R. Statist. Soc. A, 158, part 3, pp 419-466.

Defays D (1995), *'Is harmonisation possible?'*, paper presented for the conference on methodological issues in official statistics in Stockholm, Sweden, June 12-13.

Deville J.C. and Särndal C.E. (1992), *'Calibration estimators in survey sampling'*, Journal of the American Statistical Association, 87, 376-382.

Depoutot R. (1993), *'Le commerce extérieur de biens manufacturés en 1992'*, Insee Resultats, Les Comptes de l'industrie en 1992, 37-42.

Depoutot R. (1997) *'Detailed breakdown of results in the regulation on structural business statistics'* Eurostat, unpublished document.

Elvers E. and Rosén B. (1997), *'Quality Concept for Official Statistics'*, entry in the forthcoming update of the Encyclopedia of Statistical Sciences, Wiley & Sons, Statistics Sweden R&D Report, ISSN 0283-8680

Elvers E. and Lindstroem H. (1996), *'A quality concept at Eurostat for statistics from the European Statistical System'*, internal report for Eurostat.

Eurostat (1996a), *'Quality in structural business statistics'*, Document n° D3/96/02 final.

Eurostat (1996b), *'Proposal for a quality report on structural business statistics'*, Document n° D3/Quality/96/04 final.

Eurostat (1996c), *'Bibliography on quality in statistics'*, internal document.

Eurostat (1997) *'Mercure Sources - Annex to the Service Statistics 1996'* - to appear -

Eurostat (1998) *'Statistical harmonisation and quality - The case of social statistics'* - Internal report prepared for the Mondorf seminar, Jan/Feb. 1998.

Kish L.(1994), *'Multipopulation survey designs: five types with seven shared aspects'*, International Statistical Review 2, 167-186.

Laaksonen S.(1995), *'Statistical Methodology and the Principle of Subsidiarity: a challenging optimisation task for the European Statistical System'*, Methods Conference of Statistics Sweden.

Laaksonen S.(1996), *'Notes on international comparability of sample based business survey data'*, CAED, Helsinki 17-19/06/1996.

Mordant G.(1997), *'Ventilation des comptes des entreprises selon une technologie branche'*, ISI 97, Contributed papers, book 1, 369-370.

Statistics Sweden (1994), *'Quality definition and recommendations for quality declaration of official statistics'* (authors: Chris Denell, Eva Elvers and Bengt Rosén).

United Nations (1983) *'Guidelines for quality presentations that are prepared for users of statistics'*, Statistical Commission of ECE, meeting of 21-24/11/1993.

United Nations (1993) *'System of National Accounts'*.

Note: All unpublished documents can be obtained on simple request sent to raoul.depoutot@eurostat.cec.be (fax:+352 4301 34 149)

SAMPLE DEPENDENCE: THEORETICAL ASPECTS AND ILLUSTRATIONS

J.Y. Bienvenue[1], R. Depoutot[2] and M. Radjabou[3]

[1]*World Systems*[*]
[2]*Eurostat*
[3]*World Systems*[*]

1 Introduction

Using a distinction proposed by Pfeffermann and Smith (1985), statistical inferences can be classified in two types. Inferences about a known function of the finite population values (or descriptive inferences) and inferences about the model ξ (or analytic approach) thought to have generated the finite population U. ξ is referred to as a superpopulation model, the parameter is called a model parameter.

The descriptive parameter can theoretically be calculated without error in the case of a census. A model parameter being a part of a hypothetical construct can never be calculated exactly.

It is crucial to know which parameter should be the parameter of interest.

Many authors question the relevance of the finite population parameter arguing that a descriptive finite parameter has relevance only if the model associated with that parameter is true or at least well supported by available data.

In the paper mentioned above, Pfeffermann and Smith justify their positions as follows:

"We favour the analytic approach to regression analysis. We find it difficult to justify the estimation of the descriptive parameter without relying on a well-defined model and the closeness between the descriptive and the analytic parameter. We think that this inference is usually meant to refer to populations more general than the fixed finite population which existed at the time the sample was drawn."

This paper tries to highlight the interdependence of sampling and model in econometric relations. Usually in an econometric equation the standard error is defined with respect to the model (this is the standard error provided by the

[*] This paper was written within the framework of the contract OSCE n°66416 between Eurostat and World Systems ltd.

software). The superpopulation approach provides the theoretical framework to take into account the influence of both model and sampling scheme. The basic idea of this paper is that sample based relations depend both on the model and the sampling scheme. The influence of the sampling in the standard error of the parameters could prevent from drawing any valid conclusions from the equation.

There are two ways to deal with a sample data.

- The first approach could be named a bottom-up approach. We know information for a set of finite statistical units. These allow to represent the (joint) distribution of several characteristics in the reference population, with some uncertainty. For instance, we can estimate multi-dimensional moments, quantiles, etc...
- The second one is the reverse of the preceding (this approach is chosen in this paper). We want to measure some "invariants" in the reference population, in order to extend this information. An other reference population of which we know by other means that they are very similar to the one we sampled. For instance, the "other populations" can be the population at an other time, in another geographical area, in another socio-economic domain, etc...

Econometric relations are considered, here, as the result of a two-step approach:

1. First, the model is defined in the superpopulation, it represents the underlying process or the causal relations between the dependent variable and the regressors. The finite population comes from a random draw from the infinite superpopulation, hence an uncertainty appears; due to the fact that only a part of the superpopulation is considered. This is the model uncertainty (and this implies a variance with respect to the model) that will be denoted with the subscript ξ.

2. Secondly, the model is usually estimated on a sample drawn from the finite population. Thus a second uncertainty appears due to the sampling scheme. This sample uncertainty (as a consequence it exists a variance with respect to the sample) will be denoted with the subscript p.

Practically, one will apply this scheme to the modelling of the response-behaviour of enterprises in an opinion survey. On will estimate a two-step logit model using data from a European-wide survey measuring the impact of the Single Market implementation: the Eurostat Single Market Business Survey (1996). An estimation of the total variance by aggregation of its two components, will be calculated using data from the Single Market Survey, the calculation of the variance will be carried out with the bootstrap technique.

2 The superpopulation model approach

2.1 Origin of the model approach

The model-based approach has been designed to solve two imbricated practical problems:

1. The mean square errors (MSE) for classical sampling scheme have complex expressions, hence the difficulty to perform comparisons.
2. For the estimation of the precision of a parameter, there is no optimal sampling scheme, *i.e.* a scheme that gives a mean squared error lower than any other sampling scheme. Indeed the MSE values depend upon the values of the Y_k (interest variable for k=1.....N) of the N individuals of the population. For example we know that the simple random survey is optimal if the Y_k's are constant but an unequal survey with unequal probability P_k is optimal if the Y_k's are proportional to the P_k (*see Appendix 1*).

Since one cannot know all the possible distributions of the Y_k, it is useful to suppose that certain distributions are more likely to happen than others, hence a reduction of the number of unknowns. This is equivalent to assume that the finite population of size N, on which the sampling is carried out, is itself a sample drawn with replacement in one (or several) fictive populations of an infinite size, this explains the term superpopulation. A superpopulation ideally contains an infinity of individuals, they form a distribution of the interest variable Y that is exactly the distribution function that generates the random variable Y_k for the individual k. This can be viewed as the parametrisation of a non-parametric problem.

Thus, if one wanted to build the histogram of the superpopulation associated to the individual k one will use the density of the distribution function generating the random variable Y_k.

Let us suppose that we have an auxiliary information X_k on each individual of the population, one thinks *a priori* that the relation between X_k and Y_k is linear $Y_k = a + bX_k$. Then, one considers that each individual k of this population, whose auxiliary variable takes the value X_k, is the result of a random draw in a superpopulation in which the Y's are distributed, e.g. according to a Normal distribution with mean $a + bX_k$ and standard error σ .

One can then write $Y_k = a + bX_k + U_k$ where U_k is a random variable with a zero mean and a standard error σ .

The *nature of the uncertainty of* U_k is different from that of the regression residuals, as traditionally understood, indeed they express here the fact that we have an instance in the finite population of N random variables resulting from a draw from the superpopulation.

One must keep in mind that one faces a superposition of uncertainty. The first one is the classical uncertainty of a survey due to the inclusion probabilities associated to each individual k. The second level of uncertainty concerns the value of Y: one observes an instance of N random variables generated by a draw from an infinite superpopulation.

2.2 Precision in the model based approach

Let us suppose that we are interested in the inference on the superpopulation and not on the finite population U. In this case the modelisator is interested in the *underlying processes* or in the **causal relations** between Y and X.

The question now is to find the procedure to perform this inference when one observes Y and X only in the sample. One will use, here the example displayed in "Model assisted survey sampling" by Särndal, Swensson and Wretman.

Let the model $y_k = x_k'\beta + \varepsilon_k$ where $\varepsilon_1 \ldots\ldots\ldots \varepsilon_N$ are independent random variables from a normal distribution, with $E_\xi(\varepsilon_k) = 0$ and $V_\xi(\varepsilon_k) = \sigma^2$ with k=1,.....,N. One can then estimate the parameter β of the model in a two-step approach. For a census the available observations cover the whole population, the likelihood is then:

$$L(\beta) = \prod_{k=1}^{N} \left\{ \frac{1}{\sqrt{2\pi}\sigma} \exp\left[-(y_k - x_k')^2 / 2\sigma^2 \right] \right\} \qquad [1]$$

The log-likelihood is (apart from a constant),

$$h = h(\beta) = \sum_U (y_k - x_k'\beta)^2 . \qquad [2]$$

The maximisation of $h(\beta)$ leads to the estimator of β in the census case,

(first step) $\qquad \hat{\beta}_U = B = \left(\sum_U x_k x_k' \right)^{-1} \sum_U x_k y_k \qquad [3]$

However the available data are limited to a sample s; we observe (x_k, y_k) for $k \in s$ only. The π-estimator of the log-likelihood $h(\beta)$ is for any fixed β and if one denotes π_k the inclusion probability of the individual k in the sampling scheme

$$\hat{h}_\pi = \sum_s (y_k - x_k'\beta)^2 / \pi_k. \qquad [4]$$

Maximising this expression one obtains the estimator

(second step) $\qquad \hat{\beta}_s = \hat{B} = (\sum_s x_k x_k' / \pi_k)^{-1} \sum_s x_k y_k / \pi_k \qquad [5]$

this estimator is not the estimator of the finite population parameter B but of the parameter of the model in the superpopulation β.

Thus statistical properties of $\hat{\beta}_s$ can be evaluated jointly with respect to the model and sample selection.

We need to introduce the matrix notation $X = (x_1, \ldots \ldots x_n)'$ et $y = (y_1, \ldots \ldots y_n)'$ and the double subscript ξp meaning "jointly under model and design". Then, conditionally to X, $E_{\xi p}(\hat{\beta}_s) = \beta$ that is $\hat{\beta}_s$ is unbiased. Indeed:

$$E_{\xi p}(\hat{\beta}_s | X) = E_\xi \left[\sum_{s \in S} p(s)\hat{\beta}_s \right] = \sum_{s \in S} p(s) E_\xi(\hat{\beta}_s) = \beta \sum_{s \in S} p(s) = \beta \qquad [6]$$

where S denotes the set of all possible samples.

The variance, under this two-step approach has one sampling variance component (since a sample rather than the entire population is observed), and one model variance component (since the N population data points scatter according to $V_\xi(y_k | x_k) = \sigma^2$).

The decomposition is then:

$$V_{\xi p}(\hat{\beta}_s | X) = V_\xi \left[E_p(\hat{\beta}_s | y, X) \right] + E_\xi \left[V_p(\hat{\beta}_s | y, X) \right]. \qquad [7]$$

As $\hat{\beta}_s$ is approximately unbiased with respect to the design one has $E_p(\hat{\beta}_s | y, X) \approx B$. Thus the first component (that represents the model uncertainty) is roughly equal to

$$V_\xi\left[\ E_p(\hat{\beta}_s|y,X)\ \right]=V_\xi(B|X)=\sigma^2(\sum_U x_k x_k')^{-1}.$$

This represents the variance in a census case.

The second component is the mean with respect to the model of the variances according to the sampling scheme p of the parameter to estimate. Consequently, this component is exactly zero in the census case.

As the parameter β is estimated from a survey, it is natural to wonder whether one should use the sample weighted estimator shown in (5) $\hat{\beta}_s = \hat{B} = (\sum_s x_k x_k' / \pi_k)^{-1}\sum_s x_k y_k / \pi_k$ or the usual regression theory estimator:

$$\hat{\beta}_{mod} = \hat{B} = (\sum_s x_k x_k')^{-1}\sum_s x_k y_k \qquad [8]$$

Keeping in mind the model $y_k = x_k'\beta + \varepsilon_k$ with classical assumptions:
1. $\varepsilon_1........\varepsilon_N$ are independent random variables from a normal distribution,
2. $E_\xi(\varepsilon_k) = 0$ with k=1,.....,N
3. $V_\xi(\varepsilon_k) = \sigma^2$ with k=1,.....,N

Forgetting about the sampling scheme, $\hat{\beta}_{mod}$ is the best linear unbiased estimator of β (BLUE estimator). With classical assumptions on the residuals, one can prove that for any vector c, conformable with β the property of the best linear unbiased estimator implies that :

$$E_\xi\left[c'(\hat{\beta}_{mod} - \beta)^2|s, X\right] \le E_\xi\left[c'(\hat{\beta}_s - \beta)^2|s, X\right] \qquad [9]$$

Since this equality holds for every s, one can apply the operator E_p

$$E_\xi E_p\left[c'(\hat{\beta}_{mod} - \beta)^2|s, X\right] \le E_\xi E_p\left[c'(\hat{\beta}_s - \beta)^2|s, X\right] \qquad [10]$$

Therefore taking into account both the model and the sampling scheme $\hat{\beta}_{mod}$ is a better estimator of the parameter than $\hat{\beta}_s$. However $\hat{\beta}_s$ is more robust than the unweighted estimator: it is model-unbiased (if the model is true) and design-consistent for B (whether the model holds or not).

The "total" variance of $\hat{\beta}_{\text{mod}}$ can be written:

$$V_{\xi p}(c'\hat{\beta}_{\text{mod}}|s, X) = V_{\xi}(c'\hat{\beta}_{\text{mod}}|s, X) + E_{\xi}\left[V_p(\hat{\beta}_{\text{mod}}|s, X)\right] \qquad [11]$$

The first term will be lower than every variance (with respect to ξ) of another linear estimator. In particular

$$V_{\xi}(c'\hat{\beta}_{\text{mod}}|s, X) \leq V_{\xi}(c'\hat{\beta}_s|s, X) \qquad [11-a]$$

The second term can be expected to be higher than the variance of a weighted estimator indeed:

$$V_p(c'\hat{\beta}_s|s, X) \leq V_p(c'\hat{\beta}_{\text{mod}}|s, X) \quad \text{since, according to the sampling scheme}$$

the weights increase the precision.

Then $E_{\xi}\left[V_p(\hat{\beta}_s|s, X)\right] \leq E_{\xi}\left[V_p(\hat{\beta}_{\text{mod}}|s, X)\right].$ $\qquad [11-b]$

With 11-a and 11-b one cannot decide what estimator is the best in terms of precision.

2.3 Estimation of the precision

To calculate this component one should have all the possible distributions of the Y_k, one could then write:

$$E_{\xi}\left[V_p(\hat{\beta}_s|y, X)\right] = E_{\xi}\left[\sum_{s \in S} p(s)\left[\hat{\beta}_s - E_p(\hat{\beta}_s, y, X)\right]^2\right] \qquad [12]$$

It sounds natural to estimate $\sum_{s \in S} p(s)\left[\hat{\beta}_s - E_p(\hat{\beta}_s, y, X)\right]^2$ by a replication method. One suggests using for that purpose the Bootstrap. Then, using the Monte Carlo estimate of the bootstrap for a variance (see appendix 3), one gets an estimation

$$V_p(\hat{\beta}_s \big| y, X) \approx \frac{1}{R} \sum_{s=1}^{R} (\hat{\beta}_s * - \bar{\beta}*)^2 \tag{13}$$

where R is number of replications and * denotes the fact that the coefficients or their means are generated by the replication process. Besides one needs to calculate $E_\xi\left[V_p(\hat{\beta}_s \big| y, X)\right]$ one suggests evaluating this quantity with the bootstrap. The R replications constitute a distribution of the coefficients, one can therefore calculate an empirical variance. However in order to obtain the mean according to the model of this variance we must use a two-step bootstrap.

From the original sample one creates R samples S(1),....S(i).....S(R). From each R(i) one can creates R' second order replications, an empirical variance is then calculated using the approximation (9). We obtain R bootstrapped variances. The empirical mean of these variances is an approximation of

$$E_\xi\left[V_p(\hat{\beta}_s \big| y, X)\right].$$

$$E_\xi\left[V_p(\hat{\beta}_s \big| y, X)\right] \approx \frac{1}{R} \sum_{i=1}^{R} V^{S(i)}(\hat{\beta}) \quad \text{with} \quad V^{S(i)}(\hat{\beta}) = \frac{1}{R'} \sum_{s=1}^{R'} (\hat{\beta}_s * - \bar{\beta}_s *)^2 \tag{14}$$

Eventually the decomposition presented in (7) can be written

$$V_{\xi p}(\hat{\beta}_s \big| X) \approx \sigma^2 (\sum_U x_k' x_k)^{-1} + \frac{1}{R} \sum_{i=1}^{R} V^{S(i)}(\hat{\beta})$$

The implementation of a large number of replications is hampered by practical difficulties due to the needed calculation time

3 Application

The data are provided by the Single Market survey. This European-wide survey involved 13500 enterprises. It was designed to gather information, in 1995, on the European entrepreneurs' opinion concerning the measures taken for the implementation of the Single Market.

The questionnaire sought to evaluate the impact on firms of specific measures pertaining to harmonisation of technical regulations, the opening up of public procurement for example. The sampling scheme in each Member state can be regarded as a stratified sampling with a simple random draw in each stratum. In this case one will focus on a sample of 6527 enterprises of the Manufacturing industry.

The application is based on a logit model. It tries to explain the reply to the question mentioned above by qualitative covariates: the country, the size class (in terms of number of employees) and the sector (the nine manufacturing sectors defined as aggregates of Nace rev1 two-digit elements). The modelling has been carried out with the SAS software using Proc Logistic, the data-set contains 6527 observations (see description of data in annex). The application deals with the question " Please indicate whether you agree or disagree with the following statements: The Single Market programme has been a success for your enterprise". The proposed answers were " Agree, Do not agree, do not know".

A two-step logit is carried out. In a first step one seeks the determinants that condition the fact of expressing an opinion (agree or disagree).

Practically one writes:

$$P(Y_k = 1) = \frac{\exp(x_k' \beta)}{1 + \exp(x_k' \beta)}$$

Y=1 means that the enterprise expressed an opinion, Y=0 when the firm replied "no opinion", x_k being the vector of explanatory variables.

In the second step one focuses on the firms expressing opinion, and seeks the determinants of "agree" compared to "disagree". Then Y=1 means that the enterprise replied "agree", Y=0 when the firm replied "disagree",

The table 1 displays the replies to the survey, Table 2 displays the logit modelling of the original sample.

The variance provided by the software takes only into account the model error, namely the term:

$$V_\xi \left[E_p(\hat{\beta}_s \mid y, X) \right] = V_\xi(B \mid X)$$

The second part of the variance decomposition is obtained through bootstrap replications. The algorithm that has been used carries out a random draw with replacement in each stratum. A stratum is defined by the intersection of a country, a size class and a sector. To reach the asymptotic properties of a bootstrap estimate of the variance at least 200 replications are needed.

This term $E_\xi \left[V_p(\hat{\beta}_s \mid y, x) \right]$ is approximated by

$$E_\xi \left[V_p(\hat{\beta}_s \mid y, X) \right] \approx \frac{1}{R} \sum_{i=1}^{R} V^{S(i)}(\hat{\beta}) \quad \text{with} \quad V^{S(i)}(\hat{\beta}) = \frac{1}{R'} \sum_{s=1}^{R'} (\hat{\beta}_s * - \overline{\beta}_s *)^2$$

We need to use a double bootstrap one for V_p and the other for the mathematical expectation. Then for each of these bootstraps we need 200 replications.

Table 1 Results from the survey

Percentage of firms expressing the opinion	Agree	No opinion	Disagree
EUR 12	33	40	27
By Member State			
Belgium	13	66	22
Denmark	33	41	27
Germany	41	40	18
Greece	42	39	19
Spain	38	23	40
France	20	41	38
Ireland	46	38	15
Italy	54	23	23
Luxembourg	21	42	37
Netherlands	17	64	19
Portugal	12	54	34
United Kingdom	16	59	25
By Manufacturing Sector			
Food, beverages & tobacco	34	38	28
Textiles, leather & furniture	31	37	32
Wood, paper & printing/publishing	21	50	29
Chemicals, rubber & plastics	39	37	25
Non-metallic mineral products	29	51	20
Metals & metal products	31	40	28
Machinery & equipment N.E.C.	40	36	24
Electrical & optical machinery	45	32	24
Transport equipment	27	52	21
By Employment Size Class			
20-49	30	42	28
50-199	36	37	27
200-499	40	35	25
500-999	38	38	24
>= 1000	46	31	23

Table 2 Model standard error for the first logit

Variable	Parameter Estimate	Standard Error	Wald Chi-Square	Pr >Chi-Square	Standardised Estimate	Odds Ratio
INTERCEPT	-0.19	0.04	23.07	0.0001	.	.
20-49	-0.55	0.02	664.47	0.0001	-0.77	0.577
50-199	-0.17	0.02	56.79	0.0001	-0.22	0.847
500-999	-0.11	0.04	6.932	0.0085	-0.04	0.896
>1000	0.21	0.05	17.06	0.0001	0.06	1.235
NACE2*	-0.03	0.02	3.15	0.0757	-0.04	0.966
NACE3	-0.45	0.02	452.98	0.0001	-0.42	0.637
NACE4	0.07	0.02	9.16	0.0025	0.05	1.073
NACE5	-0.70	0.03	678.47	0.0001	-0.45	0.496
NACE6	-0.07	0.02	11.89	0.0006	-0.07	0.933
NACE7	0.08	0.02	13.03	0.0003	0.07	1.084
NACE8	0.32	0.02	175.54	0.0001	0.25	1.373
NACE9	-0.58	0.03	392.22	0.0001	-0.33	0.558
Denmark	1.03	0.05	410.81	0.0001	0.36	2.812
Germany	0.98	0.03	882.24	0.0001	1.13	2.676
Greece	1.09	0.05	437.83	0.0001	0.36	3.003
Spain	1.98	0.03	3071.78	0.0001	1.76	7.276
France	1.03	0.03	944.42	0.0001	1.08	2.797
Ireland	1.09	0.06	323.02	0.0001	0.29	2.975
Italy	1.96	0.03	3406.33	0.0001	2.32	7.108
Luxembourg	0.93	0.16	31.74	0.0001	0.08	2.534
Netherlands	0.14	0.04	12.62	0.0004	0.07	1.156
Portugal	0.42	0.03	122.79	0.0001	0.27	1.518
United Kingdom	0.25	0.033	58.03	0.0001	0.27	1.291

*see definition of aggregates in appendix 2.

We used for each bootstrap a paired bootstrap (see Appendix 3): the model is estimated on each replicated sample and the corresponding coefficient is kept. The moments are calculated using the empirical distribution of the replicated samples.

Now many coefficients have to be rejected, as non significantly different from zero, if we take into account the sampling standard error and under asymptotic assumptions.

Table 3 Model and sampling standard error for the first logit

Variables	Parameter Estimate	Model Standard Error	Sampling standard error
INTERCEPT	-0.19	0.04	0.29
20-49	-0.55	0.02	0.14
50-199	-0.17	0.02	0.13
500-999	-0.11	0.04	0.16
>1000	0.21	0.05	0.16
NACE2*	-0.03	0.02	0.24
NACE3	-0.45	0.02	0.24
NACE4	0.07	0.02	0.27
NACE5	-0.70	0.03	0.32
NACE6	-0.07	0.02	0.24
NACE7	0.08	0.02	0.30
NACE8	0.32	0.02	0.28
NACE9	-0.58	0.03	0.26
Denmark	1.03	0.05	0.35
Germany	0.98	0.03	0.24
Greece	1.09	0.05	0.28
Spain	1.98	0.03	0.26
France	1.03	0.03	0.23
Ireland	1.09	0.06	0.27
Italy	1.96	0.03	0.30
Luxembourg	0.93	0.16	0.34
Netherlands	0.14	0.04	0.31
Portugal	0.42	0.03	0.38
United kingdom	0.25	0.033	0.27

Table 4 Model standard error for the second logit

Variable	Parameter Estimate	Standard Error	Wald Chi-Square	Pr>Chi-Square	Standardised Estimate	Odds Ratio
INTERCEPT	-0.03	0.06	0.2393	0.6247	.	.
20-49	-0.48	0.02	337.1587	0.0001	-0.671	0.613
50-199	-0.24	0.02	77.521	0.0001	-0.312	0.786
500-999	-0.13	0.05	6.4751	0.0109	-0.052	0.873
>1000	0.13	0.06	4.7021	0.0301	0.044	1.143
NACE2*	-0.43	0.02	329.9171	0.0001	-0.517	0.645
NACE3	-0.52	0.03	332.446	0.0001	-0.433	0.596
NACE4	0.22	0.02	58.0803	0.0001	0.181	1.247
NACE5	0.08	0.04	4.7892	0.0286	0.046	1.085
NACE6	-0.24	0.02	90.3939	0.0001	-0.24	0.785
NACE7	0.09	0.03	11.2221	0.0008	0.082	1.098
NACE8	0.29	0.03	105.3741	0.0001	0.249	1.348
NACE9	-0.07	0.04	2.7147	0.0994	-0.033	0.934
Denmark	0.71	0.07	93.1557	0.0001	0.237	2.035
Germany	1.23	0.05	506.2933	0.0001	1.358	3.423
Greece	1.32	0.07	294.3074	0.0001	0.429	3.767
Spain	0.50	0.05	82.8779	0.0001	0.481	1.651
France	-0.13	0.055	6.3963	0.0114	-0.141	0.87
Ireland	1.54	0.09	290.3164	0.0001	0.414	4.687
Italy	1.48	0.05	753.0666	0.0001	1.853	4.415
Luxembourg	-0.14	0.22	0.4241	0.5149	-0.012	0.863
Netherlands	0.31	0.06	21.486	0.0001	0.128	1.365
Portugal	-0.31	0.06	25.2894	0.0001	-0.169	0.729
Un. Kingdom	0.033	0.05	0.3442	0.5574	0.0286	1.033

Table 5 Model and sampling standard error for the second logit

Variables	Parameter Estimate	Model Standard Error	Sampling standard error
INTERCEPT	-0.03	0.06	0.40
20-49	-0.48	0.02	0.16
50-199	-0.24	0.02	0.16
500-999	-0.13	0.05	0.19
>1000	0.13	0.06	0.19
NACE2*	-0.43	0.02	0.26
NACE3	-0.52	0.03	0.28
NACE4	0.22	0.02	0.28
NACE5	0.08	0.04	0.29
NACE6	-0.24	0.02	0.28
NACE7	0.09	0.03	0.37
NACE8	0.29	0.03	0.25
NACE9	-0.07	0.04	0.34
Denmark	0.71	0.07	0.48
Germany	1.23	0.05	0.38
Greece	1.32	0.07	0.42
Spain	0.50	0.05	0.37
France	-0.13	0.055	0.37
Ireland	1.54	0.09	0.42
Italy	1.48	0.05	0.43
Luxembourg	-0.14	0.22	0.49
Netherlands	0.31	0.06	0.56
Portugal	-0.31	0.06	0.49
United Kingdom	0.033	0.05	0.45

In these two examples one notices that the sampling standard error is much higher than the model error. For most of the explaining variables the sampling standard error leads to coefficients that are not significantly different from zero.

4 Conclusion

Many authors have been interested in the interdependence of model and sampling scheme. A short bibliography is proposed at the end of this paper. However some of these works deserve a particular attention.

Isaki and Fuller presented in 1982 a theoretical framework distinguishing the variance under the design from the variance under the superpopulation model. They introduced the term "anticipated variance" to identify the variance accounting for model and design. The anticipated variance at the time the survey is being constructed is differentiated from the variance realised for a particular existing finite population and survey design. Their main concern is to assess sampling designs and model unbiased estimators under different conditions.

Fuller (1975) dealt with the problem of estimating regression equations from survey data. He considered the estimation of regression equations from samples selected from finite populations, assuming that the finite population is a random sample from an infinite population. He focused mainly on the properties of the regression coefficients under different assumptions.

Nordberg (1989) used the superpopulation approach in the general case of the Generalised Linear Models. He assumed a three-step process leading to 3 sources of random variation: the superpopulation mode, the sampling design and the response model. His main concern is to obtain the best superpopulation model.

The works mentioned above illustrate how crucial it is , to increase the study on the mutual influence of model and sampling scheme. This implies further co-operation between specialists of econometrics and those of survey sampling.

Appendix 1

Comparison of two-stage sampling schemes.

One would like to compare 2 two-stage sampling schemes with a simple random survey at the last stage; and one will assume that the sizes of the *PSU* i's (primary sampling unit) are known. Let us denote M the number of PSU's and N the size of the population and

$$\overline{N} = N / M$$

$$f_1 = m / M$$

$$f_{2,i} = n_i / N_i$$

$$S_1^2 = \frac{\sum_{i=1}^{M}(T_i - \overline{T})^2}{M-1} \qquad S_{2,i}^2 = \frac{\sum_{j=1}^{N_i}(Y_{i,j} - \overline{Y}_i)^2}{N_i - 1}$$

Simple random survey of the PSU's, unbiased estimator:
The variance of the estimation of the mean is then

$$V(\hat{\bar{Y}}_1) = \left(\frac{1}{\bar{N}}\right)^2 \frac{1-f_1}{m} S_1^2 + \frac{1}{m\,M} \sum_{i=1}^{M} \left(\frac{N_i}{\bar{N}}\right)^2 (1-f_{2,i}) \frac{S^2_{2,i}}{n_i}$$

where $\hat{\bar{Y}}_1 = \dfrac{M}{Nm} \sum_{i\in s} N_i \bar{y}_i = \hat{T} / N$

Simple random survey of the PSU's, estimator by the ratio.
The idea is to use an estimator of the population size N.

$$\hat{\bar{Y}}_2 = \frac{\sum_{i\in s} N_i \bar{y}_i}{\sum_{i\in s} N_i} = \frac{m\,\hat{T}}{M \sum_{i\in s} N_i} = \frac{\hat{T}}{\hat{N}} \quad \text{where } \hat{N} = M \frac{\sum_{i\in s} N_i}{m}$$

The objective is to have an estimator more stable than $\hat{\bar{Y}}_1$ since $\hat{T}$ and $\hat{N}$ are expected to vary in the same manner. The variance is then:

$$V(\hat{\bar{Y}}_2) \approx \frac{1}{\bar{N}^2} \frac{1-f_1}{m} S_\Delta^2 + \frac{1}{m\,M} \sum_{i=1}^{M} \left(\frac{N_i}{\bar{N}}\right)^2 (1-f_{2,i}) S_{2,i}^2$$

where $S_\Delta^{\,2} = \dfrac{1}{M-1} \sum_{i=1}^{M} \Delta_i^2$ with $\Delta_i = N_i(\bar{Y}_i - \bar{Y}) = T_i - N_i \bar{Y}$

There is only one difference between $V(\hat{\bar{Y}}_1)$ and $V(\hat{\bar{Y}}_2)$: the dispersion S_1^2 of the total has been replaced by the dispersion of the variable Δ_i: a weighted dispersion of the means $\bar{Y}_i$. Then, if the PSU's have significantly different sizes N_i, S_1^2 will be larger than $S_\Delta^{\,2}$. Then according to the data $\hat{\bar{Y}}_1$ will be preferable to $\hat{\bar{Y}}_2$ and *vice versa*, and *it is not possible to decide a priori.*

Appendix2

Description of data.

Sampling Details Single Market Survey - Breakdown by Sector

STRATES Nace Rev. 1 (section)		Sample Size	Respondents	Response Rate
INDUSTRY				
DA **Nace1**	Food, beverages & tobacco	1358	773	56.9
DB+DC+DN **Nace 2**	Textiles, leather & furniture	1960	1153	58.8
DD+DE **Nace 3**	Wood, paper & printing/publishing	1458	826	56.7
DG+DH **Nace 4**	Chemicals, rubber & plastics	1286	809	62.9
DI **Nace 5**	Non-metallic mineral products	710	421	59.3
DJ **Nace 6**	Metals & metal products	1554	873	56.2
DK **Nace 7**	Machinery & equipment N.E.C.	1068	597	55.9
DL **Nace 8**	Electrical & optical machinrey	1197	690	57.6
DM **Nace 9**	Transport equipment	582	385	66.2
SUB-TOTAL INDUSTRY		**11173**	**6527**	**58.4**

Sampling Details Single Market Survey - Breakdown by Member State

MEMBER STATES		Sample Size	Respondents	Response Rate
INDUSTRY				
B	België/Belgique	594	386	65.0
DK	Danmark	467	306	65.5
D	BR Deutschland	3024	1268	41.9
GR	Elláda	474	411	86.7
E	España	1600	978	61.1
F	France	1533	957	62.4
IRL	Ireland	663	385	58.1
I	Italia	1009	669	66.3
L	Luxembourg	130	87	66.9
NL	Nederland	446	217	48.7
P	Portugal	316	228	72.2
UK	United Kingdom	917	635	69.2
SUB-TOTAL INDUSTRY		**11173**	**6527**	**58.4**

Questionnaire addressed to manufacturing firms

Q 1.   Please indicate the number of persons employed in your company (to be completed by research institute, if possible).

<50 ☐   50-199 ☐   200-499 ☐   500-999 ☐   >1000 ☐

NACE (2-letter) (to be completed by research institute)   ☐☐

NUTS (level 2) (to be completed by research institute)   ☐☐

Does your firm form part of a group of companies?   Yes   ☐   No   ☐

Q 2.1. Please state whether the following Single Market measures have had an impact on your firm's activities.	Positive Impact	No impact	Negative impact	Don't know
Harmonisation of technical regulations and/or standards	☐	☐	☐	☐
Mutual recognition of technical regulations and standards	☐	☐	☐	☐
Conformity assessment procedures	☐	☐	☐	☐
Simplified patenting procedures	☐	☐	☐	☐
The opening up of public procurement	☐	☐	☐	☐
The elimination of customs documentation	☐	☐	☐	☐
Deregulation of freight transport	☐	☐	☐	☐
The elimination of delays at frontiers	☐	☐	☐	☐
The change in VAT procedures for intra EU sales	☐	☐	☐	☐
The liberalisation of capital movements	☐	☐	☐	☐
Double-taxation agreements	☐	☐	☐	☐

Q 2.2 For each of the following aspects of your firm's operations please indicate whether the Single Market Programme has had a positive or negative impact (either directly or indirectly).	Positive impact	No impact	Negative impact	Don't know
Sales in your country	☐	☐	☐	☐
Sales in other EU countries	☐	☐	☐	☐
Sales to non-EU countries	☐	☐	☐	☐
Productivity	☐	☐	☐	☐
Profitability	☐	☐	☐	☐
Employment[1]	☐	☐	☐	☐

---

[1] If employment has increased, indicate positive impact; if employment has decreased indicate negative impact.

Q 2.3 Please indicate, for each of the following possible areas, the importance of the Single Market Programme to the development of your company's strategy in recent years.					
Strategy		Very important	Quite important	Of little or no importance	Don't know/ Not applicable
Product	Product standardisation	☐	☐	☐	☐
	Product specialisation	☐	☐	☐	☐
	Pricing	☐	☐	☐	☐
	Research and development of new products	☐	☐	☐	☐
Production	Capacity of existing domestic production plants	☐	☐	☐	☐
	Number of domestic production plants	☐	☐	☐	☐
	Establishment of production plants in other EU countries	☐	☐	☐	☐
	Lean production methods	☐	☐	☐	☐
Marketing & distribution	Penetration of markets in other EU countries	☐	☐	☐	☐
	Advertising in other EU countries	☐	☐	☐	☐
	Distribution networks in other EU countries	☐	☐	☐	☐
	Pan European labelling and packaging	☐	☐	☐	☐
Sourcing	Purchase of raw materials from other EU countries	☐	☐	☐	☐
	Purchase of components from other EU countries	☐	☐	☐	☐
	Purchase of business services from other EU countries	☐	☐	☐	☐
	Purchase of financial services from other EU countries	☐	☐	☐	☐
Acquisition Co-operation Ownership	Investment in other companies	☐	☐	☐	☐
	Investment from other companies	☐	☐	☐	☐
	Cooperation agreements with other companies (Please specify)	☐	☐	☐	☐

Q 2.4 Please indicate any change in competition levels on the domestic market which you have noticed in recent years from domestic, other EU or non-EU firms[2].	Increase	No change	Decrease
(i) from an increase in the <u>number</u> of competitors			
- domestically owned firms	☐	☐	☐
- other EU owned firms	☐	☐	☐
- non-EU owned firms	☐	☐	☐
(ii) competition <u>on the basis or price</u>			
- domestically owned firms	☐	☐	☐
- other EU owned firms	☐	☐	☐
- non-EU owned firms	☐	☐	☐
(iii) competition <u>on the basis of product quality/choice</u>			
- domestically owned firms	☐	☐	☐
- other EU owned firms	☐	☐	☐
- non-EU owned firms	☐	☐	☐

Q 3.1 To what extent, in your opinion, has the implementation of the Single Market Programme affected the unit costs of your company's typical or average product?   Don't know   ☐

Reduction >10% (Specify)	Reduction 6<10%	Reduction 2<6%	Reduction 0<2%	No change	Increase 0<2%	Increase 2<6%	Increase 6<10%	Increase >10% (Specify)
....	☐	☐	☐	☐	☐	☐	☐	......

---

[2] The distinction is based on ownership rather than location.

Q 3.2 Regarding the cost reduction/increase indicated above how important have the following been in bringing it about?

	Very important	Quite important	Of little or no importance
Production process	☐	☐	☐
Testing and certification	☐	☐	☐
Distribution costs, (including transport)	☐	☐	☐
Marketing costs	☐	☐	☐
Costs of raw materials	☐	☐	☐
Banking costs	☐	☐	☐
Insurance costs	☐	☐	☐
Other, please specify	☐	☐	☐

Q 4. Please indicate whether you agree or disagree with the following statements regarding Single Market legislation as it affects your own firm or sector.

	Agree	No opinion	Disagree
The single market programme has been a success for your firm	☐	☐	☐
The single market programme has been a success for your sector in your country	☐	☐	☐
The single market programme has been a success for your sector in the EU	☐	☐	☐
The single market programme has been successful in eliminating obstacles to EU trade in your sector	☐	☐	☐
The single market programme has been successful in creating a genuine internal market in your sector	☐	☐	☐
Additional measures are needed to eliminate obstacles to EU trade If you agree, please specify your first priority	☐	☐	☐
Additional measures are needed in this sector to create a genuine internal market If you agree, please specify your first priority	☐	☐	☐

Appendix 3

Estimation of variance with the Bootstrap

Suppose that the data $X_1 .... X_n$ are *i.i.d.* from distribution function F. This function is estimated by $\hat{F}$. Let us assume that we want to estimate a certain function T of

$$X_1 .... X_n .$$

Then the bootstrap variance estimator is

$$v_{boot} = \int \left[T_n(x) - \int T_n(y) \, d\prod_{i=1}^{n} \hat{F}(y_i) \right]^2 d\prod_{i=1}^{n} \hat{F}(x_i)$$

$$= \text{var}_* \left[T_n(X_1^* .... X_n^*) \big| X_1 .... X_n \right]$$

where $\{ X_1 .... X_n \}$ is an *i.i.d.* sample from $\hat{F}$ and is called a bootstrap sample, and $\text{var}_* \left[. \big| X_1 ...... X_n \right]$ denotes the conditional variance for given $X_1 .... X_n$. The equation above is the theoretical form of the bootstrap variance estimator for T_n. It may not be used directly when v_{boot} is not an explicit function of $X_1 .... X_n$. This is why in our case where the coefficients from the Logit cannot be written explicitly, we must use the Monte Carlo method. That is, we repeatedly draw new data sets from F and then use the sample variance of the values of T_n computed from new data sets as a numerical approximation to $\text{var}(T_n)$. This idea can be used to approximate v_{boot} since $\hat{F}$ is a known distribution. Practically we draw $\{ X_{1b}^* .... X_{nb}^* \}$, b=1,.......,B, independently from $\hat{F}$, conditioned on $X_1 .... X_n$; compute $T_{n,b}^* = T_n(X_{1b}^* .... X_{nb}^*)$ and approximate v_{boot} by the following Monte Carlo approximation:

$$v_{boot}^{(B)} = \frac{1}{B} \sum_{b=1}^{B} \left(T_{n,b}^* - \frac{1}{B} \sum_{l=1}^{B} T_{n,l}^* \right)^2 .$$

From the law of large numbers we have, $v_{boot} = \lim_{B \to \infty} v_{boot}^B$.

With the same formalism one can state the Monte Carlo approximation of the mean:

$$m_{boot}^{(B)} = \frac{1}{B}\sum_{b=1}^{B}\left(T_{n,b}^*\right) \quad .$$

REFERENCES

Fuller W. (1975) *'Regression analysis for sample survey'*, Sankhya (1975, 37)

Isaki C. and Fuller W. (1982), *'Survey Design Under the Regression Superpopulation model'*. Journal of the American Statistical Association. (1982, 77)

Laaksonen S. (CAED-1996). *'Notes on International Comparability of Sample Based Business Survey Data'* .

Nordberg.L. (1989), *'Generalized Linear Modelling of Sample Survey Data'*, Journal of Official Statistics (1989,vol 5).

Pfeffermann D. and Smith T.M.F.. *'Regression Models for Grouped Populations in Cross-Section Surveys'*. International Statistical Review (1985, 53).

Särndal C.E., Swensson B. and Wretman J.. (1992) *'Model assisted Survey Sampling.'* Springer Verlag).

Eurostat, (1996),*'The Single Market Business Survey'* in the Single Market review, Eurostat.

THE ROLE OF TECHNOLOGY IN MANUFACTURING EMPLOYMENT AND PRODUCTIVITY GROWTH: A CROSS COUNTRY MICRO DATA ANALYSIS OF JAPAN AND THE UNITED STATES

Ronald S. Jarmin[1] and Kazuyuki Motohashi[2]

[1]Center for Economic Studies, U.S. Bureau of the Census
[2]Economic Analysis and Statistics Division, Directorate for Science, Technology and Industry, OECD

1 Introduction

In recent years, establishment and firm level (micro) datasets have been compiled for research and policy analysis in a number of countries, including Canada, France, the Netherlands, Finland and the United States (OECD, 1997). A particularly important area of study using these data involves examining how innovative efforts lead to improvements in economic performance, such as productivity and employment growth.[1] A key finding of the research using micro data is that there is more variation in the characteristics and performance of establishment and firms within industries than there is across industries. Further, changes in aggregate statistics are driven largely by compositional shifts from groups of firms and establishments with one set of characteristics (e.g., low productivity) to groups with a different set (e.g., high productivity).

Although these studies have been done in several different countries, there have been no studies that directly compare how technology affects productivity and employment across different countries. In this paper, we present such a comparative analysis using firm level data from Japan and the United States.

Motivation for this cross country comparison comes from a striking difference in the pattern of productivity and employment growth for these two countries. Figure 1 shows that while manufacturing value added and labor productivity grew, over the period from 1980 to 1995, for both Japan and the U.S., manufacturing employment grew only in Japan[2]. As shown in Table 1,

---

[1] Researchers from many countries presented results from studies on topics such as these at the conference, "The Effects of Technology and Innovation on Firm Performance and Employment" in Washington DC, May, 1995.

[2] This study examines the manufacturing sector only, due to the limitations of the micro datasets.

downsizing at large establishments   drives the decrease in manufacturing employment in the U.S., while Japanese establishment does not show such pattern.

These patterns, of course, have been the subject of studies on employment and labor market differences between the two countries. The U.S. labor market is generally described as flexible, where adjustments can occur both through changes in employment and wages. On the other hand, Japanese labor markets are marked by wage flexibility, but much less downward flexibility in the number of employees. It is shown that the wage flexibility in the Japanese labor market may be due to wage setting institutions, such as annual negotiation of wages between employers and employees, called Shunto. (Hamada and Kurosaka (1986), EPA (1994)) In contrast, Doms et. al. (1995) shows that Japanese gross job flow at the plant level is significantly lower than that of France or the United States, which suggests inflexibility in the number of employment. Hence, the nature of labor markets provides one possible explanation for the different responses by American and Japanese firms to changes in demand and output.

Although labor market flexibility provides one possible explanation for the diverging picture in these countries, it is unlikely to be the singular cause and policy-makers and economists have been looking for additional structural factors. One such area is technology, and its impact on productivity and employment. Over the long-run, most economists believe that technology is a driving force behind economic growth, employment and productivity. However, the short and medium-term effects are more complicated due to a number of factors. For example, process innovation is often thought to reduce employment in the short term as productivity increases allow firms to produce current output levels with fewer workers. Further, it is believed that much of the innovation occurring in industrialized countries decreases the demand for unskilled workers relative to skilled worker (e.g., skill biased technical change). This may help explain the increase dispersion of wages between skilled and unskilled worker and in productivity and wage levels at manufacturing establishments observed in the U.S. (see Dunne, Haltiwanger and Troske, 1997). However, over the longer term, if such innovation leads to quality increases and relative price decreases which, in turn, lead to increased demand at innovating firms, these firms may have increased demand for labor. Also, product innovation may induce new demand, and lead to employment growth in a more direct way (OECD 1996).

By examining the role of technology in productivity and employment growth at the firm level, we hope to shed new light on differences in the patterns of manufacturing employment and productivity between these two countries. Another contribution of this paper is our comparative analysis using micro datasets from different countries. Indeed, this is the type of analysis that this conference (CAED 97, Bergamo) and its predecessor (CAED '96 in Helsinki) have sought to encourage.

To date, however, studies explicitly comparing results based on micro data across countries are still scarce.[3] One major obstacle to international studies is the confidential nature of micro-level datasets, which make it difficult to use these data outside national statistical offices. In this paper, we address the confidentiality constraint with both a decentralized approach, where common procedures were applied to national micro-level datasets, and an analysis based on nonconfidential aggregated data. We constructed this latter dataset by combining aggregated data from the national statistics offices in Japan (the Research and Statistics Department of MITI) and the United States (the Center for Economic Studies of the Bureau of the Census) in the course of OECD's project on micro dataset analysis on technology, productivity and employment[4].

An additional obstacle is the comparability of the micro datasets across countries. The micro datasets maintained by the various countries are composed of data collected in a variety of ways for a variety of country specific uses. Thus, these datasets contain many items that are not comparable across countries. Further, even when they contain measures of the same economic variables, cross country differences in variable definitions and the scope, coverage and methodology of the surveys used by the various national statistical agencies make international comparisons difficult.

2 Data for firm level analysis

The first task in this project was to assemble data suitable for cross-country analyses. Most national statistical offices compile micro datasets directly from business registers and statistical surveys which are not standardized internationally. In this analysis, we restrict our attention to variables that we feel have reasonably consistent definitions across the two countries.

We employ R&D intensity as our measure of the technological capability of firms. Since R&D is typically thought to be firm level activity (e.g., R&D performed at one establishment of a multi-establishment firm is very likely to benefit the firm's other establishments) and because R&D is measured in the U.S. at the firm level, we use the firm as our unit of analysis for this project.

We list the major characteristics of each of the datasets in table 2. For Japan, a firm level manufacturing survey has been conducted as a supplement to the establishment level census. Therefore, a firm level dataset is available, but only

---

[3] Exceptions include Doms et. al. (1995) who look at difference in micro economic structure of France, Japan and the United States and Baldwin, Dunne and Haltiwanger (forthcoming) who examine employment flows in Canada and the U.S.

[4] Methodology of data collection and statistical analysis for France, Japan and the United States under this project is published in OECD (1998).

for firms with more than 99 employees[5]. US establishment data (LRD[6]) are aggregated up to the firm level. The existence of firm level identifiers for each establishment makes this possible.

From the micro data available in each country, we constructed a balanced panel of data for firms from the late 1980's to the early 1990's (1987 to 1994 for Japan and 1987 to 1992 for the United States). We extracted common variables from each dataset for use in the analysis below. These included value added with appropriate deflators and number of employees for measuring labor productivity and employment growth, and R&D expenditures and total production (or sales) for measuring R&D intensity. The definitions of these variables are comparable for both countries. However, the US productivity data may suffer from a "non manufacturing establishment bias," because they are compiled only from data on manufacturing establishments.   For   example,   Some   large   firms   have establishments operating outside the manufacturing sector. These are included in the firm level R&D data, but not in the productivity measures we construct.

In addition to the two comparable firm level datasets, we also constructed an aggregate dataset based on these firm level datasets.   The micro datasets were aggregated using the same format (this procedure is described in OECD (1998)). The resulting dataset, thus, employs consistent industry classifications and size classes across the two countries. In addition, we created three R&D classes by R&D intensity. These are: firms which did not conduct R&D (no R&D firm), low R&D firms with R&D intensities below the within industry median intensity, and high R&D firms with R&D intensities above the industry median. This permits the comparison of employment and productivity performance for each of the three groupings allowing for heterogeneity of firms within industries and across size classes.

High adjustment costs and uncertainty associated with R&D investment[7] lead to relative stability in firms' R&D intensities.   This stability makes R&D intensity a practical criterion to group firms. In addition, due to the very skewed distribution of R&D intensity within industries, it is important to distinguish highly R&D intensive firms from those with low R&D intensity and those that perform no R&D.

Note that, by using R&D intensity to measure the technological capabilities of firms, we capture primarily knowledge generation and not knowledge diffusion. Although improving technological capability by capitalizing on knowledge generated by others is also an important factor for firm level competitiveness, the

---

[5] Compilation of Japanese R&D panel data is described in Motohashi (1997).

[6] Longitudinal Research Database. See McGuckin and Pascoe (1988) for details.

[7] Comparing adjustment costs associated with R&D and physical investments have been done by Kruiniger (1996). In addition, firm's R&D intensity ranking shows higher persistency than that of physical investments (Klette and Johannsen (1996)), which also suggests higher adjustment costs in R&D.

mechanism of knowledge diffusion is complicated and difficult to measure and, thus, beyond the scope of our current exercise.[8]

3 Descriptive findings on technology, productivity and employment

We begin this section by comparing relative productivity levels by industry, size class and R&D intensities across the two countries.   One well-established empirical observation is that labor productivity levels rise with firm size.   This stylized fact is true in the firm level datasets for Japan and the United States analyzed here (see Table 3 and Figure 2).   Interestingly, the size productivity premium appears to be significantly larger in the US than in Japan, while it should be noted that US data might suffer from non manufacturing establishment biases discussed in the previous section.   In addition, the distinction between firms engaged in R&D and others shows the positive link between labor productivity levels and R&D intensity.[9]   Table 3 shows that the productivity premium for R&D firms is not an industry effect, since it is observed within each industry.

Another interesting point from Figure 2 is that the size of the productivity premium for R&D firms becomes smaller as firm size increases.   That is, R&D appears to be particularly important factor in the success of SMEs relative to other SMES.   There might be financial and labor market imperfections that have adverse effects on smaller firm's R&D investments.   Further, large firms may be better able to benefit from R&D by knowing in what areas to focus its efforts, by using more developed marketing and distribution networks, and by being able to appropriate a larger share of the returns to R&D. Because it is difficult for SMEs to launch R&D investment projects, small firms that overcome such hurdles are likely to be more productive than other SMEs.   It remains the case, however, that R&D is an activity practiced mainly by large firms (see Cohen, 1996, for a review).

The main focus of this paper is to contrast the role of technology, as proxied by R&D intensities, in productivity and employment growth in Japan and the U.S. To do this we exploit the methodological framework employed by Baily et al. (1994). We, thus, classify individual firms into four different groups:

---

[8] Knowledge is diffused by being embodied in products and/or workers, or disembodied, such as information exchanges in conferences. Measurement of technology diffusion has been extensively investigated, but still there is no agreement on the best way to capture all effects (Griliches, 1992).

[9] Labor productivity could be higher for R&D firms, because they tend to be more capital intensive (Mairesse and Hall (1996)). In this sense, TFP may be a more appropriate productivity variable.   However, data constraints limit the current presentation to measures of labor productivity.

Group 1: Firms with rising labor productivity and rising employment;

Group 2: Firms with rising labor productivity, but falling employment;

Group 3: Firms with falling labor productivity and falling employment;

Group 4: Firms with falling labor productivity and rising employment.

This way of classifying firms is useful for our purposes as it allows is to examine how R&D affects both employment and productivity growth simultaneously.

Tables 4a and 4b show the share of firms falling into each of the above categories for Japan and the U.S., respectively. Comparing the two tables, the most striking features are the large shares of firms in group 1 in Japan and group 2 in the U.S. [10] The share of U.S. firms in groups 1 and 2 is much smaller than the share of U.S. manufacturing establishments in the same groups reported in Baily et. al (51.8% in table 4b compared to the 57.5% they found). Productivity measures, however, are procyclical. The period Baily et. al. examined was peak to peak, whereas the 1987-1992 period we examine for U.S. firms covers a peak to trough period. In a period such as 1987 to 1992 in the U.S., one would expect to see a relatively high share of firms in group 3, the so-called unsuccessful downsizers. Indeed, this is the case as we find 22.9% of the firms in group 3 compared to only 13.7% in Baily et. al.[11].

Nevertheless, the difference between the shares of firms in groups 1 and 2 in Japan and the U.S. is very striking. Looking only at those firms that increase productivity, in Japan 54.7% also increased employment, whereas only 37.1% did in the U.S. Similarly, for firms that decreased productivity, Japan has a larger share that increase employment, even though the U.S. has a larger absolute share in group 4.

Tables 4a and 4b also show the shares of firms in the four groups by industry, size, and R&D intensity. For R&D, we look at three classes of firms: firms that do not perform R&D[12], those performing R&D but spending less than the median

---

[10] Again, it should be noted that Japanese data are only for firms with 100 or more employee, which represents only 10.3% of total manufacturing value added in 1994. Cross country comparison after controlling for firm size is presented later.

[11] Another source of divergence from Baily et. al. comes from the difference in unit of observation, i.e., our results are based on firm level data, while establishment level data was used for Baily et. al.

[12] For the U.S., manufacturing firms classified as "no R&D" are those that do not appear in the NSF Survey of industrial R&D for either 1987 or 1992. Note that the sample for this survey over the period we are studying may have omitted some small R&D performers. Firms investing at least $1 million in R&D were included in the survey with certainty as well as some smaller performers. Not until 1992 did NSF and the Census Bureau try to more systematically assess the universe of R&D performing firms in the U.S. (see NSF, 1996).

amount, and those that spent more than the median amount. Interestingly, tables 4a and 4b indicate that, in Japan, high R&D firms were over represented in groups 1 and 4 (i.e., had employment growth) and high R&D firms in the U.S. were over represented in groups 1 and 2 (i.e., had productivity growth). Figure 3 graphically depicts the same information as the first row of tables 4a and 4b. These results provide our first indication that the role of R&D and technology in employment and productivity growth may be different across the two countries.

Another interesting fact is shown in table 5 which lists the relative R&D intensities by group and size class. Looking at firms in the larger size classes of groups 1 and 2 for which productivity increases, we see that R&D intensities are higher, within size classes, for employment upsizers in the U.S. and for downsizers in Japan. This finding is particularly intriguing given that most R&D is performed by large firms. This again suggests that there are different mechanisms of enhancing productivity growth. Namely, upsizers' achieve productivity growth via an output-enhancing effect. Product innovation that leads to new demand or process innovation with an ensuing price decrease in a price-elastic product market boosts output and, thus, demand for employment. On the other hand, downsizers' labor productivity increases may be more likely to come from non technology-related efficiency gains, such as restructuring and organizational change, coupled with labor shedding (Bartelsman, Leeuwen and Nieuwenhuijsen, 1995). Thus, the results in table 5 may indicate that successful (productivity increasers) R&D intensive firms in the U.S. focus more on product innovation, generating both productivity and employment growth, whereas less R&D intensive firms in the same size class focus more on process innovation accompanied with downsizing. In contrast, successful R&D intensive firms, in Japan, appear to follow the process innovation and downsizing model.

In Japan, higher R&D intensities are associated with declining labor productivity in some size classes. As indicated in the previous section, because wages tend to be relatively flexible, Japanese R&D firms may have sacrificed apparent labor productivity growth by hoarding labor despite the downturn of the business cycle, following the boom between 1986 and 1991. Other firms may have over-estimated their demand and still be in the process of adjusting employment in 1994. If this misjudgment of demand has been more widespread among R&D-intensive firms (perhaps because they can afford to do so), this could explain the positive link between R&D intensity and a fall in labor productivity[13]. In addition, R&D firms with more skilled workers have presumably higher cost of adjustments for hiring and firing.

It is also interesting to see how each group contributes to overall aggregate employment and productivity growth. Looking at Table 6, note the important role

---

[13]Doms et. al (1995) compared the index of plant level gross job flows in France, Japan and the United States, and found that worker mobility across plants in Japan is quite low as compared to those in the United States or France. This implies that Japanese firm's employment adjustment to the demand shock is slower.

of successful upsizers (group 1). In each country, they contribute significantly to aggregate employment and productivity growth. In Japan, group 1 is the biggest contributor to both productivity and employment growth, while the group 2 is the biggest contributor to productivity growth in the United States.

4 Regressions using country specific firm level micro data

In this section, we examine the role of technology in productivity and employment dynamics more systematically. To isolate the impact of R&D intensity, we perform a number of firm level regressions using the micro datasets from Japan and the U.S. separately. To maximize the comparability of the two datasets, we again group firms into one of the Baily et. al groups. We then run a series of probits to examine how technology effects the probability of being in each of the four groups while controlling for firm size and industry. That is we estimate the following probit regression

$$\text{Prob(Quadrant j)} = \alpha + \beta_1 \text{Industry} + \beta_2 \text{Size} + \beta_3 \text{Country} + \beta_4 \text{R\&D} + \varepsilon \quad [1]$$

where Prob (Group "j") is probability of a firm in group "j" (j=1,2,3 or 4), Industry, Size, Country and R&D are dummy variables for each class.

In table 7, we report the results of probits that compare High R&D firms to Low and No R&D firms. The main result here is in that both countries No R&D firms are significantly less likely to have increases in employment than are R&D performing firms after controlling for firm size and industry. This result is shown more clearly in table 7 where we run two probits, respectively, estimating the probability of plants exhibiting productivity and employment increases. Again the results indicate that the No R&D firms are much less likely than the High and Low R&D firms to have employment increases in both Japan and the U.S.

The productivity effects of R&D in tables 7 and 8 are much weaker. The only clear result is in table 8 which shows that, in Japan, No R&D firms are more likely to have experienced productivity increases than R&D firms. To examine the effects of R&D on productivity and employment more closely, we run the same probits on a sample restricted to R&D performing firms only. These probits compare High and Low R&D intensive firms and the results are given in tables 9 and 10. The estimates in these tables suggest that for R&D performing firms, higher R&D intensities are associated with productivity increases in the US and employment increases in Japan. This is a very intriguing and robust result that confirms the descriptive results from the last section that suggested that the role of R&D may differ substantially between the two countries.

5 Regressions using pooled aggregate data

The question now arises as to whether the differences we are observing are due to actual differences in how technology impacts productivity and employment across the two countries, or rather to some other unobserved county effects. These might include differences in market, institutional or perhaps even cultural factors that cause firms in the two countries to respond to technological change differently.

The best way to test this would be to pool the firm level micro data from the two countries and estimate equation (1) on the pooled data while controlling for country effects (i.e., include country dummies and interaction terms as well as the other right hand side variables). Unfortunately, it is not currently possible to combine micro data from these countries due to confidentiality considerations. Thus, we use standardized aggregation procedures to create a pooled dataset. Because relatively few firms, in both countries, actually perform R&D we could not construct a pooled aggregate dataset that allows us to control for industry, size, R&D and country simultaneously. There are 16 industries, 7 size classes, 3 countries and 3 R&D classes. Therefore, we control for industry and size effects separately in the following analysis based on the aggregated data. We estimate the following modified versions of (1) for industry*country*R&D class data and size*country*R&D class data:[14]

$$\text{Share}_j = \alpha + \beta_1 \text{Industry} + \beta_2 \text{Country} + \beta_3 \text{R\&D} + \varepsilon \qquad [2]$$

$$\text{Share}_j = \alpha + \beta_1 \text{Size} + \beta_2 \text{Country} + \beta_3 \text{R\&D} + \varepsilon \qquad [3]$$

where Share_j is the share of firms in group "j" for each industry*on*R&D class (or size*on*R&D class). This limited dependent variable regression is done by 2 step GLS, which make sure that results are consistent with firm level regression (1).[15] Country and R&D coefficients are presented in table 11. For

---

[14].Confidentiality constraints caused too much missing observations in industry*size*R&D data, so that we had to control industry and size effect, separately.

[15].If the share data is assumed to be an outcome by sampling from a Bernoulli population, this regression can be solved by the following heteroscedastic regression (in the case of logistic function)

$$\ln(share_j / 1 - share_j) = \alpha + \sum \beta_k x_k + u_j$$

where $E[u_j] = 0$ and $Var[u_j] = F_j(1 - F_j) / n_j f_j^2$

$(F_j = \exp(\beta x_j / 1 + \beta x_j), f_j = dF_j(x) / dx$ and n_j: the number of individual firms in each cell).

each group, two regressions are conducted; one for all firms where the R&D dummy equals one for R&D performing firms and zero for non R&D firms, and the other for R&D firms where the R&D dummy equals one for high R&D firms and zero for low R&D firms. For each regression, the country dummies are for Japan relative to the U.S.

In terms of cross country differences, the regression results in Table 11 confirm again that Japan has a higher share of successful upsizers and a smaller share of successful downsizers than the U.S. In terms of R&D classes, statistically significant coefficients are obtained for the R&D - no R&D comparisons only. These results suggest that R&D firms are more likely to be successful upsizers than non R&D firms.

For the estimated R&D coefficients there are some interesting differences between equations (2) and (3). While the estimated R&D coefficients for groups 1 and 3, the upsizers, are similar, the estimates for groups 2 and 4, the downsizers, are much smaller when we control for industry rather than size. This suggests that R&D may proxy for some industry effects in the regressions of (3) in panel b. This problem highlights the need to be able to control for both size and industry simultaneously.

Overall, however, the pooled results provide few insights that could not be had by looking at the descriptive results in section 3 or the within country analysis of sections 4 and 5. It is unlikely that pooled aggregate datasets can provide much useful new information. The advantage of micro data lies in the analyst's ability to use it i) to control for observable characteristics (and unobservable characteristics in the case of panel data) at the establishment and firm level where there is much more variation than at the industry or country level and ii) to disentangle the composition effects that determine how changes at the micro level are translated in to changes in the aggregate statistics that are typically used to compare the performance of national economies. The patterns of establishment and firm heterogeneity and compositional factors are likely to differ across countries. Pooled aggregate datasets can not possibly allow researchers to disentangle all these confounding effects.

Conclusions

In this paper, we compared the role of technology in the dynamics of productivity and employment using micro data from Japan and the United States. Our goal was to see if technology, as proxied by R&D intensity, could help explain the

---

Since var[u] is unknown, OLS is conducted at the first step for coming up with estimated weights which are used for the second step weighted least squares. (Greene (1990))

diverging pattern of aggregate manufacturing employment and productivity growth between the two countries.

For our firm level analysis, we grouped firms in each country in groups according to whether they experienced increases or decreases in employment and productivity, as in Baily et. al. (1994). Our key finding is that, over the sample period, technology is associated primarily with employment growth in Japan and primarily with productivity growth in the U.S. At first, it may seem tempting to conclude that employment growth at R&D intensive Japanese firms and productivity growth and downsizing at R&D intensive U.S. firms can explain the differences in aggregate employment and productivity growth between the two countries. This would be a mistake since the situation is much more complex as the results in table 5 suggest.

Productivity growth at the firm level can be seen as an outcome of countless firm decisions on things such as employment, training, capital investments, and R&D to name a few. Technology is an important choice variable, but only one of many, and one which involves much uncertainty about the final outcome. Non technological factors[16] are also likely to be important for explaining differences in the productivity performance of firms and countries. Our use of R&D as a proxy for technology captures only firms' knowledge generation, but not technology spillovers. Thus, it provides an incomplete picture of the role of technology.[17]

Also, in cross country studies, such as this, one needs to remember that differences in market and social institutions may affect how things like technology lead to changes in employment and productivity. In addition, different business cycle conditions may contribute to observed differences in employment and productivity. Therefore, it is important to try to control for these other factors, something we have only partially done at this point.

Indeed, it is these differences that could help researchers identify how R&D and other variables differentially affect employment and productivity growth across countries. Before this can happen, however, we must find a way to construct pooled micro datasets. These will allow researchers to estimate microeconometric models and control for country effects. Until then we are forced to compare the results of within country micro data analyses or to use pooled aggregate datasets in cross country studies such as this one.

---

[16]Possible factors include human capital (Baldwin et. al. (1995), Entorf and Kramarz (1995)), ownership of firm (McGuckin and Nguyen (1995)), human resource management (Ichniowski et. al. (1997)), and a bundle of business decisions including financial and marketing strategy (Baldwin and Johnson (1995)).

[17]As for capital embodied technology spillover, McGuckin et. al. (1996) analyzed the productivity effect of advanced manufacturing technology, Brynjolffson and Hitt (1995) worked on the productivity and computer investments. For disembodied technology spillover, Branstetter (1996) compared Japanese and US firms on the own R&D and spillover effects on productivity.

Table 1 Employment Distributions by Size - (Excluding establishments with less than 30 employees)

Country	Year	30-99	100-199	200-499	500-899	900+
Japan	82	.307	.164	.187	.106	.236
Japan	87	.314	.176	.190	.104	.216
Japan	92	.308	.177	.189	.104	.222
US	82	.188	.154	.227	.124	.308
US	87	.195	.160	.231	.122	.291
US	92	.203	.168	.239	.126	.264

Source: Doms et. al. (1995)

Table 2 Micro Datasets on R&D in Japan and the United States

	JAPAN	US
Name of Database	Japanese R&D Panel	US Longitudinal Research Database (LRD)
Unit of Analysis	Firm	Establishment, with firm identifier in every year.
Sectors	Manufacturing	Manufacturing
Years of Coverage	1987, 89, 91 and 94	1963, 1967, 1972-1992.
Sample Characteristics	All firms with 50+ employment Some cut-pff points on total capital is also applied. (20,000 firms), but R&D data are available for only 100+ firms	Census every 5 years (approx. 350,000 estabs.), probability sample in the intervening years (approx. 55,000 estabs.)
Industry Classification	3-digit Japanese SIC	4 digit ISIC revision 2
Employment Data		
Level of Employment	December 31st employment	March 12th employment
Salaries	Total annual salaries (including bonuses and other benefits, such as housing allowances.)	Total annual salaries. Also, supplemental labor costs.
Production Data		
Sales	Shipments as measured by freight on board prices	Shipments as measured by freight on board prices
Value Added	Firm level value added (total sales - all cost incurred + wage + depreciation)	Defintion of value added = sales - change in inventories - cost of purchased materials - cost of energy - cost of contract work + value of receipts of contract work performed.
Capital	Book value of machinery, equipment and buildings	Book value of machinery, equipment, and buildings. 1972-1985, ASM establishments only. 1987 and 1992 for all non-admisnistraive records.
R&D Data	R&D expenditure is surveyed	NSF R&D survey data can be lined at the firm level. (LRD data are aggregated into firm level)
R&D Expenditure	Finance Base R&D expenditure, Breakdown into activity base one and self-financed one can be done for 1991 data	Activity base R&D expenditure as well as self-financed R&D. The breakdown into basic, applied R&D and development can be done
Number of Scientist	# in head count	# in full time equivalent
Other comments	Detail technology variables, such as patent, technology licencing and use of information network, are avaialble in 1991 and 94	Survey on Advanced Manufacturing Technology can be linked at the establishment level

Table 3 Relative Labor Productivity

(All firms in each country = 1)

	Japan (1991)		US (1992)	
	R&D firms	All firms	R&D firms	All firms
Total manufacturing	1.03	1.00	1.17	1.00
Food Products	0.84	0.78	1.64	1.11
Textiles & Apparel	0.66	0.56	0.60	0.46
Wood & Furniture	0.91	0.81	0.62	0.48
Paper & Printing	1.27	1.08	1.17	0.79
Chemicals excluding Drugs	1.23	1.21	2.00	1.52
Drugs	1.19	1.17	2.57	1.87
Plastics & Rubber	0.96	0.89	0.94	0.67
Non-metallic Product	1.00	0.95	1.00	0.79
Basic Metals	1.38	1.37	0.98	0.70
Fabricated Metals	0.95	0.88	0.85	0.57
Non-electrical Machinery	0.94	0.90	0.89	0.68
Computer & Electronics	0.89	0.84	1.10	1.15
Ship, Aircraft & Rail	0.97	0.92	0.97	0.83
Motor Vehicle	0.97	0.98	1.26	1.10
Instrument	0.80	0.75	1.21	0.92
1-49	-	-	0.86	0.55
50-99	0.78	0.71	0.73	0.59
100-199	0.75	0.70	0.75	0.63
200-499	0.78	0.73	0.83	0.70
500-999	0.87	0.83	0.93	0.84
1000-	1.09	1.09	1.20	1.17

Table 4a Share by the number of firms of each group by productivity and employment growth

(Japan, 1987-1994)

	# of firms	LP>0 EMP>0	LP>0 EMP<0	LP<0 EMP<0	LP<0 EMP>0
Total manufacturing	2899	0.324	0.268	0.161	0.248
		(deviation from total manufacturing)			
Food Products	329	-0.090	-0.101	0.058	0.132
Texitles & Apparel	228	-0.179	0.061	0.159	-0.042
Wood & Furniture	74	-0.229	-0.160	0.258	0.131
Paper & Printing	230	-0.150	-0.124	0.008	0.265
Chemicals excluding Drugs	130	0.246	0.048	-0.115	-0.178
Drugs	45	0.299	0.110	-0.161	-0.248
Plastics & Rubber	164	0.091	0.001	-0.039	-0.053
Non-metalic Product	146	-0.029	0.034	0.065	-0.070
Basic Metals	142	0.050	0.021	0.008	-0.079
Fabricated Metals	181	-0.114	-0.063	0.016	0.161
Non-electrical Machinery	318	-0.173	-0.114	0.109	0.177
Computer & Electronics	476	0.160	0.113	-0.125	-0.147
Ship, Aircraft & Rail	44	-0.096	-0.177	0.066	0.207
Motor Vehicle	236	0.278	0.105	-0.153	-0.231
Instrument	94	-0.036	0.115	-0.044	-0.035
Other Manufacturing	62	-0.001	0.103	0.016	-0.119
1-49	-	-	-	-	-
50-99	-	-	-	-	-
100-199	1288	-0.029	-0.005	0.011	0.023
200-499	1024	-0.017	0.005	0.013	-0.001
500-999	352	0.103	-0.015	-0.028	-0.060
1000-1499	93	0.074	0.055	-0.075	-0.054
1500-	142	0.078	0.014	-0.077	-0.015
no R&D	910	-0.049	0.064	0.015	-0.030
low R&D	990	0.003	-0.014	-0.005	0.016
high R&D	999	0.042	-0.044	-0.009	0.012

Table 4b Share by the number of firms of each group by productivity and employment growth

(US, 1987-1992)

	# of firms	LP>0 EMP>0	LP>0 EMP<0	LP<0 EMP<0	LP<0 EMP>0
Total manufacturing	175272	0.192	0.326	0.229	0.253
	(deviation from total manufacturing)				
Food Products	8809	0.000	-0.020	-0.009	0.028
Texitles & Apparel	12536	-0.009	0.008	0.009	-0.008
Wood & Furniture	15403	-0.020	-0.007	0.036	-0.009
Paper & Printing	34547	-0.016	0.006	0.008	0.002
Chemicals excluding Drugs	4222	-0.008	-0.048	-0.003	0.059
Drugs	585	0.073	-0.090	-0.068	0.085
Plastics & Rubber	7057	0.060	-0.042	-0.058	0.040
Non-metalic Product	7354	-0.005	0.042	-0.027	-0.010
Basic Metals	3104	-0.009	-0.035	0.023	0.021
Fabricated Metals	19918	-0.008	-0.002	0.010	0.000
Non-electrical Machinery	28988	0.017	0.005	-0.011	-0.012
Computer & Electronics	8629	0.074	0.019	-0.057	-0.036
Ship, Aircraft & Rail	2085	-0.027	0.002	0.057	-0.032
Motor Vehicle	3101	0.030	-0.016	-0.005	-0.009
Instrument	4891	0.047	-0.034	-0.026	0.013
Other Manufacturing	14043	-0.046	0.019	0.025	0.002
1-49	149438	-0.008	-0.001	0.003	0.006
50-99	12832	0.039	-0.006	-0.005	-0.029
100-199	6355	0.047	-0.004	-0.014	-0.028
200-499	3889	0.043	0.020	-0.025	-0.037
500-999	1309	0.073	0.001	-0.035	-0.038
1000-1499	451	0.074	0.024	-0.076	-0.023
1500-	998	0.027	0.090	-0.042	-0.075
no R&D	173675	-0.001	0.000	0.001	0.000
low R&D	805	0.092	-0.004	-0.083	-0.005
high R&D	792	0.056	0.048	-0.059	-0.045

Table 5 Relative R&D intensity[1] by size class and group **100-199 employees in group 1=1**

| Employment size class | Productivity rises | | Productivity falls | |
	Employment rises	Employment falls	Employment falls	Employment rises
Japan				
100-199	1.00	1.24	0.77	0.91
200-499	1.50	1.33	1.18	1.48
500-999	1.94	2.69	1.34	2.77
1000-1499	2.04	2.81	2.23	2.10
1500+	3.16	4.11	5.97	4.49
United States				
1-49	0.23	0.17	0.13	0.10
50-99	0.58	0.41	0.18	0.14
100-199	1.00	1.24	1.05	0.75
200-499	4.17	1.59	1.40	1.33
500-999	3.96	2.02	2.42	2.96
1000-1499	3.81	2.82	3.50	3.50
1500-	8.94	5.56	11.91	9.32

*Notes:*1. R&D intensity is measured as R&D expenditure / value-added. All R&D intensities are expressed relative to the R&D intensity of the size class 100-199 in the group 'upsizers with productivity growth' and in each country.

Table 6 Contribution to Productivity and Employment Growth

Japan (1987-94)

	# of firm	Productivity	Employment
		(annual growth rate)	
All firms	2899	13.49%	0.65%
		(% contribution to total growth)	
LP>0, EMP>0	938	9.47%	1.14%
LP>0, EMP<0	776	5.89%	-0.94%
LP<0, EMP<0	467	-0.45%	-0.24%
LP<0, EMP>0	718	-1.42%	0.68%
All R&D firms	1989	11.00%	0.54%
LP>0, EMP>0	688	7.35%	0.95%
LP>0, EMP<0	474	5.22%	-0.81%
LP<0, EMP<0	414	-0.81%	0.29%
LP<0, EMP>0	261	-0.53%	0.23%

US (1987-92)

	# of firm	Productivity	Employment
		(annual growth rate)	
All firms	175272	2.09%	-0.32%
		(% contribution to total growth)	
LP>0, EMP>0	33601	1.67%	1.70%
LP>0, EMP<0	57152	2.56%	-2.77%
LP<0, EMP<0	40156	-0.54%	-0.87%
LP<0, EMP>0	44363	-1.28%	1.62%
All R&D firms	1597	1.72%	-0.93%
LP>0, EMP>0	424	0.96%	0.50%
LP>0, EMP<0	555	1.37%	-1.52%
LP<0, EMP<0	253	-0.37%	-0.24%
LP<0, EMP>0	365	-0.24%	0.33%

Table 7 Within Country Group Probits.

(Standard errors in parentheses)

Equation (1)

Variable	Group 1 Japan	US	Group 2 Japan	US	Group 3 Japan	US	Group 4 Japan	US
No R&D	-0.196***	-0.286***	0.389***	0.234***	0.069	0.22***	-0.279***	-0.137***
	(0.067)	(0.034)	(0.068)	(0.034)	(0.078)	(0.039)	(0.073)	(0.035)
Low R&D	-0.114**	-0.063	0.114*	-0.041	0.009	0.06	0.02	0.068
	(0.062)	(0.042)	(0.065)	(0.043)	(0.074)	(0.048)	(0.066)	(0.044)
High R&D	-	-	-	-	-	-	-	-
Dummies	Yes	Yes	Yes	Yes	Yes	Yes	Yes	Yes
N	2899	175219	2899	175219	2899	175219	2899	175219
Log L	-1641.58	-84965.5	-1592.22	-110406	-1137.93	-93944.1	-1394.33	-98851.7

Notes : Dummies control for industry and size class.
*** Statistical significance at 1% level
** Statistical significance at 5% level
Statistical significance at 10% level

Table 8 Within Country Probits for Productivity and Employment Growth (Standard errors in parentheses)
Equation (1)

Variable	LP up Japan	US	TE up Japan	US
No R&D	0.188***	-0.039	-0.125**	-0.35***
	(0.069)	(0.032)	(0.062)	(0.032)
Low R&D	-0.023	-0.092**	0.092	-0.00001
	(0.064)	(0.041)	(0.058)	(0.04)
High R&D	-	-	-	-
Dummies	Yes	Yes	Yes	Yes
N	2899	175219	2899	175219
Log L	-1552.35	-120889	-1967.59	-119877

Notes: Dummies control for industry and size class.
*** Statistical significance at 1% level
** Statistical significance at 5% level
Statistical significance at 10% level

Table 9 Within Country Probits. R&D Performing Firms Only. (Standard errors in parentheses)

Equation (1)

	Group 1		Group 2		Group 3		Group 4	
Variable	Japan	US	Japan	US	Japan	US	Japan	US
Low R&D	-0.129**	-0.036	0.122*	-0.053	0.013	0.053	0.025	0.067
	0.063	0.043	0.065	0.044	0.074	0.05	0.066	0.045
High R&D	-	-	-	-	-	-	-	
Dummies	Yes	Yes	Yes	Yes	Yes	Yes	Yes	Yes
N	1989	3805	1989	3805	1989	3805	1989	3805
Log L	-1131.08	-2294.34	-1042.78	-2211.37	-761.37	-1630.34	-986.79	-2074.91

Notes: Dummies control for industry and size class.

*** Statistical significance at 1% level

** Statistical significance at 5% level

* Statistical significance at 10% level

Table 10 Within Country Probits for Productivity and Employment Growth. R&D Performing Plants Only. (Standard errors in parentheses)

Equation (1)

	LP up		TE up	
Variable	Japan	US	Japan	US
Low R&D	-0.028	-0.085**	-0.103*	0.018
	0.064	0.042	0.058	0.042
High R&D	-	-	-	-
Dummies	Yes	Yes	Yes	Yes
N	1989	3805	1989	3805
Log L	-1051.66	-2512.99	-1339.85	-2526.53

Notes: Dummies control for industry and size class.

*** Statistical significance at 1% level

** Statistical significance at 5% level

* Statistical significance at 10% level

Table 11 Multi-Country Regression Results

(t-statistics in parentheses)

(a) Industry*Country*R&D data

		Japan (v.s. US)		R&D or high R&D	
Successful Upsizers	(all firms)	0.54 *** (	4.60)	0.39 *** (	3.69)
Successful Upsizers	(R&D firms)	0.28 ** (	2.06)	0.14 (	1.13)
Successful Downsizers	(all firms)	-0.14 (	-1.63)	-0.15 * (	-1.88)
Successful Downsizers	(R&D firms)	-0.10 (	-1.04)	-0.02 (	-0.19)
Unsuccessful Upsizers	(all firms)	0.01 (	0.10)	-0.27 ** (	-2.66)
Unsuccessful Upsizers	(R&D firms)	0.21 (	1.58)	-0.08 (	-0.62)
Unsuccessful Downsizers	(all firms)	0.22 (	1.68)	0.07 (	0.61)
Unsuccessful Downsizers	(R&D firms)	0.33 * (	2.22)	0.02 (	0.10)

(b) Size*Country*R&D data

		Japan (v.s. US)		R&D or high R&D	
Successful Upsizers	(all firms)	0.42 *** (	3.04)	0.38 *** (	3.20)
Successful Upsizers	(R&D firms)	0.24 ** (	2.39)	0.11 (	1.23)
Successful Downsizers	(all firms)	-0.26 *** (	-3.30)	-0.35 *** (	-5.24)
Successful Downsizers	(R&D firms)	-0.24 ** (	-2.53)	-0.03 (	0.41)
Unsuccessful Upsizers	(all firms)	-0.26 * (	-2.10)	-0.32 *** (	-3.22)
Unsuccessful Upsizers	(R&D firms)	-0.10 (	-1.03)	-0.05 (	-0.66)
Unsuccessful Downsizers	(all firms)	0.05 (	0.77)	0.26 *** (	4.99)
Unsuccessful Downsizers	(R&D firms)	0.07 (	0.72)	-0.04 (	-0.55)

Notes : Panel (a) gives estimates for equation (2) and panel (b) gives estimates for equation (3).

*** Statistical significance at 1% level
**   Statistical significance at 5% level
*   Statistical significance at 10% level

Figure 1: Manufacturing Employment and Productivity, Japan and the United States

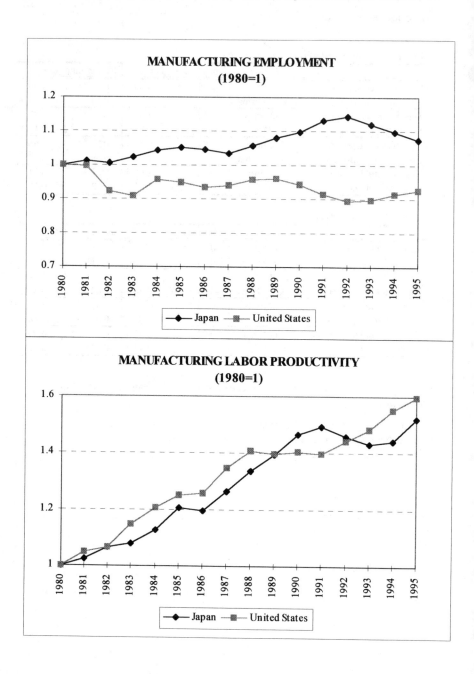

Figure 1 cont.

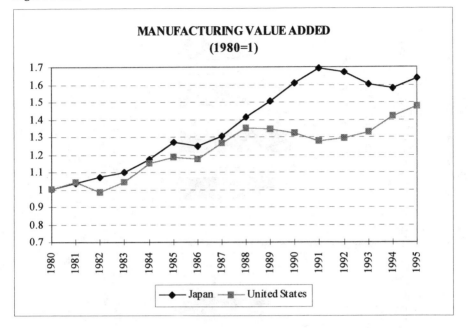

Source: OECD STAN Database

Figure 2 : Relative labor productivity level by size class
(size class = 50-99, all firms = 1)

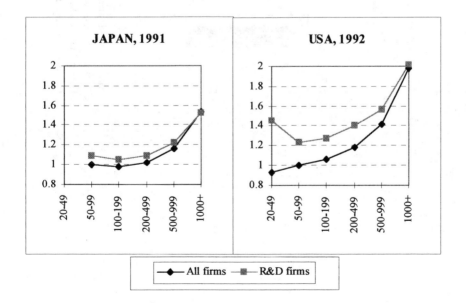

Figure 3 Share of upsizers and downsizers by R&D intensity - (firms with 50+ employees only)

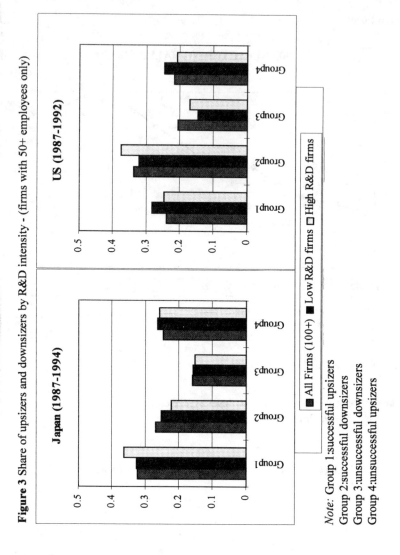

Note: Group 1:successful upsizers
Group 2:successful downsizers
Group 3:unsuccessful downsizers
Group 4:unsuccessful upsizers

REFERENCES

Baily M., Bartelsman E. and Haltiwanger J. (1994), *"Downsizing and Productivity Growth: Myth or Reality?"*, NBER Working Paper No. 4741, May 1994.

Baldwin J. and J. Johnson (1995), *"Business Strategies in Innovative and Non-innovative Firms in Canada"*, Research Paper No. 73, Analytical Studies Branch, Statistics Canada, Ottawa, Canada.

Baldwin, J., T. Dunne and J. Haltiwanger (forthcoming) *"A Comparison of Job Creation and Job Destruction in Canada and the United States"* Review of Economics and Statistics.

Bartelsman, E.J., G. Van Leeuven and H.R. Nieuwenhuijsen (1995), *"Downsizing and Productivity Growth: Myth or Reality?"*, Netherlands Official Statistics, Autumn, pp. 23-28.

Branstetter L., (1996), *"Are Knowledge Spillovers International or International in Scope? Microeconometric Evidence from the U.S. and Japan"*, NBER Working paper #5800.

Brynjolfsson E. and L. Hitt (1995), *"Information Technology as a Factor of Production: The Role of Differences Among Firms"*, Economics of Innovation and New Technology, 1995 vol. 3, pp183-199.

Cohen, W (1996), *"Empirical Studies of Innovative Activity"*, in Handbook of Economics of Innovation and Technological Change, Stoneman ed. Blackwell Publishers, Oxford, UK.

Doms, M., Jensen, J., Kramarz, F., Motohashil, K., and Nocke, V. (1995), *"A Micro Economic Comparison of the Manufacturing Sectors in France, Japan and the United States"*, a paper presented for the NBER Summer Institute, Productivity Workshop, July 1995, Cambridge, USA.

Dunne, T., Haltiwanger, J. and K. Troske, (1997), *"Wage and Productivity Dispersion in U.S. Manufacturing: The Role of Computer Investment"*, mimeo Center for Economic Studies, Washington, DC.

Economic Plannig Agency (1994), *"The White Paper of the Japanese Economy"*, 1994, the Japanese Government.

Entorf, H and F. Kramarz (1995), *"New Technologies, Wages and Worker Selection"*, a paper presented at the conference on *"The Effects of Technology and Innovation on Firm Performance and Employment"*, Washington, May 1995.

Greene, W. H. (1990), *Econometric Analysis*, Second Edition, Prentice Hall Inc.

Griliches, Z. (1992), *"The Search for R&D Spillovers"*, Scandinavian Journal of Economics, vol. 94, supplement, pp. 29-47.

Hamada K. and Kurosawa Y. (1986), *"Trends in Unemployment, Wages and Productivity: The Case of Japan"*, Economica, Supplement, 1986, 53(210), pp. S275-296.

Ichniowski C., Shaw K. and Prennushi G. (1997), *"The Effects of Human Resource Management Practices on Productivity: A Study on Steel Finishing Lines"*, American Economic Review, vol. 87, no. 3, pp. 291-313

Klette, T. and Johanssen, F. (1996), *"The Accumulation of R&D Capital and the Dynamic Performance of Manufacturing Firms"*, a paper presented for the International Conference : The Economics and Econometrics of Innovation", June 1996, Strasbourg

Kruininger H. (1996), *"Consequences of Capital Market Imperfections for the Adjustment of the Stocks of Physical Capital and R&D"*, a paper presented for the International Conference: The Economics and econometrics of Innovetion, June 1996, Strasbourg.

Mairesse J. and B. Hall (1996), *"Estimating the Productivity of Research and Development in French and United States Manufacturing Firms: An Exploration of Simultaneity Issues with GMM Methods"*, mimeo

McGuckin R. and Pascoe G. (1988), *"The Longitudinal Research Database: Status and Research Possibilities"*, Survey of Current Business, vol. 68, November, pp. 30-37

McGuckin R. and Nguyen S. (1995), *"On the Productivity and Plant Ownership Change: New Evidence from the LRD"*, Rand Journal of Economics, vol. 26, No. 2, pp. 257-276

McGuckin R., Streitwieser M. and Doms M. (1996), *"The Effect of Technology Use on Productivity Growth"*, CES Discussion Papers, CES 96-2, Center for Economic Studies, US Bureau of Census, Washington, DC.

Motohashi K. (1997), *"Japanese Experience of Longitudinal Dataset Analysis and International Perspectives"*, in The Evolution of Firms and Industries, S. Laaksonen ed., Statistics Finland Research Report, no. 223, Helsinki, Finland

National Sciences Foundation, (1996), *Research and Development in Industry*: 1993, NSF 96-904.

OECD (1998), *"Technology, Productivity and Employment: Insights from Firm Level Datasets in France, Japan and the United States"*, forthcoming STI Working Paper

OECD (1997), *"Use of Firm-Level Datasets for Policy Analysis"*, report to Japan Economic Foundation, April, mimeo

OECD (1996), *Technology, Productivity and Job Creation*, vol. 2: Analytical Report, OECD, Paris

QUALITY INDICATORS FOR STATISTICAL SURVEYS

Luigi Badaloni[1], Giuseppina Galante[2] and Francesca Gallo Baldessarri[3]

[1]*Andersen Consulting S.p.A.., Roma*
[2]*ISTAT, Roma*
[3]*Dip. Statistica, Probabilità e Statistiche Applicate, Univ. "La Sapienza" Roma*

1 Introduction

To know a phenomena means to know the laws which control it. Nevertheless, the first step in the study of the controlling laws is to look for evenness and unevenness of the phenomena itself having in mind a model.

All this is possible after the crucial stage of the "collection of the observations", that is the microdata. As a matter of fact this stage by itself can decide of the success or failure of the entire project.

Generally, the collection of the observations is realized through a number of complex operations that are called a "production process" or "collection process".

The study can be either a total one, that is concerning the population as a whole, or a partial one, that is a concerning a population sample which is selected following a sample design; in any case the survey will be affected by all the accidental and systematic errors that the different steps of the collection process may bring in.

The aim of this paper is to point out a way to monitor each step of the collection process to achieve the most reliable information and also to illustrate a different way to estimate the missing answers.

2 The collection process

The following diagram represents graphically the different steps of the collection process (Fig.1).

The monitoring process starts from the questionnaire realization and ends with the formalization of results.

At each step of the collection process there are a number of human interventions which rely, for the most, on common sense and on experience.

Nevertheless such interventions allow for unreliability of the statistical information quality the survey will be able to produce.

At this point it is necessary to define what *information quality* means. In this contest we wish microdata to:

1. contain the required information;
2. be collected in the time interval expected;
3. be representative of the population or of the defined sample.

In this paper indicators are defined which are suitable to test *efficacy and efficiency* of the survey. Here *efficacy* is intended as the competency of the survey to achieve the intended target" and *efficiency* is intended as the competency of the collection process to carry out it with the minimum waste of resource".

3 Efficacy indicators

The competency of a survey to grasp the intended target may be progressively evaluated using two indicators defined in two specific steps of the process:

- a) a representativeness indicator;
- b) a reliability indicator.

The first is designed to represent the efficacy level of the information in the first step of the collection process: "Collection and first check"; the second is intended to represent a measure of the efficacy of the step "Second check and formalization".

3.1 The representativeness indicator

The purpose of such and indicator is to control that the number of collected questionnaires is the one necessary for the sample. It is defined as the ratio between the number of questionnaires collected after the i-th letter of reminder and the total number of questionnaires sent.

If,

D_i = number of questionnaires collected after the i-th letter of reminder;

N = number of questionnaires sent;

this indicator may be written:

$$I_{C_i} = \frac{D_i}{N} \qquad (i = 1,2,3,\ldots,r) \tag{1}$$

Generally in each survey a maximum number r of reminders is provided and if the letters of reminder are sent to those who have not replied the indicator takes the form

$$I_C = \frac{D_r}{N} = \frac{D}{N} \qquad [2]$$

with $D_r = D$.

To ensure representativeness this indicator should be close to 1.

3.2 Reliability indicator

Even if I_C is close to 1 (that is the number of replies is close to the number of questionnaires sent), it is not possible to state that the survey has been successful; it is necessary to check that each questionnaire has been drawn up correctly and carefully. It is necessary to check that the final information is exhaustive.

First of all it is worthwhile to point out that in the model there are different types of questions:
– *fundamental questions*: the answers are essential for the targets of the survey;
– *alternative questions*: answers that can stand in place of the fundamental ones (because they may be considered a good approximation of the first ones).
First of all, let us consider that on answer it is always truthful and let:
F = the number of fundamental questions;
F = the number of alternative ones;

$$k_{ij} = \begin{cases} 1 & \text{if on the i-th questionary there is an answer to the j-th question;} \\ 0 & \text{if on the i-th questionary there is no answer to the j.th question.} \end{cases}$$

We have for the i-th questionnaire that the answers to fundamental or alternative questions are in total:

$$\sum_{j=1}^{F} \left[k_{ij} + (1 - k_{ij}) k_{i,j+F} \right]. \qquad [3]$$

If we consider the all collected questionnaires the reliability indicator is defined as

$$I_A = \frac{\sum_{i=1}^{D}\sum_{j=1}^{F}\left[k_{ij} + (1-k_{ij})k_{i,j+F}\right]}{FD} \qquad [4]$$

which is the ratio between the total number of answers to the fundamental or alternative questions and the total number of answers expected to these questions and it has to be near to 1.

The $(1-k_{ij})k_{i,j+F}$ are the answers to the alternative questions.

In defining I_A we consider that for each fundamental question there is an alternative one; if that is not true it is necessary to consider a partition of $\sum_{j=1}^{F}$ in two sums: the first one will concern the fundamental question with alternative answers, $\sum_{j=1}^{F'}\left[k_{ij} + (1-k_{ij})k_{i,j+F}\right]$, the second one will concern the questions for which an alternative answer is not foreseen, $\sum_{j=F'+1}^{F}k_{ij}$.

Therefore we have

$$I_A = \frac{\sum_{i=1}^{D}\left[\sum_{j=1}^{F'}\left[k_{ij} + (1-k_{ij})k_{i,j+F'}\right] + \sum_{j=F'+1}^{F}k_{ij}\right]}{FD} \qquad [5]$$

4 Optimization of the survey

The previous indicators are instruments useful to check for the reliability of the survey and they may be useful during the preparation of the survey itself because they point out critical points:

- representativeness indicator points out: *Dysfunctions on operative organization: incorrect survey unit*; incorrect location of survey unit; questionnaire not drawn up in the best way.
- reliability indicator points out: *Dysfunctions on the questionnaire.*

While the dysfunctions on operative organization are generally solvable, the structural dysfunctions of the questionnaire are essentially due to the peculiarity of the questions.

To check for peculiarities a low-satisfaction indicator:

$$I_j = 1 - \frac{\sum_{i=1}^{D} k_{ij}}{D} \qquad [6]$$

has been proposed by G. Galante, P. Anitori in the paper: A statistical indicator for monitoring microdata quality.

The indicator I_j checks the "non answers" for each question and allows to analyse the peculiarities of "non answering persons" so to optimize:
- the bearing of the question to the target of the survey;
- the easiness of the answering;
- the clarity of the question;
- the confidentially.

To find out and to correct such peculiarities, in progress of work, makes the difference between success and failure of the survey.

5 Efficiency indicator

The second property required for the microdata quality is connected strictly to the efficiency of the survey; expected times of accomplishment are closely connected to the resources allocated and, then, to the expected costs.

Generally speaking the planned time T_p , and the planned cost, C_p , are fixed beforehand.

Let,

T_C = final time for the survey

C_C = final cost of the survey;

the two efficiency indicators we propose are:

$$I_{ET} = \frac{T_P}{T_C} \qquad [7]$$

$$I_{EC} = \frac{C_P}{C_C} \qquad [8]$$

which should be ≥ 1 for a good performance of the survey.

The importance of these two indicators is in relation to the survey taken into consideration: if the timeliness of the information is essential one must check for realization time; if not one may try a fair balance between the two indicators.

It is worthwhile to point out that these two indicators are definable for each step of the process and that it is wise to proceed to their computing in order to know how much a setback will cost in terms of time and resources and eventually to bound this cost by means of a different use of resources.

6 Conclusions

To define synthetic indicators of efficacy and efficiency of a survey means to make comparable different surveys by means of indicators.

For the efficacy we state

$$I_{efficacy} = I_C \ I_A \qquad \qquad [9]$$

and if we consider on a Cartesian plane their maximum value, that is one, we have

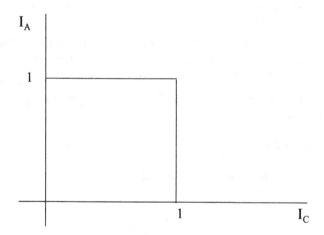

To compare different surveys we may, then, compare different areas: to equal areas correspond surveys of equal performance on efficacy. In any case to fix the admittable limits of I_C and I_A is a charge of the experts of the survey.

For a synthetic indicator of efficiency let us consider

$$\Delta T = 1 - \frac{T_C}{T_P} \tag{10}$$

$$\Delta C = 1 - \frac{C_C}{C_P} \tag{11}$$

and we define

$$I_{efficiency} = \Delta T + \Delta C \tag{12}$$

Let us consider a plane $(\Delta T, \Delta C)$; the ideal maximum of the two variable separately are one and one respectively:

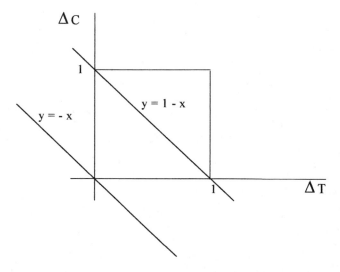

To consider different surveys which give the efficiency equal one, we have to take the straight lines of equation $y=1-x$; all the straight lines parallel to this one give equal values of efficiency. Also negative values of ΔT or ΔC may be considered if they are admittable for the experts of the survey which, in any case, are the one to fix the admittable range of ΔT and ΔC.

DYNAMIC LABOUR DEMAND MODEL FOR HETEROGENEOUS PANELS

J.-Y. Bienvenue

World Systems

1 Introduction

In the "European Panels Project"[1] Dr Andrew Hildreth[2] has assisted Eurostat. In particular, he has presented the panel estimation techniques proposed by Arellano and Bond (1991) and the associated Gauss program: the "Dynamic Panel Data" program. These two authors have adapted to panel data a method proposed by Hansen (1982). They use a Generalised Method of Moments (GMM) in order to estimate consistently the parameters of a dynamic linear equation. This method relies on a number of orthogonality conditions between some instrumental variables and the error term. It generalises the estimation methods by Instrumental Variables (IV) proposed by Balestra and Nerlove (1966) and Anderson and Hsiao (1981, 1982). This method has been tested by estimating dynamic models using panel data for eleven countries. Some of these results focusing on the estimate of employment equations have been taken into account in this paper to illustrate the problem of estimating a dynamic linear model on heterogeneous panels. This paper is organised in three sections.

The general framework usually used to specify an employment function by a linear equation is described in a first section. The theoretical foundations of dynamic labour demand models are briefly presented. We are focused on a particular dynamic structure by the intermediate of hiring and firing costs and their implications for the time path of employment. To obtain a simple linear employment relation, we retain a dynamic labour demand model based upon the quadratic adjustment costs and rational expectations assumptions. The first assumption is useful to write down the representative firm's employment behaviour as a linear function of predetermined variables and expectations. The rational expectations are useful to specify unobserved expectations in terms of observable variables. Finally, we take into account the two justifications suggested by Nickell (1984,1986) to have an explicit dynamic theory underlying the empirical model. Firstly, a dynamic equation is deduced from a log-linear

---

approximation of the Euler equations. In this context, the basic estimating equation may be defined by an unrestricted vector auto-regressions (VAR's) where short-run effects and long-run effects are represented by the lagged endogenous variable and by current and lagged exogenous variables, respectively. Secondly, at least two lags on the dependent variables are specified to capture possible large differences in adjustment costs between different groups of workers.

In the traditional panel procedures using the fixed effects and random effects models, the heterogeneity may be considered in the intercept term. For example, panel data regressions with cross-country data all rely on some pooled estimates. The pooling is often done either under the assumption of complete homogeneity of all the parameters or under the assumption that some heterogeneity is allowed in the intercept term. To discuss the problem of heterogeneity in a second section, we will use the simplified model considered by Pesaran and Smith (1995). Using this particular case, these authors show that when the number of time-periods is small or large (even if the number of individuals is large), the un-modelled slope heterogeneity yields in general inconsistent estimated coefficients. The application of alternative methods such as Instrumental Variables (IV) or Generalised Method of Moments (GMM) to a pooled model is applicable under some conditions. In order to consistently estimate the dynamic employment equation, we will use predetermined variables as valid instruments. This procedure proposed by Arellano and Bond (1991) , Arellano and Bover (1995) is also described in this section.

Using Eurostat Panel of Enterprises, econometric results are reported in section 3. Two approaches are considered. First, under the homogenous parameter assumption, we estimate the labour demand model independently on each country panel data. Secondly, under the heterogeneous parameter assumption, the model is estimated across six countries (or six panel data). The difference between these two procedures will enable us to illustrate the presence of a bias when the heterogeneity of the parameters is ignored in the pooled regressions.

2 Dynamic models of labour demand

We consider a model of labour demand in presence of uncertainty. Our attention mainly focuses on its dynamic aspects using a basic adjustment model. The dynamic nature of the demand takes into account the fact that hiring and firing generate costs for the firm. These costs ensure that the demand for labour depend both on current exogenous factors, initial level of labour factor and on expectations about the future levels of these factors.

In general, observed employment is assumed to be the outcome of an optimisation procedure adopted by the firms. Labour demand function is derived from the solving of a problem where firms are assumed to maximise their present discounted value of expected profits over an infinite horizon. Let us A_t $(A_t > 0)$, a random variable defining all macro-economic shock and assume that firms choose the levels of long-term and short-term employment after the current realisation of this shock is observed. In this context, a labour demand can be derived from

$$\left\{ Max\ E_t \left\{ \sum_{i=0}^{\infty} \left(\frac{1}{1+r} \right)^i \left(p_{t+i} Q_{t+i} - c_{t+i} K_{t+i} - w_{t+i} L_{t+i} - g\left(K_{t+i}, L_{t+i} \right) \right) \right\} \right.$$
$$\text{subject to } Q_{t+i} = f(A_{t+i}, K_{t+i}, L_{t+i})$$

where $E_t \left\{ X_{t+i} \right\}$ denotes the expectation formed at time t of X at $t+i$, r is the discount rate, p_t is the product price, Q_t is the production, c_t is the user's capital cost, K_t is the capital stock, w_t is the wage, L_t is the labour input, and where the function g represents others costs which are limited here to the existence of hiring or firing costs associated with employment changes.

To keep the presentation as straightforward as possible, we will ignore the hours dimension of labour input and consider and consider that labour input and employment are the same thing. However, the distinction between the labour defined in hours and the employment (measured in jobs or number of employees) is important for several reasons. In particular, it permits the link between an approach around a steady state (see 1.4.1) and the economic approach in terms of equilibrium (see 1.4.2). As most of surveys[3], we will not taking into account the rules which determinate the wages and assume that costs which are associated to changes in employment are not dependant of labour costs.

Different specifications of dynamic models can be obtained. They mainly depend on three sets of assumptions respectively made about the structure of the adjustment costs facing employers (sub-section 1.1), about the way decision-makers form their expectations (sub-section 1.2), and about the determinants of the labour demand (sub-section 1.3). The first set is crucial because it describes the temporal pattern of labour demand in response to exogenous shocks. The second set defines the specification of the adjustment process. With this two steps, the change in employment may be followed by the intermediate of a distance measuring the deviation between the level of the observed employment and the value corresponding to the steady state (sub-section 1.4.1). The third set is used to follow the employment strategy of firms in the neighbourhood of

---

[3] For example, see Bresson, Kramarz and Sevestre (1995). The survey of Nickell (1986) seems to be an exception.

equilibrium and by the intermediate of partial adjustment mechanism (sub-section 1.4.2). Most of empirical studies prefer to study this deviation in referencing to equilibrium state. In this case, a correct presentation implies to make the distinction between the labour input and the level of employment. As the aim of this paper is not to present a survey on the theory of wage, we prefer to keep an relatively incorrect approach.

2.1 The symmetric quadratic adjustment costs hypothesis

Labour is not considered as a perfectly flexible production factor. We assume the presence of adjustment costs, in particular hiring and firing costs[4]. Following Eisner and Strotz (1963), these gross (or net) adjustment costs[5] are approximated analytically by a symmetric quadratic function defined as:

$$g(V_t) = \frac{b}{2}(V_t)^2 \ , \ b \geq 0 \qquad\qquad [1.1]$$

where $V_t < 0$ defines a volume of employment destroyed (or firing) and $V_t > 0$ a volume of created employment (or hiring) in period t. Even though this assumption can be unrealistic[6], we will use it to derive an explicit partial adjustment model of labour demand, then a closed form which can be estimated by econometric methods. Others functions can be used to describe different possible structures of hiring and firing costs, but quadratic function is the only form which leads to a simple linear relation, as it is described in sub-section I.4.1.

---

[4] See Oi (1962).

[5] No empirical study tries to distinguish between gross and net adjustment costs empirically, and no theorical study examines their different implications. This tradition is respected in this study.

[6] Most of empirical studies (see Hamermesh (1993) for a summary of English and American major studies) noticed three important features:

i)   - Hiring and firing costs are not equal;

ii)   - The discrepancy between costs associated with the hiring of skilled workers and those induced by hiring unskilled workers is large;

iii) - Firing costs do not depend as much on the skill level of workers but have mainly institutional origins.

2.2 Uncertainty and rational expectations

When there is uncertainty, the standard way of dealing with this problem is to specify the complete underlying structure of the model as quadratic. With this quadratic assumption and using standard certainty equivalence result, future random variables may be replaced by their expectations. The most often used representation is based on the rational expectations assumption which states that the expectation about a variable X (noted $E_t\{X_{t+i}\}$ with $i \geq 0$) is just the expectation formed at time t of its generating process at time $t+i$, conditional on the available information at the time when the expectation is formed. We will assume that all firms know the generating process of the expected variable and that they elaborate their expectations accordingly. This hypothesis is useful to build a model written in terms of observable variables. For example, these future expectations may be modelled in specifying models for each of the exogenous variables determining X. Imposing a quadratic structure on all the model (in particular, on the revenue function and on the cost function), an obvious specification technique is to use vector auto-regressions[7]. In terms of econometric methodology, the model can be estimated in the short term by instrumental variables (IV) or generalised method of moments (GMM) where instruments belong to the information set of the firm at time t.

2.3 The determinants of the long-run labour demand

The specification of dynamic labour demand models also depends on the assumption made about the predetermination of production, of capital stock and about function of production. Three types of models[8] are often presented in the literature.

In a first class of models, the firms are output-constrained and they determine the optimal path of their employment by minimising their cost, subject to their technological constraint (defined by a production function).

$$\left\{ Min\ E_t \left\{ \sum_{i=0}^{\infty} \left(\frac{1}{1+r}\right)^i \left[c_{t+i}K_{t+i} + w_{t+i}L_{t+i} + g\left(L_{t+i}, K_{t+i}\right) \right] \right\} \atop under\ Q_{t+i} = f\left((A_{t+i}, K_{t+i}, L_{t+i}\right) \right. \tag{1.2}$$

---

[7] Current decisions are based on unobserved expectations and , observed values of period (t+1) are substituted for their expectations of one period ahead.

[8] See Nickell (1986), Bresson, Kramarz and Sevestre (1995).

The first order conditions give the so-called Euler equations given by

$$
\left\{
\begin{array}{l}
E_t\left\{ w_{t+i} + \lambda_{t+i} \dfrac{\partial f}{\partial L_{t+i}} + \dfrac{\partial g}{\partial L_{t+i}} - \dfrac{1}{1+r} \dfrac{\partial g}{\partial L_{t+i+1}} \right\} = 0 \, , \forall i \\[4mm]
E_t\left\{ c_{t+i} + \lambda_{t+i} \dfrac{\partial f}{\partial K_{t+i}} + \dfrac{\partial g}{\partial K_{t+i}} - \dfrac{1}{1+r} \dfrac{\partial g}{\partial K_{t+i+1}} \right\} = 0 \, , \forall i
\end{array}
\right.
\qquad [1.3]
$$

and to which the production function must be added. In such a model , employment mainly depends on expected output and relative capital/labour costs[9] . The demand of labour determines the employment strategy of a representative firm in the region of long run equilibrium. Using a multivariate partial adjustment mechanism, the change in employment is described as a function both of the distance of employment from its equilibrium and of the distance of capital stock from its equilibrium level.   This first approach is often followed in American and French studies[10].

A second category of models retained in this study is to assume that firms are not output constrained but that their capital stock is predetermined. The decision program can then be written as

$$
\text{Max } E_t\left\{ \sum_{i=0}^{\infty} \left(\frac{1}{1+r} \right)^i \left(p_{t+i} Q_{t+i} - w_{t+i} L_{t+i} - g(L_{t+i}) \right) \right\}
\qquad [1.4]
$$

and the Euler equations are

$$
E_t\left\{ -w_{t+i} + p_{t+i} \frac{\partial Q}{\partial L_{t+i}} - \frac{\partial g}{\partial L_{t+i}} + \frac{1}{1+r} \frac{\partial g}{\partial L_{t+i+1}} \right\} = 0 \, , \forall i
\qquad [1.5]
$$

The partial labour demand appears to be related to the marginal productivity of labour (which depends on the installed capital stock) and to the real wage. The investment may be introduced in assuming that its determination is independent of all others inputs.

A third type of models is to assume that firms operate on markets where monopolistic competition prevails. The interest of this assumption, the industry

---

[9] Employment also depends on relative adjusment/labour costs.
[10]See Hamermesh (1989, 1993), Dormont and Sevestre (1986).

output can be included as a supplementary argument for explained variations in employment. The expected profit maximisation of the *price-maker* firm can be defined by

$$Max\ E_t\left\{\sum_{i=0}^{\infty}\left(\frac{1}{1+r}\right)^i\left(\left(\frac{Q_{t+i}}{Q_{t+i}^S}\right)^{-\eta^{-1}}p_{s,t+i}-w_{t+i}L_{t+i}-c_{t+i}K_{t+i}-g(\Delta L_{t+i},\Delta K_{t+i})\right)\right\} \quad [1.6]$$

and the Euler equation for employment is given by

$$E_t\left\{\frac{\eta-1}{\eta}\frac{\partial Y_{t+i}}{\partial L_{t+i}}\left(\frac{Q_{t+i}}{Q_{t+i}^S}\right)^{-\eta^{-1}}p_{s,t+i}-w_{t+i}-\frac{\partial g}{\partial L_{t+i}}+\frac{1}{1+r}\frac{\partial g}{\partial L_{t+i+1}}\right\}=0,\forall i \quad [1.7]$$

The assumption that firms operate in imperfectly competitive markets is often used in English studies[11].

2.4 Labour demand model and homogeneous groups of workers

Note that if the revenue function (or the production function f) and the adjustment costs are quadratic and under the rational expectation assumption, an explicit model for labour and capital can be directly derived from these Euler equations[12] where the actual level of employment (or its variations) is expressed as a function of its determinants in long-run on the one hand, and depends on lagged values of employment and on the same determinants in short-run on the other hand.

2.4.1 Dynamic of employment around steady state

Our reference theoretical model is defined by the equations $[1.4]$ and $[1.1]$. We assume that voluntary quits induce no direct costs and take place at a proportional rate q $(q>0)$ where we add the evolution rule following:

---

[11] See Arellano and Bond (1991), Burgess (1988).

[12] In the other cases, an explicit model can be defined in making some linear approximations, step by step (see Nickell, 1986).

$$L_t = (1-q)L_{t-1} + V_t , \quad \forall t \geq 1 \text{ and for } L_0 \text{ given.} \qquad [1.8]$$

At time t, the expected profit is defined by

$$\Pi_t = E_t \left\{ \sum_{i=0}^{\infty} \left(\frac{1}{1+r} \right)^i \left[R(A_{t+i}, L_{t+i}) - w_t L_{t+i} - \frac{b}{2} V_{t+i}^2 \right] \right\}$$

Under the rational expectations and if we assume that the production function is defined by a linear quadratic function, an explicit model for labour demand can be directly derived from Euler equations. Let

$$R(A_t, L_t) = p_t f(A_t, L_t) = A_t L_t - \frac{B}{2} L_t^2 , \quad A_t > w_t \text{ and } B > 0. \qquad [1.9]$$

Euler equations are given by:

$$A_t - BL_t - w_t - b(L_t - L_{t-1}) + \frac{b(1-q)}{1+r} E_t \{ L_{t+1} - L_t \} = 0 , \quad \forall t \geq 1 \qquad [1.10]$$

which can be rewritten as:

$$L_t = a_t + a_1 L_{t-1} + a_0 E_t \{ L_{t+1} \} \qquad [1.11]$$

with $\qquad a_0 = \dfrac{b(1-q)}{(B+b)(1+r) + b(1-q)}, \qquad a_1 = \dfrac{1+r}{1-q} a_0 \qquad$ and

$a_t = \dfrac{(A_t - w_t)}{b} a_1$. Equation [1.11] can be solved by the "undetermined coefficients" method[13]. It consist in letting a particular form for the solution of [1.11], then, to identify the unknown parameters verifying [1.11]. In our case, as

---

[13] See Sargent(1986, chap.14).

L_t is function of L_{t-1} and $E\{a_{t+i}\}$, we can search a solution which is a linear expression of these three quantities. Let

$$L_t = \lambda L_{t-1} + \sum_{i=0}^{\infty} \mu_i E_t \{a_{t+i}\} \qquad [1.12]$$

where λ and μ_i $(i \geq 0)$, are unknown parameters. Given $[1.12]$, we can write

$$E_t\{L_{t+1}\} = \lambda L_t + \sum_{i=0}^{\infty} \mu_i E_t \{a_{t+i+1}\} \qquad [1.13]$$

Substituting $[1.13]$ in $[1.11]$ gives a linear form for the solution of $[1.11]$:

$$L_t = \frac{1}{1 - \lambda a_0} \left(a_t + a_1 L_{t-1} + a_0 \sum_{i=0}^{\infty} \mu_i E_t \{a_{t+i+1}\} \right) \qquad [1.14]$$

With the identification of coefficients of L_{t-1} and a_{i+1}, $(i \geq 0)$, in $[1.12]$ and $[1.14]$, we can obtain the value of coefficients λ and μ_i $(i \geq 0)$. We have

$$\lambda = \frac{a_1}{1 - \lambda a_0}, \quad \mu_0 = \frac{1}{1 - \lambda a_0} \quad \text{and} \quad \mu_i = (a_0 \mu_0)^i \mu_0, \forall i \geq 1. \text{ As } \lambda \text{ is a root}$$

of polynomial $a_0 \lambda^2 - \lambda + a_1$ which has two positive real roots:

$$\lambda_1 = \frac{1 - \sqrt{1 - 4a_0 a_1}}{2a_0} \quad \text{and} \quad \lambda_2 = \frac{1 + \sqrt{1 - 4a_0 a_1}}{2a_0}.$$

In order to have a stationary solution, we keep the value of λ which is less than one $(\lambda = \lambda_1)$. Finally, when we introduce in $[1.12]$ the value of the coefficients calculated above, we have:

$$L_t = \lambda L_{t-1} + \frac{1}{1 - \lambda a_0} \sum_{i=0}^{\infty} \left(\frac{a_0}{1 - \lambda a_0} \right)^i E_t \{a_{t+i}\} \, , \quad \lambda = \frac{1 - \sqrt{1 - 4a_0 a_1}}{2a_0} \qquad [1.15]$$

It is easy to verify that the value of λ increases with the parameter b which is a measure of the adjustment cost. This implies that variations of labour demand are less important when the adjustment costs are important.

Finally, in a uncertainty context and under rational expectations hypothesis, the level of present employment L_t is given by L_{t-1} and the expectations on economic shocks a_{t+i} $(i \geq 1)$. With some supplementary assumptions, $E_t\{a_{t+i}\}$ can be substituted by predicted values given by the estimated process. For example, if the process generating a_t is AR(1)

$$a_t = \alpha a_{t-1} + \varepsilon_t \, , \, 0 < \alpha < 1$$

where ε_t is a white noise, we have $E_t\{a_{t+i}\} = \alpha^i a_t$ and the expression of equation $[1.15]$ is

$$L_t = \lambda L_{t-1} + \frac{\mu_0}{1-\gamma\alpha}a_t = \lambda L_{t-1} + \frac{1}{1-a_0(\lambda+\alpha)}a_t \qquad [1.16]$$

As all variables in $[1.16]$ can be observed at time t, this equation can be estimated. In general, when the random variable a_t follows a more complex process, it is always possible to obtain an equation which builds a link between the present employment and the observable values of past and present shocks.

2.4.2 Dynamic of employment around short/long-run equilibrium

Another approach suggested by Nickell (1984) is to consider a more general non-static model in terms of the equilibrium employment level L_t^*. He assumes that actual employment L_t never tracks L_t^* closely, and that L_t^* follows a cyclical path. Under the assumption of strictly convex adjustment costs, the fluctuations in L_t follow those in L_t^* but with a smaller amplitude. In this context, the actual employment level is described by a partial adjustment relationship of behaviour which implies that current employment will be some convex combination of a target level and employment last period. In the neighbourhood of short period equilibrium, the employment path is indeed defined approximately by the partial adjustment equation

$$L_t - L_{t-1} = \lambda\left(L_t^* - L_t\right)$$ [1.17]

As in sub-section [1.4.1], we consider a discrete time version where we impose quadratic structures on the adjustment costs and on the revenue function respectively given by [1.7] et [1.9]. Assuming $q = 0$, the first-order conditions are given by

$$A_t - BL_t - w_t - b\left(L_t - L_{t-1}\right) + \frac{b}{1+r}E_t\left\{L_{t+1} - L_t\right\} = 0, \ \forall t \geq 1.$$ [1.18]

From [1.18], the short period equilibrium levels of employment L_t^* are defined by the quantities which would adopt in the absence of adjustment costs (b=0) and are determined by the condition

$$A_t - BL_t = w_t$$ [1.19]

A relationship between L and L^* may be obtained by a linear approximation of the first terms in [1.18].Let:

$$A_t - BL_t = A_t - BL_t^* - B\left(L_t - L_t^*\right)$$ [1.20]

The introduction of [1.20] in [1.18] gives the linear difference equation with constant coefficients:

$$\frac{b}{1+r}E_t\left\{L_{t+1}\right\} - \left[\left(1 + \frac{1}{1+r}\right)b + B\right]L_t + bL_{t-1} = -BL_t^*, \ \forall t \geq 1.$$ [1.21]

The solution to the fundamental [1.21] may be derived using the lag operator ℓ. In this case, [1.21] may be written

$$\alpha b \ell^{-1} - \left(\left[(1+\alpha)b - \theta\right] + b\ell\right)L_t = \theta L_t^*, \ \forall t \geq 1.$$ [1.22]

with $\theta = -B$, $\alpha = (1+r)^{-1}$, $\alpha > 0$, $\theta < 0$ and $b > 0$.

Noting μ the stable root given by

$$\mu = \frac{1}{2}\left(1+\alpha^{-1}\right) + \frac{|\theta|}{2\alpha b} - \left(\left[\frac{1}{2}\left(1+\alpha^{-1}\right) + \frac{|\theta|}{2\alpha b}\right]^2 - \alpha^{-1}\right)^{\frac{1}{2}} \qquad [1.23]$$

Equation $[1.24]$ can be written

$$-\frac{b}{\mu}\left(1-\alpha\mu\ell^{-1}\right)\left(1-\mu\ell\right)L_t = \theta L_t$$

or

$$L_t = \mu L_{t-1} - \frac{\mu}{b}\frac{\theta L_t^*}{\left(1-\alpha\mu\ell^{-1}\right)} = \mu L_{t-1} + \left(1-\mu\right)\left(1-\alpha\mu\right)\frac{\theta L_t^*}{\left(1-\alpha\mu\ell^{-1}\right)} \qquad [1.24]$$

$[1.24]$ may be expanded to obtain the basic equation which describes the optimal path for labour:

$$L_t = \mu L_{t-1} + \left(1-\mu\right)\left(1-\alpha\mu\right)\sum_{i=0}^{\infty}\left(\alpha\mu\right)^i L_{t+i}^* \qquad [1.25]$$

If we rewrite $[1.25]$ as

$$L_t - L_{t-1} = \left(1-\mu\right)\left[\left(1-\alpha\mu\right)\sum_{i=0}^{\infty}\left(\alpha\mu\right)^i L_{t+i}^* - L_{t-1}\right] \qquad [1.26],$$

we see that L_t follows a partial adjustment process (where the target is a weighting convex combination of all future expected values of L^*). From $[1.22]$, the speed of adjustment $\left(1-\mu\right)$ is decreasing in the level of adjustment cost b and consequently increases in b add relatively more weight to the future.

Sims (1974) use $[1.25]$ to analyse the relation[14] between output and employment. To obtain more or less any short or indeed long-run elasticity

---

[14] In his paper, Sims is particularly concerned with the empirical phenomenon of short-run increasing returns to labour: elasticity of demand for aggregate labour with respect to output is smaller than unity and less than the long run elasticity.

depending on the time series process generating output, he proposes to take the log linear form. Nickell suggests to follow this approach.

For example, divide [1.26] by L_{t-1}, we obtain

$$\frac{L_t - L_{t-1}}{L_{t-1}} = (1-\mu)(1-\alpha\mu)\sum_{i=0}^{\infty}(\alpha\mu)^i \frac{L^*_{t+i} - L_{t-1}}{L_{t-1}} \qquad [1.27]$$

Then, following Bresson, Kramarz and Sevestre (1995) which consider the case where the relative changes in employment are small from period to period, we can use the first order development of the logarithm function and approximate [1.27] by

$$\log\left(\frac{L_t}{L_{t-1}}\right) = (1-\mu)(1-\alpha\mu)\sum_{i=0}^{\infty}(\alpha\mu)^i \log\left(\frac{L^*_{t+i}}{L_{t-1}}\right)$$

which can be rewritten as

$$\log L_t = \mu \log L_{t-1} + (1-\mu)(1-\alpha\mu)\sum_{i=0}^{\infty}(\alpha\mu)^i \log L^*_{t+i} \qquad [1.28]$$

Then, by some linear approximations, we can therefore determine a situation without adjustment costs, then study the deviation with the case where these costs are signifiant. By example, the determinants of the desired levels of employment L^*_{t+i} may be derived from the solution of the firm program without adjustment costs, and describe in function of the expected production level Q^*_t, on the expected labour cost w^*_t and on economic shocks defined by time dummies D_t. Let:

$$\log L^*_{t+i} = b_1 \log Q^*_{t+i} + b_2 \log w^*_{t+i} + c_{1,t+i}D_{t+i} + a_4 + \varepsilon_{t+i} \qquad [1.29]$$

In assuming that the logarithms of the exogenous variables $\left(Q_{t+i} \text{ and } w_{t+i}\right)$ follow an AR(1) process, equation [1.28] become:

$$\log L_t = \mu \log L_{t-1} +$$

$$+ (1-\mu)(1-\alpha\mu)\sum_{i=0}^{\infty}(\alpha\mu)E_t\{b_1\log Q^*_t + b_2\log w^*_t + c_{1,t+1}D_{t+1} + a_1 + \varepsilon_{t+1}\} \qquad [1.30]$$

At last linear approximation, if we assume that $\varepsilon_t = \rho\varepsilon_{t-1} + u_t$, $\forall t$, the final equation in terms of observable variables is

$$\log L_t = \mu \log L_{t-1} + \beta_0 \log Q_t + \alpha_0 \log w_t + \gamma_t D_t' + \delta + \omega_t \qquad [1.31]$$

with

$$\beta_0 = \frac{(1-\mu)(1-\alpha\mu)}{(1-\alpha\mu b_1)} \; , \; \alpha_0 = \frac{(1-\mu)(1-\alpha\mu)}{(1-\alpha\mu b_2)} \; , \; \omega_t = \frac{(1-\mu)(1-\alpha\mu)}{(1-\alpha\mu\rho)} u_t$$

The partial adjustment model [1.31] can be interpreted as an error correction model. More generally, if the logarithms of exogenous variables follow an AR(p) process, the expression of the final equation is given by

$$\log L_t = \mu \log L_{t-1} + \sum_{l=0}^{p} \beta_l \log Q_{t-l} + \sum_{l=0}^{p} \alpha_l \log w_{t-l} + \gamma_t D_t' + \delta + \omega_t$$

2.5 Labour demand models and heterogeneous workers

The labour demand models described above is based, at least implicitly, on the assumption that the groups of workers are homogeneous. Most of empirical studies are based on aggregated employment data. When there are large differences in adjustment costs between several groups of workers (skilled and unskilled, for example), this heterogeneity can be captured in the specification of the aggregated equation. Under some restrictive assumptions[15], Nickell (1984,1986) has proposed to take into account implicitly the heterogeneous nature of workers by means of a more complex dynamic model of total employment. For that, he considers that differing adjustment costs for k distinct categories of workers lead to different dynamic adjustment for the employment of these groups and this is consistent with the k-th order nature of aggregate employment dynamics. In specifying a linear dynamic labour demand model and

---

[15] These assumptions are mainly that:
i)   - The structure of employment between different categories is constant over time;
ii)   - There are no cross-adjustment costs between different categories of workers;
iii) - The relationship between the expected average wage and those of the different categories of workers is constant over time.

in assuming that the ratio of the desired levels of employment in these categories remains constant over time, he has shown how to exactly aggregate the k models to get a correct representation of the dynamics of total employment.

For the sake of simplicity and under the assumption of quadratic adjustment costs, assume that there are two categories of workers for which the adjustment processes of employment L_1, L_2 to their desired levels L_1^* and L_2^* can be represented as $L_t = \mu\left(L_t^* - L_{t-1}\right)$ with $L_t = \begin{pmatrix} L_{1t} \\ L_{2t} \end{pmatrix}$

$\mu = \begin{pmatrix} \mu_{11} & \mu_{12} \\ \mu_{21} & \mu_{22} \end{pmatrix}$, $L_t^* = \begin{pmatrix} L_{1t}^* \\ L_{2t}^* \end{pmatrix}$ and $L_{t-1} = \begin{pmatrix} L_{1t-1} \\ L_{2t-1} \end{pmatrix}$ which can be

rewritten as $\left(I - \mu B\right)L_t = \mu L_t^*$ where B is the lag operator.

Aggregation over the two categories of workers then leads to $cL_t = c(I - \mu B)^{-1}\mu L_t^*$ with $c = (1,1)$, that is,

$$cL_t = \left(\mu_{11} + \mu_{22}\right)cL_{t-1} - \left(\mu_{11}\mu_{22} - \mu_{12}\mu_{21}\right)cL_{t-2} + \left(\mu_{11} + \mu_{21}\right)L_{1t}^* + \left(\mu_{22} + \mu_{12}\right)L_{2t}^*$$
$$- \left(\mu_{21}^2 - \mu_{11}\left(\mu_{22} + \mu_{21} - \mu_{12}\right)\right)L_{1,t-1}^* - \left(\mu_{12}^2 - \mu_{22}\left(\mu_{11} + \mu_{12} - \mu_{21}\right)\right)L_{2,t-1}^*$$

To aggregate the desired levels of employment L_{1t}^* and L_{2t}^* as well as their lags, Nickell 's approach is based on the assumption that the structure of desired employment is constant over time. Thus, if we let

$\left(\dfrac{L_{1t}^*}{L_{2t}^*}\right) = h$, $\forall t$, we can write $cL_t^* = L_{1t}^* + L_{2t}^* = \beta cL_t^* + \left(1 - \beta\right)cL_t^*$ where

$h = \dfrac{\beta}{1 - \beta}$.

The expression of the aggregated labour demand model is

$$cL_t = \left(\mu_{11} + \mu_{22}\right)cL_{t-1} - \left(\mu_{11}\mu_{22} - \mu_{12}\mu_{21}\right)cL_{t-2} + \left(\mu_{11} + \mu_{21}\right)L_{1t}^* +$$
$$\left(\mu_{22} + \mu_{12}\right)L_{2t}^* - \left(\mu_{21}^2 - \mu_{11}\left(\mu_{22} + \mu_{21} - \mu_{12}\right)\right)L_{1,t-1}^* -$$
$$- \left(\mu_{12}^2 - \mu_{22}\left(\mu_{11} + \mu_{12} - \mu_{21}\right)\right)L_{2,t-1}^*$$

If the total employment is composed of two categories of workers (skilled and unskilled labour) with different partial adjustment processes and if the ratio h is constant over time, the model for total employment can be defined as an autoregressive model of order 2 (AR(2) model) with lags on the exogenous variables. Second-order lags on the dependent variable are described as the consequence of aggregating two first-order processes on aggregated data. More generally, when there are k basic AR(1) models relative to k categories of workers, with different adjustment lags, total employment follow an AR(k) model. If the exogenous variables appear with p lags in the basic models, there are specified with p+k-1 lags in the aggregated model. If we apply this approach on model [1.31] we have

$$\log L_t = \sum_{l=1}^{k} \mu_l^* \log L_{t-l} + \sum_{l=0}^{k+p-1} \beta_l^* \log Q_{t-l} + \sum_{l=0}^{k+p-1} \alpha_l^* \log w_{t-l} + \gamma_t D_t' + \delta + \omega_t \qquad [1.32]$$

Under this standard specification of dynamic labour models, the parameters of interest are the "short-run" coefficients $\sum_{l=1}^{k} \mu_l^*$, $\sum_{l=0}^{k+p-1} \beta_l^*$, $\sum_{l=0}^{k+p-1} \alpha_l^*$ and in particular, the mean adjustment coefficient defined by

$$\mu^{LR^*} = \frac{\displaystyle\sum_{l=1}^{k} \mu_l^*}{1 - \displaystyle\sum_{l=1}^{k} \mu_l^*} \qquad\qquad [1.33]$$

An alternative interpretation of the model is to make appear the long-run effects with respect to real wages and output respectively given by

$$\beta^{LR^*} = \frac{\displaystyle\sum_{l=0}^{k+p-1} \beta_l^*}{1 - \displaystyle\sum_{l=1}^{k} \mu_l^*} \quad\text{and}\quad \alpha^{LR^*} = \frac{\displaystyle\sum_{l=0}^{k+p-1} \alpha_l^*}{1 - \displaystyle\sum_{l=1}^{k} \mu_l^*} \qquad [1.34]$$

Note that similar implications arise with aggregation across enterprises which differ in adjustment costs. However, the interpretation proposed by Nickell is not the only reason. The k-order lags on the dependent variable may be justified as arising from a serially correlated unobservable characteristics. Thus, the estimated coefficients of lagged dependent variable would be the consequence of misspecification[16].

3 Pooled regressions and the problem of parameter heterogeneity

3.1 The problem of parameter heterogeneity when T is large

To discuss the problem of heterogeneity, Pesaran and Smith (1995) consider a model of the form:

$$y_{it} = \delta_i + \mu_i y_{it-1} + \beta_i' x_{it} + v_{it}, \quad -1 < \mu_i < 1, \ i = 1,...,N; \ t = 1,...,T.$$

[2.1]

with the following assumptions:
- the coefficients are constant over time but differ randomly across individuals;
- the distribution of the coefficients is independent of the exogenous regressors and error terms;
- v_{it} is i.i.d $(0, \sigma_i^2)$ and is distributed independently of $(\delta_i, \beta_i, \mu_i)$ and x_{it} ;
- the initial observed value of y for individual i exists and is noted y_{io}.
- the Between- individuals disturbance covariances are zero:

$$E(v_{it} v_{i't'}) = 0, \quad \forall t \text{ and } t' \text{ and } i \neq i';$$

- the parameters μ_i and β_i are random and are characterised respectively by $\mu_i = \mu + \eta_{1i}$ and $\beta_i = \beta + \eta_{2i}$. We assume that η_{1i} and η_{2i} have zero means and a constant variance covariance matrix $\Omega = \begin{pmatrix} \omega_{11} & \omega_{12} \\ \omega_{12}' & \omega_{22} \end{pmatrix}$.

- the higher order moments of η_{1i} and η_{2i}, and their cross-moments exist and are finite;

---

[16] See Sargent (1978).

– the parameters of interest $\beta = E(\beta_i)$, and $\mu = E(\mu_i)$, $\theta = E\left(\dfrac{\beta_i}{1-\mu_i}\right)$

and $\phi = E\left(\dfrac{\mu_i}{1-\mu_i}\right)$ exist.

– Under these assumptions, the pooled regression is given by

$$y_{it} = \delta_i + \mu_i y_{it-1} + \beta_i' x_{it} + \left(\eta_{1i} y_{it-1} + \eta_{2i}' x_{it} + v_{it}\right),\ i = 1,...,N;\ t = 1,...,T. \qquad [2.2]$$

where different group-specific fixed or random effects can be included through the intercept terms δ_i which are allowed to differ across groups. As $y_{i,t-1}$ and x_{it} are correlated with v_{it}, the estimates of μ and β from [2.2] are biased.

In the static case[17] $\left(\mu_i = 0\right)$, where the regressors are strictly exogenous and the coefficients differ randomly and are distributed independently from the regressors across individuals, the pooled regressions provide consistent (and unbiased) estimates of the coefficient means $\left(\mu,\beta\right)$. For dynamic models $\left(\mu_i \neq 0\right)$, Pesaran and Smith (1995) show that the estimates of coefficients from a pooled regression are not consistent, even for large N and T. The problem arises in models with lagged dependent variables because when the regressors are serially correlated, ignoring coefficient heterogeneity induces serial correlation in the disturbance.

To give some idea of these biases, Pesaran and Smith propose to determine the probability limits of the fixed effects estimators of μ and β in the particular following case. They consider the case where the variation in β_i across groups is the only source of heterogeneity $\left(\mu_i = \mu,\ \forall i\right)$, and assume that the model [2.2] contains only one exogenous variable which follows a stationary AR(1) process defined by:

$$x_{it} = a_i\left(1-\rho\right) + \rho x_{i,t-1} + \varepsilon_{it},\ |\rho| < 1 \qquad [2.3]$$

---

[17] See Zelllner (1969).

where a_i is the mean of x_{it} and $\varepsilon_{iti} \approx i.i.d(0, c_i^2)$. Assuming that the variations in σ_i^2 and c_i^2 across groups i are independent of μ_i and β_i, and noting by σ^2 and c^2, the means of σ_i^2 and c_i^2 respectively, the probability limits given by the authors are[18]:

$$\plim_{\substack{N\to\infty \\ T\to\infty}} \hat{\mu}_{FE} = \mu + \frac{\rho(1-\mu\rho)(1-\mu^2)w_{22}}{\left(\sigma^2\!/_{c^2}\right)(1-\rho^2)(1-\mu\rho)^2 + (1-\mu^2\rho^2)w_{22} + (1-\rho^2)\beta} \qquad [2.4]$$

$$\plim_{\substack{N\to\infty \\ T\to\infty}} \hat{\beta}_{FE} = \beta - \frac{\beta\rho^2(1-\mu^2)w_{22}}{\left(\sigma^2\!/_{c^2}\right)(1-\rho^2)(1-\mu\rho)^2 + (1-\mu^2\rho^2)w_{22} + (1-\rho^2)\beta} \qquad [2.5]$$

These two results show the complex nature of these biases which depend here on ρ, w_{22} (the variance of β_i), μ, β and $\sigma^2\!/_{c^2}$. When $\rho > 0$, the asymptotic bias of $\hat{\mu}_{FE}$ is positive while $p\lim \hat{\beta}_{FE} < \beta_{FE}$. For the limit case where $\rho \to 1$, we have

$$\plim_{\rho\to 1} \hat{\mu}_{FE} = 1 \text{ and } \plim_{\rho\to 1} \hat{\beta}_{FE} = 0$$

The asymptotic biases may disappear when $\rho = 0$ or $w_{22} = 0$. When $\rho \neq 0$ or $w_{22} \neq 0$, they vanish only when $\mu \to 1$. Note that this results implies that the fixed estimator of the long run effect, θ is also asymptotically biased. It also over-estimates the long run effect when $\rho > 0$ and under-estimates it when $\rho < 0$. The authors obtain similar (but more complex) results in more general models. They conclude that the inconsistency of the pooled estimators vanishes only under the parameter homogeneity assumption.

To solve the problem of heterogeneity when $T \to \infty$, the coefficients in a dynamic model can be consistently estimated by a mean group procedure: separate regressions are estimated for each group, then the averages of the estimated group-parameter and their standard errors may be calculated . When T

---

[18] For the demonstration, see Pesaran and Smith (1995), appendix A, pp.103-108.

is relatively small, the bias associated to the parameter heterogeneity becomes a more serious problem.

3.2 The problem of parameter heterogeneity when T is small

For T small, the fixed effects estimator is not used in dynamic models because it is also inconsistent[19]. In this case, there are a large variety of alternatives estimators based on the Instrumental Variables method (IV) or the Generalised Method of Moments (GMM). These methods may be used to estimate a pooled regression if two conditions are verified. First, instrumental variables must not be correlated with the error term. Second, they must have a non-zero correlation with the included regressors. We refer to the procedure presented in Arellano and Bond (1991) and Arellano and Bover (1995).

These authors suggest a two step procedure. Firstly and following Anderson and Hsiao (1982), the equation is written in first difference to remove the individual specific intercepts. In general, their procedures are presented using a dynamic model defined by:

$$y_{it} = \delta + \mu y_{i,t-1} + \beta x_{it} + (\eta_i + v_{it}), \; |\mu| < 1 \qquad\qquad [2.6]$$

under the assumptions (when the exogenous variables are predetermined[20]):

$$\begin{cases} \eta_i \approx iid\left(0, \sigma_\eta^2\right) \\ v_{it} \approx iid\left(0, \sigma_v^2\right) \\ E\left(v_{it}, v_{is}\right) = 0 \text{ for } t \neq s \\ E\left(x_{it}, v_{is}\right) \neq 0 \text{ for } s < t \text{ and } E\left(x_{it}, v_{is}\right) = 0 \text{ for } s \geq t, \; \forall s, t = 1, \dots, T \end{cases}$$

Under parameter homogenous assumption, the estimated equation is:

---

[19] See Nickell (1981).
[20] We refer to the equation [1.31]

$$\Delta y_{it} = \delta + \mu \Delta y_{i,t-1} + \beta \Delta x_{it} + \Delta v_{it} \qquad\qquad [2.7]$$

The second step consists in selecting a set of instruments z_{it} for consistent estimation of the pooled regression [2.3]. To be valid, z_{it} must be serially uncorrelated with the Δv_{it} ($E(\Delta v_{it} z_{it}) = 0$), and correlated with the lagged endogenous dependant variable ($E(\Delta y_{it-1} z_{it}) \neq 0$) and current and lagged exogenous variable ($E(\Delta x_{it-1} z_{it}) \neq 0$). To verify these three conditions, they propose to use a set of instrumental variables defined for the i-th group, by :

$$z_i = diag\left[y_{i1}, y_{i2}, ..., y_{is}, x_{i1}', x_{i2}', ..., x_{i,s+1}'\right], \ s = 1,2,...,T-2. \qquad [2.8]$$

and which verifies the moments conditions:

$$E\left(\left(\Delta y_{it} - \delta \Delta y_{i,t-1}\right) y_{i,t-j}\right) = 0, \ j = 2,..,t-1; t = 3,..,T \qquad [2.9]$$

and

$$E\left(x_{it} v_{is}\right) = 0, \ \forall s < t, \ s,t = 1,...,T \qquad\qquad [2.10]$$

Then, equation [2.7] may be consistently estimated by the Generalised Method of Moments.

For Pesaran and Smith, it is not always possible to obtain consistent estimates in presence of parameter heterogeneity.

If we apply this procedure to estimate the coefficients of the model, the transformed model is defined by:

$$\Delta y_{it} = \mu \, \Delta y_{it-1} + \beta' \Delta x_{it} + \left(\eta_{1i} \Delta y_{it-1} + \eta_{2i}' \Delta x_{it} + \Delta v_{it}\right), \ i = 1,...,N; \ t = 1,...,T. \qquad [2.11]$$

The selection of a valid set of instrumental variables to estimate the first difference formulation is only possible in the two following cases:

- when μ is homogenous $\left(\mu_i = \mu \text{ for each i}\right)$;
- when μ_i vary across groups and are independently distributed from β_i .

In the others cases, the transformation in first difference does not eliminate all sources of heterogeneity.

4 Application

To illustrate this problem of parameter heterogeneity in dynamic models, employment equations have been estimated for a panel of six Member-States of the European Union over the five years 1989-1993. The logarithm of employment (l_{it}), measured in number of employees, is explained by current and lagged values of the logarithms of real turnover (q_{it}), real labour cost (w_{it}), real investment (k_{it}), together with two lags of log employment, an intercept and time dummies. Two approaches have been considered.

First, under the homogenous parameter assumption, a labour demand model has been estimated independently for each of six countries by the Generalised Method of Moments. The columns 1 to 6 of table 1 provide estimates using the equation in first difference given by

$$l_{it} = \mu_1 l_{it-1} + \mu_2 l_{it-2} + \beta_0 q_{it} + \beta_1 q_{it-1} + \alpha_0 \omega_{it} + \alpha_1 \omega_{it-1} + \gamma_t + v_0 k_{it} + \delta + v_{it}$$

$$i = 1,...,N \; ; t = 1,...,T$$

Secondly, to integrate a possible source of heterogeneity, we have estimated the model given by the equation [1.31], by a pooled GMM estimator across the six countries (or six panel data). The three last columns give the results on the basis of the pooled regressions using the equation

$$\dot{l}_{it} = \mu_1 \dot{l}_{it-1} + \mu_2 \dot{l}_{it-2} + \beta_0 \dot{q}_{it} + \beta_1 \dot{q}_{it-1} + \alpha_0 \dot{w}_{it} + \alpha_1 \dot{w}_{it-1} + \gamma_t + v_0 \dot{k}_{it} + \delta_j + \dot{v}_{it} ,$$

$$i = 1,..., \sum_{j=1}^{6} N_j \; ; t = 1,...,T; j = 1,...,6$$

To allow some heterogeneity in the intercept term, different country-specific fixed effects are included through the three following specifications:

$$\delta_j = \delta + \eta_{tj}, j = 1,...,6. \; ; \text{(individual and time dummies)}$$

$\delta_j = \delta + \eta_j$, $j = 1,...,6$ (individual dummies)

$\delta_j = \delta$, $j = 1,...,6$

Table 2 gives the estimate of these dummies. We note that in general time dummies and or individual dummies are significant.

To compare the difference between these two approaches, the estimates of the long run effects are reported in Table 3. It seems that long run effects are overestimated, in particular concerning the labour cost. We note also that the results of the pooled regressions are unstable.

Table 1: Labour demand estimation: GMM estimates.

Explanatory variables	BE	F	DK	NL	UK	IT	EUR6 $\delta_j = \delta + \eta_{ij}$	EUR6 $\delta_j = \delta + \eta_j$	EUR6 $\delta_j = \delta$
$\dot{l}_{t-1}$	0.737	0.593	0.657	0.590	0.390	0.645	0.744	0.683	0.649
	(0.032)	(0.044)	(0.052)	(0.049)	(0.051)	(0.045)	(0.038)	(0.036)	(0.034)
$\dot{l}_{t-2}$	-0.053	0.071	0.025	-0.020*	0.130	0.162	0.127	0.128	0.095
	(0.018)	(0.016)	(0.022)	(0.018)	(0.024)	(0.024)	(0.017)	(0.016)	(0.016)
$\dot{q}_t$	0.511	0.239	0.557*	0.173	0.411	0.265	0.310	0.332	0.327
	(0.036)	(0.038)	(0.038)	(0.026)	(0.041)	(0.028)	(0.032)	(0.030)	(0.029)
$\dot{q}_{t-1}$	-0.278	-0.120	-0.341	0.007*	-0.145	-0.086	-0.182	-0.136	-0.131
	(0.022)	(0.025)	(0.037)	(0.020)	(0.031)	(0.019)	(0.021)	(0.018)	(0.018)
$\dot{q}_{t-2}$	0.016*	-0.038	-0.027*	0007*	-0.041	-0.019*	-0.065	-0.060	-0.034
	(0.016)	(0.013)	(0.021)	(0.015)	(0.016)	(0.013)	(0.011)	(0.011)	(0.010)
$\dot{w}_t$	-0.631	-0.358	-0.657	-0.537	-0.374	-0.380	-0.523	-0.567	-0.441
	(0.051)	(0.050)	(0.044)	(0.072)	(0.099)	(0.067)	(0.042)	(0.037)	(0.037)
$\dot{w}_{t-1}$	0.353	0.115	0.380	0.262	0.225	0.134	0.225	0.138	0.117
	(0.031)	(0.031)	(0.035)	(0.044)	(0.066)	(0.036)	(0.028)	(0.018)	(0.017)
$\dot{w}_{t-2}$	0.052	0.061	0.023*	-0.029*	0.047*	0.031*	0.070	0.067	0.004*
	(0.023)	(0.019)	(0.029)	(0.024)	(0.037)	(0.029)	(0.020)	(0.015)	(0.011)
$\dot{i}_t$	0.014	0.010	0.023	0.005*	0.023	0.047	0.029	0.028	0.028
	(0.005)	(0.004)	(0.004)	(0.003)	(0.006)	(0.014)	(0.005)	(0.004)	(0.004)
Wald[1]	7.10*	31.05	25.52	62.38	10.72	46.40	6.23	65.23	31.82
	(9.49)	(9.49)	(9.49)	(9.49)	(9.49)	(9.49)	(9.49)	(9.49)	(9.49)
Wald[2]	-	-	-	-	-	-	-	74.94	-
								(11.10)	
Wald[3]	-	-	-	-	-	-	149.11	-	-
							(31.4)		
Wald[4]	-	-	-	-	-	-	177.91	105.74	-
							(36.4)	(16.9)	
Sargan[5]	68.09	85.66	73.09	70.05	83.26	68.38	73.3	93.36	128.45
	(75.26)	(75.26)	(75.26)	(75.26)	(75.26)	(75.26)	(75.26)	(75.26)	(75.26)
N	304	800	282	157	340	773	2656	2656	2656
T	4	4	4	4	4	4	4	4	4

Estimation period: 1990-1993. Time dummies are included in all equations Asymptotic standard errors robust to cross-section and times series heteroskedacticity are reported in parenthesis. Instruments are the logarithms of all exogenous variables. As instrument for the lagged dependent variable, levels of the own lags dated two periods or earlier are used. The basic instrument set used is of the form:

* The coefficient is not significant (5%).

1 Value of the Wald statistic of joint significance of time dummies. The $\chi^2_{5\%}$ for the appropriate degree of freedom is reported in brackets.

2 Value of the Wald statistic of joint significance of individual dummies. The $\chi^2_{5\%}$ for the appropriate degree of freedom is reported in brackets.

3 Value of the Wald statistic of joint significance of individual/time dummies. The $\chi^2_{5\%}$ for the appropriate degree of freedom is reported in brackets.

4 Value of the Wald statistic of joint significance of all dummies. The $\chi^2_{5\%}$ for the appropriate degree of freedom is reported in brackets.

5 Value of the Sargan statistic for instrument validity test. For each test the $\chi^2_{5\%}$ for the appropriate degree of freedom is reported in brackets.

Table 2: Estimated dummies.

Dummies	EUR6 $\delta_j = \delta + \eta_{tj}$	EUR6 $\delta_j = \delta + \eta_j$	EUR6 $\delta_j = \delta$
Intercept	0.021* *(0.011)*	0.032 *(0.007)*	0.018 *(0.006)*
Time dummies			
D91	-0.008* *(0.014)*	0.003* *(0.007)*	0.004 *(0.007)*
D92	-0.017* (0.012)	-0.031 *(0.006)*	-0.018 *(0.005)*
D93	-0.019* (0.012)	-0.037 *(0.007)*	-0.020 *(0.005)*
Individual dummies			
IF	-	0.015 *(0.004)*	-
IDK	-	0.003* *(0.003)*	-
INL	-	0.006* *(0.004)*	-
IUK	-	-0.014 *(0.004)*	-
IT	-	-0.016 *(0.017)*	-
Ind./Times dummies			
IF-D90	0.078 *(0.015)*	-	-
IF-D91	0.026 *(0.012)*	-	-
IF-D92	0.001* *(0.008)*	-	-
IF-D93	-0.003* *(0.008)*	-	-
IDK-D90	-0.024* *(0.013)*	-	-
IDK-D91	0.020* *(0.013)*	-	-
IDK-D92	-0.002* *(0.011)*	-	-
IDK-D93	0.024* *(0.013)*	-	-
INL-D90	0.018* *(0.014)*	-	-
INL-D91	0.005* *(0.013)*	-	-
INL-D92	-0.009* *(0.012)*	-	-
INL-D93	0.015* *(0.014)*	-	-
IUK-D90	-0.023* *(0.015)*	-	-
IUK-D91	0.002* *(0.013)*	-	-
IUK-D92	-0.021* *(0.012)*	-	-
IUK-D93	-0.006* *(0.016)*	-	-
IT-D90	-0.013* *(0.012)*	-	-
IT-D91	0.023 *(0.011)*	-	-
IT-D92	-0.026 *(0.010)*	-	-
IT-D93	-0.050 *(0.013)*	-	-

Asymptotic standard errors robust to cross-section and times series heteroskedacticity are reported in parenthesis.

*The coefficient is not significant (5%).

Table 3:Estimates of long-run labour demand elasticities.

Country	Turnover	Labour cost	Investment	Weight
BE	0.788	-0.715	0.044	0.11
F	0.241	-0.542	0.030	0.30
DK	0.594	-0.799	0.072	0.11
NL	0.435	-0.707	0.011	0.06
UK	0.469	-0.212	0.048	0.13
IT	0.829	-1.114	0.243	0.29
EUR6 (weighted sum)	0.552	-0.722	0.099	1.00
EUR6 $\delta_j = \delta + \eta_{tj}, \forall j, \forall t$	0.488	-1.767	0.225	1.00
EUR6 $\delta_j = \delta + \eta_j, \forall j$	0.715	-1.905	0.147	1.00
EUR6 $\delta_j = \delta, \forall j$	0.628	-1.246	0.109	1.00

5 Conclusion

In this study, two sources of heterogeneity are considered to estimate a dynamic model of labour demand. First, the possible presence of several categories of workers is implicitly taken into account by specifying a more complex dynamic model . Secondly, the possibility that the firms are not in the same phase of the business cycle is captured by differences between countries. For that purpose, some heterogeneity has been allowed in the intercept term using time and/or country dummies. The unstable results presented in section 3 indicate that others sources of heterogeneity must be specified in order to consistently estimate a pooled regression under the parameter homogeneous assumption.   As last conclusion, and given the importance of the heterogeneity , it would be necessary to test for it (by an Hausman type tests for example). As far as we know, such a test is not yet available when T is relatively small .

REFERENCES

Ahn S. C. and Schmidt P. (1995), *"Efficient Estimation of Models for Dynamic Panel Data"*, Journal of Econometrics, 68, 79-113.

Anderson T. W. and Hsiao C. (1981*)*, *"Estimation of Dynamic Models with Error Components"*, Journal of the American Statistical Association, 76, 598-606.

Anderson T. W. and Hsiao C. (1982), *"Formulation and estimation of dynamic models using panel data"*, Journal of Econometrics, 18, 578-606.

Arellano M. and Bond S. (1991), *"Some tests of specification for panel data: a Monte Carlo evidence and an application to employment equations"*, Review of Economic Studies, 58, 277-297.

Arellano M. and Bover O. (1995), *"Another look at the instrumental variable estimation of error-components models"*, Journal of Econometrics, 68, 29-51.

Balestra P. and Nerlove M. (1966), *"Pooling cross-section and time-series data in the estimation of a dynamic model"*, Econometrica, 34, 585-612.

Baltagi B. H. and Griffin J.M. (1984), *"Short and long run effects in pooled models"*, International Economic Review, 25, 631-645.

Bresson G., Kramarz F. and Sevestre P. (1995), *"Dynamic labour demand models"*, in The Econometrics of Panel Data, eds. By Matyas L. and Sevestre P., Kluwer Academic Publishers, London, Second Revisited Edition.

Broze L., Gourieroux C. and Szafarz A. (1985), *"Solutions of linear rational expectations models"*, Econometric Theory, 1, 341-368.

Burgess S. M. (1988), *"Employment adjustment in UK manufacturing"*, Economic Journal, 98, 81-103.

Dormont B. and Sevestre P. (1986), *Modèles dynamiques de demande de travail: spécification et estimation sur données de panel*, Revue Economique, 37, 3.

Eisner R. and Strotz R. (1963), *"Determinants of business investment "*, in Impacts of Monetary Policy, Englewood Cliffs, New York.

Gourieroux C., Laffont J-J. and Monfort A. (1982), *"Rational expectations in dynamic linear models "*, Econometrica, 50, 409-425.

Griliches Z. (1967), *"Distributed lags: A survey"*, Econometrica, 35, 16-49.

Hamermesh D. (1989), *Labor Demand and the structure of adjusment costs*, American Economic Review, 79, 674-689.

Hamermesh D. (1993), *Labour Demand*, Princeton University .

Hansen L.P. (1982), *"Large Sample Properties of Generalized Method of Moments Estimators "*, Econometrica, 50, 1029-1054.

Hansen L. P. and Singleton K. J. (1982), *"Generalised instrumental variables estimation of nonlinear rational expectations models"*, Econometrica, 50, 1269-1286.

Hausman J. A. (1978), *"Specification Tests in Econometrics"*, Econometrica, 46(6), 1251-1271.

Holt C., Modigliani F., Muth J. and Simon H. (1960*), Planning Production, Inventories and Workforce*, Prentice-Hall, Englewood Cliffs, New York.

Machin S., Manning A. and Meghir C. (1993), *"Dynamic models of employment based on firm level panel data, in Labour Demand and Equilibrium Wage Formation"*, edited by J. C. Van Ours, G. A. Pfann and G. Ridder, North-Holland.

Nerlove M. (1971), *"Further evidence on the estimation of dynamic economic relation from a time-series of cross-sections"*, Econometrica, 39, 359-382.

Nerlove M. (1972), *"Lags in economic behaviour"*, Econometrica, 40, 221-251.

Nickell S. (1984), *"An Investigation of the Determinants of Manufacturing Employment in the United Kingdom"*, Review of Economic Studies, vol. LI(4), 167, 529-558.

Nickell S. (1986), *"Dynamic Models of Labour Demand "*, in Handbook of Labour Economics , vol. I, Edited by Ashenfelter O. and Layard R., Elsevier Science Publishers, 473-522.

Oi W. Y. (1962), *"Labour as a Quasi-Fixed Factor"*, Journal of Political Economy, vol. LXX, 6, 538-555.

Pesaran M. H. and Smith R. (1995), *"Estimating long-run relationships from dynamic heterogeneous panels"*, Journal of econometrics, 68, 53-78.

Sargent T.J. (1978), *"Estimation of dynamic labour demand schedules under rational expectations"*, Journal of Political Economy, 86.

Sargent T. J. (1979), *Macroeconomic Theory*, Academic Press.

Sims C. A. (1974), *"Ouput and labor input in manufacturing"*, Brookings Papers on Economic Activity, 3.

Zellner A. (1969), *"On the aggregation problem: A new approach to a troublesome problem"*, in K. A. Fox et al., eds., Economic models, estimation and risk programming: Essays in honor of Gehard Tintner, Springer-Verlag, Berlin, 365-378.

White H. (1982), *"Instrumental Variables Regression with Independent Observations"*, Econometrica, 50, 483-499.

PRODUCTIVITY AND SPECIFICITY IN FACTOR INPUTS[1]

Eric J. Bartelsman

Ministry of Economic Affairs, the Netherlands, and ALERT, Free University of Amsterdam

This paper evaluates the macroeconomic importance of specificity in factor markets by considering the effects of wage moderation in the Netherlands on productivity growth since 1982. The analysis is based on a vintage model of capital with embodied technology. In a traditional vintage model, a decline in wages relative to cost of capital will delay scrapping and postpone new investment, thus reducing productivity growth. In recent models that take into account the specific production relationship between capital and labor and the problem associated with appropriability of rents, institutionalized wage moderation will increase new investment and improve productivity. A preliminary analysis of micro-level data of industrial firms does not yet lead one to reject the role of specificity.

1 Introduction

This paper presents preliminary results of an empirical evaluation of the macroeconomic importance of specificity in factor markets. The paper compares the model of specificity with a base model by considering the different short- and medium-term effects on productivity growth of wage moderation that took place in the Netherlands after 1982. An analysis also is made of differential behavior under the two models of a collection of indicators on investment, employment, and capital stocks in individual industrial firms in the Netherlands. In particular, observed micro-level lumpiness in capital input allows one to distinguish between the two competing hypotheses.

The first model is based on a production structure with technology embodied in vintage capital. In this model, wage moderation leads to a short- and medium-term reduction in productivity growth (see Kleinknecht (1994)). The mechanism is that reduced wage pressure reduces incentives for firms to invest in new capital, and delays scrapping of old capital, thus allowing a decline in the

---

[1] The paper reflects my personal opinions and not necessarily those of my employers.

capital-labor ratio. The second model has a similar vintage production structure, but posits the existence of a rent-appropriation problem associated with specificity of labor and capital in the production relationship (see Caballero and Hammour (1996)). In this model, wage moderation via consensus act as a fortuitous institutional advance that reduces the appropriability problem. In the model, reductions in specificity curb opportunism and pull resources into production, thus increasing productivity. While empirical testing of the hypotheses is not based on estimation of a structural model of firm dynamics, the empirical findings are supportive of the macro-economic importance of specificity as described by Caballero and Hammour, and point towards a significant role of wage moderation in boosting employment as well and productivity.

Although the paper is primarily concerned with evaluating the relevance of specificity problems in macroeconomics, it does so by considering the effects of wage moderation. A short digression on the institutional setting of wage moderation and on the channels through which wage moderation is thought to effect the economy is thus in order. Wage moderation has been credited with the extraordinary growth in hours worked in the Dutch economy since 1983. During the first Lubbers administration, wage bargaining between social partners was replaced with consensus building over common policy goals. The social partners (confederation of unions and employers organization) provided qualitative recommendations on specific issues, while sectoral trade unions took into account sector specific conditions that allowed variation within the central guidelines. Wage moderation affects more than 80~percent of workers who were directly covered through collective agreements or through mandatory extension (see CPB (1997)). Following the 'Agreement of Wassenaar' of 1982, the common policy goal became employment creation, and the common vehicle wage moderation.

According to Bovenberg (1997), three main channels exist through which lower wages led to employment growth. First, profitability of firms improved, creating the financial room and incentives to invest. Next, the competitive position of firms improved on world markets, raising exports. Finally, production became more labor intensive. While the effects on employment are clear, the effects on total factor productivity (TFP) are not. In a vintage capital model with embodied technology, the first channel leads to more new capital, thus to higher TFP. The second channel is ambiguous, because it is not clear which firms raise output to meet export demand. If existing firms with old technology increase utilization and output, or delay scrapping, TFP will be held back, while if firms with new capital gain market share, TFP will improve. The third channel lowers labor productivity, and may retard TFP growth if increased demand is met by adding labor to existing capital (with embodied technology).

The combined effect on productivity (TFP) of wage moderation through the three channels above is ambiguous, because different models underlie the analysis. In essence, the direction of TFP growth following wage moderation can be used to distinguish the models and test whether specificity plays an important role. We will look at the macro, sectoral, and micro-level implications of wage moderation under the two competing models. We will show why sectoral data cannot be used to disentangle the effects of wage moderation on productivity. Instead, we will assess whether findings from the micro data are consistent with the implications of one of the two hypotheses.

The organization of the paper is as follows: First, the two models are presented. Next, a macro- and sectoral overview is presented of wage moderation and its implications under the competing hypotheses, followed by implications at the micro level. The empirical section starts with a discussion of the macro- and sectoral evidence, or lack thereof. Finally, summary statistics on investment behavior and age of the capital stock, and some indicators of TFP and capital growth are shown which are consistent with the model of specificity. A final section concludes and sketches an outline for a structural model that nests the two hypotheses.

2 Productivity and factor inputs: two models

What are the determinants of technological change? In this paper, we assume for both models that the growth rate of available technology is exogenous. We further assume that available technology is embodied in capital, and that all investment is in new capital which embodies the best available technology. Once capital is in place, it cannot costlessly be shifted to another use. The vintage structure of capital and the embodied nature of technology is common to both models.

2.1 Traditional vintage model

In a traditional vintage model (VM), lower wages have a clear short-and medium-term effect on the actions of the representative firm. First, the age at which old vintages cease to be profitable, at the margin, increases. Second, all the existing vintages will be used in production with a higher level of associated labor. Output can thus increase somewhat without adding newer vintages of capital with their embodied technology. Depending on the direction of demand--- lower owing to a reduction of domestic income, higher owing to a boost in export demand from lower production costs---the lull in new capital spending may be longer or shorter.

2.2 Specificity in input markets

In a production relationship, capital and labor join forces to produce more output than they could generate independently. The production function, with its associated properties of scale and substitution elasticities and diminishing marginal returns have been well described in the literature. More recently, another aspect of joint production has come to the forefront in (macro)economics, namely the temporary nature of the production relationship. Jobs are created and destroyed, firms come and go, capital is put in place and scrapped.[2] Each discrete decision has irreversible elements because investments in the relationship are sunk. The types of investments in a production relationship include search costs for the employment match, job-training, sunk investments in capital, etc.

The costs incurred in the specific relationship need to be recouped during the lifetime of the joint effort; when the relationship is broken, a remainder is lost. The economic problem is that it is difficult to form ex-ante contracts to cover the division of the flow of rents which are generated to cover the fixed costs. In words of Caballero and Hammour (1997), the "...specific quasi-rents may not be divided *ex post* according to the parties' *ex ante* terms of trade." This problem, known in the literature as the "hold-up" problem occurs when one party to a transaction can appropriate a portion of the quasi-rents associated with the relationship.[3]

In a particular market, the hold-up problem leads to an undercommitment of resources, because the factor is concerned that future quasi-rents may be appropriated by others. An introduction of a new technology which is profitable given factor prices, may not lead to its adoption if the benefits cannot be shielded from future opportunism of other contracting parties. Institutional arrangements are thought to evolve in order to compensate for the hold-up problem, although they are generally acknowledged not to solve the problem completely.[4] In the empirical section of this paper, we evaluate if the wage moderation in the Netherlands in early 1982 can be seen as an institutional change that reduced the hold-up problem in the eyes of the market participants.

In the model of Caballero and Hammour (1996) (CH) the hold-up problem plays a central role in the functioning of the macro-economy. In particular, "...a highly inefficient macro 'solution' to the unresolved microeconomic contracting problems" results as the problem of deciding on investments and sharing the benefits on an individual level spreads throughout the economy. The basic macro implications are that the market for the appropriating factor is segmented and that the productive structure is sclerotic. In other words, if workers attempt to get

---

[2] See Dunne *et al.* (1988), Davis *et al.* (1996), and Caballero *et al.* (1995) for examples of plant dynamics, employment gross flows, and micro capital behavior.

[3] An overview of the problem as related to labor markets is presented by Malcomson (1997).

[4] See CPB (1997), chapter 2.

more than what was predicated on their ex-ante terms of trade, involuntary unemployment will occur and too many low productivity units will be kept in operation.

In the CH model of the economy there are two factors of production that can either produce in autarky or commit to joint production relationships with partly irreversible fixed costs. The ex-ante terms of trade are derived from their autarky options; when operating jointly the factors are complementary and cannot be given payments based on marginal products. The quasi-rents arising from a specific relationship is the difference between the value of the joint product and the sum of the autarky products. The hold-up problem occurs because a party can threaten to break the relationship, leaving the other with a loss. In the equilibrium outcome, division of rents and allocation of factors to joint production is such that no party has an incentive to deviate from its choices, given the choices of others. In the general framework of Caballero and Hammour, the factors labor and capital are symmetrical, and only differ in the value of the outside option (autarky) and the amount lost if the relationship ends. An interpretation of the autarky option may be unemployment with benefits for workers, and flight to international assets for capital. Specificity for capital may arise from hiring (and firing) costs and investment in training embodied in the worker. Specificity for labor may arise from search costs and from acquisition of firm-specific knowledge. Net specificity combines the outside options and potential losses, and points to the factor that is subject to appropriation, or opportunism, by the other factor.

The model is otherwise akin to the vintage model, with a distribution of productivity among the existing production units, a lower bound on productivity below which the unit is scrapped, and a free entry condition for creating new units with the best technology.

If the interplay between outside options and sunk costs are such that specificity in factors is not balanced (net specificity points to one factor), an inefficient equilibrium will result with underemployment (positive allocation of resources to autarky), and market segmentation (the appropriated factor will always receive its autarky marginal product, while the appropriating factor will earn less in autarky). This latter effect can be thought of as involuntary unemployment for the appropriating factor. The number of joint production jobs is limited by the low allocation of the appropriated factor to the joint sector, which is their response to the appropriability problem. Next, in this model, the scrapping margin is at a lower level of productivity than would occur if specificity were balanced or if complete enforceable contracts could be made. This happens because resources freed up by scrapping the marginal unit would not receive the benefits from the new technology with certainty, but would have a probability of earning less in autarky. Finally, the model shows that in equilibrium creation will be insufficient and destruction excessive. The latter occurs because the social opportunity cost of labor (return in autarky) is lower than the wage in joint production.

So far, the model does not say much about the capital-labor ratio. The model posits fixed proportions in the short run. In the long run, the model allows for technological choices from a range of proportions, with perfect substitutability. In equilibrium the appropriated factor chooses the technology. The direction of the capital-labor ratio following a change in specificity depends on the extent to which net specificity itself varies with the capital-labor ratio. For example, if specificity is caused by severance pay, a higher capital-labor ratio for a given level of output reduces the magnitude of the problem. In this case an exogenous increase in specificity of capital leads to lower employment and a higher capital labor ratio for new vintages. If on the other hand, specificity does not depend on the capital-labor ratio, the earlier described mechanism of withdrawing capital to autarky will dominate after an exogenous increase in capital specificity, reducing the capital-labor ratio of new vintages. In either case, the capital-labor ratio is sub-optimal, given outside factor prices.

3 Implications of wage moderation

This paper attempts to distinguish between the two models. The method is to find an economic event that generates a different response under the two models. The following sections show that the two models predict different outcomes for a few indicators following a change in wages. However, two obstacles cloud the ability to distinguish between the two models. First, what is the nature of the wage reduction? Is it an exogenous occurrence, for example caused by a helicopter drop of highly educated workers. Or is it caused by an institutional change in the way in which wages are negotiated? If so, is the implication that the specificity of labor was reduced? One path for this reduction would be in the lowering of the value of the outside option, which lowers the bargaining power of labor. Another path is more direct through the belief that market parties have that the consensus agreement will be honored, and that opportunistic behavior will be limited. The second obstacle is the level at which the models generate differences in outcomes. Possibly, a difficulty could exist in isolating the theoretical differences in outcomes of indicators at the sectoral level from observed differences. At the micro-level, such problems of interpretation may be less severe.

The importance of micro-level data in distinguishing between sources of changes in aggregates lies at the heart of the above problem. As an example, the evolution of aggregate TFP is broken down into its micro-components. Aggregate or sectoral productivity (TFP) growth is the result of both the development of productivity at each production unit, and of the allocation, usually through market mechanisms, of sectoral or aggregate output across firms. Aggregate TFP is thus a weighted average of the productivity level associated with technology embodied in each unit of capital, with the weight being equal to the share of output produced by that unit of capital (together with associated labor). Firm level TFP can only change with a change in the age structure of its capital, either through the introduction of new units of capital or the scrapping of old units. Aggregate TFP can increase without changes in productivity at the firm level, for example if more productive firms gain market share, new firms enter the industry, or less productive firms exit the industry. We will see below how knowledge of micro-level developments in indicators indeed can aid in understanding the channels through which effects occur in the two models.

3.1 Aggregate and sectoral indicators

Table 1 shows the short- and medium-term effect on a selection of macro (or sectoral) variables following wage moderation under the two models, the traditional vintage model (VM) and the model of specificity (CH). For the purpose of the table, it is assumed that wage moderation also lowered net specificity of capital. The first line shows the effect on output. In VM, the reasonable assumption is made that the export boosting effect dominates the direct effect of lower wages on domestic expenditures. In the CH model, output grows because of the increase in resources drawn to joint production. Labor increases in VM, through an increase in labor intensity, while employment grows in CH because of a reduction in market segmentation. The effect on the capital-labor ratio in the CH model is ambiguous, because even though capital is drawn into joint production, the choice of technique might favor labor if the degree of specificity depends on factor intensity. Labor productivity is depressed in VM because of the higher labor intensity and because of the postponement of purchases of new vintages. In the CH model, labor productivity may decline if the effects of new vintage purchases are offset by the possible decline in capital intensity.

Table 1 Aggregate and sectoral indicators

Indicator	VM	CH
Output	+	+
Employment	+	+
Capital-labor ratio	–	±
Labor productivity	–	±
Labor share of income	–	–
Investment	–	+
TFP	–	+

The next line shows labor share of income, which is related to both the cause, wage moderation, and the effects, output and employment. The fall in labor share resulting from a decline in product wages (wage deflated by output price), partly can be offset by the fall in labor productivity under VM, but could be strengthened by an increase in labor productivity under CH. The institutional setting of wage moderation in the Netherlands ensures that labor share of income will fall, under both models. This occurs because product wage increases are negotiated within boundaries of the 'wage-space,' namely some proportion of labor productivity growth. The first five rows of the table do not provide indicators that can be used to distinguish the two models.

The models do have distinct effects on investment spending and TFP. Investment clearly goes through a lull in VM as the stock sits around waiting until the new, increased, obsolescence age is reached.[5] In the CH model, scleroris is reduced and new vintages are purchased as capital is drawn into joint production. Unfortunately, the very cyclical nature of investment makes it hard to determine whether the movements in investment over time are the results of the change in wages, or because of other (international) macroeconomic disturbances. Similarly, the different prediction for TFP, a decline under VM and an improvement under CH, may be hard to distinguish in practice because one does not know what the direction of TFP would have been in the absence of wage moderation. Of course, a structural model with appropriate instruments for other effects could be used, but in practice such instruments are difficult to find. Nonetheless, we will briefly describe the aggregate and sectoral indicators in the section 4.

3.2 Micro-level indicators

The richness of micro-level data provides dimensions which aid in distinguishing between the two models. Individual firms vary significantly from each other in many ways, whether size, age, technology, profitability, productivity, cyclicality, etc. This heterogeneity seems to be the one constant found by analysts looking at longitudinal micro datasets, i.e. datasets that cover a large sample of all firms or establishments over time, and that form the basis for the official sectoral and aggregate statistics.[6]

---

[5] In the earlier discussion of the analysis of Bovenberg (1997) on the employment effects of wage moderation, the first channel was an increase in investment. This channel is important when firms are credit constrained and need cash-flow for investment. The other explanation for increased investment, namely improvements in expected profits, are related to the CH model.

[6] For surveys of the burgeoning literature, see e.g. McGuckin (1995) and Bartelsman and Doms (1997).

Some of the stylized facts from analysis of longitudinal micro datasets (LMDs) in various countries fit the theoretical constructs in the CH model quite nicely. Table 2 shows the direction of certain measurable quantities from the micro data following wage moderation under the two models. Before discussing the table, it is helpful to introduce some terminology which has become standard in the analysis of LMDs. First, measurements can take place along the 'within' or 'between' dimension. 'Within' productivity growth, for example, shows a weighted average of firm level productivity, with initial input shares as weights. 'Between' productivity growth shows how much aggregate productivity changes through a shift in output shares, given initial productivity levels. Next, a cross-term shows the contribution to the aggregate of the covariance between changes in productivity and changes in shares. Finally, entry and exit affect aggregate productivity.

Another term to be used is a difference-in-differences estimator (DD). This method looks at differences in outcomes of a group which is influenced by an effect before and after the effect occurred, with differences before and after in a group which is not influenced. A concrete example: If wage moderation only can have influence on a firm's technology choice if they are at the vintage stage where they are ready to implement a new technology, we can compare outcomes of firms which do major re-tooling before and after wage moderation, with outcomes of firms which are not at the re-tooling stage. This technique can be argued to provide a 'control group' to filter out influences of other factors.

First, we review some general features of the data, and what they would look like under the two models. The degree of factor substitutability depends on the dimension along which it is measured. Substitution occurs 'within' micro-units, takes place over time as older units are replaced (entry-exit) or cross-sectionally through reallocation of output shares across micro-units with different factor intensities ('between'). For capital-energy substitution in the U.S. industrial sector it is well documented (see Doms (1993)) that the 'within' dimension shows little action. This fact also fits the modern views in energy modelling (see Koopmans (1997)). Little 'within' substitutability of capital and labor at a particular firm in the short-run, and possibly even complementarity, would fit the CH model nicely. In the long run both the VM and CH models exhibit substitutability between capital and labor.

Next, investment behavior is analyzed by counting the number of firms that experience a 'major investment project' in a particular year, where 'major investment project' is defined as investment expenditures that make up a significant portion of total investment spending of the firm over a long horizon (see for example, Doms and Dunne (1993), or Cooper et al. (1994)). Both models should show significant lumpiness in investment, because in a vintage model a period of inaction follows after a new unit of capital has been put in place.

Productivity (TFP) growth only changes in the within dimension following an investment spike of a firm, under both models. Between effects, and entry and exit contributions also play a role in both models.

Table 2 Micro-level indicators

Indicators	VM	CH
Model features		
Factor substitution		
short-run	yes	no
long-run	yes	yes
Lumpy investment	yes	yes
TFP growth		
within	after spike	after spike
between, entry, exit	yes	yes
Wage moderation		
Firms with spike	−	+
Average age of capital	+	−
DD estimate of effect		
TFP growth	−	+
Capital growth	−	+

The next rows of the table show the effects of wage moderation on certain indicators. The first effect is the number of investment spikes in the years following moderation, which should go up under CH as expected realizable profits increase and scrapping age decreases, and decline under VM as more firms will find themselves in the range of inaction. Next, the within measure of the age of the capital stock should decline under CH and increase under VM. The lowering of opportunistic behavior of labor creates an incentive for investments in new, highly productive capital. Further, the scrapping age decreases leaving many firms with capital which can be scrapped immediately.

An investment spike of a firm gives the econometrician a nice tool to see what choices a firm has made for capital investment and for the implementation of new technology. The last two rows of the table show the expected difference-in-differences estimates for the effect of wage moderation on changes in capital and on TFP growth.

The capital stock clearly is boosted following a spike in investment at the firm. Changes in the capital stock in firms in years where no major investment project takes place could be positive if investment is larger than the amount of scrapping, or could be negative, but in any case is smaller than for firms with spikes. Capital stock growth following wage moderation will be different under the two models, and will depend on whether spikes occur. More spikes are expected under CH, but even under VM spikes will occur with a positive probability. Conditional on a spike occurring, the growth in capital will be lower following moderation under VM, all else equal, because desired capital stock is reduced. Under VM, capital growth for firms without a spike will be higher than before, all else equal, because the scapping margin is extended. Under CH, growth at firms without spikes will decline, because more scrapping takes place, and growth at firms with spikes will increase because firms desire to draw more capital into joint production. Thus, under CH, the relative growth of spike to non-spike firms increases following wage moderation, while it declines under VM. The difference in differences estimate helps in the 'all else equal' clause, because external influences, such as an exogenous increase in the cost of capital, will affect aggregate investment, and the probability of the spike, but will have no, or less, effect on the relative change of spike to non-spike firms.

For TFP, we look at the contribution to total TFP growth of the firms with a spike compared with firms without a spike, before and after wage moderation. Although we thereby implicitly take into account the number of firms which have a spike, we are able to correct for underlying differences in technological opportunity because we use the control group of firms without a spike. The expectation is that the relative contribution to TFP of firms with a spike increases following wage moderation under CH, and decreases under VM.

4 Empirical evidence

4.1 Aggregate and sectoral data

The empirical section starts with a cursory glance at aggregate and sectoral data. Sources and definitions of the data are provided in appendix A. Chart 1 shows four panels with the developments in the industrial sector between 1975 and 1995. The top left panel shows labor share of income on the left scale and the minimum wage (deflated with product prices) on the right scale. These indicators show the policy shift following the agreement of Wassenaar in 1982. The top right panel shows the development of output---the solid line, hours worked—the declining dotted line, and investment. A clear shift takes place in the trend of hours worked, starting in 1985, although an increase in investment is far more prominent. Bottom left, we see the developments of wages and user cost of capital, both relative to the output deflator. The turning point in the trend of product wages takes place in 1985. Wages relative to user cost of capital actually are increasing until around 1985. Desinflation and reductions in nominal interest rates surpress the cost of capital significantly throughout the decade. Finally, the bottom right chart shows the developments in (log) of TFP, (log) of labor productivity, and the capital-labor ratio. TFP shows a noticeable upturn after 1983, although cyclical factors are notorious in bouncing around measured TFP.

The following charts show the same indicators for selected industries, Metal and electronics (ME), and Food, alcohol, and tobacco (VG). The layout of the charts is the same. It should be noted that the minimum wage is deflated with the relevant output prices deflator, thereby exhibiting a different pattern in each chart. The metal sector shows an earlier turnaround in labor income share than aggregate industry, and also an earlier recovery in investment.

Overall, the data do not provide evidence to support one model over the other. The movement in TFP and investment would have provided evidence, if one had information on their development in the absence of wage moderation. Of course, instrumental variable techniques could provide an empirical means for filtering out unwanted effects, such as exogenous shifts in export demand, consumer confidence, state of the business cycle, and others. While instrumental variables techniques are quite standard in many econometric analyses, direct access to micro-data can provide more robust identification.

4.2 Micro-level data

The simplicity of the empirical tests applied to the micro-data belies the considerable amount of datawork needed to construct the relevant measures. Table 3 shows the number of firms with investment spikes in each year. The table is constructed from investment data from a balanced panel of firms, namely firms which occur in all available survey years of the investment statistics database. Next, for each firm a sum is created for deflated investment in transport vehicles and in equipment. A spike occurs if the investment of a firm on the relevant asset type is more than 25 percent of total investment on that asset type over time.

It should not be surprising to those who have followed the recent literature on investment that such spikes occur with the frequency they do (see e.g. a survey by Caballero (1997)). In fact, in the Netherlands, half the firms spend more than 25 percent of their total investment in transport vehicles over a 16 year span in one year. For equipment investment the size of the median spike is 20 percent. These figures are roughly the same as for US manufacturing firms, where the median spike is 25 percent (see Doms and Dunne (1993)), which is surprising since the unit of observation in the U.S. is an establishment, while it is a firm in the Netherlands. The difference lies in the fact that firms could smooth necessary lumpiness in plant investment by shifting resources across plants over time, if they want to.

Table 3 Investment indicators

Year	Transport vehicles		Equipment	
	Spikes[a]	Investment[b]	Spikes	Investment
1980	37	101	20	1215
1981	20	90	17	1093
1982	25	84	10	1103
1983	21	86	12	1260
1984	22	90	18	1876
1985	49	112	26	1947
1986	40	99	31	1947
1987	39	97	32	1613
1988	37	106	29	1535
1989	48	117	33	1880
1990	53	115	55	1955
1991	58	110	40	1954

Source: Authors's calculation at CeReM, panel of 1351 firms.
a: Number of firms with > 25% of 16 years of Inv in a year
b: Inv.; total investment for firms in panel, 1985 guilders.

The data in table 3 indeed show a significant increase in the number of firms that have a spike in 1985. This is the same year that aggregate hours increased, and lags the Wassenaar agreement by three years. The increase in spikes goes against the VM model and is not contradictory to the CH model.

Next, table 4 shows the average age of the stock of transport vehicles and equipment over time. After increasing through 1983, the age starts declining. The fact that age falls reflects both an increase in investment as well as a reduction of the scrapping age under CH. In the previous table we saw that investment does not pick up until 1985; the margin of rejuvenation therefore initially took place through scrapping. It should be noted that aggregate industrial investment picked up sooner than investment in the balanced panel, reflecting the fact that many smaller firms and entrants boosted their investment at an earlier stage.

Finally, table 5 shows the difference in differences estimates of the effects of wage moderation on TFP growth and capital growth. Consistent with the CH model, it is seen that the contribution to aggregate TFP growth of firms in the years surrounding an investment spike minus the contribution of the firms which had no spike in that year increased following wage moderation. Spikes are considered in the years 1979, 80 and 81 for before moderation, and in 1983, 84, and 85 following moderation; firm level TFP growth is calculated from the year prior to the spike to two years following the spike.

The difference in differences growth of capital also exhibits the pattern expected under CH. In this case, the figures are based on weighted average growth rates, rather than on contributions to aggregate growth used, as was for TFP. In other words, they reflect the within behavior of capital stock growth. It is seen that changes in growth rates for firms with a spike relative to those without, increased following wage moderation, reflecting both a reduction in scrapping age, and an improvement in profitability outlook for investments as expected under CH.

Table 4 Average of capital stock

Year	Transport Vehicles	Equipment
1978	7.9	8.6
1979	8.3	8.9
1980	8.6	9.1
1981	8.7	9.2
1982	8.6	9.2
1983	8.3	9.2
1984	8.2	9.1
1985	8.2	8.8
1986	7.0	8.6
1987	7.6	8.1
1988	7.3	7.6
1989	7.0	7.4
1990	6.6	7.3
1991	6.3	6.9

Source: Author's calculation at CeReM, 1435 firms.

Table 5 Effects of wage moderation

Difference-in-differences estimates (Growth rate differences in percentage points).

Indicator	Before moderation	After moderation
Relative change in TFP[a]	.13	.42
Relative change in K[b]	8.1	16.0

Source: Author's calculation at CeReM, 1350 firms.
a: Average TFP growth of firms with spike in year t minus TFP growth firms with no spike.
b: Average K growth of firms with spike in year t, minus K growth firms with no spike.

5 Conclusions and suggestions for further research

In this paper some preliminary results are presented of an empirical test of the relevance of specificity in macroeconomics. The very elegant theory of Caballero and Hammour, of course, is based partly on empirical observation, but, as yet, no rigorous empirical testing has taken place. The preliminary results presented here do not meet standards of rigor, but are suggestive that future research will be fruitful.

The methodology used in the paper to assess whether specificity plays a role in macroeconomics is to see how wage moderation in the Netherlands has affected productivity (TFP) growth. Using a vintage model (VM) as the null hypothesis and a vintage model with appropriability of quasi-rents (CH) as a description of the world with specificity, we see whether the development of certain indicators leads us to reject the CH model.

The paper discusses why it is difficult to make assessment concerning the role of specificity with aggregate and sectoral data. Further a preview is given of the possibilities to distinguish the models using micro-level data. Especially the ability to make non-standard aggregations and make special queries allows one to tailor series to conform to indicators which are expected to differ between both models on theoretical grounds. The number of firms which show an unusually large investment in a particular year is such a statistic; the figure would not have been generated through the traditional process of statistics bureaus, but requires retrospective analysis of the micro data.

The paper is still in a very preliminary form. Much work remains to be done to assess the robustness of the indicator on capital age to changes in methodological assumptions, selection of firms, changes in aggregation of asset categories, etc. Further work remains to be done on evaluating the short-term substitutability of capital and labor. Finally, the paper still requires some general statistics on the behavior of the chosen sample compared with the behavior of the universe of industrial firms, let alone the rest of the economy.

Beyond the preliminary nature of this paper, one can think of extensions which would make a more rigorous test of the two models possible. The VM model can be thought of as a special case of CH, namely the case where specificity between the factors is perfectly balanced so that no appropriation takes place. The hypothesis would then be that net specificity of capital in the economy was reduced following wage moderation. An open question would be whether institutional arrangements in the Netherlands have resulted in balanced specificity, thus solving the macroeconomic problems flagged by Caballero and Hammour.

Appendix A

Aggregate and sectoral data

The aggregate and sectoral data are sourced from the sectoral timeseries database of CPB, and are based on efforts to put National Income Accounts data from Statistics Netherlands on a common basis over time. The capital stock data are created using timeseries on investment by type and sector from 1950 through 1995, using the perpetual inventory method. Initial stocks (1948) are provided by Statistics Netherlands, along with information on mean service life. The PIM method using a stochastic mean service life, with a truncated normal distribution centred about the mean life, with a variance of one quarter the mean life, and truncation at 50 percent above and below the mean. Further, a beta-decay function using ϑ =.90 is applied to the remaining stock to reflect efficiency loss. Capital stock by type are aggregated to the sectoral level using expenditure shares, in order to create a measure of capital service inputs, following the methodology of Jorgenson et al (1987}. The user cost of capital needed to compute user-cost of capital is based on a long-bond and equity returns, and tax rate information from the CPB macro model FKSEC (1992) and sectoral information on tax deductability, accelerated depreciation allowances, and investment tax credits.

Micro-level data

The micro-level datasets are available on-site at CeReM, Statistics Netherlands. The data used in the study come from three sets of surveys, the production statistics (PS), the investment statistics (IS) and the capital stock survey (CS). The PS are an annual census of large manufacturing firms, and a survey of small firms (10 employees). Firms are queried about employment (in workers), sales, production, inventories, materials and energy use. Each year, on the order of 10000 firms are in the dataset. A balanced panel of firms from 1978 through 1993 can be made with about 6000 firms.[7]

The investment statistics, available from 1980 through 1993 provide information on investment spending by asset type by firm. The survey is smaller, with an integral count of the largest firms (500). A balanced panel containing observations of a firm for all years results in a selection of about 1400 firms.

The CS survey is a small sample of very large firms, with information on capital stocks, by asset type and by vintage. The sample is drawn from a rotating selection of industries (SBIs) and contains between 150 and 400 firms per year,

---

[7] See Abbring and Gautier (1997) for some notes on panel linking.

from 1983 through 1995. Owing to the sample selection method, only roughly 600 firms are sampled more than once throughout the period, usually with a 5 year span in-between observations.

Deflators for output, and materials are available at a 3-digit level, from Statistics Netherlands. Investment deflators by asset type also are from Statistics Netherlands.

Construction of timeseries of the capital stock for as large a group as possible occurs in steps. The reader should be warned that the methodology contains many untested assumptions. Results have not been tested as extensively for robustness to assumptions as I would like.

The first step was to use all firms that were observed twice over time to estimate the parameters for a mean stochastic service life PIM methodology. This can be done by using information on the quantity of capital in firm i of type j and vintage $\therefore$ observed in year $\therefore_0$ and comparing it to the quantity observed in $\therefore_1$. This can be done for all $i, j, \therefore$ observed in t_0. Stacking the observations over survey pairs, allowing for differences in time-span between observation allow one to run a non-linear regression to fit the chosen functional form (Truncated Normal).

The next step is to extend an observed vintage/type capital structure backwards in time for each firm by blowing up observed values with the estimated scrapping function. Then, a beta-decay is applied to vintage structure to create an annual stock for each firm for all years prior-and up to the survey year. The average age of the stock of a firm in each year is a (post-decay) stock weighted average of the age of each vintage. For years following the survey date, the scrapping function is applied to earlier vintages, and the investment data from IS is used for the latest vintage. All vintage values are than summed, after applying beta-decay. Age is a (post-decay) stock weighted average of age in each vintage. The above process is applied to aggregates of asset type, namely transport vehicles which is a sum of vehicles for internal and external use, and equipment.

TFP is constructed as a Solow residual, using cost-shares rather than expenditure shares as weights for factor inputs. Output is measured as value added, and factors of production are labor, transport vehicle stock and equipment stock.

Chart 1   Industry (IN)

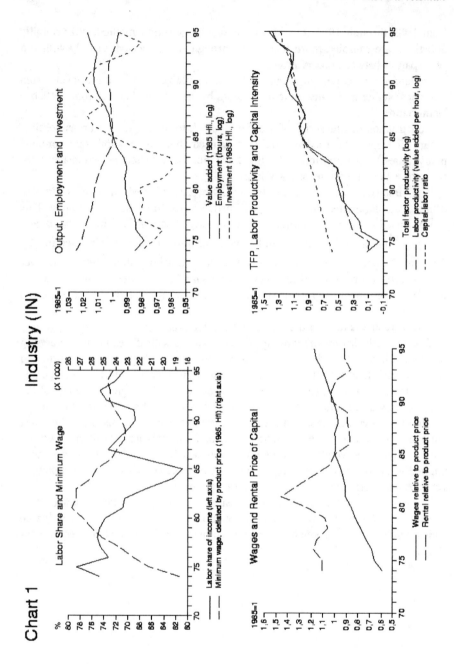

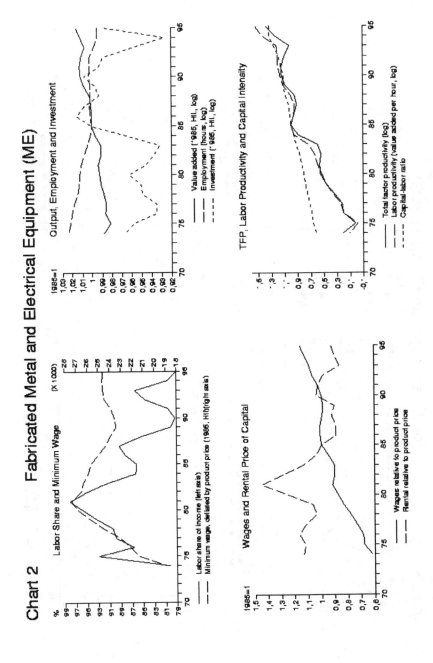

Chart 2   Fabricated Metal and Electrical Equipment (ME)

Chart 3   Food, Beverages and Tobacco (VG)

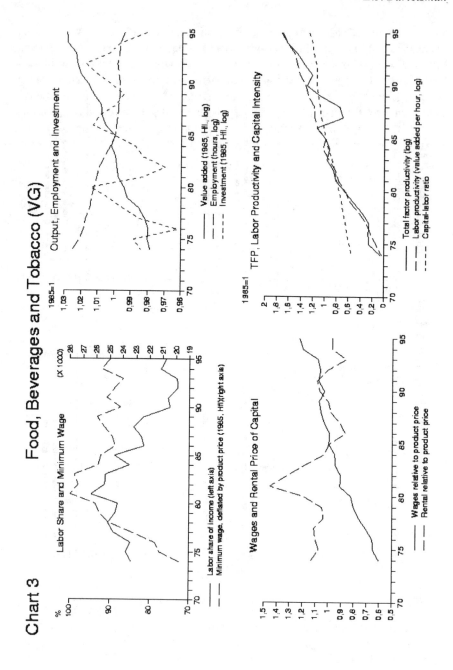

REFERENCES

Abbrin, J.H. and P.A. Gautier (1997), *"Gross Job Flow in Netherlands Manufacturing: A Panel Data Analysis,"* mimeo.

Bartelsman, E. J. and M. E. Doms (February 1997), *"Understanding Productivity: Lesson from Longitudinal Mirco Datasets"*, Proposal for review article.

Bovenberg, Lans A (september 1997)., *"Dutch employment growth: an analysis"*, CPB-report, 2 (2), 16-24.

Caballero, R.J. (May 1997), *"Aggregate Investment, a 90's View,"* mimeo.

____ and M.L. Hammour, (September 1996) *"The macroeconomics of specificity"*, NBER Working Paper Series 5757.

____ , E.M. Engel and J.C. Haltiwanger (1995), *"Plant-level Adjustment and Aggregate Investment Dynamics"*, in "Brookings Papers on Economic Activity" Washington, D.C. pp. 1350-1368.

Cooper, R., J. Haltiwanger and L. Power (1994), *"Machine replacement and the business cycle: Lumps and bumps"*, mimeo.

CPB (1992),. *FKSEC: A macro-econometric model of the Netherlands*, Nijmegen: Stenfert-Kroese.

____ (1997), *Challenging Neighbours*, Berlin: Springer Verlag.

Davis, S., J. Haltiwanger and S. Schuh (1996), *Job Creation and Job Destruction*, Cambridge, MA: MIT Press

Doms, M. E. (1993), *"Inter Fuel Substitution and Energy Technology Heterogeneity in U.A. Manufacturing"*, discussion paper CES 93-5, U.S. Bureau of Census, Center for Economic Studies March.

Dunne, T. and M.e. Doms (1993), *"An Investigation into Capital and Labor Adjustment at the Plant Level"*, mimeo, Center for Economic Studies.

Dunne, T., M. Roberts and L. Samuelson (1988), *"Patterns of Firm Entry and Exit in U.S. Manufacturing Industries"*, RAND Journal of Economics, *19* (4), pp. 495-515.

Fare R. (March 1994), *"Productivity Growth, Technical Progress, and Efficiency Change in Industrialized Countries"*, American Economic Review, *84* (1), pp. 66-83.

Jorgenson, D., F. Gollop and B. Fraumeni (1987), *Productivity and U.S. Economic Growth*, Cambridge: Harvard University Press.

Kleinknecht, A.H.(1994), *"Heeft Nederland een loongolf nodig?"*, Economisch Statistische Berichten, pp. 5-24.

Koopmans, C.l, (1997), *"Nemo: CPBs new energy model"*, CPB-report, *2* (2), 34-38.

Malcomson, J.M. (1997), *"Contracts, Hold-up and Labor Markets"*, Journal of Economic Literature, 35(4), 1916-57.

McGuckin, R.H. (1995), *"Establishment Microdata for Economic Research and Policy Analysis: Looking beyond the Aggregates"*, Journal of Business and Economic Statistics, *13* (1), 121-26.

IS MAXIMAL EFFICIENCY NECESSARILY OPTIMAL FOR FIRMS? A PANEL DATA ANALYSIS OF FIRMS TECHNICAL EFFICIENCY WITHIN AN EFFICIENCY WAGE FRAMEWORK

Pierre Blanchard[1] and Patrick Sevestre[2]

[1,2]*Erudite, Université Paris XII Val de Marne*

1 Introduction

There is a great amount of literature about the problem of measuring the firms relative technical efficiency. Indeed, productivity is a key factor in the determination of many fundamental variables in the economy, among which prices and wages. In a competitive market context, inefficient firms are likely to disappear and studying the origin of such inefficiencies can help in understanding the firm's destruction process. In non competitive markets, when a regulation exists, the evaluation of the relative productive efficiency of firms can be the base for pricing decisions: prices will equal marginal costs if the firm is efficient while if it is not, prices will be cut-off as an incentive for the firm to become more efficient. The implicit assumption made in this literature is that the greatest its technical efficiency, the better-off the firm is.

Besides this literature, another one exists which focuses on the question of the labour input efficiency. In particular, many studies have shown that there exists a link between the level of wages in a firm (relatively to the expected outside wage) and labour efficiency: the wage efficiency hypothesis, which can be justified on several grounds (cf. Akerloff and Yellen (1986)), cannot be ruled out, i.e. other things being equal, firms paying higher wages benefit from a more efficient labour input. In that context, the optimal behaviour of firms is not to reach the maximum possible efficiency in their use of labour, but the one which corresponds to the unity of the elasticity of the efficiency function with respect to the wage.

The aim of this paper is then to try to answer the following question which, to our knowledge, has been previously addressed in only one paper by Kumbhakar (1991): If the firms do have an efficiency wage policy, how does this policy affect their productive efficiency? In particular, are the most technically efficient firms necessarily at an optimum from the efficiency wage policy point of view? The structure of the paper is as follows: in section 2, we present the general theory of firms efficiency and how it can be combined with the efficiency wage hypothesis. Section 3 will be devoted to an econometric analysis of this issue, based on a panel of French firms. Section 4 will conclude.

2 Technical efficiency and the efficiency wage hypothesis

2.1 The technical efficiency of firms: a brief reminder

Allowing for possible technical inefficiency of firms leads to write their production function as:

$$Y_{it} = a_{it} \cdot f(X_{it}; \beta) \cdot \exp(\eta_{it}) \qquad 0 \le a_{it} \le 1$$

where a_{it} accounts for this potential inefficiency and η_{it} is a disturbance term. As noted in Cornwell and Schmidt (1995), most empirical models consider a logarithmic transformation of the production function, which leads to write the firm production function as:

$$\ln(Y_{it}) = \ln(f(X_{it}; \beta)) - \alpha_{it} + \eta_{it}$$

where $\alpha_{it} = -\ln(a_{it})$ represents the technical inefficiency of the firm, i.e. the amount of "lost output" due to its technically bad use of its inputs. The estimation of α_{it} (or that of a_{it}) raises two problems. First, α_{it} is obviously not identifiable in such a model if one does not make any further assumption. Identification relies on various possible assumptions: either distributional ones (e.g. see Aigner, Lovell and Schmidt (1977)) or, using panel data, assuming time constancy ($\alpha_{it} = \alpha_i$) or that α_{it} is a simple function of time (e.g. see Kumbhakar (1990)). Second, one has to ensure that the estimates are such that $\alpha_{it} \ge 0$, $\forall i, t$. This can be done by considering the difference $u_{it} = \max(\alpha_{it}) - \alpha_{it}$ or again, by making distributional assumptions (see Cornwell and Schmidt (1995) for a survey on these issues).

Once α_{it} is estimated, one can evaluate the relative efficiency of firms by computing $a_{it} = \exp(-u_{it})$.

2.2 The efficiency wage hypothesis

Ignoring, for the moment, the question of technical efficiency, let the production function of a firm be

$$Y_{it} = f(K_{it}, L_{it}^*, Z_{it}; \beta) \cdot \exp(\eta_{it})$$

where Y is the output, K the capital stock, Z stands for other variables such as capital vintage, technical progress, and so on,. and L^* for the quantity of labour measured in efficient units. Assuming that there exists an efficiency-wage relationship amounts to consider that L^* is defined as $L \cdot e(w)$ where L is a physical measure of the quantity of labour used (e.g. the number of employees or that of work hours) and $e(w)$ is the efficiency function. $e(w)$ accounts for the fact that the same physical quantity of labour can be more or less efficient, depending on its "productive" characteristics; characteristics which are supposed to depend on the wage w; more specifically, the firm can have interest in setting the wage above the market level, because of this positive relationship between the wage and workers efficiency. Besides the original justification proposed by Leibenstein (1957), this relationship can be justified on several grounds. According to Shapiro and Stiglitz (1984), the firm can set the wage above the market level in order to discourage its workers to shirk. Another justification rests on the existence of labour turnover costs (cf. Stiglitz (1974)). A third one is proposed by Weiss (1980): it assumes that firms suffer from an imperfect information about the quality of applicants to the jobs they offer and that an higher wage increases the probability of recruiting a good candidate. Finally, Akerlof (1984) justifies the efficiency wage policy on sociological grounds.

Following Solow (1979), let L_e the quantity of labour measured in efficiency units be defined as $L \cdot e(w)$ where L is the actual number of workers and $e(w)$ is the efficiency (or effort) function which depends on the wage w. Moreover, suppose that the effort function is such that $e'(w) > 0$ and $e''(w) < 0$, it can be shown that the optimal behaviour of firms is to set the wage at a level where the elasticity of $e(w)$, the efficiency function, with respect to the wage, equals unity,

$$\varepsilon_{e/w} = \frac{\partial e(w)}{\partial e} \frac{w}{e} = 1 \qquad [1]$$

At this point, it is interesting to note that there is no reason for all firms to face the same effort function (because of differences in the possibility to control the workers effort or in the turnover costs for example). Then, two firms using the same amount of physical inputs will not necessarily have the same level of production. This does not mean that one is technically efficient while the other one is not. Indeed, the difference in their productive performance may reflect the fact that they do not apply the same efficiency wage policy. On the other hand, it is difficult to suppose that all the efficiency (or inefficiency) differences between firms come only from the efficiency wage policy chosen by firms. It is likely that some unobserved factors (like managerial ability, random productivity shocks and so on, may explain a part of the observed differences in their productivity level.

2.3 Technical efficiency and the efficiency wage hypothesis

As said above, the optimal behaviour of firms is to set up the wage at a level where the elasticity of $e(w)$, the efficiency function, with respect to the wage, equals unity. Again, because this function is not the same for all firms, the wage level may differ across firms. Moreover, since the efficiency is an increasing function of the paid wage, and that the optimal wage is not infinity, the optimal efficiency does not correspond to its maximum. Indeed, firms paying their employees above the efficiency wage level will benefit from a greater productive efficiency but this will not be optimal, i.e. this will not correspond to their maximum possible profit. On the other hand, firms paying wages under the "efficient level", will suffer from an insufficient level of labour efficiency, which will be part of their apparent technical inefficiency. Then, in this context, the measure of the optimal level of efficiency is not necessarily the maximum. Indeed, it should rather be the *maximum one among firms in which the elasticity of the labour efficiency with respect to the wage is unity.* This way of measuring the optimal efficiency presents the advantage of avoiding to (implicitly) assume that attaining the maximum efficiency is necessarily optimal footnote In this respect, our approach differs from that adopted by Kumbhakar (1991). In a context where firms do have an efficiency wage policy, this can no more be considered as true.

3 The evaluation of the optimal level of efficiency

Let us consider the following translog production function, where the efficiency wage assumption is taken into account by including the firm relative wage, RW, i.e. the ratio of the wage paid by the firm to the outside option wage[1]:

$$
\begin{aligned}
\ln(Y_{it}) = & a_0 + a_1 \ln(L_{it}) + a_2 \ln(RW_{it}) + a_3 \ln(K_{it}) + a_4 \cdot (t - A_{it}) + b_1 (\ln(L_{it}))^2 \\
& + b_2 (\ln(RW_{it}))^2 + b_3 (\ln(K_{it}))^2 + b_4 \cdot (t - A_{it})^2 + c_1 \ln(L_{it}) \cdot \ln(RW_{it}) \\
& + c_2 \ln(L_{it}) \cdot \ln(K_{it}) + c_3 \ln(L_{it}) \cdot (t - A_{it}) + c_4 \ln(RW_{it}) \cdot \ln(K_{it}) \\
& + c_5 \ln(RW_{it}) \cdot (t - A_{it}) + c_6 \ln(K_{it}) \cdot (t - A_{it}) - \alpha_{it} + \varepsilon_{it}
\end{aligned}
\tag{2}
$$

where Y_{it} is the value-added of the firm i at time t, L_{it} accounts for its labour input (in terms of physical units - in our case the number of employees in the firm), K_{it} for its capital stock and A_{it} the age of the equipments (so that $t - A_{it}$ accounts for the technical progress incorporated in these equipments).

Estimating this production function allows us to get estimates of the two following elasticities, i.e. omitting the indexes i and t:

$$
\varepsilon_{Y/RW} = a_2 + 2b_2 \ln(RW) + c_1 \ln(L) + c_4 \ln(K) + c_5 (t - A)
\tag{3}
$$

and

$$
\varepsilon_{Y/L} = a_1 + 2b_1 \ln(L) + c_1 \ln(RW) + c_2 \ln(K) + c_3 (t - A)
\tag{4}
$$

Then, one can get a measure of the elasticity of the labour efficiency function by noting that:

$$
\varepsilon_{Y/RW} = \varepsilon_{Y/e} \cdot \varepsilon_{e/RW}
\tag{5}
$$

and noting that $\varepsilon_{Y/e} = \varepsilon_{Y/L}$ as long as, as usually assumed (cf. Solow (1979)), the production function is initially expressed in terms of the efficient amount of labour, which is obtained by multiplying the physical measure of

---

[1] We could also include other factors affecting the efficiency of workers, such as the unemployment level (see Shapiro and Stiglitz (1984)), or the rate of supervisors in the firm (see Leonard (1987))

labour (here the number of workers) by the efficiency function $e(RW)$. Then, *without assuming any particular form of the efficiency wage function*[2], one can get an estimate of its elasticity by simply computing:

$$\varepsilon_{e/RW} = \frac{\varepsilon_{Y/RW}}{\varepsilon_{Y/L}} \qquad [6]$$

It must be noticed that this elasticity is firm specific and does not require the efficiency-wage relationship to be the same across firms.

The estimation of this production function also allows to evaluate the relative technical efficiency of firms. Indeed, let us first assume that the inefficiency is constant ($\alpha_{it} = \alpha_i$). Then, using panel data, one can obtain an estimate of α_i as:

$$
\begin{aligned}
\hat{\alpha}_i = \ln(\overline{Y_i}) - (\hat{a}_0 + \hat{a}_1 \overline{\ln(L_i)} + \hat{a}_2 \overline{\ln(RW_i)} + \hat{a}_3 \overline{\ln(K_i)} + \hat{a}_4 \cdot \overline{(t-A_i)} + \hat{b}_1 \overline{(\ln(L_i))^2} \\
+ \hat{b}_2 \overline{(\ln(RW_i))^2} + \hat{b}_3 \overline{(\ln(K_i))^2} + \hat{b}_4 \cdot \overline{(t-A_i)^2} + \hat{c}_1 \overline{\ln(L_i) \cdot \ln(RW_i)} \\
+ \hat{c}_2 \overline{\ln(L_i) \cdot \ln(K_i)} + \hat{c}_3 \overline{\ln(L_i) \cdot (t-A_i)} + \hat{c}_4 \overline{\ln(RW_i) \cdot \ln(K_i)} \\
+ \hat{c}_5 \overline{\ln(RW_i) \cdot (t-A_i)} + \hat{c}_6 \overline{\ln(K_i) \cdot (t-A_i)})
\end{aligned}
\qquad [7]
$$

where $\overline{Z_i}$ is the mean over the T_i observations of the variable Z for each firm i.

Then, an estimate of the usual relative efficiency measurement is obtained by computing $Eff_i = \exp(-(\max(\alpha_i) - \alpha_i))$.

Again, this is not necessarily the best way to evaluate the distance of firms efficiency from its optimal level since, as said above, the latter does not necessarily correspond to the maximum observed efficiency. To be more concrete, a firm can reach an high level of labour efficiency by paying high wages but this does not necessarily leads to its maximum profit. In that case, it seems preferable to compute the distance from the optimal efficiency by evaluating $Eff_i = \exp(-(\max\big|_{\varepsilon_{e/RW}=1}(\alpha_i) - \alpha_i))$. Then, it can appear that firms with the maximum technical efficiency are not necessarily in a better situation than firms with a lower efficiency. Indeed, firms can appear to be "over-productive", in that their productive efficiency relies on too high wages, with respect to the optimal level, given by the condition $\varepsilon_{e/RW} = 1$. Then, one should try to

---

[2] Levine (1992) also specified an efficiency wage model without an explicit effort function, although his model rests on a Cobb-Douglas production function.

disentagle the true "technical inefficiency" from the over or under wage efficiency.

4 The econometric model and its estimation

4.1 The data

The data we use comes from an unbalanced sample of 824 different firms (5201 observations) observed over the period 1979-1988. There are about 500 firms by year (cf. table 1).

Table 1 Number of firms by year

1979	1980	1981	1982	1983	1984	1985	1986	1987	1988
546	527	485	528	487	524	524	530	511	539

In order to estimate our model, we extract from the previous sample all the firms observed on a minimum of 3 years. We obtain an unbalanced sample of 615 firms, observed over the same period; the total number of observations is reduced to 4869. The following table provides some information about this sample:

Table 2 Definition and descriptive statistics for main variables

Variable	Definition	Mean	Std. Dev.
Y	Real value added	168290	311750
L	Nb of workers	1171.50	1917.56
L_s	Nb of skilled workers	329.33	723.68
L_u	Nb of unskilled workers	842.16	1321.95
K	Real capital stock	361664	900096
$t\text{-}age$	Year less age of equipments	76.34	4.19
W_s	Real wage for skilled workers	107.7	26.97
W_u	Real wage for unskilled workers	53.87	12.22
Y/L	Average productivity of labour	138.66	49.75
K/L	Capital to labour ratio	266.23	294.22
Qual	% of skilled workers in total employment	0.28	0.155
RW_s	Relative real wage for skilled workers	1.0235	0.255
RW_u	Relative real wage for unskilled workers	1.0635	0.221

Our sample consists of large firms as shown by table 3.

Table 3 Distribution of firms size in 1988

Size	% of firms	% of firms in BIC 1988[3]
]0,20[	0.2	30.2
[20-50[	3.0	46.3
[50-200[	20.0	18.1
[200-500[	18.7	3.5
[500 and more[	58.7	2.0

One point must be noted in the computation of the real relative wage for skilled and unskilled workers. If we note AW_s the alternative (real) mean wage for skilled workers computed as the (real) mean wage of firms belonging to the same quartile of labour force skill level, U_s the national unemployment rate for skilled employees and UB_s the unemployment benefits by unemployed for the skilled workers scaled by the ratio W_s/W, the workers's outside opportunities (OO_s) is computed as $(1 - U_s) \cdot AW_s + U_s \cdot UB_s$. The real relative wage for skilled workers, RW_s, is then computed as OO_s/W_s. For unskilled workers, the same principle is applied.

4.2 The econometric model

The model we estimate is an extension of the Translog production function that we have presented above. Indeed, we split the worforce into two categories of workers, the skilled ones (mainly technicians, commercial and administrative managerial staff, engineers and executives), and "unskilled ones", who mainly regroup the blue collars as well as the unskilled administrative and commercial staff. We consider that these two groups of workers have specific efficiency functions so that we include the relative wages of these two categories in the Translog production function. The estimation results are presented in the table below:

---

[3] BIC, Déclarations Bénéfices Industriels et Commerciaux (BIC) is a database of balanced sheets about firms with 20 employees or more, built up by INSEE, from which our sample is extracted. These data were completed by information about employment structure by skill (from the surveys "Structure des Emplois" (ESE), INSEE) and about wages by skill (from the survey "Déclarations Annuelles de Données Sociales, (DADS), INSEE) in addition to data on value added by sector and year and on unemployment rates by year.

Table 4 Estimation results[4]

Variable	All variables		Insignificant variables removed (at 5%)	
	$\hat{\beta}$	$s_{\hat{\beta}}$	$\hat{\beta}$	$s_{\hat{\beta}}$
$\ln L_s$	0.3696	0.0864	0.3185	0.0600
$\ln L_u$	0.7204	0.0942	0.5995	0.0651
$\ln K$	-0.1563	0.1082	-	-
t-age	0.0289	0.0200	0.0194	0.0063
$\ln^2 L_s$	0.0766	0.0045	0.0746	0.0038
$\ln^2 L_u$	0.1025	0.0063	0.1056	0.0060
$\ln^2 K$	0.0307	0.0068	0.0241	0.0041
$(t$-age$)^2$	-0.00007	0.00011	-	-
$\ln L_s \ln L_u$	-0.1571	0.0083	-0.1614	0.0070
$\ln L_s \ln K$	-0.0095	0.0076	-	-
$\ln L_s (t$-age$)$	0.0036	0.00084	0.0034	0.0007
$\ln L_u \ln K$	-0.00472	0.0106	-0.0469	0.0100
$\ln L_u (t$-age$)$	-0.0013	0.00097	-	-
$\ln K (t$-age$)$	-0.0015	0.00096	-0.0023	0.0067
$\ln RW_s$	0.1338	0.2234	-	-
$\ln RW_u$	-1.1092	0.2803	-	-
$\ln^2 RW_s$	0.0977	0.0306	0.0954	0.0300
$\ln^2 RW_u$	0.1032	0.0428	0.1001	0.0427
$\ln L_s \ln RW_s$	0.1737	0.0164	0.1706	0.01147
$\ln L_s \ln RW_u$	-0.2070	0.0223	-0.2158	0.0213
$\ln L_u \ln RW_u$	0.1478	0.0218	0.1394	0.0214
$\ln L_u \ln RW_s$	-0.1428	0.0190	-0.1451	0.0145
$\ln RW_s \ln RW_u$	-0.0634	0.0547	-0.1769	0.0524
$\ln K \ln RW_s$	-0.0078	0.0164	-	-
$(t$-age$) \ln RW_s$	0.0042	0.0023	0.0052	0.0008
$\ln K \ln RW_u$	0.02789	0.0198	0.0450	0.0178
$(t$-age$)\ln RW_u$	0.0177	0.0028	0.0175	0.0027
	R^2=0.609		R^2=0.608	
	F=221.48		F=341.66	
	4869 obs.		4869 obs.	

Using these estimates, we have been able to compute the elasticities of production to changes in the various inputs. These estimates being firm (and time) specific, we have evaluated them, for each firm, at its own mean value of

---

[4] The regression also contains 9 industry and 10 time dummies. Due to space, their coefficient estimates and standard errors are not reported here.

the variables; e.g. for the elasticity of production with respect to the skilled labour, we have computed:

$$\varepsilon_{(Y/L)i} = a_{ls} + 2b_{ls}\overline{\ln(L_s)}_i + c_{ws}\overline{\ln(RW_s)}_i + d_{ls}\overline{\ln(RW_u)}_i + e_{ls}\overline{\ln(L_u)}_i + f_{ls}\overline{\ln(K)}_i \qquad [8]$$
$$+ g_{ls}\overline{(t-A)}_i$$

where $\overline{Z}_i$ is the mean of the variable Z for each firm. The following table presents the mean and standard errors of these individual elasticities[5].

Table 5 Statistics about the estimated firm level elasticities

elasticity	mean	std. dev.	minimum	maximum
ε_{Y/L_s}	0.344	0.133	0.008	0.744
ε_{Y/L_u}	0.534	0.145	0.111	0.958
$\varepsilon_{Y/K}$	0.096	0.050	-0.051	0.259
$\varepsilon_{Y/t-age}$	0.0097	0.0046	-0.003	0.023
ε_{Y/RW_s}	0.360	0.133	-0.017	0.771
ε_{Y/RW_u}	0.446	0.155	-0.014	0.871

As can be seen, although there is obviously some variation in the individual estimates, these elasticities take quite plausible values which we take as an indication that subsequent calculations can be considered as reliable. Indeed, in order to answer the question of the possible existence of a difference between the maximum and the optimal productive efficiency of firms, we need to estimate the elasticity of the efficiency functions of our two groups of workers with respect to their relative wage. This estimation just amounts to compute, for skilled workers:

$$\varepsilon_{e_s/RW_s} = \varepsilon_{Y/RW_s} / \varepsilon_{Y/L_s} \qquad [9]$$

with

---

[5] The complete distributions of these elasticities are presented in an appendix.

$$\varepsilon_{Y/RW_s} = a_{ws} + 2b_{ws} \ln(RW_s) + c_{ws} \ln(L_s) + d_{ws} \ln(RW_u) + e_{ws} \ln(L_u) + f_{ws} \ln(K)$$
$$+ g_{ws}(t - A) \qquad [10]$$

and

$$\varepsilon_{Y/RW_s} = a_{ls} + 2b_{ls} \ln(L_s) + c_{ls} \ln(RW_s) + d_{ls} \ln(RW_u) + e_{ls} \ln(L_u) + f_{ls} \ln(K)$$
$$+ g_{ls}(t - A) \qquad [11]$$

and accordingly for the unskilled workers. The obtained elasticities are summarized in the table below:

Table 6 Statistics about the estimated firm level elasticities of effort

elasticities	mean	std. dev.	minimum	maximum
ε_{e/RW_s}	1.060	0.231	-2.073	3.326
ε_{e/RW_u}	0.825	0.172	-0.059	1.415

What we can observe from these figures is that the elasticity of the efficiency function of unskilled workers is, on average, below unity while that of skilled workers is, on the contrary, just above 1. In order to test whether these elasticities are significantly different from 1, which is the optimal value, we have computed their standard error and tested their value for unity. It appears that we must reject the hypothesis that both elasticities are not unity in 61% of cases. We reject it in 23% of cases for the skilled workers and in 49% of cases for unskilled workers. Only 11% of firms are not at an optimum for the 2 categories of workers.

Table 7 Optimality in the efficiency wage policy: Mean elasticity of effort with respect to the relative wage for skilled and unskilled workers[6].

	N	ε_e / RW_s	ε_e / RW_u
optimality for s and u	239	1.027	0.947
optimality for s only	233	1.080	0.715
optimality for u only	76	1.047	0.905
optimality for none	67	1.125	0.681

This means that most firms have an optimal efficiency wage policy for their skilled workers. On the contrary, an unoptimal efficiency wage policy seems to be quite frequent for unskilled workers. Moreover, it appears a slight negative correlation (-0.08, significantly different from 0) between these two elasticities: a too large elasticity of the efficiency of skilled workers seems to be associated with a too low one for unskilled workers. In other words, since the difference to one of the values taken by these elasticities reflect the difference between the optimal value of the efficiency wage and the paid wage, it seems that firms compensate the "too high" relative wages of their skilled workers by "too low" ones for unskilled workers.

At this point, we are able to compute different measures of the firms relative efficiency. First, we have computed several measures of their technical efficiency by taking as "the best" either the observed absolute maximum in the sample, or, to avoid dependency on possible outliers, on the 95th and the 90th percentiles of the efficiency. We have also considered relative efficiency with respect to the same references but within the sub-sample of firms having an optimal efficiency wage policy, i.e. of firms for which the elasticities of the efficiency functions for the two groups of workers is not significantly different from one.

---

[6] The sample has been split on the basis of a test of unity of the elasticities of the efficiency function for skilled and unskilled workers, at the firm level, i.e. we have computed the statistic $\left| (\varepsilon_e / RW - 1) / \sigma_s \right|$ for each firm and compared it to the theoretical value of the Student, where σ_ε .is the estimated standart error of the elasticities estimated firm by firm.

Table 8 Relative technical efficiency and optimality of the efficiency wage policy

category	N	mean Max	mean $P95$	mean $P90$	mean $Max_{|WE}$	mean $P95_{|WE}$	mean $P90_{|WE}$
Max		5.75	5.27	5.16	5.67	5.36	5.19
full sample	615	0.453	0.730	0.816	0.490	0.670	0.795
optimality for s and u	239	0.463	0.746	0.834	0.501	0.685	0.813
optimality for s only	233	0.439	0.707	0.790	0.474	0.649	0.771
optimality for u only	76	0.467	0.751	0.840	0.504	0.690	0.819
optimality for none	67	0.450	0.725	0.810	0.486	0.665	0.789

The main conclusion that can be drawn from these estimates is that the differences between the two evaluations of the relative efficiency of firms are not very strong. This seems to indicate that most efficient firms (from the technical point of view) also have an optimal efficiency wage policy. Then, the possibility that we considered that some firms could be "over-efficient" appears to be non relevant. On the contrary, firms which are technically inefficient are, for a non negligible part of them, also "inefficient" in their way of optimizing the efficiency of their workers.

5 Conclusion

This paper aims at evaluating the impact of a wage efficiency policy on the relative technical efficiency of firms. We estimate a translog production function including an efficiency wage argument. The advantage of this production function in comparison with a Cobb-Douglas one that the former allows more flexibility in the representation of the production technology and in the wage efficiency argument. It also allows to take into account firms heterogeneity in a better way. In particular, the wage efficiency relationship may be different across firms. The model is estimated on an unbalanced panel data of 615 French firms observed at least 3 years between 1979 and 1988. Due to the short period covered, the model allows only for time-invariant inefficiency. Four mains results are found.

First, an optimal wage efficiency policy for the two categories others we consider (skilled and unskilled) is applied by 39% of firms. This figure goes up to 77% for the skilled labour force and to 51% for the unskilled one.

Second, including a wage efficiency argument in the production function leads to an estimate of the mean relative technical efficiency of firms which is larger than the one we obtain without taking it into account (45,3% versus 36%). Again, this is an illustration that differences in the wage-efficiency relationship may explain why two firms using the same amount of physical inputs will not necessarily have the same level of production.

Third, from a theoretical point of view, it appears preferable to calculate the technical efficiency by reference to the maximum technical efficiency for the firms which are optimal in their wage efficiency policy. In doing so, relative technical efficiency grows from 45.3% to 49%. This difference is not very strong but indicates that firms having an optimal efficiency wage policy are slightly more efficient than others.

Last, an optimal wage efficiency policy for unskilled workers seems to be applied in only 51% of firms. This surprisingly low proportion has to be studied more thoroughly.

Indeed, this is probably not the whole story. This last result may reflects that firms, due to labour adjustment costs, cannot adjust their physical amount of inputs (mainly for unskilled workers) instantaneously, which we do not take into account here. Moreover, we have modelled only a kind of inefficiency, the one coming from the wage policy, which has both technical and allocative efficiency consequences; but we have ignored the question of the optimality in the physical inputs choices by firms (i.e. the more usual allocative efficiency question). In fact, a full joint treament of all aspects of allocative and technical efficiencies within a wage efficiency framework, is clearly required.

Appendix

Figure 1 Elasticity of work effort for skilled workers with respect to skilled workers relative wage

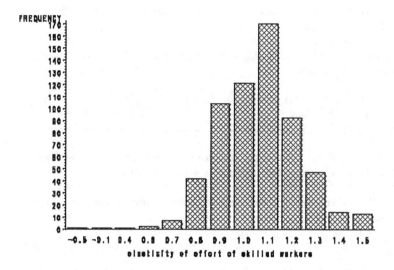

Figure 2 Elasticity of work effort for unskilled workers with respect to unskilled workers relative wage

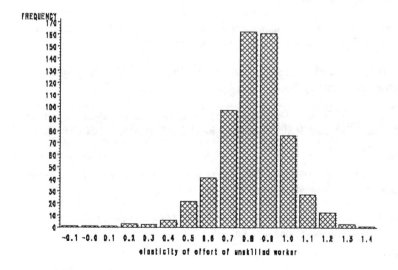

REFERENCES

Aigner D., C.A.K. Lovell, P. Schmidt (1977), *"Formulation and Estimation of Stochastic Frontier Production Function Models"*, Journal of Econometrics, 6, pp. 21-37.

Akerlof G. A, (1984), *"Gift Exchange and Efficiency Wages: Four Views"*, American Economic Review, 74, May.

Akerlof G. A., J. L. Yellen, (1986), *Efficiency Wage Models of the Labour Market*, Cambridge University Press.

Cornwell C., P. Schmidt, (1996) *"Production Frontier and Efficiency Measurement"*, chapter n°32 in L.Matyas and P. Sevestre (eds), The Econometrics of Panel data, A Handbook of the Theory with Applications, 2nd edition, Kluwer Academic Publishers.

Kumbhakar S. B., (1990), *"Production Frontiers, Panel Data and Time-Varying Technical Inefficiency"*, Journal of Econometrics, 46, pp. 201-212.

Kumbhakar S. B., (1991), *"Work Effort, Technical Efficiency and Productivity Growth"*, Econometric Review, 10(1), pp. 101-123.

Leibenstein H., (1957), *Economic Backwardness and Economic Growth*, New-York, Wiley.

Levine D. I. (1992*), "Can Wage Increases Pay for Themselves? Tests with a Production Function"*, Economic Journal, September, pp. 1102-1115.

Leonard J.S., (1987), *"Carrots and Sticks: Pay, Supervision and Turnover"*, Journal of Labor Economics, 5(4), October, pp. S136-S152.

Shapiro C., J.E. Stiglitz, (1984), *"Equilibrium Unemployment as a Worker Discipline Device"* American Economic Review, 74,June, pp. 433-444.

Solow R. (1979), *"Another possible Source of Wage Stickiness"*, Journal of Macroeconomics, Winter, pp. 79-82.

Stiglitz J.E., (1974), *"Alternative Theories of Wage Determination and Unemployment in LDC's: the Labor Turnover Model"*, Quarterly Journal of Economics, LXXXVIII, 2, pp. 194-227.

Wadhwani S. B., M. Wall, (1991), *"A Direct Test of the Efficiency Wage Model Using Micro-Data"*, Oxford Economic Papers, 43, pp. 529-548.

Weiss A., (1980), *"Job Queues and Layoffs in Labor Markets with Flexible Wages"*, Journal of Political Economy, June, pp. 526-538.

PRODUCTIVITY, COMPETITION, FINANCIAL PRESSURE AND CORPORATE GOVERNANCE - SOME EMPIRICAL EVIDENCE·

Mogens Dilling-Hansen[1], Tor Eriksson[2], Erik Strøjer Madsen[3] and Valdemar Smith[4]

[1]Dept. of Management, Un. of Aarhus; Centre for Industrial Economics, Un. of Copenhagen.
[2] Dept. of Economics, Aarhus Sch. of Business; Centre for Labour Economics and Social Research (CLS), Un. Of Aarhus and Aarhus Sch. of Business.
[3] Dept. of Economics, Aarhus Sch. of Business; Centre for Industrial Economics, Un. of Copenhagen.
[4]The Danish Inst. for Studies in Research and Research Policy, Un. of Aarhus; Centre for Industrial Economics, Un. of Copenhagen.

1 Introduction

In this paper we examine the relationship between the productivity of firms and the pressure from their shareholders, debtholders and the competitors in their product market. There are remarkably few empirical studies on firm productivity[1] compared to the large number of empirical studies on other firm performances - profitability in particular - and market competition carried out in the sixties and up through the eighties. This lack of empirical studies on firm level productivity differentials is surprising for two reasons.

Firstly, the theoretical discussions among economists on firm productivity and competition are almost as old as economics itself. It was discussed already when Adam Smith wrote in his Wealth of Nations that monopoly is a great enemy to good management and has since then constituted one of the perennials in economic analysis. More recently in the sixties, Leibenstein (1966) invented the term X-efficiency for situations, where firms have high costs due to a weak

---

· Acknowledgements: We are grateful to participants at CAED'98 Conference in Bergamo for comments and to Torben T. Pedersen for excellent research assistance.

[1] There are surprisingly few studies of the relationship between competition and productivity at firm or establishment levels; see Haskel (1992), Nickell, Wadhwani and Wall (1992) and Blanchflower and Machin (1996) for some notable exceptions. These studies, as well as Nickell (1996), have been concerned with productivity developments in the UK during the Thatcher era.

external competitive pressure in their markets. Besides external market conditions, also the internal organization of firms may affect their productivity. Baumol (1959) was the first who studied how the separation of ownership from control of the firm may affect the behavior of the firm, when profit maximization is substituted with maximization of the firms turnover. Another important strand in the literature is Oliver Williamson's (1964) pioneering work which began the opening of the black box of firms among economists. Despite the theoretical developments and the lively debates associated with them, evidence based on quantitative analyses of the relationship between competition and corporate performance has been relatively scant.

Secondly, from an economic perspective changes in firms' productivity are more important than changes in firm performance as measured by their profit rate or mark-up rate. The main theoretical idea behind the studies on firm performance is that firms with substantial market power will benefit from this. The monopoly rents captured in the market can then be shared among the shareholders, managers and other employees in the firm. Beside the inefficiency of a lower output in the monopolised industries, the result is merely a problem of distribution of monopoly rents between the consumers and the different agents within the firm. The impact on firm productivity of market competition or the organisation of the firms also have a more direct effect on the efficient use of the resources in the firms. Moreover, changes in total factor productivity are important for economic growth; in fact, according to a large number of growth accounting studies it is the key component in growth in the developed countries.

One major advantage of the data set used in this study is that it covers a broad cross-section of firms of different sizes. A major criticism of earlier studies of the performance of firms is that they have predominantly been concerned with large firms. This is likely to give rise to severe sample selection problems. For example, owner-controlled firms which grow large over time while their owners retain control of the firm are likely to be exceptionally well run. Thus, sampling only big firms means that you end up with the most efficient owner-controlled firms in the sample. This will, of course, distort any inference regarding comparisons of manager and owner-controlled firms.

Another limitation of previous studies is that they are concerned with only one potentially important factor at a time. Thus, they do not take into account that in practice many factors external to the firm may affect its performance and that they may reinforce or act as substitutes for each other. The latter may be important not least from a policy perspective. The remainder of the paper is organized as follows. The data set and the empirical model used in this study are presented in section 3. The empirical results are presented and discussed in section 4, and section 5 concludes the paper.

2 Theoretical background

In this section we discuss the different theories which have focused on the development in firms' productivity and its relation to market competition and the organisation or management of the firm. Some of the new empirical studies in this field are briefly discussed as well.

2.1 Competition

The literature on competition (see *e.g.* Short (1994) and Nickell (1995)) focuses on two main mechanisms whereby competition influences firm behaviour. The first is that competition improves managerial performance and the second is that competition may be good for firms' innovation activities.

Lack of competition gives rise to monopoly rents which in turn leads to slacking managers and as a consequence of that, lack of effort from other employees as well. However, owners of monopolistic firms are also interested in reducing managerial slack and one way to accomplish that is to set up incentive schemes which link managerial and firm performance to managerial compensation. In order for these incentives to be effective, the owners have to be able to assess the performance of the managers. As shown by *e.g.* Holmström (1982), the comparison possibilities are greater the more managers there are in comparable firms (in the same industry).[2]

Another effect of competition discussed in the literature (see *e.g.* Martin (1993)) starts off from the plausible assumption that as competition is increased, firms' profits become more sensitive to the actions of their managers. Thus, if increased competition gives rise to an increase in the firm's demand elasticity, this may cause owners to try to induce the managers to put forth more effort and reduce inefficiency. But increased competition may also lead to a reduction in demand for the individual firm which results in lower managerial effort. The net effect of these two impacts (increased demand elasticity and reduction in demand) is *a priori* ambiguous. If the demand reduction effect dominates, the outcome may actually be lower managerial effort and hence a worsening of corporate performance.

Although most research has focused on the behaviour of management, monopoly rents may also affect the performance of other employees. The recent

---

[2] As discussed by Nickell (1995) referring to an unpublished paper by John Vickers, there does not have to be an explicit reward scheme. If current performance influences future earnings via its signal of managerial ability, the existence of other firms in the industry generates shaper incentives because unobserved productivity shocks are likely to be correlated across firms in the industry.

literature on rent sharing in the labour market has produced some empirical evidence indicating that rent sharing is quite important for wage determination; see Oswald (1996) for a survey and a discussion. Of course, another form in which rents can be captured is reduced effort. Thus, this is another mechanism through which lack of competition may lead to lower productivity.

2.2 Innovation activities

The Schumpeterian view that competition is not necessarily good for innovation (rather the reverse as firms in concentrated markets can more easily appropriate the returns to their R&D investments) has spurred a huge, still growing number of studies of the relationship between market structure and R&D investments or innovation activities of firms. As already noted by Arrow (1962), there are two opposing forces at work here. There is, on one hand, the replacement effect from the competitive firm gaining more at the margin from innovating than a monopoly, and on the other hand, the efficiency effect due to strategical innovating behaviour of monopolists to raise the barriers for new entrants into their markets. Accounting for the possibility of spillover effects suggests that the competitive firms have less incentives to innovate than monopolies which appropriate all the gains. However, if innovation activities are associated with learning by doing elements, they may still be worthwhile pursuing and spillovers may be less a problem. *A priori* the net effect remains ambiguous, though.

2.3 Financial pressure

Beginning with Baumol (1959), numerous studies have documented and explained how firms and their managers are allowed to engage in non-present value maximising behaviour such as bad acquisitions and other bad investments (so called pet projects). Jensen's (1986, 1988) free cash flow theory offers an explanation for such behaviour. In short, the theory says that weak owner control of management leads to the free cash flow (that is, earnings in excess of that required to finance projects with positive net present value) being wasted rather than returned to the investors.

Free cash flow theory also implicates that debt may have a disciplinary effect on managerial performance. This is because interest payments on debt have to be paid (and therefore reduce the free cash flow), whereas dividend payments to the owners are at least to some extent decided upon by the top management of the firm. Debt, therefore, restricts the discretion of managers and increases the threat of bankruptcy. Consequently, the theory predicts that a higher debt burden is associated with better firm performance.[3] Testing this prediction is complicated by the fact that if managers want to avoid being closely monitored by their debtholders, they have an incentive to finance projects internally. As a result, (especially large) manager controlled firms may have a higher degree of retained earnings, a lower debt ratio and a lower return on investments.

2.4 Corporate governance

The growing body of corporate governance studies[4] suggests that it does matter whether a firm is controlled by the managers or by the owners. Due to the differences in the objective functions of owners and managers, the separation of ownership from control may have behavioural implications for the firms. However, there is a continuing debate about the limits to managerial discretion imposed by the competition in managerial labour market and compensation packages with explicit rewards for firm performance. As noted above, there may also be other stakeholders than the owners of the firm, in particular banks and other debtholders, who may exercise control and need to be considered in a full analysis.

3 The empirical model and data

The empirical model, following Nickell (1996) and Nickell, Nicolitsas and Dryden (1997), is a standard Cobb-Douglas production function (in natural logarithms) augmented with variables for competition in the product market, financial pressure and corporate governance:

$$y_{it} = \beta_1 n_{it} + \beta_2 k_{it} + \beta_3 h_{jt} + X'\gamma \qquad [1]$$

where y_{it} is the ith firm's turnover in year t deflated by a 3-digit (when available, 4-digit) industry-specific price deflator, n_{it} is the number of employees in the firm, k_{it} is the firm's capital stock deflated by an aggregate capital goods

---

[3] The alternative here is the famous Modigliani-Miller theorem according to which the financial structure of a firm in equilibrium is independent of its performance (and market value).

[4] See Short (1994), Mayer (1996), Berglöf (1996) and Shleifer and Vishny (1997) for some recent surveys.

price index, h_{jt} is an index of capacity utilisation in industry j, and X is a vector of firm characteristics (ownership type and size) and a number of other factors expected to affect productivity growth. Among the latter we have included the market share of the firm, the degree of financial solvency, measured as equity capital divided by the total balance, firm rent, measured as the ordinary result divided by the annual turnover (deflated by the same price indices as turnover) and the Herfindahl-index as a measure of market concentration. We have used three alternative competition measures as there is no "perfect" measure reflecting all aspects of competition. The main limitation of the market share variable is of course that it does not pick up foreign competition. The advantage with the rent variable is that it is an *ex post* measure and may therefore capture some of the hard-to-measure factors like collusion or potential competition.

The data set used in this study is constructed from public accounts of Danish firms over the period 1990 to 1995[5]. The data come from a private company (*Købmandsstandens Oplysnings-bureau A/S*) and are based on firm-specific information derived from the firms' legal obligation to submit accounts reports to the authorities. In principle, all Danish firms are included in the database which takes the form of an unbalanced longitudinal data set. However, personally owned firms with less than 10 employees are not obliged to publish information on turnover, number of employees and so on, and so these companies are not included in our data set.

The sample used in this paper is restricted to the manufacturing sector including industries ranging from 1500 to 3800 at a 4-digit level of the NACE-industry code. We have furthermore excluded firms with an annual turnover less than DKK 500,000. This gives a sample of a little less than 3,000 firms per annum. About half of the firms are limited liability companies (Ltd.'s) and the rest are funds, partnerships and so on. In the latter, there are normally only one or a few owners of the firm.

A summary description of the data used in the estimations is given in *Table 1*. Productivity is measured as the annual turnover for a given labour force and capital stock, and the explanatory variables are partly firm-specific information and partly industry-specific information. The information about market concentration (the Herfindahl index) is generated at the industry level from the micro data (public information on economic performance) and the information on capacity utilisation, which is also available at the industry level only, is obtained from the Danish Bureau of Statistics (various issues of '*Månedlig ordre- og omsætningsstatistik for industrien*'). Full information for the variables presented in Table 1 in the period 1990-95 is available for between 1,800 and 3,000 firms per annum and pooling the data for all six years in an unbalanced data set gives almost 16,000 observations.

---

[5] A fuller description of the data set is found in Dilling-Hansen et al. (1997).

Table 1 Descriptive statistics for the sample of Danish firms, 1993

Variable	Number of obs.	Mean	Stand. Deviation
Annual turnover	3337	86,502.6*	424,377.6*
Number of employees	2923	89.1	351.7
Capital (*'anlægsaktiver'*)	3214	40,135.3*	304,790.1*
Market share	3337	0.062	0.162
Financial solvency	3337	0.339	0.221
Result of the year/invested capital	3334	0.057	0.270
Concentration ratio (Herfindahl)	3337	19.58	19.40
Capacity utilisation rate	3337	77.45	5.60
Limited liability company (dummy)	3337	0.533	-
Younger than 20 years (dummy)	3337	0.563	-

Note: * Figures indicate DKK million.

The real turnover for the firms in our sample rose by 2.9% per annum during the period 1990 to 1995. The 'average firm' in the sample has almost 80 employees and the high standard deviation compared to the relatively low mean value together with the fact that the typical information about the firm is non-negative indicates that the distributions of the variables have a long tail to the right due to the large companies. The largest company in the sample has about 8,000 employees in 1993 and the highest annual turnover is about DKK 10,000 million. Only firms with a positive equity capital are considered as valid observations in the models and hence, the variable 'financial solvency' is non-negative. The variable 'rent' (the result of the year relative to the annual turnover) has significant variation from the mean (10%) and can take on negative as well as positive values.

For many firms, part of their current performance reflects decisions which may have been made much earlier (Kay, 1993). Some of these decisions and factors (like reputation, organisation of production, potential competition, technological opportunities to innovation) are unobserved (to the econometrician) and would be hard to operationalize, anyway.[6] However, many of the relevant unobserved factors are likely to vary substantially across industries but not across firms within the same sector or industry. Consequently, in order to capture them, one should try to control for industry effects. As will be seen below, we have included industry dummies in the estimations and we have also checked for their importance by running specifications where they are omitted. Furthermore, any remaining firm-specific, time-invariant unobserved factors will be captured by firm-level fixed effects in the estimations.

In interpreting results from analyses like those presented in this paper, a major problem is that competition in the long run is unlikely to be independent of the behaviour of the firms. Clearly, firms which have performed well may gain market power and so because of the endogeneity of the market structure there is a danger of drawing false conclusions. This problem which was first pointed out by Demsetz (1973) is known as the efficiency hypothesis. Unfortunately, there are no straightforward solutions to the problem, although having access to longitudinal information the firms is likely to help a lot.

4 Empirical results

We first estimated the production function augmented with the firm's market share, rents and solvency, the Herfindahl index, and a dummy for whether the firm is a limited liability company and another for firm size (firms with more than 75 employees are taken as big companies[7]) for each year. The estimation results, which are set out in the appendix, were strikingly similar across years. All explanatory variables, except the product market concentration index,[8] differed significantly from zero and attached coefficients of reasonable magnitude.

Firms' rents and market share both carry positively signed coefficients whereas solvency has a negative effect on productivity. According to these cross-sectional results large and limited liability companies have higher total factor

---

[6] This pertains also to the resources and capabilities emphasized by the so called Aresource based A view of the firm found in the management literature; see for example Barney (1991).

[7] About 17 per cent of the firms in our sample are 'big' according to this definition.

[8] Note, however, that as a consequence of excluding the market share from the equation, the Herfindahl index becomes significantly different from zero. This is in line with a large number of studies of corporate performance; see for example Scherer and Ross (1990). In our data there is a relatively strong association between the concentration and the market share variables; the correlation coefficient is about 0.5 for each year.

productivity than other firms. Note that estimations with the lagged output included as an explanatory variable to pick up partial adjustment yields qualitatively unchanged results (not shown).

We find that limited liability companies (Ltd.'s) are more productive than firms with other ownership structures. This is rather surprising in view of the fact that Ltd. companies often have a more dispersed ownership than the other firms in which owners are much more present, thereby reducing the discretion of the managers. Indeed in many cases owners and managers coincide. In future analyses we plan to employ a further distinction between firms the stock of which is publicly held and those in which it is not. We would expect the latter to be controlled more directly by the owners (and in many cases to be family firms with the owners present as managers).

Table 2 contains the results from estimations on the unbalanced panel for the years 1990 to 1995. The first column gives the estimates from pooling the cross-sections and entering year dummies to account for overall productivity growth. The estimates are quite similar to those obtained from the cross-sections and so, there is nothing new worth airing here.

Turning next to the second column where the longitudinal character of the data is recognised for the first time by the inclusion of firm-level fixed effects, some noteworthy changes can be observed. Firstly, the returns estimates to both labour and capital drop considerably indicating diminishing returns. However, this is in all likelihood due to measurement errors accentuated by the fixed effects methodology. Secondly, our product market concentration now carries a negative and statistically significant coefficient. Thus, accounting for fixed effects and following firms over a somewhat longer time period leads to a change in the sign to the coefficient in the direction suggested by received theory. Thirdly, as a result of entering fixed effects the coefficient to our financial pressure variable, the solvency of the firm, is more than halved and at the same time loses a lot of its significance. In the third column we include in addition to firm-level fixed effects also 14 industry dummies. As can be seen, the estimates remain strikingly similar to those in column (2).

Table 2 Estimations on the period 1990-95[*].

	(1)	(2)	(3)
Labour	0.857	0.593	0.591
	(0.005)	(0.008)	(0.008)
Capital	0.148	0.078	0.078
	(0.004)	(0.004)	(0.004)
Utilisation rate	0.007	0.002	0.002
	(0.001)	(0.001)	(0.001)
Market share	0.514	0.790	0.849
	(0.039)	(0.043)	(0.045)
Rents	0.401	0.621	0.620
	(0.030)	(0.018)	(0.018)
Concentration	0.084	-0.319	-0.348
	(0.030)	(0.038)	(0.040)
Solvency	-0.194	-0.062	-0.057
	(0.023)	(0.023)	(0.024)
R^2 (adj.)	0.895	0.99	0.99
N	15,713	15,713	15,713

[*] Columns (1) - (3): year dummies are included but not reported; (2): estimation with firm-level fixed effects; (3): in addition to year and fixed effects, 14 (2-digit NACE) industry dummies are included as well.

Table 3 provides some further estimations based on the balanced panel. Here the unobserved firm-specific fixed effects are accounted for by estimating the models on first difference form. Note that this differences on differences formulation provides us with the effects of the explanatory variables on the total factor productivity levels.

Table 3 Estimations on first differences.

	(1)	(2)	(3)*
Constant	0.017	0.018	0.017
	(0.003)	(0.002)	(0.003)
①Labour	0.574	0.541	0.487
	(0.009)	(0.009)	(0.010)
②Capital	0.054	0.053	0.034
	(0.005)	(0.005)	(0.006)
③Utilisation rate	0.005	0.004	0.004
	(0.001)	(0.001)	(0.001)
①Market share		0.856	0.822
		(0.047)	(0.053)
②Concentration		-0.421	-0.412
		(0.042)	(0.050)
①Rents		0.670	0.761
		(0.020)	(0.023)
①Solvency		-0.079	-0.068
		(0.025)	(0.028)
Ltd. company			0.006
			(0.016)
R^2 (adj.)	0.273	0.357	0.561
N	11,494	11,428	11,428

* Industry dummies were included but are not reported.

The statistical fit of the difference estimations is good. The basic production function "explains" 27 per cent and the augmented versions as much as 36 and 56 per cent of the variation in productivity levels across firms. Again the inclusion of fixed effects leads to a substantial decline in the returns to the factors of production. Also the other estimates are in line with those in Table 2. Thus, increases in market shares and rents are associated with higher total factor productivity whilst increasing solvency and product market concentration is harmful for productivity.

The third column presents results from a specification with industry dummies and a dummy for limited liability companies. The industry dummies, which in a first difference model correspond to industry-specific trends, turn out to be very important. Their inclusion does not affect the estimates of the other regressors, although it should be noted that the returns to labour and capital are even lower than in earlier specifications, but they do give rise to a significant increase in the model's explanatory power.[9] The limited company dummy is totally insignificant implying that there is no difference in productivity growth between firms with different ownership structures.[10]

We have found that both higher rent and market share have a stable, statistically significant, and *positive* effect on total factor productivity. On the other hand, the market concentration ratio as an indicator of competition in the firm's product market turned out *negative* and significant in the estimations which made use of the panel structure of the data set.

It should be noted that these results differ partly from those of Nickell *et al.* (1997), who found a strong *negative* relationship between the growth in firm productivity and competition, as measured by a concentration index at the industry level or market share or average rent at the firm level, for a sample of 670 UK firms over the period 1985-94. This could of course be due to the fact that Nickell (1996) and Nickell *et al.* (1997) have observations from longer time periods (but also samples with less dispersion in firm size). For data availability reasons our period is only six years. Thus, we cannot completely rule out the possibility that the positive relationships between productivity and market share or rent are merely a result of a spurious correlation due to the endogeneity of competition. However, it is unlikely that higher total factor productivity causes less concentration in product markets and less financial solvency of firms.

In accordance with the theoretical discussions above, a higher debt burden appears to restrain managerial behaviour and hence improves firm performance. The size of the estimated effect shrinks considerably as firm-specific fixed effects are allowed for. Still, the results imply that a reduction in the free cash flow and the threat of bankruptcy may have an important effect on the behaviour of firms.

Estimation results from specifications with interaction effects between ownership, product market concentration, firm rents and solvency are set out in

---

[9] It should be noted that here our results differ substantially from those obtained from cross-sections; see Dilling-Hansen et al. (forthcoming). In the cross-section estimations, industry differences are of minor importance for explaining differences in levels across firms. In the panel setting, industry dummies are important for understanding inter-firm differences in productivity growth.

[10]Note, that as this variable measures firm type only once, it captures the effect on growth.

Table 4. We begin by looking at the interactions with firm type. From column (1) we can see that Ltd. companies with a high degree of solvency have a lower level of productivity. Thus, a high degree of solvency is more damaging for a limited liability company's productivity performance. This is consistent with our earlier conjecture that some of the Ltd. companies may be less productive, especially the bigger ones which are less owner-controlled, and hence, there might be greater scope for slack in these companies. The interaction between the Ltd. company dummy and firm rents is completely insignificant; see column (4).

As can be seen from column (2), solvency interacted with the Herfindahl index is negative indicating that the more concentrated the product market of the firm, the larger is the negative impact of solvency on the firm's total factor productivity. Consequently, financial pressure and product market concentration are to some extent substitutes for each other.

From column (3) we can note that the interaction term for solvency and market share is also significantly negative, again implying that financial pressure and market concentration appear to be substitutes. However, the interaction term for solvency and rents (see column (4)) is completely insignificant. In both columns (3) and (4) there is a small positive interaction between Ltd.'s and market share.

Our results for the interaction effects resemble those obtained by Nickell *et al.* (1997), who also found strong evidence of substitution between debt payments and competition and between competition and shareholder control. Their competition measure was average profits over value added during the whole ten year period under study, whereas our measure is on an annual basis. In future work we will attempt to distinguish more carefully than at present between different types of owners and owner control.

Table 4 Interactions*.

	(1)	(2)	(3)	(4)
Ltd. Company	0.363	0.324	0.300	0.304
	(0.018)	(0.015)	(0.012)	(0.012)
Solvency	-0.085	-0.109	-0.140	-0.177
	(0.052)	(0.031)	(0.024)	(0.022)
Market share			0.772	0.550
			(0.080)	(0.064)
Concentration		0.115		
		(0.056)		
Rents				0.461
				(0.075)
Interactions:				
Ltd. * Solvency	-0.171			
	(0.044)			
Concentration * Solvency		-0.346		
		(0.112)		
Ltd. * Concentration		-0.088		
		(0.050)		
Solvency * Market share			-0.640	
			(0.140)	
Ltd. * Market share			0.147	0.139
			(0.066)	(0.066)
Ltd. * Rents				-0.048
				(0.064)
Solvency * Rents				0.004
				(0.098)

* In addition to input of production, market share, rents, the Herfindahl index, solvency and a Ltd. dummy, year industry dummies were included in the estimations. Only the main effects and the interactions associated with them are reported in the table.

5 Conclusions

The estimated production functions fit the data on Danish manufacturing sector firms very well explaining more than ninety per cent of the variation in turnover across firms during the years 1990 to 1995. Higher rents and larger market shares have significant positive effects on total factor productivity. The estimated coefficient to the market concentration index suggests that firms in concentrated industries are less productive. These results differ somewhat from those obtained in recent studies of productivity in UK firms (Nickell (1996), Nickell *et al.* (1997)). However, these studies use data from longer periods than ours, and hence our results can be due to the endogeneity of market structure and firm productivity which we cannot address in our short data period. On the other hand, the sample used in this paper is not only much larger, but also covers a broader spectrum of firms of different size. Except for the two studies mentioned above, good comparisons simply do not exist. Consequently, it is difficult to determine the sources of our differences in results.

Financial pressure as measured by financial solvency turned out to have a significant effect on the productivity of firms. The less the firm is dependent upon external financial sources, the less pressure on management to improve productivity. This result also implies that the threat of bankruptcy may have an important positive effect on the productivity performance of firms.

Firms organised as limited liability companies were found to have a significantly higher total factor productivity, but there is also evidence that total factor productivity is lower in the more solvent Ltd.'s. The interaction between solvency and concentration, measured either by the Herfindahl index or the firm's market share, turned out negative. This suggests that external financial pressure and product market competition are substitutes.

Table A-1 Estimations on cross-sections, 1990-95.

	1990	1991	1992	1993	1994	1995
Labour	0.762	0.801	0.801	0.794	0.786	0.779
	(0.016)	(0.015)	(0.015)	(0.015)	(0.016)	(0.019)
Capital	0.141	0.131	0.134	0.130	0.127	0.126
	(0.010)	(0.009)	(0.009)	(0.009)	(0.010)	(0.011)
Utilisation rate	0.004	0.006	0.006	0.013	0.002	0.009
	(0.003)	(0.003)	(0.002)	(0.002)	(0.002)	(0.003)
Market share	0.650	0.535	0.503	0.577	0.583	0.411
	(0.092)	(0.192)	(0.093)	(0.093)	(0.095)	(0.100)
Rents	0.500	0.410	0.424	0.482	0.259	0.322
	(0.064)	(0.070)	(0.059)	(0.074)	(0.090)	(0.107)
Concentration	0.060	0.114	0.084	-0.003	-0.007	0.160
	(0.073)	(0.073)	(0.074)	(0.074)	(0.078)	(0.083)
Solvency	-0.186	-0.245	-0.177	-0.198	-0.254	-0.307
	(0.058)	(0.053)	(0.053)	(0.052)	(0.059)	(0.066)
Ltd. companies	0.320	0.295	0.297	0.293	0.332	0.346
	(0.028)	(0.027)	(0.027)	(0.028)	(0.030)	(0.037)
Big (> 75 employees)	0.199	0.136	0.171	0.194	0.187	0.225
	(0.046)	(0.044)	(0.044)	(0.043)	(0.046)	(0.051)
R^2 (adj)	0.887	0.894	0.898	0.903	0.898	0.919
N	2,575	2,892	2,921	2,865	2,677	1,777

REFERENCES

Arrow, J. (1962), *"Economic Welfare and the Allocation of Resources for Invention"*, in NBER: The Rate and Direction of Inventive Activity: Economic and Social Forces. Princeton University Press, Princeton.

Barney J. (1991), *"Firm resources and sustained corporative competitive advantage"*, Journal of Management, 17, 99-120.

Baumol, W. (1959), *Business Behavior, Value and Growth*. Macmillan, New York.

Bergölf, E. (1996), *"Reforming corporate governance: redirecting the European agenda"*, Economic Policy.

Blanchflower, D. and Machin, S. (1996), *"Product Market Competition, Wages and Productivity: International Evidence from Establishment-Level Data"*. Centre for Economic Performance Discussion Paper No. 286.

Demsetz, H. (1973), *"Industry structure, market rivalry and public policy"*, Journal of Law and Economics, 16, 1-9.

Dilling-Hansen, M., Madsen, E.S. and Smith, V. (1997), *"Entry into Danish Manufacturing Industries"*, in S. Laaksonen (ed.): *The evolution of firms and industries. International Perspectives*. Statistics Finland, Helsinki, 180-193.

Dilling-Hansen, M., Eriksson, T., Madsen, E.S. and Smith, V. (1998), *"Firm Productivity Growth and Competition"*, Nationaløkonomisk Tidskrift (Danish Journal of Economics), forthcoming.

Green, A. and Mayes, D.G. (1991), *"Technical Inefficiency in Manufacturing Industries"*, Economic Journal, 101, 523-38.

Haskel, J. (1992), *"Imperfect Competition, Work Practices and Productivity Growth"*, Oxford Bulletin of Economics and Statistics, 53, 265-279.

Holmström, B. (1982), *"Managerial Incentive Problems - a Dynamic Perspective"*, in: Essays in Economics and Management in Honor of Lars Wahlbeck. Swedish School of Economics, Helsinki.

Jensen, M. (1986), *"Agency Costs of Free Cash Flow, Corporate Finance and Takeovers"*, American Economic Review, 76, 323-329.

Jensen, M. (1988), *"Takeovers: Their Causes and Consequences"*, Journal of Economic Perspectives, 2, 21-48.

Kay, J. (1993), *Foundations of Corporate Success*. Oxford University Press, Oxford.

Leibenstein, H.(1966), *"Allocative Efficiency vs. 'X-Efficiency'"*, American Economic Review, 56, 392-415.

Levine, R. (1997), *"Financial Development and Economic Growth: Views and Agenda"*, Journal of Economic Literature, 35, 688-726.

Martin, S. (1993), *"Endogenous Firm Efficiency in a Cournot Principal-Agent Model"*, Journal of Economic Theory, 59, 445-450.

Mayer C. (1996), *"Corporate Governance, Competition and Performance"*, OECD Economic Studies, No. 27, 8-34.

Modigliani, F. and Miller, M.(1958*), "The Cost of Capital, Corporation Finance and the Theory of Investment"*, American Economic Review, 48, 261-297.

Nickell S.J. (1995), *The Performance of Companies*. Blackwell, Oxford.

Nickell S.J. (1996), *"Competition and Corporate Performance"*, Journal of Political Economy, 104, 724-746.

Nickell S.J., Wadhwani, S. and Wall, M. (1992), *"Productivity Growth in UK Companies*, 1975-86", European Economic Review, 36, 1055-92.

Nickell S.J., Nicolitsas, D. and Dryden, N. (1997), *"What Makes Firms Perform Well?"*, European Economic Review, 41, 783-796.

Oswald, A. (1996), *"Rent-Sharing in the Labor Market"*. Warwick Economic Research Papers No. 474.

Schere, F.M. and Ross, D. (1990), *Industrial Market Structure and Economic Performance*, Houghton Mifflin, Boston.

Shleifer, A. and Vishny, R. (1997), *"A Survey of Corporate Governance"*, Journal of Finance, forthcoming.

Short, H. (1994), *"Ownership, Control, Financial Structure and the Performance of Firms"*, Journal of Economic Surveys, 8, 203-249.

Williamson, O. (1964), *The Economics of Discretionary Behaviour: Managerial Objectives in a Theory of the Firm*. Prentice-Hall, New York.

CHANGING NATURE OF JAPANESE FIRM?: TECHNOLOGY ADOPTION, ORGANIZATIONAL STRUCTURE AND HUMAN RESOURCE STRATEGY

Kazuyuki Motohashi

Economic Analysis and Statistics Division, Directorate for Science, Technology and Industry, OECD

1 Introduction

It is perceived that adoption of new technology (particularly information technology) causes significant changes in firm's organization structure and human resource strategy. A considerable number of case studies address this point, and a general conclusion of IT's impact on its organizational characteristics has been drawn, such as IT's essential role in "business process re-engineering" (Hammer and Champy (1993)) and IT's enhancement of flexible adjustment to dynamic business environments (Davidow and Malone (1993)). A recent study in the U.S. shows that only IT investments do not provide a whole solution of firm's productivity growth, but that it is also needed an appropriate human resource strategy, such as commitment to skill development of its workers, decentralized decision making mechanism and performance base incentive system (Brynjolfsson and Hitt (1996)).

In a broader context, innovative work practices can enhance firm's adaptive capability of new technology (Vickery and Wurzburg (1996)). Innovative work practices refers to worker involvement systems, such as work team (e.g. QC circle), employee stock ownership program and flexible and broader job assignment (Ichniowski et. al. (1996)). Theoretical support to the complementarity of technology, firm's business strategy and its organization is presented in Milgrom and Roberts (1990) and Milgrom and Roberts (1995). They stress the importance of coordination among various functions inside a firm, such as engineering, production, shipping and marketing to achieve efficient and flexible "modern manufacturing" operation.

This paper provides some empirical evidence on the complementarity of technology adoption, organizational characteristics and human resource strategy of Japanese firms. After the burst of "economic bubbles" in the early 1990's, Japanese firms faced a strong pressure for rationalization of their business activities, number of them have gone through significant restructuring processes.

In this sense, a major motivation of organizational changes in this period is improving efficiency by suppression of workforce. In this paper, how such effort is related to technology use and its consequences to human resource strategy is investigated.

In addition to this adverse economic environment, there are also some structural factors, such as technological development and globalization of firm's activities, which may affect "Japanese human resource management system", i.e., long-term employer employee relationship, seniority payment and promotion, firm specific skill development, etc. These elements are in the relationship of strategic complementarity (Aoki and Okuno (1996)), while this system was challenged by firm's efforts of workforce rationalization. In addition, an advance of information and knowledge based economy may require a firm to re-allocate its resources quickly, which cannot be achieved by consensus based decision making system inside Japanese firms (Motohashi and Nezu (1997)). How Japanese firms coped with such difficulty, as well as opportunity, is also addressed in this paper.

2 Data and Issues for measuring organizational characteristics

This study is based on the survey data designed by MITI and the Ministry of Labor (MOL), and conducted by the Japan Productivity Center for Socio-Economic Development in 1995. This survey (MITI-MOL survey, hereafter) covers a broad range of questionnaire, including technology adoption, organizational structure change, human capital development and incentive system for workers, during the period from 1991 to 1994.[1] The survey was conducted to 6,622 firms, publicly traded in Japanese stock markets or by over the counter market, and 1206 firms responded.

There are some points to be noted for this survey. First, the unit of observation of MITI-MOL survey is firm, instead of establishment, which is often taken by this type of survey, such as Brynjolfsson and Hitt (1996), NUTEK (1996) and Osterman (1994). The main advantage of establishment over firm is that a respondent is more likely to know details of work practices, as compared to that of firm (Osterman (1994)). This is true for surveying detail work practices, which apply individual workers of each organization, such as TQC and team base management. In contrast, MITI-MOL survey concentrates on firm wide human resource strategy and organizational change, such as wage policy and changing organizational hierarchy.

---

[1] List of variables and summary statistics is available in the Government of Japan (1996).

The second issue is measurement error. Non-response biases might exist, because the response rate of very low (18.2%).[2] One way to correct such bias is to conduct a follow up survey to sampling of non respondees, as is shown in NUTEK (1996), while such kind of survey has not been conducted in this case. In addition, another type of error is rooted in questionnaire itself, because substantial number of questions require qualitative and subjective responses. Although there is no clear and agreed definition of "organizational structure", one have to ask a question like "has your organization been flattered?" to capture such important organizational aspect. In this sense, it is important to come up with coordinated conceptual framework and survey methodology for further development of this area (Vickery and Wurzburg (1996)).

3 Building blocks

3.1 Basic settings; technology adoption and organizational change

In this section, statistical analysis on technology adoption, organizational changes and human resource strategy is provided. The relationship between technology adoption and organizational changes is investigated first, then bundles of work practices, i.e., skill development, incentive system and job security, are interacted with technology and organizational variables.

Core variables of this study are technology adoption and organizational changes. As regards technology adoption, MITI-MOL survey asked whether a firm introduced the following three kinds of IT related technology in 1991 and 1994.

- Intra-firm network system : Information network system inside a firm, such as LAN (local area network), POS (point of sales system) and information system to control production and distribution
- Inter-firm network system : Information network system between firms, such as distribution network between suppliers and customers
- Office automation system : Information system to improve efficiency either of production sites or of back offices, such as CAD/CAM, flexible manufacturing system and accounting management system

As is seen from Table 1, the penetration rate of all three kinds of technology increased significantly from 1991 to 1994.

---

[2] It is also noted that there might be selection biases, because samples are drawn from the list of publicly traded firms, instead of entire population. This can be treated econometrically, such as by Heckman's two step method. (Heckman (1979)).

MITI-MOL survey also asked whether a firm conducted the following seven kinds of organizational change from 1991 to 1994.
- flattering the structure of firm (FLAT)
- integrating divisions or departments of firm (INT-D)
- suppression of back office staffs (CUT)
- diversification of office location (DIV)
- integrating office location (INT-O)
- enhancing flexible work time system (FLEX)
- active use of outsourcing (OUT)

Table 2 provides a first cut information on this organizational variable in relation to technology adoption. Technology variable is presented by the number of technology introduced in 1991 and 1994, respectively.

A positive association between technology and organizational change can be shown both in technology level (the number of technology adopted in 1991 or 1994) and in changes in the level (the number of technology introduced between 1991 and 1994). Information technology use may be a precondition for organizational transformation of firm, or a firm's managerial decision for IT investment and organizational change may be done simultaneously. To see which factor is dominant, the following descriptive regression is conducted.

$$\Pr(org\_change) = \alpha + \beta_1 tech91 + \beta_2 tech\_change + \beta_3 ind + \beta_4 size + \varepsilon$$

Tech91 and Tech_change is a set of dummy variables for the number of technologies in 1991 and the number of technology introduced from 1991 to 1994. It is also controlled for industry and size effects.[3] Table 3 shows coefficients of technology variables for each 7 organization variable.

In general, regression results suggest that technology level in 1991 has more explanatory power. Specifically, a firm with all three technologies in 1991 is more likely to go through organizational change in all types, while a statistical significant coefficient can be found in only two types of organizational change for variables of technology adoption from 1991 to 1994. These two types of organizational change ("suppression of back office staffs" and "enhancing of flexible work time") are not really organizational transformation, but rather changes in work practices. Therefore, a firm with IT adoption is likely to go through major organizational transformation, such as changes of the firm structure, while chances of an opposite causality are small.

In the following sections, human resource variables (human capital development, incentive system and job security) are interacted with firm's characteristics of technology adoption and organizational changes. To keep simplicity of analysis, each type of human resource strategy is regressed by both

---

[3] There are 16 industry types (roughly 2 digit level JSIC) and 4 size classes by the number of employees. The same control variables are applied to the following regressions as well.

technology and organizational variables. As regards technology adoption, the following 4 categories of firms are created to capture the difference in human resource practices both by the number of technologies adopted in 1991 and by the number of technologies adopted during the period from 1991 to 1994.
- High-tech firm : a firm with all three technologies in both 1991 and 1994
- Low-tech firm : a firm with 1 or 2 technologies in both 1991 and 1994
- Change-tech firm : a firm which introduced one or more technology during the period from 1991 to 1994
- No-tech firm : a firm with no technology in either 1991 or 1994

As regards organizational variable, the first principal component of seven organizational variable is used. Because its eigenvectors are all positive, ranging from 0.359 to 0.395, and its eigenvalue is 3.04, as compared to 0.93 for the second principal one, the transformed variable by the first principal component works very well as a proxy of the degree of overall organizational change. In contrast, the ratio of noise to information is quite high for the second or lower components.

3.2 Human capital development

Human capital development is an important factor to make most of new technology adoption, and a positive link between technology and worker's skill have been supported by "skill biased technical progress " literature. (Doms et al. (1997), Krueger (1993), etc.) At the micro level, computers are supposed to substitute for "routine jobs", and workers can concentrate on more difficult jobs requiring higher skills. However, this does not work well without a proper system of worker's motivation for skill development (Levy and Murnane (1996)). The relationship between organizational change and human capital development is more complicated, because workforce rationalization may do harm to worker's incentive for long term skill development.

MITI-MOL survey has qualitative questions on changes in the need for skill level by five occupation categories, managers, administrative, R&D, sales and production workers. It should be noted that skill level here is measured by respondee's perception (upskill, no change or downskill) on each type of jobs, instead of objective scales such as educational attainments and years of work experience. Four kinds of skill type in an original questionnaire are aggregated into two, IT related skill and non-IT related skill, then the following regression is conducted by occupation and by skill type.[4]

$$\Pr(skill\_change) = \alpha + \beta_1 tech + \beta_2 org + \beta_3 ind + \beta_4 size + \varepsilon$$

---

[4] Regressions are done by ordered probit model.

Regression is conducted for two kinds of samples, all firms (upper panel of Table 4) and only firms with technology in either 1991 or 1994 (lower panel of Table 4). The first result shows a general association of skill, technology and organizational change, while the second one shows the effect of technology adoption when restricting samples to only technology firms. The first panel suggests positive link of upskilling with both technology and organizational change. According to the manager's perception, coping with new IT system needs higher skill level not only in IT related skill, but also non IT related one, such as general planning and coordination ability. In addition, a positive link between the need for high skills and organizational change is found. Due to the long economic depression in Japan in the early 1990's, Japanese firms faced a strong pressure for downsizing. In fact, a firm with organizational change shows relatively larger employment loss, as is shown later. It is interesting to see that managers which have gone through such tough restructuring process perceive the necessity to skill upgrading more than the others.

According to the lower panel of Table 4, positive and significant coefficients with organization variable are found, even for only technology firms. As regards technology variables, it is found that skill upgrading for tech-change firms is perceived as much as that for high-tech firms, but more than that of low-tech firm, particularly for managers. In addition, in high tech firms, non IT related skills for sales and production workers are perceived to be more upgraded, as compared to those in tech change firms.

The MITI-MOL survey asked respondee's opinion on obstacles for human capital development and desirable measures to help firms to conduct training. Table 5 and 6 are regression results of each choice of questionnaire as a dependent variable.[5] There are some interesting observations. For example, the size effect[6] cannot be found in some obstacles, such as financial difficulty. Instead, smaller firms are likely to list lack of human resources for training and know-hows as an obstacle. This point should be taken into account in policy making of human capital development in SMEs. There is very small technology effect, and only one significant coefficient is found in organization variable with financial difficulty. However, this needs careful interpretation, because a firm with organizational changes is supposed to face severe financial difficulty, as compared to the others. As for the desirable measure regressions, some positive coefficients of technology and organization are found for financial incentives, such as subsidy and tax treatment.

---

[5] This is a multiple choice question with a list of obstacles or measures for training.

[6] Negative coefficient means as the firm size increases, the probability of recognizing each obstacle becomes small.

3.3 Incentive system

Wage and promotion are important instruments for workers to work hard and improve productivity, and an appropriate incentive system is critical to firm's success. Incentive system is related to the organizational structure of firm. For example, if a firm transforms its organization to flatter one and delegates responsibility to individual workers, decentralized incentive system (pay for individual performance) may be better fitted. Use of information technology is also related. IT leads to increasing monitoring ability in employer, who can delegate more responsibility to employees, and a wage contract linked with individual workers becomes more efficient (Brynjolfsson and Hitt (1996)).

One of key issues in incentive system for Japanese firms is either performance based pay or seniority based pay. It is believed that seniority based pay and promotion is a key element of "Japanese employment system". Job vacancy is filled by an internal candidate, and promotion of worker (linked with wage) is considered, only when his just one step senior position becomes open. There is no leap frog in this promotion ladder. This kind of system used to work in Japan due to demographic characteristics (relatively abundant young workforce) and high growth expectation (EPA (1994)). However, it becomes harder for a firm to maintain it, and increasing number of firms have introduced performance based wage setting systems such as yearly contract base payment.

In the MITI-MOL survey, two questions are asked to see whether a firm will enhance performance linked wage system. The first question asks whether a firm strengthen wage's link with performance, for its base salary and bonus, respectively. Bonus is often linked with the performance of firm, and it has served as an instrument to keep flexibility of labor cost for Japanese firms (Hamada and Kurosaka (1986)). This question also distinguishes bonus's link with overall firm's performance and individual worker's performance. The second question asks the same kind of question, but for five different occupation categories, respectively. The following descriptive regression is conducted to see how incentive system changes are related to technology and organizational characteristics. Results are presented at Table 7a and 7b.

$$\Pr(increase\_performance\_payment) = \alpha + \beta_1 tech + \beta_2 org + \beta_3 ind + \beta_4 size + \varepsilon$$

In general, it is found that technology and organizational variable are positively correlated with firm's propensity to incentive payments, and it is more likely for bonuses to be used as an instrument for performance based payment. Therefore, it is confirmed that a firm with organizational change is more likely to depart from traditional Japanese seniority wage system, and seeking for new style of human resource management style. It is also noted that a positive link seems to be found more with the organization variable than with technology variables. For the regression by occupation, technology variables have a positive and significant coefficient in managers, and partly in R&D and sales workers, and there is no positive sign for administrative workers, while the organizational variable has a positive and significant coefficient for all occupations.

3.4 Job security

Job security, or limited port of entry into internal labor market is a crucial element for "Japanese employment management system". It is found that the wage profile by age for Japanese firms is steeper than that of the United States and some European countries (EPA (1994)). This implies that younger workers are paid less than their marginal productivity, while older ones are paid more. This inter-generation wage subsidization is possible, because employment opportunity is limited to new graduates for most of Japanese firms. In addition, younger workers are motivated to work for promotion competition and rapid salary increase. However, this system is questioned as well, by increasing number of firms applying performance based incentives and active external labor market policy by the government.

Changes in the job rotation system have some skill development implications as well. Job security enables worker to invest in firm specific human capital for efficient communication between colleagues and enhancing team work for firm's success. Swedish study shows that a firm with more manager's commitment to worker's skill development has lower job turnover rate (NUTEK (1996)). However, US study shows no significant relationship between high performance workplaces and job security, and it is interpreted that segmentation of internal labor market into "core workers" and "contingent workers" occurs in such organization (Osterman (1994)).

MITI-MOL survey asks whether a firm increases, does not change or decreases each of seven types of ways in coping with labor demand changes, as is shown in Table 8. To see how firm's preference of each type is related to technology and organizational characteristics, the following regression is conducted.

$$\Pr(type\_of\_workforce\_change) = \alpha + \beta_1 tech + \beta_2 org + \beta_3 ind + \beta_4 size + \varepsilon$$

It is found that there is very little impact of technology, while some significant coefficients can been seen for the organizational variable. That is, a firm with organizational change is less likely to increase full time workers by cutting down the number of hiring new graduates, and maintain its flexibility by increasing in-house or cross firm labor transferring. It should be noted that there is not significant association between increasing number of temporary or contract workers and organizational change. Even for a firm with organizational changes, it tries to keep its internal employment system by internal rotation to cope with labor demand changes.

4 Labor productivity and employment growth

In this section, the relationship with firm level performance is investigated. The focus of this section is changes in labor productivity[7] and employment, instead of level, because there is no variable for the level of organizational characteristics. First cut information on technology and firm performance can be found in Table 9. It looks that labor productivity loss is less for higher technology level firms, while it is worse for firms with technology adoption from 1991 to 1994. On the other hand, there seems to be a positive employment effect of technology.

Next, statistical significance of this observation is tested by a fixed effect model (Table 10). The sign of coefficients is consistent with observations from Table 9, but statistical significance cannot be found for labor productivity regressions. There are number of potential reasons. One is data problem with productivity measurement (Baily and Gordon (1991)). Another is due to real effects, such as lags and mismanagement of information technology (Brynjolfsson (1993)). It is also found that productivity impact of IT depends on its application. For example, IT use for production management has more impacts, as compared to back office applications such as accounting system (Motohashi (1998a)). It is not necessary to go through whole discussion on "Solow's Productivity Paradox" here[8], but it is worthwhile to note that this is not a strange result in empirical literature (McGuckin et al. (1996)).

In contrast, there is very clear employment effects by technology. As compared to no-technology firms, positive and statistically significant coefficients are found, not only in tech-change firms, but also in high-tech and low-tech firms. Therefore, employment growth by technology adoption is not just a temporary one as a result of adjustment of firms into new environment.[9] On the other hand, organizational change leads to employment reduction, which may be due to an outcome of corporate restructuring in severe economic condition.

Detail look at employment impacts is done by the type of occupation. Empirical literature of skill biased technical progress suggests that technology adoption leads to relatively higher growth rate of white collars, as compared to

---

[7] Value added for labor productivity is calculated from operating profit + labor compensation, because depreciation data is not available. This definition is different from typical definition of gross value added, which include the amount of depreciation.

[8] Solow's paradox is extensively investigated in OECD (1996).

[9] According to comparative study of France, Japan and the United States, the positive association between technology and employment growth is stronger in Japan than in the other two (Motohashi (1998b)).

blue collars (Berndt et al. (1992)). However, the results are not consistent with such literature. The sign of coefficients (not statistically significant) shows that administrative jobs seems to decrease by technology, as compared to other job categories.[10] Organizational change works employment loss for all categories, except sales workers. Again, the impact on administrative job is the greatest. To investigate employment impacts of information technology, it is necessary to depart from traditional view of job category (production workers vs non-production workers), and to take a detail look at inside white collar categories as well (Bresnahan (1997)).

5 Synthesis and concluding remarks

The followings are main points of changes in human resource strategy of Japanese firms.

- Skills: Greater needs of skill upgrading for every type of worker is found in a firm with technology adoption and/or organizational changes.
- Incentive system: Increasing number of firms apply performance based wage system, and this is more likely for a firm with technology and/or organizational changes.
- Job security: Japanese firms still manage to keep job security for existing workers by restricting new graduate hiring and shifting labor forces internally to cope with negative labor demand changes.

These elements of human resource strategy have to be treated as a system, and the Japanese management style is characterized as a complement relationship of firm specific skill development, seniority based incentive system and high job security by long term employment.[11] As is described before, an employee for Japanese firm (particularly white collar worker in large firm) can invest in firm specific human capital, which contributes to efficient internal communication and share the same value with colleagues, by long term employment. Due to the high retention rate of workers, subjective performance evaluation by supervisor is relatively easily introduced, and wage, as well as promotion is linked with seniority (with adjustment by supervisor's evaluation), instead of short term

---

[10] Since only qualitative data (increase, no change or decrease) are available for changes in employment by occupation, this results are not so efficient as those from actual number data.

[11] Aoki and Okuno (1996) extensively discuss complementarity of internal labor market system for Japanese firms. Milgrom and Roberts (1992) also present systematic nature of human resource policy by using an example of Japanese system.

performance of workers. Seniority based payment also reduces over-competition among colleagues and encourage team works.[12]

MITI-MOL survey shows some changes in these compliment elements. First, technology adoption leads to higher skill requirement for every types of occupation. MITI-MOL survey distinguishes IT related skills and non-IT related skills. It should be noted that information technology opens up an opportunity of new work style, which requires higher IT skill. Since IT skill can be classified into general purpose human capital rather than firm specific human capital, increases in such skill requirement may affect complimentarities of Japanese system. Second, a firm with new technology is shifting its incentive system from seniority to performance based one. Due to relative changes in skill requirement, it is assumed that technology based firms begin to focus on objective performance evaluation system, instead of seniority system with subjective performance evaluation by supervisors.

On the other hand, difference in job security between technology based firms and non-technology ones cannot be found. Even for firms with organizational changes which mainly lead to workforce rationalization, they cope with labor demand changes by internal labor force movements. This can be interpreted that internal labor market policy is not easily affected. In addition, job security, or lower labor turnover is found to have a positive effect on worker's motivation and performance (Ichniowski et. al. (1997), Brynjolffson and Hitt (1996) and NUTEK (1996)). High retention rate of Japanese is difficult to be sustained without lack of active external labor market, while this is changing now by active labor market policy by the government and increasing number of mid-career hiring by firms in IT related high growth industry. In this sense, Japanese firm is supposed to face strong pressure to modify its human resource management strategy.

Organizational inertia and complementarity of various elements impede rapid adjustment in human resource strategy for Japanese firms. However, there are some signs of systematic changes. Severe economic situation after the burst of "bubbles" in Japanese economy causes firms to rationalize their business activities. Restructuring efforts leading to labor force suppression are one of main factors behind changes in human resource practices. Another one is technological progress, particularly in IT, which opens up substantial opportunity of new business style, requiring different kind of worker skills and incentive systems. One unsolved problem in this paper is the relationship of new work practices with firm's performance. Productivity impact may be revealed in a longer timeframe and with detailed look at systematic interactions of each components.

---

[12] Because decision making on promotion involves large number of individuals, it may induce a worker to spend substantial time to influence supervisors about his reputation. The opportunity cost associated with such influence activities can be mitigated by seniority system (Milgrom and Roberts (1992)).

Table 1 The share of firms adopting new technology (for 1182 firms)[13]

	1991	1994
Intra-firm network	34%	57%
Inter-firm network	16%	27%
Office Automation system	50%	70%

Table 2 The share of firm with organizational change by its technology adoption

Tech 91	Tech 94	# of firms	FLAT	INT-D	CUT	DIV	INT-O	FLEX	OUT
all	all	1182	29%	38%	50%	14%	18%	22%	21%
0	0	247	15%	26%	26%	6%	10%	9%	15%
0	1	159	26%	26%	41%	8%	13%	13%	14%
0	2	86	35%	41%	53%	17%	15%	31%	29%
0	3	32	28%	41%	66%	13%	19%	31%	13%
1	1	211	24%	38%	49%	14%	13%	18%	18%
1	2	90	41%	43%	69%	21%	29%	33%	33%
1	3	22	36%	55%	82%	27%	59%	41%	50%
2	1	174	37%	48%	57%	17%	25%	26%	23%
2	2	46	41%	65%	70%	26%	28%	30%	28%
3	3	115	35%	46%	68%	17%	26%	37%	26%

---

[13]Since all respondees of survey do not always give their answers to all questions, this number is different from the number of respondees. The same as follows.

Table 3 Regression : organizational change = f(technology adoption) [14]

	technology level in 1991			technology adopted during 91-94		
	0	1	2	0	1	2
flattering organization	-0.45***	-0.19	0.00	-0.26	0.04	0.16
	0.16	0.15	0.15	0.26	0.26	0.27
integrating divisions	-0.37**	-0.06	0.17	-0.28	-0.19	0.05
	0.15	0.15	0.15	0.24	0.25	0.26
supression of back office staffs	-0.88***	-0.26*	-0.22	-0.88***	-0.47*	-0.25
	0.15	0.15	0.16	0.25	0.25	0.27
diversification of office location	-0.64***	-0.11	-0.01	-0.41	-0.17	0.21
	0.19	0.18	0.18	0.31	0.32	0.33
integrating office location	-0.53***	-0.14	-0.01	-0.34	-0.09	0.13
	0.17	0.16	0.16	0.28	0.28	0.30
enhancing of flexible work time	-0.72***	-0.38**	-0.27	-0.64**	-0.45*	-0.04
	0.17	0.16	0.16	0.27	0.27	0.28
active use of outsourcing	-0.36**	-0.05	-0.12	0.23	0.39	0.76**
	0.16	0.16	0.16	0.31	0.32	0.33

Note :   *** : statistical significance at 1% level
          ** : statistical significance at 5% level
          * : statistical significance at 10% level

---

[14]Dummy variables are arranged by setting the number of technologies = 3 as a base.

Table 4 Regression results; Skill change = f (technology, organizational change)

(For all firms: No-tech firms as a base)

		High-tech firm		Low-tech firm		Tech-change firm		Organization	
Manager	IT related skill	0.627***	(0.155)	0.477***	(0.112)	0.800***	(0.112)	0.106***	(0.024)
	non IT skill	0.398***	(0.138)	0.143	(0.100)	0.352***	(0.100)	0.059***	(0.021)
Administrative	IT related skill	0.805***	(0.170)	0.856***	(0.115)	0.949***	(0.116)	0.119***	(0.028)
	non IT skill	0.524***	(0.139)	0.376***	(0.102)	0.604***	(0.102)	0.071***	(0.021)
R&D	IT related skill	0.666***	(0.181)	0.484***	(0.126)	0.649***	(0.125)	0.049*	(0.026)
	non IT skill	0.54***	(0.159)	0.288**	(0.117)	0.424***	(0.116)	0.029	(0.023)
Sales	IT related skill	0.813***	(0.164)	0.507***	(0.113)	0.574***	(0.113)	0.140***	(0.025)
	non IT skill	0.622***	(0.141)	0.254**	(0.103)	0.429***	(0.103)	0.068***	(0.021)
Production	IT related skill	0.807***	(0.182)	0.390***	(0.127)	0.671***	(0.127)	0.056***	(0.026)
	non IT skill	0.696***	(0.168)	0.228*	(0.122)	0.359***	(0.122)	0.047*	(0.024)

Table 4 Continued

(For tech firms only: Tech-change firms as a base)

		High-tech firm		Low-tech firm		Organization	
Manager	IT related skill	-0.190	(0.138)	-0.330***	(0.091)	0.111***	(0.026)
	non IT skill	0.049	(0.123)	-0.212***	(0.082)	0.055**	(0.023)
Administrative	IT related skill	-0.141	(0.162)	-0.098	(0.105)	0.087***	(0.031)
	non IT skill	-0.068	(0.123)	-0.236***	(0.082)	0.060***	(0.023)
R&D	IT related skill	-0.018	(0.168)	-0.165	(0.106)	0.061**	(0.029)
	non IT skill	0.120	(0.141)	-0.128	(0.094)	0.035	(0.025)
Sales	IT related skill	0.226	(0.150)	-0.065	(0.094)	0.117***	(0.027)
	non IT skill	0.212*	(0.126)	-0.171**	(0.084)	0.056**	(0.023)
Production	IT related skill	0.149	(0.164)	-0.277***	(0.103)	0.075***	(0.028)
	non IT skill	0.356**	(0.148)	-0.132	(0.098)	0.047*	(0.026)

Note :
*** : statistical significance at 1% level
** : statistical significance at 5% level
* : statistical significance at 10% level

Table 5 Regression : Obstacle for HRD = f (technology, organizational change)

	% of firm	Size effect	High-tech	Low-tech	Tech-change	Organization
Lack of personel working for coordination of training	40%	—		+		
Lack of time for training	38%	—				
Lack of know-how for training	30%	—	—			
Lack of instructor	26%	—		+		
Lack of knowledge on the contents of training	23%					
Lack of in-house training center	18%	—				
Financial difficulty	15%					++
Lack of training center nearby	5%					
Lack of institution for consultation on training	4%	—				

Note :   +++ : positive significant coefficient at 1 % level
        ++ : positive significant coefficient at 5 % level
        +   : positive significant coefficient at 10 % level
        --- : negative significant coefficient at 1 % level
        -- : negative significant coefficient at 5 % level
        -   : negative significant coefficient at 10 % level

Table 6 Regression : Measures for training = f (technology, organizational change)

	% of firm	Size effect	High-tech	Low-tech	Tech-change	Organization
Subsiaries to training	42%					++
Increasing opportunity of training	40%	—				+
Increasing information dissemination	38%		+			
Diversifying training contents in public institution	35%	—				
Tax measures for training	33%			+	++	+
Official evaluation for training outcomes	20%	—				

Note :   +++ : positive significant coefficient at 1 % level
        ++ : positive significant coefficient at 5 % level
        +   : positive significant coefficient at 10 % level
        --- : negative significant coefficient at 1 % level
        -- : negative significant coefficient at 5 % level
        -   : negative significant coefficient at 10 % level

Table 7a Regression by wage and performance type

	base salary		bonus	
	worker's	firm's	worker's	firm's
High-tech firm	0.202	0.324**	0.377**	0.271
	0.146	0.144	0.169	0.176
Low-tech firm	0.289***	0.049	0.265**	0.238**
	0.104	0.102	0.113	0.118
Tech-change firm	0.170*	0.082	0.344***	0.276**
	0.102	0.101	0.112	0.117
Organization	0.063***	0.074***	0.118***	0.090***
	0.023	0.022	0.028	0.029

Note : *** : statistical significance at 1% level
       **   : statistical significance at 5% level
       *   : statistical significance at 10% level

Table 7b Regression by occupation

	manager	administrative	R&D	sales	production
High-tech firm	0.175	0.027	0.021	0.135	0.169
	0.163	0.155	0.174	0.167	0.172
Low-tech firm	0.353***	0.152	0.153	0.218*	0.206*
	0.114	0.109	0.124	0.117	0.120
Tech-change firm	0.228**	0.166	0.289**	0.227*	0.155
	0.112	0.108	0.124	0.116	0.119
Organization	0.070***	0.081***	0.067**	0.077***	0.058**
	0.026	0.024	0.027	0.026	0.026

Note : *** : statistical significance at 1% level
       **   : statistical significance at 5% level
       *   : statistical significance at 10% level

Table 8 Regression results : the style of labor force increases = f (technology, organization)

	High-tech firm		Low-tech firm		Tech-change firm		Organization	
Hiring new graduates	0.084	(0.137)	0.061	(0.098)	0.100	(0.097)	-0.086***	(0.021)
Hiring mid-careers	0.068	(0.141)	0.029	(0.099)	0.059	(0.099)	-0.030	(0.021)
Teporary staff contract	0.154	(0.158)	0.075	(0.115)	0.187	(0.114)	0.013	(0.023)
Part time workers	0.047	(0.147)	-0.051	(0.104)	-0.096	(0.103)	0.003	(0.022)
In-house transfer	0.257*	(0.153)	0.105	(0.111)	0.214*	(0.109)	0.079***	(0.023)
Cross-firm transter-1	-0.089	(0.156)	-0.091	(0.117)	0.105	(0.115)	0.069***	(0.024)
Cross-firm transfer-2	0.025	(0.181)	0.036	(0.137)	0.188	(0.135)	0.057***	(0.027)

Note :   *** : statistical significance at 1% level
         ** : statistical significance at 5% level
         *   : statistical significance at 10% level

Table 9 Summary statistics of labor productivity and employment by technology

Tech 91	Tech 94	# of firms	EMP91	LP91	lpgr	empgr
all	all	1182	5.69	1.99	-6.19%	0.89%
0	0	247	5.07	2.01	-3.46%	-2.20%
0	1	159	5.26	1.97	-6.87%	1.84%
0	2	86	5.84	2.09	-8.94%	4.97%
0	3	32	6.08	2.04	-15.94%	0.25%
1	1	211	5.39	1.97	-8.23%	-1.16%
1	2	90	6.05	2.03	-7.11%	3.29%
1	3	22	6.70	1.67	-0.74%	0.94%
2	1	174	6.09	1.94	-5.99%	3.60%
2	2	46	6.19	1.86	-2.03%	1.93%
3	3	115	6.59	2.08	-4.38%	0.87%

Table 10 Regression results : productivity and employment by technology and organizational change

Dependent variable=labor productivity growth

	(1)	(2)	(3)
High-tech firm	0.0053	0.0004	-
	0.0561	0.0562	-
Low-tech firm	-0.0190	-0.0256	-
	0.0407	0.0411	-
Tech-change firm	-0.0188	-0.0245	-
	0.0368	0.0372	-
Organization	-	0.0099	0.0090
	-	0.0099	0.0085
N=	745	745	745

Dependent variable=employment growth

	(1)	(2)	(3)
High-tech firm	0.0476**	0.0530**	-
	0.0231	0.0232	-
Low-tech firm	0.0489***	0.0531***	-
	0.0173	0.0173	-
Tech-change firm	0.0434***	0.0486***	-
	0.0158	0.0159	-
Organization	-	-0.0092**	-0.0077**
	-	0.0036	0.0036
N=	745	745	745

Note : *** : statistical significance at 1% level
   ** : statistical significance at 5% level
   * : statistical significance at 10% level

Table 11 Regression results: Employment effect by occupation

	manager	administrative	R&D	sales	production
High-tech firm	0.077	0.032	-0.004	-0.158	0.018
	0.134	0.135	0.138	0.135	0.141
Low-tech firm	0.070	-0.104	0.065	0.097	-0.001
	0.095	0.095	0.099	0.097	0.099
Tech-change firm	0.123	-0.044	0.249**	0.111	0.114
	0.095	0.094	0.099	0.096	0.099
Organization	-0.074***	-0.113***	-0.047**	-0.009	-0.090***
	0.021	0.021	0.021	0.021	0.021

Note :   *** : statistical significance at 1% level
        ** : statistical significance at 5% level
        *   : statistical significance at 10% level

REFERENCES

Aoki M. ,Okuno M. (1996), *Comparative Institutional Analysis: A New Approach to Economic Systems* (In Japanese), University of Tokyo Press, Tokyo.

Berndt E., Morriron C., Rosenalum L. (1992), '*High-tech Capital, Economic and Labor Composition in U.S. Manufacturing Industries: An Explanatory Analysis*', NBER Working Paper #4010.

Bresnahan T. (1997), '*Computerization and Wage Dispersion: An Analytical Reinterpretation*', a paper presented at NBER Productivity Workshop, Cambridge USA, August 1997.

Brynjolfsson E. (1993), '*Productivity Paradox of Information Technology*', Communications of ACM, December 1993 pp. 66-77.

Brynjolfsson E. , Hitt L. (1996), '*Information Technology, Organizational Architecture and Productivity: Firm Level Evidence*', mimeo.

Doms M., Dunne T., Troske K. (1997), '*Workers, Wages and Technology*', Quarterly Journal of Economics, vol. 112, pp. 253-290.

Davidow W., Malone P. (1993), *The Virtual Corporation: Structuring and Revitalizing the Corporation for 21st Century*, Harper Business.

Economic Planing Agency (1994), *The White Paper of Japanese Economy, 1994*, The Japanese Government.

Gordon R., Baily M. (1991), *'Measurement Issues and the Productivity Slowdown in Five Major Industrial Countries'*, in G. Bell ed. Technology and Productivity: The Challenge for Economic Policy, OECD, Paris, pp. 187-206.

Government of Japan (1996), *'Outline of Results of "Questionnaire for Influences on Enterprise'* Employment by Technological Innovation', January, 1996, unpublished paper.

Hamada K., Kurosaka Y. (1986), *'Trends in Unemployment, Wages and Productivity: The Case of Japan'*, Economica, Supplement, 1986, 53(210), pp. S275-296 .

Hammer M., Champy J. (1993), *Reengineering the Corporation: A Manifesto for Business Revolution*, Harper Collins.

Heckman J. (1979), *'Sample Selection Bias as a Specification Error'*, Econometrica, vol. 46 no 6, pp. 1251-711.

Ichniowski C, Kochan, T. A., Levine D., Olson C., Strauss G.(1996), *'What Works At Work: Overview and Assessment'*, Industrial Relations, vol. 35 no. 3, July 1996, pp. 299-333.

Ichniowski C., Shaw K., Prennushi G. (1997), *'The Effects of Human Resource Management Practices on Productivity: A Study on Steel Finishing Lines'*, American Economic Review, vol. 87, no. 3, pp. 291-313.

Krueger A. (1993), *'How Computer Have Changed the Wage Structure? Evidence from Micro Data'*, Quarterly Journal of Economics, vol. 108, pp. 33-60.

Levy F., Murnane R.J. (1996), *'With What Skills Are Computers a Complement?'*, American Economic Review, vol. 86, no. 2, May, pp. 258-262.

McGuckin R., Streitwieser M., Doms M. (1996), *'The Effect of Technology Use on Productivity Growth'*, CES Discussion Papers, CES 96-2, Center for Economic Studies, US Bureau of Census, Washington, DC.

Milgrom P., Roberts J. (1990), *'The Economics of Modern Manufacturing: Technology, Strategy and Organization'*, American Economic Journal, June 1990, pp. 511-528.

Milgrom P., Roberts J. (1992), *Economics, Organization and Management*, Prentice Hall, Englewood Cliffs, New Jersey.

Milgrom P., Roberts J. (1995), *'Complementarities and Fit Strategy, Structure, and Organizational Change In Manufacturing'*, Journal of Accounting and Economics, vol, 19, pp. 179-208.

Motohashi K (1998a), *'Economic Analysis of Information Network Use : Organizational and Productivity Impacts on Japanese Firms'* mimeo.

Motohashi K (1998b), *'Technology, Productivity and Employment: Insights from Firm Level Datasets in France, Japan and the United States'*, forthcoming STI Working Paper, OECD, Paris.

Motohashi K, Nezu R. (1997), *'Why Do Countries Perform Differently?'*, OECD Observer, no. 206, June/July, pp. 19-22, OECD, Paris.

Nutek (1996), *Towards Flexible Organizations*, Swedish National Broad for Industrial and Technical Development, 1996:6.

OECD (1996b), *Technology, Productivity and Job Creation, vol. 2: Analytical Report*, OECD, Paris.

Osterman P. (1994), *'How Common Is Workplace Transformation and Who Adopt It?'*, Industrial and Labor Relations Review, vol. 47 no. 2, January 1994, pp.173-188.

Vickery G., Wurzburg G. (1996), *'The Challenge of Measuring and Evaluating Organizational Change in Enterprises'*, a paper presented at the Conference of New S&T Indicators For the Knowledge Based Economy.

PARAMETRIC ESTIMATION OF TECHNICAL AND ALLOCATIVE EFFICIENCIES AND PRODUCTIVITY CHANGES: A CASE STUDY[*]

Bert M. Balk[1] and George Van Leeuwen[2]

[1,2]*Department of Statistical Methods, Statistics Netherlands*

1 Introduction

The increased availability of firm level data has led to a renewed interest in the components of productivity change in different sectors of the economy. Simultaneously, recent years have seen a rapid development of efficiency and productivity change measurement techniques. Nonparametric methods like DEA became increasingly popular, and parametric models became sufficiently elaborate to capture other sources of productivity change than technological change[1]. At present parametric models are able to distinguish between technological change (the movement of the technological frontier through time) and the change of allocative and technical efficiency. Allocative efficiency is related to sub-optimality of the input mix. A firm may improve its efficiency (reduce its cost) by adapting its input mix to prevailing market prices. Technical efficiency is related to slacks in inputs: the actual level of output can be achieved with less inputs. It is well known that both kinds of efficiency cannot be estimated simultaneously unless panel data are available. For this reason early studies that estimated allocative efficiencies had to assume that firms were fully technically efficient (see e.g. Atkinson and Halvorsen 1984, 1986 for examples of estimating allocative efficiencies from cross-sectional data and Oum and Zhang 1995 for a time series example). Furthermore, in the absence of panel data, estimates of technical efficiencies can only be obtained by imposing some structure on the disturbances of the model (the stochastic frontier approach).

With panel data available, less restrictive models can be applied which include both kinds of efficiency as well as technological change. Recent examples are

---

[*] The authors thank Henry R. Nieuwenhuijsen for the data preparation and the DEA calculations. The views expressed in this paper are those of the authors and do not necessarily reflect the policies of Statistics Netherlands.
[1] Recent developments in this area are documented in the October 1996 issue of The Journal of Productivity Analysis.

Atkinson and Cornwell (1994a), (1994b). These studies model efficiencies as firm-specific fixed effects. For technological change it is common practice to assume Hicks-neutral or factor augmenting change. Baltagi et al. (1995) followed an alternative approach by assuming the parameters of the cost-system to be time-dependent and technical efficiencies to be firm-specific fixed effects. However, up to our knowledge, no attempt has been made that allows time-patterns of allocative and technical efficiencies to differ among firms alongside with movements of the frontier.

This paper presents a first attempt to estimate simultaneously shifts in the frontier while allowing for moving distances to the frontier, by assuming that both technical and allocative efficiencies are driven by firm-specific levels and trends. To this end we use the modified version of the standard augmented cost system, as proposed by Balk (1997). We apply a highly parameterized model to panel data of the Dutch rubber-processing industry and compare our results with the efficiency scores and productivity change figures obtained by Data Envelopment Analysis (DEA).

DEA offers an interesting framework for comparisons. Amongst other things it will be shown that the parametric estimates of the technical efficiencies are rather similar to the scores obtained by DEA, when we assume that the firms are allocatively efficient and the technical efficiencies fixed. However, assuming both allocative and technical efficiencies to be firm- and time-dependent lowers technical and cost efficiencies. It is also shown that the two methods yield exactly the same cost efficiencies (after rescaling) in constant-returns-to-scale models that allow for both types of efficiency. Firm averages across time of cost efficiencies derived from parametric estimates using pooled data appear to be equal to the results built up from yearly DEA applications. However, this conclusion does not hold for variable-returns-to-scale models. This paper also contributes to the literature by investigating the consequences of the misspecification of models for the decomposition of productivity changes. It is shown that imposing restrictions on models may lead to different conclusions with respect to the decomposition of productivity changes.

The plan of the paper is as follows. In section 2 we discuss the specification of the parametric models and the decomposition of cost efficiency into technical and allocative efficiency. The estimates of the technology parameters are given in section 3, the efficiency scores for different models in section 4 and the decomposition of productivity changes in section 5. Section 6 closes with a summary and presents some conclusions.

2 The model

2.1 Derivation of the cost and share equations

The econometric model to be used for parametric estimation consists of a modified version of the shadow or augmented cost system. Early applications of the model can be found in Atkinson and Halvorsen (1984), (1986). The shadow cost system has been developed in answer to the limitations of the traditional cost minimization problem. At the beginning the model has been applied to capture changes in the regulatory environment of firms, e.g. due to government policies. In the course of time it has been given a broader economic content by assuming that firms may not react properly to price signals and as a consequence may incur losses in cost efficiency. The model can be extended further by allowing for a varying degree of technical efficiency. Technical efficiency may be looked upon from the input side or from the output side. Input technical efficiency is related to the largest possible proportional reduction of all inputs that still satisfies the input requirements for a given level of output. Output technical efficiency is measured via the largest possible output expansion given available inputs.

Consider a single firm and let x_t, y_t denote the N-vector of observed input quantities and scalar output quantities respectively during time period t. Let w_t denote the vector of corresponding input prices. The period t technology, to which this firm has access, will be represented by the cost function $C^t(w, y)$. $C^t(w, y)$ is the minimum cost of producing y when the input prices are w. The conventional cost minimization model of firm behaviour assumes that observed cost is equal to minimum cost, that is

$$w_t x_t = C^t(w_t, y_t), \qquad [1]$$

where $w_t x_t \equiv \sum_{n=1}^{N} w_{nt} x_{nt}$ is observed cost. Thus input quantities x_t are assumed to be optimal and the firm is said to be fully efficient. In our model, however, we allow for two types of inefficiency.

Technical inefficiency means that $ITE_t x_t$, where input technical efficiency[2] $ITE_t \leq 1$, is just able to produce y_t. Allocative inefficiency means that $ITE_t x_t$ is not optimal for prices w_t. One can show (see Balk 1997) that under weak regularity conditions there exists a w_t^* such that

---

[2] Notice that *ITE* is the reciprocal of the input distance function.

$$w_t^* ITE_t x_t = C^t(w_t^*, y_t).$$ [2]

The vector w_t^* is called the vector of shadow prices. The shadow prices are those prices that make the technically efficient input quantity vector $ITE_t x_t$ the least cost solution for producing y_t. One can normalize w_t^* such that

$$w_t^* x_t = w_t x_t.$$ [3]

Then,

$$w_t ITE_t x_t = C^t(w_t^*, y_t).$$ [4]

Shephard's Lemma applied to [2] yields

$$ITE_t x_{nt} = \frac{\partial C^t(w_t^*, y_t)}{\partial w_n} \quad (n = 1, \cdots, N),$$ [5]

which implies, by using [4], that

$$\frac{\partial \ln C^t(w_t^*, y_t)}{\partial \ln w_n} = \frac{w_{nt}^*}{C^t(w_t^*, y_t)} \frac{\partial C^t(w_t^*, y_t)}{\partial w_n} = \frac{w_{nt}^* x_{nt}}{w_t x_t} = \frac{w_{nt}^*}{w_{nt}} \frac{w_{nt} x_{nt}}{w_t x_t} = \theta_{nt} s_{nt}$$

where $s_{nt} \equiv \dfrac{w_{nt} x_{nt}}{w_t x_t}$ $(n = 1, \cdots, N)$ are   observed   cost   shares

and $\theta_{nt} \equiv \dfrac{w_{nt}^*}{w_{nt}}$ $(n = 1, \cdots, N)$ are price distortion factors. Rearranging the last expression, we obtain

$$s_{nt} = \frac{\partial \ln C^t(w_t^*, y_t)}{\partial \ln w_n} \frac{1}{\theta_{nt}}.$$ [6]

Notice that, due to the linear homogeneity in prices of the cost function,

$$\sum_n s_{nt}\theta_{nt} = 1.$$ [7]

After rewriting [4] as

$$\ln c_t \equiv \ln w_t x_t = \ln C^t(w_t^*, y_t) + \ln(\frac{1}{ITE_t}),$$ [8]

an empirical specification for the model can be obtained by choosing a functional form for $\ln C^t(w,y)$. An appropriate choice is the translog functional form which is frequently applied in other studies. In the empirical application we use one output and three inputs: capital, material inputs (including energy) and labour. A balanced panel is available which tracks 18 firms over a period of 15 years. Then, appending also firm subscripts, the cost system reads

$$\ln c_{kt} = \alpha_0 + G(t) + \sum_n \alpha_n \ln w_{nkt}^* + (1/2)\sum_n \sum_{n'} \alpha_{nn'} \ln w_{nkt}^* \ln w_{n'kt}^* + \beta_1 \ln y_{kt}$$

$$+ (1/2)\beta_{11}(\ln y_{kt})^2 + \sum_n \gamma_n \ln w_{nkt}^* \ln y_{kt} + \ln(\frac{1}{ITE_{kt}}),$$ [9]

where $\ln w_{nkt}^* = \ln \theta_{nkt} + \ln w_{nt}$, $k = 1,\cdots,18$, $t = 1,\cdots,15$, and $n = 1,\cdots,3$.

In [9] $G(t)$ denotes a general representation of disembodied technological change. Using [6] and [9], a parametric expression for the (observed) cost shares can be obtained as

$$s_{nkt} = [\alpha_n + \sum_{n'} \alpha_{nn'} \ln w_{nkt}^* + \gamma_n \ln y_{kt}] / \theta_{nkt} \quad (n, n' = 1,\cdots,3).$$ [10]

In [9] and [10] y_{kt} and c_{kt} denote actual real output and actual cost of firm k in year t, and s_{nkt} denotes the actual cost share of input n for firm k in year t. Furthermore, w_{1t}, w_{2t} and w_{3t} refer to observed prices for capital, material inputs and labour respectively, which are assumed to be the same for all firms.

The following usual restrictions are imposed in estimating [9] and [10]:

$$\sum_n \alpha_n = 1, \sum_{n'} \alpha_{nn'} = 0 \ (n = 1, \cdots, 3), \ \sum_n \gamma_n = 0 \ \text{and} \ \alpha_{nt} = \alpha_{n'n} \qquad [11]$$

Input homotheticity requires the following restrictions

$$\gamma_n = 0 \ (n = 1, \ldots, 3). \qquad\qquad\qquad\qquad\qquad\qquad\qquad\qquad [12]$$

Global constant-returns-to-scale requires in addition to [12]

$$\beta_1 = 1 \ \text{and} \ \beta_{11} = 0. \qquad\qquad\qquad\qquad\qquad\qquad\qquad\qquad [13]$$

Notice that [9] and [10] differ from the system used by Atkinson and Cornwell (1994a) and Oum and Zhang (1995). The last term in their specification of the cost function does not appear in our specification. Similar conclusions hold for the denominators of their cost share equations. These simplifications are due to the different normalization rule adopted here. Furthermore, [7] implies that we only need to specify two price distortions per period t and firm k. We use labour as the dependent input factor in the normalizations [7] and [11].

We now turn to dynamics. In [9] and [10] we assumed that the price distortion factors are input-, firm- as well as time-specific. Our primary objective is to estimate technical and allocative efficiencies simultaneously, relaxing the assumption of Atkinson and Cornwell (1994a) that both components of cost efficiency are constant through time. But we do not - in addition - allow technological change to interact with other explanatory variables, and we explicitly assume technological change to be disembodied. Three specifications for $G(t)$ will be explored in section 3. When, in addition, technical efficiencies are to be different across firm, it is not possible to estimate [9] and [10] as such. Additional restrictions are required to keep things tractable. A convenient assumption seems to be the hypothesis that both technical and allocative efficiencies differ across firms in their initial state and that both efficiencies follow a firm-specific long run time trend. Thus we assume the firm-specific paths of technical efficiencies to be driven by

$$\ln(\frac{1}{ITE_{kt}}) = \varsigma_1^k + \varsigma_2^k t, \qquad\qquad\qquad\qquad\qquad\qquad\qquad [14]$$

and the paths of the input price distortions by

$$\theta_{nkt} = \theta_{n1}^k + \theta_{n2}^k t .$$ [15]

For identification of the model it is necessary to set $ITE_{kt} = 1$, and thus $\zeta_1^k = \zeta_2^k = 0$, for one of the firms. As will be shown in section 4, the choice of the reference firm appears to be not trivial in case of estimating both allocative and technical efficiencies. It should be noted that, as an implication of this identification restriction, technical efficiencies are estimated relative to the reference firm.

Model [9] - [10] will be called the *input* model, because of its orientation to input technical efficiency. Orientating instead to output technical efficiency ($OTE_{kt} \leq 1$), we obtain under weak regularity conditions (see again Balk 1997) the *output* model. The only difference with [9] - [10] pertains to the additive input technical efficiency term, which disappears from the cost function equation. Instead output is now multiplied by $1/OTE_{kt}$. Then, maintaining the same notation for the other parameters, the output model reads

$$\ln c_{kt} = \alpha_0 + G(t) + \sum_n \alpha_n \ln w_{nkt}^* + (1/2) \sum_n \sum_{n'} \alpha_{nn'} \ln w_{nkt}^* \ln w_{n'kt}^*$$
$$+ \beta_1 \ln(\frac{y_{kt}}{OTE_{kt}}) + (1/2)\beta_{11}(\ln\frac{y_{kt}}{OTE_{kt}})^2 + \sum_n \gamma_n \ln w_{nkt}^* \ln(\frac{y_{kt}}{OTE_{kt}}),$$ [16]

$$s_{nkt} = [\alpha_n + \sum_{n'} \alpha_{nn'} \ln w_{nkt}^* + \gamma_n \ln(\frac{y_{kt}}{OTE_{kt}})] / \theta_{nkt} \quad (n,n' = 1,\cdots,3)$$ [17]

with $\ln(\frac{1}{OTE_{kt}}) = \mu_1^k + \mu_2^k t$. Again, for identification of the model, it is necessary to set $OTE_{kt} = 1$ for one of the firms.

2.2 The derivation of efficiency scores

Estimates of allocative and technical efficiencies can be derived after estimating [9] or [16]. Because all parameters appear in the cost function, it would suffice to estimate the cost function for both models only. However, using a cost system, by including also two of the three share equations (omitting the third to circumvent the singularity problem), one can expect a gain in precision of the estimates (see Atkinson and Cornwell 1994a). This is the procedure we followed.

After eliminating labour by using the various restrictions, we estimated various versions of the cost system of both models. The differences are related to assumptions concerning the efficiencies. It can be verified that imposing in the input model $\theta_{n1}^{k} = \theta_{n2}^{k} = 0$ $(n = 1,\cdots,3)$ invokes technical efficiencies only (as assumed in Atkinson and Cornwell 1994b), and letting $\zeta_{1}^{k} = \zeta_{2}^{k} = 0$ boils down to a model with allocative efficiencies only. Furthermore, with $\theta_{n2}^{k} = 0$ $(n = 1,\cdots,3)$ and $\zeta_{2}^{k} = 0$ imposed, the cost system collapses into a model with fixed firm-specific allocative and technical efficiencies as investigated by Atkinson and Cornwell (1994a)[3]. All models can be estimated in the unrestricted variable-returns-to-scale (VRS) form or - by imposing [12] and [13] - in the constant-returns-to-scale (CRS) version.

In the full input model, the following expressions can be derived for the efficiency scores. Expanding equation [9], using $\ln w_{nkt}^{*} = \ln \theta_{nkt} + \ln w_{nt}$, one can easily verify that

$$\ln c_{kt} = \ln c_{kt}^{0} + \ln c_{kt}^{\theta} + \ln(\frac{1}{ITE_{kt}}) \qquad [18a]$$

with

$$\ln c_{kt}^{0} = \alpha_{0} + G(t) + \sum_{n}\alpha_{n}\ln w_{nt} + (1/2)\sum_{n}\sum_{n'}\alpha_{nn'}\ln w_{nt}\ln w_{n't}$$
$$+ \beta_{1}\ln y_{kt} + (1/2)\beta_{11}(\ln y_{kt})^{2} + \sum_{n}\gamma_{n}\ln w_{nt}\ln y_{kt} \qquad [18b]$$

$$\ln c_{kt}^{\theta} = \sum_{n}\alpha_{n}\ln \theta_{nkt} + \sum_{n}\sum_{n'}\alpha_{nn'}\ln w_{nt}\ln \theta_{n'kt} + \sum_{n}\gamma_{n}\ln y_{kt}\ln \theta_{nkt}$$
$$+ \sum_{n}\sum_{n'}\alpha_{nn'}\ln \theta_{nkt}\ln \theta_{n'kt}. \qquad [18c]$$

If all parameters are estimated, then expressions [18b] and [18c] can be seen as estimates of (the logs of) the minimum cost and the potential cost reduction pertaining to achieving full allocative efficiency and $\ln(1/ITE_{kt})$ represents the estimate of the potential cost reduction (in logs) obtainable by achieving full technical efficiency. Equation (18a) also provides a representation of the decomposition of cost efficiency (CE) into input technical efficiency (ITE) and input allocative efficiency (IAE). It is immediately clear that

---

[3] It should be remembered that Atkinson and Cornwell (1994b) used a different normalization.

$$CE_{kt} = \frac{\exp\{\ln c_{kt}^0\}}{\exp\{\ln c_{kt})}, \qquad\qquad 0 < CE_{kt} \leq 1 \qquad\qquad [19a]$$

$$ITE_{kt} = \exp\{-\varsigma_1^k - \varsigma_2^k t\}, \qquad\qquad 0 < ITE_{kt} \leq 1 \qquad\qquad [19b]$$

$$IAE_{kt} = \exp\{-\ln c_{kt}^\theta\}, \qquad\qquad 0 < IAE_{kt} \leq 1 \qquad\qquad [19c]$$

and that

$$CE_{kt} = ITE_{kt} IAE_{kt}. \qquad\qquad\qquad [19d]$$

To derive estimates of the efficiency scores from the output model, a different route has to be followed. First we estimate [16] - [17] and apply [18b] and [19a] to obtain an estimate of CE_{kt}. Secondly we evaluate

$$\ln c_{kt}^e = \alpha_0 + G(t) + \sum_n \alpha_n \ln w_{nt} + (1/2)\sum_n \sum_{n'} \alpha_{nn'} \ln w_{nt} \ln w_{n't}$$
$$+ \beta_1 \ln(\frac{y_{kt}}{OTE_{kt}}) + (1/2)\beta_{11}(\ln\frac{y_{kt}}{OTE_{kt}})^2 + \sum_n \gamma_n \ln w_{nt} \ln(\frac{y_{kt}}{OTE_{kt}}) \qquad 20]$$

Then the dual measure of output technical efficiency (*DOTE*) is given by

$$DOTE_{kt} = \frac{\exp\{\ln c_{kt}^0\}}{\exp\{\ln c_{kt}^e\}}. \qquad\qquad\qquad [21]$$

In section 4 estimates will be presented for the three efficiency scores, with CE_{kt} derived from [19a] for both models, ITE_{kt} from [19b] for the input model and $DOTE_{kt}$ from [21] for the output model. Finally estimates of IAE_{kt} for both models are derived by applying equality constraint (19d) with ITE_{kt} replaced by $DOTE_{kt}$ in case of the output model. Notice that our approach yields estimates for all three scores for every year and every firm in our data set. This enables us to look at efficiencies in the firm dimension as well as in the time dimension of the data. Firm averages across time and the time paths of average efficiency scores are compared with the average scores based upon a DEA model.

3 Empirical results

3.1 Data

To estimate the models we use data on real output, prices and cost shares for capital, material inputs (including energy) and labour for the rubber processing industry. This data set tracks the performance of 18 firms over the period 1978 - 1992. Real output is calculated by deflating gross output values by firm-specific, weighted sectoral output price index numbers for home sales and exports. Sectoral deflators for material inputs and contract wages are used as material and labour price index numbers. For capital we calculated the user cost of capital by using firm and time specific depreciation cost and sectoral data on scrapping rates, corporate tax rates and the long-term interest rate. Capital price index numbers were calculated from sectoral price index numbers of investment goods by applying a rental cost formula. Total cost is obtained by adding the user cost of capital to the wage bill (including social security contributions) and the cost of material inputs which are readily available from the Production Surveys used in constructing the panel.

The cost equations, [9] and [16] respectively, and the cost share equations for capital and material inputs, [10] and [17] respectively, were jointly estimated after appending disturbance terms to each equation. As usual we assumed that the disturbances are of the SUR-type: contemporaneously correlated but uncorrelated across firms and time. The correlations were assumed to be constant through time. Estimates were obtained from the maximum likelihood estimation method of TSP 4.3A. In estimating we imposed restrictions [7] and [11]. Labour has been used as the input which could be factored out[4]. The input model as well as the output model has been estimated under variable-returns-to-scale (labeled VRS) and constant-returns- to-scale (labeled CRS).

3.2 Estimates of technology parameters for the various models

A distinct feature of our approach is that technical and allocative efficiencies are treated as entities which are allowed to vary over time. This enables a direct estimation of efficiency scores from the parameters of the models, provides a framework for testing different model assumptions, and also enables us to assess their implications for the efficiency scores and rankings. Models with firm-specific and time-varying technical efficiencies are not entirely new. For instance, Cornwell et al. (1990) estimated production frontiers with cross-sectional and

---

[4] Using instead of labour one of the other two inputs leads to estimates which are not statistically different.

time-series variation in technical efficiency levels by adopting a second-order polynomial of time with firm-specific parameters. In the estimation procedure the production function parameters were estimated after projecting out the time-varying and firm-specific effects. Subsequently, firm-specific and time-varying efficiency levels were derived from the predictions of a regression of the production function residuals on a constant, time and time squared term[5]. This procedure implicitly assumes that the residual part of the regression represents technical efficiency only.

The models we propose here are highly parameterized. This has the potential of taking into account an additional purifying of the residuals. However, this advantage comes at a price. The models chosen, the parameterization of efficiencies and the restrictions [7] and [11] require maximum likelihood estimation on highly nonlinear models. Furthermore, allowing for technical as well as allocative efficiency simultaneously limits the range of tractable specifications with regard to the dynamics. We are aware of the fact that the models proposed are encompassing with respect to the components of productivity change, but - on the other hand - may be too restrictive with respect to the specification of dynamics. For instance, due to data availability, it is not possible to allow the cost function parameters to vary so freely in time as proposed by Baltagi et al. (1995)[6]. Instead we investigated three specifications of disembodied technological change[7]:

$$G(t) = \delta t \qquad \qquad [22a]$$

$$G(t) = \delta_1 t + \delta_2 t^2 \qquad \qquad . \quad [22b]$$

$$G(t) = \delta \sqrt{t} \, . \qquad \qquad [22c]$$

As mentioned in the preceding section we also had to select the most efficient firm. For reasons of identification we have to pinpoint for one firm its efficiency parameters ζ_1^k and ζ_2^k at zero. As a consequence levels and trends of technical efficiencies of the other firms are relative to the firm chosen. Deciding which firm to choose appears to be not trivial. The proposed models aim at estimating allocative and technical efficiencies simultaneously. Therefore, the choice of the firm which is technically fully efficient has to be made conditional on assuming

---

[5] In Cornwell et al. (1992) it has been shown that this method can be extended to systems of equations with time-varying fixed effects.

[6] We used sectoral price indices as exogenous prices. Therefore, the Baltagi approach would give rise to singularity problems when estimating firm-specific trends for technical efficiencies and price distortions.

[7] In principle - following Cornwell et al. (1990) - we could also use (22b) for the technical efficiencies and the price distortions. We did not choose this route because it would increase the number of parameters to be estimated by 54 !

the possibility of allocative inefficiency. Excluding the price distortions, that is assuming allocative inefficiency away, does not lead to the same choice of the technically fully efficient firm, because in this case technical efficiency scores may not be purely 'technical' as can be easily verified from [18a] and the foregoing discussion. The technically fully efficient firm may not be allocatively efficient at the same time.

In the estimation procedure we followed a sequential approach. Limiting the specification search for disembodied technological progress and the fully efficient firm to the input model, we first estimated simple cost systems assuming all inefficiencies away by imposing $\zeta_1^k = \zeta_2^k = 0$ and $\theta_{n1}^k = \theta_{n2}^k = 0 \ (n = 1,2)$ for all k. This provided starting values for the second round estimates including firm-specific fixed technical and allocative efficiencies (imposing $\zeta_2^k = \theta_{12}^k = \theta_{22}^k = 0$ for all k). This in turn provided information on the technically most efficient firm in our data set, conditional on the assumption of fixed allocative and technical efficiencies. Finally, we allowed for firm-specific differences in time-paths of efficiencies, relaxing the last assumption and pinpointing ζ_1^k and ζ_2^k at zero for the technically most efficient firm of the second round[8]. The last stage has been repeated for each of the specifications [22a] - [22c], yielding the preferred specification of disembodied technological change in the fully specified input model. The choice of the specification of disembodied technological change has been guided by the likelihood of the models. For specification [22b] the likelihood was slightly higher than for [22a], which in turn outperformed [22c][9]. Because of the small difference between [22a] and [22b] we adopted [22a] as the preferred specification. Next we compared the input model and the output model, investigated differences between the restricted and unrestricted forms of the cost system and the implications of imposing restrictions on the parameters related to the efficiency scores.

Table 1 presents the estimates for the cost function parameters in the restricted and unrestricted forms of the cost systems at the final stage. As can be seen in table 1, the estimates for the input model and the output model almost coincide in the constant-returns-to- scale version, but they don't do so for the unrestricted form of the models. The Wald statistic for testing constant-returns-to-scale strongly rejects this, with $\chi_5^2 = 213$ for the input model and $\chi_5^2 = 210$ for the output model, while the critical value $\chi_5^2 (0.01)$ equals 15.1. Since the data clearly reject linear homogeneity in output it can be concluded that the two models yield different representations of the efficiencies under variable-returns-to-scale. To save space we do not present estimates of the parameters related to efficiency. It suffices to note that the

---

[8] This appeared to be firm 1.

[9] The (log) likelihoods for the three specifications were 1824, 1826 and 1754 respectively.

Table 1 Estimates of the technology parameters under various assumptions[a]

Model	Input VRS		Output VRS		Input CRS		Output CRS	
Param	Est.	SE	Est.	SE	Est.	SE	Est.	SE
α_0	2.29531	.77930	1.64226	.63518	-1.14911	.12417	-1.15205	.12452
α_1	0.02189	.00507	0.00630	.00694	0.29663	.00923	0.29727	.00923
α_2	-0.03115	.04207	0.01969	.04697	0.07694	.02040	0.07662	.02038
α_3	1.00930	.04392	0.97400	.04701	0.62643	.01559	0.62611	.01555
β_1	0.62358	.16041	0.76222	.12280	1.00000		1.00000	
β_{11}	0.00902	.01642	-0.00446	.01156	0.00000		0.00000	
α_{11}	0.00855	.00242	0.00181	.00268	0.10619	.00528	0.10658	.00528
α_{12}	-0.01574	.00443	-0.00367	.00540	0.00477	.00370	0.00476	.00370
α_{13}	0.00719	.00209	0.00186	.00273	-0.11096	.00509	-0.11134	.00508
α_{22}	-0.02124	.01194	-0.03294	.01248	-0.04279	.01136	-0.04259	.01133
α_{23}	0.03698	.01198	0.03662	.01308	0.03802	.00873	0.03784	.00871
α_{33}	-0.04418	.01243	-0.03848	.01414	0.07294	.01071	0.07350	.01069
γ_1	0.00030	.00025	0.00016	.00023	0.00000		0.00000	
γ_2	0.03082	.00503	0.02784	.00498	0.00000		0.00000	
γ_3	-0.03112	.00516	-0.02800	.00499	0.00000		0.00000	
δ	0.02263	.00350	0.01931	.00352	0.02163	.00920	0.02169	.00923
Log likelihood	1824		1822		1740		1740	
R^2 cost function	.998		.998		.992		.992	
R^2 share capital	.867		.873		.886		.886	
R^2 share material	.752		.808		.925		.925	

[a] Firm 1 taken to be technically efficient in all years.

parameters referring to the initial states of technical efficiency (ζ_1^k or μ_1^k) were significantly different from 0 for all firms (except, of course, firm 1), with a lowerbound for the t-values of 3 in the VRS models and 4 in the CRS models. An exception must be made for firm 13 which appeared to be close to the frontier in the VRS models. The trend parameters of technical efficiency (ζ_2^k or μ_2^k) were also statistically significant at level 0.05, except for firm 18 (and except, of course, firm 1). A striking result is that all trend parameters were negative, indicating that - on average - the distance to the technical frontier decreased during the years under consideration. In the second stage of the estimation

332 B.M. Balk, G. Van Leeuwen

procedure it was also found that the assumption of full allocative efficiency was strongly rejected by the data[10].

In table 2 arithmetical averages (across time) of price distortions are reported for material inputs, capital and labour, with the results for the latter derived from the normalization [7]. An estimate < 1.0 implies over-utilization and > 1.0 under-utilization of inputs. Material and capital inputs appear to be over-utilized and labour to be under-utilized in the rubber-processing industry in the years under consideration. The results show that the sources of allocative efficiency are widely dispersed between firms. In particular the price distortions for capital differ widely between firms and also between models. Notice also that firms 1 and 13 - which were on or close to the frontier - are the only two firms with under-utilization of capital in the input model.

Table 2 Average price distortion factors

	Material		Capital		Labour	
Firm\Model	IVRS	OVRS	IVRS	OVRS	IVRS	OVRS
1	.40	.45	1.52	.34	3.02	3.01
2	.77	.80	.10	.02	1.41	1.41
3	.53	.59	.50	.11	2.48	2.42
4	.79	.85	.09	.02	1.46	1.42
5	.57	.64	.45	.09	1.57	1.55
6	.66	.73	.24	.05	2.02	1.93
7	.56	.63	.53	.11	1.57	1.54
8	.75	.83	.09	.02	1.97	1.85
9	.58	.64	.27	.06	1.92	1.88
10	.57	.64	.44	.10	2.04	1.98
11	.74	.76	.05	.01	1.48	1.47
12	.66	.71	.14	.03	2.05	1.99
13	.41	.46	1.08	.22	2.39	2.40
14	.73	.78	.05	.02	1.67	1.62
15	.55	.60	.29	.06	2.06	2.03
16	.50	.58	.84	.16	1.64	1.61
17	.77	.84	.06	.02	1.81	1.73
18	.57	.60	.18	.04	2.04	2.05
mean	.62	.67	.38	.08	1.92	1.88

[10] The likelihood ratio test statistic for both models strongly indicates rejection of the null hypothesis of full allocative efficiency.

We also tested for the time constancy of technical efficiencies and price distortions in the input and the output model. The null hypotheses considered are

$H_0 : \zeta_2^k = 0$ or $\mu_2^k = 0$ (all $k \neq 1$), for input or output technical efficiencies,

$H_0 : \theta_{12}^k = 0$ (all k), for the trends of the price distortions of capital, and

$H_0 : \theta_{22}^k = 0$ (all k), for the trends of the price distortions of material inputs.

The Wald test statistic strongly rejects time constancy for the technical efficiencies with $\chi_{18}^2 = 270$ for the VRS input model and $\chi_{18}^2 = 149$ for the VRS output model, with the critical value of $\chi_{18}^2(0.01) = 34.8$. A different picture emerged for the trends of the price distortions. Time constancy of the material input price distortions was rejected by the data with $\chi_{18}^2 = 52$ for the input model and $\chi_{18}^2 = 54$ for the output model. However, H_0 was not rejected (at significance level .05) for the trends of the capital price distortions in both models.

Finally, table 3 presents estimates of the elasticities (evaluated at the average sample point) derived from the technology parameters of the models under variable-returns-to-scale, including time-varying technical efficiencies as well as allocative efficiencies. Notice that all price elasticities are estimated precisely, that own price elasticities have the expected sign and that the differences between the input model and the output model are not statistically significant. This conclusion also holds for the elasticities of substitution and the output and (inverse) scale elasticities, the latter indicating that our data exhibit strongly increasing returns-to-scale.

Table 3 Estimates of elasticities for VRS models

	Input model		Output model	
	Est.	SE	Est.	SE
(Cross) price elasticities of demand				
Capital	-.815	.025	-.886	.028
Capital-Material inputs	.385	.046	.511	.057
Capital-Labour	.430	.022	.374	.029
Material inputs-Capital	.067	.008	.089	.010
Material inputs	-.489	.022	-.510	.023
Material inputs-Labour	.422	.022	.421	.024
Labour-Capital	.116	.006	.101	.008
Labour-Material inputs	.654	.034	.653	.037
Labour	-.770	.035	-.754	.040
Allen-Uzawa elasticities of substitution				
Capital-Material inputs	.700	.084	.930	.102
Capital-Labour	1.212	.062	1.055	.080
Material inputs-Labour	1.190	.061	1.188	.067

	Input model		Output model	
	Est.	SE	Est.	SE
Morishima elasticities of substitution				
Capital-Material inputs	.874	.055	1.021	.063
Capital-Labour	1.200	.047	1.128	.059
Material inputs-Capital	.882	.033	.974	.038
Material inputs-Labour	1.192	.057	1.175	.063
Labour-Capital	.931	.020	.986	.020
Labour-Material inputs	1.143	.055	1.163	.058
Scale- and output elasticities				
Inverse scale	.711	.023	.718	.023
Output-Capital	.715	.023	.719	.023
Output-Material inputs	.767	.025	.768	.025
Output-Labour	.624	.026	.639	.027

4 Estimates of technical and allocative efficiencies

4.1 Technical efficiencies

In this section we look at the efficiency scores arising from the models presented in the preceding section. We focus on the input models. In table 4A geometric firm-specific averages of the estimated *ITE's* are presented for models reflecting different assumptions with respect to inefficiencies. It should be noted that no rescaling has been done. In addition we compare the parametric estimates with the results of DEA[11]. At the outset it should be noted that all efficiency index numbers are smaller or equal than 100 in all years and for all firms, corroborating a priori theoretical reasoning. An exception is the average *ITE* score of firm 13 in the VRS model with time varying technical and allocative efficiency (column 5).

To clarify this result we recall the sequential procedure described in subsection 3.2. Each column of table 4A represents the average efficiency scores arising from a particular model estimated. Several notable conclusions can be drawn. Firstly, when assuming allocative inefficiency away, the parametric estimates of the technical efficiencies are relatively close to the DEA results (col. (1) - (2) and (9) - (10)). On average, the parametric scores are lower than the DEA scores, which should not surprise us because the latter are coming from more flexible frontiers. In the parametric method we have only one firm on the frontier. In the nonparametric case the number of technically efficient firms varies between the years with a lower bound of four[12]. When assuming allocative inefficiency away in the parametric method, firm 11 appears to be the most efficient firm. This result is corroborated by the nonparametric method. Here the average efficiency score is also 100, indicating that firm 11 is on the frontier in all years. An other interesting result reported in table 1 is that with DEA, according to theoretical expectations, the efficiency scores are invariably lower in the constant-returns-to-scale model than in the variable-returns-to-scale model. This is, however, not so with the parametric method. Taking into account that the constant-returns-to-scale assumption was rejected by the data, this indicates that invalidly imposing constant-returns-to-scale apparently biases technical efficiencies upwards.

When allowing for the possibility of allocative inefficiency, firm 11 was no longer technically efficient, but its role was taken over by firm 1 (col. (3) - (4)). Under this assumption, firm 13 also appeared to be very close to the frontier. Similar to other firms, in the course of time firm 13 experienced an increase of technical efficiency relative to firm 1, and since its initial score was very close to 100, this leads to *ITE* scores higher than 100 in the course of time (see col. (5)).

---

[11] See Appendix B for details on the computation.

[12] The number of firms on the frontier varies between 4 in 1979 and 10 in 1984.

Table 4A Average technical efficiencies (x 100) from various input models

Firm	Fixed TE AE = 100		Fixed TE/AE		Time varying TE/AE (I)[a]		Time varying TE/AE (II)[b]		DEA	
	VRS	CRS	VRS	CRS	VRS	CRS	VRS	CRS	V	CR
	(1)	(2)	(3)	(4)	(5)	(6)	(7)	(8)	(9)	(10)
1	**86.1**	83.4	**100.0**	100.0	100.0	100.0	**85.8**	113.1	99.	99.0
2	**95.3**	97.7	**61.1**	71.7	55.3	48.6	**47.4**	54.9	99.	97.9
3	**87.5**	94.1	**71.5**	99.6	53.3	78.1	**45.8**	88.2	98.	98.3
4	**86.0**	94.5	**50.1**	71.1	39.1	48.2	**33.6**	54.4	10	92.6
5	**91.7**	90.9	**67.7**	69.6	71.4	60.9	**61.3**	68.8	93.	91.3
6	**73.3**	90.6	**45.6**	86.1	31.4	62.3	**27.0**	70.3	99.	90.3
7	**98.2**	97.3	**71.8**	74.9	73.6	64.0	**63.1**	72.3	98.	97.6
8	**66.5**	86.1	**38.7**	78.7	26.6	50.0	**22.8**	56.4	99.	87.1
9	**86.2**	87.4	**65.2**	75.6	57.6	55.0	**49.4**	62.0	88.	86.0
10	**87.0**	91.8	**64.6**	84.3	51.8	67.9	**44.4**	76.7	96.	93.9
11	**100.0**	100.0	**68.9**	73.1	69.7	56.7	**59.8**	64.0	10	99.9
12	**87.5**	93.5	**62.2**	83.0	48.9	57.3	**42.0**	64.7	95.	94.1
13	**92.9**	90.2	**97.9**	90.3	116.6	88.5	**100.0**	100.0	10	98.9
14	**88.1**	91.0	**59.5**	72.0	51.4	46.7	**44.1**	52.7	91.	88.7
15	**92.9**	93.0	**75.9**	83.7	70.4	60.8	**60.4**	68.7	94.	93.1
16	**79.6**	78.5	**64.3**	61.5	76.7	62.9	**65.8**	71.1	98.	89.0
17	**68.4**	86.9	**39.0**	76.3	27.0	49.2 .	**23.1**	55.5	96.	85.2
18	**97.7**	96.9	**83.7**	83.0	90.9	57.2	**78.0**	64.6	98.	93.8
mean	**86.4**	91.2	**63.9**	79.1	57.0	60.5	**48.9**	68.4	97.	93.1

[a] Technical efficiencies relative to firm 1.
[b] Technical efficiencies relative to firm 13.

This is clearly an undesirable outcome. We therefore re-estimated the full model, taking firm 13 as technically efficient during all years[13]. The results are presented in col. (7) - (8).

A striking result of table 4A is that the technical efficiencies drastically decrease when allocative inefficiency is allowed for. In particular firms 4, 6, 8 and 17 show small technical efficiencies. These firms were already among the least technically efficient ones under the assumption of fixed technical efficiency only, but they become even less technically efficient when adopting the possibility

---

[13] The estimates of the technology parameters are reported in Appendix A. This model leads to the same elasticities as those reported in table 3. Notice that the estimates of δ now appear to be not significantly different from 0. Notice further, that in this case imposing constant returns to scale leads to an average efficiency score for firm 1 that is larger than 100 (see col. (8)).

of allocative inefficiency. Thus it is the simultaneous approach that reduces technical efficiencies substantially.

4.2 Allocative efficiencies

Allocative efficiency scores arising from the various input models are presented in table 4B. It can be seen that for all firms the allocative efficiencies decrease by imposing constant- returns-to-scale in the full model, whereas the same does not happen when assuming technical and allocative efficiencies to be constant. An other interesting result is that re-estimating the model, taking firm 13 as the technically efficient firm, does not alter the allocative efficiencies both in the restricted and the unrestricted form of the model. Finally, notice that our allocative efficiencies are substantially lower than those obtained by applying DEA.

4.3 Comparing parametric and nonparametric cost efficiency scores

Table 4A showed that parametric efficiency scores arising from a model assuming fixed technical efficiency only, were relatively close to DEA scores for technical efficiency. On average the former were slightly lower, but the differences seem to be reasonable, if we take into account that with DEA the data are fitted to more flexible frontiers and that in the parametric model we have only one firm on the frontier. The DEA results reveal that several firms are on the frontier in different years. In the parametric method cost efficiency equals technical efficiency when allocative inefficiency is assumed away. In the DEA approach cost efficiencies are computed by solving a linear programming problem and then - similar to the parametric method - allocative efficiencies are calculated by dividing cost efficiencies by technical efficiencies. In table 4B it can be verified that DEA allocative efficiency scores are much closer to 100 than parametric allocative efficiencies. Furthermore, averages of DEA allocative efficiencies across time show less dispersion than their parametric equivalents. An other feature of DEA allocative efficiencies is that in every year at least one of the technically efficient firms is also allocatively efficient. With other firms being more close to the allocatively efficient firm than in the parametric case, this reflects the result that cost efficiencies from DEA are larger than their parametric equivalents.

Table 4B Average allocative efficiencies (x 100) from various input models

Firm	Fixed TE/AE		Time varying TE/AE (I)[a]		Time varying TE/AE (II)[b]		DEA	
	VRS	CRS	VRS	CRS	VRS	CRS	VRS	CRS
	(1)	(2)	(3)	(4)	(5)	(6)	(7)	(8)
1	**55.1**	59.9	59.2	36.5	**59.2**	36.4	90.4	88.0
2	**82.2**	82.3	87.9	74.1	**87.9**	74.0	88.9	87.7
3	**63.0**	64.5	70.9	50.2	**70.9**	50.1	98.5	95.1
4	**81.2**	81.1	87.6	73.0	**87.6**	72.9	88.4	90.7
5	**81.1**	83.9	85.7	58.6	**85.7**	58.4	94.8	93.2
6	**70.3**	68.7	79.3	58.0	**79.3**	57.9	98.7	95.8
7	**81.5**	84.3	86.1	60.2	**86.1**	60.0	96.7	94.2
8	**69.2**	67.4	77.9	64.8	**77.9**	64.7	98.3	89.1
9	**72.2**	74.2	78.2	62.4	**78.2**	62.3	95.9	95.4
10	**70.8**	72.2	77.9	54.7	**77.9**	54.6	94.6	94.6
11	**82.7**	84.6	87.9	66.6	**87.9**	66.5	92.9	90.4
12	**69.2**	70.5	75.7	62.4	**75.7**	62.3	92.9	90.7
13	**63.6**	69.2	66.9	43.2	**66.9**	43.0	99.9	92.1
14	**75.9**	76.7	81.8	72.2	**81.8**	72.1	90.3	91.0
15	**69.5**	72.2	75.3	60.6	**75.3**	60.5	96.4	94.5
16	**79.6**	84.0	83.3	50.1	**83.3**	49.9	90.2	84.7
17	**72.0**	70.2	80.7	66.5	**80.7**	66.4	95.8	91.6
18	**69.0**	72.9	73.9	64.5	**73.9**	64.4	94.2	94.0
mean	**72.3**	74.0	78.3	59.0	**78.3**	58.9	94.3	91.8

[a] Technical efficiencies relative to firm 1.
[b] Technical efficiencies relative to firm 13.

A comparison between the cost efficiency scores arising from the two methods seems to be more appropriate after rescaling the parametric results. This comparison is presented in table 5 for both the restricted and the unrestricted form of the input model. For every year, parametric cost efficiency scores derived from [19a] were rescaled relative to the highest score[14].

In this way the rankings of the cost efficiencies were not altered, but the parametric results made more comparable to the nonparametric results[15]. Then, averaging across years yields the results presented in table 5.

---

[14] We recall that in DEA one of the firms always has a *CE* equal to 100 because this firm is technically as well as allocatively efficient.
[15] It should be noted that rescaling distorts the comparison between the restricted and unrestricted forms of the parametric method.

Table 5 Average cost efficiency scores (x 100) from two methods[a]

Firm	Parametric method				Nonparametric DEA			
	VRS	Rank	CRS	Ran	VRS	Rank	CRS	Rank
	(1)	(2)	(3)	(4)	(5)	(6)	(7)	(8)
1	75.1	(7)	**87.1**	(8)	89.7	(11)	**87.1**	(8)
2	61.7	(9)	**85.9**	(10)	88.3	(16)	**85.9**	(10)
3	48.0	(13)	**93.4**	(1)	97.1	(4)	**93.4**	(1)
4	43.5	(15)	**83.9**	(13)	88.4	(14)	**83.9**	(13)
5	77.7	(6)	**85.1**	(12)	88.4	(15)	**85.1**	(12)
6	32.1	(16)	**86.8**	(9)	98.4	(2)	**86.8**	(9)
7	80.6	(4)	**92.0**	(2)	94.9	(5)	**92.0**	(2)
8	26.4	(18)	**77.6**	(17)	97.6	(3)	**77.6**	(17)
9	57.4	(10)	**82.0**	(14)	84.4	(17)	**82.0**	(14)
10	51.3	(12)	**88.8**	(5)	91.1	(9)	**88.8**	(5)
11	77.8	(5)	**90.3**	(4)	92.9	(6)	**90.3**	(4)
12	47.1	(14)	**85.3**	(11)	89.1	(12)	**85.3**	(11)
13	98.9	(1)	**91.1**	(3)	99.9	(1)	**91.1**	(3)
14	53.5	(11)	**80.7**	(15)	83.0	(18)	**80.7**	(15)
15	67.5	(8)	**88.0**	(7)	90.8	(10)	**88.0**	(7)
16	81.1	(3)	**75.1**	(18)	89.0	(13)	**75.1**	(18)
17	27.7	(17)	**78.1**	(16)	92.4	(8)	**78.1**	(16)
18	85.8	(2)	**88.2**	(6)	92.7	(7)	**88.2**	(6)
mean	60.7		**85.5**		91.6		**85.5**	

[a] Parametric method: CE's rescaled in every year.

A most striking result, for which no theoretical explanation is known to the authors, is that in the restricted model after rescaling, the average parametric and non-parametric cost efficiencies are exactly the same for all firms. Computing cost efficiencies from independent yearly DEA applications and taking firm-specific averages of them yields the same result as estimating a parametric model including technical and allocative efficiencies on pooled data, when assuming the technology to be linearly homogeneous in output. However, this conclusion does not hold for the unrestricted form of the model. It can also be seen that, as a consequence of imposing the linear homogeneity restriction, the cost efficiency rankings change substantially, and that the rescaled cost efficiencies are considerably lower with the parametric method than with DEA. The latter results reflects the main message from tables 4A and 4B, namely that simultaneously estimating allocative and technical efficiencies constitutes the main difference between the two methods for the decomposition of cost efficiency.

5 The decomposition of productivity change

The efficiency scores in tables 4A and 4B were derived by averaging firm- and time-specific efficiencies across time. With the adopted specifications for the efficiencies, the models generate both estimates of initial efficiencies and trend estimates describing the patterns of efficiency change in the period under consideration. Therefore, an other route is to look at the time-paths of the different components of efficiency, and the consequences of imposing different model assumptions for the decomposition of productivity change. Taking into account that all time-paths are relative to the firm on the frontier, we present results for the average change of technical efficiencies relative to firm 1 and relative to firm 13.

We can also compare the parametric model based decomposition of productivity change, here understood as the combination of technical efficiency change and technological change, with the results from using DEA. The DEA based decomposition of productivity change for 1978 - 1992 uses the index of technical efficiency change and a primal index of technological change. The index of efficiency change compares for each firm the distances to the frontier in 1978 and 1992. The index of technological change computes a distance between the two frontiers. Multiplication of the two index numbers yields the Malmquist index number of productivity change[16]. We take geometric averages across firms and convert the resulting index numbers into yearly percentage changes. In the parametric method, the average yearly efficiency change can either be inferred directly from the trend parameters of the model $(-\zeta_2^k)$ or be computed via [21]. In both cases the technological change is given by $-\delta \times 100$ %.

We summarize the results concerning the decomposition of productivity change for the various input and output models in table 6. The table presents average technical efficiencies for 1978, 1985 and 1992, and estimates of average annual growth rates of technical efficiency change (*EC*), technological change (*TC*) and productivity change (*PC*) over the whole period. We also present estimates of the returns-to-scale coefficient (*RTS*). We noticed already that our data exhibit strongly increasing returns-to-scale.

Several notable conclusions can be drawn from table 6. Firstly, the differences between the results from the input and the output models are rather small. Corresponding to theoretical reasoning, the results are identical in the CRS forms, irrespective of the reference firm chosen. We notice further that the choice of the reference firm affects the time-paths of efficiency change and - consequently - the contribution of efficiency change to productivity change. If the technically efficient firm is chosen to be firm 1, then we see increasing efficiency and technological regress.

---

[16] See Appendix B for further details on the computation.

Table 6 The decomposition of average productivity change, 1978 - 1992

	Fixed TE		Fixed TE/AE		Time varying time varying (I)[a)]		Time varying (II)[b)]		DEA	
	AE = 100				TE/AE (I)[a]		TE/AE (II)[b]			
Year	VRS	CRS	VRS	CRS	VRS	CRS	VRS	CRS	VRS	CRS
	(1)	(2)	(3)	(4)	(5)	(6)	(7)	(8)	(9)	(10)
Average technical efficiency scores (x 100) from input models										
1978	86.4	91.2	63.9	79.1	50.0	51.2	**49.8**	74.4	95.8	87.9
1985	86.4	91.2	63.9	79.1	57.0	60.5	**48.9**	68.4	99.5	96.2
1992	86.4	91.2	63.9	79.1	65.0	71.6	**48.1**	62.8	96.9	94.8
Average annual changes (percentages)										
EC	0	0	0	0	1.9	2.4	**-0.3**	-1.2	0.1	0.5
TC	-0.4	-0.4	0.2	0.4	-2.3	-2.2	**0.1**	1.5	-0.4	-0.9
PC	-0.4	-0.4	0.2	0.4	-0.4	0.2	**-0.2**	0.3	-0.3	-0.3
Returns-to-scale										
RTS	1.05	1	1.18	1	1.40	1	**1.39**	1		
Average technical efficiency scores (x 100) from output models										
1978	82.8	91.2	63.8	79.1	52.2	51.1	**49.8**	74.5		
1985	82.8	91.2	63.8	79.1	58.2	60.5	**48.3**	68.4		
1992	82.8	91.2	63.8	79.1	65.4	71.6	**47.5**	62.9		
Average annual changes (percentages)										
EC	0	0	0	0	1.6	2.4	**-0.3**	-1.2		
TC	-0.5	-0.4	0.2	0.4	-1.9	-2.2	**0.1**	1.4		
PC	-0.5	-0.4	0.2	0.4	-0.3	0.2	**-0.2**	0.2		
Returns-to-scale										
RTS	.87	1	1.18	1	1.39	1	**1.39**	1		

[a] Technical efficiencies relative to firm 1.
[b] Technical efficiencies relative to firm 13.

However, if the reference firm is chosen to be firm 13, a small decrease of efficiency and a negligable technological change results. In the latter case, the decomposition of productivity change appears also to be rather sensitive to the returns-to- scale assumption. Thus, after invalidly imposing constant returns-to-scale, the decomposition of productivity change shows decreasing efficiency but technological progress, indicating that returns-to-scale effects are absorbed in the estimates of technological change. However, this conclusion does not hold when the reference firm has been chosen without taking into account inter-firm differences in efficiency change. In this case, that is when firm 1 acts as a reference, imposing constant returns-to-scale does not affect the decomposition of productivity change very much.

We can also compare the parametric model based and the DEA based decomposition of productivity change. It can be seen that the two methods yield estimates of productivity change that are similar. Both DEA and the parametric method show that productivity change was negative (annually about -0.3 % for the unrestricted form of the models). However, the two methods arrive at a rather different decomposition of productivity change, with less pronounced differences for the decomposition in case of firm 13 as the reference firm, than in the alternative with firm 1 acting as the reference firm.

6 Summary and conclusions

In this paper the approach presented in Balk (1997) has been implemented on a data set of 18 rubber-processing firms during the period 1978 - 1992. We performed a sensitivity analysis of the components of cost efficiency scores and productivity change, using different parametric models, and also compared the parametric results with those from nonparametric DEA. It was not our primary objective to provide the ultimate wisdom concerning the productivity change of the rubber-processing industry as such.

In this paper the core elements of the comparison were the estimates of efficiency scores based on a highly parameterized and nonlinear cost system, the nonlinearity arising from the introduction of time-varying and firm-specific allocative and technical efficiencies. We distinguished between the output and the input representation of technical efficiency. A distinct feature of our approach is that both types of efficiency are explicitly modeled with parameters. We estimated initial states of efficiencies and firm-specific trends for technical efficiencies and price distortion factors. This enabled a precise computation of technical efficiencies and a decomposition of productivity change into technical efficiency change and technological change.

With the fully specified models serving as a frame of reference we performed a specific-to- general specification search in order to identify the technically most efficient firm and the preferred specification of disembodied technological change. Two alternatives for the reference firm were explored. The first represents the firm which is technically most efficient over the whole period. This firm has been identified by estimating the model under the assumption of firm-specific fixed allocative and technical efficiencies. Using this firm as the reference firm we re-estimated the model, relaxing the assumption of fixed technical and allocative efficiencies, tested for the preferred specification of technological change and for the time-constancy of allocative and technical efficiencies and linear homogeneity in output. The test statistics showed a strong rejection of the time-constancy of the efficiency parameters and also a rejection of the constant-returns-to-scale assumption. Finally, we re-estimated the model after re-selecting the reference firm, allowing for differences in technical efficiency change, and performed a sensitivity analysis for the efficiency scores and the decompositions of productivity change by imposing restrictions on the fully specified models.

The most important findings of the sensitivity analysis are:

- Efficiency scores from the input and output models appeared to be very similar in the unrestricted form of the models and were identical under the constant-returns-to-scale assumption.
- Parametric model based technical efficiencies were relatively close to the DEA estimates when assuming allocative inefficiency away, but allowing for allocative inefficiency reduces them considerably.
- Parametric model based allocative efficiencies are substantially smaller than their DEA equivalents.
- The simultaneous estimation of technical and allocative efficiencies causes the cost efficiencies to be much smaller than those obtained by DEA.
- Conditional on assuming constant returns-to-scale, the re-scaled parametric model based cost efficiencies appeared to be exactly the same as their DEA equivalents. Computing cost efficiencies from independent yearly DEA applications and taking averages over time yields the same result as estimating a parametric model with technical and allocative inefficiencies on pooled data, thereby assuming the technology to be linearly homogeneous in output.
- Our data appear to exhibit strongly increasing returns-to-scale. Then, invalidly imposing constant returns-to-scale biases estimates of technical efficiencies upwards.
- The choice of the firm that is to be on the frontier appears to be important for the decomposition of productivity change. When the reference firm is chosen by neglecting inter-firm differences in efficiency change, then the decomposition shows an average efficiency change which is biased upwards and technological change which is biased downwards.
- When the reference firm is chosen while taking into account inter-firm differences in efficiency change, then imposing constant returns-to-scale increases the magnitude of technological change.

Appendix A: Estimates of the technology parameters under various assumptions[a]

Model	Input VRS		Output VRS		Input CRS		Output CRS	
Parameter	Est.	SE	Est.	SE	Est.	SE	Est.	SE
α_0	2.31217	.76099	1.98225	.00669	-0.74057	.08808	-0.73803	.08776
α_1	0.02189	.00574	0.00883	.00560	0.29734	.00923	0.29663	.00923
α_2	-0.03115	.04207	-0.01135	.04677	0.07659	.02038	0.07694	.02040
α_3	1.00926	.04392	1.00252	.04746	0.62607	.01555	0.62643	.01559
β_1	0.62358	.16041	0.69115	.12387	1.00000		1.00000	
β_{11}	0.00902	.01642	0.00207	.01139	0.00000		0.00000	
α_{11}	0.00855	.00242	0.00300	.00261	0.10664	.00528	0.10619	.00528
α_{12}	-0.01574	.00443	-0.00602	.00518	0.00472	.00369	0.00477	.00370
α_{13}	0.00719	.00209	0.00303	.00259	-0.11137	.00508	-0.11096	.00509
α_{22}	-0.02124	.01194	-0.02955	.01228	-0.04249	.01131	-0.04279	.01136
α_{23}	0.03698	.01198	0.03557	.01271	0.03776	.00870	0.03802	.00873
α_{33}	-0.04418	.01243	-0.03860	.01362	0.07361	.01069	0.07294	.01071
γ_1	0.00030	.00025	0.00026	.00023	0.00000		0.00000	
γ_2	0.03082	.00535	0.02895	.00486	0.00000		0.00000	
γ_3	-0.03112	.00516	-0.02922	.00489	0.00000		0.00000	
δ	-0.00138	.00344	-0.00070	.00341	-0.01448	.00815	-0.01442	.00811
Log likelihood	1824		1823		1740			1740
R^2 cost function	.998		.998		.992			.992
R^2 share capital	.867		.872		.886			.886
R^2 share material	.818		.812		.925			.925

[a] Firm 13 taken to be technically efficient in all years.

Appendix B: The computation of efficiency scores and productivity change by DEA.

The input technical efficiency scores ITE_{kt} for all firms and all years were obtained as solutions of the following linear programming problem:

$$ITE_{kt} = 1 / D_i^t(x_{kt}, y_{kt})$$

$$= \min_{z,\lambda} \lambda \quad \text{subject to}$$

$$\sum_{k'=1}^{18} z_{k'} x_{k't} \leq \lambda x_{kt} \quad , \qquad y_{kt} \leq \sum_{k'=1}^{18} z_{k'} y_{k't} , \qquad z_{k'} \geq 0 \quad (k' = 1, \cdots, 18) ,$$

$$[\sum_{k'=1}^{18} z_{k'} = 1] .$$

The restriction between brackets must be deleted when imposing constant-returns-to-scale (CRS). The cost efficiency scores were obtained as ratios

$$CE_{kt} = \frac{C^t(w_t, y_{kt})}{c_{kt}} ,$$

where

$$C^t(w_t, y_{kt}) = \min_{z, x} w_t x \quad \text{subject to}$$

$$\sum_{k'=1}^{18} z_{k'} x_{k't} \leq x \ , \quad y_{kt} \leq \sum_{k'=1}^{18} z_{k'} y_{k't} , \quad z_{k'} \geq 0 \ (k' = 1, \cdots, 18) , \quad [\sum_{k'=1}^{18} z_{k'} = 1] .$$

The allocative efficiency scores were obtained by using [19d]. The technical efficiency change, going from year 1 (1978) to year T (1992), was computed as

$$EC_k = \frac{ITE_{kT}}{ITE_{k1}} .$$

Technological change was computed as

$$TC_k = \left[\frac{D_i^T(x_{k1}, y_{k1})}{D_i^1(x_{k1}, y_{k1})} \frac{D_i^T(x_{kT}, y_{kT})}{D_i^1(x_{kT}, y_{kT})} \right]^{1/2} ,$$

where

$$1 / D_i^T(x_{k1}, y_{k1}) = \min_{z, \lambda} \lambda \quad \text{subject to}$$

$$\sum_{k'=1}^{18} z_{k'} x_{k'T} \le \lambda x_{k1} \quad , \qquad y_{k1} \le \sum_{k'=1}^{18} z_{k'} y_{k'T}, \qquad z_{k'} \ge 0 \quad (k' = 1,\cdots,18),$$

$$[\sum_{k'=1}^{18} z_{k'} = 1],$$

and $1/D_i^1(x_{kT}, y_{kT})$ was calculated by the same formula after replacing "$k'T$" by "$k'1$" and "$k1$" by "kT".

REFERENCES

Atkinson, S.E., Halvcrsen, R. (1984), *'Parametric Efficiency Tests, Economies of Scale, and Input Demand in U.S. Electric Power Generation'*, International Economic Review 25, 647-662.

Atkinson, S.E., Halvcrsen, R. (1986), *'The Relative Efficiency of Public and Private Firms in a Regulated Environment: The Case of U.S. Electric Utilities'*, Journal of Public Economics 29, 281-294.

Atkinson, S.E., Cornwell, C. (1994a), *'Parametric Estimation of Technical and Allocative Inefficiency with Panel Data'*, International Economic Review 35, 231-243.

Atkinson, S.E., Cornwell, C. (1994b), *'Estimation of Output and Input Technical Efficiency using a Flexible Functional Form and Panel Data'*, International Economic Review 35, 245-255.

Balk, B.M. (1997), *'The Decomposition of Cost Efficiency and the Canonical Form of Cost Function and Cost Share Equations'*, Economics Letters 55, 45-51.

Baltagi, B.H., Griffin, J.M., Rich, D.P. (1995), *'The Measurement of Firm-Specific Indexes of Technical Change'*, The Review of Economics and Statistics, 654-663.

Cornwell, C., Schmidt, P., Sickles, R.C. (1990), *'Production Frontiers with Cross-sectional and Time-series Variation in Efficiency Levels'*, Journal of Econometrics 46, 185-200.

Cornwell, C., Schmidt, P., Wyhowski, D. (1992), *'Simultaneous Equations and Panel Data'*, Journal of Econometrics 51, 151-181.

Kumbhakar, S.C. (1996), *'Efficiency Measurement with Multiple Outputs and Multiple Inputs'*, The Journal of Productivity Analysis 7, 225-255.

Oum, T.H., Zhang, Y. (1995), *'Competition and Allocative Efficiency: The Case of the U.S. Telephone Industry'*, The Review of Economics and Statistics, 82-96.

EFFICIENCY OF THE ITALIAN BANKING SECTOR VIA A PARAMETRIC APPROACH

Silvia Biffignandi[1], Sergio Bonzani[2] and Barbara Rizzi[3]

[1,3] *Department of Mathematics, Statistics, Computer Science and Applications, Università degli Studi di Bergamo, Bergamo, Italy*
[2] *NIELSEN, Milan, Italy*

1 Foreword

The analysis of productivity and efficiency of manufacturing activities is a well-known field of research. The recent structural changes of the economic systems have contributed to move researchers' attention from goods production activities to the services sector and among them to the banking activity, object of this study.

Productivity and efficiency analysis is a crucial aspect both from a macroeconomic point of view (since it is gives information for political economic decisions) and for individual enterprises (since it is useful for benchmarking purposes and for identifying tools for improving their performance). In addition, this kind of analysis is a basic reference for international comparisons of economic systems and of their competitiveness.
Empirical analysis of productivity and efficiency in the services sector is affected by two kinds of difficulties:
- first, the are great differences among countries since its rate of development, also within Europe, has been highly heterogeneous;[1]
- secondly, many methodological aspects have to be considered to settle adequate measurement techniques of input and output and suitable models of analysis.

Therefore, in order to improve international comparisons of the economic systems, we need to proceed working towards the direction of settling analyses which understand sectoral development, efficiency and performances within each country. In fact, this studies are a good starting point to identify the basis of the theoretical economic framework for international analysis. In this context, our paper limits the attention to a specific sector, the banking one, and country, Italy.

---

[1] For an analysis on the models of development of the services sector in the European Union countries, see Commission of the European Community (1993).

As specified in the following paragraph, in fact, the international differences among banking sectors of various countries are linked both to economic characteristics and national regulations which, however, the globalization process of the economy will progressively reduce, making it possible, in the short run, to carry out international comparisons of the sector efficiency.

2 International comparability of the banking sector

The financial integration process, begun in 1993, among the European Community countries, is only a part of the markets integration process, but it represents the most innovative aspect.

The creation of a single market in the financial sector led to two structural changes:
- the free circulation of capitals, begun in 1990, which eliminated the restrictions imposed on financial flows among the member-countries and increased the choices for savers and credit users;
- the free offer of financial services, begun in 1993, which allowed each bank operating in a country of the Community to carry out, all over the European banking market, those activities already practised in the country of origin.[2]

These changes are determining an increasing competition among the financial institutions of the various countries of the Community and are raising the problem of the efficient behaviour of these operators.

However, the creation of a single market in the financial sector did not require a total harmonization of the financial regulations among the member-countries. In fact the private laws concerning the single financial operations were not harmonized. As a consequence, the financial operations carried out by banks within their country of origin are still disciplined by the contractual regulation of that country and, therefore, differences still remain among the various national regulations.

These differences caused enormous difficulties to those analyses which tried to compare banking sectors among countries. In particular, problems are due to:
- structural and environmental differences among the various systems. For example, in Germany, Austria, Norway and France the banking laws establish the principle of the "universal bank", that is a multi-output bank which can carry out diversified activities, while in Italy, Belgium and UK, the principle of the "specialised bank" is still prevailing;
- lack of homogeneity on the operative conditions of the financial institutions. The banks of a country belonging to a financial category (for example the saving banks) do not operate under the same conditions of the same kind of

---

[2] For a study on the consequences of the financial integration in the European Community, see Masera (1991).

banks of another country: owing to different national regulations they can not offer the same services and can not carry out the same financial operations;
- different fiscal and civil laws which, in the various countries, regulate the compilation of Income Statements and Balance Sheets. Sometimes, some aggregates of the Balance Sheet or Income Statement of a bank operating in a country have the same name of similar aggregates recorded in the Balance Sheet or Income Statement of a bank operating in another country, but the contents may refer to very different entities.

Due to the difficulties arisen from the comparisons among different banking systems, an efficiency analysis of the Italian banking sector based on the comparison with the situation of the foreign banking sectors would be not only very difficult, but also unreliable.

Since a good starting point for settling models of international comparison is surely the knowledge of the single national realities and the direction towards which their efficiency is developing, in the following we analyze the Italian situation. In this country during the last years the implementation of efficiency measurement techniques to the banking sector has become a theme of particular interest arisen from the need to improve the performance of the Italian credit institutions. Moreover, the sectoral efficiency analysis is a benchmarking tool for individual credit institutions[3].

The first aim of this analysis is to estimate the efficiency of the Italian banking sector using 1995 Balance Sheet data relative to 89 Italian banks.

The second aim is to verify, comparing our results with those of previous studies (in particular with the study of Cardani, Castagna and Galeotti in 1991):
- if the Italian banking system has become more or less efficient than it was in the past;
- if the statistical hypotheses previously made about the kind of functional form used to represent the banking production technology and about the distribution of inefficiency are still acceptable or not.

3 Parametric models and efficiency analysis

As it is well-known, efficiency measurement techniques are based on the estimation of a frontier.

By the term "frontier" we mean:
- the whole maximum productions which banks can realize using a certain quantity of inputs, (in this case the frontier is said to be a "production-frontier");

---

[3] The results of this paper has been further developd for benchmarking purposes in a local context.

- the whole minimum costs which banks are able to bear, given the volume of production and the input prices, (in this case the frontier is said to be a "cost-frontier").

In literature, there are many models which can be referred to in order to estimate a frontier. Each of these models is based on particular hypotheses giving different evaluations of the performance of the institutions analyzed.

Unfortunately it is very difficult to establish which model is the best, since a model could be better than others to represent a particular situation, but could be worse in other cases. However it is possible to classify the existing models with respect to some characteristics.

The more general classification is: parametric models and non-parametric models. The first models are those in which the frontier is represented through a functional form (Cobb-Douglas, Translog, etc...), while the second ones are models in which no functional forms are assumed on the frontier.

According to the constraints imposed on the distribution of the error term, parametric models may be distinguished between:

1. deterministic models.[4]

   They assume that the distance of each observation from the efficient frontier is due only to inefficiency without considering the possible existence of random errors and, hence, making hypothesis of a one-sided error term. Deterministic models may be estimated by statistic methods, and by mathematical programming procedures, such as linear programming (minimizing the sum of the absolute values of the residuals, subject to the constraint that each residuals be non-positive) or quadratic programming (minimizing the sum of the squared residuals, subject to the same constraint). The mathematical programming approach makes no assumption on the distribution of the error term, but it produces estimates which have no statistical properties and, therefore, inferential results cannot be obtained,

2. stochastic models.[5]

   They are not characterized by the same limitation as deterministic models because they assume that the error term is composed of the sum of two components: the first component which is one-sided and the second one which is normally distributed. In this manner, the distance of each observation from the efficient frontier is due both to inefficiency and to random errors. The main limitation of these models is the impossibility to estimate separately the two error components unless some specific hypotheses are made on the distribution of such components. However, it has been demonstrated that, using panel data, it is possible to overcome this last limit without formulating hypotheses on the distribution of the two error components (see Baltagi, 1995).

---

[4] For deterministic models see, for instance, Aigner and Chu (1968).

[5] For stochastic models see Aigner, Lovell and Schmidt (1977) and Meeusen and Van Den Broeck (1977). For a comparison between deterministic and stochastic models, see Forsund, Lovell and Schmidt (1980).

Most of the parametric models on the efficiency of the Italian banking sector are based on a cost frontier rather than a production frontier, since from a macroeconomic point of view, the major purpose is not to maximize the production capacity of the banking system but to minimize the intermediation costs.

Parametric models may be distinguished according to:

- the kind of variables used to formulate the cost frontier. There are studies which adopt the intermediation approach, based on the assumption that Deposits are an input of the banking production process. Other studies, instead, adopt the production approach which considers Deposits as an output;[6]
- the kind of variables used to measure outputs. Some studies apply stock variables, while others apply flow variables.[7]
- the distribution of the error term. Authors who are interested in measuring only scale and scope economies, adopt models estimated by usual methods such as Ordinary Least Squares, Seemingly Unrelated Regression or Maximum Likelihood, that is classical models in which the error term is random and, hence, normally distributed.[8] Authors interested in estimating efficiency adopt stochastic models estimated by Corrected Ordinary Least Square or Maximum Likelihood. In these models the error term is composed of a random component, which is normally distributed and a one-sided component which may be half-normal, truncated-normal, exponential or gamma.[9]

Actually, previous parametric analyses studied, above all, scale and scope economies rather than banking efficiency. This choice depends on the influence that scale and scope economies have on the decisions of the Central Authorities. The only study that focused on the problem of Italian banking efficiency is that of Cardani, Castagna and Galeotti (1991).[10]

---

[6] Among authors who adopt the intermediation approach we remember Lanciotti and Raganelli (1988); Cossutta, Di Battista, Giannini and Urga (1988); Conigliani, De Bonis, Motta and Parigi (1991); Cardani, Castagna and Galeotti (1991); Berger, Hanweck and Humphrey (1987). Production approach is followed by Baldini and Landi (1990).

[7] Most of stock variables used are: Total Assets, Total Loans, Total Deposits and so on. Authors who use stock variables, such as Conigliani, De Bonis, Motta and Parigi (1991), consider that these kind of measures are able to represent banking output because they require the management of the financial flows which arise from credit decisions. Flow variables are usually: Value Added and Interests on Assets. Cardani, Castagna and Galeotti, for example, adopt the weighted sum of Interests on Assets because they consider that stock variables are inadequate to measure banking output which has the nature of a flow quantity.

[8] See, for example, Baldini and Landi (1990) for an OLS estimation and Conigliani, De Bonis, Motta and Parigi (1991) for a SUR estimation.

[9] See Cardani, Castagna and Galeotti (1991) for an ML estimation.

[10] These authors carried out such an analysis using 1986 Balance Sheet data relative to a sample of 94 Italian banks.

4 An empirical analysis through a stochastic model

This analysis estimates the current efficiency of the Italian banking sector through a sample of 89 Italian banks.

To carry out the study, 1995 Balance Sheet data are used relative to each credit institution considered in the sample.[11] The sample of firms is divided into 4 groups according to the size of banks, measured through the number of branches. In particular, the sample is composed as shown in Table 1.

Table 1 Groups of banks according to size.

GROUPS OF BANKS	NUMBER OF BRANCHES
MAJOR	from 617 to 1.276
LARGE	from 105 to 586
MEDIUM	from 50 to 98
SMALL	from 29 to 48

The composition of each group is shown in Table 2.

The 1995 Balance Sheet data relating each bank are:
- EXPENSES: Interest expenses; Valuation Adjustments; Labour expenses; Amortization of Fixed Assets.
- INCOMES: Interests on Assets; Income on Services.
- ASSETS: Customers Loans; Due from Central Banks; Due from other Banks; Securities; Fixed Assets (plant and equipment).
- LIABILITIES: Total Deposits.
- NUMBER OF EMPLOYEES; NUMBER OF BRANCHES.

Average values of the above mentioned variables relative to each group of banks are shown in Table 3 and Table 4.

The starting point of our analysis is to decide which variables apply to represent the outputs and the inputs of the banking production process and to measure them, working on all the possible amounts reported in Balance Sheets and Income Statements of the 89 banks. More specifically, from Income Statements, we derive the amount of banking output and the amount of the shares of Total Cost referring to each banking input, as shown in Table 5.[12]

---

[11] The data source is the Electronic Archive of the Banking Balance Sheets of the Centrale dei Bilanci S.r.l.. We wish to thank Maurizio Zucchi and the Credito Bergamasco Bank for having kindly supplied us the data.

[12] Each share of Total Cost can be divided into the product between the Input Price and the Input Quantity. In our case:
- Interest Expenses = (Price of Deposits) x (Quantity of Deposits)
- Labour Expenses = (Price of Labour) x (Quantity of Labour)
- Valuation Adjustments and Amortizations = (Price of Capital) x (Quantity of Capital).

Table 2 Sample of 89 Italian Banks.

7 MAJOR	34 LARGE	33 MEDIUM	15 SMALL
Istituto Banc. S. Paolo-To	Rolo Banca 1473	Banca Pop. di Brescia	Banca Fideuram - Milano
Banca Commerc. Italiana	Banco Ambrosiano Veneto	Banca Pop.Commer. e Ind.	C.R. Pisa S.p.A.
Banca di Roma SpA	Banco di Sicilia SpA	Banca Pop. di Sondrio	Banco di Desio e Brianza
Banca Naz.le del Lavoro	Banca Pop. di Novara	Cassamarca S.p.A.	Credito Artigiano
CARIPLO S.p.A.	Banca CRT S.p.A.	Banca Sella SpA	Banca di Piacenza
Credito Italiano	Banca Naz.le Agricoltura	C.R. Reggio Emilia S.p.A.	Banca Agric. Pop.Ragusa
Monte Dei Paschi - Siena	Banca Pop. di Milano	Banca del Salento	Banca Pop. di Cremona
	Caviverona Banca S.p.A.	Banca di Legnano	Banca Pop. Luino e Varese
	Banca Pop. di BG - C. V.	C.R.Trento e R. S.p.A.	C.R. Rimini S.p.A.
	Deutsche Bank SpA	C.R. Lucca S.p.A.	Banca Pop. di Ravenna
	Banca Toscana	Credito Valtellinese	Banca Pop. di Intra
	Banca Pop.VR-Banco S.G.	CRTrieste - Banca S.p.A.	C.R. Cesena S.p.A.
	C.R.Parma e Piacenza SpA	Banca Pop. di Ancona	Banca Pop. Abbiategrasso
	Carisbo S.p.A.	C.R. Perugia S.p.A.	Banca di Sassari SpA
	C.R. Firenze S.p.A.	C.R. Bolzano S.p.A.	C.R. Savona S.p.A.
	Banco di Sardegna SpA	Banco di Chiavari-Riv. Lig.	
	C.R. Padova e R. S.p.A.	C.R. Pistoia e Pescia S.p.A.	
	Banca Carige S.p.A.	Banca Agricola Milanese	
	Cab S.p.A.	Banca Pop.Puglia-Basilic.	
	Credito Bergamasco	Banca C.R. Asti S.p.A.	
	B.R.E.Banca S.p.A.	Banca Pop. Friuladria	
	Banca delle Marche S.p.A.	C.R. Udine e P. S.p.A.	
	Banca Agricola Mantovana	C.R. San Miniato S.p.A.	
	Banca Antoniana	C.R. Ferrara S.p.A.	
	Banca San Paolo di Brescia	Banca di Trento e Bolzano	
	Carical S.p.A.	Banca Pop. dell'Alto Adige	
	Banca Pop. Veneta	Banca Pop. Pugliese	
	Credito Emiliano SpA	Banca Mediterranea SpA	
	Banca Pop. Di Lodi	C.R. Teramo S.p.A.	
	Caripuglia S.p.A.	C.R. La Spezia S.p.A.	
	Banca Pop. Etruria-Lazio	C.R. Alessandria S.p.A.	
	C.R. Venezia S.p.A.	Banca Pop. Asolo-Monteb.	
	Banca Pop. Vicentina	C.R. Ravenna S.p.A.	
	Banca Pop. Dell'Adriatico		

Table 3 Average values of Expenses and Incomes.

Banks	EXPENSES*:				INCOMES*:	
	Interest Expenses	Valuation Adjustments	Labour Costs	Amortizations	Interest on Assets	Income on Services
MAJOR	8.616.551	368.415	2.031.377	683.807	11.627.300	1.086.584
LARGE	1.173.434	57.815	389.421	134.169	1.817.389	203.327
MEDIUM	231.692	13.728	91.668	25.621	402.701	47.994
SMALL	145.000	8.554	61.541	23.901	260.569	40.372
Average of the sample	387.532	112.128	643.502	216.875	3.526.990	344.569

(*) Data are divided by 1.000.000.

Table 4 Average values of Assets and Liabilities.

ASSETS*:						LIAB.* :	
Banks	Customer Loans	Due from Central B.	Due from other B.	Securities	Fixed Assets	Total Deposits	Emplo-yees
MAJOR	71.172.661	3.766.467	27.699.375	23.621.105	6.943.444	75.062.754	18.320
LARGE	9.869.069	847.000	3.428.346	4.670.739	981.400	13.236.250	3.584
MEDIUM	1.969.047	91.662	572.370	1.318.398	195.346	3.071.964	875
SMALL	1.236.348	139.456	447.554	722.140	133.099	1.957.340	609
Average of the sample	21.061.781	1.236.146	8.036.911	7.583.096	2.063.322	23.332.077	5.847

(*) Data are divided by 1.000.000.

Table 5 Income Statement.

INCOME STATEMENT

Description of the Expenses reported in the Income Statement:	EXPENSES:	INCOMES:	Description of the Incomes reported in the Income Statement:
Share of Total Cost relative to Deposits	Interest Expenses	Interest on Assets and Income on Services	Banking output
Share of Total Cost relative to Labour	Labour Expenses		
Share of Total Cost relative to Capital	Valuation Adjustments and Amortizations		
	Total Cost		

As regards banking outputs, this study adopts the intermediation approach[13] and a single-output cost frontier.[14] Moreover, banking output is measured through a flow variable, the average interests weighted by single assets plus Income on Services.

Weights are obtained through a regression of a constant and three Assets (three banking outputs) on Total Interests, as follows:

Total Interests on Assets = $\alpha_0 + \alpha_1*x_1 + \alpha_2*x_2 + \alpha_3*x_3$

where : α_0 = constant;

x_1 = Customers' Loans;

x_2 = Due from Central Banks and other Credit Institutions;

x_3 = Total Securities.[15]

Regression results are shown in Table 6.

Table 6 Regression results.

Variables	Coefficients	t-statistics
constant	-0,357	-6
x_1	0,503	19,97
x_2	0,179	10,34
x_3	0,288	11,45
$R^2 =$	99,36	
D-W =	2,21	
F(3,85)=	4413,4	
Log-lik=	160,675	

---

[13] Deposits are considered an input.

[14] Output is measured through a weighted product index which allows the aggregation of different banking outputs in a unique variable.

[15] Before proceeding in the regression, normality and independence hypotheses on the variables are tested.

Normality hypothesis is tested through a chi-squared statistic. Test results force us to reject this hypothesis and to transform all variables by logarithms. After transformations, frequency distributions of all variables becomes more normal. A multicollinearity problem is evident, due to a dimensionality matter, i.e. a strong interrelation among the three indepentent variables which share common information. In fact, in order to overcome the correlation problem we carry out both a principal component analysis and a ridge regression procedure. The first analysis shows that the variability is explained mainly (93,4%) by the first principal component. The second analysis shows that OLS regression coefficients are stable except the intercept. These results lead us to the conclusion that correlation among variables is due to the fact that they hold the same information about banking output. They are, in fact, three kinds of assets which generate interests and, hence, which can be considered three banking outputs.

From an economic point of view, regression coefficient estimates tell us about the average income rates relative to the three assets considered as independent variables. In particular, it can be seen that the asset which provides most of the income is Customers Loans, while the least profitable one, is Due from Central Banks and other Credit Institutions.[16]

After evaluating banking output, we need to measure Labour, Capital and Deposits which stand for banking inputs.[17] From Balance Sheets we derive two banking inputs, Capital[18] and Deposits, as shown in Table 7.

Table 7 Balance Sheet.

	BALANCE	SHEET	
Description of Assets reported in the Balance Sheet:	ASSETS:	LIABILITIES:	Description of Liabilities reported in the Balance Sheet:
Input Quantity of Capital	Customers Loans	Total Deposits	Input Quantity of Deposits
Input Quantity of Capital	Due from Central Banks		
Input Quantity of Capital	Due from other Banks		
Input Quantity of Capital	Securities		
Input Quantity of Capital	Fixed Assets		
	Total Assets		

Quantity of Labour, instead, is measured by the number of Employees.

[16] Regression results are similar to those obtained by Cardani, Castagna and Galeotti (1991), who measured banking output by the same procedure.

[17] We recall that each share of Total Cost reported in the Income Statements can be divided into the product between the Input Price and the Input Quantity, where the Input Quantity corresponds to a variable reported in the Balance Sheet.

[18] Studies on industrial firms usually consider Fixed Assets (plant and equipment) as a measure of the Input Quantity of Capital. Moreover, Fixed Assets are normally greater than Net Worth because they are financed by long-term Liabilities. In case of banks, on the contrary, Net Worth is bigger than Fixed Assets since it finances not only Fixed Assets, but also those Assets which are kept fixed for precautional purposes. For this reason, some authors such as Garcia and Vilarino (1992) adopt Net Worth as Input Quantity of Capital. Unfortunately, in this study, the Net Worth of each bank is not available, so we estimate it through the difference between Total Assets and Total Deposits.

After evaluating input and output quantities, input prices[19] are calculated dividing the shares of Total Cost relative to each input by the corresponding input quantity, i.e.:

p_L = Price of Labour = (Labour expenses / n° of Employees);

p_K = Price of Capital = (Valuation Adjustments and Amortizations / (Total Assets - Total Deposits));

p_D = Price of Deposits = (Interest expenses / Total Deposits).

In our study we test two functional forms on the cost frontier: a Cobb-Douglas and a Translog. First of all we formulate a Cobb-Douglas cost function because it is simpler, self-dual and can be transformed, by logarithms, in a function which is linear in its parameters so that classical estimation methods (such as OLS) can be applied to it. This kind of functional form has been very popular in the past and has been used by the previous analyses basically for studying returns to scale.

In linear form the Cobb-Douglas cost function is:

$$\log C(y, p_L, p_K, p_D) = b_0 + b_L \log (p_L) + b_K \log (p_K) + b_D \log (p_D) + b_Q \log (Q) + \varepsilon$$

where: $C(y, p_L, p_K, p_D)$ = Total Cost obtained as the sum of: Interest Expenses, Labour Expenses, Valuation Adjustments and Amortizations;

Q = banking output;

$\varepsilon = u + v$ = error term composed of the sum of a one-sided component, u, which reflects inefficiency and a random component, v, which reflects random errors outside firms' control (see Annex 1).

The above mentioned function is estimated, by a TSP 4.3 Program, following a three-step procedure.

1st STEP: OLS estimation is carried out under the assumption that there is no inefficiency and that the error term is only random, with a normal distribution, ($u=\underline{0}$; $\varepsilon=v$).

This step provides the starting values to carry out the other steps of the estimation procedure and OLS estimates can be compared with the final estimates in order to verify if the hypothesis of presence of inefficiency among firms must be accepted or rejected.[20]

---

[19] We, in fact, estimate a cost frontier in which inputs are considered with respect to their own prices.

[20] The test on the hypothesis of presence of inefficiency against the hypothesis of absence of inefficiency is carried out subsequently through a chi-square test. However, comparing OLS and ML estimates obtained from the estimation procedure, we can express a preliminar judgement. In particular, in case of no significant difference between OLS estimates (which imply the hypothesis of absence of inefficiency) and ML

2 [nd] STEP: Assuming the presence of inefficiency among firms, we must consider that OLS estimators, obtained in the first step, are likely to be unbiased with the exception of the intercept. The bias of the constant term corresponds to the mean of ε, as demonstrated by Richmond (1974) (see Annex 2).

We apply the Corrected Ordinary Least Squares method to have an unbiased intercept and to estimate the variance components of the error term, σ_u^2, σ_v^2. With the parameters (except b_0) set to the OLS values and b_0, σ_u^2 and σ_v^2 parameters adjusted according to the COLS formula, we derive the log likelihood function for the cost frontier model (see Stevenson, 1980):

$$\log L = \log(\mathbf{b}, \sigma^2, \lambda, \mu) = -(n/2)\log \sigma^2 -(n/2)\log 2\pi -(n/2\sigma^2)\log \sum (\varepsilon-\mu)^2 + \sum \log [1-F^*(-\mu/\lambda\sigma-\varepsilon/\sigma)] -n \log [1-F^*(-\mu/\sigma(\lambda^2+1)^{1/2})]$$

As it is well known sometimes the log-likelihood is concave, in which case there is only one maximum; in other cases, there are many local maxima so that it is difficult to find the global maximum if the starting values are too far away from it.

In order to consider the possibility that the log-likelihood function is not concave, we carry out a grid search across the parameter space of $\gamma = \sigma_u^2/\sigma^2$. This last parameter, in fact, takes values between 0,00..1 and 0,99..9, consequently we search for the global maximum of the function varying γ from 0,00001 to 0,9999 in increments of size 0,0001.

3 [rd] STEP: The values selected in the grid search are used as starting values in an iterative procedure (using the Davidon-Fletcher-Power Quasi-Newton method) to obtain the final maximum likelihood estimates.[21]

The parameters of the Cobb-Douglas cost function, estimated by the three-step procedure, are shown in Table 8.

Looking at the results in Table 8 we observe that:

1. comparing the three models, stochastic frontier models are superior to the non-stochastic model. The first model shows, in fact, lower t-statistics (for all the parameters with exception of the constant term) than those of the second and the third models. Moreover, we carry out a joint test on the significance of the one-sided component **u** using the generalized-likelihood ratio.

Proved, in fact, that if the variable **u** is absent from the model, ($\lambda=u=\varnothing$), then

---

estimates (which imply the hypothesis of presence of inefficiency distributed half-normally or truncated-normally), we will reject the second hypothesis.

[21] Many of the gradient methods, used to obtain maximum likelihood estimates, such as the Newton-Raphson method, require the matrix of second partial derivatives to be calculated. Quasi-Newton methods, instead, require only the vector of first partial derivatives be derived. Among these methods, the Davidon-Fletcher-Powell has been successfully used in a wide range of econometric applications and was also recommended by Pitt and Lee (1981) for stochastic frontier function estimation. See Bernt, Hall and Hausman (1974) for a description of this method.

the ordinary least squares estimators of the remaining parameters of the cost function are maximum-likelihood estimators. Therefore, the negative of twice the logarithm of the generalized-likelihood ratio for the first and the third models has approximately chi-square distribution with parameter equal to two (see Battese and Coelli, 1988).

$$\chi^2 = -2[\text{Log-Lik}_{\text{ML}(\mu \neq \varnothing)} - \text{Log-Lik}_{\text{OLS}}]$$

Test statistic results: $H_0 = \mu = \lambda = \varnothing$;

$$H_1 = \mu \neq \varnothing \wedge \lambda \neq \varnothing.$$

$\chi^2_{0,05}$ (critical value) $= 5,99$ χ^2 (calculated value) $= 31,13$

The value of the test statistic is 31,13 and, hence, highly significant. According to this result, we conclude that the hypothesis regarding the presence of inefficiency among firms must be accepted and, also, that the frontier models (the second and the third models) are significant at a five percent level to describe the production technology of the banks considered;
2. of the two stochastic frontier models, the latter is surely to prefer since it shows higher t-statistics values. Furthermore, proved that if the parameter μ has value zero, then the negative of twice the logarithm of the generalized-likelihood ratio for the restricted ($\mu = \varnothing$) and the unrestricted ($\mu \neq \varnothing$) frontier models has approximately chi-square distribution with parameter equal to one (see Battese and Coelli, 1988).

Test statistic results: $H_0 = \mu = \varnothing$;

$$H_1 = \mu \neq \varnothing.$$

$\chi^2_{0,05}$ (critical value) $= 3,84$ χ^2 (calculated value) $= 18,91$

In our case, the test statistic shows a value of 18,91 which is significant at a five percent level. This result means that, assured a certain level of inefficiency among firms, this level is truncated-normally distributed, as confirmed by the value of the parameter μ which is different from zero.[22] From the result of this test we conclude that the best model to represent the banking production process is the third one, based on the hypothesis that most of the banks considered are inefficient. This prevalent behaviour is probably due to the adoption of long period strategies which prevent banks from choosing the input combinations which minimizes Total Costs in the short run;
3. according to the chosen model, returns to scale are about 1,006 (constant returns to scale). Coefficients relative to input prices are highly significant. In particular, the most significant one is that of Deposits, while the least

---

[22] Note that the asymptotic t-test on the estimated μ value doesn't indicate that μ is significantly different from zero at a five percent level, but at a fifteen percent level. Obviously, this difference is due to the fact that the test obtained from the generalized-likelihood ratio is less precise than the t-test which is focused on a single parameter.

significant one is that of Capital. These estimates confirm that the banking production process is labour-intensive rather than capital intensive and that Deposits are the main financial resources used by banks to realize banking outputs. We also note that the maximum likelihood value of $\lambda^{\frac{1}{2}}$ is 1,068 reflecting $\sigma_u{}^2 = 0,0054$ and $\sigma_v{}^2 = 0,0042$. This is the evidence that the error term is composed, in equal proportions, by components $\mathbf{u}$ (=inefficiency) and $\mathbf{v}$ (=random errors) without prevalence of one component over the other. After estimating the Cobb-Douglas cost function we assume a more complex functional form like the Translog.[23]

The Cobb-Douglas specification, based on the hypothesis that elasticities of substitution among inputs are constant and unitary, is able to represent only simple production technologies   characterized by replaceable inputs. The Translog functional form is, conversely, very flexible because it allows the elasticities of substitution to vary among inputs and, hence, it can represent sophisticated production technologies, characterized by complementary inputs. Its formulation is as follows:

$\log C = b_0 + b_L \log p_L + b_D \log p_D + b_Q \log Q + \frac{1}{2} b_{LL} (\log p_L)^2 + b_{LD} (\log p_L) (\log p_D) + \frac{1}{2} b_{DD} (\log p_D)^2 + \frac{1}{2} b_{QQ} (\log Q)^2 + b_{LQ} (\log p_L) (\log Q) + b_{DQ} (\log p_D) (\log Q) + \varepsilon$ (see Annex 3).

The variables used in this second cost function are the same as in the Cobb-Douglas. Moreover we estimate the Translog parameters by the same three-step procedure obtaining the results shown in Table 9 .

On the basis of the results reported in Table 9, we note that:
1. all the three estimated models satisfy the concavity condition requested by the duality theory. From an economic point of view this condition assures that when the price of an input increases, the Total Cost of production increases and the demand for that input decreases[24];
2. as in the Cobb-Douglas formulation, also for the Translog the stochastic frontier models are superior over the non-stochastic one. In fact, the test on the significance of the one-sided component $\mathbf{u}$ shows a value for χ^2 of 60,26 which is significant at a five percent level;

---

[23] The Translog is a second-order expansion, with Taylor's formula, of a generic function in which all variables are in logarithms. Moreover, in order to make easier the maximum likelihood estimation of the function through iterative algorithms, input Prices and output are scaled subtracting their corresponding sample means.

[24] The concavity condition is satisfied when:
1) $b_{LL} < \emptyset$;

2) $\det \begin{bmatrix} b_{LL} & b_{LD} \\ b_{DL} & b_{DD} \end{bmatrix} < \emptyset$

In our case we find that all the three models considered satisfy the two inequalities.

3. between the two stochastic models, that reported in the third column of the table, is preferable since it has higher t-statistic values. Furthermore, the test on the significance of the parameter μ shows a value for χ^2 of 54,44 which is significant at a five percent level. Consequently, like the Cobb-Douglas, also the Translog stochastic cost function leads us to the conclusion that the one-sided component reflecting inefficiency, is truncated-normally distributed;

4. according to the chosen model we note that some second-order parameters, like b_{DQ} and b_{LQ}, are statistically significant and, hence, we establish that the Translog formulation is the best functional form to represent the banking production technology. The second-order parameters b_{LL}, b_{LD} and b_{DD}, represent the input price elasticities. In particular, b_{LL} is negative. If the Price of Labour increases, while the other input prices remain constant, the demand for that input decreases; b_{LD} is positive, showing that the Labour input and the Deposits input are substitutes; b_{DD}, at last, is positive establishing that an increase in the Price of Deposits leads to an increase in the demand for that input. This result is reasonable considering that an increase in the interest rate on Deposits leads customers to deposit more and more. Parameters b_Q, b_{QQ}, b_{LQ} and b_{DQ} tell us about returns to scale. Their values (1,25 on average) assure the presence of increasing returns to scale, conversely to the result given using a Cobb-Douglas cost function which shows constant returns to scale. Finally we note that $\lambda^{\frac{1}{2}} = 1,173$ with $\sigma_u^2 = 0,0052$ and $\sigma_v^2 = 0,0038$, reflecting again that there is no prevalence of one component error over the other and, hence, that the error term is composed both by inefficiency and by random errors.

Table 8 Cobb-Douglas estimation.

Variables	OLS estimates u=0	ML estimates u=half-normal	ML estimates u=truncated-normal
b_0	18,870 (1499,2)*	18,869 (3,008)	18,857 (379,733)
b_L	0,396 (6,110)	0,395 (11,157)	0,388 (8,011)
b_D	0,508 (9,106)	0,507 (15,833)	0,513 (11,017)
b_Q	0,987 (86,953)	0,99 (140,971)	0,994 (102,279)
μ	-	-	-0,110 (-1,007)
σ	-	0,060 (0,496)	0,098 (2,015)
$\lambda^{1/2}$	-	-0,154 (-0,0004)	1,068 (1,565)
$R^2 =$	99,60 %	-	-
Log-lik =	83,85	58,829	68,286

* t-statistics in parentheses.

Table 9 Translog estimation.

Variables	OLS estimation u=0	ML estimation u=half-normal	ML estimation u=truncated-normal
b_0	18,870 (933,915)*	18,869 (5,309)	18,861 (554,683)
b_L	0,586 (5,917)	0,561 (4,538)	0,581 (6,730)
b_D	0,383 (4,703)	0,400 (4,121)	0,387 (5,371)
b_Q	0,977 (74,740)	0,981 (81,349)	0,978 (74,920)
b_{LL}	-0,340 (-0,541)	-0,344 (-0,467)	-0,334 (-0,738)
b_{LD}	0,018 (0,033)	0,011 (0,016)	0,012 (0,031)
b_{DD}	0,216 (0,442)	0,217 (0,366)	0,221 (0,587)
b_{QQ}	-0,009 (-0,389)	-0,010 (-0,481)	-0,008 (-0,445)
b_{LQ}	0,226 (2,656)	0,208 (2,212)	0,223 (3,089)
b_{DQ}	-0,165 (-2,210)	-0,146 (-1,664)	-0,162 (-2,551)
μ	-	-	-0,047 (-0,333)
$\lambda^{1/2}$	-	0,231 (0,002)	1,173 (2,054)
σ	-	0,073 (0,465)	0,095 (2,289)
$R^2 =$	99,70 %		
Log–Lik=	92,210	89,302	62,081

* t-statistics in parentheses.

Once the efficient frontier is estimated, we can calculate the economic inefficiencies of each group of banks and the mean inefficiency relative to the whole sample (see Annex 4).

In order to estimate the economic inefficiencies, for all the reasons already discussed, we choose the Translog cost function to represent the production technology and the maximum likelihood estimates provided by the model which assumes a truncated-normal distribution for **u**.

Since the inefficiencies are captured by the one-sided component of the error term, **u**, they are measured as:

INEFF = $(1-e^{-u})$

The three-step procedure provides the values of the estimated residuals, ε, for each observation, but is not able to decompose such residuals in separated estimates of the components **u** and **v**. Since to calculate the individual inefficiencies we need an estimate of **u** for each observation, we adopt the solution suggested by Jondrow, Lovell, Materov and Schmidt (1982).

These authors demonstrated that, assuming a particular distribution for **u** and formulating the probability density function of **u** conditioned to ε, than the mode of this last function corresponds to the maximum likelihood estimator of **u**.[25]

Results are shown in Table 10.

Table 10 Percentage of economic inefficiencies.

Groups of banks	Inefficiencies
MAJOR	23,5 %
LARGE	1,4 %
MEDIUM	17,4 %
SMALL	29,8 %
AVERAGE OF SAMPLE	18,05 %

---

[25] In case of assuming a half-normal distribution for **u**, the probability density function of **u** conditioned to ε is:

$f(u/\varepsilon) = [(2\pi)^{1/2} \sigma_*^2]^{-1} [1-F^*(-\varepsilon\lambda/\sigma)]^{-1} e^{[-1/(2\sigma^{*2})(u-(\varepsilon \sigma u^2/\sigma^2))^2]}$

where : $\sigma_*^2 = \sigma_u^2 \sigma_v^2 / \sigma^2$; $\lambda = \sigma_u /\sigma_v$.

The mode of this function and ML estimator of **u** is:

$M(u/\varepsilon) = u^\wedge = \varepsilon(\sigma_u^2 / \sigma^2)$

In case of a truncated-normal distribution for **u**:

$f(u/\varepsilon) = [(2\pi)^{1/2} \sigma_*^2]^{-1} [1-F^*(-\mu/\sigma\lambda-\varepsilon\lambda/\sigma)]^{-1} e^{[-1/(2\sigma^{*2})(u-(\varepsilon \sigma u^2 + \mu\sigma v^2)/\sigma^2)^2]}$;

$M(u/\varepsilon) = u^\wedge = (\varepsilon\sigma_u^2 + \mu\sigma_v^2) / \sigma^2$.

Figure 1 Percentage of inefficiencies.

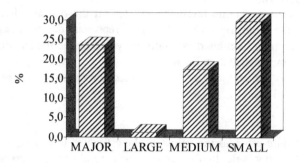

Table 10 presents interesting results. The most efficient banks are the large and the medium ones, while the least efficient banks are the small and the major ones.

Overall, the credit institutions of our sample could reduce their costs by 18,05 % eliminating all inefficiencies due to a waste of inputs or to a wrong mix of them.

5 Concluding remarks

In the present analysis we study the economic inefficiency of the Italian banking sector through a sample of 89 Italian banks using 1995 Balance Sheet data.

Following a parametric approach we test two kinds of hypotheses concerning the functional form representing the banking production technology and the kind of distribution assumed by the inefficiency among firms.

These hypotheses were already tested, in the past, by Cardani, Castagna and Galeotti (1991) which refer to year 1986 and, however, found results that are quite different from ours. In particular:

- as regards the first kind of hypotheses, we observe that the most suitable function for representing the actual banking production process is the Translog, confirming the considerations made by the above-mentioned authors. As already anticipated by the previous study, we reaffirm that actual banking production process requires complex and flexible functional forms, like the Translog, to represent it. Cobb-Douglas and other inflexible forms (used in the past by some other authors) do not consider the presence of complementary inputs;
- for what concerns the second kind of hypotheses, it seems, according to our study, that the inefficiency among firms is truncated-normally distributed

conversely to the results of Cardani, Castagna and Galeotti who confirm a half-normal distribution for it. Our results might be explained by the fact that most banks, following long-period strategies, choose a combination of inputs which is different from the one that minimizes the Total Cost.

Overall, looking at the Italian banking system, we find that, while the previous study estimated a 7 per cent economic inefficiency, our analysis shows a higher level of inefficiency (18 %). The most efficient banks are no more the major and the small, but the large and the medium ones.

This study is affected by some limitations due to the fact that some aspects have not been considered. For example, we use data referring to only one year and, so, we do not consider the evolution in time of the phenomenon.

Secondly, we estimate the whole economic inefficiency without splitting it into its two components: the technical and the allocative inefficiency.

All these limitations make this analysis suitable to be improved by future researches.

Annex 1

It's original formulation is:

$$C(y, p_L, p_K, p_D) = a_0 \ p_L^{bL} \ p_K^{bK} p_D^{bD} \ Q^{bQ}$$

The Cobb-Douglas functional form assures that a Cobb-Douglas cost function is dual to a Cobb-Douglas production function since it is based on the hypothesis that elasticities of substitution among inputs are constant and unitary.

Actually, duality theory demonstrates that a Cobb-Douglas cost function is dual to its Cobb-Douglas production function if and only if the first is: non-negative; non-decreasing in input prices and in output; concave and linearly homogeneous in input prices (see Burgess 1975, Diewert 1971a and 1974b, Shephard 1953).

Given the properties of a Cobb-Douglas functional form, it can be simply verified that it surely satisfies the first and the second condition, but not the third one. Linear homogeneity condition comes from the proof, given in the duality theory, that the first partial derivatives calculated with respect to input prices of a cost function dual to its production function are equal to the shares of Total Cost relative to each input. This means that the sum of the first partial derivatives must be equal to one.

In the Cobb-Douglas case this condition is satisfied when:

$$\partial C/\partial p_L + \partial C/\partial p_K + \partial C/\partial p_D = 1 \qquad b_L + b_K + b_D = 1$$

In order to be sure that the Cobb-Douglas cost function is dual, we estimate it imposing the constraint derived from linear homogeneity condition.

Substituting $b_K = 1 - b_L - b_D$ in the function, we obtain:

$$\log (C/p_K) = b_0 + b_L \log (p_L/p_K) + b_D \log (p_D/p_K) + b_Q \log Q + \varepsilon$$

Annex 2

The intercept is corrected adding to the OLS estimate of the constant, the mean of ε. In fact: $E(\varepsilon) = E(\mathbf{u+v}) = E(\mathbf{u}) + E(\mathbf{v}) = E(\mathbf{u}) + \varnothing = E(\mathbf{u})$.

The COLS formula, in case of a half-normal distribution for $\mathbf{u}$, is:

$$b_{0<COLS>} = b_{0<OLS>} + E(\varepsilon) \qquad \text{with } E(\varepsilon) = (2/\pi)^{1/2} \, \sigma_{\mathbf{u}}$$

In case of a truncated-normal distribution for $\mathbf{u}$:

$$E(\mathbf{u}) = E(\varepsilon) = (\mu a/2) + (\sigma_{\mathbf{u}} \, a/(2\pi)^{\frac{1}{2}}) \, e^{[-\frac{1}{2}(\mu/ \, \sigma u)^a]}$$

where : μ = mode of the distribution of $\mathbf{u}$;

$$a = [1 - F^*(-\mu/\sigma_{\mathbf{u}})]^{-1}$$

F^* = distribution function for a standard normal random variable.

As regards the variances $\sigma_{\mathbf{u}}^2$ and $\sigma_{\mathbf{v}}^2$, it was demonstrated by Aigner, Lovell and Schmidt (1977) and confirmed by Olson, Schmidt and Waldman (1980) that if a specific distribution is assumed for $\mathbf{u}$, than it is possible to estimate the parameters of this distribution from the higher-order (second, third and so on) central moments of the OLS residuals.

In particular, in case of a half-normal distribution for $\mathbf{u}$:

$$\sigma_{\mathbf{u}}^2 = [(\pi/2)^{1/2} \, (\pi/(\pi-4)) \, m_3]^{2/3}$$

$$\sigma_{\mathbf{v}}^2 = m_2 - ((\pi-2)/\pi) \, \sigma_{\mathbf{u}}^2$$

where : m_2 = second central moment of the OLS residuals;

m_3 = third central moment of the OLS residuals.

In case of a truncated-normal distribution for $\mathbf{u}$:

$$\sigma^2 = \sigma_{\mathbf{v}}^2 + \sigma_{\mathbf{u}}^2 \; ;$$

$$\sigma_{\mathbf{v}}^2 = m_2 - (a/2)\mu^a \, (1 - a/2) - a/2 \, ((\pi-a)/\pi).$$

Annex 3

The original formulation of the function is:

$$\log C = b_0 + b_L \log p_L + b_K \log p_K + b_D \log p_D + b_Q \log Q + \tfrac{1}{2} b_{LL} (\log p_L)^2 + \tfrac{1}{2} b_{LK} (\log p_L)(\log p_K) + \tfrac{1}{2} b_{KL} (\log p_K)(\log p_L) + \tfrac{1}{2} b_{LD} (\log p_L)(\log p_D) + \tfrac{1}{2} b_{DL} (\log p_D)(\log p_L) + \tfrac{1}{2} b_{KK} (\log p_K)^2 + \tfrac{1}{2} b_{DK} (\log p_D)(\log p_K) + \tfrac{1}{2} b_{KD} (\log p_K)(\log p_D) + \tfrac{1}{2} b_{DD} (\log p_D)^2 + \tfrac{1}{2} b_{QQ} (\log Q)^2 + b_{LQ} (\log p_L)(\log Q) + b_{KQ} (\log p_K)(\log Q) + b_{DQ} (\log p_D)(\log Q) + \varepsilon$$

Unfortunately, in this original form, the Translog is not "self-dual" and requires some restrictions to be imposed on its parameters in order to satisfy the symmetry and linear homogeneity conditions requested by the duality theory (see Burgess, 1975). The restrictions are:

1) $b_{LK} = b_{KL}$; $b_{LD} = b_{DL}$; $b_{DK} = b_{KD}$ (to satisfy the symmetry condition);
2) $b_L + b_K + b_D = 1$; $b_{LL} + b_{LK} + b_{LD} = \varnothing$; $b_{KK} + b_{KL} + b_{KD} = \varnothing$; $b_{DD} + b_{DL} + b_{DK} = \varnothing$; $b_{LQ} + b_{KQ} + b_{DQ} = \varnothing$ (to satisfy the linear homogeneity condition).

Substituting these constraints in the original function we obtained the restricted form above-mentioned. In few words, to make sure that the Translog cost function is dual to its corresponding Translog production function, it is necessary that Total Cost and input prices are normalized with respect to an input price. In our analysis we choose the Price of Capital for proceeding in the normalization, but it was demonstrated by the duality theory that the choice of one price rather than another, doesn't influence the parameters estimates.

Annex 4

By the term "economic inefficiency" we mean a total inefficiency which is able to be decomposed in two particular kinds of inefficiency:

a) technical inefficiency, measured by the distance between the observed production and the production which lies on the efficient production frontier;
b) allocative inefficiency, measured by the distance between the production which lies on the efficient production frontier and the production which lies on the efficient cost frontier.

The distance is calculated by a radial measure, that is, reducing equiproportionally all inputs quantities.

Figure 2 Economic inefficiency and its decomposition.

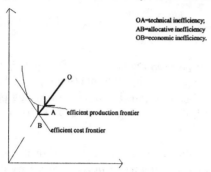

From an economic point of view, the presence of economic inefficiency indicates the fact that inputs are wasted (technical inefficiency) and/or that inputs are chosen in the wrong manner with respect to their prices (allocative inefficiency).

REFERENCES

Aigner D., Chu S. (1968), *"On estimating the industry production function"*, American Economic Review, Vol.53.

Aigner D., Lovell K.C.A., Schmidt P. (1977),*"Formulation and estimation of stochastic frontier production function models"*, Journal of Econometrics, Vol. 6.

Baldini D., Landi A. (1990), *"Economie di scala e complementarietà di costo nell'industria bancaria italiana"*, L'Industria, Vol. 1.

Baltagi B.H. (1995), *"Econometric Analysis of Panel Data"*.

Battese G.E., Coelli T.J. (1988),*"Prediction of firm-level technical efficiencies with a generalized frontier production function and panel data"*, Journal of Econometrics, Vol.38.

Berger A.N., Hanweck G.A., Humphrey D.B. (1987), *"Competitive Viability in Banking. Scale, Scope and Product Mix Economies"*, Journal of Monetary Economics, Vol.20.

Berndt E.K., Hall B.H., Hausman J.A. (1974), *"Estimation and Inference in Non-linear Structural Models"*, Annals of Economic and Social Measurement, Vol.3.

Burgess D.F. (1975),   *"Duality theory and pitfalls in technologies"*, Journal of Econometrics.

Cardani A.M., Castagna M., Galeotti M. (1991),*"La misurazione dell'efficienza economica : un'applicazione al sistema bancario italiano"*, Ricerche Economiche, Vol. XLV(1).

Commission of the European Community (1993), *"European Economy. Social Europe. Market Services and Europe integration"*, Report and Studies, N. 3.

Conigliani C., De Bonis R., Motta G., Parigi G. (1991),*"Economie di scala e di diversificazione nel settore bancario"*, Temi di Discussione, Vol.150, Banca D'Italia, Roma .

Cossutta D., Di Battista M.L., Giannini C., Urga G. (1988), *"Processo produttivo e struttura dei costi nell'industria bancaria italiana"* in Cesarini F., Grillo M., a cura di Banca e Mercato, Bologna, Il Mulino.

Diewert W.E. (1971a) *"An application of the Shephard duality theorem : a generalized Leontief production function"*, Journal of Political Economy, Vol.79.

Diewert W.E. (1974b) *"Applications of duality theory"*, Frontiers of Quantitative Economics, editors: Intrilligator M.D., Kendrick D.A., Vol. II.

Forsund F.R., Lovell C.A.K, Schmidt P. (1980) , *"A survey of frontier production functions and their relationship to efficiency measurement"*, Journal of Econometrics, Vol. 13.

Garcia F.P., Vilarino R.D. (1992),*"La produttività del sistema bancario spagnolo negli anni '80, un confronto internazionale"*, Moneta e Credito, BNL n°178, Vol. 6.

Jondrow J., Lovell C.A.K., Materov I.S., Schmidt P. (1982),*"On the estimation of technical inefficiency in the stochastic frontier production function model"*, Journal of Econometrics, Vol. 19.

Lanciotti G., Raganelli T. (1988), *"Funzioni di costo e obiettivi di efficienza nella produzione bancaria"* , in "Temi di discussione", n. 99, Roma, Banca d'Italia.

Lee K.F., Pitt M.M. (1981) *"Measurement and Sources of Technical Efficiency in the Indonesian Weaving Industry"*, Journal of Development Economics, Vol. 9.

Masera R. (1991), *"Intermediari, mercati e finanza d'impresa. Prospettive dell'integrazione finanziaria in Europa e della globalizzazione"*, Roma-Bari, Laterza.

Meeusen W., Van Den Broeck J. (1977), *"Efficiency Eestimation From Cobb-Douglas Production Functions With Composed Errors"*, International Economic Review, Vol. 18.

Olson J.A., Schmidt P., Waldman D.M. (1980),*"A Monte Carlo study of estimation of stochastic frontier production functions"*, Journal of Econometrics, Vol. 13.

Shephard R.W. (1953), *"Cost and Production Functions"*, Princeton, N.J.: Princeton University Press

Stevenson R.E. (1980), *"Likelihood functions for generalized stochastic frontier estimation"*, Journal of Econometrics, Vol.13

Paper prepared within the research project C.N.R. 97,00963.ct10

ANALYSIS OF EFFECTS OF RECONSTRUCTED BUSINESS UNITS ON EMPLOYMENT AND PRODUCTIVITY LONGITUDINAL STUDY USING SYNTHETIC UNITS OF FINNISH MANUFACTURING

Seppo Laaksonen[1] and Ismo Teikari[2]

[1,2]*Statistics Finland*

1 Introduction

This study has the three major targets. First, it is a methodological and conceptual contribution to the problems arising from the changes of enterprises and other business units over time. We use a certain enterprise concept, so that all manufacturing establishments/plants of an enterprise constitute this 'enterprise.' Such an enterprise may be referred to as a kind-of-activity unit with its broadest meaning. As is well-known, it is not easy to follow business units consistently over time. The tracking of an enterprise unit is usually more difficult than that of a plant. Although our study is concerned only to the manufacturing plants of enterprises, the tracking is difficult enough. In order to understand the demographic events of these enterprises we have analyzed the units based on initial survey information. Utilizing a cohort approach we have then constructed so-called synthetic enterprises, if we have observed a reasonable continuity. We believe that these synthetic units give a better understanding than the initial survey units do.

Our second major target is to use this new data set to facilitate the analysis of consequences of reconstruction's of enterprises, such as merger, split-off and takeover, and also consequences of births and deaths. We have provided comparative results using both demographic approaches. Furthermore, we have analyzed the reconstruction effects to the labor productivity and to the employment; this has been done both before and after this reconstruction. We have provided many interesting findings although the time period is very short. On the other hand this period is very interesting, because it was very dramatic for Finland and its economy. The year 1990 was the first recession year after the long and strong overheating growth in the late 1980s. The deepest recession years were 1991 and 1992, but 1994 was already somewhat better. Our third target is to analyze the effects of the recession.

The paper is organized so that in the next section we introduce the concepts of the enterprise demography and present the practical creation of the data file. Section 3 gives some comparative results using both types of enterprise concepts. We preliminarily also present some effects which may arise from the changes in business units. Many effects of the recession are observed as well. In the 4th section we present some background for empirical analysis of Section 5. We have not seen any exactly similar approach in the previous research, but some concerning for instance to ownership changes looks of the same kind. These have been taken into account.

2 Business demography

The rapidly changing structure of population is a special feature in business surveys. Continuously new enterprises and establishments enter to the population and numerous establishments and enterprises ceases their activities. At the same time some persistent businesses change their industrial group and grow and decrease in their sizes. The research topic studying this phenomenon is called the business demography.

In this section we present how the enterprise demography is constructed (see Eurostat 1996). There are three basic changes which continually take place in the business population (Struits and Willeboordse 1995):
1. *The change of characteristic*: This means that the identity of the enterprise has not changed but the main activity or the size class or some other important character has changed. The number of units before and after this change remains the same and the identity of the enterprise continues.
2. *Changes of existence*: These changes involve units that are not related to any unit of the population to which they could be compared. In the case of *birth* there is no enterprise related to this enterprise before the change and in the case of *death* there is no related enterprise after the change. Of course the identity does not continue in either of these cases.
3. *Changes of structure*: These changes involve more than one unit before or after the change. *Concentration* means that two or more units combine to one unit. The unit emerging from the concentration may or may not be essentially the same as one unit before the change. In the case of *take-over* one unit continues its identity whereas other units lose their identity. In the case of *merger* all units lose their identity and a new enterprise appears after the change. During the *deconcentration* a unit either *breaks up* without any one retaining the identity of the original unit or one or more units *split of* from one unit which retain its identity. This case is the reverse of concentration. *Restructuring* involves the more complex changes of the structure.

In addition to these cases a new registration can occur when an enterprise changes its legal form. All of these changes except the change of characteristic creates the administrative birth or death of an enterprise in administrative registers. A question arises: how the changes above can be identified in the administrative register?

In Finland, the tax authority gives an ID-number for an enterprise when it appears to the register. This ID-number disappears in the cases of administrative deaths and appears in the cases of administrative births. The business register which investigate the number and the location of establishments of these new enterprises when they appears, gives the ID-number for an establishment. This ID-number is independent of the enterprise number and in general does not alter in the cases of administrative births and deaths. So using the enterprise number and the establishment number jointly, it is possible, exploiting the knowledge of continuity of the enterprise after the change and information of the existence of the new enterprise before the change, to classify some demographic events:

1. An enterprise disappears; the establishment remains; A new owner of an establishment is a new registration. This case involves three possible events:
   a) two or more enterprises have *merged* and all have changed their identity,
   b) one enterprise has *split off* and ceased
   c) an enterprise has *changed its legal form*.
2. An enterprise disappears; an establishment remains, a new owner of an establishment is a remaining enterprise. This is a case of take-over.
3. An enterprise stays and an establishment stays but moves to a new enterprise which is a new registration. This is a case of break up.
4. A new enterprise and a new establishment appears.
   This is a case of *pure birth* of an enterprise.
5. An enterprise and an establishment disappears:
   This a case of *pure death* of an enterprise.
6. An enterprise stays and an establishment stays but move to a new owner; a new owner is a retaining enterprise.

This is a *movement of an establishment* and may have some results in the change of characteristic of an enterprise but does not have any result on the enterprise demography.

In cases 1-3 we have prepared *a synthetic enterprise* which describes the changes in establishments only, not the changes which are results of the reconstruction of the businesses. A synthetic enterprise can be a combination of establishments which do not belong to it in the real world. Below are some examples to enlighten this problem.

1. In the case of *merger*, enterprises A and B disappear and a new enterprise C appears as a combination of these two enterprises in the real world. In the world of synthetic enterprises A and B stay alive and the changes in the time period could be described as those changes that take place in the original establishments of enterprises A and B. Enterprise C does not exist in the world of synthetic businesses.

2. In the case of *split-off*, enterprise A is divided into enterprises B and C in the real world. In the world of synthetic enterprises A stay alive and businesses B and C does not exist. The changes that take place in the time period could be described as those changes that take place in the establishments that constitute the original enterprise A.
3. In the case of *take-over*, enterprises A and B disappear and join as establishments to the enterprise C which includes the establishments X and Y previously. In the world of synthetic enterprises A and B stay alive and an enterprise C includes the establishments X and Y only.

Using the information in two alternative worlds it is possible to estimate the changes that are not effected by the changes in size due to the structural changes. In the next chapter we present some differences which occur between the changes in the real world and in the world of synthetic enterprises.

Below our interest concerns to cases 1 and 3; cases 2 were not possible carefully to analyze because of a too low number of such observations. In case 1 there are in fact three alternatives which are not separable. However the weight of the merger is so strong that it is possible to call this case a merger. It must be remembered however that the few cases of split of are the reverse of a merger so that the estimates will be slightly bias. The cases of legal form changes are neutral and very few because data consists of only a few micro businesses where these cases mainly take place.

In this study we consider a merger as a case of kindly change of ownership. Because all identities of businesses disappear there must be some combined advantages between the joined businesses. A take-over we consider a hostile acquirer. An identity of an acquirer stays and the identity of the acquired enterprises disappears.

3 Comparisons using the two alternative demographic measures

We use standard demographic measures and rates in our analysis (see e.g. Davis and Haltiwanger 1990, Vainiomäki and Laaksonen 1997). The job creation rate is the sum of the birth rates in new enterprises and the growth rate in increasing enterprises. The job destruction rate is respectively the sum of the death rates and the declining rates. The minus sign is often used for the job destruction, so that the sum of these rates is the net rate. This sum is called the turnover rate if the plus sign is used also for the job destruction rate. Tables 1 and 2 describe some comparisons over the period 1990 - 1994.

Table 1 Net rates from 1990/91 to 1993/94 for synthetic enterprises

1990/91	0.069
1991/92	0.097
1992/93	0.064
1993/94	0.004
1990/94	0.064

These net rates show that the worst decline in employment occurred in the period from 1991 to 1992, and the second worst from 1990 to 1991.

Table 2 Average demographic rates from 1990 to 1994 in size classes within the initial and synthetic longitudinal data. Size is the average value over the whole period.

Size Class ..	Ceation		Dstruction		Trnover		Net	
	Synth.	Init	Synth	Init.	Synth.	Init.	Synth.	Init.
- 9.9	0.139	0.154	-0.203	-0.209	0.342	0.363	-0.064	**0.055**
10.0- 19.9	0.125	0.148	-0.167	-0.181	0.292	0.328	**-0.042**	-0.033
20.0- 49.9	0.088	0.121	-0.153	-0.185	0.241	0.307	-0.065	-0.064
50.0- 99,9	0.069	0.104	-0.135	-0.178	0.204	0.282	-0.066	-0.073
100.0-249.9	0.052	0.105	-0.119	-0.169	0.171	0.274	-0.067	-0.064
250.0-499.9	0.029	0.103	-0.106	-0.197	0.135	0.300	-0.077	-0.094
500+	0.017	0.107	-0.064	-0.187	0.080	0.294	-0.047	-0.081

In Table 2 it can be seen that synthetic enterprises provide lower job creation and job destruction rates (in absolute values) than the initial enterprises do. This is due to the fact that the pure enterprise births and deaths gives much lower job creation and destruction rates than the initial administrative births and deaths ones do. There is also a systematic difference in net rates: the initial rates overestimate the net rates for the small enterprises and underestimate those for the larger enterprises. The sign even changes in the case of micro enterprises.

We approach to our basic research targets in Table 3, which gives demographic rates for some specific sub-populations of synthetic enterprises. The job destruction rates of mergers are above the average over the whole period, but the creation rates after the first year. This is to some extent the implication of the two kind of mergers: some of these have been created jobs very well, the others destructed.   The takeovers have in all years created relatively little jobs, but destructed relatively much. The table also shows that the exported enterprises have succeeded better than the average in job creation losing the jobs no more than the average at the same time. The implication is much lower net decrease than in average.

Table 3 Average job creation, destruction and net rates from 1990 to 1994 for some enterprise groups using synthetic longitudinal data. The bold text if the rate better than the average for all enterprises.

Creation	Destruction	Net	
All enterprises	0.044	-0.101	-0.058
Mergers			
90/91	0.016	-0.117	-0.101
91/92	**0.045**	-0.171	-0.126
92/93	**0.052**	-0.138	-0.086
93/94	**0.073**	-0.128	**-0.055**
90/94	0.039	-0.136	-0.098
Takeovers			
90/92	0.015	-0.161	-0.146
92/94	0.035	-0.138	-0.103
90/94	0.023	-0.153	-0.131
Non-mergers			
and non-takeovers			
90/94	0.045	-0.093	-0.048
Exported enterprises			
90/94	**0.065**	**-0.100**	**-0.036**

4 Impact of concentrations (mergers and take-overs) on enterprise performance - previous approaches and findings

Dickerson et al (1997) discuss about the enterprise behavior in view of the growth and the profitability. The modern theories of the enterprise performance provide a more explicit role for growth in the enterprises strategy than do the neo-classical models where the growth plays only an incidental role in profit maximization. Enterprises try to maximize the profits in the long run investing in all projects which gives a positive net present value. However, the managerial constraints puts a limit on growth. This results from the fact that if the enterprise expands too fast, the management is not able to manage the growth efficiently.

Little attention is paid to the relative advantages and disadvantages due to the internal growth and acquisition growth, even in modern theories. Firstly, acquisition growth allows a company to acquire a ready-made investment including employees required to operate it. Secondly, acquisition can provide an enterprise with new internal investment opportunities by facilitating entrance into new product areas and by providing new information in those areas.

Using the data of synthetic enterprises in the longitudinal data it is possible to study some sources of the productive growth at enterprise level. Otherwise it should be used the establishment level data because the enterprise level data hide many important features. We have not seen any other just the similar approach to analyze the evolution of enterprises, but there is much theoretical and empirical research which helps us in such an analysis. The theory of Lichtenberg and Siegel (1989) and the matching theory of job turnover developed by Jovanovic (1979) are consistent with the observation that plant productivity is negatively related to ownership change and that ownership change is then positively related to productivity growth. This means that ownership change is often signal of high business quality but there are inefficiencies in management. Changing owners have a much more negative effect on employment growth in central offices than it is in manufacturing plants. Central offices changing ownership had on the other hand slower growth in wages. In this study we were not able to distinguish central offices and other plants, but we deduce that there are analogous effects due to mergers and takeovers.

McGuckin et al (1993 and 1995) analyze the impact of ownership change in a more general framework using both enterprise and plant level longitudinal data. They particularly concentrate on productivity, wages and employment in the US food manufacturing. They got three principal results. First ownership change (acquiring enterprises) is positively associated with productivity and wage growth, although these effects are significantly smaller for large plants. Second, ownership change appears to be associated with increases, not decreases, in employment at operating plants. Third, plants changing ownership show a greater likelihood of survival than those that do not change owners. These results means that ownership change is generally associated with the transfer of plants with above average productivity, not poorly performing ones. Thus synergy's and related efficiencies are important motives for the ownership change.

Dickerson et al 1997 examine the impact of acquisitions (takeovers) on company performance using a panel of UK enterprises. Their results show no evidence that acquisition has a net beneficial effect on company performance as measured by profitability. On the contrary they found that acquisitions have a systematic detrimental impact on company performance. Not only is the coefficient on acquisition growth much lower than that on internal growth but there is an additional and permanent reduction in profitability following acquisition. Enterprise level data have given the same results because some important characteristics are hidden at this level.

Baldwin (1996) considers from the Canada's perspective associations between job creation, wages and productivity. Although he does not exactly consider the importance of acquisition, his analysis emerges some interesting points on growth of small and large enterprises. As he mentions, small enterprises are often seen as the engines of growth because they have created more new jobs than large enterprises. However they have not increased their shipments much more than the great enterprises. This means that they have not become much more important as producers and their relative labor productivity has fallen.

There are various methodological approaches to this type of analysis, which necessarily leads to use longitudinal data. We apply several methods, starting from the approach presented by Baily et al (1994). Briefly described it is as follows.

Because the previous studies have shown that the productivity growth and downsizing/upsizing are in some connection, Baily et al (1994) divide the data into four productive and employment quadrants.

(i) *Quadrant 1* consists of the *successful upsizers*, enterprises that were able to raise both labor productivity and employment. Enterprises can be found in this quadrant if it has had a long run increase (in this case only 4 years) in both labor productivity and employment and it is consistent with increased demand for its products combined with increasing returns of technology. Also enterprises can be found of this quadrant if they have actually moved their production frontier outward through technological innovation, while facing elastic product demand.

(ii) *Quadrant 2* consists of the *successful downsizers*, the enterprises that were able to raise productivity by reducing employment. This pattern is consistent with technological innovation combined with either falling demand or very inelastic demand.

(iii) *Quadrant 3* consists of *unsuccessful downsizers*, the enterprises that faced reductions in both productivity and employment. Enterprises can be found in this quadrant if the employment and productivity behavior is consistent with one of following: a) falling demand and increasing returns to scale, b) negative productive shock and elastic demand, c) falling demand and incomplete adjustment of employment.

(iv) *Quadrant 4* consists of *unsuccessful upsizers,* the enterprises raised employment but at the expense of productivity. This pattern is consistent with a negative productivity shock and inelastic demand or rising demand and diminishing returns. Alternatively, these plants could have shifted to lower quality employees, which could be observed by falling wages.

In the other parts of this study we apply longitudinal GEE models (GEE = Generalized Estimating Equations, see McCullagh and Nelder 1989, SAS Users' Guide 1997). We have exploited previous research of McGuckin et al (1993 and 1995) and Dickerson et al (1997), for instance, in the specifications of these models including the selection of the explanatory variables. Our data set would have given opportunity to other types of approaches (see Annex) as well.

5 Effects of mergers/takeovers on employment and productivity

This section analyses the effects of mergers and takeovers from the several perspectives. It begins from the cross-classifications, using the approach of Baily et al to some extent. Next we construct a number of multivariate models which aim at illustrating these effects in a broader sense, including some control variables and other interesting variables. Few comparisons by both data sets (initial and synthetic) are given in Table 4, where we mainly use synthetic data. The differences between these techniques are more dramatic in smaller groups and in specific groups close to this reconversion.

It seems that the growth of the labour productivity has been faster among large enterprises than in small enterprises. That is because the small enterprises can be found in the group 'unsuccessful' more often than the large enterprises. *The smallest enterprises* in this group tend to be unsuccesful downsizers which means that they have met reductions in both productivity and employment. They have met either falling demand of products combined with increasing returns to scale or negative production shock combined with elastic labour demand or falling demand of products combined with incomplete adjustment of employment.

The medium size enterprises tend to be successful upsizers which means that they have been able to raise both labour productivity and employment. These enterprises may have moved their production frontiers outward through technological innovation, or they have had a long run increase in both labour productivity and employment which is consistent with increased demand of its products combined with increasing returns of technology. *The large enterprises* tend to be successful downsizers where also typically lies the enterprises which have met with *merger* or *take-over,* and the exporting enterprises. These enterprises have been able to raise their productivity by reducing employment. Often this is consistent with technological innovation combined with falling demand of inelastic demand of employment.

Table 4 Cross-classification of enterprises by their growth/decline employment (called upsizers/downsizers) and their labor productivity growth/decline (called successful/unsuccessful) (% of the whole panel). The balanced panel for 1990-94. The bold text used for the figures above the average.

Group	Upsizer/ Successful	Upsizer/ Unsucc.	Downsizer /Successful	Downsizer/ Unsucc.	All
	%	%	%	%	%
ALL					
Synthetic	14.7	8.6	53.2	23.4	100
Initial	15.5	9.2	51.3	24.0	100
Size class					
(synthetic)					
- 9.9	7.3	**11.6**	48.9	**32.4**	100
10.0- 19.9	12.9	**9.8**	48.3	**29.1**	100
20.0- 49.9	**17.7**	**9.2**	51.1	22.0	100
50.0- 99.9	**16.2**	7.8	**58.6**	17.4	100
100.0-249.9	**20.8**	4.6	**62.3**	12.3	100
250.0-499.9	14.7	2.6	**69.8**	12.9	100
500+	14.3	1.7	**70.6**	13.5	100
Mergers					
90/92	12.2	6.3	**62.9**	18.6	100
92/94	10.7	**8.8**	53.2	**27.3**	100
90/94	11.5	7.6	**58.0**	23.0	100
Takeovers					
90/92	**15.4**	5.1	**59.0**	20.5	100
92/94	5.1	2.7	**65.4**	**26.9**	100
90/94	9.7	3.9	**63.1**	23.3	100
Exported	**17.7**	7.8	**54.7**	19.9	100
enterprises					
Industries					
in R&D survey					
- No R&D	10.3	**9.6**	**55.9**	**24.2**	100
expenditure					
- R&D	**24.4**	8.1	55.6	11.9	100
expenditure					

Table 5 presents the results of the five models which are based on the analysis of the relative labor productivity RLP for the enterprises being survived over the whole period 1990 - 1994 (balanced panel).

$$RLP_{ij} = \frac{LP_{ij}}{ALP_j}$$

where i and j denote plant i and industry j, LP is plant labor productivity and ALP is average industry labor productivity (2- or 3-digit level depending on the number of observations). This is a standard regression model, where the relative labor productivity of each year, relative to the average of the same industry group, (see McGuckin et al 1993&1995 who also use this concept) is the response variable. Model 1b of Table 5 is based on the initial enterprises, the five others on the synthetic enterprises.

Table 5 Regression models for labor productivity growth (log %) for the synthetic manufacturing enterprises survived from 1990 to 1994

Estimates (and p-values)

Explanatory variables	Model 1a -Synthetic All enterprises n = 3343	Model 1b -Initial All enterprises n = 3343	Model 2 All enterprises n = 3343	Model 3 All enterprises n = 3343	Model 4 R&D Survey industries n = 921	Model 5 R&D Survey industries n = 921
Intercept	0.138 (0.0081)	0.147 (0.4210)	0.136 (0.0002)	0.134 (0.0104)	0.126 (0.2042)	0.250 (0.0240)
Empl Growth (log %)	-0.063 (0.0001)	-0.034 (0.0102)	-0.063 (0.0001)	-0.063 (0.0001)	-0.089 (0.0027)	-0.084 (0.0046)
Wage Growth	0.697 (0.0001)	0.715 (0.0001)	0.718 (0.0001)	0.695 (0.0001)	0.698 (0.0001)	0.695 (0.0001)
Exported enterprise			0.066 (0.0001)	0.033 (0.0239)		
R&D expenditure enterprise					0.080 (0.0089)	0.085 (0.0057)
Merger 90-92	0.056 (0.0257)	-0.185 (0.2046)	0.060 (0.0168)	0.055 (0.0239)	0.112 (0.0222)	0.091 (0.0657)
Merger 92-94	-0.001 (0.9858)	0.216 (0.0298)	-0.000 (0.9929)	0.001 (0.9710)	-0.053 (0.3222)	-0.045 (0.4002)
Takeover 90-94						0.144 (0.0119)
Size class	Higher for larger enterprises	Higher for larger enterprises			Higher for larger enterprises	Higher for larger, highest for 2nd largest	Higher for larger, highest for 2nd largest
Industry	Highest for electronics	Highest for electronics		Highest for electronics	Highest for electronics	Highest for electronics
R-Square	0.182	0.175	0.168	0.183	0.207	0.212

The sign of employment growth is negative in all models. This is going in the same direction as in the previous model where it was noted that the most general case was the successful downsizer. The possible productivity growth has been achieved by reducing employment in a general case. The average wages per worker have not been decreased, but instead increased. This is a new evidence of the rigidity of the Finnish wage bargaining system which has been welcome for employed people, but not for unemployed (see Laaksonen and Vainiomäki 1997). From the previous results it is also not surprising that the export and the R&D enterprises have increased their productivity.

There are not much differences in estimates of wage or employment whether used initial or synthetic data, but much more when comparing estimates of the effects of mergers, even the signs differ. We here believe more in the synthetic figures which show in all models a positive effect on productivity if the merging has occurred in the early (1990-92) recession. There is no significant effects instead for later (1992-94) merged enterprises. This means that there has been a different target in mergers of these periods. It is obvious that the productivity growth in early phase has been done mainly destructing actions/jobs with low productivity; it has been necessary in order to survive.

Since the number of take-overs is relatively small, we have only such a model for this group which concerns take-overs during the whole period. The estimate of model 5 is positive and higher than for mergers. Acquisition has thus improved the performance more than that of mergers.

Table 6 gives results of our following modeling technique which is based on the unbalanced panel over the whole period 1990 - 1994. We mainly have estimated GEE estimates but model 1A gives the standard regression estimates based on the pooled data. These pooled data estimates show the estimated relative labor productivity 'rates.'

Table 6 Cross-sectional estimates and longitudinal GEE estimates when explaining relative labor productivity (log %) by synthetic data for the unbalanced panel from 1990 to 1994. Poisson distribution and logarithmic link function are applied, correlation structure is exchangeable.

Estimates (and p-values[1])

	Model 1 Cross-section All enterprises n=24176	Model 2A Longitudinal All enterprises n=24176	Model 2B Longitudinal All enterprises n=24176	Model 3 Longitudinal R&D Survey enterprises n=6439	Model 4A Longitudinal, average size <100 n=22087	Model 4B Longitudinal average size >=100 n=4615
Explanatory variables etc.						
Intercept	7.087	7.521	8.178	8.038	7.623	8.327
	(0.0001)	(0.0001)	(0.0001)	(0.0001)	(0.0001)	(0.0001)
Employment	0.015	-0.083	-0.213	-0.070	-0.133	-0.102
(log %)	(0.0001)	(0.1869)	(0.1037)	(0.1702)	(0.1206)	(0.1211)
Exported	0.249	0.157	0.226	0.1622	0.159	0.085
enterprise	(0.0001)	(0.0001)	(0.0001)	(0.0001)	(0.0001)	(0.0018)
R&D				0.3550		
expenditure				(0.0001)		
enterprise						
Merger	-0.143	-0.126	-0.121	-0.071	-0.144	-0.087
90-91	(0.0001)	(0.0459)	(0.0924)	(0.6594)	(0.0090)	(0.5563)
Merger	0.005	0.061	0.086	0.350	0.035	0.171
91-92	(0.0001)	(0.3297)	(0.2996)	(0.0205)	(0.6049)	(0.1215)
Merger	-0.023	0.003	0.031	0.014	0.017	0.315
92-93	(0.0001)	(0.9621)	(0.7142)	(0.9434)	(0.8277)	(0.0216)
Merger	-0.063	-0.026	-0.026	0.186	-0.066	0.124
93-94	(0.0001)	(0.7401)	(0.7850)	(0.1971)	(0.4724)	(0.2790)
Take-over 90-94	0.259	0.323	0.418		0.310	0.156
	(0.0001)	(0.0001)	(0.0001)		(0.0004)	(0.1058)
Closed during	-0.077	-0.088				
90-94	(0.0001)	(0.0091)				
Years						
1990	-0.237	-0.179	-0.253	**-0.218**	-0.154	-0.235
1991	**-0.239**	**-0.223**	**-0.299**	**-0.216**	**-0.207**	**-0.307**
1992	-0.180	-0.181	-0.249	-0.136	-0.178	-0.217
1993	-0.091	-0.091	-0.126	-0.069	-0.096	-0.106
1994	0.000	0.000	0.000	0.000	0.000	0.000
Industry	Included in the model but details excluded here	Included in the model but details excluded here	Included in the model but details excluded here	Included in the model but details excluded here	Included in the model but details excluded here	Included in the model but details excluded here
Number of clusters	No	6389	6389	1696	5944	1032

---

[1] except for variable year, for which the most estimated values are significant compared to the reference year 1994.

Model 1 is based on the cross-sectional analysis of the data for 1990 - 1994. Models 2A an 2B are based on the longitudinal analysis of the same data, but models 1 and 2A only have the exactly same explanatory variables, that is, include the 'closed enterprise' dummy. Model 3 is based on the data for R&D enterprises. Models 4A and 4B are based on the longitudinal analysis in the data consisting the enterprises with less than 100 employees in model 4A and the enterprises with 100 or more employees in model 4B, correspondingly.

Models 2,3 and 4 are estimated by the GEE procedure (General Estimating Equations method). When the responses are correlated and discrete and the normality assumption may not be reasonable GEE provides a practical method with reasonable statistical efficiency to analyze such data. This extends the traditional linear model and is applicable to a wider range of data analysis problems. The response variable is RLP.

The most explanatory variables are categorical, not changing during this period. The productivity itself and employment are the exceptions. We can see that the sign of the employment parameter is positive for the pooled data model. Thus the larger enterprises are more productive although a number of other (controlling) variables have been taken into account. Instead, this sign is slightly but not very significantly negative in other (longitudinal) models. This shows that the productivity growth is rather due to the reduction in employment than to other factors, but not very significantly. In the balanced panel results (Table 5) this effect is more significant.

Mergers 90-91 seem to be fairly different from other mergers. Their productivity level was relatively low, the productivity growth not much higher. This means that enterprises which merged in the early years of the recession have not been very productive and even the growth of the labor productivity has been lower than in average. The later mergers have been more productive but not as productive as non-mergers in average. The growth does not differ much from non-mergers. The exceptions are mergers 91-92 of R&D enterprises (see model 3), the productivity growth is significantly positive. In models 4A and 4B we can see the significant growth of the large enterprises which have merged in 92-93. In all cases the growth has been faster in the large merged enterprises than it has been in small ones. This results is in the same direction as obtained by Lichtenberg and Siegel (1989.).

The behavior of take-overs is interestingly different from mergers. Their productivity level has been fairly high, but it has improved fast during the period. Obviously a typical takeover is more strongly associated with the reorganization of the acquired parts. It is also worthy of consideration to note that the productivity growth in merged large enterprises has been significant whereas in merged small enterprises it has not been significant.

Some of the productivity changes may be explained by production changes. Production declined during the early recession in many companies and productivity as well. This emerged the reduction in employment but growth in productivity, if the enterprise was still alive.

It is fortunately so that the closed enterprises were before this occurrence less productive than the continuing enterprises. Correspondingly, the exported and R&D enterprises have in this context improved their productivity relatively well. This was also concerned opened enterprises, but not very significantly (this is not included in the table).

6 Discussion

The focus in this paper is to analyze the effects of changes in enterprise status's regarding their possible new construction due to mergers and take-overs on employment, wages and productivity. This required first to build a new type of longitudinal data set which standardize better than the original one these enterprise units over time.

We use this data set to give the first results on the two types of demography for enterprises, and secondly, we make attempts to analyze the impact of changes in the nature of enterprises. Our results signalize that a user should be careful with enterprise demographic figures in particular, if the unit is enterprise. The use of establishment/plant data does not arise as bad problems. The worst problems are met when creation, destruction and turnover figures have been used and their level compared. The use of net rates or changes over time is not as problematic.

Our analysis on the effects of mergers/take-overs is concerned a very interesting time in the history of Finland, since our first year 1990 was the first recession year, and our last reference year 1994 the last recession year, respectively. Of course, the consequences for the recession are derived from late 1980s, and the influence of the recession remains several years after the real recession. However, our target population, manufacturing industries, is a predecessor in many respects.

The share of mergers and take-overs has not been high (on average for mergers 2.8% and for take-overs 0.7%), and because of that we have not been able to analyze every-year effects for take-overs, and there have been difficulties in such analysis for mergers as well. However, we have found interesting aspects, many of which are in the same direction as obtained by few other researchers in this field.

Based on our results, it seems that when the recession begun (varying since 1989 to 1991, depending on the industry, for example), it was not really understood. Production declined but works were done by about same employees. Hence productivity declined as well, but soon enterprises started to react mainly reducing employment, closing plants in some cases as well. It was maybe the simplest way to rapidly improve productivity and the competitiveness - as drifted in 'straitened circumstances.' Later also other types of improvements in these enterprises were done, and some enterprises made attempts to take advantage of mergers, take-overs and other new constructions of enterprises. The productivity growth of the average manufacturing enterprise was good during this period, but it was even better if a take-over and a merger had taken place.

We hope to deepen our analysis for example making more comparisons with other research. Our data set gives also opportunities for other analyses, for example concerning the changes in investments due mergers and take-overs as Dickerson et al (1997) have done.

Annex: Data Description

The construction of the data was motivated by the agreement with Eurostat.

Two types of units:
- Initial 'enterprise' that consists of all the manufacturing plants of an enterprise.
- Synthetic enterprise, constructed as presented in the text
  The number of units:
- Full pooled data from 1990 to 1994: 24500
- Data from which R&D expenditure information was available.
- Other data sets, see the text

Coverage
- Manufacturing establishments with at least 5 employees

List of the variables used:
- Establishment/plant code
- Initial enterprise code
- Longitudinal identifier for constructing synthetic units
- Year
- Industry classification (Nace code), 5-digit levl, and its aggregation for partly to 2-digit- and partly to 3-digit level
- Total turnover
- Number of employees
- Labour productivity = total turnover per number of employees
- Size class of the enterprise based on the average during the whole period survived
- Wages and other labout costs
- Wages per employee
- R&D expenditure but here it is used as a dummy
- Exports but here used as a dummy
- Dummy of mergers
- Dummy of takeovers
- Dummy of closed enterprises

The following variables have not been used in real analysis so far:
- Production value, excluding VAT
- Gross value added at factor cost
- Total investments
- Stocks of semi- or furnished products and goods for resale

REFERENCES

Baily, M.N., Bartelsman, E.J. and Haltiwanger J. (1994). *"Downsizing and Productivity Growth: Myth or Reality"*. Center for Economic Studies. Discussion Paper 4. U.S. Department of Commerce.

Baldwin, J. (1996). *"Job Creation, Wages and Productivity in Manufacturing."* Canadian Economic Observer, November.

Davis, S.J. and Haltiwanger, J. (1990). *"Gross Job Creation and Destruction: Microeconomic Evidence and Macroeconomic Implications"*. NBER Macroeconomic Annual, Davis, S.J. and Haltiwanger, J. (eds.).

Dickerson, A.P. and Gibson, H.D. (1997). *"The Impact of Acquisitions on Company Performance: Evidence from a Large Panel"* of UK Enterprises. Oxford Economic Papers 49, 344-361.

Eurostat (1996). *"SME Project: The Longitudinal Study Request"*. Unpublished Paper. Available from Unit D2 or from the authors.

Jensen, J.B. and McGuckin, R.H. (1997). *"Enterprise Performance and Evolution: Empirical Regularities in the US Micro Data."* In: Laaksonen, (Ed.). S. The Evolution of Enterprises and Industries. Statistics Finland Research Reports 223, 24-49.

Jovanovic, B. (1979). *"Job Matching and the Theory of Turnover"*. Journal of Political Economy 87, 972-90.

Laaksonen, S. and Vainiomäki, J. (1997). *"The Effects of Technology on Wages in Finnish Manufacturing"* 1974-93. In: Laaksonen, S. (Ed.). The Evolution of Enterprises and Industries. Statistics Finland Research Reports 223, 454-475.

Lichtenberger, F.R. and Siegel, D. (1989). *"The Effect of Takeovers on the Employment and Wages of Central-Office and Other Personnel"*. Center for Economic Studies. Discussion Paper 3. U.S. Department of Commerce.

McCullagh, P. and Nelder, J.A. (1989). *"Applied Life Data Analysis."* John Wiley & Sons. New York.

McGuckin, R.H.. and Nquyen, S.V. (1993). *"On Productivity and Plant Ownership Change: New Evidence from the LRD."* Center for Economic Studies. Discussion Paper 15. U.S. Department of Commerce.

McGuckin, R.H., Nquyen, S.V. and Reznek, A.P. (1995). *"The Impact of Ownership Change on Employment, Wages and Labor Productivity in U.S. Manufacturing 1977-87"*. Center for Economic Studies. Discussion Paper 8. U.S. Department of Commerce.

SAS Users' Guide (1997). *"The Genmod Procedure."*

Struits, P. and Willeboordse, A. (1995*). "Changes in Populations of Statistical Units, Business Survey Methods."* John Wiley & Sons, inc..

Vainiomäki, J. and Laaksonen, S. (1997).*"The Effects of Technology on Job Creation and Destruction in Finnish Manufacturing."* 1986-93. In: Laaksonen, S. (Ed.). The Evolution of Enterprises and Industries. Statistics Finland Research Reports 223, 234-253.

FACTORS OF PERFORMANCE BY PLANT GENERATIONS. SOME FINDINGS FROM FINLAND

Mika Maliranta

Statistics Finland

1 Introduction

As plant-level data sets have become available to researchers, it has become possible to study some important factors of growth more comprehensively than before. This paper deals with such factors as technology vintages (or generations), learning by doing and spillovers. These are of interest, for example, when the process of the evolution among the new plants is explored.

The newly established plants account for only a minor share of the total labour input in the manufacturing. With this in mind, it can be argued that job creation in the new manufacturing plants is insignificant for an economy's employment. Furthermore, as the labour productivity is typically lower among the entrants than among the older ones, the creation of new plants does not seem very beneficial for the real competitiveness of a sector.

However, a part of the newly established plants are capable of rapid growth in the years to come. The labour share of the successful new plants increases considerably during a decade as is illustrated by Baldwin (1995, 208-238) and Maliranta (1997b, 17). In addition, the performance level of the newly established plants is underrated when evaluated with labour productivity measures, as the capital intensity is relatively low among these plants. As it is pointed out in Maliranta (1997a), the total factor productivity is reasonably high among the new plants. Some indications were also obtained that the new plants are able to improve their capability of using the resources productively quite rapidly. To sum up, the importance of the emergence of new plants should be viewed from a wider and longer perspective as the share of new plants increases and the performance level improves over time.

A large number of studies have been made by using firm-level data. The performance and growth of small and medium-sized enterprises has been of an extensive interest in recent years. Also the analysis of globalisation is typically based on the framework where the enterprise is the statistical unit under focus. However, essentially the enterprise is an organisation whose major role is to own and co-ordinate those units where the production process ultimately takes place.

What occurs at the enterprise level is heavily dependent on the acquisitions or divestitures. However, the effect of the plant opening, plant closing and the expanding or downsizing at the production unit level is generally much more important as far as employment, productivity or wealth of a nation or a region is concerned.

The units under the control of an enterprise may operate in quite different kinds of industries. In practice the units may be rather independent in relation to their parents in many respects. In this study the statistical unit is the plant, which is a local kind-of-activity unit.

2 Factors of performance level of interest for new plants

2.1 Vintage (or generation) effect

As some irreversibility is involved in the investments, new plants may obtain benefits from being able to choose new vintages of physical capital during the construction process. As the new plants have a relatively larger share of new vintages of physical capital that are more productive than the vintages used in the older plants, the production frontiers of the new plants may be wider (see Hulten, 1992). This may appear to be the case especially when the deflators for investment equipment inadequately take into account the improvement in efficiency, as seems to be the case in the light of the results given by Gordon (1990) or by Greenwood et al. (1997).

In addition, the construction of an organisation involves sunk costs of many kinds. Thus the new plants may gain advantage over older ones from being able to choose the skill structure of employees that match with the modern technology. They may be better able to develop operation models to the direction that is in keeping with the requirements of that time regarding technology and management, for example. Moreover, the founder of a new production unit has an option to choose the site that is most favourable to those activities in question at that time. The role of vintage or generation for productivity level and productivity growth is studied empirically, for instance, in Baily et al. (1992), Griliches and Regev (1995) and Jensen et al (1998).

2.2 Learning by doing

On the other hand, the efficient use of production potentials requires knowledge. Some of this disembodied technology element is plant-specific. That kind of knowledge may be acquired possibly best through learning by doing. The stock of this kind of knowledge apparently accumulates most rapidly in the beginning and thus the performance level should improve especially rapidly among the new generation plants. In a sense, the lack of plant-specific experience can be interpreted as one of the potential sources of technical inefficiency.

Some of the knowledge acquired through experience is more general than plant-specific in the sense that it can be made use of in the other production units operating in the same industry. This kind of firm- or industry-specific knowledge may be captured by firm managers, for example. With this in mind, we may expect that the plants built in the event of the greenfield entry tend to have lower performance levels than those belonging to a mature firm. On the other hand, the growth rate of the performance level of the new plants in the greenfield firms should be especially rapid, as they are capturing both plant- and firm-specific knowledge.

2.3 Spillovers

Plants interact among themselves and as a consequence externalities are involved in the production. This may create a problem when the analysis is performed with aggregated data. Caballero and Lyons (1990) have argued that conventional estimates of returns to scale made at the industry level are biased because the productivity of each industry is affected by total industrial production (see discussion for example in Honkatukia, 1997).

Knowledge that is more general than plant-specific can be acquired through spillovers that play a central role in the R&D literature. It seems that R&D of a certain firm (industry) increases also production potential in many other firms (industries) and thus the social return of R&D investments may be higher than private return, leading to a potential market failure (see Griliches, 1992).

Akerlof (1997) provides an extensive discourse on social interactions of individuals and their importance for social decisions. There is a rather close analogy with the behaviour of production units or plants. As the utility of a person may be dependent on the utility or actions of the others, the performance level of the neighbourhood or the other plants in the same firm may be related with the performance level of a plant in various ways. Technology spillovers are an apparent candidate for a link between production units that are separated by only a short distance in the business environment. By short distance it is meant here that the plants in the same industry are near to each other either geographically or organisationally, i.e. they are located in the same region or they belong to the same enterprise.

There are various reasons why performance of a plant may be correlated with that of the other plants at a short distance. By following reasoning made by Akerlof, the neighbourhood characteristics may be indicative of unobservable and exogenously determined factors that affect the performance level. For example, some regions may provide an exceptionally suitable environment (availability of raw material, employment, industrial tradition etc.) for productive operations in that industry. Similarly, high productivity in the plants that belong to a certain firm may be a result of efficient management, which is typically unobservable. It may be profitable for these kinds of firms to establish more production units. Thus we may expect that the creation of new plants is concentrated on the high productivity businesses. The omitted variable problem may easily create spurious relationships. This risk should be reduced by controlling plant characteristics as comprehensively as possible. It is also possible that some unobservable plant characteristics vary systematically between regions and consequently there may be a spurious relationship between plants' performance levels with each other. Controlling plant characteristics more comprehensively can reduce this risk.

Competition is another explanation for the correlation between performance of a plant and performance of the other plants at a short distance. In addition, operating in those regions where the plants generally have a high performance level may call forth abnormal effort and productivity for an individual plant (see discussion in Liu, 1993, 218-220).

It is important to realise for policy considerations, for example, that the observed background group effect may also be an indication of the fact that technology and the ideas spill in the interactions of the plants that are near to each other geographically or organisationally. R&D spillovers within geographical areas are considered by Audretsch and Feldman (1996). All in all, information on the importance of neighbourhood or firm characteristics is valuable when assessing the costs and benefits of hampering the geographical concentration, obstructing mergers, and favouring decentralisation and small businesses.

One question of interest in this paper is what is the importance of spillovers for the new plants relative to that of the older ones. As the new plants are lacking knowledge that is accumulated through the learning by doing, the spillovers may be expected to provide a useful substitute for them. The availability of useful knowledge from the near distance may be expected to discriminate between the plants, especially among the recent generations. On the other hand, the implementation of the knowledge obtained from neighbours or other plants in the same firm may take time. In other words, there may be some convergence in the performance levels of the continuing plants within firms over time. Consequently, the performance level of the other plants in the same firm may be a good predictor of a plant's productivity, especially for the old plants. A similar kind of reasoning can be given, of course, to the importance of regional spillovers for different age groups. On the other hand, the relevant plant-specific knowledge available in the same region or in the same firm may be scarce for those plants that have recently chosen modern technology.

3 Methodology

In this paper we make use of a type of multilateral total factor productivity indicator suggested by Caves et al. (1981). The difference in total factor productivity between a plant i in period t (TFP_{it}) and the benchmark representative plant is:

$$\ln TFP_{it} = \ln\left(\frac{Y_{it}/L_{it}}{\widetilde{Y}/\widetilde{L}}\right) - \frac{S_{it} + \overline{S}}{2} \cdot \ln\left(\frac{K_{it}/L_{it}}{\widetilde{K}/\widetilde{L}}\right), \qquad [1]$$

where Y is the output and L and K are labour and capital input, respectively. The benchmark plant is defined by using geometric means of the output ($\widetilde{Y}$) and inputs ($\widetilde{L}$ and $\widetilde{K}$). To implement this indicator, the cost share of capital input for each plant in each year (S_{it}) and the arithmetic mean of the sample's cost shares ($\overline{S}$) have to be determined. These are estimated by using both plant-level information from the industrial statistics and industry-level information from the national accounts (for details, see Maliranta, 1997a).[1]

This kind of indicator of performance is a sort of weighted average of the labour and capital productivity. If the production units face competitive output and factor markets and if the constant returns to scale prevail, this indicator provides a measure of technical (in)efficiency. If there are increasing returns to scale in the production in reality, the technical efficiency of the relatively large plants will be overrated. To control or (detect) this possibility, some variables for size effects should be included in the model. This kind of approach where an indicator of total factor productivity is used as the dependent variable is applied also in Baily et al. (1992).

As our goal is to investigate explanations for differences in the quality of the technology or technical (in)efficiency between plants, the analysis should be based on the variation within industry. The total factor productivity indicator is defined separately for each industry. Industries are pooled but dummy variables for industries are included in the model. Furthermore, the time trend that is supposed to capture technical change in the plants is allowed to vary between

---

[1] In the determination of total factor productivity indicator it is assumed that the real interest rate is 5 per cent. In this case the average cost share of capital input is somewhat lower than that obtained by using income shares. In Maliranta (1997a), an interest rate (some 13 per cent) was used that is consistent with income share at the aggregate level. The results did not seem to be very sensitive to the choice of interest rate.

industries. Thus, we are assuming that the effect of learning by doing among the new generation relative to that of the older ones is similar across the industries.

4 Data sets

The main data source is industrial statistics that are supplemented with 2-digit industry price deflator series for output and investments that are obtained implicitly from the national accounts (15 industries). Data sets are cleaned conservatively from the most exceptional observations (the very extreme tails of the distribution of some important ratios are cut off) at stages by using a similar kind of approach as used by Mairesse and Kremp (1993) (for details see Maliranta, 1997a, 3-4). In addition, we have removed those plants that have changed industries during the time span under study. We have not allowed 'holes' in the plant's record: observations after the first disappearance of a plant are not included.

We perform separate analysis for two periods: 1975-1984 and 1981-1994. A multilateral total factor productivity indicator is constructed by using different types of measures of capital input. For the period from 1975 to 1984 the fire insurance value of the total capital stock is available for a large number of plants. For the period from 1981 to 1994 the capital input is measured with an estimate of machinery and equipment stock (including transport and other equipment) derived by the perpetual inventory method (PIM) (for details, see Maliranta, 1997a and 1997b).

The plant is the statistical unit under investigation in the following analysis. It corresponds to a local kind-of-activity unit. Furthermore, at times we mention 'firm' but the meaning of this concept is quite particular here: by firm we refer to a group of plants that operate in the same 2-digit industry and under the control of the same enterprise. In other words, here the 'firm' corresponds to a kind-of-activity unit.

5 Some descriptive analyses of the new plants

Because some irreversibility is involved, the behaviour and characteristics of the new plants may be particularly revealing.[2] One way to assess the importance of the firm or geographical spillovers is to study what sort of firms construct new plants and what kind of geographical locations are chosen for the new plants. If some of the technology features are such that they can be transferred within firms

---

[2] A similar kind of reasoning is also used by Gort et al. (1993, 223).

within some time period, we may expect that it is profitable for high productivity firms to establish more new plants. Thus, new plants are likely to be under the control of high productivity firms.

To explore the emergence of plants in the different types of firm, for each plant we have calculated a weighted average of the total factor productivity level[3] of the other plants that belongs to the same firm *(FIRMTFP)*.[4] Plants are weighted by total nominal costs by which we mean the sum of labour costs (wages and supplements) and estimated nominal capital costs (see Maliranta, 1997a, 8-9 and 27). For those plants that do not have a 'sister' (single unit firms, for example) *FIRMTFP*=0. The plants where *FIRMTFP*>0 are sorted in each year and in each industry by the *FIRMTFP* variable into five equal-sized groups that are in ascending order: group 1 consists of plants that have low productivity 'sisters' and the plants in group 5 have high productivity 'sisters'. Thus, in each group the share of all the plants is 20 per cent.

Next we have investigated the relative frequencies of the new plants (age not more than five years) in the groups defined above for each industry and for each year. Figure 1 points out that the new plants are clearly overrepresented in the groups where the average total factor productivity of the rest of the firm is relatively high. The new plants are typically underrepresented in the low productivity groups. Those enterprises that have high productivity plants in some industry deem themselves capable of constructing new high productivity and thus profitable plants. Presumably transferable firm-specific technology or knowledge plays some role here.

A similar kind of exercise is carried out in order to explore the importance of geographical location. For each plant we have calculated an indicator, which measures the total nominal-cost weighted average of the total factor productivity of the other plants that operate in the same region and in the same industry *(REGTFP)*. As above, we have ranked plants in each year and in each industry in ascending order by *REGTFP* variable and then grouped them into five groups. As Figure 2 shows there does not seem to be a similarly clear pattern in the distribution of the shares of the new plants as above. The new plants seem to be surrounded by plants that usually have a rather low as opposed to a relatively high performance level.

---

[3] In this case we use an industry-specific multilateral total factor productivity index for the period from 1975 to 1984 where capital input is measured with fire insurance value (in real terms) of the total capital stock. (For methodology and details, see Maliranta, 1997a.)

[4] It is worth repeating that according to the concept of the firm employed here, all other plants in the same firm operate in the same industry.

Figure 1 Distribution of the new plants according to the performance level of the rest of the kind-of-activity unit

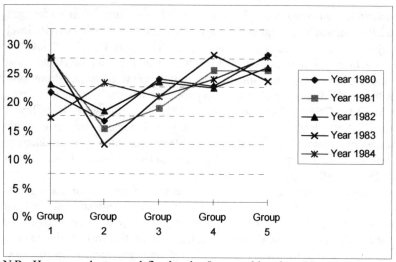

N.B.: Here new plants are defined to be 5 years old or less. Note that the share of all plants is 20 per cent in each group. See text.

Figure 2 Distribution of new plants according to the performance level of the other plants that operate in the same region and in the same 2-digit industry

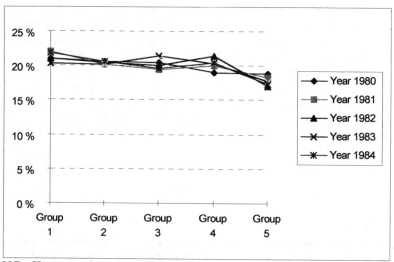

N.B.: Here new plants are defined to be 5 years old or less. Note that the share of all plants is 20 per cent in each group. See text.

There may be two conflicting aspects in the consideration of the best location. When the plant is constructed in the middle of the high productivity plants it may gain benefits from being able to capture positive spillovers from the surroundings. Exceptionally high productivity levels of the plants in a certain region may also reflect the fact that the operative environment may be favourable for that industry because of suitable infrastructure or services. With these in mind one may expect the new plants are constructed in the neighbourhood of the high productivity plants. On the other hand, local competition may be hard among the high productivity plants and thus it may be rational to be situated far from such a concentrated group.

Another point under investigation here is the learning by doing. One way to evaluate its importance is to compare the total factor productivity percentage change within plants between new and old plants. We have used the same decomposition of total factor productivity growth as in Maliranta (1997b), but now separately for relatively new and old plants (see also Bernard Jones, 1996, 140).

Plants are sorted with the plant codes by their age into three equal sized groups in each year and in each industry: new, medium-aged and old plants. For each group, for each industry and for each pair of successive years we have used the following formula for those plants that stay two consecutive years in question:

$$\frac{TFP_t^S - TFP_{t-1}^S}{TFP_{t-1}^S} = \sum_i \left(\frac{TFP_{i,t} - TFP_{i,t-1}}{TFP_{i,t-1}} \right) \cdot \left(\frac{TFP_{i,t-1}}{TFP_{t-1}^S} \right) \left(\frac{w_{i,t} + w_{i,t-1}}{2} \right)$$

$$+ \sum_i \left(w_{i,t} - w_{i,t-1} \right) \cdot \left(\frac{(TFP_{i,t} + TFP_{i,t-1})/2}{TFP_{t-1}^S} \right), \qquad [2]$$

where TFP_t^S is total factor productivity (derived with industry and time-specific income shares) among stayers (denoted by symbol S) in year t. Weight $w_{i,t}$ is the ratio of an index of inputs (calculated by income shares) in plant i to an aggregate index of inputs. Industry results are aggregated to the total manufacturing level by using nominal value added shares as weights.

The term on the right-hand side is the within effect, which aims to measure the productivity growth at the plant level. It comprises such factors as general micro-level technological change and learning by doing. The term below is the share effect, which captures the contribution of aggregate productivity growth that arises from the fact that input shares are changing among the plants (see Maliranta, 1997b).

Decompositions are carried out by using two different kinds of measures of capital input: with the machinery and equipment stock derived with the perpetual inventory method and with the usage of electricity (in mwh). The results obtained with these measures of capital are shown in Figure 3.

As the figure shows the within effect seems to be slightly larger in the case of the new plants than that of the old plants in the period from the mid 70's to the mid 80's but since then the positions have been reversed. Consequently, in the first half of our period we have obtained some (weak) support for the view that new plants are able to improve their performance better than the older ones. It should be noted that we have split the plants into generation groups in a broad outline. In this setting the group of new plants contains relatively experienced units but later a more detailed classification will be used.

However, an important point regarding the evolution of the new plants becomes clearly evident with this kind of decomposition. The positive share effect component demonstrates that the low productivity plants lose their capital input shares to the new high productivity plants. The so-called creative destruction is especially influential among the new plants, as the share effect components in Figure 3 indicate. It seems that especially during the 80's the contribution of the share effect increased among the new plants. In the other words, a substantial and systematic adjustment in the microstructures seems to be occurring among the plants that are taking the first steps in the course of evolution. There may be a great heterogeneity in the performance levels of newcomers and those unlucky in the choice of technology, production site, labour force etc. are compelled to vanish in the competitive business environment. Therefore, in the analysis of performance of the new plants, a need to control for unsuccessful outcomes becomes under consideration. This is especially the case here, as we are attempting to assess the potentials absorbed in the emerging plants.

Figure 3 Decomposition of aggregate total factor productivity growth among continuing plants

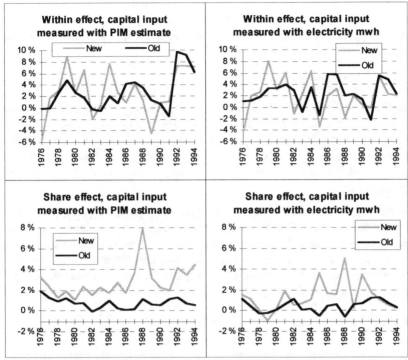

N.B.: See text.

6 Estimation of the factors of performance level

First we study those plants that existed in 1975. The first look covers the period from 1975 to 1984. It is required that observations in each plant are continuous, but the plants are allowed to disappear during the period under investigation.[5] In addition, we have run a regression for the balanced panel set in order to explore how the results are affected when the failed plants are removed entirely.

---

[5] However, we do require that there are at least three observations per plant.

6.1 Key variables

We have run several regression equations to study factors of performance level. The dependent variable is the log of the multilateral total factor productivity indicator. The explanatory variables of special interest are the following.

Vintages (or generations)

The justification for much that is to come in the following analysis is based on the idea that the date of birth of the plant determines many important and invariant factors of performance. We were not able to determine the year of birth for most of the plants. Therefore we make use of cohorts. With the plant code it is possible to rank plants from newest to oldest as the latest plant has the highest code number etc.

For the year 1975 we have formed six generation groups separately for each industry on the basis of the order of appearance. The latest two groups (the very new and new generation plants) are decile classes and the rest of the classes are quintile groups (see Table 1). In practise, the shares may differ from the ones that can be inferred from Table 1 as some observations are removed from the sample (see results in the appendix).[6]

Table 1 Plant generations formed for each industry by age

Generation group	Dummy variable	Percentiles
Generation A (the very new plants)	*GENA*	0-10
Generation B (the new plants)	*GENB*	10-20
Generation C	*GENC*	20-40
Generation D	*GEND*	40-60
Generation E	*GENE*	60-80
Generation F (the old plants)	*GENF*	80-100

N.B.: Classification is made for the first year of the period under investigation. The group of each plant is kept for the whole period.

In addition, generation *A* and generation *B* are split into two parts by the generation of the firm. The generation of a firm is determined here by the age of its oldest plant. The firms are ranked from newest to oldest and grouped into three equal sized groups for each industry and for each year separately. The firms

---

[6] Those plants that are not found for more than two years or have changed the industry in the period under study are removed. A small number of plants are removed as they have some very unreasonable values of variables. Furthermore, those plants are excluded that are the only plants operating in that particular region and industry.

in the first group are called new (group denoted by A) as distinct from 'not new' (denoted by B) (see Table 2). Linear time trend (*TREND*) is allowed to vary between different generations.

Table 2 Classification of new plants according to the age of the firm

Group	Dummy variable	Definition
Generation AA	*GENAA*	Plant is a member of A generation, and the firm is new
Generation AB	*GENAB*	Plant is a member of A generation, and the firm is not new
Generation BA	*GENBA*	Plant is a member of B generation, and the firm is new
Generation BB	*GENBB*	Plant is a member of B generation, and the firm is not new

N.B.: See text.

Spillover effects

As mentioned earlier, we have constructed a variable that describes the total factor productivity level of the rest of the firm (*FIRMTFP*). In order to analyse the relationship between a plant and the total factor productivity of the rest of the firm in greater detail, also this variable is allowed to interact with binary variables that denote generation groups. There are a number of plants, which are the sole units in the kind-of-activity units in question. These are controlled by dummy variables that are constructed separately for each generation group.

In a similar vein, the relationship between a plant's performance and the performance of the geographically surrounding plants is investigated by constructing the *REGTFP* variable. In the regression models it is allowed to interact with dummy variables that denote the generation group.

Other variables

To avoid the omitted variable bias imminent in the following kind of analysis we have included a large number of control variables. Separate intercepts and trends are allowed for each industry. An important factor is the region controlled by binary variables constructed for each region ('vanha lääni' for the period from 1975 to 1984 and 'maakunta' for the period from 1981 to 1994). Variables controlling for the relative size are included. We have also tried to capture the effect of the following factors; foreign ownership, 'the shadow of the death' (see Griliches Regev, 1995, 193-195), the extent of rents, recent investments, the share of female employment, white collar employment, capacity utilisation, export and outsourcing of service operations (see comprehensive list of variables in the appendix).

6.2 Results

The main results for the period from 1975 to 1984 obtained from pooled regressions are reported in Table 3 and 4 and illustrated in Figure 4 and 5. First column in Table 3 shows that there are substantial differences in the performance level between different generations. There seems to be a general tendency that the total factor productivity level decreases when it is moved towards the older generations (generation C is an exception to this tendency here). Various interpretations may be given to this result, as mentioned earlier. The new plants have a relatively more modern capital stock, which may be more effective in relation to the older vintages. The problem may lie in the investment deflators that may ignore or underrate investment-specific technological change. In other words, the price increase of the tangible capital goods may be overrated due to the unrecorded quality improvement.

The results in column (1) show the average relative positions in the period from 1975 to 1984, but the relative positions may vary over time because of the different rates of productivity growth between generations. The second column provides some indication that the rate of growth is the strongest among the very new generation plants. This may be a result of the decreasing technical inefficiency among newcomers or learning by doing (see Bahk et al., 1993 and Gort et al., 1993), depending on the way of thinking. The relative total factor productivity levels of the plant generations during the period from 1975 to 1984 according to the model (2) are outlined in Figure 4. At the beginning of the period generation B is superior to the others but loses its positions to the newest generation in a decade. Generally each generation seems to be superior to the previous one; generation C being an exception to this rule here.

According to the estimates, the firm spillover effect tends to increase when moved towards the older generations.[7] Thus, although the performance level of the rest of the firm is typically relatively high in the case of the newcomers as we saw in Figure 1, the relationship between a plant and firm's performance level is the stronger the older the plant is.

As far as regional spillover effects are concerned, the pattern of the effects is different from that of the firm spillover effects. Quite interestingly, the relationship seems to be particularly strong for the newest and the latest generation group.

The results obtained with a balanced data set are reported in columns from (4) to (6). As is to be expected, the R^2 value of the model estimated with balanced data is somewhat higher than that obtained with unbalanced data albeit still very small.

---

[7] Generation D seems to be a group out of the ordinary. We do not know the reason for this peculiar finding.

Generally speaking, the findings made with unbalanced panels are still valid. The total factor productivity of the new generation plants is relatively high. The growth rate of *TFP* is bigger among the very new plants than in the other generations, although the statistical support is weak. Also the profile of the firm spillover effect is unaltered. On the other hand, the relationship between the plant and the region's performance becomes considerably stronger when the failed plants are removed from the data set.

Table 4 shows the estimates when the groups of the new plants are studied more comprehensively. Column (1) provides some support to the view that especially those new plants that are established by an experienced firm (*GENAB*=1 and *GENBB*=1) are relatively strong in total factor productivity, when compared with the older plants or with greenfield entries. On the other hand, the results in column (2) indicate that the very new plants in the young firms tend to increase especially rapidly their performance level relative to the older generation plants. This is illustrated in Figure 5.

Column (3) in Table 4 points out that as far as new generations (generations A and B) are concerned the relationship between the plant's and firm's performance level is stronger among older firms than among the newer ones. This is suggested by the observation that the coefficient of ln(*FIRMTFP*)*GENAB is substantially larger than that of ln(*FIRMTFP*)*GENAA and the coefficient of ln(*FIRMTFP*)*GENBB is larger than that of ln(*FIRMTFP*)*GENBA. We also gain some evidence that this applies also for the regional spillovers.

The analysis is repeated for the period from 1981 to 1994. Now the total factor productivity indicator is constructed by using the PIM estimate of machinery stock as a measure of capital input, instead of the fire insurance value of the total capital stock earlier (which is not available since 1985).

The results largely corroborate the main findings made earlier (see Table 5): New plants provide a positive contribution to the evolution of productivity performance, but it takes a period of years before the potential hidden in the new plants comes into sight. As Figure 6 seems to suggest the relative growth rate decreases generation by generation at the beginning of the evolution process.

The relationship with firm's productivity performance is generally weaker among the new generation plants than among the older generations. However, the relationship with region total factor productivity seems to be important among the very new plants just as is the case with the oldest plants, too.

Table 3 OLS regression estimates for the period from 1975 to 1984, dependent variable: ln(*TFP*)

	Unbalanced			Balanced		
	(1)	(2)	(3)	(4)	(5)	(6)
Intercept	-0.948**	-0.993**	-1.599*	-0.956**	-0.992**	-1.760**
	(-5.515)	(-5.776)	(-5.442)	(-5.068)	(-5.246)	(-5.115)
GENB	-0.023	0.039	1.093*	-0.013	0.044	1.344**
	(-1.527)	(1.455)	(3.080)	(-0.788)	(1.349)	(3.408)
GENC	-0.090**	-0.034	0.627*	-0.095**	-0.058*	0.450
	(-7.521)	(-1.551)	(2.246)	(-6.843)	(-2.106)	(1.379)
GEND	-0.052**	-0.015	0.578*	-0.040**	-0.004	0.465
	(-4.308)	(-0.716)	(2.069)	(-2.884)	(-0.137)	(1.437)
GENE	-0.060**	-0.014	0.425	-0.055**	-0.013	0.388
	(-4.901)	(-0.657)	(1.490)	(-3.860)	(-0.461)	(1.176)
GENF	-0.071**	-0.025	-0.004	-0.083**	-0.055*	0.032
	(-5.742)	(-1.109)	(-0.012)	(-5.775)	(-1.982)	(0.094)
TREND*GENB		-0.015**	-0.009		-0.013*	-0.004
		(-2.863)	(-1.531)		(-2.103)	(-0.598)
TREND*GENC		-0.014**	-0.009		-0.008	-0.005
		(-3.263)	(-1.785)		(-1.668)	(-0.852)
TREND*GEND		-0.009*	-0.003		-0.008	-0.003
		(-2.196)	(-0.651)		(-1.670)	(-0.569)
TREND*GENE		-0.011**	-0.009		-0.009	-0.007
		(-2.704)	(-1.837)		(-1.906)	(-1.179)
TREND*GENF		-0.012**	-0.013**		-0.006	-0.008
		(-2.708)	(-2.684)		(-1.262)	(-1.348)
ln(FIRMTFP)*GENA			0.090			0.108
			(1.884)			(1.774)
ln(FIRMTFP)*GENB			0.198**			0.203**
			(5.355)			(4.689)
ln(FIRMTFP)*GENC			0.190**			0.223**
			(4.842)			(5.375)
ln(FIRMTFP)*GEND			-0.079			-0.096
			(-1.758)			(-1.904)
ln(FIRMTFP)*GENE			0.259**			0.159**
			(7.721)			(4.872)
ln(FIRMTFP)*GENF			0.271**			0.277**
			(12.211)			(11.515)
ln(REGTFP)*GENA			0.153**			0.205**
			(2.830)			(3.164)
ln(REGTFP)*GENB			-0.091			-0.093
			(-1.544)			(-1.516)
ln(TFPGRE)*GENC			0.008			0.094**
			(0.259)			(2.741)
ln(REGTFP)*GEND			0.021			0.101**
			(0.629)			(2.941)
ln(REGTFP)*GENE			0.059			0.120**
			(1.640)			(3.287)
ln(REGTFP)*GENF			0.149**			0.188**
			(4.203)			(4.862)
Adjusted R²	0.0965	0.0968	0.1112	0.1042	0.1043	0.1202
No. of obs.	35161	35161	35161	26860	26860	26860

N.B.: Standard errors and t-values (t-values in parentheses) are adjusted for heteroskedasticity according to White (1980). Furthermore, a number of other variables are included in all models in order to control for heterogeneity: see table in appendix. The capital input for *TFP* indicator is measured by the fire insurance value of the total capital stock.

* Denotes significant estimate for the coefficient at a 5 per cent risk level.

** Denotes significant estimate for the coefficient at a 1 per cent risk level.

Table 4 OLS regression estimates for the period from 1975 to 1984 where the groups of new generation plants are split into two parts by the firm generation, dependent variable: ln(*TFP*)

	Unbalanced			Balanced		
	(1)	(2)	(3)	(4)	(5)	(6)
Constant	-0.915**	-0.909**	-1.799**	-0.937**	-0.900**	-2.408**
	(-5.305)	(-5.215)	(-4.179)	(-4.956)	(-4.987)	(-4.640)
GENAA	-0.052*	-0.140**	0.289	-0.030	-0.157**	1.102
	(-2.490)	(-3.385)	(0.577)	(-1.228)	(-2.987)	(1.847)
GENBA	-0.111**	-0.094*	1.662**	-0.077**	-0.069	2.525**
	(-4.978)	(-2.250)	(2.940)	(-3.048)	(-1.348)	(3.981)
GENBB	0.000	0.022	1.149*	0.008	-0.013	1.790**
	(-0.002)	(0.488)	(2.189)	(0.323)	(-0.245)	(2.970)
GENC	-0.120**	-0.127**	0.817	-0.111**	-0.153**	1.092*
	(-6.982)	(-3.549)	(1.946)	(-5.709)	(-3.423)	(2.158)
GEND	-0.082**	-0.109**	0.773	-0.057**	-0.099*	1.115*
	(-4.725)	(-3.041)	(1.837)	(-2.887)	(-2.226)	(2.203)
GENE	-0.089**	-0.106**	0.617	-0.070**	-0.107*	1.035*
	(-5.089)	(-2.963)	(1.448)	(-3.542)	(-2.384)	(2.028)
GENF	-0.098**	-0.114**	0.191	-0.097**	-0.147**	0.679
	(-5.640)	(-3.168)	(0.448)	(-4.933)	(-3.290)	(1.324)
TREND*GENAA		0.025**	0.026**		0.031**	0.038**
		(3.237)	(2.947)		(3.362)	(3.726)
TREND*GENBA		-0.007	0.002		-0.005	0.011
		(-0.872)	(0.253)		(-0.604)	(1.012)
TREND*GENBB		-0.005	0.000		0.004	0.015
		(-0.600)	(0.055)		(0.414)	(1.427)
TREND*GENC		0.001	0.004		0.008	0.013
		(0.147)	(0.578)		(1.080)	(1.507)
TREND*GEND		0.006	0.010		0.008	0.015
		(0.951)	(1.354)		(1.126)	(1.782)
TREND*GENE		0.003	0.004		0.007	0.012
		(0.575)	(0.548)		(0.936)	(1.367)
TREND*GENF		0.003	0.000		0.010	0.011
		(0.527)	(-0.031)		(1.356)	(1.242)
ln(FIRMTFP)*GENAA			-0.091			0.048
			(-0.693)			(0.280)
ln(FIRMTFP)*GENAB			0.138**			0.118
			(2.742)			(1.845)
ln(FIRMTFP)*GENBA			0.098			0.072
			(1.426)			(0.852)
ln(FIRMTFP)*GENBB			0.223**			0.225**
			(5.218)			(4.600)
ln(FIRMTFP)*GENC			0.190**			0.223**
			(4.852)			(5.378)
ln(FIRMTFP)*GEND			-0.079			-0.096
			(-1.764)			(-1.907)
ln(FIRMTFP)*GENE			0.259**			0.159**
			(7.725)			(4.882)
ln(FIRMTFP)*GENF			0.271**			0.277**
			(12.214)			(11.513)
ln(REGTFP)*GENAA			0.124			0.092
			(1.823)			(1.166)
ln(REGTFP)*GENAB			0.200*			0.357**
			(2.288)			(3.339)
ln(REGTFP)*GENBA			-0.179*			-0.212*
			(-1.975)			(-2.270)
ln(REGTFP)*GENBB			-0.049			-0.046
			(0.627)			(-0.567)
ln(REGTFP)*GENC			0.008			0.094**
			(0.250)			(2.731)
ln(REGTFP)*GEND			0.019			0.098**
			(0.590)			(2.877)
ln(REGTFP)*GENE			0.058			0.119**
			(1.624)			(3.247)
ln(REGTFP)*GENF			0.148**			0.187**
			(4.175)			(4.828)
Adjusted R²	0.0975	0.0981	0.1123	0.1047	0.1054	0.1213
Num. Of Obs.	35161	35161	35161	26860	26860	26860

N.B.: See notes for Table 3.

Figure 4 Log-differences in TFP level between generations, generation A = 0

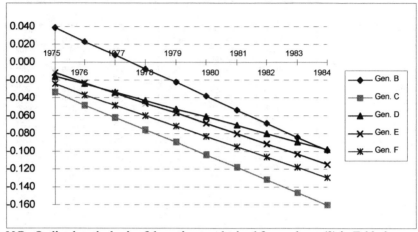

N.B.: Outlined on the basis of the estimates obtained from column (2) in Table 3.

Figure 5 Log-differences in *TFP* levels between generation groups, generation AB = 0

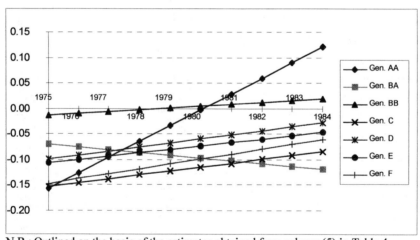

N.B.: Outlined on the basis of the estimates obtained from column (5) in Table 4.

Table 5 OLS regression estimates for the period from 1981 to 1994, dependent variable: ln(*TFP*)

	Unbalanced			Balanced		
	(1)	(2)	(3)	(4)	(5)	(6)
Intercept	-0.735**	-0.821**	-1.092**	-1.0345**	-1.112**	-0.417
	(-7.599)	(-8.421)	(-6.324)	(-7.893)	(-8.206)	(-0.898)
GENB	-0.024*	0.000	0.357	0.010	0.047	0.185
	(-2.313)	(-0.002)	(1.807)	(0.353)	(1.071)	(0.364)
GENC	-0.040**	0.030	0.168	0.017	0.074	-0.684
	(-4.500)	(1.837)	(0.989)	(0.642)	(1.880)	(-1.473)
GEND	-0.099**	-0.013	0.237	-0.050	0.005	-0.561
	(-11.367)	(-0.793)	(1.415)	(-1.933)	(0.123)	(-1.225)
GENE	-0.106**	-0.007	-0.206	-0.040	0.012	-1.151*
	(-12.243)	(-0.460)	(-1.248)	(-1.531)	(0.302)	(-2.533)
GENF	-0.137**	-0.050**	-0.012	-0.060*	-0.006	-0.928*
	(-14.982)	(-2.979)	(-0.069)	(-2.291)	(-0.159)	(-2.026)
TREND*GENB		-0.004	-0.003		-0.027	-0.028
		(-1.649)	(-1.052)		(-1.771)	(-1.856)
TREND*GENC		-0.012**	-0.013**		-0.032*	-0.040**
		(-5.279)	(-4.651)		(-2.159)	(-2.748)
TREND*GEND		-0.015**	-0.014**		-0.031*	-0.035*
		(-6.573)	(-4.936)		(-2.142)	(-2.415)
TREND*GENE		-0.017**	-0.019**		-0.031*	-0.040**
		(-7.544)	(-6.980)		(-2.107)	(-2.748)
TREND*GENF		-0.015**	-0.019**		-0.031*	-0.040**
		(-6.621)	(-6.844)		(-2.130)	(-2.739)
ln(FIRMTFP)*GENA			-0.027			-0.025
			(-0.594)			(-0.359)
ln(FIRMTFP)*GENB			0.161**			0.134**
			(4.403)			(2.686)
ln(FIRMTFP)*GENC			0.168**			0.138**
			(5.396)			(3.469)
ln(FIRMTFP)*GEND			0.093**			0.080*
			(2.974)			(2.165)
ln(FIRMTFP)*GENE			0.017			0.086**
			(0.578)			(3.009)
ln(FIRMTFP)*GENF			0.195**			0.088**
			(11.394)			(4.336)
ln(REGTFP)*GENA			0.076*			-0.137
			(2.281)			(-1.384)
ln(REGTFP)*GENB			-0.001			-0.173**
			(-0.037)			(-3.099)
ln(REGTFP)*GENC			0.045*			0.031
			(2.221)			(1.005)
ln(REGTFP)*GEND			0.022			-0.012
			(1.135)			(-0.445)
ln(REGTFP)*GENE			0.124**			0.129**
			(6.846)			(6.114)
ln(REGTFP)*GENF			0.077**			0.077**
			(3.609)			(2.968)
Adjusted R²	0.16694	0.16822	0.17553	0.18519	0.18527	0.19429
No. of obs.	63863	63863	63863	28084	28084	28084

N.B.: Standard errors and t-values (t-values in parentheses) are adjusted for heteroskedasticity according to White (1980). Furthermore, a number of other variables are included in all models in order to control heterogeneity: see table in appendix. Capital input for the *TFP* indicator is measured by the PIM estimate of the machinery and equipment stock (inc. transport equipment).
* Denotes significant estimate for the coefficient at a 5 per cent risk level.
** Denotes significant estimate for the coefficient at a 1 per cent risk level.

Figure 6 Log-differences in *TFP* level, generation A = 0

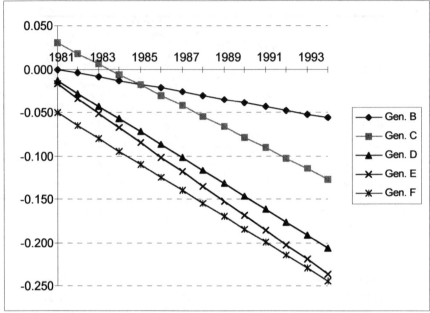

N.B.: Outlined on the basis of the estimates obtained from column (2) in Table 5.

There are several econometric problems involved in the analysis of this kind. Given that the cost shares render the appropriate weight for each input in our *TFP* indicator, many problems inherent in the widely used production function approach can be evaded. These include concerns about suitable functional form, simultaneity and coefficient bias due to the errors in capital input variable (see discussion in Baily et al., 1992, Griliches Mairesse, 1995 and Griliches Regev, 1995). One great advantage of the approach applied here is that it conveniently allows us to pool many different industries. This is not, however, done without costs; the analysis is exposed to other caveats. Implicitly we are assuming that there are constant returns to scale and thus the size effect is not captured within our indicator. The variables aimed to control for the size effect seem, however, to suggest that there are not any significant size effects to be controlled. In this respect our findings are very much in keeping with the ones obtained by Baily et al. (1992) with plant-level data. Indications of increasing returns are reported by Hall (1988) and Honkatukia (1997) based on the results from industry-level data. These findings may derive its origin from externalities prevailing at the micro-level.

Heteroskedasticity poses potential problems for inferences based on least squares in this kind of setting used here. We obtained clear evidence of heteroskedasticity in our models. The Breusch and Pagan (1980) Lagrange multiplier test was performed and the hypothesis of homoskedasticity was strongly rejected for all models. Therefore we have made the standard error correction suggested by White (1980).

7 Conclusions and discussion

There is an abundant body of literature on the factors of continuous productivity growth that is visible in the aggregate data sets here, there and everywhere. The distinction made between embodied and disembodied technological change in the analysis of sources of economic growth is widely known. The former is typically associated with the improvement of input quality, that is, labour skills and the characteristics of the new investment goods. The latter is commonly assumed to arise from the increases in the stock of knowledge. Knowledge relevant to the production process may be acquired by managers, labour or teams through training, learning by doing or spillovers. As a result the production unit is capable of producing more with a given (quality adjusted) amount of inputs.

The distinction between embodied and disembodied is, however, ambiguous in many important aspects of productivity as noted by Gort et al. (1993). The characteristics of inputs are interrelated with the knowledge relevant for the utilisation of those particular inputs. However, the distinction is unquestionably valuable as it brings up the view that it may be useful to interpret technology more broadly than that of comprising solely properties of machinery and equipment.

This paper leans very much on the view that the date of birth of a plant is important for many reasons. It determines the availability of the technology embodied in the investment goods. Thus the very new plants may be expected to have superior production potential because of the modern equipment. At the same time plants aspire to obtain such skill structure of employment that supports the technology cost efficiently. The choice of skill structure made at the beginning may be critical in the sense that the radical changes through churning, i.e. via hiring and firing, or retraining may be costly (see Bellman, Kölling, 1997). Also the management practises should suit the technology that is chosen for that particular type of new plant (and with skill structure). Practices optimal for a new type of technology may differ from that of the older types.

On the other hand, the dominant proportion of capital expenditures is usually spent on the existing plants, as we are reminded by Gort et al. (1993, 227). Thus also some old plants may have reasonably new equipment and modern technology as shown by Dunne (1991). On the other hand, the characteristics of the new assets acquired for new plants may differ from that acquired for established plants as in the latter case the new assets have to be incorporated with old assets and technology. In addition, the new integrated whole of tangible assets from different vintages has to be matched with the skill structure that is collected in the past.

It is worth of noting that the process of constructing a new plant is often long as there may be uncertainty regarding the conditions for success with that particular type of new technology or there may be adjustment costs. Although some acquisitions of assets are registered for the later periods, they may closely match the blueprint made at the date of birth of that plant (or actually some time before that).

Our simple analysis with plant-level data from Finnish manufacturing indicated that the date of birth is an important explanatory factor of productive performance. The total factor productivity among the new generation plants seems to be high relative to that of older generations. On the other hand, it appears that not all potentials are utilised in the first phases of the course of the evolution. In addition to the general improvement of total factor productivity experienced among all the plants over time, there seems to be some supplementary growth especially among the newest plants. This may be due to the learning by doing regarding the technology at hand, i.e. plant-specific learning by doing. Furthermore, the increase of total factor productivity may be abnormally high among the newest plants because they may operate below the optimal scale at the beginning. All in all, despite the fact that initially the emergence of new plants may be inconsequential for a sector's aggregate performance many of the newly established plants will give a substantial positive contribution later.

Plant-specific learning by doing is one aspect of disembodied technological change. In addition, there are other forms of accumulation of knowledge that may help to produce more with given bundle of inputs. Thanks to the spillovers within the same organisation, a certain local kind-of-activity unit may gain advantage from the knowledge possessed by other units in the same kind-of-activity unit. The analysis indicated that the newer the plant, the weaker is the evidence on the importance of spillovers within the same kind-of-activity unit. One explanation for this finding may be that the relevant achievable knowledge may be scarce as far as new technologies are concerned. Alternatively, the process of implementation of knowledge that is acquired elsewhere may take time. As a result, the relationship between the performance levels among the units that operate under the control of the same management may be weak at first.

We observed that new plants are established especially in those kind-of-activity units that already have high productivity (see Figure 1). This may be a reflection of the fact that the high productivity firms realise some chances for extra profits. They may have some factors of success in some industry for that they are able to incorporate into the new production units. They behave accordingly and expand by plant openings.

We have also studied other forms of spillovers, i.e. those prevailing within geographical regions. Quite interestingly, for the relatively new and relatively old generations there seems to be substantially and statistically significant positive relationships with the total factor productivity of the other plants that operate in the same region (and in the same 2-digit industry). As far as the plants that belong to the middle generation groups are concerned, the relationship with surroundings in terms of performance level appears to be lacking. These patterns recurred regardless of analysing the period from 1975 to 1984 or from 1981 to 1994 or analysing with an unbalanced or with a balanced panel set. Convincing explanations for this kind of finding is difficult to find. It is important to note that in the above analysis the general region effect is controlled with binary variables. It turned out that the total factor productivity level is generally high in the south and in the south-west.

Our investigations did not give much support for the view that the new plants are established relatively more frequently in those regions where the average productivity is already higher than in those of low productivity areas. Of course, the ability to continue production may differ in different kind of areas.

The analysis in this study was performed with pooled data sets that cover very heterogeneous groups of plants. The results obtained here are crude averages from total manufacturing. We obtained some indication that the new generations are especially heterogeneous. The decomposition of aggregate total factor productivity demonstrated that the growth effect resulting from the changes in the microstructure play a relatively important role for the new generations. This implies that there is substantial creative destruction going on among the new plants; the low productivity plants lose input shares to the better candidates or disappear entirely.

This is what is predicted by the theory of Jovanovic (1982). According to it new firms expand or contract depending on what they learn by experience about their ability to make a profit. This ability is assumed to be fixed. According to the results obtained here, the ability to make extra profit with the help of superior technology is provisional as it will be taken by the generations to come with more modern technology.

Furthermore, it was discovered that there are some differences among the new plants in respect of the age of the firm (or kind-of-activity unit to be precise). It was observed that the total factor productivity level of those new plants that belong to an established firm is higher than that of those belonging to a relatively new firm. The former plants may be the ones who can make use of some valuable general knowledge. On the other hand, some indication was obtained that the plants involved in the greenfield entry are capable of exceptionally fast growth of performance, possibly because these plants accumulate both plant- and firm-specific knowledge.

There may also be interesting differences between industries depending on the nature of technological change experienced in that industry worth considering in the future. It may be expected that the gap between new and old plants is especially wide in those industries where the changes in the technology and business environment have been the severest. This paper focuses on the intra-industry differences and the inter-industry differences are left to be looked at in the future.

We have tried to control for a wide set of plant characteristics but much has certainly remained unobserved. For instance, the quality of labour input may differ between plants. This may be an important issue to be investigated, as it is possible that there are systematic differences in labour characteristics between different generations as there seems to be differences in technology. We hope that in the future we are able to control for labour characteristics by linking information on the individuals to the plant panel. In addition, it is useful to control for technology more directly by using data from technology surveys.

The results obtained here suggest that part of the fruits involved in the new technology can be reaped later with the help of knowledge that is accumulated at plants. This is one of the explanations given for the so-called productivity paradox, i.e. an answer to the important question why heavy investments on the information and communication technology have had so modest productivity effects.

The findings concerning the importance of spillovers are not only interesting but also important. The results are valuable when evaluating the costs and benefits of the policies aimed at favouring or supporting small kind-of-activity units or peripheral regions. The advantage of large kind-of-activity units is that they provide a convenient vehicle for transferring knowledge that is accumulated in the otherwise isolated production units. There are, of course, other alternatives for co-operation between plants like networks. Geographical concentration may also be useful as it makes it possible for each unit to make use of the knowledge and experiences of the others. This may apply especially at the industry level, as more general knowledge may be more easily transferred from the longer distances.

Appendix

Description of variables

TFP   Industry specific total factor productivity indicator.

FIRMTFP   Average total factor productivity of the other plants in the same firm that operate in the same industry, weighted by nominal costs of capital and labour input.

REGTFP   Average total factor productivity of the other plants that are located in the same region ('vanha lääni') and operate in the same industry.

CAPACITY   An industry- and year-specific estimate of capacity utilisation. It is derived on the basis of variation electricity consumption per capital stock at the industry level. Capacity utilisation is 100 per cent in that year when the electricity consumption per capital stock is at its highest in the period from 1975 to 1984 in that industry.

FOREIGN   Indicator for plants that belong to a foreign-owned firm; the share of foreign ownership is at least 20 per cent in the firm.

MULTI   Indicator for plants that belong to a multi-unit firm.

OUT01   Indicator for plants that are to disappear next year or the year after (one year left at most). For the year 1993 and 1994 it is assumed that OUT12=0.

OUT23   Indicator for plants that are to disappear after two or three years (exists two or three more years). For the years from 1991 to 1994 it is assumed that OUT23=0.

RENTSH   Rent per capital stock.

INVSH   Investments (total investments for the period 1975-84 and machinery investments for the period 1981-94) per capital stock.

FEMALESH   Females per total employment.

WCS   White collar workers per total employment.

AHOUR   Total hours per employment.

DINDxx   Set of dummy variables that indicate the 2-digit industry.

DREGxx   Set of dummy variables that indicate the region ('vanha lääni').

DEXPSMALL   The export share in the industry is relatively small.

DEXPSMEDIU   The export share in the industry belong to the medium group.

DMEDIU   Indicator for plants that are relatively medium-sized plants; the size of these plants is at least one half of the median-sized plant but not more. Median size for each industry and for each year is determined so that one half of the persons is working in the plants that are smaller and one half is working in the plants above this size.

DSMALL   Indicator for plants that are relatively small plants; the size of these plants is smaller than the median determined in a way described above.

M6AGA   Indicator for plants that are the only production units in that particular kind-of-activity unit in the group of generation A (*FIRMTFP*=0).

M6AGB   Indicator for plants that are the only production units in that particular kind-of-activity unit in the group of generation B (*FIRMTFP*=0).

M6AGC   Indicator for plants that are the only production units in that particular kind-of-activity unit in the group of generation C (*FIRMTFP*=0).

M6AGD   Indicator for plants that are the only production units in that particular kind-of-activity unit in the group of generation D (*FIRMTFP*=0).

M6AGE   Indicator for plants that are the only production units in that particular kind-of-activity unit in the group of generation E (*FIRMTFP*=0).

M6AGF   Indicator for plants that are the only production units in that particular kind-of-activity unit in the group of generation F (*FIRMTFP*=0).

Furthermore the following binary variables are included for the controlling differences in the rate of outsourcing (see details from Maliranta, 1997a).

DO2SMALL   Indicator for plants where the ratio (Costs of non-industrial services - receipts from non-industrial services)/labour costs is relatively low.

DO2MEDIU   Indicator for plants where the ratio (Costs of non-industrial services - receipts from non-industrial services)/labour costs is at a medium level.

DO3SMALL   Indicator for plants where the ratio of costs of non-industrial services per total costs of intermediate inputs is relatively low.

DO3LARGE   Indicator for plants where the ratio of costs of non-industrial services per total costs of intermediate inputs is at a medium level.

Estimation results, dependent variable natural log of TFP. Model in column (1) in

Table 6

Variable	Coefficient	Standard Error	z=b/s.e	.P-value	Mean of X
Constant	-0.94819	0.17193	-5.515	0.00000	
GENB	-0.22560E-01	0.14776E-01	-1.527	0.12680	0.7955E-01
GENC	-0.89879E-01	0.11951E-01	-7.521	0.00000	0.1959
GEND	-0.51687E-01	0.11998E-01	-4.308	0.00002	0.2140
GENE	-0.59986E-01	0.12239E-01	-4.901	0.00000	0.2071
GENF	-0.71294E-01	0.12416E-01	-5.742	0.00000	0.2195
ln(CAPACITY)	0.21950	0.37309E-01	5.883	0.00000	4.416
FOREIGN	0.10052	0.18536E-01	5.423	0.00000	0.3407E-01
MULTI	-0.36171E-01	0.72037E-02	-5.021	0.00000	0.3642
OUT01	-0.11653	0.15050E-01	-7.743	0.00000	0.4499E-01
OUT23	-0.10748	0.13494E-01	-7.965	0.00000	0.5697E-01
RENTSH	-0.18155E-02	0.32740E-03	-5.545	0.00000	0.2177
RENTSH^2	0.10456	0.14104E-01	7.414	0.00000	0.4663E-01
INVSH	0.44960E-01	0.32184E-01	1.397	0.16243	0.7201E-01
FEMALES	-0.32355	0.15145	-2.136	0.03265	0.3894
FEMALES^2	-0.27681	0.66392	-0.417	0.67673	0.2361
FEMALES^3	1.8917	1.0534	1.796	0.07253	0.1691
FEMALES^4	-1.4367	0.54305	-2.646	0.00815	0.1317
WCS	-0.28436	0.52882E-01	-5.377	0.00000	0.1922
WCS^2	0.98605	0.73317E-01	13.449	0.00000	0.5990E-01
ln(AHOUR)	0.50034	0.15118	3.310	0.00093	0.5612
ln(AHOUR)^2	-0.65852	0.14066	-4.681	0.00000	0.3262
TREND	0.33763E-01	0.25015E-02	13.497	0.00000	4.113
DI320	-0.10586E-01	0.18498E-01	-0.572	0.56713	0.1483
DI330	0.75725E-01	0.20676E-01	3.662	0.00025	0.1434
DI341	-0.19851E-01	0.37515E-01	-0.529	0.59670	0.3450E-01
DI342	-0.11136	0.20495E-01	-5.434	0.00000	0.9351E-01
DI351	-0.13406	0.35980E-01	-3.726	0.00019	0.3976E-01
DI353	0.52011	0.12134	4.286	0.00002	0.4323E-02
DI355	-0.72557E-01	0.32371E-01	-2.241	0.02500	0.1687E-01
DI360	-0.66466E-02	0.23786E-01	-0.279	0.77991	0.6979E-01
DI370	-0.46995E-01	0.42707E-01	-1.100	0.27117	0.1487E-01
DI381	-0.16476	0.20630E-01	-7.987	0.00000	0.6979E-01
DI382	-0.16355	0.20566E-01	-7.952	0.00000	0.8862E-01
DI383	-0.29899E-02	0.25753E-01	-0.116	0.90757	0.3549E-01
DI384	0.36444E-01	0.28316E-01	1.287	0.19808	0.3367E-01
DI390	-0.98218E-01	0.34876E-01	-2.816	0.00486	0.1806E-01
DI320*TREND	0.12911E-01	0.32631E-02	3.957	0.00008	0.5856
DI330*TREND	-0.13678E-01	0.36267E-02	-3.772	0.00016	0.5794

DI341*TREND	*-0.10276E-01*	*0.70715E-02*	*-1.453*	*0.14620*	*0.1464*
DI342*TREND	-0.15265E-01	0.38142E-02	-4.002	0.00006	0.3982
DI351*TREND	-0.37357E-02	0.72549E-02	-0.515	0.60661	0.1675
DI353*TREND	-0.11624	0.20499E-01	-5.671	0.00000	0.1866E-01
DI355*TREND	0.13826E-01	0.59009E-02	2.343	0.01912	0.7122E-01
DI360*TREND	-0.12613E-01	0.42067E-02	-2.998	0.00271	0.2895
DI370*TREND	-0.73389E-02	0.79041E-02	-0.929	0.35315	0.6155E-01
DI381*TREND	0.20838E-01	0.39451E-02	5.282	0.00000	0.2911
DI382*TREND	0.22002E-01	0.39219E-02	5.610	0.00000	0.3680
DI383*TREND	-0.17999E-01	0.49755E-02	-3.618	0.00030	0.1514
DI384*TREND	-0.86671E-02	0.54748E-02	-1.583	0.11340	0.1388
DI390*TREND	0.23468E-01	0.68106E-02	3.446	0.00057	0.7494E-01
DR02	-0.10011	0.87612E-02	-11.426	0.00000	0.1824
DR04	-0.85381E-01	0.88564E-02	-9.641	0.00000	0.1847
DR05	-0.17167	0.13451E-01	-12.763	0.00000	0.6041E-01
DR06	-0.17994	0.15618E-01	-11.521	0.00000	0.4087E-01
DR07	-0.17000	0.18591E-01	-9.144	0.00000	0.2577E-01
DR08	-0.16729	0.16097E-01	-10.393	0.00000	0.3746E-01
DR09	-0.13206	0.14590E-01	-9.051	0.00000	0.4027E-01
DR10	-0.16366	0.11149E-01	-14.679	0.00000	0.1118
DR11	-0.15275	0.13566E-01	-11.260	0.00000	0.5640E-01
DR12	-0.13892	0.20158E-01	-6.891	0.00000	0.2099E-01
DEXPSMALL	-0.10974	0.86393E-02	-12.703	0.00000	0.2398
DEXPMEDIU	-0.71567E-02	0.10292E-01	-0.695	0.48684	0.9627E-01
DSMALL	-0.84030E-02	0.88268E-02	-0.952	0.34110	0.2377
DMEDIUM	-0.10593E-01	0.70036E-02	-1.513	0.13039	0.3317
DOS2SMALL	-0.74762E-01	0.81920E-02	-9.126	0.00000	0.4721
DOS2MEDIU	-0.10330	0.92584E-02	-11.157	0.00000	0.1332
DOS3SMALL	0.49566E-01	0.91079E-02	5.442	0.00000	0.3254
DOS3MEDIU	0.22173E-01	0.74015E-02	2.996	0.00274	0.3363

Observations = 35161; adjusted R^2 = 0.09650; Breusch - Pagan chi-squared = 5242.8463 (68 d.f.).

Estimation results, dependent variable natural log of TFP. Model in column (3) in

Table 7

Variable	Coefficient	Standard Error	z=b/s.e.	P-value	Mean of X
Constant	-1.5988	0.29380	-5.442	0.00000	
GENB	1.0927	0.35483	3.080	0.00207	0.7955E-01
GENC	0.62660	0.27898	2.246	0.02470	0.1959
GEND	0.57777	0.27919	2.069	0.03850	0.2140
GENE	0.42512	0.28540	1.490	0.13635	0.2071
GENF	-0.35455E-02	0.28686	-0.012	0.99014	0.2195

TREND*GENB	-0.90728E-02	0.59252E-02	-1.531	0.12571	0.3253
TREND*GENC	-0.86021E-02	0.48203E-02	-1.785	0.07433	0.8005
TREND*GEND	-0.30987E-02	0.47631E-02	-0.651	0.51533	0.8890
TREND*GENE	-0.88139E-02	0.47987E-02	-1.837	0.06625	0.8468
TREND*GENF	-0.12994E-01	0.48405E-02	-2.684	0.00726	0.9177
FTFP*GENA	0.90412E-01	0.47999E-01	1.884	0.05962	0.1319
FTFP*GENB	0.19802	0.36980E-01	5.355	0.00000	0.1424
FTFP*GENC	0.19008	0.39254E-01	4.842	0.00000	0.1693
FTFP*GEND	-0.79071E-01	0.44980E-01	-1.758	0.07876	0.1138
FTFP*GENE	0.25943	0.33599E-01	7.721	0.00000	0.2136
FTFP*GENF	0.27112	0.22202E-01	12.211	0.00000	0.5160
M6AGA	-0.33902	0.21751	-1.559	0.11909	0.2878E-01
M6AGB	-0.71580	0.16942	-4.225	0.00002	0.3137E-01
M6AGC	-0.86655	0.17886	-4.845	0.00000	0.3729E-01
M6AGD	0.41188	0.20151	2.044	0.04096	0.2489E-01
M6AGE	-1.1544	0.15591	-7.404	0.00000	0.4707E-01
M6AGF	-1.1580	0.10207	-11.345	0.00000	0.1136
RTFP*GENA	0.15290	0.54033E-01	2.830	0.00466	0.3859
RTFP*GENB	-0.91085E-01	0.58985E-01	-1.544	0.12254	0.3653
RTFP*GENC	0.83636E-02	0.32267E-01	0.259	0.79548	0.8984
RTFP*GEND	0.20667E-01	0.32850E-01	0.629	0.52926	0.9934
RTFP*GENE	0.58966E-01	0.35946E-01	1.640	0.10092	0.9593
RTFP*GENF	0.14902	0.35454E-01	4.203	0.00003	1.018
ln(CAPACITY)	0.19226	0.37179E-01	5.171	0.00000	4.416
FOREIGN	0.10192	0.18389E-01	5.543	0.00000	0.3407E-01
MULTI	-0.77509E-01	0.11390E-01	-6.805	0.00000	0.3642
OUT01	-0.11915	0.15000E-01	-7.943	0.00000	0.4499E-01
OUT23	-0.10864	0.13368E-01	-8.127	0.00000	0.5697E-01
RENTHS	-0.18645E-02	0.33088E-03	-5.635	0.00000	0.2177
RENTSH^2	0.10705	0.14281E-01	7.496	0.00000	0.4663E-01
INVSH	0.45128E-01	0.31505E-01	1.432	0.15204	0.7201E-01
FEMALES	-0.27637	0.15034	-1.838	0.06601	0.3894
FEMALES^2	-0.52471	0.66034	-0.795	0.42685	0.2361
FEMALES^3	2.3331	1.0501	2.222	0.02630	0.1691
FEMALES^4	-1.6791	0.54258	-3.095	0.00197	0.1317
WCS	-0.28928	0.52665E-01	-5.493	0.00000	0.1922
WCS^2	0.98869	0.72886E-01	13.565	0.00000	0.5990E-01
ln(AHOUR)	0.49341	0.14937	3.303	0.00096	0.5612
ln(AHOUR)^2	-0.65050	0.13905	-4.678	0.00000	0.3262
T	0.38918E-01	0.48700E-02	7.991	0.00000	4.113
DI320	0.10543E-01	0.18506E-01	0.570	0.56887	0.1483
DI330	0.10191	0.20414E-01	4.992	0.00000	0.1434
DI341	0.46976E-03	0.37831E-01	0.012	0.99009	0.3450E-01
DI342	-0.95815E-01	0.20568E-01	-4.658	0.00000	0.9351E-01

DI351	-0.67107E-01	0.35915E-01	-1.869	0.06169	0.3976E-01
DI353	0.51539	0.11199	4.602	0.00000	0.4323E-02
DI355	-0.25243E-01	0.32855E-01	-0.768	0.44230	0.1687E-01
DI360	0.16117E-01	0.23739E-01	0.679	0.49718	0.6979E-01
DI370	0.22611E-01	0.42317E-01	0.534	0.59312	0.1487E-01
DI381	-0.12229	0.21000E-01	-5.823	0.00000	0.6979E-01
DI382	-0.12946	0.20521E-01	-6.309	0.00000	0.8862E-01
DI383	0.26804E-01	0.25814E-01	1.038	0.29910	0.3549E-01
DI384	0.58702E-01	0.28465E-01	2.062	0.03918	0.3367E-01
DI390	-0.69818E-01	0.35019E-01	-1.994	0.04618	0.1806E-01
DI320*TREND	0.11640E-01	0.32692E-02	3.561	0.00037	0.5856
DI330*TREND	-0.15791E-01	0.35867E-02	-4.403	0.00001	0.5794
DI341*TREND	-0.12906E-01	0.71142E-02	-1.814	0.06966	0.1464
DI342*TREND	-0.14054E-01	0.37654E-02	-3.732	0.00019	0.3982
DI351*TREND	-0.71190E-02	0.71541E-02	-0.995	0.31969	0.1675
DI353*TREND	-0.10660	0.19126E-01	-5.574	0.00000	0.1866E-01
DI355*TREND	0.11589E-01	0.59011E-02	1.964	0.04954	0.7122E-01
DI360*TREND	-0.14460E-01	0.41697E-02	-3.468	0.00052	0.2895
DI370*TREND	-0.11913E-01	0.77079E-02	-1.546	0.12221	0.6155E-01
DI381*TREND	0.18515E-01	0.39654E-02	4.669	0.00000	0.2911
DI382*TREND	0.19461E-01	0.38899E-02	5.003	0.00000	0.3680
DI383*TREND	-0.19312E-01	0.49660E-02	-3.889	0.00010	0.1514
DI384*TREND	-0.82088E-02	0.54723E-02	-1.500	0.13360	0.1388
DI390*TREND	0.22683E-01	0.67907E-02	3.340	0.00084	0.7494E-01
DR02	-0.91851E-01	0.88078E-02	-10.428	0.00000	0.1824
DR04	-0.69281E-01	0.90018E-02	-7.696	0.00000	0.1847
DR05	-0.14905	0.14025E-01	-10.628	0.00000	0.6041E-01
DR06	-0.15596	0.16044E-01	-9.720	0.00000	0.4087E-01
DR07	-0.15071	0.18926E-01	-7.963	0.00000	0.2577E-01
DR08	-0.14689	0.16353E-01	-8.983	0.00000	0.3746E-01
DRO9	-0.11393	0.14823E-01	-7.686	0.00000	0.4027E-01
DR10	-0.14496	0.11438E-01	-12.673	0.00000	0.1118
DR11	-0.12875	0.13962E-01	-9.222	0.00000	0.5640E-01
DR12	-0.11461	0.20632E-01	-5.555	0.00000	0.2099E-01
DEXPSMALL	-0.10985	0.86565E-02	-12.689	0.00000	0.2398
DEXPMEDIU	-0.82858E-02	0.10293E-01	-0.805	0.42080	0.9627E-01
DSMALL	-0.33009E-02	0.87234E-02	-0.378	0.70514	0.2377
DMEDIUM	-0.65517E-02	0.69380E-02	-0.944	0.34500	0.3317
DOS2SMALL	-0.68255E-01	0.81087E-02	-8.418	0.00000	0.4721
DOS2MEDIU	-0.96825E-01	0.91836E-02	-10.543	0.00000	0.1332
DOS3SMALL	0.47355E-01	0.90198E-02	5.250	0.00000	0.3254
DOS3SMEDIU	0.21515E-01	0.73392E-02	2.931	0.00337	0.3363

Observations = 35161; adjusted R^2 = 0.11120; Breusch - Pagan chi-squared = 5313.7659 with 91 degrees of freedom.

Estimation results, dependent variable natural log of TFP. Model in column (2) in

Table 8

Variable	Coefficient	Standard Error	z=b/s.e.	P-value	Mean of X
Constant	-0.82095	0.97486E-01	-8.421	0.00000	
GENB	-0.42107E-04	0.19414E-01	-0.002	0.99827	0.9961E-01
GENC	0.30477E-01	0.16592E-01	1.837	0.06623	0.1973
GEND	-0.12958E-01	0.16342E-01	-0.793	0.42781	0.1981
GENE	-0.74853E-02	0.16258E-01	-0.460	0.64524	0.2041
GENF	-0.49849E-01	0.16731E-01	-2.979	0.00289	0.2092
*TREND*GENB*	-0.43252E-02	0.26222E-02	-1.649	0.09905	0.5972
*TREND*GENC*	-0.12091E-01	0.22902E-02	-5.279	0.00000	1.178
*TREND*GEND*	-0.14833E-01	0.22565E-02	-6.573	0.00000	1.163
*TREND*GENE*	-0.16868E-01	0.22358E-02	-7.544	0.00000	1.201
*TREND*GENF*	-0.14994E-01	0.22645E-02	-6.621	0.00000	1.243
ln(*CAPACITY*)	0.15443	0.22227E-01	6.948	0.00000	4.367
FOREIGN	0.90766E-01	0.13077E-01	6.941	0.00000	0.3491E-01
MULTI	0.79186E-01	0.56700E-02	13.966	0.00000	0.2935
OUT01	-0.18048	0.12919E-01	-13.970	0.00000	0.3362E-01
OUT23	-0.85589E-01	0.87264E-02	-9.808	0.00000	0.7061E-01
RENTSH	0.25135E-01	0.21349E-02	11.773	0.00000	0.2051
RENTSH^2	-0.10346E-03	0.27665E-04	-3.740	0.00018	2.679
INVSH	-0.31683E-02	0.11330E-02	-2.796	0.00517	0.1686
WCS	-0.13623	0.31921E-01	-4.268	0.00002	0.2225
WCS^2	0.75286	0.36286E-01	20.748	0.00000	0.8799E-01
ln(*AHOUR*)	0.34320	0.63689E-01	5.389	0.00000	0.5255
ln(*AHOUR*)^2	-0.50218	0.64685E-01	-7.764	0.00000	0.2923
TREND	0.37861E-01	0.24195E-02	15.648	0.00000	5.915
DI320	0.14966E-01	0.14563E-01	1.028	0.30410	0.1171
DI330	0.90931E-02	0.16277E-01	0.559	0.57639	0.1502
DI341	-0.10730	0.27242E-01	-3.939	0.00008	0.2910E-01
DI342	-0.22012	0.14886E-01	-14.786	0.00000	0.1129
DI351	-0.14930	0.29002E-01	-5.148	0.00000	0.3953E-01
DI353	-0.42224	0.10228	-4.128	0.00004	0.2846E-02
DI355	-0.10381	0.23719E-01	-4.377	0.00001	0.2416E-01
DI360	-0.51318E-01	0.19320E-01	-2.656	0.00790	0.6628E-01
DI370	-0.69641E-01	0.41857E-01	-1.664	0.09616	0.1008E-01
DI381	-0.94156E-01	0.15138E-01	-6.220	0.00000	0.1015
DI382	-0.46352E-01	0.16987E-01	-2.729	0.00636	0.9480E-01
DI383	-0.48929	0.20571E-01	-23.786	0.00000	0.4944E-01
DI384	0.10225	0.23231E-01	4.402	0.00001	0.3402E-01
DI390	-0.10774	0.29341E-01	-3.672	0.00024	0.1460E-01
*DI320*TREND*	0.11898E-01	0.20647E-02	5.763	0.00000	0.6221
*DI330*TREND*	0.66190E-02	0.20735E-02	3.192	0.00141	0.8671

*DI341*TREND*	0.14566E-01	0.35781E-02	4.071	0.00005	0.1734
*DI342*TREND*	0.83291E-02	0.19900E-02	4.185	0.00003	0.6864
*DI351*TREND*	0.65604E-02	0.36598E-02	1.793	0.07305	0.2443
*DI353*TREND*	0.68765E-01	0.14703E-01	4.677	0.00000	0.1662E-01
*DI355*TREND*	0.15584E-01	0.30526E-02	5.105	0.00000	0.1534
*DI360*TREND*	0.21641E-02	0.28333E-02	0.764	0.44499	0.3923
*DI370*TREND*	0.11052E-01	0.57207E-02	1.932	0.05337	0.6151E-01
*DI381*TREND*	0.16542E-01	0.20466E-02	8.083	0.00000	0.6306
*DI382*TREND*	0.11596E-01	0.23778E-02	4.877	0.00000	0.5825
*DI383*TREND*	0.67118E-01	0.28234E-02	23.772	0.00000	0.3213
*DI384*TREND*	-0.71317E-02	0.31846E-02	-2.239	0.02513	0.1954
*DI390*TREND*	0.26177E-01	0.43411E-02	6.030	0.00000	0.8637E-01
DRO02	-0.69995E-01	0.78548E-02	-8.911	0.00000	0.1036
DRO03	-0.14306	0.97894E-02	-14.614	0.00000	0.5762E-01
DRO04	-0.85079E-01	0.11116E-01	-7.654	0.00000	0.3846E-01
DRO05	-0.78448E-01	0.74503E-02	-10.530	0.00000	0.1192
DRO06	-0.10186	0.93412E-02	-10.904	0.00000	0.5385E-01
DRO07	-0.12673	0.12392E-01	-10.226	0.00000	0.3562E-01
DRO08	-0.73785E-01	0.13748E-01	-5.367	0.00000	0.2339E-01
DRO09	-0.16678	0.12396E-01	-13.455	0.00000	0.2883E-01
DRO10	-0.12091	0.11153E-01	-10.841	0.00000	0.4137E-01
DRO11	-0.16547	0.12759E-01	-12.969	0.00000	0.2730E-01
DRO12	-0.14569	0.10117E-01	-14.401	0.00000	0.4565E-01
DRO13	-0.16187	0.98658E-02	-16.407	0.00000	0.5862E-01
DRO14	-0.11173	0.10855E-01	-10.292	0.00000	0.4534E-01
DRO15	-0.12834	0.18348E-01	-6.995	0.00000	0.1614E-01
DRO16	-0.12575	0.10669E-01	-11.787	0.00000	0.5005E-01
DRO17	-0.12959	0.19624E-01	-6.604	0.00000	0.1135E-01
DRO19	-0.14165	0.14296E-01	-9.908	0.00000	0.2431E-01
DRO22	-0.86806E-01	0.16378E-01	-5.300	0.00000	0.1832E-01
DEXPSMALL	-0.11486	0.21076E-01	-5.450	0.00000	0.1265E-01
DEXPMEDIU	-0.23741E-01	0.58596E-02	-4.052	0.00005	0.3634
DSMALL	0.16817E-01	0.63347E-02	2.655	0.00794	0.3203
DMEDIUM	-0.37655E-02	0.54210E-02	-0.695	0.48730	0.3318
DOS2SMALL	-0.16316	0.68932E-02	-23.670	0.00000	0.3912
DOS2MEDIU	-0.12426	0.55371E-02	-22.441	0.00000	0.2731
DOS3SMALL	0.12544	0.71103E-02	17.642	0.00000	0.3321
DOS3MEDIU	0.33809E-01	0.53243E-02	6.350	0.00000	0.3343

Observations=63595; adjusted R^2 =0.16822; Breusch-Pagan chi-squared=6586.6370 with 77 degrees of freedom.

REFERENCES

Akerlof, G. A. (1997), *"Social Distance and Social Decisions"*, Econometrica, 65, 5, 1005-1027.

Bahk, B. H. Gort, M. (1993), *"Decomposing Learning by Doing in New Plants"*. Journal of Political Economy, 101, 4, 561-583.

Baily, M. Hulten, C. Campbell, D. (1992), *"Productivity Dynamics in Manufacturing Plants"*, Brookings Papers: Microeconomics 1992.

Baldwin, J. R. (1995), *"The Dynamics of Industrial Competition "*, Cambridge University Press.

Bellmann, L. Kölling, A. (1997), *"Technology, Wages and Churning in Western Germany: Estimates from the IAB-Establishment Panel"*, in Laaksonen (ed.): "The Evolution of Firms and Industries; International Perspectives" Research Reports 223, Statistics Finland.

Bernard, A. Jones, C. (1996), *"Productivity Across Industries and Countries: Time Series Theory and Evidence"*, The Review of Economics and Statistics, 78, 1, 135-146.

Breusch, T. Pagan, A. (1980*), "The LM Test and its Application to Model Specification in Econometrics"*, Review of Economic Studies, 47, 239-254.

Caballero, R. J. Lyons, R. K. (1990), *"Internal vs External Economies in European Industry"*, European Economic Review, 34, 805-830.

Caves, D. W. Christensen, L. R. Trethway, M. W. (1981), *"U.S. Trunk Air Carriers, 1972-1977: A multilateral comparison of total factor productivity"*, in Cowing, T. G. Stevens, R. E. (eds.), "Productivity measurement in regulated industries", New York, Academic Press, 1981.

Dunne, T. (1991), *"Technology Usage in U.S. Manufacturing Industries: New Evidence from the Survey of Manufacturing Technology"*, Discussion Paper CES 91-7, Center for Economic Studies, Bureau of the Census.

Gordon, R. J. (1990), *"The Measurement of Durable Goods Prices"*, University of Chicago Press, Chicago.

Gort, M. Bahk, B. H. Wall, R. A. (1993), *"Decomposing Technical Change"*, Southern Economic Journal, 60, 1, 220-234.

Griliches, Z. (1992), *"The Search of R&D spillovers"*, The Scandinavian Journal of Economics, 94, Supplement, S29-S47.

Griliches, Z. Mairesse, J. (1995), *"Production Functions: The Search for Identification"*, NBER Working Paper Series, Working Paper No. 5067.

Griliches, Z. Regev, H. (1995), *"Firm Productivity in Israeli Industry 1979-1988"*, Journal of Econometrics, 65, 175-203.

Greenwood, J. Hercowitz, Z. Krusell, P. (1997), *"Long-Run Implications of Investment-Specific Technological Change"*, The American Economic Review, 87, 3, 342-362.

Hall, R. E. (1988), *"The Relation between Price and Marginal Cost in U.S. Industry"*, Journal of Political Economy, 96, 921-947.

Honkatukia, J. (1997), *"The Transmission and Effects of Monetary Fluctuations under Intraindustry Trade"*, Helsinki School of Economics and Business Administration, A-125.

Hulten, C. R. (1992), *"Growth Accounting When Technical Change is Embodied in Capital"*, The American Economic Review, 82, 4, 964-979.

Jensen, J. B. McGuckin, R. H. Stiroh, K. J. (1998), *"The Impact of Vintages and Age on Productivity: Evidence from Cohorts of U.S. Manufacturing Plants"*. Mimeo, January 1998.

Jovanovic, B. (1982), *"Selection and the Evolution of Industry"*, Econometrica, 50, 649-670.

Liu, L. (1993), *"Entry-exit, Learning, and Productivity Change Evidence from Chile"*, Journal of Development Economics, 42, 2, 217-242.

Mairesse, J. Kremp, E. (1993), *"A Look at Productivity at the Firm Level in Eight French Service Industries"*, The Journal of Productivity Analysis, 4, 211-234.

Maliranta, M. (1997a), *"Plant Productivity in Finnish Manufacturing Characteristics of High Productivity Plants"*, Discussion Papers No. 612, The Research Institute of the Finnish Economy.

Maliranta, M. (1997b), *"The Determinants of Aggregate Productivity The Evolution of Microstructures and Productivity within Plants in Finnish Manufacturing from 1975 to 1994"* Discussion Papers No. 603, The Research Institute of the Finnish Economy.

White, H. (1980), *"A Heteroskedasticity-Consistent Covariance Matrix Estimator and A Direct Test for Heteroskedasticity"*, Econometrica, 48, 817-838.

EFFICIENCY AND OPTIMAL SIZE ESTIMATION WITH PANEL DATA: THE CASE OF BUSINESS SERVICE AND BUILDING SECTOR IN ITALY**

Fabio Bacchini[1] and Alessandro Zeli[2]

[1,2]*Istituto Nazionale di Statistica (Istat)*

1 Introduction

Different evolution characterise Building sector and Information technology over the period 1991-94. A decreasing of the average level of profit on turnover associated to an increasing level for the tangible assets and the turnover per head characterise Building sector. On the contrary Information technology is characterised by increasing in profit, decreasing in tangible assets and in turnover.

To relate these features of the two sectors to difference in the performance of the firms, we evaluate a stochastic frontier production for each sector.

Use of stochastic frontier production to estimate firm-level technical efficiencies was proposed independently by Aigner, Lovell and Schmidt (1977) and Meeusen and van den Broeck (1977).

This kind of model "involves the specification of the error term as being made up of two components, one normal and the other from a one-sided distribution" (Aigner, Lovell and Schimdt, 1977 page 21). This involves that first we estimate a frontier production function with respect to which individual inefficiency are defined as a residual. The residuals are composed by two elements: a noise, symmetrically distributed and a measure of technical inefficiency asymmetrically distributed, because every firm lie on or below the frontier. It is necessary the choice of some distribution for the two random components.

Several works have investigated the behaviour of the model and in particular the choice of one-side distribution that is not innocuous for the robustness of estimation (Stevenson, 1980, Greene, 1980). In this context, estimation of a stochastic frontier model from cross-section data requires the assumption that technical inefficiency is independent of the inputs.

** Comments by Duccio Gazzei and Piero Taccini are gratefully acknowledged. We thank Carla Schiattone for assistance with data compilation and Roberta Garofalo for the editing. None of them should be responsible for any errors remaining.
Chapters 1,3,5 by A. Zeli, 2,4,7 by F. Bacchini, 6 by A. Zeli and F. Bacchini.

Panel data allows this independence assumption to be relaxed, in fact firms may know their level of inefficiency in relation to the others firms and they change the behaviour in consequence. Technical inefficiency can be estimated more precisely by observing the firms more than ones. Furthermore, recent literature using panel data models has sought to relax the assumption that technical inefficiency is time-invariant (Cornwell, Schmidt and Sickles, 1996, Coelli, 1995).

In this framework, we estimate two kinds of models using the program Frontier (ver. 4.1). The first one permits to test the time-varying efficiency. In the second one, following Battese and Coelli (1995), we investigate a model specification in which the firm effects are directly influenced by firms size.

This paper is organised as follows: in section 2 we discuss the choice of the model, the database is presented in section 3, while in section 4 and 5 are reported the empirical results. Section 6 presents some observations about the differences between the building and information sectors. Section 7 concludes.

2 Inefficiency stochastic frontier model for panel data

2.1 The general model

The general model specification, for N firms and T periods, is:

$$Y_{it} = x_{it}\beta + (V_{it} - U_{it}) \qquad\qquad i=1,....., N \quad t=1,.........,T \qquad\qquad [1]$$

where, the V term represents the noise, U represents the firm technical inefficiency, X inputs quantities β is the vector of coefficients of production function and Y is the output.

In literature, different distribution have been used for the U_i: half-normal, exponential, gamma and truncated normal distribution. This last case, which is implemented in FRONTIER program (Coelli, 1996) and the U_{it} can assume the following form:

$$U_{it} = (U_i \ exp(-\eta(t-T)) \qquad\qquad [2]$$

the U_i are non negative and are assumed to be iid as truncation at zero of the $N(\mu,\sigma_u^2)$ distribution and they are also permitted to vary systematically with time.

We utilise the same parametrisation of FRONTIER. In this way we replace σ_v^2 and σ_u^2 with $\sigma^2 = \sigma_u^2 + \sigma_v^2$ and $\gamma = (\sigma_u^2 / \sigma_u^2 + \sigma_v^2)$ in order to estimate (indirectly) the U_i (or better $E(U_i | E_i)$).

The interpretation of γ is easy because its range of variation is between 0 and 1; when γ is equal 1 it means that all deviations from the frontier are due entirely to technical inefficiency; if γ is equal 0 it means that the choice of the model was wrong. In that case there are not inefficiency effects and the model can be estimate consistently by ordinary least squares (OLS).

The imposition of one or more restriction upon this model formulation can provide a number of the special cases of this particular model which are appeared in literature.

For example if we impose $\eta = 0$, $\mu = 0$ and $T = 1$ we return to the original cross-sectional, half-normal formulation of Aigner, Lovell and Schimdt (1977)[1].

2.2 A model with firm-specific variables

In the formulation of model (1)-(2) there is no exploration of the reason that can explain the difference in predicted efficiencies between firms.

Battese and Coelli (1995) propose a model where the inefficiency effects (U_i) are expressed as an explicit function of a vector of firms-specific variables and a random error.

In this case the U_i term could be expressed by:

$$U_{it} = z_{it}\,\delta + W_{it} \qquad\qquad [3]$$

with W_{it}, distributed as a truncation of the normal distribution with zero mean[2].

In order to estimate the parameters we use the maximum-likelihood estimator (MLE) implemented by program FRONTIER. The use of MLE is due to the statistical proprieties of this estimator.

In fact Coelli (1995) proved that the MLE is significantly more efficient then corrected least squared estimator (COLS) in presence of:
(i) a contribution of technical inefficiency to the error term (γ) greater than 0.5 and
(ii) when the sample is greater than 50.

---

[1] We label the model (1)-(2) as "model-1" in the estimate in paragraph 3-4.

[2] We label the model (1)-(3) as "model 2" in the estimate in paragraph 3-4.

2.3 Technical efficiency

Following Battese-Coelli (1988, page 389) we define "the technical efficiency (*T.E.*) of a given firm as the ratio of firms mean production (in original units), given its realised effect, to the corresponding mean production if the firm effect was zero. Thus the technical efficiency of i *th* firm, denoted by TE_i is defined by:

$$TE_i = E(Y^*_{it}/U_{it},x_{it}\, t=1,2,....)/\, E(Y^*_{it}/U_i=0,\, x_{it},\, t=1,2...) \qquad [4]$$

where Y^*_{it} denotes the value of production (in original units) for the i *th* firm in the t *th* period.

TE is a measure that has value between zero and one. If the frontier production function is defined for the logarithm of production, then the production for the firm in t*th* period is $exp(Y_{it})$, thus the TE is now defined by:

$$TE_i = exp(-U_i) \qquad [5]$$

Almost all empirical models involve logarithm transformation of (1). In this work we choice the Cobb-Douglas formulation for model (1)[3].

3 The data set

We focus the investigation on Building (Nace 45) and Information Technology (Nace 72) sectors that were not included in precedent works.

We investigate this sectors because they are very different each other: one is a market characterised by the presence of an high number of firms (Building) and "traditional" activity. The other is a market characterised by an high technical level and a smaller number of firms.

The data are taken from Istat "Systems of the Enterprises Accounts Italian" Annual survey about all Italian enterprises with 20 or more employees for the period 1991-1994.

The panel is retrospective: we started with 1994 observations and then we verified the presence/absence of every firm in the previous years. We take off only the enterprises that were present in every year.

---

[3] We have observed that the results with a Translog formulation of model (1) are quite similar.

The data are book items of all firms which employs more then 20 employees, the items are submitted to an homogeneous treatment. We have obtained at last 1816 firms in the building sector and 217 in the information technology sector[4].

We considered the Y (turnover) as a proxy of output, K (tangible assets) as a proxy of capital and L (number of employees) as a proxy of labour.

Moreover, for the second model we use the class of employees as variable z. In particular we classify the firms by the number of employees in the following way: 20-49 employees; 50-99 employees; 100-199 employees; 200-499 employees; 500-999 employees; 1.000 and over.

Description of some important relation (firm distribution by firm size, turnover per head, tangible assets per head and profits per head) for the two sectors are provided in the appendix.

4 Building sector

The results of "model-1" estimation are showed in table 1. We note difference between OLS estimation and ML estimation only in the intercept term associate with a significative value of $\mu \neq 0$.

The elasticity parameter for capital and labour are significant and the sign are as we expected.

Table 1 Parameter estimates for frontier production function for Building sector - Model 1

	Variable			Variance parameter				Log-
	Intercept	Capital	Labour	σ^2	γ	μ	η	likelihood
O.L.S.	3.60	0.25	0.86	0.40	..	..	..	-7153,9
T-ratio	(77,7)	(29,3)	(62,0)					
M.L.	4.7	0.25	0.82	0.40	0.5	0.9	0.006	-6134.3
T-ratio	(57,0)	(22,1)	(42,5)	(21,3)	(34,3)	(21,2)	(1,2)	
L.R. test	2039.3							
	Year 1	Year 2	Year 3	Year 4				
Mean TE	0.4067	0.4086	0.4104	0.41				

---

[4] The choice of economic activity, to be take out, was restricted to NACE 72 (Information technology) because of problems of homogeneity throughout the sector of business service (NACEK).

Parameter η is not significant. Thus the hypothesis of time-varying effects is not verified. However, the sign of the parameter is positive (the value is slightly over zero). This is reflected also in the dynamic of the *TE* mean during the period, that is increasing.

The significant value of γ is an indicator for the preference of ML estimator instead of COLS estimator (Coelli 1995).

Null hypothesis that inefficiency effects are absent strongly rejected.

Estimation of the mean technical efficiencies, indicate the firms in building sector are about 41% technical efficient. We report in table 2 the prediction of technical efficiencies of individual firm that were obtained using the estimated parameter values for the frontier production function.

About 73% of firm are at a technical efficient level that is low than 60% and only 3,1% of firms are a technical level more than 80%.

Table 2 Frequencies and percentage of technical efficiency within decile ranges for Building sector (1994)

Technical efficiency	Frequencies	Percentage
Below 0.2	71	3.8%
0.2-0.3	381	20.5%
0.3-0.4	574	30.8%
0.4-0.5	400	21.5%
0.5-0.6	200	10.7%
0.6-0.7	118	6.3%
0.7-0.8	59	3.2%
0.8-0.9	43	2.3%
0.9-1.0	15	0.8%
Total	1861	

In table 3 there are the results of estimation of "model-2". Dimensional size is influent for building sector. Intercept term is lower than in model-1 and the elasticity of capital is bigger than in the previous case. Moreover the value of parameter γ is significant and close to 1 (0,9): which indicates that the inefficiency effects are likely to be highly significant in the analysis of turnover (mean *TE* pass from 41% to 76%). The coefficient δ_l is positive, which indicates that big firms are more inefficient than the small and the medium ones.

This result is confirmed by the analysis of predicted efficiency level of the firms. From the 15 more efficient firms (table 2), 7 are included in the class 50-99 employees and 4 in the class 100-199 employees. Moreover, all firms with more then 1.000 employees have an efficient level less than 60%. Summing up, small and medium firms seems more efficient then the others.

5 Information technology sector

The results of estimation are showed in table 4, we can note that the coefficient of η is not statistically significant. Thus the hypothesis of time-varying effects, i.e. variation of the efficient coefficients in the time is not verified. We can note, anyway, that the sign of the parameter is negative, and the value is slightly over zero. The value of μ (1.13) is low but significant, thus the distribution of efficiency is not zero-mean.

Table 3 Parameter estimates for frontier production function for Building sector Model 2

	Variable			Variance parameter		Z's parameter		Log-
	Intercept	Capital	Labour	σ^2	γ	δ_0	δ_1	likelihood
O.L.S.	3.60	0.24	0.85	0.40	..	..	..	-7153,9
T-ratio	(77,7)	(29,3)	(62,0)					
M.L.	3.5	0.25	0.96	6.0	0.9	-22.5	2.9	-6871.5
T-ratio	(74,7)	(34,1)	(98,4)	(10,4)	(204,8)	(-9,5)	(10,3)	
L.R. test	564.9							
Mean TE	0.76							

Table 4 Parameter estimates for frontier production function for the Information Technology sector Model 1

	Variable			Variance parameter				Log-
	Intercept	Capital	Labour	σ^2	γ	μ	η	likelihood
O.L.S.	3.39	0.22	0.93	0.22	..	..	..	-567.77
T-ratio	(45,00)	(18,4)	(45,04)					
M.L.	5.55	0.18	0.77	0.36	0.89	1.13	0.02	-163.87
T-ratio	(35,59)	(12,39)	(32,39)	(10,01)	(129,87)	(14,39)	(-2,50)	
L.R. test	807.8							
	Year 1	Year 2	Year 3	Year 4				
Mean TE	0.35	0.34	0.34	0.33				

We can point out that the coefficients are all significant, the signs of the stochastic frontier are as expected. We can note a strong influence of the labour cost on the production function. In fact, this is a labour intensive sector where the presence of skilled employees is really relevant, increasing the productivity.

Also γ coefficient is strongly significant, and the value is closer to one, it means that the 89% of the variance is represented by the inefficiency effects, and the model is a view of the reality. Generalised likelihood-ratio test of null hypothesis that inefficiency effects are absent or that they have simpler distribution is also presented; the null hypothesis is strongly rejected.

The technical efficiency values are very low, the mean efficiency estimation for the four years is showed in table 5. The efficiency has, also, a slight decrease in the period.

Table 5 Frequencies and percentage of technical efficiency within decile ranges for Information Technology sector (1994)

Technical efficiency	Frequencies	Percentage
Below 0.2	48	22.1%
0.2-0.3	63	29.0%
0.3-0.4	48	22.1%
0.4-0.5	31	14.3%
0.5-0.6	14	6.5%
0.6-0.7	3	1.4%
0.7-0.8	4	1.8%
0.8-0.9	2	0.9%
0.9-1.0	4	1.8%
Total	217	

The points are more crowded under the line of $TE=0.5$; the mean is slight over the line of $TE=0.3$.

The results of the second model are described in table 6, we can note that the LR test now accept the null hypothesis, the γ coefficients is not significant like the δ_0 and δ_1 ones.

Table 6 Parameter estimates for frontier production function for the Information Technology sector Model 2

	Variable			Variance parameter		Z's parameter		Log-
	Intercept	Capital	Labour	σ^2	γ	δ_0	δ_1	likelihood
O.L.S.	3.39	0.22	0.93	0.22	..	..	..	-567.77
T-ratio	(45,00)	(18,4)	(45,04)					
M.L.	3.02	0.22	1.05	0.22	5E-07	-0.09	0.09	-566.12
T-ratio	(12,86)	(17,65)	(15,75)	(20,62)	(0,0002)	(-1,12)	(1,82)	
L.R. test	3.29							
Mean T.E.	0,92							

This kind of results provide in a large evidence the lack of influence of the firms size influence respect to inefficiency, i.e. the dimension of the enterprises does not affect their performance.

This result is confirmed by the analysis of predicted efficiency level of the firms. From the 6 more efficient firms (table 5), there is no a dimension size that emerges, summing up there is no evidence that one dimension size performs better than the others.

6 Comparison of the results between building and information technology sectors

Results from the estimation of stochastic frontier model in both sectors suggest some differences in the average efficiency during the period. In particular, building sector shows a slight increasing in the average meanwhile information technology has a slight decrease during the period . Moreover in building sector the class of employees results significant in the explication of the efficiency (table 3).

These two evidence could be related with the differences that emerging in the two markets over the period 1991-1994 (Figure 1-6).

Building sectors is characterised by a decreasing of the average level of profit on turnover (Figure 3) associated to an increasing level for the tangible assets per head (Figure 2) and the turnover per head (Figure 1). On the contrary information technology sectors shows increasing in profit (Figure 6), decreasing in tangible assets (Figure 5) and in the turnover (Figure 4).

These stylised facts could indicate a relation between the results of the estimated stochastic frontier and the degree of selection present in the market. In this way if we regard to information technology as an emerging market with growing level of profit we could account for a low degree of selection and then more inefficiency.

In the building sector the declining in the level of profits is associated to some form of re-structuration in term of more intensive investment in tangible assets. In fact in the first half of '90 in Italy the building sector was invested by a particularly strong crisis, which increased the competitiveness and the market selection. It is not suprising if the firms of building sector look like more efficient then information technology ones.

7 Conclusion

The results of our application seems confirm the relation between   sector evolution and firm-level technical efficiencies. Particularly building sector shows a slight increasing in the average meanwhile information technology has a slight average decreasing during the period.

The results of our application illustrate that for both sectors the time-varying technical inefficiency is no significant: in the case of building sectors exists a slight average increasing meanwhile in the case of information technology there is a slight decreasing.

We test also the influence of dimensional size in error components that is only significant for building sector. This result is confirmed by the analysis of predicted efficiency level of the more efficient firms.

Finally we try to argue that this results is related to different levels of selection in the two sectors.

Figure 1 - Turnover per head
Buildings - 1991-1994

Figure 4 - Turnover per head
Information Technology -1991-1994

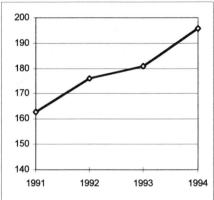

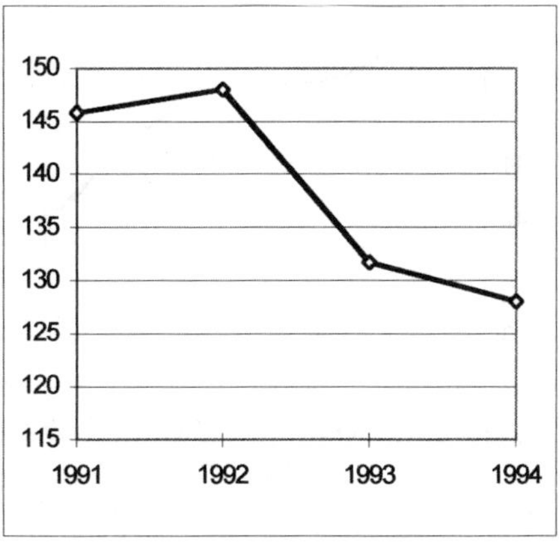

Figure 2 Tangible assets per head
Buildings - 1991-1994

Figure 5 Tangible assets per head
Information Technology 1991-1994

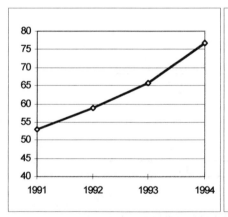

Figure 3 Profits on turnover -   **Figure 6** Profits on turnover

Buildings - 1991-1994   Information Technology - 1991-1994

Statistical Appendix

Table 1 Building sector - Firm distribution by size

Size	Frequencies
<50	1149
50-99	423
100-199	170
200-499	79
500-999	28
1000 and over	12
Total	1861

Table 2 Building sector - Turnover per head distribution by size and year

Size	1991	1992	1993	1994
<50	146,6	162,0	162,5	176,6
50-99	177,4	177,4	191,5	218,0
100-199	191,6	213,9	234,2	265,0
200-499	225,0	262,0	290,3	303,6
500-999	277,9	274,5	305,0	349,7
1000 and over	152,4	236,2	263,5	175,3
Total	163,0	176,1	181,0	195,9

Table 3 Building sector - Tangible assets per head distribution by size and year

Size	1991	1992	1993	1994
<50	45,9	52,0	59,4	70,3
50-99	59,0	61,3	68,4	81,2
100-199	64,3	76,8	85,5	99,2
200-499	90,7	99,6	116,1	144,9
500-999	78,5	75,9	85,0	79,8
1000 and over	67,0	87,1	90,7	104,4
Total	53,1	58,8	65,8	76,9

Table 4 Building sector - Profits on turnover distribution by size and year

Size	1991	1992	1993	1994
<50	0,035	0,035	-0,007	0,013
50-99	0,031	0,012	-0,006	-0,005
100-199	0,025	0,277	0,007	-0,017
200-499	0,019	0,035	-0,006	-0,143
500-999	0,044	0,012	-0,014	-0,015
1000 and over	0,014	-0,005	-0,011	-0,058
Total	0,032	0,048	-0,006	0,002

Source: Istat - Panel Sci 1991- 1994

Table 5 Information technology sector - Firm distribution by size

Size	Frequencies
<50	126
50-99	37
100-199	27
200-499	17
500-999	7
1000 and over	3
Total	217

Table 6 Information technology sector - Turnover per head distribution by size and year

Size	1991	1992	1993	1994
<50	132,8	138,7	111,6	112,6
50-99	160,4	162,5	148,7	138
100-199	160,2	158,8	159	155,5
200-499	148,7	139,9	162,7	152,4
500-999	161	159	148,2	144,3
1000 and over	287,1	276,9	250,6	227,6
Total	145,8	148,1	131,8	128

Table 7 Information technology sector -Tangible assets per head distribution by size and year

Size	1991	1992	1993	1994
<50	36,8	34,1	37,8	33,7
50-99	92	91,6	79,7	70,1
100-199	35,4	35,2	38,5	39,5
200-499	48,1	42,8	50,6	44,9
500-999	68,7	53,2	47,7	45,8
1000 and over	30,7	35,1	36	35,4
Total	50	46,9	46,6	41,9

Table 8 Information technology sector - Profits on turnover distribution by size and year

Size	1991	1992	1993	1994
<50	1,83	1,33	2,34	1,72
50-99	-3,51	-3,14	-3,60	-0,83
100-199	2,41	2,19	0,80	1,44
200-499	-2,26	-0,83	0,23	1,60
500-999	-13,57	-2,03	2,07	0,22
1000 and over	-0,52	0,03	-1,51	1,41
Total	-0,13	0,21	0,86	1,19

Source: Istat - Panel Sci 1991-1994

REFERENCES

Aigner D.J., Lovell C.A.K., Schmidt P. (1977), *"Formulation and estimation of stochastic frontier models"*, Journal of Econometrics, 6, 21-37.

Battese G. E., Coelli T. (1988), *"Prediction of firm-level technical efficiencies with a generalised frontier production function and panel data"*, Journal of Econometrics, 38, 387-399.

Battese G. E., Coelli T. (1995), *"A model for technical inefficiency effects in a stochastic frontier production function for panel data"*, Empirical Economics, 20, 325-332.

Coelli T. (1995), *"Estimators and hypothesis tests for a stochastic frontier function: a Monte Carlo analysis"*, Journal of Productivity Analysis, 6, 247-268.

Coelli T. (1996), *"A Guide to FRONTIER Version 4.1: A Computer Program for Stochastic Frontier Production and Cost Function Estimation"*, CEPA Working Paper 96/07.

Cornwell C., Schmidt P. Sikles R. (1996), *"Production frontiers and efficiency measurement"* in Matyas L., Sevestre P. (eds), The econometrics of panel data: handbook of the theory applications, Kluwer Academic Publishers

Greene W. H. (1980), *"Maximum Likelihood Estimation of Econometric Frontier Functions"*, Journal of Econometrics, 13, 27-56.

Greene W. H. (1993), *"The econometric approach to efficiency analysis"* in Fried H., Lovell K., Schmidt S. (eds), The measurement of productive efficiency: techniques and applications, Oxford University Press.

Olson J.A., Schmidt P. and Waldman D.M. (1980), *"A Monte Carlo Study of Estimators of Stochastic Frontier Production Functions"* Journal of Econometrics, 13, 67-82.

Meeusen W., Van den BroekJ. (1997), *"Efficiency Estimation from Cobb-Douglas Production Functions with Composed error"*, International Economic Review , 18, 435-444.

Stevenson R. E. (1980), *"Likelihood functions for generalised stochastic frontier estimation"*, Journal of Econometrics, 13, 57-66

INFORMATION CONTENT OF BALANCE SHEETS FOR QUANTITATIVE ANALYSIS OF INDUSTRIAL DISTRICTS*

Guido Ferrari[1], Piero Ganugi[2] and Giorgio Gozzi[3]

[1]University of Florence
[2,3]University of Parma

1 Introduction

Italian Companies Balance-Sheet Items (ICBI) of CERVED represent an important source of information to develop quantitative economic studies at microarea level, particularly, if the area overlaps with an Industrial District.

Starting from the consideration of the very limited utilization of this source of data, this paper aims to underline its potentiality for some specific topics. At the same time we will try to emphasize its information benefits which are, without any doubt, higher than its costs both in terms of purchase expenditure and in terms of carrying out an essential preliminary screening of each Balance Sheet.

As we shall check, the information power of ICBI File proves to be increased if it is integrated with other Administrative Files.

In this paper, after discussing the main features of the ICBI File, we will consider the following five topics:
1. evaluation of the industrial Gross Product at provincial level;
2. construction of four (ESA) accounts for Textile Non Financial Corporations Sector. That is: Production Account, Distribution of Gross Product Account, Capital Account, Financial Account;
3. Assets Account for the same Sector;
4. estimation of Cost and Production functions;
5. distress analysis.

*The authors acknowledge financial support from Ministry of University (MURST). Despite being the result of a common work, section 2 was written by G. Ferrari, sections 3-5 were written by P. Ganugi and section 6 was written by G. Gozzi.

2 Characteristics of ICBI File

CERVED (an information company of The Italian Chambers of Commerce) manages ICBI File (CERVED FILE). This is an informative service that gives access to the most salient data of a Balance Sheet of a company. Since the end of 1992 this data bank is accessible on line. It is possible to get data also on magnetic support (Floppy Disk for example). In Paniccia (1993), it is possible to find a complete description of this data bank and important information about the characteristics and quality of the data. The content of each record, restricted to only one item, is reported in Table 1. In the field "C-ATTIVITÀ" we find the code ATECO [1] of the prevailing economic activity of the company. It is necessary to point out that when a 4 digit code is considered, sometimes the identification of the economic activity may be difficult. In this case, a check with other sources of information becomes necessary. CERVED FILE lacks some information that can constitute elements of weakness and restrict the fields of use for the analysis as regards the five topics outlined above. The most important gap is the absence, for many companies, of the indication of the number of the employees. Moreover, it is not possible to obtain, from this File, information on the date of birth and on the state of activity (active, in liquidation, failed) at the time the File is read. In order to obtain the number of the employees, it is necessary to integrate the CERVED FILE with the INPS FILE of employees. [2] In fact, the chance of finding this information through personnel expenditure registered in the Balance-Sheet is very low, given the deep differences in productivity and duration of the working day among the companies of a sector. The key for the integration of two Files is the Fiscal Code.

Table1 Example of a structure of a record in the ICBI File.

CCIA	NRD	DENOMINAZ	C_ATTIVITA'	VOCE_BIL	IMP_BIL
Chamber of Commerce	Company Code	Company Name	Economic Activities Code ATECO	Balance Sheet Item	Balance Sheet Value

Further information can be obtained through the integration of CERVED FILE with the Business Register of Chambers of Commerce CCIAA FILE[3]. In this way,

---

[1] We refer to classification of economic activities ATECO91, that is the Italian version of the EEC classification NACE Rev. 1.

[2] With INPS FILE we refer to the Italian Social Security (INPS) Archive built up using data on individual employees taken from Model DM10. See: Billia, G. (1993), pp. 139-149.

[3] Business Register (BR) is a register which is held by the Chamber of Commerce. For its characteristics, see: Biffignandi S., Martini M. (1995), pp.167-198.

it is possible to acquire the date of constitution (and therefore the age) and the effective state of the company. The key of intersection is always the Fiscal Code. The integration of the CERVED FILE with the INPS FILE and CIAA FILE[4] provides a not negligible information advantage. In fact, the number of employees, the state and the age of the company may be considered very interesting variables for quantitative analysis. These seem to be at most three important uses:

1. the number of employees is not only the best proxy of the size of the company, but it can also be used to build up important productivity ratios;
2. the age can reasonably be considered a meaningful variable of the economic and financial strength of the firm;
3. through the joint use of age and number of employees, we can use the location model as monitoring tool of the companies.

It is neccesary to stress that the integration of CERVED FILE with INPS FILE and CCIAA FILE implies a wide reduction of the number of companies contained in the CERVED FILE. In fact:

- integration with INPS FILE implies the cutting of companies without any employees, which are a lot in Industrial Districts;
- integration with CCIAA FILE involves the exclusion of the companies which do not appear in the Business Register, brought up to date at least one year later than CERVED FILE. But this integration is not completely free from drawbacks: the companies can register a change of company form and this involves the exclusion of the same unit from the Intersection of the three Files.

3 Direct Evaluation of Gross Product

As it is known, in Italy there is no survey at provincial level for the direct evaluation of Gross Product. To solve this problem, the statisticians have implemented indirect methods based on the sharing out regional Gross Product evaluated by ISTAT at Industry level to the different provinces according to analytical indicators extracted from the Census of Industry (for Tuscany see IRPET, 1991). This approach should not be confused with the indirect but synthetic methodology of evaluation of Disposable Income (see Marbach, 1983).

In this section we suggest a procedure for obtaining a direct evaluation of Industrial Gross Product at factor cost at province level.

The possibility of integrating the evaluation of Gross Product with the Profit and Loss Account (Economic Account) of Balance Sheet was known to ISTAT from the 70s. For some classes of companies, ISTAT arranged special sets of

---

[4] On the possible methodological approach for the integration of administrative business registers, refer to Aimetti, P. (1995).

questions about specific items of the Economic Account (see: Siesto, 1973, p. 181).

In spite of this, there were two precise obstacles to a systematic use of the Balance Sheet for a direct evaluation of Gross Product:

1. the lack of strict laws for the compilation of the Balance Sheet;
2. the absence in Economic Account of an economic framework like that of Production Account in SNA through which to clearly obtain the Gross Product produced by a company.

According to the Fourth EEC Directive, the firm Profit and Loss Account finally takes a structure of National Accounts. The most evident proof of this fact is the new questionnaire of the ISTAT annual survey on the Gross Product called "Sistema dei Conti delle Imprese (SCI)". In the questionnaire the "Economic Account" appears like a multiple-step form account that accurately follows the Profit and Loss of the firm. In fact, "it allows identification of the contribution of the different operational phases to the running outcome; as a consequence, it facilitates the determination of economic aggregates used for business analysis: Production, Gross Product, Gross Operating Surplus and Net Operating Surplus" (See: Predetti, 1994, p.217).

In the first part of the Balance Sheet supplied by CERVED, Total Production (Net from proceeds that do not result from specific production activity of the firm) is made up of: Consumption of Materials; General Expenditure (that include payments on external workmanships and the expenses for machinery rental); the Gross Product at Factor Cost subdivided in compensation for employees and Gross Operating Surplus[5]. As is known, the subdivision of the items is not arbitrary but is clearly fixed by the Civil Code.

On the basis of the items, we obtain the Gross Product at Factor Cost as sum of Compensation for employees and Gross Operating Surplus. It is necessary to remark that CERVED is inaccurate in the definition of Gross Product because it erroneously includes the General Expenditure, but fortunately it correctly calculates the Gross Operating Surplus by deducting from this definition of Gross Product, not only Compensation Expenditure but also General Expenditure erroneously added before.

CERVED FILE does not include the Non Companies and the Individual Firms that represent a significant share of the productive units. A solution to the problem of calculating Gross Product for Non Companies with employees can be found using the information originating from the intersection of CERVED FILE and INPS FILE, that is the number of employees.

The intersection of the two Files is in fact the universe of the companies with employees of the province (see Figure 1) from which it is possible to get the productivity (Gross Product per employee) by size of companies (no. of employees). Such productivities can be used for the estimate of Gross Product for

---

[5] We use the expression "Gross Operating Surplus" as a translation of the Italian "Margine Operativo Lordo (MOL)."

each company (by size of employees) not belonging to CERVED FILE but with employees. This, of course, in the hypothesis, very likely in our case, that the productivity does not change, when given the same class of employees, we move from Companies to Non Companies.

Figure 1 Integration of Files used for the estimation of Industrial Gross Product at province level

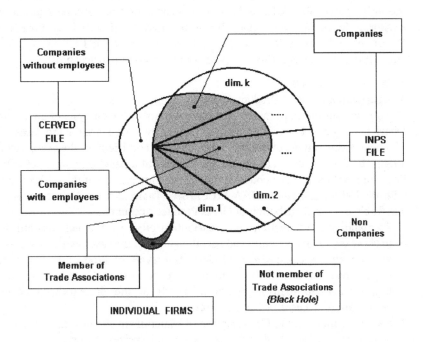

However, the intersection of CERVED FILE with INPS FILE does not include Firms without employees. Because of their usually very small size they do not keep double-entry books but only a simple Income Tax Return. This inconvenience can be overcome with the collaboration of Craftsmen Associations if they supply (anonymously) the Income Tax Returns of their members where it is possible to extract the Gross Product.

Our procedure does not include Individual Firms which are not members of Trade Associations. This is not a great problem as in an Industrial District this kind of firm is a very low percentage. (In Figure 1 they are shown as Black-Hole).

4 The System of Accounts

4.1 Production Accounts and Distribution of Gross Product Account

As it has been said above we are able to evaluate Industrial Gross Product through the integration of CERVED FILE with INPS FILE and the collaboration of the Trade Association. Next step is to analyse the possibility of building - on the only source, the Balance Sheet, - a system of ESA accounts at the same territorial level. We have just shown the overlap (induced by Fourth EEC Directive) of Balance Sheet in the ESA model used by ISTAT to evaluate the Gross Product. Consequently it is possible to construct two accounts:

- Production Account;
- Distribution of Gross Product Account.

To point out the importance of these accounts in the analysis of an Industrial District, we have obtained, as an esercise, the two accounts for the Textile Non Financial Corporations of the provinces of Prato and Biella in the years 1994 and 1995. The data we used are the Balance Sheets of a panel of companies (602 for Prato and 200 for Biella) obtained through the integration of the CERVED FILE with the INPS FILE and CCIAA FILE. (See: Tables 2-5 for Production Account and Table 6-9 for Distribution of Gross Product Account).

Availability of Production and Distribution of Gross Product Account allows us to show the main economic and social features of the two Textile Districts:

1. with an almost equal Gross Product, the levels of Production and General Expenditure (which include the payment for external production) are far higher in Prato than in Biella as result of the decentralized economic organisation of Tuscany Textile Discrict;
2. a stronger incidence of Consumption of Materials in Biella than in Prato (45% against 36%) as result of higher average import prices of wool;
3. a different structure of Gross Product distribution, as a consequence of a widespread micro entrepreneurship in Prato. At the same time, the model of distribution of Biella tends to keep the same pattern as Prato.

Table 2 Production Account for Textile Non Financial Corporations Sector of Prato in 1994 - At current prices *(million lire)*

Uses		%	Resources	
Consumption of raw Materials	1,830,874	36.3	Production	5,040,862
General Expenditure	2,050,988	41.7		
Gross Product at factor cost	1,159,000	23.0		

Table 3 Production Account for Textile Non Financial Corporations Sector of Biella in 1994 - At current prices *(million lire)*

Uses		%	Resources	
Consumption of raw Materials	1,501,394	44.6	Production	3,371,177
General Expenditure	863,894	25.6		
Gross Product at factor cost	1,005,889	29.8		

Table 4 Production Account for Textile Non Financial Corporations Sector of Prato in 1995 - At current prices *(million lire)*

Uses		%	Resources	
Consumption of raw Materials	1,903,328	36.5	Production	5,225,806
General Expenditure	2,089,944	40.0		
Gross Product at factor cost	1,232,535	23.5		

Table 5 Production Account for Textile Non Financial Corporations Sector of Biella in 1995 - At current prices *(million lire)*

Uses		%	Resources	
Consumption of raw Materials	1,802,549	45.8	Production	3,936,077
General Expenditure	958,035	24.3		
Gross Product at factor cost	1,175,493	29.9		

Table 6 Distribution of Gross Product Account for Textile Non Financial Corporations Sector of Prato in 1994 - At current prices (*million lire*)

Uses		%	Resources	
Compensation of employees	595,153	51.3	Gross Product at factor cost	1,159,000
Gross Operating Surplus - of which Consumption of Fixed Capital	563,847 127,160	49.7		

Table 7 Distribution of Gross Product Account for Textile Non Financial Corporations Sector of Biella in 1994 - At current prices (*million lire*)

Uses		%	Resources	
Compensation of employees	579,774	57.6	Gross Product at factor cost	1,005,889
Gross Operating Surplus - of which Consumption of Fixed Capital	426,115 173,083	42.4		

Table 8 Distribution of Gross Product Account for Textile Non Financial Corporations Sector of Prato in 1995 - At current prices (*million lire*)

Uses		%	Resources	
Compensation of employees	631,391	51.2	Gross Product at factor cost	1,232,535
Gross Operating Surplus - of which Consumption of Fixed Capital	601,144 129,986	49.8		

Table 9 Distribution of Gross Product Account for Textile Non Financial Corporations Sector of Biella in 1995 - At current prices (*million lire*)

Uses		%	Resources	
Compensation of employees	637,891	54.2	Gross Product at factor cost	1,175,493
Gross Operating Surplus - of which Consumption of Fixed Capital	537,602 188,489	45.8		

4.2 Capital Account

The construction of the Capital Formation Account appears far less a direct one. In fact, contrary to what happens for production and distribution of Gross Product, in the company Balance Sheet, the flows of Investment and Saving and their financial offsets are not framed in an ESA pattern.

Investment is not shown by Balance Sheet and the same is true for Saving. The loss of information caused by this divergence between Balance Sheet and ESA is quite heavy. At district level, the gap between Saving and Investment cannot be grasped and it is not clear how far the District has been able to feed its Capital formation with its own resources, and, on the other hand, how much it has drawn from other Sectors and different industries.

Due to this "shortfall" of information of Balance Sheet and, on the contrary, the clearness of ESA in describing the whole process of Capital accumulation and its financing, the translation of business accountancy to macroeconomic accounts is fruitful for quantitative analysis of Industrial Districts.

If we extended this work of translation into the process of Redistribution of Income, the importance of this commitment would be more powerful. In fact, it would become clear how the share of Gross Product earned by the company is modified through its activities and liabilities towards banking and insurance systems, General Government and also its employees for the disbursement of Social benefits.

It is important to recall that more than twenty years ago, two Italian statisticians (Cao-Pinna, 1974 and Siesto, 1973) remarked this work of translation of business accountancy into SNA as one of the most fertile topics in the field of a National Accounts.

Given the dramatic difficulties of interpretation of the Balance Sheet, as compared to the Redistribution process, in this paper we do not construct the Income Account.

For modelling Capital Formation Account, we get Investment as a difference between the Stocks of Fixed and Intangible Assets and Inventories of two years supplied by the Asset and Liability Statement.

As, according to recent rules, depreciation is yearly deduced from the value of Fixed Assets, the Investment we obtain through the flows of funds is net.

As regards to Saving it is necessary to remember that in ESA such a flow is provided by identity [1] or, alternately, by identities [2] and [3] (in our case Net Capital Transfers are equal to zero):

$$S \equiv Y - C \tag{1}$$

$$S \equiv I + L \tag{2}$$

$$\Delta AF - \Delta PF \equiv S - I \tag{3}$$

where: S, Y, and C are respectively, Gross National Saving, Gross National Disposable Income and National Consumption. I and L are, respectively, Gross Investment and Balance of Capital Formation Account and (in absolute value) of Financial Account, ΔAF and ΔPF are changes of financial Activities and Liabilities.

Through identity [1], S is the balance of National Income and Consumption. We are not allowed to choose this procedure because, as we have hinted above, the construction of the Income Account via Balance Sheets is quite tricky.

On the basis of identities [2] and [3] and remembering the particular new treatment of depreciation, Saving is obtained as net variation of Worth (defined as the sum of Fixed and Intangible Assets, Inventories and Net Financial Activities).

It is interesting to observe that, as the resulting Investment is net, Saving is net as well. The same effect took place in the Capital Formation Account of Italy before ESA (Ferrari, 1991, pp 129-136).

4.3 Financial Account

As Regards the construction of the Financial Account for an Industrial District, it is necessary to notice the absence of companies on the Stock Exchange. As it happens, at National level, for the Financial Account of Producer Families supplied only by Bank of Italy, also in our case we do not face the problem of the valuation of the Nominal Share Capital of the company. Financial Account can then be formed on the basis of the flows of funds relative to Financial Activities and Liabilities.

Since Balance Sheet supplied by CERVED show a certain aggregation with regards to some Financial Items as compared to the Account of the Bank of Italy, our Financial Account for the sector of companies of the District Industry is much poorer. In fact, Cash and Coins, Sight Deposits and Other Deposits are not available. Furthermore Financial Activities are not divided among Medium and Long Securities and Shares. On the other hand, our Account has an information content which is not without any meaning.

Its most interesting feature is the availability of trade debt, which does not appear in the account of the Bank of Italy, but plays a relevant role in short term finance of Industrial District. Short debt is separated from the long debt and accrued TFR (Retirement Fund) is divided from that of taxes.

Finally, it is necessary to clarify the information content of our Accounts. As for Prato these have been constructed on the basis of the intersection of three FILES and not on the whole of the companies, their structure is more important than their level.

Capital and Financial Account of Textile Non Financial Corporations Sector of Prato and Biella are supplied for years 1994 and 1995 (see: Tables 10-17)

Table 10 Capital Account for Textile Non Financial Corporations Sector of Prato in 1994
– At current Prices *(million lire)*

Changes in Assets		*Changes in Liabilities*	
Net Fixed Capital Formation	25,825	Saving, Net	90,972
Changes in Inventories	153,152		
Changes in Intangible Assets	-1,365		
Net lending(+)/Net borrowing(-)	-86,640		

Table 11 Capital Account for Textile Non Financial Corporations Sector of Biella in 1994
– At current Prices *(million lire)*

Changes in Assets		Changes in Liabilities	
Net Fixed Capital Formation	-7,212	Saving, Net	65,325
Changes in Inventories	193,098		
Changes in Intangible Assets	-7,319		
Net lending(+)/Net borrowing(-)	-113,242		

Table 12 Capital Account for Textile Non Financial Corporations Sector of Prato in 1995
– At current Prices *(million lire)*

Changes in Assets		Changes in Liabilities	
Net Fixed Capital Formation	75,571	Saving, Net	88,404
Changes in Inventories	-21,800		
Changes in Intangible Assets	1,162		
Net lending(+)/Net borrowing(-)	33,471		

Table 13 Capital Account for Textile Non Financial Corporations Sector of Biella in 1995
– At current Prices *(million lire)*

Changes in Assets		Changes in Liabilities	
Net Fixed Capital Formation	61,761	Saving, Net	103,479
Changes in Inventories	105,461		
Changes in Intangible Assets	-1,854		
Net lending(+)/Net borrowing(-)	-61,889		

Table 14 Financial Account for Textile Non Financial Corporations Sector of Prato in 1994 – At current prices *(million lire)*

Changes in Assets		Changes in Liabilities	
Credits (Share Holders)	138	Contingency funds	6,399
Credits (Owned and Shared Companies)	14,307	TFR	11,240
Short and Trade Credits	212,756	Debts	345,515
		Of which:Trade Debts	185,304
		Medium/Long term(Banks)	-990
		Short term (Banks)	153,782
Currency and Sight deposits	39,773	Other Financial Liabilities	-6,208
Other Financial Assets	3,332	Net lending(+)/Net borrowing(-)	-86,640

Table 15 Financial Account for Textile Non Financial Corporations Sector of Biella in 1994 – At current prices *(million lire)*.

Changes in Assets		Changes in Liabilities	
Credits (Share Holders)	1,337	Contingency funds	4,558
Credits (Owned and Shared Companies)	57,885	TFR	9,698
Short and Trade Credits	149,868	Debts	374,878
		Of which:Trade Debts	199,276
		Medium/Long term(Banks)	41,356
		Short term (Banks)	29,841
Currency and Sight deposits	76,147	Other Financial Liabilities	-6,932
Other Financial Assets	-2,413	Net lending(+)/Net borrowing(-)	-113,242

Table 16 Financial Account for Textile Non Financial Corporations Sector of Prato in 1995 – At current prices *(million lire)*

Changes in Assets		Changes in Liabilities	
Credits (Share Holders)	368	Contingency funds	639
Credits (Owned and Shared Companies)	71,947	TFR	14,735
Short and Trade Credits	22,012	Debts	79,120
		Of which:Trade Debts	-57,745
		Medium/Long term(Banks)	38,056
		Short term (Banks)	354
Currency and Sight deposits	18,702	Other Financial Liabilities	-408
Other Financial Assets	14,528	Net lending(+)/Net borrowing(-)	33,471

Table 17 Financial Account for Textile Non Financial Corporations Sector of Biella in 1995 – At current prices *(million lire)*

Changes in Assets		Changes in Liabilities	
Credits (Share Holders)	-1,473	Contingency funds	-2,266
Credits (Owned and Shared Companies)	5,231	TFR	17,782
Short and Trade Credits	82,457	Debts	175,931
		Of which:Trade Debts	67,795
		Medium/Long term(Banks)	48,522
		Short term (Banks)	67,433
Currency and Sight deposits	35,584	Other Financial Liabilities	-1,141
Other Financial Assets	6,618	Net lending(+)/Net borrowing(-)	-61,889

5 Assets Accounts and Production Analysis

Recently, Scafuri (1996) has produced Patrimonial Accounts *à la* Goldsmith for the Italian Private and Public Companies Sector.

At a District level, the formation of the Assets Account for the company Sector might provide important information. Through this particular Balance Sheet of Economy, we are able to know the "economic" value of Assets and so of Net Worth. As it is known, in Assets Account, Capital Goods are registered according to an economic statistic procedure, frequently the method of Perpetual Inventory and Net Worth is affected consequently.

There are two basic reasons that prevent the "passage" from Balance Sheet to the Assets Account, both dependent on the procedure of entering Capital goods in the Asset and Liability Statement:

1. historical costs and therefore the possibility, particularly heavy during inflation periods, of considering equal plants with very different productive capacity;
2. the recent rule of deducing yearly depreciation from Fixed Assets, with the consequence of the total disappearance of the entire value of Capital Good after some years.

In order to overcome these difficulties, it is necessary to resort to the depreciable Assets Book, where the Capital good is recorded according to its Brand Name, date of purchase and the kind of good.

Unlike the Balance Sheet, the Depreciable Assets Book is not public and can be only consulted on permission of the company.

At a District level, some Craftsmen Associations and other Associations of entrepeneurs belonging to different segments of Industry, began to put Files of Depreciable Assets Books on magnetic support.

The same problem of Capital affects the possibility of estimating Cost and Production Functions. Unlike Cost Functions, which use the Personnel outlay as costs, Production Functions directly require the number of employees. In addition to Depreciable Assets Books, we need to integrate Balance Sheets with INPS FILE.

6 Distress Analysis

The evaluation of economic and financial strength of each company and, along as this, the forecast of bankruptcy, represents a fundamental tool, both for banking and analysis of industry.

Regular Monitoring of companies is useful for estimating the eventual loss of jobs caused by failing firms.

Since the late 1960s to the present days, a number of studies have been devoted to assessing one's ability to combine publicly available data with statistical classification techniques in order to predict business failure. Altman (1968) provides stimulus for a number of additional papers.

It is not the aim of our paper to discuss the different statistical techniques for the classification of the companies. For an international survey of business failure classification models, see, for exemple, Altman and Narayanan (1996). In this work, it is more interesting to analize more closely the problems faced by distress analysis at District level. In fact, monitoring of industry, might be biased by a weak approach to the solution of these problems.

A first problem is the widespread presence of marginal companies with Balance Sheets characterized by anomalous items affecting the quality of monitoring.

In order to overcome this inconvenience, it may be profitable to integrate CERVED FILE with INPS FILE. The intersection produces a selection of companies with employees necessarily more organized and structured than those without employees. It is quite intuitive that in this way the weight of "outliers" is strongly reduced. However a complete solution to this problem can be obtained through the use of suitable statistical techniques.

A second problem is the non availability of failed companies Balance Sheets. As a matter of fact, researchers share a striking similarity in their approach to distress prediction. Nearly every study contrasts the profile of failed firms with that of healthier firms, to draw conclusions about the coincident factors of failure. At district level (and for the same Industry) the number of bankrupted companies is usually quite low and the problem is made more difficult due to the strong propensity of distressed companies not to hand over their Balance Sheets. As in many areas of empirical research, the sophistication of the techniques is often non matched by the availability of good data, especially data on failed firms.

In this situation of little accounting information, the problem of classification of firms and forecast of bankruptcy can not be faced with the usually multivariate statistical techniques (discriminant analysis, neural networks, etc.). In this condition, we are compelled to use procedures entirely based on Balance Sheets of healthy companies. Ganugi, Gozzi, (1997), offer a new alternative approach in distress prediction based on Mahalanobis distance from weighted centroids.

At the end of this section devoted to the use of the Balance Sheet FILE in monitoring companies, we want to highlight a promising field of research which can be explored by the integration of different FILES. As through the integration of CERVED FILE with INPS FILE and CCIAA FILE it is possible to get a partition of healthy and failed company Balance Sheets according to age and dimension (measured with the number of employees), the problem of monitoring can be formulated in terms of "location models" (see Krzanowsky, 1988). This statistical model combines the traditional multivariate discriminant analysis function approach within each partition of companies (healthy and failed). Our preliminary application of this model displays a promising discriminant ability.

REFERENCES

Aimetti P. (1995), *"Aspetti metodologici dell'"integrazione di archivi in Italia"*, in Biffignandi S., Martini M. (a cura di) (1995), Il registro statistico europeo delle imprese. Esperienze e metodi per la sua costruzione in Italia. Franco Angeli, Milano.

Altman E. I. (1968), *"Financial ratios, discriminant analysis and the prediction of corporate bankruptcy"*, Journal of Finance, 23, 589-609.

Altman E. I., Narayanan, P. (1996), *Business Failure Classification Models: An International Survey*, New York University Salomon Center, Working Paper Series S-96-34.

Biffignandi S., Martini M.,a cura di, *Il registro statistico europeo delle imprese. Esperienze e metodi per la sua costruzione in Italia*, Franco Angeli, Milano, pp. 239-263.

Billia G. (1993), *"Stato e prospettive delle banche dati dell'INPS"*, Società Italiana di Statistica, Atti del Convegno: La Statistica nel mondo della produzione e dei servizi reali e finanziari, Roma, 25-26 Marzo 1993, Rocco Curto Editore, Napoli.

Cao-Pinna V. (1973), *Bilanci Aziendali e Contabilità Nazionale*, Franco Angeli, Milano.

Ferrari G. (1991), *Introduzione ai sistemi di contabilità nazionale*, Libreria Editrice Courier, Firenze.

Ganugi P., Gozzi G. (1997), *"Il monitoraggio delle imprese in presenza di limitata informazione contabile"*, Società Italiana di Statistica, Atti del Convegno: La Statistica per le imprese, Torino, 2-4 Aprile.

IRPET (1991), *Reddito prodotto e disponibile nei comuni Toscani* – anno 1989, Economia Toscana , n. 5.

ISTAT (1990), *Nuova contabilità nazionale*, Annali di Statistica, Roma.

Krzanowski W. J. (1988) *Principles of Multivariate Analysis: A User's Perspective*, Clarendon Press, Oxford.

Marbach G. (1983), *"Per una stima del reddito e dei consumi delle famiglie italiane"*, in Il reddito dei comuni italiani 1981, Quaderni del Banco di S. Spirito, Vol. I, Utet, Torino.

Paniccia U. (1993), *"La produttività statistica dei dati gestionali"*, Società Italiana di Statistica, Atti del Convegno: La Statistica nel mondo della produzione e dei servizi reali e finanziari, Roma, 25-26 Marzo 1993, Rocco Curto Editore, Napoli.

Predetti A. (1994), *L'informazione economica di base*, Giuffè, Milano.

Scafuri E. (1996), *"The Balance Sheet of Italian Non Financial Enterprises"*, Proceeedings of I.A.R.I.W., Lillehammer.

Siesto, V. (1973), *Teoria e Metodi di Contabilità Nazionale*, Giuffrè, Milano.

EFFICIENCY AND LOCALISATION: THE CASE OF ITALIAN DISTRICTS

S. Fabiani[1], G. Pellegrini[2], E. Romagnano[3] and L.F. Signorini[4]

[1,2,3,4]*Servizio Studi - Banca d'Italia*

1 Introduction

Italy is peculiar among large industrialised countries because of the overwhelming dominance of small firms and traditional sectors in the manufacturing industry. According to one comparison, for example, the textile and clothing industry employs almost a quarter of the manufacturing labour force in Italy, as against 10 per cent in the US, 6 per cent in Japan and 5 per cent in Germany (Signorini and Visco, 1997); also, in 1991 71 per cent of the Italian manufacturing labour force was employed by firms with fewer than 250 employees, as against, say, 38 per cent in Germany, 47 in France, 45 in U.K., 37 in USA (Brusco and Paba, 1997).

This kind of industry and size specialisation makes Italy much more similar to many emerging economies than to the average G-7 country. This has long been considered both a *puzzle* and (to many) a source of *concern*. First of all, why is Italy so different, i.e. what makes such a specialisation efficient, in some sense, for Italy? And, secondly, how can its manufacturing industry ultimately face the double competition of low-cost NICs and hi-tech, large-scale productions in other advanced countries?

The concern has so far proved unfounded. In the long run, Italy has grown more than most other G-7 countries (though, of course, less than many NICs); and small firms have remained, by and large, the most dynamic part of the Italian manufacturing industry. Despite occasional setbacks in some regions and/or industries, their share of the manufacturing labour force has continued to grow, at least, until the latest industrial census. Many light industries, where the predominance of small firms is even more marked than in manufacturing as a whole, have consistently generated trade surpluses, and made a decisive contribution to the substantial surplus of the current-account balance that Italy enjoys since 1993. The day of reckoning may yet come; but, so far, the peculiar industry and size structure of Italy's manufacturing sector has not seriously hindered its development.

Which leaves us with the puzzle about the efficiency of such a structure. To solve it, industrial district theorists have long claimed that looking at firms in isolation may be misleading, and using only industry classifications even more so (see, for instance, Becattini 1990 and Brusco 1986). In certain industries, *internal* economies of scale may be more or less irrelevant beyond a (small) threshold; much more important are the *external* economies produced by the special 'industrial climate' which is said to predominate in certain local agglomerations of small firms, all specialised in one industry and sharing idiosyncratic, community-dependent competitive advantages. Following early descriptions by Marshall, these agglomerations are called industrial districts (ID). In this view, generic statements about 'small firms' or 'traditional sectors' are largely meaningless; it is the interplay between size, industry and location that determines the competitiveness and development potential of industry.

While the early literature on IDs was almost exclusively qualitative and case-based, the more recent literature has also a quantitative dimension. One aspect of this is an attempt to measure the *share* of ID production in the Italian manufacturing industry. This implies the difficult task of specifying which areas qualify as districts in the strict Marshall-Becattini sense. The Sforzi (1990) -Istat (1996) classification is based on local labour systems (LLSs), defined as areas which are more or less closed with respect to daily commuting trips. An LLS is then classified as an industrial district if it meets some criteria (manufacturing vocation, industry specialisation, small firm size, and so on), judgmentally specified in advance by the authors in a way that is compatible, in some general sense, with the qualitative descriptions of IDs usually found in the relevant literature. Sforzi and Istat find that over 40 per cent of Italian manufacturing (measured in terms of labour) is concentrated in industrial districts.

On the other hand, there are very few attempts to measure the size of the supposed *competitive advantages* of IDs with respect to other forms of productive organisations. This is surprising, given the large body of qualitative literature on Italian industrial districts that has amassed over the last two decades, where such an advantage was always assumed but never empirically demonstrated. One of us (Signorini, 1994) has tried to measure an 'industrial district effect' in one specific instance (the wool textile industry), by comparing several measures of performance between district and non-district firms in this industry. We are aware of no comprehensive quantitative study of the existence and size of 'district effects' in Italy.

This paper (which is part of a wider Bank of Italy research project on regional and local development) makes a first attempt at such a comprehensive study. Basically, using the Centrale dei Bilanci database, we take balance-sheet data on about 10,900 small and medium-sized firms belonging to all branches of the manufacturing industry and all regions of Italy. We classify each firm as ID or non-ID ("isolated"), on the basis of the Sforzi-Istat map, with a compex matching procedure based on the postal code of each firm. We compare a number of key firm-level characteristics in ID and isolated firms. The methodology adopted for the identification of ID firms and the construction of the database are presented in Section 2.

The main object of analysis is the economic efficiency of industrial districts production. If ID external economies exist, they should be detectable in some measures of productivity and/or profitability. As a first step, in Section 3 we try to detect the 'district' effect from balance-sheet data, on profitability as well as on some key variables which can be   influenced by the characteristics of the organisation of the productive process in IDs (high labour quality and hence cost, capital stock, cost of credit). The data mainly refer to 1995, although for some particularly relevant variables we present evidence for the period 1982-1995.

The results on productivity and profitability are striking. In almost each industry considered, both appear to be considerably higher for ID firms. To investigate the efficiency effect in a rigorous framework, in Section 4 we estimate industry-level stochastic frontier production functions, with random inefficiency terms which are assumed to depend, among other things, on whether a firm belongs to an ID or not. The estimation is based on balanced panels covering the period 1991-1995. Being in a district generally improves technical efficiency (closeness to the frontier) of the firm in a strongly significant way. The few cases where this does not occur in a sense reinforce the result, as they are related to industries (such as transportation equipment and chemicals productions) where districts are known to be largely irrelevant.

2 The matching between firm and district: some methodological problems

There are two main problems that have hindered the quantification of district effects: the spatial identification of the district area and the evaluation of the industrial structure in the district.

The concept of industrial district is well defined in the Italian economic literature: a district is a local agglomeration of small and medium sized independent firms, all specialised in one industry, and enjoying idiosyncratic, community-dependent externalities. Unfortunately, this definition does not lead to a clear, unique way to assess whether an agglomeration of firms in a limited area is an industrial district or not, and which are its precise boundaries. Recently, Sforzi (1990) and Istat (1996) have proposed a statistical approach for the identification of districts, based on a complex multi-step procedure[1]. The methodology is based on the so-called "sistemi locali del lavoro" (local labour systems, LLS): the Italian territory is partitioned in 784 LLSs, i.e. groups of neighbouring municipalities (comuni), joined together on the basis of the degree

---

[1] For a detailed description of the procedure see also Brusco and Paba (1997) and Appendix 1 in Baffigi, Pagnini and Quintiliani (1997).

of daily-commuting by the local population due to work reasons, estimated using the Population Census of 1991. Each LLS is defined as an ID if (1) it is more industrialised than the average (i.e. the share of workers in the manufacturing sector is greater than the national share); (2) it is specialised in a manufacturing sector; (3) there is a high concentration of employment in small-medium sized productive plants (with no more than 250 employees). We have chosen the results of this procedure as a basis for our analysis.

The Sforzi-Istat criteria lead to the identification of 199 industrial districts for 1991, with 42,5 per cent of the total labour force in manufacturing. Clearly, the procedure adopted can be criticised from several points of view: for instance, the method is quite mechanical, and it does not consider the social environment in which firms are involved; all the big and medium sized cities are excluded, because of the high share of employment in services (Brusco and Paba, 1997); specialisation may not be well captured by only one sector (if there is vertical specialisation, like the case of the production of shoes and of machinery for shoes industry). On the other side, the methodology is not only close to the concept of ID proposed by Becattini, but also it is widely adopted in the recent quantitative analyses of districts.[2]

The identification of the structure of the district would require data on the location of single production plants and on their productive characteristics (production, workers, capital stock, financial variables). However, this information is available only at the firm level. Moreover, data on productive activity are produced by Istat or other agencies only at the regional or provincial level, that is, too aggregate to capture the distinctive features of IDs. Therefore, the analysis must be based on enterprise micro data, aggregated by districts.

The collection of micro data at the district level is not an easy task. An approach used in a stream of recent studies (for example, Brusco and Bigarelli, 1997) is to collect data by interviewing relevant actors in the district specialisation field. The problem is that this kind of analysis is clearly limited both in the extension and the statistical significance of the sample, and in the amount of quantitative information that can be collected. Another approach, experimented only in Signorini (1994), is to use a large enterprise database, like Centrale dei Bilanci, and select the firms that belong to districts. The problem is how to identify such firms. Signorini considers all the firms operating in a specific province in the specialisation sector of the main district in the same province (in the specific case, Firenze for the Prato wool district) as district firms. However, this approach cannot be generalised, for two main reasons: first, the district map does not overlap with the provincial one, because several districts belong to more than one province; second, as we noted before, several district firms produce in sectors that differ from the one in which they are specialised. Therefore, as a first approach, we decided to aggregate all the small and medium sized firms (with no more than 250 employees) in local labour markets, and to

---

[2] See Brusco and Paba (1997), Baffigi, Pagnini and Quintiliani (1997).

identify as district firms all the ones that are in a local labour market defined as an ID.

This approach does not completely solve the problem. Firms located in a district may produce goods that are not related to the district specialisation. For example, transport vehicle firms producing in Prato wood district. Our prior is that this specific problem is not so important, for a double reason: first, the share of firms producing in sectors that are not related to the district specialisation is lower than the average, because of the statistical definition of district; second, the favourable socio-economical environment originated by the district is enjoyed by all the firms located in the district area. However, the distortion can be relevant in sectors where the share of correctly defined district firms is low, like in chemicals, transport vehicles, paper, electrical equipment.

The selection, for each district, of the firms producing goods which are related to the district specialisation is quite complex, and we are planning to present some results in this direction in a new version of the paper. A safe approach could be to consider only the sectors in which the share of district firms is overwhelming (i.e. textile, leather industries, wood, mechanical equipment). For this reason, our results are always disaggregated by sector.

The aggregation of firms in local labour systems cannot be carried out using the denomination of the municipality. In administrative databases, the name of several municipalities can be written in different ways (with abbreviations, blank inside, small differences), and it is not possible to correct or homogenise the data. The approach we have developed to overcome this problem is to use the postal code, that differs by municipality.[3] This is a numeric code of five figures and therefore it is less prone to typing and other kind of errors. We performed a double check by postal code and denomination of the municipality, that allowed to solve most of the ambiguous cases.

The information by firm is drawn from the Centrale dei Bilanci company account database (CB).[4] CB covers about 30,000 firms in all sectors of the Italian economy. It is not by any means a statistical sample, because the selection criteria are not rigorously defined (Cannari, Pellegrini and Sestito, 1996). The coverage decreases with size: with respect to the Census of 1991, CB covers 16 per cent of the firms with more than 9 workers (45 per cent of total workers), but only 6 per cent of the firms with more than 10 and less than 19 workers. Considering the core of the firms analysed in this paper (20-99), the coverage is more than one quarter (28 per cent of the firms, 29 per cent of workers).

The sample is likely to be statistically representative of the small and medium sized firms, if there are no other important sources of distortion apart from the size of the distribution itself. Since firms are originally chosen by CB if they have multiple relations with the bank system, it is plausible that the more efficient

---

[3] Only in the big cities the postal code can be different by groups of streets.

[4] For more information on Centrale dei Bilanci see Centrale dei Bilanci (1991), Signorini (1994),Cannari, Pellegrini and Sestito (1996).

firms are overrepresented in the sample. This bias should not affect district and non district firms. However, the distortion being stronger among small firms, we decided to separate the results obtained for small firms (10-19 workers) from the others.

3 The difference between district and non district firms: some descriptive evidence

This section presents some empirical evidence on the differences in the real and financial structure of firms located in a district versus firms not located in a district.

The analysis is based on the firms sampled in the CB database. The use of company accounts for economic analysis is always troublesome: not only because the accounting of some variables (like sales, expenses, fixed assets) can be modified by tax rules and fiscal contingencies, but also because exceptional events, mistakes in reporting, errors in filling and editing the balance sheet can affect the registered firm accounts. A way to deal with the problem is to introduce tests for excluding clear errors and extreme values. However, this approach suffers from the fact that the selection of the boundaries is arbitrary, and different boundaries lead to different results. Therefore, we used a two-step approach: first, we excluded all the firms with signals of potential troubles in the balance sheet. We choose only firms with more than 9 workers, with a complete balance sheet in the year, not affected by mergers or acquisitions, with employment, production, capital stock, value added, revenues and net assets greater than one. Second, we calculated a synthetic indicator using the median, that is a more robust statistic estimator that the mean in presence of outliers. Being interested in industrial districts, we selected firms in sectors that are involved, even if partially, in this phenomenon. Therefore, we considered only the manufacturing sector, without the energy and mining industry.

In 1995 (latest year for which complete information is available in the CB database) we sampled 10,939 firms, 70 per cent of which in the 20-99 class, 21 per cent in the 100-250 class and the others in the 10-19 class. The details are in table A1 in the Annex. The highest shares are in the machinery industry (15 per cent), in textile (14), in the electric and electronic industry (13), in the food and beverage industry (11); the lowest share is in the wood industry (2 per cent).

Of 10,939 firms, 6,389 (58 per cent) are in a district (table A2 in the Annex). They employ the 57 per cent of the 747,000 workers in the sampled firms. The ID firms are concentrated in the 20-99 class (71 per cent of district firms, 42 of the whole sample). Moreover, they have a lower average size than the non-ID firms (67 versus 70 average workers). The share of ID firms is higher than 60 per cent in the textile, leather, wood, mechanical equipment and other manufacturing sectors. Also in the Istat data for the 1991 the share of employment in district firms is particularly high in these sectors.[5] The share of ID firms is lower than 45 per cent only in paper and printing, chemicals, transport vehicles.

The empirical analysis of the district effect is based on three main aspects: profitability, cost of labour and labour productivity, financial costs.

The positive externalities in the district could increase the profitability of firms with respect to the non district ones. This is clearly the case in our sample, where the profitability indicators show always higher values in districts, for each dimensional class and sector (tables 1-3). The profitability is measured by return on investment (ROI), return on equity (ROE) and the share of gross operating profits on value added. On average, in 1995, ROI is higher in district firms by two points, ROE by more than four points, the share of profits by two and a half points. Only large firms in few sectors (food, wood, transport) show higher profitability in non district areas.

The results obtained for 1995 are not a cyclical coincidence: figures 1 and 2 show that profitability has been higher in district firms always from 1982 to 1995. Moreover, there are signals that the size of the gap is procyclical in favour of ID firms.

The higher profitability can derive from efficiency gains (higher productivity), from lower costs, or both. The efficiency analysis is presented in the next section. As a first step, a simple, rough measure of labour productivity (per capita revenues) shows a slightly higher value in district firms (table 4). This is confirmed in all sectors but the wood one, in which it is true only for small and medium sized firms.

A high profit share could be due to low per capita labour cost. Actually, if human capital is higher and more sector-specific in district firms, one expects wage to be higher in such firms. The empirical evidence is not so clear cut: in the whole manufacturing sector, per capita labour costs are lower in district firms (table 5), and this is always true from 1982 to 1995 (figure 2). Probably, the higher share of small and medium sized firms in districts can affect the level of wages. However, in sectors like food, textile, leather, plastic product, non metallic mineral product, where the presence of district firms is strongly relevant, the labour costs are higher.

Higher gross profits could not be translated in higher net profit if the share of capital is large. Per capita gross fixed assets are on average lower in district firms, even if there are strong differences across sectors (table 6).

Another factor that can reduce the importance of a higher share of gross profits in IDs is the cost of debt. In the whole sample, the weight of interest on financial debts on operating revenues is lower for the medium and large sized district firms (table 7). This is partially due to a slightly lower cost of debt (table 8), that is affected by the stronger social relationships and the higher social knowledge in the district environment.

---

[5] Baffigi, Pagnini and Quintiliani (1997).

The overall results deriving from the descriptive analysis confirm that district firms are more profitable than non district ones. This is due to higher productivity, but also to slightly lower cost of labour and capital. Anyway, the dominant district effect seems to arise from efficiency: this is the issue considered in the next section.

4 Technical efficiency and industrial districts

4.1 Modelling and measuring firms' efficiency

Firms' performance can differ across district and non-district firms and across industries for various reasons. For example, they may use different technologies or operate at different scales. Even allowing for such differences, however, there may still be considerable gaps in the quantity of output firms can produce from the same level of inputs. The failure to produce the maximum possible output for any chosen combination of inputs is denoted in the literature as technical inefficiency. This concept embodies also the sources of inefficiency arising from the managerial and organisational structure and the socio-economic environment in which firms operate.

This section aims at capturing the presence of district effects on the productive performance of firms. In principle, such effects, due to the externalities arising from the organisation of the labour market, the diffusion of knowledge and the social environment favouring integration among small and medium sized firms, should reflect in a higher technical efficiency with respect to firms that are not located in districts. The major problem involved in the evaluation of such effects lies in the possibility of isolating them from the multiplicity of other factors that can influence firms' efficiency, and in the related choice of the model and of the estimation method.

The literature on Italian IDs is mostly qualitative and it presents quite few attempts to measure localisation effects on firms' economic or financial perfomance. Signorini (1994) provides one of the first quantitative tests of the predictions of district theory, focused on the Italian wool textile industry, finding that the productivity of firms located in districts is significantly higher than elsewhere. His approach for isolating localisation factors is based on the cross-section estimation of a production function that includes district dummies (both in level and interacted with factors' coefficients) among the variables explaining output. This method, based on ordinary least squares, does not allow to capture the presence of firm specific fixed effects and time effects in the structure of production, which could instead be investigated by applying standard econometric techniques on panel data. Moreover, the approach, by including the variables that may affect technical efficiency among the factors of the production function, does not allow to explicitly model efficiency itself and hence to evaluate which are the main determinants of more or less efficient performances.

In order to overcome these drawbacks, the method adopted in this work for the evaluation of the productive performance of ID firms as compared to non-ID ones is based on recent developments of the theoretical and empirical literature on technical inefficiency.[6] The crucial issue in this approach is the definition of 'efficiency', that is, the frontier or best-practice technique. This can be either based on the theoretical construct of a production function, or expressed in terms of the best performances actually observed within a sector or an industry. As a reflection, the statistical methods for the analysis of efficiency can be classified under two different categories: parametric and nonparametric.

The first is based on the formalisation of a frontier production function, with respect to which individual inefficiencies are defined as a residual, either deterministic or stochastic. In the latter case, such a residual is assumed to comprise two independent elements, a symmetrical random one, as it is quite common in economic behavioural relations, and an asymmetrical one, explicitly due to technical inefficiency. This second term has mean greater than zero because each firm has to lie on or below the frontier after allowing for purely random disturbances. The solution of the model requires, in order to obtain consistent and efficient estimates, the specification of the distribution of both residual components.

The alternative non-parametric approach does not require the choice of a particular functional form for the production function. The computation of the frontier is based on the most efficient units - the ones with the highest level of production for a given combination of inputs or with the lowest use of inputs for a given level of output - using linear programming techniques or simple comparisons of data. Efficiency is then measured as the distance from the frontier.[7]

It is quite difficult to assess with certainty which approach and statistical technique perform better. The empirical evidence provided by the literature varies according to the choice of the measurement of technical inefficiency, of the definition of the variables to be included, of the form of the production function and of the method for evaluating inefficiency. Overall, non-parametric methods, despite being very sensitive to the presence of outliers, are statistically robust to the choice of the model. Conversely, parametric methods have the advantage of providing an economic interpretation for the coefficients of the frontier production function, and hence a theoretical framework for the analysis of

---

[6] See, among others, Jondrow, Lovell, Materov and Schmidt (1982), Battese and Coelli (1988, 1995).

[7] The most widely used methods for this purpose are FDH (Free Disposable Hull) and DEA (Data Envelopment Analysis), where the latter requires the assumption of a convex set of attainable input-output combinations. See Farrell (1957), Deprins, Simar and Tulkens (1984), Deprins and Simar (1989), Tulkens (1993).

efficiency. Moreover, unlike non-parametric techniques, they allow for high variation across firms due to random non-identifiable reasons, hence avoiding to consider as "best" some unusually large outlier. However, they depend on the assumptions concerning the functional form of the stochastic frontier and the distribution of the residual component due to inefficency.

For the analysis presented here we choose, as a first approach, to investigate the relevance of localisation effects on efficiency using parametric techniques on panel data, which provide evidence on the production process across firms and over time.[8] The basic model for panel data can be written as:

$$y_{it} = \beta'x_{it} + v_{it} - u_{it} \qquad\qquad [1]$$

where y_{it} denotes the production of the ith firm at time t (i=1,...,N; t=1,...,T), x_{it} is a vector of inputs and other explanatory variables associated with the ith firm at the tth observation, β is a vector of unknown parameters. v_{it} and u_{it} are two residual independent components, the former being a purely random term and the latter a non-negative one which reflects inefficiency with respect to the frontier. The estimation of the model requires precise assumptions on the distribution of the two residual components. Although the central limit theorem can be invoked in order to assume that v_{it} is iid $N(0,\sigma^2_v)$, the choice of the distribution of the one-sided component u_{it} is quite crucial. In the literature, the truncated normal, the normal, the exponential and the gamma are the most commonly adopted distributions.

The specification allows to investigate the factors underlying technical inefficiency.[9] Battese and Coelli (1995) propose a model in which u_{it} is assumed to be independently distributed as truncation at zero of a normal distribution with variance σ^2_u and mean $m_{it} = z_{it}\delta$, where z_{it} is a vector of variables that influence individual inefficiencies and δ a vector of unknown parameters. The model can be estimated simultaneously by maximum likelihood methods, which, despite being based on nonlinear optimisation techniques and hence quite complex, provide efficient estimates of the parameters of interest. The likelihood function to be maximised is expressed in terms of the variance parameters $\sigma^2=\sigma^2_v+\sigma^2_u$ and $\gamma=\sigma^2_u/\sigma^2$, and the predicted measures of inefficiency, which take a value between zero and one, are derived as:

---

[8] When the analysis is carried out on cross-sectional data, the estimates of individual efficiency measures are based on only one observation and hence have uncertain statistical properties.

[9] Until recent developments of the literature (Battese and Coelli, 1995), applied works on stochastic frontier production functions have dealt with this issue mainly by adopting a two-stage approach in which the inefficiency effects predicted in the first step are regressed, in the second step, against some explanatory variables.

$$EFF_i = \frac{E(y_i|u_i,x_i)}{E(y_i|u_i = 0,x_i)} \qquad [2]$$

which depend on the conditional probability function $f(u_i|v_i - u_i)$ and hence on the joint distribution assumed for $(u_i, v_i\text{-}u_i)$.[10] The estimated value and the significance of the parameter γ allow to assess whether a stochastic frontier production function is required at all. The acceptance of the null hypothesis that the true value of the parameter equals zero implies that σ^2_u is zero and hence that the inefficiency term should be removed from the model.

4.2 Efficiency in Italian manufacturing firms and localisation effects: some results

The econometric analysis focuses on 13 manufacturing industries (the ones considered in the previous section). The balanced panel selected for each industry, drawn from the CB database for the period 1991-1995 applying the same filtering rules as the ones described above, contains a varying number of firms and of ID and non-ID firms, as described in the following table:

The panel selected for each sector and its composition (1991-1995)

MANUFACTURING SECTOR	TOTAL	DISTRICT	NON-DISTRICT
Food, beverages and tobacco	724	350	374
Textile	1025	772	253
Leather industries	339	274	65
Wood and wood products	150	107	43
Paper, paper products, printing and publishing	413	193	220
Chemicals	394	168	226
Rubber and plastic products	407	255	152
Non-metallic mineral products	449	238	211
Metal and metal products	949	585	364
Mechanical equipment	878	541	337
Electrical equipment	440	231	209
Transport (vehicles)	134	58	76
Other manufacturing	385	284	101

For each of these industries the following stochastic frontier production function, specified as a Cobb-Douglas, is estimated:

---

[10] The expressions for the conditional expectations, given the assumptions of the model, are presented in Battese and Coelli (1993).

$$\ln(y_{it}) = \beta_0 + \beta_1 \ln(labour_{it}) + \beta_2 \ln(capital_{it}) + v_{it} + u_{it}, \qquad [3]$$

where y indicates value added, *labour* the numer of employees, *capital* the value of fixed assets net of depreciation, v_{it} iid $N(0, \sigma_v^2)$, and the technical inefficiency effects u are specified as:

$$u_{it} = \delta_0 + \delta_1(district_{it}) + \delta_2(year_{it}) + \omega_{it}, \qquad [4]$$

with *year* indicating the year of the observation involved and *district* taking the value one if the firm belongs to a district and zero otherwise. These two variables allow inefficiency to vary linearly with respect to time and to depend on the firm being located in a district or not. The expected sign of both coefficients is negative, meaning that district firms are expected to be less inefficient and that, in general, their inefficiency is expected to decrease with time.

For the industries where the above specification is rejected by the data and by tests of the skewness of the residuals, a different and simpler model is estimated, in which the inefficency random component is not explicitly modelled as a function of the variables considered in this work. In this case, the specification allows for the presence of individual inefficiency effects which are assumed to be distributed as truncated normal random variables and also permitted to vary systematically over time:

$$\ln(y_{it}) = \beta_0 + \beta_1 \ln(labour_{it}) + \beta_2 \ln(capital_{it}) + (v_{it} - u_{it}), \qquad [5]$$

$$v_{it} \text{ iid } N(0, \sigma_v^2),$$

$$u_{it} = u_i \exp(-\eta(t - T)) \text{ and } u_i \text{ iid } N^+(\mu, \sigma_u^2).$$

In this case, the correlation between the time varying estimated measures of technical inefficiency and the district dummy can be computed to investigate whether district economies are somehow related to firms' performance in the industries of interest.

The maximum likelihood estimates, the standard errors and the variance parameters, obtained using an updated version of the computer program FRONTIER developed by Coelli (1992) are presented in Tables 9 and 10. The results show that, for 8 out of the 13 industries considered in the analysis, the fact that a firm is located in an ID significantly improves its efficiency with respect to the frontier production function. The industries in which this phenomenon seems to be particulary relevant are the ones predicted by theoretical and qualitative studies on industrial districts, i.e. the light manufacturing sectors such as textile, leather, wood, rubber and plastic products. The few cases where this does not occur, and the parameter of interest is either significant but with the wrong sign or not significantly different from zero, in a sense reinforce the result, as they are related to industries (such as transportation and electrical equipment, paper and paper products, chemicals productions) where districts are known to be largely irrelevant.

5 Conclusions

The results of this work suggest that the external economies enjoied by firms located in industrial districts can be quantified and measured in a precise way. The 'district effect' on the profitability of ID firms is strongly evident by sector, dimension and also year, and it can be evaluated, on average, around two to four percentage points. The econometric analysis shows that this effect has a relevant impact on technical efficiency: this seems to be the main channel of transmission of external economies to firms' profitability.

We presume that these results are quite robust: they are stronger in sectors characterized by a stronger presence of industrial districts. Further investigation could, however, improve the database used and, in particular, remove some noise in the data. Firstly, the definition of ID firms used here is debatable, as we classify firms only on the basis of location, regardless of product specialisation. Districts are, by definition, strongly specialised; while it may be argued that some district economies are likely to spill-over to non-specialised local firms, they are probably more relevant for core-industry firms. We suspect that some of the less easily interpretable results in this paper may be due to problem of classification, especially in non-ID-intensive industries. Thus, for a future extension of this research we plan to see what happens if an alternative classification (one which makes reference to industry as well as location) is employed.

Secondly, it may be useful to enrich the strictly dichotomous classification of local system as either districts or non-districts; moreover, the Sforzi-Istat classification used here is based on certain quantitative thresholds which, though reasonable, are unavoidably arbitrary to some extent. One possible line of research is to employ alternative, possibly non-dichotomous, classifications of local systems, to see whether our results are robust to changes in the operational definition of districts. Another is to include in the analysis interactions between observable characteristics of the local structure (such as the Census data on which the Sforzi-Istat classification is based) and the broad geographical area in which a local system is located (such as Northwest, Northeast, South, etc.), to account for some idiosyncratic features of local economic and social interactions. Related research (see e.g. Cannari-Signorini, 1997, on the informative advantages of locally based banks in loan contracts) suggests that informal networks and information flows between small firms and other agents may work very differently in different contexts. Still another line of research would decompose, so to speak, the district effect into the separate effects of various characteristics of the local economic structure (such as average firm size, share of manufacturing, industry specialisation, pure agglomeration effects, and so on), to identify the factors, or combinations of factors, that mostly contribute to the competitive edge of districts.

This paper is therefore a progress report along an ongoing research project. However, we feel that the main results presented here are sufficiently clear-cut and robust to provide a first significant and broad-based empirical corroboration to the vast qualitative literature on industrial districts: which, in our opinion, much needed it.

Figure 1 Return on investment (ROI) and return equity (ROE) in ID and non-ID firms

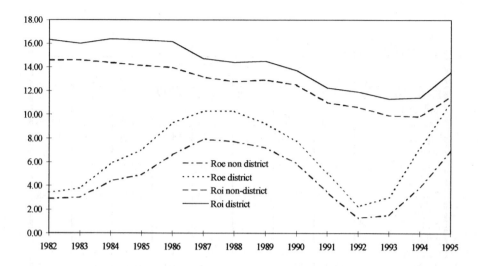

Figure 2 Gross operating margin/value added and per capita labour costs in ID and non-ID firms

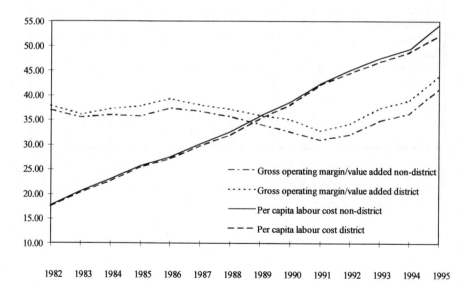

Table 1 Return on investment - 1995

Manufacturing Sector	Non-district				District			
	10-19	20-99	100-250	Total	10-19	20-99	100-250	Total
Food, beverages and tobacco	9.38	8.31	7.88	8.43	11.17	9.73	8.62	9.65
Textile	13.08	11.53	9.79	11.36	16.71	13.69	10.93	13.29
Leather industries	13.86	13.70	12.52	13.78	14.20	15.29	13.87	14.59
Wood and wood products	13.76	11.72	13.14	12.10	10.25	12.47	10.42	12.24
Paper, paper products, printing and publ.	14.70	11.98	9.42	11.74	18.74	13.88	13.34	13.88
Chemicals	14.85	11.96	8.55	8.27	14.12	13.53	8.94	8.82
Rubber and plastic products	16.30	13.66	13.48	13.78	21.18	16.01	15.38	16.07
Non-metallic mineral products	10.25	8.85	8.45	8.88	14.05	11.79	10.69	11.78
Metal and metal products	16.83	14.90	11.96	14.52	19.82	15.59	14.87	15.55
Mechanical equipment	21.97	13.77	12.81	13.67	18.59	15.40	13.95	15.19
Electrical equipment	16.80	12.18	9.92	11.98	19.08	14.38	13.08	14.44
Transport (vehicles)	9.92	14.83	14.78	14.48	13.93	14.88	14.56	14.56
Other manufacturing	10.62	10.70	13.21	10.91	10.62	11.36	11.24	11.28
Total	12.77	11.71	10.56	11.55	15.25	13.66	12.39	13.54

Table 2 Return on equity - 1995

Manufacturing Sector	Non-district				District			
	10-19	20-99	100-250	Total	10-19	20-99	100-250	Total
Food, beverages and tobacco '	2.01	2.54	1.89	2.40	7.33	4.23	3.69	4.37
Textile	4.90	6.39	6.23	6.23	10.69	10.26	7.15	9.46
Leather industries	16.17	10.37	6.43	10.12	13.33	12.25	9.79	11.48
Wood and wood products	15.11	7.56	5.64	6.92	2.67	8.62	5.05	7.78
Paper, paper products, printing and publ.	9.55	5.83	4.55	5.82	13.46	13.08	14.07	13.52
Chemicals	11.38	5.99	6.22	6.36	7.88	12.59	3.08	10.91
Rubber and plastic products	7.24	9.43	15.40	11.02	16.51	16.89	18.08	16.91
Non-metallic mineral products	3.37	2.22	3.74	2.34	15.57	6.86	9.01	7.89
Metal and metal products	13.84	12.77	9.10	11.70	19.72	15.07	17.44	15.98
Mechanical equipment	10.59	11.26	9.18	10.11	16.50	12.70	12.38	12.73
Electrical equipment	9.53	8.93	7.12	8.29	24.65	11.84	14.45	12.94
Transport (vehicles)	6.34	12.53	14.49	12.56	4.64	16.17	13.70	14.44
Other manufacturing	5.12	6.27	9.77	6.73	3.58	4.14	9.60	4.58
Total	6.36	6.89	7.04	6.90	11.15	11.12	10.41	11.01

Table 3 Gross operating profits/value added - 1995

Manufacturing Sector	Non district				District			
	10-19	20-99	100-250	Total	10-19	20-99	100-250	Total
Food, beverages and tobacco	53.81	44.39	39.62	45.35	56.89	48.00	38.22	47.92
Textile	64.11	44.23	34.45	44.61	61.89	46.85	36.18	46.52
Leather industries	54.87	41.84	26.20	40.42	58.47	43.39	37.16	44.05
Wood and wood products	66.56	47.32	44.75	49.63	64.01	47.60	40.51	47.31
Paper, paper products, printing and publ.	57.11	39.52	30.18	39.52	60.81	47.52	44.17	48.20
Chemicals	60.36	45.46	35.53	45.32	57.11	48.20	39.13	46.89
Rubber and plastic products	56.36	44.10	39.00	43.96	62.98	46.98	40.95	46.82
Non-metallic mineral products	49.61	42.94	36.92	42.42	65.54	43.82	33.13	42.83
Metal and metal products	60.61	42.94	33.82	42.85	61.25	45.06	41.66	45.13
Mechanical equipment	53.97	35.77	32.91	35.78	52.22	38.39	34.88	37.92
Electrical equipment	59.20	38.64	29.14	37.66	60.87	39.88	39.55	40.44
Transport (vehicles)	33.72	36.37	37.19	36.95	33.93	41.20	36.57	40.02
Other manufacturing	54.22	38.94	34.80	38.96	53.77	40.54	35.95	40.53
Total	57.29	41.77	34.64	41.40	59.15	44.18	38.15	44.03

Table 4 Per capita revenues - 1995

Manufacturing Sector	Non district				District			
	10-19	20-99	100-250	Total	10-19	20-99	100-250	Total
Food, beverages and tobacco	914.30	523.29	442.27	565.19	944.10	567.14	591.23	616.81
Textile	959.57	355.32	217.11	346.90	815.92	376.95	228.55	376.95
Leather industries	653.93	385.37	208.08	386.11	755.31	427.56	248.34	437.64
Wood and wood products	723.42	326.07	259.66	366.01	649.30	343.50	305.02	345.67
Paper, paper products, printing and publ.	812.90	348.73	294.86	369.93	819.06	385.94	358.33	402.87
Chemicals	690.43	436.72	378.15	454.32	727.80	496.66	480.17	523.82
Rubber and plastic products	628.97	343.31	284.75	349.30	1054.88	381.57	319.29	381.01
Non-metallic mineral products	634.00	274.23	290.25	285.64	573.56	325.02	253.40	314.60
Metal and metal products	880.00	326.80	259.48	335.15	831.54	333.98	292.60	339.99
Mechanical equipment	672.56	320.24	260.28	312.31	831.23	321.54	287.74	318.71
Electrical equipment	725.05	301.86	262.29	301.81	893.02	317.00	283.07	323.44
Transport (vehicles)	639.17	283.44	260.87	285.64	1266.79	301.49	282.79	301.49
Other manufacturing	780.73	288.52	291.10	291.50	887.80	291.95	303.18	308.37
Total	783.52	350.69	282.92	359.77	838.29	358.51	290.18	364.85

Table 5 Per capita labour costs - 1995

Manufacturing Sector	Non district				District			
	10-19	20-99	100-250	Total	10-19	20-99	100-250	Total
Food, beverages and tobacco	50.43	51.41	57.35	51.63	56.14	54.48	60.35	55.26
Textile	48.07	46.02	46.00	46.06	51.46	47.25	47.42	47.63
Leather industries	47.68	42.56	43.60	43.22	44.79	43.82	42.86	43.83
Wood and wood products	44.93	45.37	46.84	45.61	43.80	44.86	50.60	45.10
Paper, paper products, printing and publ.	60.62	56.75	62.91	57.82	49.00	53.34	57.82	53.77
Chemicals	61.22	64.62	72.39	66.81	64.35	59.03	69.52	61.34
Rubber and plastic products	45.30	50.43	55.87	51.24	53.34	51.14	54.42	51.64
Non-metallic mineral products	57.00	51.94	61.39	54.53	55.95	56.74	57.57	56.81
Metal and metal products	51.79	54.11	58.30	54.83	53.05	53.98	58.18	54.58
Mechanical equipment	56.16	59.43	60.69	59.94	52.88	57.08	59.32	57.41
Electrical equipment	58.18	57.06	59.79	57.53	61.13	51.23	54.53	52.09
Transport (vehicles)	55.90	48.88	55.30	51.64	47.67	50.34	51.15	50.48
Other manufacturing	48.68	46.21	47.96	46.86	45.93	42.80	46.89	43.80
Total	52.66	53.28	58.04	54.25	51.58	51.62	54.37	52.17

Table 6 Per capita gross capital - 1995

Manufacturing Sector	Non district				District			
	10-19	20-99	100-250	Total	10-19	20-99	100-250	Total
Food, beverages and tobacco	259.30	211.40	203.94	215.64	236.22	204.93	194.82	206.36
Textile	86.31	95.78	100.33	95.86	63.60	104.88	111.70	99.95
Leather industries	66.52	63.25	46.39	63.20	65.85	60.83	56.38	60.62
Wood and wood products	107.96	122.93	99.69	109.32	184.29	114.14	124.76	118.18
Paper, paper products, printing and publ.	93.75	132.34	154.13	132.06	216.37	166.51	211.28	172.72
Chemicals	176.34	157.90	148.08	156.78	185.10	167.25	163.38	168.90
Rubber and plastic products	137.21	144.90	163.98	146.40	183.75	140.57	176.10	146.34
Non-metallic mineral products	213.14	199.23	188.05	198.39	174.40	170.35	143.53	165.84
Metal and metal products	163.78	139.79	129.68	139.66	195.69	141.04	142.72	142.81
Mechanical equipment	78.24	86.00	101.33	89.03	102.38	82.01	97.59	86.88
Electrical equipment	61.46	74.69	93.80	80.77	91.58	78.95	105.60	85.68
Transport (vehicles)	70.00	90.11	103.38	92.95	76.61	102.39	109.26	95.95
Other manufacturing	105.59	89.76	86.10	89.52	95.21	85.73	112.35	88.80
Total	138.40	123.58	124.86	124.88	126.98	115.92	123.58	118.29

Table 7 Financial debt/gross operating profits - 1995

Manufacturing Sector	Non district				District			
	10-19	20-99	100-250	Total	10-19	20-99	100-250	Total
Food, beverages and tobacco	46.59	37.52	40.92	38.60	37.98	35.47	43.15	36.73
Textile	48.15	40.19	33.42	39.95	39.59	32.45	31.81	33.11
Leather industries	39.49	29.91	41.69	32.98	48.36	37.27	26.66	37.27
Wood and wood products	43.26	39.60	53.96	40.63	58.89	37.61	28.58	37.61
Paper, paper products, printing and publ.	28.32	28.28	33.74	29.98	27.83	25.13	19.71	23.48
Chemicals	24.98	29.53	27.56	28.69	23.39	22.50	30.16	24.79
Rubber and plastic products	49.83	26.95	18.08	26.14	19.77	25.64	21.58	25.16
Non-metallic mineral products	55.96	30.80	29.51	30.96	20.76	26.33	24.58	25.68
Metal and metal products	27.31	27.70	33.64	29.04	28.36	25.04	21.87	24.69
Mechanical equipment	31.84	27.02	30.29	27.94	37.00	27.93	26.89	28.03
Electrical equipment	32.92	30.79	29.72	30.73	13.91	27.73	19.50	26.03
Transport (vehicles)	37.09	25.33	21.85	26.12	67.63	23.43	22.65	23.43
Other manufacturing	47.57	37.46	40.14	39.55	51.48	35.40	30.93	35.27
Total	35.27	31.33	31.84	31.78	36.64	29.55	26.91	29.52

Table 8 Cost of debt - 1995

Manufacturing Sector	Non district				District			
	10-19	20-99	100-250	Total	10-19	20-99	100-250	Total
Food, beverages and tobacco	8.58	8.68	9.21	8.76	8.49	9.08	9.64	9.06
Textile	6.28	7.62	8.77	7.78	5.36	7.69	8.28	7.62
Leather industries	6.38	7.55	8.08	7.53	7.23	6.66	7.26	6.75
Wood and wood products	7.23	7.78	7.12	7.55	7.47	7.86	7.95	7.91
Paper, paper products, printing and publ.	6.61	8.01	9.39	8.20	6.83	8.26	8.34	8.08
Chemicals	5.75	7.72	8.84	8.03	6.75	8.02	8.44	7.92
Rubber and plastic products	7.27	7.21	8.33	7.49	6.13	7.52	8.62	7.68
Non-metallic mineral products	6.91	8.10	8.54	8.07	6.85	8.30	9.38	8.49
Metal and metal products	8.41	7.71	9.10	8.21	6.34	7.52	8.72	7.87
Mechanical equipment	7.24	7.32	8.37	7.70	5.72	7.07	8.54	7.25
Electrical equipment	5.29	7.81	8.92	7.86	8.39	8.07	9.41	8.25
Transport (vehicles)	8.26	7.73	7.86	7.79	8.50	7.86	7.84	7.88
Other manufacturing	8.06	7.78	8.11	7.89	7.68	7.34	8.79	7.51
Total	7.46	7.85	8.83	8.03	6.96	7.71	8.64	7.84

Table 9 MLE efficiency estimation results

Model specification 1:

$$\ln(Y_{it}) = \beta_0 + \beta_1 \ln(L_{it}) + \beta_2 \ln(K_{it}) + (v_{it} - u_{it})$$

$$v_{it} \text{ iid } N(0, \sigma_v^2) \qquad u_{it} \text{ iid } N^+(m_{it}, \sigma_u^2) \qquad m_{it} = z_{it}\delta$$

$$\gamma = \sigma_u^2 / (\sigma_u^2 + \sigma_v^2)$$

Sector	β_0	β_1	β_2	δ_0	δ_1	δ_2	γ
Food, beverages and tobacco	4.111 (0.047)	0.680 (0.011)	0.232 (0.008)	19.85 (3.718)	-0.013 (0.002)	-5.787 (0.823)	0.943 (0.009)
Textile	5.032 (0.069)	0.659 (0.014)	0.105 (0.007)	-2.935 (1.131)	-2.841 (1.004)	-	0.789 (0.046)
Leather industries	4.541 (0.054)	0.622 (0.013)	0.189 (0.008)	-5.631 (3.368)	-3.233 (2.359)	-	0.921 (0.047)
Wood and wood products	4.475 (0.092)	0.698 (0.022)	0.147 (0.013)	-2.152 (1.165)	-3.607 (1.903)	-	0.822 (0.058)
Rubber and plastic products	3.978 (0.061)	0.682 (0.012)	0.229 (0.009)	125.2 (32.4)	-3.483 (0.761)	-0.066 (0.017)	0.936 (0.012)
Non-metallic mineral products	4.014 (0.063)	0.733 (0.014)	0.219 (0.009)	8.746 (1.479)	-5.926 (0.635)	-0.008 (0.001)	0.966 (0.003)
Metal and metal products	4.176 (0.040)	0.759 (0.008)	0.171 (0.005)	-8.502 (1.517)	-0.239 (0.052)	-	0.914 (0.014)
Mechanical equipment	4.587 (0.039)	0.829 (0.009)	0.085 (0.006)	-8.471 (1.310)	-0.545 (0.116)	-	0.928 (0.009)
Electrical equipment	4.666 (0.048)	0.743 (0.014)	0.124 (0.007)	36.96 (9.716)	1.252 (0.237)	-0.023 (0.006)	0.919 (0.015)
Transport (vehicles)	4.311 (0.125)	0.882 (0.029)	0.092 (0.018)	7.915 (3.633)	3.412 (1.295)	-0.010 (0.004)	0.944 (0.020)

Table 10 MLE efficiency estimation results

Model specification 2:

$$\ln(Y_{it}) = \beta_0 + \beta_1 \ln(L_{it}) + \beta_2 \ln(K_{it}) + (v_{it} - u_{it})$$

$$v_{it} \text{ iid } N(0, \sigma_v^2) \qquad u_{it} = u_i \exp(-\eta(t - T)) \quad u_i \text{ iid } N^+(\mu, \sigma_u^2)$$

$$\gamma = \sigma_u^2 / (\sigma_u^2 + \sigma_v^2) \qquad \rho = corr(-u_{it}, district\ dummy)$$

Sector	β_0	β_1	β_2	μ	η	γ	ρ
Paper, paper products, printing and publishing	5.503 (0.409)	0.789 (0.072)	0.111 (0.017)	0.817 (0.145)	0.098 (0.006)	0.745 (0.031)	-0.082
Chemicals	5.413 (0.001)	0.914 (0.026)	0.058 (0.012)	0.721 (0.036)	0.065 (0.006)	0.703 (0.014)	-0.102
Other manufacturing	5.459 (0.179)	0.595 (0.032)	0.159 (0.013)	0.666 (0.044)	0.053 (0.005)	0.743 (0.011)	-0.123

ANNEX

Table A1 Distribution of firms in 1995 by sector and dimensional class

Sector	Dimensional class			Total	%
	10-19	**20-99**	**100-250**		
Food, beverages and tobacco	232	748	192	1172	10.7
Textile	198	1053	326	1577	14.4
Leather industries	73	383	88	544	5.0
Wood and wood products	20	172	35	227	2.1
Paper, paper products, printing and publ.	67	452	139	658	6.0
Chemicals	76	436	135	647	5.9
Rubber and plastic products	42	516	133	691	6.3
Non-metallic mineral products	39	500	134	673	6.2
Metal and metal products	116	1162	357	1635	14.9
Mechanical equipment	62	1032	351	1445	13.2
Electrical equipment	54	535	193	782	7.1
Transport (vehicles)	12	158	74	244	2.2
Other manufacturing	44	494	106	644	5.9
Total	1035	7641	2263	10939	100

Table A2 Distribution of firms by sector and dimensional class IN 1995: districts vs non-districts (percentages)

Sector	District				Non-district				Total
	10-19	20-100	100-250	Total	10-19	20-100	100-250	Total	
Food, beverages and tobacco	8.70	30.38	7.25	46,33	11.09	33.45	9.13	53.67	100
Textile	10.21	49.21	15.03	74,45	2.35	17.56	5.64	25.55	100
Leather industries	11.76	52.57	12.50	76,84	1.65	17.83	3.68	23.16	100
Wood and wood products	3.08	53.74	10.13	66.96	5.73	22.03	5.29	33.04	100
Paper, paper products, printing and publ.	3.95	31.00	8.51	43.47	6.23	37.69	12.61	56.53	100
Chemicals	5.56	27.51	8.04	41.11	6.18	39.88	12.83	58.89	100
Rubber and plastic products	3.76	44.14	10.27	58.18	2.32	30.54	8.97	41.82	100
Non-metallic mineral products	2.67	39.08	10.10	51.86	3.12	35.22	9.81	48.14	100
Metal and metal products	3.67	44.10	12.05	59.82	3.43	26.97	9.79	40.18	100
Mechanical equipment	2.21	44.50	14.05	60.76	2.08	26.92	10.24	39.24	100
Electrical equipment	2.30	33.63	12.02	47.95	4.60	34.78	12.66	52.05	100
Transport (vehicles)	1.64	31.15	9.84	42.62	3.28	33.61	20.49	57.38	100
Other manufacturing	4.35	56.52	10.71	71.58	2.48	20.19	5.75	28.42	100
Total	5.32	41.66	11.40	58.38	4.14	28.19	9.29	41.62	100

REFERENCES

Baffigi, Pagnini and Quintiliani (1997), *"Industrial Districts and Local Bank: Do the Twins ever Meet?"*, Paper presented at the XXXVII ERSA Congress, Siracusa, October 1997.

Battese and Coelli (1988), "Prediction of firm-level technical efficiencies: with a generalised frontier production function and panel data", Journal of Econometrics, Vol.38, pp. 387-99.

Battese and Coelli (1993), *"A stochastic frontier production function incorporating a model for technical inefficiency effects"*, Working Papers in Econometrics and Applied Statistics, N.69, University of New England, Armidale.

Battese and Coelli (1995), *"A model for technical inefficiency effects in a stochastic frontier production function for panel data"*, Empirical Economics, vol. 20(2), pp. 325-32.

Becattini (1990), *"The Marshallian districts as a socio-economic notion"* in Pyke, Becattini and Sengenberger (eds.), Industrial districts and inter-firm co-operation in Italy, Geneva, pp. 37-51.

Brusco, S. (1986), *"Small firms and industrial districts: The experience of Italy"*, Economia internazionale, No. 2, pp. 85-97.

Brusco S. and Bigarelli D. (1997), *"Regional productive systems in the knitwear and clothing sector in Italy: Industrial structure and training needs"*, ESRC Centre for Business Research Working Paper No. 51, March 1997.

Brusco and Paba (1997), *"Per una storia dei distretti industriali italiani dal secondo dopoguerra agli anni novanta"* in F. Barca (ed.) Storia del capitalismo italiano dal dopoguerra a oggi, Donzelli, pp. 265-334.

Cannari, Pellegrini and Sestito (1996), *"L'utilizzo di microdati d'impresa per l'analisi economica: alcune indicazioni metodologiche alla luce delle esperienze in Banca d'Italia"*, Temi di discussione, Banca d'Italia, No. 286.

Cannari and Signorini (1997), *"La geografia economica italiana: nuovi strumenti per la classificazione dei sistemi locali"*, mimeo.

Centrale dei Bilanci (1991), Economia e finanza delle imprese italiane, Milano, Il Sole-24 Ore.

Coelli (1992), *"A computer program for frontier production estimation: FRONTIER Version 2.0"*, Economic Letters, Vol. 39, pp. 29-32.

Deprins, Simar and Tulkens (1984), *"Measuring labor inefficiency in post offices"*, in Marchand, Pestieau and Tulkens (eds.), The Performance of Public Enterprises: Concepts and measurement, Amsterdam, North-Holland, pp. 243-67.

Deprins and Simar (1989), *"Estimating technical inefficiencies with correction for environmental conditions with an application to railways companies"*, Annals of Public and Cooperative Economics, Vol. 60, pp. 81-102.

Farrell (1957), *"The measurement of productive efficiency"*, The Journal of the Royal Statistical Society, A(120), pp. 253-81.

Jondrow, Lovell, Materov and Schmidt (1982), *"On the estimation of technical inefficiency in stochastic frontier production models"*, Journal of Econometrics, Vol. 19, pp. 233-38.

Istat (1996), *Rapporto annuale. La situazione del Paese nel 1995*. Istituto Poligrafico dello Stato.

Sforzi (1990), *"The quantitative importance of Marshallian industrial districts in the Italian Economy"*, in Pyke, Becattini and Sengenberger (eds.), Industrial districts and inter-firm co-operation in Italy, Geneva.

Signorini L. F. (1994), *"The price of Prato, or measuring the industrial district effect"*, Papers in Regional Science, No. 73, pp. 369-92.

Signorini, L.F. and I. Visco (1997), *L'economia italiana*, Bologna, Il Mulino.

Tulkens (1993), *"On FDH efficiency analysis: some methodological issues and application to retail banking, courts, and urban transit"*, Journal of Productivity Analysis, Vol. 4, pp. 183-210.

GROUPS, SME, AND TERRITORIES: A STATISTICAL TYPOLOGY OF THE LOCAL INDUSTRIAL STRUCTURES IN FRANCE[1]

Vincent Hecquet[1] and Frédéric Lainé[2]

[1]INSEE - Direction Générale, Division Synthèse des Statistiques d'Entreprises
[2]INSEE - Direction Générale, Division Statistiques et Études Régionales

1 Introduction

In this paper, we aim to analyse through a statistical study the local features of the French industrial system. On the overall map of France, we try to recognize typical industrial organizations and their underlying territories, such as the areas dominated by an important group, or on the contrary, those with a tissue of small and medium enterprises (SME). We try then to evaluate the economic evolution of the different types of industrial systems drawn from our analysis.

Several studies have ever tried to recognize typical productive systems on the French territory. Some authors have classed the areas according to the activities practised by the firms (A. Lipietz, or the GIP-RECLUS [1991]). In other papers, the productive systems are characterised by the proportion of the different functions of their jobs (F. Moaty, A. Valeyre [1991]). The territories may also be described by the forms of employment and wages relationships (F. Lainé [1994]). Besides, several economists in France and in other countries have studied peculiar forms of productive systems, especially the industrial districts (C. Courlet, B. Pecqueur [1993] in France, Sforzi [1990, 1995] in Italy).

Compared to these studies, our paper has two characteristics: First this statistical study claims to be exhaustive. We have taken into account all of the local units of the industrial sector, on the overall French territory. Secondly, the territories are characterized by the different forms of their productive units. We were able to elaborate this information thanks to the data produced by the French statistic system.

---

[1] This working paper does not reflect the position of INSEE but only the authors' views.

2 An approach by the different forms of productive units

Processing data from the French state statistic system, we made up a file with all the local units set up in France. (around 2.4 millions local units, in 1995). In each area, the set of local units defines a productive system that we analyse, through data analysis. In this paper, we focus on industrial structures.

We firstly aim to describe the territories by the size of the firms which are set in them. It is well known that the kinds of the economic relationships within a territory are strongly connected to the size of the firms. In the industrial districts, the small size of the firms, their employment practices and the co-ordination between them closely links up. Moreover for each territory, the size of a firm compared to the others directly indicates its importance in the local economy. Big firms may bring a way of development for the smaller ones, but they cause at the same time a dependence of the area. Besides the size of a firm is a key factor of its economic evolutions. Such as their activities, the size of the firms, which are set in a territory determines its economic growth.

As we aim to appreciate the degree of autonomy of local productive systems, we consider the firms which have a real autonomy. In France, the enterprise is the productive unit which is autonomous from a legal point of view, for the accounts and the juridical personality. An enterprise may have one local unit, or several ones.

Some enterprises may be connected by financial links within a group. Though these enterprises are juridicaly autonomous, the group forms a whole for its economic evolutions. An enterprise which is controlled by a group is not able to choose alone its strategy.

Thanks to the data produced by the French statistic system, we are able to link the local units to the enterprise which manages it. We can also reconstitute the groups.

The SIRENE register records all of the local units set up in France, and links them to the enterprises. Of each local unit we particularly know the address, the number of people employed, the activity and the one of the enterprise which manages it.

Concerning the groups, the INSEE holds a yearly survey about the financial links between the enterprises (survey LIFI). Moreover, the foreign companies which invest in France have to declare their investment to the French Treasury.

Processing these data, we are able to evaluate the proportion of the different forms of productive units in the French industry. We have characterized the industrial structure of each territory by the proportions of the different forms of productive units : small enterprises, SME, and the different kinds of groups.

3 Five forms of productive units studied in the French industry

3.1 The importance of groups in the French industry

The groups have a dominating place in the French industry. If we consider only the enterprises of which French or foreign groups own more than 50% of the capital, we note that they employ 57% of the industrial workers [2](Table 1).

One knows that a group may rule an enterprise even by owning less than 50% of its capital. To take account of this influence, we may also count the enterprises of which the groups own at least 20% of the capital. Nevertheless, these enterprises are few: they employ only 2% of the industrial workers. The groups indeed use to control the enterprises by holding a majority of their capital, in order to secure their leadership.

It has to be pointed out that above 200 people employed, the enterprises which are not a part of a group are seldom seen. In the industrial sector, the enterprises of this kind employ only 3% of the workers (5% for all the productive system). In France, only a few people are aware of this sort of concentration. Public opinion still keeps in mind the model of the uncontrolled big SME, while this kind of firm is very unusual.

---

[2] In all this paper, we study all the industry, including the food industry. We have nevertheless excluded the production of gas and electricity, which in France is performed by the national electrical company. We have also excluted the supply of water, which may be performed by public services.

Table 1 Proportion of the different types of productive units in the industrial sector (31/12/1994)

Productive unit	Size (workers)	number of industrial enterprises	proportion of the industrial enterprises	number of local units	proportion of the local units	proportion of the industrial employment
uncontrolled enterprises	< 10	127990	72.1	132469	63.5	10.3
	10 to 199	38435	21.6	48400	23.2	27.4
	200 to 499	398	0.2	1134	0.5	2.7
	≥ 500	32	0.0	215	0.1	0.7
enterprises with minority investement of groups	all sizes	1228	1.7	1745	0.8	1.9
French groups	< 200	1720	1.0	2487	1.2	2.1
	200 to 499	1204	0.7	2168	1.0	3.4
	500 to 1999	1476	0.8	3676	1.8	6.9
	2000to 9999	990	0.6	3498	1.7	7.9
	≥10 000	1057	0.6	4811	2.3	19.0
foreign groups	all sizes	2 942	1.7	7938	3.8	17.7
all	all sizes	177 532	(100.0)	208 541	(100.0)	(100.0) 4 125 970

Data : Insee, data Sirène LIFI Trésor, 1994

Reading : In the industrial sector (excluding production of gas electricity and supply of water) 127 990 enterprises employ less than 10 people. They are 72.1% of the industrial enterprises. They have 132 469 local units, that is to say 63.5% of the whole. They employ 10.3% of the industrial workers.

3.2 The productive units observed in this study

The spatial spread of the groups in the French territory may be appreciated by the implantation of their local units. We have already studied this point in previous papers (Hecquet, Lainé, 1997). In this typology, we have distinguished the groups in accordance with the aim to appreciate the autonomy of the territories:

– The foreign groups are considered separately. In spite of the internationalisation of the economy, most of the groups make the biggest part of their capital for one country. Moreover, the nationality of group still remains an important factor of its implantation policy.

In the French industry, 18% of the workers are employed by enterprises which belong to foreign groups. This high proportion is connected to the deep internationalisation of the French economy. The industry is far more internationalised than the other sectors. For the whole of the productive system (without agriculture and public services) the foreign groups employ only 9% of the workers.

According to their spatial implantation, we distinguish two types of French groups
- First we consider the «regional groups». At least 80 % of the people they employ work in a one region. In France the region is an administrative part on the territory, and there are 22 regions on the overall map of the country (see map 1).
- If its workers are more scattered in space, we call the group «supra-regional».
- We also describe the territory by the local units of the «uncontrolled» enterprises, that is to say the enterprises which are not controlled by groups. We distinguish small enterprises and SME.

3.3 A survey of the industrial activities

The proportion of the different types of productive units differs from an industrial activity to the next one.

In the French industrial system, several activities are chiefly controlled by foreign groups. Foreign groups employ a majority of the French workers in the industries of mechanical equipments, computers, production of paper and oil refining. The production of locomotives is mainly controlled by the european group GEC-ALSTHOM. Besides, foreign groups employ more than 40% of the French workers in several sectors of the chemicals industry.

Supra-regional French groups employ virtually all the workers in the industries of steel, cars, aircraft, and arms. The regional groups employ 7% of the workers for all the industry. The proportion is around 20% in the sectors of glass working, fabric and wearing, shipbuilding industry. In several industries of food, about 20% of the workers are also employed by regional groups.

Uncontrolled SME employ a majority of the workers in the following sectors: working of wood, toy industry, metallurgical industry and boilermaking. Lastly, small enterprises employ around 30% of the workers in ironwork, agricultural equipments, furnitures and reprocessing of scrap.

Map 1 The administrative regions of France

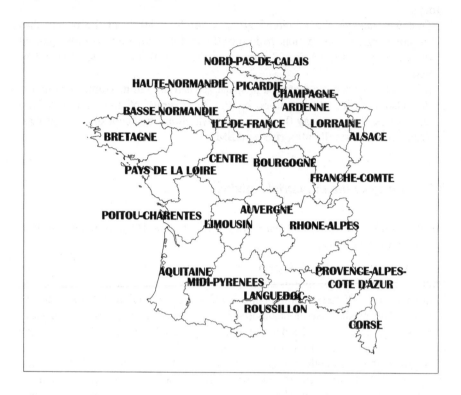

4 A typology of the local features of the industrial productive system

We consider the «employment areas», which are the result of a geographic partition used by the French administration. Theses areas are a division of the regions. On the overall map of France, there are 348 employment areas.

To draw up a typology of the employment areas, we consider three kinds of indicators characterizing their productive system.
– To characterize the local productive systems of the areas, one of the main features to take into account is merely their density. The distribution of economic activities in relation to space, like that of people, is obviously very unequal. The importance of a firm for local activity directly depends on the number of units. We firstly take into account the industrial density of each area, in terms of the average number of local units for a square kilometre.
– A second set of indicators is composed of the employment in the area among the five kinds of firms we consider. We take into account the importance of

uncontrolled SME, regional group, and French supra-regional groups and foreign ones in the local economy.

- For a same proportion of employees controlled by groups, we may have two very different situations. Either the groups control many small local units, or they control a few big local units. To take into account the ways in which groups are set up in the area, we consider the proportion of the local units they control. We distinguish the proportion of French supra-regional groups and foreign groups' one.

All the variables of the typology are represented in the following table :

The variables of the typology

Industrial density of the area
- number of local units controlled by groups for a square kilometer. - number of local units controlled by uncontrolled SME for a square kilometer.
Share of the local employment controlled by the different kinds of firms
Another set of indicators shares out the total employment of the area among the five kinds of firms we consider : - small entreprises uncontrolled by the groups (enterprises of less than 10 employees) - medium entreprises uncontrolled by groups (enterprises from 10 to 500 employees) - French groups of a regional extent (80% of their employment are set within a single region) - french group of a supra-regional extent - foreign groups
Share of the local units controlled by supra regional groups
- share of the local units from 10 employees which are controlled by French group of a supra-regional extent - share of the local units from 10 employees which are controlled by foreign groups

5 The results of the typology

A first glance at the results of the typology shows that the overall map of France is divided into three main types of areas (see map 2).

Half of the French territory, that is to say the southern part, is mainly occupied by areas with a low industry density. On the contrary, on the north of a line from Nantes to Valence, the territory is more industrialised. In a large basin around Paris, and in the regions near the borders, the industrial productive system is chiefly dominated by French supra-regional groups and by foreign ones.

Lastly, other areas show both a high industry density and a kind of local autonomy of firms. In Brittany (region Bretagne) and in Rhône-Alpes, many local units are still controlled by local SME or by regional groups. In a smaller proportion, such local autonomy may be observed in the North of France or in the environs of Nantes.

5.1 The densely industrialised areas with supra-regional groups

The areas with a high density of industry and supra regional groups are chiefly situated in the northern half of France. This localisation may be explained by several reasons. One knows that some of these territories lie in the birthplace of the French capitalism. The regions Nord Pas-de-Calais and Lorraine were in the past mining areas, and the main industries of the 19th century had been established there, such as iron, steel and textile. At their beginning in France, the car and the aircraft industries were born in Paris and in its neighbourhood. Since the fifties, the basin around Paris has been more and more industrialised, because of the general rise of industry and the implanting of foreign firms.

Among the densely industrialised areas with supra-regional groups, we may distinguish five classes according to our typology.

Map 2 Industrial density and local autonomy

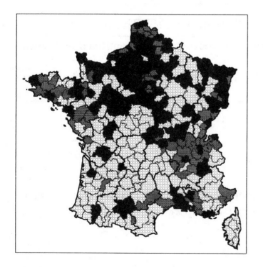

bright grey : sparcely industrialised areas
dark grey : densely industrialised areas with local firms
black : densely industrialised areas with supra-regional groups

– *the areas with both French and foreign groups*

Absent from the southern half of France, these areas are concentrated in a large basin around Paris. In these territories 36% of the industrial workers are on average employed by French groups, and 27% by the foreign ones. In the Parisian basin, the groups take advantages of the nearness of big markets, such as the metropolis of Paris and Lille, and the countries of northern Europe. There, they are also set up near the political and economic centers of decision.

Moreover in the Ile-de-France, the groups may count on a industrial tradition, and a high density of subcontractors. Others areas farther from the capital also have local units because of the decentralisation of the French groups, as in Picardie, Normandie and Centre.

Map 3 The densely industrialised areas, with both French and foreign groups

– *the areas in which foreign groups dominate*

In these areas the foreign groups control on average 38% of the industrial employment and 14% of the local units. 13 of these territories are situated near the eastern borders, especially in Alsace, Lorraine and Franche-Comté where German groups are set up. 18 others areas of this kind are situated in a large basin around Paris.

Besides, in three areas the foreign groups dominate, but the local SME employ a big number of the workers. Two of them are situated in Alsace, where the industrial know-how is traditionaly established. The other one is in Roissy, where the Paris international airport attracts foreign implantations next to the local SME.

Map 4 The densely industrialised areas, with foreign groups dominating

– *the areas in which French groups dominate, but with many foreign local units*

In this class a big share of the industrial employment is controlled by French groups (49% on average), but many small local units belong to foreign companies. Many of these areas are in Lorraine.

It has to be pointed out that many metroplis of the southern France have this kind of productive system, especially Bordeaux and Toulouse. Their industrial system is dominated by French groups, and local firms are few and far between. Nevertheless, foreign groups have set up local units, probably in order to take advantage of the growth of the local market, and industrial amenities.

Map 5 The densely industrialised areas, with French groups dominating and foreign local units

– *the areas in which French groups dominate*

Half of the industrial workers of these areas is on average employed by French groups of a supra regional extent. Opposite to the previous classes, foreign companies are weakly present.

Compared to the territories with both French and foreign groups, these areas are more scattered on the overall map of France. Some activities strictly managed by French groups have to be situated in peculiar areas, such as the shipbuilding industry in the ports of Brittany. Besides, many areas of this class result from the policies of decentralisation followed by the French groups from the fifties to the eighties. These groups have moved local units into the western regions, following the governement's recommendations and looking for areas where wages were lower.

Map 6 The densely industrialised areas with French groups dominating

5.2 The densely industrialised areas, with local firms

Only several territories show both a high density of industry and a local autonomy of firms. These areas are situated in precise regions, such as Brittany, the Rhône-Alpes and the Nord Pas-de-Calais. They have kept a kind of local autonomy, since many of their local units belong to regional groups or to local enterprises.

We distinguish three kinds of areas, according to the respective proportions of regional groups and SME. Whatever the organization of the firms, these areas are next to each other. A high density of uncontrolled SME or of regional groups are both the reflection of local dynamism. According to region and to the activities of the firms, this local dynamism takes different forms.

− the densely industrialised areas, with regional groups
In such areas, around a third of the industrial workers are employed by regional groups. Many of these territories are in Brittany, and in the environs of Nantes. The regional groups which are established there belong to sectors of the naval industy and the food industry, especially the production of meat. The high density of regional groups in Brittany may also be connected to the strong identity of this region.

Many regional groups are also located in the Nord Pas-de-Calais. Since the 19th century, this region has been known for its tradition of local capitalism, ruled by a few families of employers.

Map 7 The densely industrialised areas, with regional groups

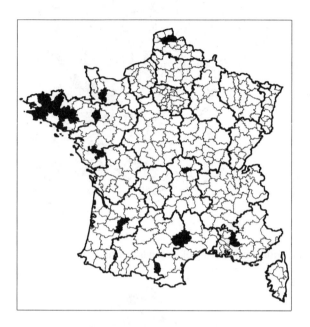

— the areas with a high density of uncontrolled SME
These areas are mainly concentrated in the region Rhône-Alpes. In this class we notably find the industrial districts, which have been well described in many studies. For example, in the Arve valley many industrial SME practice the décolletage (production of thin pieces of steel). The plastic industry of Oyonnax is also famous in France (map 8).

— the areas with a high density of all kinds of firms
These territories enjoy a high density of industrial local units which are managed by all kinds of firms, such as groups, small enterprises and SME. They are frequently situated next to the areas of the two previous classes.

Many metropolis belong to this class: Paris and several of its suburbs, Lille-Roubaix-Tourcoing, Strasbourg, Montpellier, Nice and Nantes. Nevertheless, one has to bear in mind that other southern metropolis do not show a similar structure, because their local firms are insufficiently developed.

Apart from metropolis, a large part of the Rhône-Alpes has such an industrial system. Since this region is very industrialised, all kinds of firms are situated there (map 9).

Map 8 The areas with a high density of uncontrolled SME

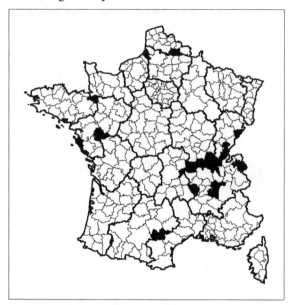

Map 9 The areas with a high density of all kinds of firms

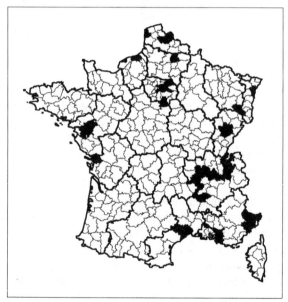

5.3 The sparcely industrialised areas

The areas with a low density of industry are chiefly situated in the southern half of the country. The general geographical features of France partly explain this situation. Some of these areas have a very weak density of population, such as Corsica or Limousin. Other places, such as the French Riviera, are densely populated, but their productive system is mostly composed of services.

The small number of industrial firms in a territory may proceed from various reasons, and have opposite results for development. In this paper we do not consider these questions, contenting ourselves with describing the different types of sparcely industrialised areas. Our typology divides them into five classes.

– the sparcely industrialised areas, with small enterprises or SME
These areas are mainly located in the south of France. Some of them are particularly underpopulated or agricultural, such as Medoc above Bordeaux. Others are strictly devoted to services, such as Menton on the Riviera. The whole of Corsica is notably without industrial enterprises.

Map 10 The sparcely industrialized areas, with small enterprises

Another class includes the areas where only a few industrial SME may be seen. Most of them are also in the South (map 11).

– *the sparcely industrialised areas, with groups and SME*

Nearly all these territories are situated in the south-west of France, in the regions of Aquitaine, Midi-Pyrenées and Limousin. In this class we find, for example, Mont-de-Marsan, Cahors and Tulle (map 12).

Map 11 The sparcely industrialised areas, with SME

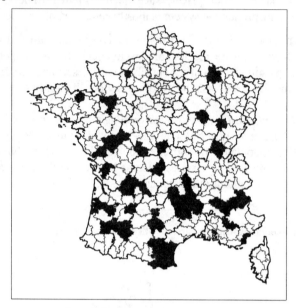

– *the sparcely industrialised areas, with all kinds of firms*

This class is well distributed over the overall map of France. Its economic meaning is ambiguous. Some areas have a low density of industrial local units, because they have also other activities. This is probably the situation in Troyes, Champagne-Ardennes. Since this area is very large, it probably contains agricultural space. On the contrary, other areas of this class have an industrial system which used to be flourishing but is nowadays in a state of crisis. This may be the situation in Vierzon in the region Centre (map 13).

Map 12 The sparcely industrialised areas, with groups and SME

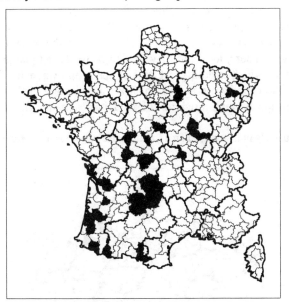

Map 13 The sparcely industrialised areas, with all kinds of firms

– the sparcely industrialised areas, dominated by groups of a national extent

In these areas a few groups employ a large number of the industrial workers, while other firms employ few. In every case these groups are French, and their status is supra-regional. Most of them as situated near the montains in the Alps and the Pyrenees. There, local industry used to be weak, but plants have been set up by companies which need a great deal of space and water for their activities (for example, the chemical industry). Such a concentration of the supra-national groups may obviously cause a risk for these territories (map 14).

Map 14 The sparcely industrialised areas, dominated by groups of a national extent

5.4 The proportion of the different types of productives systems in the industrial employment

In the following table are registred the proportion of the 12 types of areas revealed by our typology in the industrial employment.

We note that only 8% of the French industrial workers are situated in areas which have an high density of uncontrolled SME or regional groups. As far as we may compare to other studies, this proportion is very weak, compared to Sforzi's results for Italy.

Table 2 Number of areas and proportion of the industrial employment in the different types

	number of employment areas	proportion of the employment in French industry
sparcely industrialised areas with small enterprises	12	0.2
sparcely industrialised areas with SME	40	3.9
sparcely industrialised areas with groups and SME	27	2.2
sparcely industrialised areas supra-regional groups dominating	30	4.4
sparcely industrialised areas all kinds of firms	34	7.0
densely industrialised foreign groups dominating	40	8.2
densely industrialised both foreign and French groups	31	16.6
densely industrialised French groups dominating and foreign local units	29	15.1
densely industrialised French groups dominating	32	10.7
high density of regional groups	17	2.8
high density of uncontrolled SME	19	5.7
high density of all kinds of firms	37	23.2
total	348	(100.0)

6 Industrial structures and dynamic of territories

In this part of the paper, we try to evaluate the economic evolution of the different types of industrial systems revealed by our typology. In order to do this, we have choosen as a indicator the evolution of industrial employment from 1989 to 1994. This data comes from the UNEDIC, the French administration for unemployment insurance.

We have first measured the evolution of industrial employment for each of the 13 classes of areas. We have then divided this evolution into a structural effect and a residual one, by a shift and share analysis. In this analysis we start by considering the proportion of the different industrial activities in the jobs in each area. We calculate a theorical evolution, which would be observed for the area if all its activities grew according to the national average. This calculation gives the structural effect, while the residual one is the difference in terms of the evolution which has really happened.

Here are the first results of this analysis :

- *The areas with foreign groups or regional groups get a better evolution of the employment than the national average*
- *The areas with a high density of industrial SME well resist*

The areas with a high density of SME show a good residual effect. This could corroborate the idea that the industrial districts are rather efficient, compared to the productive systems devoted to the same activities.

Nevertheless, the general evolution of these areas is less favorable, because of a harmful structural effect. Indeed, many industrial districts practice activities which are now threatened by foreign trading, such as textile production and the plastics industry.

- *The areas ruled by both French and foreign groups suffer the industrial restructurations*

In the classes in which the supra-regional French groups and foreign groups are well established, industrial employment particulary decreased. This fall could reflect the restructurations put into operation by the companies during the last decade.

Table 3 Evolution of employment in the different types of areas, from 1989 to 1994

	evolution of industrial employment	relative evolution	difference in terms of the national average	structural effect	residual effect
sparcely industrialised areas with small enterprises	-1098	-12.0	-0.3	2.2	-2.5
sparcely industrialised areas with SME	-13015	-7.7	+3.0	-0.6	+3.6
sparcely industrialised areas with groups and SME	-9979	-10.3	+1.4	-0.3	+1.7
sparcely industrialised areas supra-regional groups dominating	-18716	-9.9	+1.8	-0.2	+2.0
sparcely industrialised areas all kinds of firms	-25495	-8.5	+3.1	-0.8	+3.9
densely industrialised foreign groups dominating	-23814	-6.9	+4.8	+0.4	+4.4
densely industrialised both foreign and French groups	-111608	-15.3	-3.7	+1.0	-4.7
densely industrialised French groups dominating and foreign local units	-68860	-10.8	+0.8	+0.6	+0.2
densely industrialised French groups dominating	-35065	-8.0	+3.6	0.4	3.2
high density of regional groups	-2550	-2.3	+9.4	+0.2	+9.2
high density of uncontrolled SME	-19631	-8.0	+3.6	-3.0	+6.6
high density of all kinds of firms	-175314	-16.5	-4.8	-0.3	-4.5

7 Conclusion

The first result of this statistical study is to identify several industrial systems, and to evaluate their proportion in industrial employment.

Several results corroborate general geographical features of France. Groups are mainly situated on the north of a line from Nantes to Valence. The southern half of the country is less industrialised. Only a few regions have both a high density of industry and a local autonomy of firms. This is the situation in Brittany, the Rhône-Alpes and the Nord-Pas-de-Calais. These types of densely industrialised areas with a local autonomy of the firms probably represent a smaller proportion of employment than in other countries.

From 1989 to 1994 the areas with a high density of regional groups and SME had a more favourable evolution of employment than the national average. Further investigations would be interesting to explain the dynamic of territories.

REFERENCES

Courlet C., Pecqueur B. [1993] *"Systèmes productifs localisés et industrialisation"*, Industries et territoires en France, La documentation française.

Gip-Reclus [1991] *"Le développement des branches d'activité en France"*, in Réalités industrielles, série des annales des mines, nov. 1991.

Guegan J-C., Rousier N. [1989] *Sur l'organisation territoriale de l'industrie française*, Note de recherche IREPD, Grenoble.

Hecquet V., Laine F.[1997] *Inscription territoriale des groupes et indentité des systèmes productifs locaux* , Document de travail E9705/H9701, Direction des Statistiques d'Entreprises/Direction de la Diffusion et de l'Action Régionale.

Lainé F. [1994] *Formes de rapport salarial, systèmes d'emploi et structures de l'espace économique*, Thèse de doctorat , Université de Picardie-Jules Verne.

Moatty F., Valeyre A.[1991] *"Division spatiale du travail industriel et organisation des entreprises"*, Travail et emploi, n°50/4.

Moatty F., Valeyre A.[1991] *"La division spatiale du travail entre zones d'emploi"*, Revue d'économie régionale et urbaine n°5.

Sforzi F.[1990] *"The competitive Importance of Marshallian Industrial Districts in the Italian Economy"* in Pyke F. et al., eds, Industrial Districts and Firm Cooperation in Italy, International Institute for Labour Studies, Genève.

Sforzi F. [1995] *"Local systems of small and medium-sized firms in Italy"*, International seminar on local systems of small firms and job creation, OCDE, Paris, juin 1995.

ECONOMETRIC ISSUES IN THE ANALYSIS OF LINKED WORKER-EMPLOYER SURVEYS*

Andrew Hildreth[1] and Stephen Pudney[2]

[1]*Dept. of Economics and Institute for Labour Research, Un. of Essex*
[2]*Public Sector Economics Research Centre, Dept. of Economics, Un. of Leicester*

1 Introduction

Outside of labour demand models, it is only recently that economists have started to seriously consider the role of employers within the labour market using formal models. Employer behaviour in determining the employment and remuneration of individuals has become a concern in models of wage determination, worker turnover, and worker selection. If we are to avoid using a small case study approach to empirically examine theories of the labour market, using representative matched panels is one means by which such tests might be undertaken. The degree to which data are representative depends on the sampling structure of the data, the success of the survey in obtaining sufficient response, and the variables available within the survey design. A natural avenue to explore in obtaining representative matched data lies in the use of Government surveys and administrative records.[1]

For many areas in labour economics matched worker-employer data offers the opportunity that we might understand the selection and matching of individuals to employers. Questions on specific against general human capital, the incidence of unemployment as a result of employer decisions, and the employment opportunities that different employers present are possible areas that matched worker-employer data can address. This paper examines the implications of matching worker and employer data in cross-sections for estimating equations

---

* We thank the conference participants at CAED '97, University of Bergamo, Italy. We are grateful to the ONS for access to respondent-level data from the New Earnings Survey and Annual Census Of Production, and for their efforts in implementing the linking process. All the views in this paper are our own and not necessarily those of the ONS. This research was supported by the ESRC through grant no. R000222231.

[1] Work along such lines has already been carried out in France and the USA. For France see work by Abowd, Kramarz, and Margolis (1996), Entorf and Kramarz (1997), and Margolis (1996). For the US, see work by Troske (1998b). Also see a survey of the literature in Abowd and Kramarz (1997).

that contain individual and establishment dependent or independent variables. We present some econometric theory that argues that when conditioning on the match between workers and employers in equations with a worker variable as the dependent, there should be no bias in the estimated coefficients. By comparison, equations with an employer dependent variable are likely to have biased coefficients. Even in samples where both the worker and employer samples are individually representative, the matching of the two surveys can create a bias in the estimated coefficients for the employer equations.

The analysis of matched worker-employer data is a relatively new phenomenon. The resources required to match in workers to their employers have not been made available before, and the computing power necessary to analyse the large size of the matched files has not existed on a large enough scale. Abowd and Kramarz (1997) survey the extent of what is available is the way of worker data matched to employers. There are, at present, only a few countries in the world that have such resources available. If such data are available, then there are a number of possible avenues to explore in re-examining issues in labour economics: job specific returns, seniority, trade union membership and recognition, gender and racial differences in remuneration, the returns to new technology, and job mobility.[2] In all of these cases, the inclusion of firm or establishment variables into worker equations, or the estimation of establishment level relationships, proceeds without recourse to possible inference or bias induced by the matching process itself. It is not straightforward to assume that if there is a large random sample drawn in both cases, on workers and employers, that the estimated coefficients in any model will automatically be consistent. In this paper we examine for a limited range of cross-section models the possible bias in the coefficients from matching Government surveys on workers and employers.

The models we examine are the remuneration to individual and employer characteristics, transitions into or out of unemployment, and the labour demand of employers. As such, the models taken as a whole, even though they are estimated separately, do give a picture of a matched labour market involving workers and employers in the production sector in Great Britain for 1994 and 1995. If labour economists are to use the new statistical resources some attention should be given to the underlying distributions of the variable under consideration. We provide some words of warning on the implementation of standard reduced form models with matched worker-employer cross-sections. The bias arises not from choice-based sampling (see Imbens and Lancaster, 1996), but from not conditioning on the selection of employers through the match with workers.

---

[2] See papers, *inter alia*, by Abowd, Kramarz, and Margolis (1997), Cahuc and Kramarz (1997), Carrington and Troske (1998), Doms, Dunne and Troske, (1997), Entorf and Kramarz (1997), Hildreth and Pudney (1997) and Troske (1998).

At first glance, the use of administrative Government data would appear to be without fault. Government agencies have access to more complete sampling frames covering the population and they have the legal powers to compel respondents to complete the questionnaire. Even in cases where surveys and administrative records have been sampled according to random rules, the merging of the data sets by some identification criteria can create a non-representative sample of labour market activity. Irrespective of the size of the sample (by number of respondents) inconsistency in the model parameters still results.

Despite the possibility of linking individuals across employers, and into and out of unemployment spells, there are still missing aspects of labour market behaviour that are not known from such a match. One notable example is missing household information. We do not know how employment opportunities, or hours of work, affect the labour market experience of the other partner within the household (if there is one). Other problems are that Government data, usually collected to compile macroeconomic aggregates, may not have all the variables required to examine a particular economic phenomena that a researcher wishes to investigate. Information on the type of technology adopted, product market prices, or the labour relations structure of the enterprise are information categories that are not necessarily present on employers.[3]

There are a number of ways around such dilemmas if Government data are to be used for analysis. One possibility would be to use existing survey sampling frames and extend the sphere of interest for the survey design. For example, the NES sampling frame could be used to extend the questionnaire to include household questions. Alternatively, if related enterprise surveys are undertaken, they use a common sampling frame and design, so that links can be made to existing surveys.[4]

The paper first discusses the sampling and nature of the survey design for each part of the matched data. We then discuss how the linkages between data sets are made and the problems this creates. Once the matched data are assembled we discuss the sampling problems and their implications for models of labour market behaviour. We find that when using matched data, that including employer data in individual level equations does not give biased estimates. However, the matching of individuals and employers does give rise to potentially biased estimates if employer equations are estimated. Corrections can be made with suitably weighted maximum likelihood estimation.

---

[3] See Hildreth (1996) and Hildreth and Pudney (1996).
[4] Work using the French matched panel has already shown this to good effect: see Entorf and Kramarz (1997), and Cahuc and Kramarz (1997).

2 The NES-JUVOS-ACOP matched survey

The possibility to construct this matched data comes from the development of the IDBR (Inter-Departmental Business Register) at the Office for National Statistics (ONS). The register was developed because of inconsistencies that occurred between the maintenance of separate sampling frames between the ONS (formerly the CSO - Central Statistical Office) and the Employment Department. In particular, the maintenance of the Annual Census of Production (ACOP) by the ONS and the New Earnings Survey (NES) by the Employment Department was done from two separately maintained registers of businesses in the United Kingdom. Differences in classification and coverage between the two registers led to different estimates of key economic indicators, especially employment. The main administrative sources that comprise the sampling frame for the IDBR are the VAT (value added tax) and PAYE (pay as you earn) registers for tax purposes. The only sectors that are not covered are some parts of agriculture, and some other very small businesses, for example the self-employed and some non-profit making organisations. The statistical unit for both registers is an enterprise. An enterprise can be a single entity or a group of legal units. The IDBR has been used for sampling purposes for both the NES and ACOP since 1994. Our work concerns the two cross-sections for 1994 and 1995.

2.1 The New Earnings Survey (NES)

The NES is an annual sample survey of earnings in Great Britain of employees in employment.[5] The survey is based on a one percent sample of employees who are members of the PAYE tax scheme. Questionnaires are sent to employers to be filled out on employees selected as part of the sample. Individuals are identified by means of their national insurance number (NINO) and the sample selected is based on the last two digits. NINO's are randomly allocated to individuals when they attain working age. All individuals whose NINO ends with the number 14 are selected as the sample. Although national insurance numbers are individual specific, and might be deemed to be a unique identifier, they are not in practice. A very small number of national insurance numbers are allocated to more than one individual through administrative re-using of the same number. Since 1975 the same last two digits have been used with each successive wave of the NES.

Employees are identified in the survey by one of two methods. About 90 percent of the sample is identified from lists supplied by the Inland Revenue containing the selected national insurance numbers and the names and addresses

---

[5] Details of the difference between the questionnaires issued and the survey response can be found in New Earnings Survey, Part A, 1994 and 1995.

of the employers. To the employers, an enterprise reference (ENTREF) number is attached that can be taken directly from the IDBR. The remaining percentage of the information required for the NES sample is obtained directly from the large organisations who employ the employees. Once again, these enterprises will carry an ENTREF.

The information collected in the NES concerns earnings for a particular pay period (determined and reported by the employer). Other information is limited to hours worked per week (basic and overtime), age, occupation, industry, collective agreement coverage, and location. The gender of the respondents is not actually recorded as part of the NES. Gender records are provided by the Inland Revenue to the NES as part of the initial sample check list. Inland Revenue provide a new list each year. Where there is a change in gender, or the record is missing, the record is checked against a DSS (Department of Social Security) file called 'Ledger 14'. Ledger 14 gives a complete listing of all NINO's ending in 14 and the gender of the individual.

2.2 The Joint Unemployment and Vacancies Operating System (JUVOS)

As the same set of national insurance numbers have been used for the NES since 1975, the same set of individuals should be in the sample from one year to the next. Non-response on the part of an employer about an individual should occur for one of two principal reasons. First, the individual may no longer be part of the labour force. The individual may have retired, been on maternity leave, or absent for other reasons. Second, the individual may be unemployed. If the individual falls into this latter category, and registers as being unemployed, then the unemployment record is recorded against an individual's national insurance number as they collect unemployment benefit. These records are maintained by the Department of Trade and Industry (DTI). The unemployment benefit (UB) records provide information on a quarterly basis on whether a spell of registered unemployment occurred and how long (in days per quarter) it lasted. The computer records are up-dated on a monthly basis.

The UB records are taken from JUVOS (Joint Unemployment and Vacancies Operating System). The JUVOS cohort is a five percent sample of all computerised claims for unemployment benefit in the first quarter of 1983. The records for JUVOS are up-dated each quarter. The sample chosen is based on the last two digits of the NINO with 14, 24, 44, 64, and 84 as the selected numbers. Individuals whose NINO ends in 14 are the same as those individuals included in the NES sample. If an individual has claimed unemployment benefit since the computerised records began, then their unemployment history is known. The one variable we use off the JUVOS records is the number of days within a quarter that an individual is unemployed, and this denotes both whether an unemployment spell occurred and the proportion of a year that an individual is unemployed.

2.3 The Annual Census of Production (ACOP)

The ACOP is not a true census, but rather a sample survey. Each year, the COP samples approximately 20000 establishments (reporting units) in the energy and utility, manufacturing, mining, and construction sectors. The sampling probability for the establishments for 100 plus employees is one. Below this sample size cut off, establishments are sampled on a stratified basis with probabilities differing across size and industry classification. Reporting units are drawn from the IDBR via the ENTREF. As such, the enterprise unit from the IDBR is at a greater level of aggregation than the reporting unit. For each ENTREF, there are reporting and local units that have their own reporting reference (RUREF). The basis for sampling in the ACOP is done using the RUREF. The RUREF is a unique identifier for each reporting unit. The reporting unit is essentially the mailing address for the ACOP forms. A separate mailing address should be given for each type of activity at the enterprise. Information at the reporting unit level is collected on a number of variables, for example, employment, turnover, value added, stocks of goods or materials, wages, and capital expenditure.

2.4 Linking workers and employers

Linking individual records between NES and JUVOS is straightforward. Selecting only those individuals from JUVOS whose NINO ended in 14, the match is then simply one obtained in terms of the NINO. Where individuals do not have an unemployment record, the number of days spent unemployed in any quarter of the year is assumed to be zero.

Linking across the NES and ACOP data sets is problematic. Although in principal it should be possible to create a known unique match from individual to establishment, there are problems in creating this unique match. First, the link between individual and establishment has to be made via the ENTREF. An ENTREF, as it refers to an enterprise, is not unique for any individual/establishment pair. To create the unique match it has to be inferred from the IDBR records. As a reporting unit is supposed to be, by definition, an activity at a particular address, the combination of an enterprise reference by industrial activity, given by the five digit SIC92 (1992 edition of the Standard Industrial Classification) code, should provide a unique identification of an establishment. This same identification is then available on each individual in the

NES. This identification in the NES assumes that the SIC92 code used in the NES is the same as that used in the ACOP. Given that both surveys are derived from the same sampling frame (IDBR) that carries an industry identification, this is a relatively safe assumption to make.

In creating this match across the NES and ACOP a number of observations were lost from multiple entries for individuals according to their national insurance number, and incidences where the ENTREF and SIC92 code did not create a unique identification. Table 1 summarises the information loss from matching according to these criteria. Information from non-unique national insurance numbers in each wave contributes to only a 1-2 percent loss of information. In the 1994 NES, a greater amount of information is lost from the ENTREF being missing for a number of NES respondents. The missing ENTREF was the result of some organisations (public authorities and national corporations) being contacted directly because of their prominence in the labour market. The 1995 NES does not contain this missing information problem. Without the ENTREF, no link can be made between NES respondents and ACOP establishments.

Once the NES and ACOP were matched, it gave individuals at establishments where we knew that the match was unique. There were some sampling anomalies to this match because of sampling and survey dates. For example, in the 1995 NES/ACOP link, some establishments have a zero employment at the mailing address (RUREF) because of the timing between surveys. The NES survey issues the sample and carries out the survey in the first quarter of the year. The ACOP draws the sample from the IDBR and carries out the survey in the final quarter of the year. For the 1995 NES/ACOP link there were 69 individuals that are matched to 17 establishments that existed when the NES was undertaken and had more than one employee when the ACOP95 sample was drawn (this can be ascertained from the employment figures kept on the IDBR), but by the end of the last quarter in 1995 had no employees. The final two rows of Table 1b show that about 66 percent of establishments in the ACOP respondents could be matched to NES respondents. In approximately 30 percent of the cases there were more than one worker per establishment. Figures 1 and 2 present the distributions of workers per establishment for the two years. The number of workers per establishment shows a distribution that is approximately log-normal.

Figure 1 Distribution of Workers per Establishment: NES/ACOP 1994

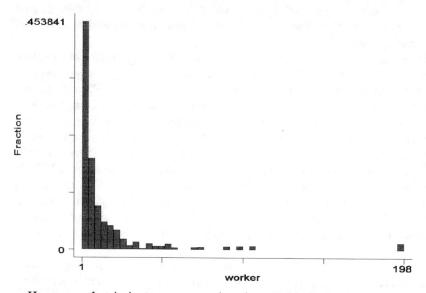

However, what is important to notice about Table 1c is the change in the number of observations on establishments once they have been matched to NES respondents. The differential sampling in the size classes shows how matching reduces the probability of observing smaller establishments that were not sampled with certainty. Matching establishments to observed employees over emphasises the larger sized employers. The impact of this differential sampling can also be gleaned from Tables A1 and A2 in the Appendix. The remaining observations provided on the smaller establishments are not necessarily representative of the sample that results from the ACOP survey.

Figure 2 Distribution of Workers per Establishment : NES/ACOP 1995

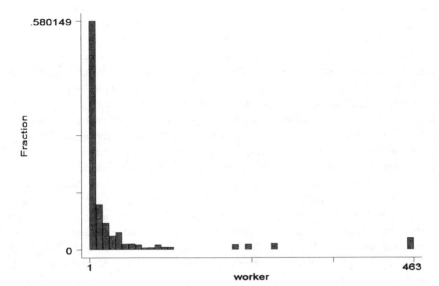

3 A model of the sampling/linking process

Given that the sample statistics in Tables 1, A1 and A2 show that the matching process introduces a potential bias in the distribution of worker and employer variables, we now model the matching process and investigate if it implies biased coefficients for models of the labour market.

3.1 The cross-section sample distribution

We define the following notation relating to a single survey year. There are three sources of information:

(i)   NES information on individuals who are in employment, denoted ω;
(ii) JUVOS information on individuals' current and past experience of unemployment, denoted u;
(iii) ACOP information on the characteristics of the employer, denoted (f,S), where S is firm size measured by employment and f is a vector containing all other firm characteristics.

Our task is now to derive the sample distribution of the observations from a single year's data on employees and their employers, to provide a basis for drawing inferences about the processes of pay determination, job loss and unemployment. From the viewpoint of the theoretical statistician, there is a serious problem to be overcome in analysing the dataset that results from the firm-worker matching process described in Section 2. The techniques customarily used to model survey data are based on the assumption of an underlying continuous distribution. For example, probit or Tobit analysis requires that behavioural disturbances are drawings from a normal distribution; logit analysis is based on the logistic distribution. But a distribution can only be continuous if the population it describes is infinite. Since the total number of firms and workers in existence at any time is very large, one usually feels safe in using these infinite-population methods for analysing company or worker cross-sections. However, with matched data, this is more problematic. If there are infinite numbers of firms and workers, then the probability of observing even a single firm-worker match is essentially zero in any finite sample, unless there exist firms of infinite size. There is a further problem in the case of the ACOP, since the survey design requires that every firm in the target production sectors is sampled with probability 1 if its workforce exceeds a pre-specified threshold size. In an infinite population of firms, this would generally imply an infinite sample of large firms.

Fortunately, a suitable theoretical framework is available for situations like this. Superpopulation theory (Cassel *et. al*, 1977; Pudney, 1989) allows us to work with a finite population, by postulating the existence of an underlying infinite superpopulation from which the actual finite population is assumed to have been drawn at random by "nature". Essentially, the superpopulation describes the set of possible forms the actual finite population might have taken. The objective of our statistical analysis is then to estimate fundamental relationships present in the superpopulation - in other words the (random) processes that govern the nature of the actual population we see around us. Since the superpopulation is infinite, it is admissible to estimate these statistical relationships using techniques which assume continuous distributions. However, in doing so, it is necessary to take proper account of the fact that the process generating our data has two stages - a draw (made by "nature") from the superpopulation, followed by a second draw (made by the survey designer) from the finite population.

At any particular time, the superpopulation consists of an infinite set of elements, each corresponding to a manufacturing firm and its workforce. The size of the firm's workforce is s, and the information set describing the firm and its S workers is denoted $X=\{S,f,w^1...w^S\}$.[6]

---

[6] For the purposes of cross-section analysis, the unemployment information u can be treated in exactly the same way as the NES information w, so there is no loss of generality if we omit u for the sake of notational simplicity.

In the superpopulation, the distribution of these firm/workforce clusters is described by a probability density/mass function (pdf) $g(X)$. Our sample falls into two parts: an exhaustive sample of firms in the section of the population for which $S \geq C$; and a random sample (without replacement) from the section of the population for which $s < C$, where C is a pre-selected threshold that may be a function of other firm variables (specifically, C depends on SIC sector for the 1995 ACOP). The total sample size and the numbers of observations from these two parts of the population are $n = n^* + n^{**}$. We consider the two parts of the sample separately. Henceforth, we use the symbol $g(.)$ as generic notation for any distribution that describes the superpopulation; the symbol $h(.)$ is used to represent sample distributions.

Large firms

Let the size of the actual population be N firms, and let $P = \Pr(S > C) = 1 - E_C(G_S(S|C))$ be the frequency of large firms in the superpopulation, where $G_S(S|C)$ is the conditional cumulative distribution function (cdf) of firm size in the superpopulation. The number of large firms in the actual population, N^*, is therefore random and distributed as binomial (N, P). Exhaustive sampling implies that the number of sampled large firms, n^*, is exactly equal to N^*. Conditional on this number, we can regard the sampled large firms as a simple random sample of size n^*, drawn directly from the superpopulation. Thus, the joint distribution of all potentially observable information relating to the sampled large firms is:

$$h(n^*, X_1 \ldots X_{n^*}) = \binom{n^*}{N} P^{n^*} (1-P)^{N-n^*} \prod_{j=1}^{n^*} g(X_j | S_j \geq C_j) \qquad [1]$$

However, in general the collection of variables X is not fully observable, since the NES is a 1 in (approximately) 100 random sample of NI numbers. Thus, any particular worker has a known probability $\rho \approx 0.01$ of being observed in the NES. Conditional on the size of the firm, S, the number of workers captured by the NES (q) therefore has a binomial (S, ρ) distribution. Letting the symbol $\tilde{X}$ denote the part of X that is observed, the joint sample distribution for large firms is therefore:

$$h(n^*, \tilde{X}_1 \ldots \tilde{X}_{n^*}) = \binom{n^*}{N} P^{n^*} (1-P)^{N-n^*}$$

$$\times \prod_{j=1}^{n^*} g(f_j | S_j \geq C_j) \binom{q_j}{S_j} \rho^{q_j} (1-\rho)^{S_j - q_j} \prod_{i=1}^{q_j} g(w_j^i | f_j, S_j) \qquad [2]$$

The remainder of the sample is a set of n^{**} small firms, where n^{**} is a fixed number chosen as part of the survey design. Under the superpopulation approach, observations on small firms ($S<C$) are viewed as being generated as a random sample (without replacement) drawn from a random sample drawn from the relevant part of an underlying infinite population. But a random sample of a random sample is itself a random sample, so the joint distribution of information relating to sampled small firms is:

$$h(X_{n^*+1}...X_n) = \prod_{j=n^*+1}^{n} g\left(X_j | S_j \geq C_j\right) \qquad [3]$$

Taking account of the random sampling of workers within firms as we did before, the full sample distribution for all observed firms and workers is:

$$h(n^*, X_1...X_n) = \binom{n^*}{N}(1-P)^{N-n}$$

$$\times \prod_{j=1}^{n^*} g\left(f_j, S_j\right)\binom{q_j}{S_j}\rho^{q_j}\left(1-\rho\right)^{S_j-q_j} \prod_{i=1}^{q_j} g\left(w_j^i | f_j, S_j\right) \qquad [4]$$

where we have used the relationships $g(f,S|S \geq C)=g(f,S)/P$ and $g(f,S|S<C)=g(f,S)/(1-P)$.

4 Cross-section estimation

We now consider the implications of the sample distribution [4] for some simple estimation purposes.

4.1 Estimating a cross-section earnings equation

For some practical purposes, we may be interested in the distribution of one or more worker variables conditional on the characteristics of the firm and remaining characteristics of the worker. This is so, for example, if we use the data to estimate an earnings regression. To find this conditional distribution, we divide the worker variables w into an endogenous variable w^* (earnings) and the remaining conditioning variables w^{**} (age, gender, unemployment history, etc.). We then need to integrate out the endogenous worker variable w^* to derive the marginal distribution of the conditioning variables $\{f,s,w^{**},q,n^*\}$, and then divide the full sample distribution by this marginal. When this is done, many terms in the sample distribution [4] cancel, and the result is the following conditional sample distribution:

$$h\left(w^*|f,s,q,n^*,w^{**}\right) = \prod_{j=1}^{n}\prod_{i=1}^{q_j} \frac{g(w_j^i|f_j,s_j)}{g(w_j^{**i}|f_j,s_j)} =$$

$$\prod_{j=1}^{n}\prod_{i=1}^{q_j} g\left(w_j^{*i}|f_j,s_j,w_j^{**i}\right)$$

[5]

The important result here is that this is essentially identical to the distribution of w^* conditional on $\{f,s,w^{**}\}$ in the superpopulation. Thus, the usual type of sample analysis of earnings conditional on firm and worker characteristics will give valid inferences about the underlying (super)population.

Table 2 gives the results of estimating conventional semi-log wage equations separately for 1994 and 1995, using a conventional set of explanatory covariates from the NES and JUVOS datasets, supplemented by ACOP firm characteristics.[7]

The earnings equation is standard apart from the inclusion of the employer variables and the before and after unemployment indicators. Similar such equations can be found in Hildreth (1996) and Troske (1998a). In all Tables to follow, the number next to the estimated coefficient is the asymptotic t-ratio unless otherwise indicated.

The results from Tables 2 and 3 provide results consistent with others in the literature. The age-earnings profile is unusual as even the third and fourth power terms are significant for men and women (although only for 1994 for women). Murphy and Welch (1990) argue that in the absence of detailed human capital control variables, a quartic in age approximates the empirical age-earnings profile. A collective bargaining agreement has a positive and significant effect for men, but a positive and insignificant effect (at normal levels) for women. All two digit occupation and industry dummy variables are significant, as are the 17 location dummies.

The unemployment variables show a varied pattern across time and across gender. Unemployment incidence before the job has a negative effect for men in 1994. The proportion of the year spent in unemployment has a negative and well determined effect on wages for men. For women, the effect is also negative, but not so significant. Unemployment incidence the following year also has a significant negative effect for men, but only for 1994 for women. The proportion of the following year unemployed for women shows the most surprising results. For 1994, the coefficient was well determined and positive. For 1995, the coefficient was negative and significant. Such a change in the coefficient is probably the effects of matching and obtaining a different cohort of individuals in

---

[7] Given that there are approximately 50 percent of the observations in either cross-section that have employers where more than 1 individual is observed at that establishment, it would be possible to recover an estimate of employer fixed effects. Hildreth (1996) provides an example of such an estimation. Such an exercise is not undertaken here.

1994 against 1995. Combining the two waves into a matched panel is the only means by which such effects can be disentangled.

Three employer variables were included in the wage equations: log number of employees, profit per employee, and capital expenditure per employee. All coefficients are positive, well determined (apart from capital expenditure per employee for females in 1995), and show that employers have significant effects on an individual's wage. As it might be expected that correlation between the employer variables might exist, because number of employees is common to each term, separate equations with only one employer term were estimated. The result of such an exercise showed that the sign, size, and significance of the employer terms did not change. It also showed that the coefficients on the individual specific components did not change. Employer effects on the wage appear independent and supplemental to individual characteristics.

The coefficients on employer variables are similar to those in Hildreth (1996) or Troske (1998a). If we concentrate on the rent-sharing parameter for Table 2 (estimated without instruments and so might therefore contain some endogeneity bias) we can illustrate some of the problems on reading the rent-sharing effect (see Hildreth, 1996; Hildreth and Oswald, 1997).[8]

The profit-per-employee coefficient implies an elasticity of 1.9 percent if we use the mean for the NES/ACOP link in 1994, or an elasticity of 2.6 percent for the same mean in 1995. It should be noted that the elasticities in both instances would be lower if we had used a properly weighted profit-per-employee term from the ACOP part of the sample. To further compound the differences from using the matched distribution of profit-per-employee over the ACOP distribution, we examine how much of the wage distribution the rent-sharing parameter explains. For 1994, the difference between the matched profit-per-employee distribution and the ACOP distribution is negligible. For 1995, the choice of profit-per-employee distribution to evaluate the elasticity matters a great deal. The ACOP sample standard deviation is twenty times larger than the matched NES/ACOP sample. The implications of the sample statistics are that the rent-sharing parameter explains nearly all the distribution in wages in either 1994 or 1995 if the matched NES/ACOP standard deviation is used. For 1995, if we use the standard deviation from the ACOP sample then the rent-sharing parameter explains an infeasibly large distribution for wages.[9] Matching workers and employers in 1995 only picks up on the larger (and more profitable) employers. This biases the inference on the extent of the wage distribution explained by rent-sharing. How the sample has been constructed can influence the conclusion on the rent-sharing effect in matched cross-section data.

---

[8] Hildreth and Oswald (1997) do this as 4 times the standard deviation of the profit-per-employee variable (move from bottom to top of distribution because of volatility of profits), multiplied by the elasticity to give the wage increase.

[9] Note that it does not matter if the average wage for establishments is used, or the average wage for the workers at establishments (scaled up to the annual level)

4.2 Estimating the probability of a transition to unemployment

The JUVOS dataset provides details of any spells of registered unemployment in the period following each of the NES/ACOP surveys. This allows us to estimate a model of the probability of a separation from the firm with a period of unemployment. Since JUVOS information is available in principle for each of our NES subjects, this entails no further sampling complications. We use a simple probit model of the probability that there is at least one spell of registered unemployment in the year following the NES (specifically 1994q3-1995q2 and 1995q3-1996q2 for the 1994 and 1995 samples respectively). In each case we use the base year's ACOP as the source for our firm-specific data, thus avoiding the need to link successive years' ACOP samples.

The estimating equation was a simple probit where the dependent variable equalled one if an unemployment spell occurred, and zero otherwise.[10]

The same individual and establishment characteristics were included in the probits as in the wage equation. The coefficients on Tables 4 and 5 are the differentiated coefficients so that they can be read directly as a one unit change in the variable of interest on the probability of an unemployment spell occurring.[11]

Tables 4 and 5 show that for men, the wage earned and a previous history of unemployment have a significant effect on the probability of being unemployed in the year succeeding a job. The higher the weekly wage, the less likely a male worker is unemployed. A previous spell, in either incidence or duration, has a positive effect.[12]

In general, no workplace variables were significant, although the industry dummies failed to reject the null that they were jointly zero. This tends to indicate that there are important sectoral differences. For 1995, capital expenditure per employee by an employer has a negative and well determined effect on the probability that a male worker will be unemployed in the succeeding year. Although capital expenditure is not necessarily tied to technology, the coefficient implies that any effects are not negative on employment.

The pattern of coefficients for females indicates that only the incidence of unemployment in the previous year has a significant and positive effect on the probability of a succeeding unemployment spell. Otherwise, collective bargaining helps female workers retain employment, and a large employer is more likely to have a negative effect on a female worker being unemployed.

---

[10] The individual could be unemployed on more than one occasion in the period following an NES employment spell, but we are only concerned if one occurred or not.

[11] In other words, if the probit model is defined as $Pr[y_i \neq 0 | X_i, Z_i] = \Phi(X_i\beta + Z_i\gamma)$ then the change in the probability for a given change in one element in X is: $\dfrac{\delta\Phi}{\delta X_i} = f(X_i\beta)\beta_i$.

[12] This is not counted as a lagged endogenous variable in this instance, although it is undoubtedly a dynamic event. We are concerned with the cross-section analysis for a single year.

4.3 Estimating the propensity to hire from the pool of unemployed

As the cross-section for each year effectively allowed unemployment experience to be recorded before and after the job spell. Using exactly the same estimating techniques as before, we estimated the probability of having an unemployment spell before finding a job. The before period was counted as 1993q2-1994q1 and 1994q2-1995q1 for the 1994 and 1995 samples respectively. The results are presented on Tables 6 and 7 and give the differentiated coefficients, so the estimates can be read directly (again as before).

For men (Table 6) the probability that an unemployment spell will precede a job is significant and increasing in age and the propensity to become unemployed after employment. The probability is decreasing in a collective bargaining workplace, where there is greater profit per employee, or if the employer is larger. In short, large, high profit employers do not hire men from the unemployed pool. The chi-squared tests indicate that there are important occupational and industrial differences in the propensity to be hired from unemployment.

Table 7 provides the results for women. The results show that there is little in the way of a consistent pattern between the two matched cross-sections. The general pattern is that being selected from the unemployment pool in this year is positively correlated with the probability that an unemployment spell will follow once the job is terminated. For 1994, the employer characteristics are well determined: profit per employee and size of employer having a negative effect, the capital expenditure per employee having a positive impact. For 1995, the industry dummy variables no longer fails to reject the null that they are all insignificantly different from zero. Sectoral effects that were captured in 1994 by employer characteristics were no longer significant in 1995.

Although it is supposed to apply at the regional level, there is a question of whether these results would confirm or cast doubt on a 'wage curve' (Blanchflower and Oswald, 1995). A wage curve would be consistent with an unemployment spell before the wage earning job. An unemployment effect that is negatively related to the previous job implies that there is a reverse causation: that as the wage falls an individual will enter unemployment. This is a competitive view of the world rather than one which postulates that unemployment has a negative effect on the wage. In fact, the results, both from the wage equations on Tables 2 and 3, and the results on unemployment on Tables 4 - 7 indicate that wages are procyclical (Bils, 1985). The results also give some evidence in favour of state dependence in unemployment.[13]

---

[13] See Hildreth *et al* (1997) for a test on state dependence in unemployment using individual lifetime work histories.

4.4 Estimating a cross-section model of firm variables

The same general conclusion is true if we derive the distribution of some firm characteristic f^* (such as profitability) conditional on firm size S and other firm characteristics f^{**}. However, any use of the ACOP data to analyse firm size, either unconditionally or conditional on other firm characteristics will produce biased results unless we make some allowance for the non-uniform ACOP sampling rates. For example, the distribution of the S_j conditional on the f_j is:

$$h\left(S_1...S_n|f_1...f_n,n^*\right) = \prod_{j=1}^{n} \frac{g\left(S_j|f_j\right)}{G_{S|f}\left(C_j\right)^{\left(1-\xi_j\right)}\left[1 - G_{S|f}\left(C_j\right)\right]^{\xi_j}} \neq \prod_{J=1}^{n} g\left(S_j|f_j\right) \qquad [6]$$

where $\xi_j=1$ if $S_j \geq C_j$ and $\xi_j = 0$ otherwise. Thus, conventional unweighted sample-based models of firm size would give biased inferences about the (super)population distribution $g(S_j \mid f_j)$, and bias-corrected methods such as weighted ML or truncated regression based on [6] are appropriate.

One estimate that is important in the context of a general labour analysis is the demand for labour by firms. In particular, the literature (reviewed by Hamermesh, 1993) shows a number of estimates for the constant output elasticity for homogeneous labour. Even ignoring the basic problems outlined by Hamermesh (1993) in estimating a cross-section labour demand equation, without accounting for the sampling effect from matching workers and employers, the estimates are going to be biased. The bias arises from the differential sampling probabilities for the ACOP data against the NES data. Table 1c provides evidence on the effect of the different sample that arises from matching employees with their employers.

The cross-section labour demand model used here is standard. The basic form includes the value-added per employee and the annual average wage as well as sectoral (26) and location (17) dummies. In estimating equation (6) we use weighted maximum likelihood and compare this with estimating the simple labour demand model using ordinary least squares (OLS). Table 8 presents the results.

Estimation of the model by either method gives parameters on the two variables of interest that are similar. The constant output elasticity of labour demanded is approximately 0.8. The elasticity with respect to the average wage is negative and approximately -0.9. Both coefficients are well determined. The difference by estimation method is only slight, but it is significant. A test on the equality of coefficients rejects the null that they are the same in both years. However, in terms of determining the economic variable of the constant output elasticity, there is little advantage to be gained from consideration of the sampling structure in cross-section equations.

The difference between methods can be gleaned from the coefficients on the industry dummy variables. For 1994 there are notable differences between the industries of extraction, food products, wood products, and chemicals, among others. The simple sampling scheme for the ACOP in that year (only establishments of 100+ employees sampled with a probability of 1) provided a noted difference between using OLS and weighted maximum likelihood. For 1995, when the sampling scheme had changed so that the threshold for exhaustive sampling was dependent on industry as well as size, there was little difference between the coefficients estimated by either method. This indicates that the extent of theoretical bias can be reduced through a representative sampling scheme.

5 Conclusions

This paper has three objectives. Firstly, we have described the construction of a new dataset formed from the British New Earnings Survey (NES) of employees, the Annual Census of Production (ACOP), covering manufacturing firms, with national insurance records (JUVOS) used to provide additional information on periods of registered unemployment. This linked dataset is in effect a panel, with two waves in the years 1994 and 1995, but we have restricted attention here to its use for cross-section analysis.

Secondly, using a theoretical foundation in superpopulation sampling theory, we have considered the methodological problems raised by the linking process and the non-uniform sampling design of the ACOP. We have established that, for the purpose of estimating a cross-section relationship such as an earnings equation relating the level of pay to firm and worker characteristics, conventional methods such as multiple regression will not be biased by the NES/ACOP sampling scheme, provided the estimated relationship is interpreted as holding only for jobs in manufacturing industry. However, any model with firm size (employment) as an endogenous variable will in general be affected by sample selection bias as a result of the non-uniform ACOP sampling rate. Thirdly, we have presented some estimation results for simple models of earnings, job separations and employment. In the first two cases, these demonstrate the importance of including in the analysis variables that can typically only be supplied by this sort of linked dataset. The employment model illustrates that although serious bias can result from ignoring the employment-related nature of the ACOP sampling scheme, for the simple model that was estimated, the effects were very limited.

Table 1a Observation Loss from the NES by National Insurance

Source	NES 1994	NES 1995
Sample issued	209900	213500
Response	166634	162068
Observations lost from repeat NINO	4021	2112
Observations available for matching to JUVOS	162613	159955
Observations lost from missing ENTREF	46941	1980
Observations remaining for match to ACOP	115672	157975
Manufacturing observations remaining for match to ACOP	36153	34641

Table 1b Observation Loss from the JUVOS by National Insurance number (NINO).

Source	JUVOS NES 94	JUVOS NES 95
NINO records available on JUVOS file	201648	202595
Number of unemployment records	73350	73180
NES observations available for match to JUVOS	162613	159956
Number of records	61145	60668
Number of records for 1993-96 period	23195	24050

Table 1c Observation Loss from the ACOP by Reporting Unit reference number (RUREF).

Source	ACOP 94	ACOP 95
Sample issued: total	16035	15458
Sample issued: <100 employees	8496	9140
Sample issued: 100+ employees	7539	6318
Response: total	13031	12617
Response: <100 employees	6591	7090
Response: 100+ employees	6443	5527
Number of establishments matched to NES	4490	3824
Number of observations on establishments matched to NES	13910	16016
Matched to NES: <100 employees	1534	1389
Matched to NES: 100+ employees	12376	14627

Table 2 Estimated log wage equations for Males: NES-JUVOS-ACOP 1994/5

Covariate	1994 sample		1995 sample	
constant	0.866	1.356	0.671	1.302
age/100	43.536	6.161	42.730	7.674
age^2	-142.469	5.020	-141.787	6.459
age^3	208.248	4.310	210.621	5.715
age^4	-115.387	3.905	-118.554	5.304
collective bargaining agreement	0.018	1.511	0.032	2.463
proportion of last year unemployed	-0.266	3.018	-0.595	2.838
unemployment during last year	-0.033	2.298	0.045	0.998
proportion of following year unemployed	0.073	1.077	0.004	0.037
unemployment during following year	-0.136	4.273	-0.107	3.945
profit per employee	0.0001	8.413	0.0001	10.701
capital expenditure per employee	0.002	4.170	0.001	3.101
log number of employees	0.031	9.150	0.041	12.713
F test on occupational dummies [p-value]	130.89	[0.000]	151.67	[0.000]
F test on industry dummies [p-value]	35.82	[0.000]	8.53	[0.000]
F test on location dummies [p-value]	8.75	[0.000]	6.45	[0.000]
R^2	0.305		0.368	
n	9861		11660	

Table 3 Estimated log wage equations for Females: NES-JUVOS-ACOP 1994/5

Covariate	1994 sample		1995 sample	
constant	3.084	4.062	3.597	5.144
age/100	15.572	2.134	9.974	1.358
age^2	-55.629	1.983	-30.337	1.076
age^3	91.717	1.992	43.608	0.944
age^4	-59.229	2.163	-26.377	0.958
collective bargaining agreement	0.012	0.446	0.064	2.020
proportion of last year unemployed	-0.389	1.322	-0.146	0.628
unemployment during last year	-0.022	0.294	0.050	0.786
proportion of following year unemployed	0.256	2.070	-0.418	2.104
unemployment during following year	-0.104	2.206	-0.006	0.134
profit per employee	0.0002	5.210	0.0002	5.362
capital expenditure per employee	0.003	2.696	0.001	1.054
log number of employees	0.053	7.157	0.045	6.058
F test on occupational dummies [p-value]	47.55	[0.000]	37.77	[0.000]
F test on industry dummies [p-value]	6.81	[0.000]	7.28	[0.000]
F test on location dummies [p-value]	5.71	[0.000]	4.20	[0.000]
R^2	0.318		0.279	
n	3821		4063	

Table 4 Estimated probits for Males for unemployment in the succeeding year: NES-JUVOS-ACOP 1994/5

Covariate	1994 sample		1995 sample	
age/100	-0.694	0.470	0.201	0.120
age^2	0.495	0.090	-4.270	0.640
age^3	2.013	0.210	12.171	1.060
age^4	-2.382	0.420	-9.801	1.390
collective bargaining agreement	-0.001	0.110	-0.003	0.540
log weekly wage	-0.033	6.410	-0.019	5.310
proportion of last year unemployed	0.102	3.470	0.080	3.050
unemployment during last year	0.080	4.860	0.070	4.650
profit per employee	0.001	0.250	-0.001	0.750
capital expenditure per employee	-0.001	0.370	-0.001	2.660
log number of employees	0.002	1.290	0.001	0.630
χ^2 test on occupational dummies [p-value]	13.37	[0.343]	23.04	[0.083]
χ^2 test on industry dummies [p-value]	39.04	[0.020]	89.29	[0.000]
χ^2 test on location dummies [p-value]	24.46	[0.080]	20.00	[0.220]
pseudo R^2	0.092		0.093	
n	9782		11519	

Table 5 Estimated probits for Females for unemployment in the succeeding year: NES-JUVOS-ACOP 1994/5

Covariate	1994 sample		1995 sample	
age/100	0.505	0.160	2.151	0.590
age^2	-7.070	0.530	-12.132	0.800
age^3	19.074	0.780	25.686	0.960
age^4	-15.450	0.960	-18.364	1.070
collective bargaining agreement	0.020	1.950	0.018	1.710
log weekly wage	-0.006	0.990	-0.009	1.630
proportion of last year unemployed	0.034	0.730	0.116	2.160
unemployment during last year	0.094	3.590	0.081	3.040
profit per employee	0.001	0.090	-0.002	1.510
capital expenditure per employee	0.002	0.560	-0.001	1.410
log number of employees	-0.005	2.000	0.004	1.530
χ^2 test on occupational dummies [p-value]	14.75	[0.255]	10.51	[0.571]
χ^2 test on industry dummies [p-value]	25.04	[0.295]	40.18	[0.015]
χ^2 test on location dummies [p-value]	17.14	[0.377]	21.05	[0.177]
pseudo R^2	0.114		0.093	
n	3761		4004	

Table 6 Estimated probits for Males for unemployment in the preceding year: NES-JUVOS-ACOP 1994/5

Covariate	1994 sample		1995 sample	
age/100	5.332	3.310	0.804	1.850
age^2	-23.846	3.520	-3.854	2.090
age^3	43.377	3.580	7.448	2.230
age^4	-28.044	3.590	-5.093	2.340
collective bargaining agreement	-0.011	2.670	-0.002	2.230
proportion of following year unemployed	0.001	0.020	0.037	11.410
unemployment during following year	0.115	8.360	0.135	16.430
profit per employee	-0.001	1.840	-0.001	2.070
capital expenditure per employee	-0.001	0.080	0.001	1.320
log number of employees	-0.005	3.800	-0.001	1.860
χ^2 test on occupational dummies [p-value]	59.32	[0.000]	14.17	[0.512]
χ^2 test on industry dummies [p-value]	43.24	[0.003]	28.68	[0.278]
χ^2 test on location dummies [p-value]	9.45	[0.894]	15.62	[0.480]
pseudo R^2	0.165		0.621	
n	9367		11658	

Table 7 Estimated probits for Females for unemployment in the preceding year: NES-JUVOS-ACOP 1994/5

Covariate	1994 sample		1995 sample	
age/100	0.619	0.210	0.911	0.910
age^2	-7.351	0.560	-5.144	1.150
age^3	19.905	0.820	11.428	1.340
age^4	-16.650	1.020	-8.824	1.500
collective bargaining agreement	-0.015	2.080	0.004	1.320
proportion of following year unemployed	0.030	1.110	0.039	5.780
unemployment during following year	0.072	3.530	0.113	9.360
profit per employee	-0.001	1.790	-0.000	0.060
capital expenditure per employee	0.001	1.970	-0.000	0.210
log number of employees	-0.005	2.220	-0.001	1.210
χ^2 test on occupational dummies [p-value]	13.30	[0.208]	10.74	[0.466]
χ^2 test on industry dummies [p-value]	20.15	[0.512]	99.57	[0.000]
χ^2 test on location dummies [p-value]	9.33	[0.859]	6.82	[0.977]
pseudo R^2	0.148		0.472	
n	3590		3886	

Table 8 Difference between Labour Demand models by method of estimation: NES/ACOP 1994 and 1995. (Standard errors)

Covariate 1994	Weighted ML		OLS	
log value added per employee	0.796	0.005	0.790	0.005
log average annual wager	-0.918	0.026	-0.924	0.025
Extraction	-0.535	0.154	-0.364	0.150
Mining quarrying	-0.227	0.133	-0.017	0.129
Food products	-0.853	0.330	-0.618	0.221
Tobacco	-0.241	0.136	-0.008	0.131
Textiles	-0.078	0.142	0.096	0.133
Apparel	-0.233	0.148	-0.013	0.136
Leather	-0.257	0.142	-0.074	0.136
Wood products	-0.275	0.136	-0.015	0.131
Paper	-0.177	0.135	0.024	0.130
Printing	-0.456	0.145	-0.163	0.153
Chemicals	-0.291	0.135	-0.070	0.130
Chemical products	-0.272	0.136	-0.056	0.130
Rubber & plastic	-0.174	0.136	0.008	0.131
Non-metal mineral	-0.179	0.135	0.063	0.131
Basic metals	-0.212	0.135	-0.007	0.129
Fabricated metals	-0.163	0.134	0.050	0.129
Metal machinery	-0.053	0.144	0.138	0.144
Office machinery	-0.161	0.136	0.064	0.131
Electrical machinery	-0.134	0.137	0.075	0.133
Machinery not specified	-0.138	0.136	0.053	0.131
Communication equipment	-0.132	0.137	0.092	0.131
Precision instruments	0.046	0.138	0.263	0.133
Motor vehicles	-0.153	0.137	0.053	0.131
Other transport	-0.731	0.392	-0.337	0.312
Furniture	-0.109	0.180	0.130	0.221
Energy supply	-0.575	0.165	-0.388	0.150
n	4399		4399	

Covariate 1995	Weighted ML		OLS	
log value added per employee	0.802	0.005	0.806	0.005
log average annual wager	-0.833	0.027	-0.875	0.029
Extraction	0.840	0.614	1.135	0.450
quarrying	-0.200	0.093	-0.241	0.099
Food products	0.372	0.074	0.354	0.075
Tobacco	-0.095	0.255	-0.029	0.234
Textiles	0.352	0.081	0.373	0.079
Apparel	0.468	0.091	0.490	0.087
Leather	0.488	0.110	0.516	0.100
Wood products	0.222	0.086	0.236	0.090
Paper	0.327	0.082	0.305	0.079
Printing	0.231	0.077	0.279	0.076
Chemicals	0.035	0.088	0.098	0.113
Chemical products	0.214	0.075	0.222	0.077
Rubber & plastic	0.339	0.081	0.373	0.077
Non-metal mineral	0.287	0.080	0.273	0.079
Basic metals	0.269	0.078	0.285	0.079
Fabricated metals	0.364	0.079	0.389	0.077
Metal machinery	0.437	0.077	0.438	0.075
Office machinery	0.484	0.097	0.478	0.097
Electrical machinery	0.419	0.082	0.440	0.079
Machinery not specified	0.373	0.085	0.401	0.083
Communication equipment	0.404	0.082	0.406	0.079
Precision instruments	0.436	0.086	0.436	0.079
Motor vehicles	0.660	0.080	0.626	0.083
Other transport	0.395	0.083	0.407	0.079
Furniture	-0.100	0.135	-0.120	0.195
Energy supply	0.357	0.113	0.348	0.123
n	3739		3739	

Appendix A: Additional Tables

Table A1 Descriptive Statistics 1994: Means and Standard Deviations.

	NES for JUVOS	NES for ACOP	ACOP	ACOP <100	ACOP 100+	NES/ACOP	NES/ACOP<100	NES/ACOP 100+
N	162612	115672	15945	8761	7187	15261	1906	13355
wage (week)	269.162	268.295				302.922	280.637	306.103
	(206.481)	(211.565)				(186.772)	(236.697)	(178.296)
age	38.445	38.639				39.247	39.993	39.141
	(12.283)	(12.500)				(11.929)	(12.809)	(11.794)
coll.barg	0.326	0.207				0.172	0.201	0.168
	(0.469)	(0.405)				(0.378)	(0.401)	(0.374)
female	0.473	0.443				0.264	0.237	0.268
	(0.499)	(0.497)				(0.441)	(0.425)	(0.443)
pre unemp	0.051	0.057				0.045	0.058	0.043
	(0.221)	(0.233)				(0.207)	(0.233)	(0.203)
post unemp	0.055	0.060				0.053	0.047	0.054
	(0.227)	(0.237)				(0.224)	(0.212)	(0.225)
π/n (000's)			10.557	7.763	13.958	18.257	9.161	19.556
			(27.932)	(29.513)	(25.461)	(30.702)	(23.259)	(31.408)
employment			220.557	41892	438.301	1109.564	57.892	1259.657
			(809.654)	(25.668)	(1169.337)	(2267.062)	(24.387)	(2361.756)
sales (million)			26.442	2.899	50.885	153.548	4.264	172.051
			(155.994)	(6.201)	(220.088)	(360.585)	(4.768)	(378.194)
K/n (000's)			2.542	1.978	3.230	4.683	2.025	5.062
			(8.703)	(9.606)	(7.395)	(11.505)	(4.848)	(12.114)

Table A2 Descriptive Statistics 1995: Means and Standard Deviations.

	NES for JUVOS	NES for ACOP	ACOP	ACOP 100	ACOP 100+	NES/ACOP	NES/ACOP<100	NES/ACOP 100+
N	159955	115672	12579	7052	5527	15731	1277	14454
wage (week)	278.120	267.742				333.689	282.277	338.232
	(220.001)	(212.725)				(197.454)	(167.641)	(199.242)
age	38.596	38.457				39.283	39.373	39.276
	(12.198)	(12.529)				(11.535)	(12.900)	(11.407)
coll.barg	0.297	0.294				0.146	0.080	0.152
	(0.457)	(0.456)				(0.353)	(0.271)	(0.359)
female	0.475	0.475				0.259	0.281	0.257
	(0.499)	(0.499)				(0.438)	(0.450)	(0.437)
pre unemp	0.049	0.050				0.036	0.052	0.035
	(0.216)	(0.216)				(0.186)	(0.223)	(0.183)
post unemp	0.051	0.051				0.049	0.060	0.048
	(0.221)	(0.221)				(0.216)	(0.237)	(0.214)
π/n (000's)			23.767	28.748	17.413	24.858	13.240	14.777
			(1148.478)	(1533.621)	(33.266)	(39.162)	(34.082)	(26.550)
employment			233.025	35.791	486.036	3206.875	56.425	446.752
			(830.806)	(26.588)	(1208.714)	(9226.446)	(25.925)	(1223.354)
sales (million)			29.018	3.218	62.114	623.818	6.031	682.484
			(178.418)	(9.460)	(265.728)	(1985.720)	(8.665)	(2068.298)
K/n (000's)			9.783	14.008	4.391	6.840	3.490	3.841
			(662.518)	(884.800)	(9.936)	(12.053)	(11.615)	(7.742)

REFERENCES

Abowd, J. M. and Kramarz, F. (1997) *"The Analysis of Labor Markets using Matched Employer-Employee Data"*, in Ashenfelter, O. and Card, D., Handbook of Labor Economics, Vol III, North-Holland, Amsterdam.

Abowd, J. M., Kramarz, F. and Margolis, D. (1997) *"High Wage Workers and High Wage Firms"*, Econometrica.

Bils, M. (1985) *"Real Wages over the Business Cycle: Evidence from Panel Data"*, Journal of Political Economy, 93, 666-689.

Cahuc, P. and Kramarz, F. (1997) *"Voice and Loyalty as a Delegation of Authority: A Model and a Test on Matched Worker-Firm Panels"*, Journal of Labor Economics, 15.

Blanchflower, D. G. and Oswald, A. J. (1994) *The Wage Curve* (MIT Press, Mass., Camb. USA).

Carrington, W. J. and Troske, K. R. (1998a*) "Interfirm Racial Segregation and the Black/White Wage Gap"*, Journal of Labor Economics.

Carrington, W. J. and Troske, K. R. (1998b) *"Sex Segregation in U.S. Manufacturing Industry"*, Industrial and Labor Relations Review.

Cassel, C., Särndal, C. E. and Wretman, J. H. (1977) *Foundations of Inference in Survey Sampling.* New York: Wiley.

Entorf, H. and Kramarz, F. (1997) *"Does Unmeasured Ability explain the Higher Wage of New Technology Workers?"* European Economic Review, 41, 1489-1509.

Gregory, M. and Jukes, R. (1997) *"The Effects of Unemployment on Subsequent Earnings: A Study of British Men 1984-94"*, mimeo, Oxford University.

Hamermesh, D. S. (1993) *Labor Demand. Princeton*: Princeton University Press.

Hellerstein, J. K., Neumark, D., and Troske, K. R. (1998) *"Wages, Productivity, and Worker Characteristics: Evidence from Plant-Level Production Functions and Wage Equations"*, mimeo, University of Missouri.

Hildreth, A. K. G. (1996) *"Rent-Sharing and Wages: Product Demand or Technology Driven Premia?"* Paper given at the STEP Conference, National Academy of Sciences, Washington.

Hildreth, A. K. G., Mortensen, D. T., Millard, S. P. and Taylor, M. P. (1997) *"Wages, Work, and Unemployment"*, Applied Economics.

Hildreth, A. K. G. and Oswald, A. J. (1997) *"Rent-Sharing and Wages: Evidence from Company and Establishment Panels"*, Journal of Labor Economics, 15.

Hildreth, A. K. G. and Pudney, S. E. (1996) *"Employers, Workers and Unions: An Analysis of a Firm-Worker Panel with Endogenous Sampling, Attrition and Missing Data"*, University of Leicester Discussion Paper in Economics no. 96/15.

Imbens, G. W. and Lancaster, T. (1996) *"Efficient Estimation and Stratified Sampling"*, Journal of Econometrics, 74, 289-318.

Murphy, K. M. and Welch, F. (1990) *"Empirical Age-Earnings Profiles"*, Journal of Labor Economics, 8, 202-229.

Pudney, S. E. (1989). *Modelling Individual Choice. The Econometrics of Corners, Kinks and Holes.* Oxford: Blackwell.

Troske, K. R. (1998a) *"Evidence on the Employer Size-Wage Premium from Worker-Establishment Matched Data"*, Review of Economics and Statistics.

Troske, K. R. (1998b) *"The Worker Establishment Characteristic Database"*, in Haltiwanger, J., Manser, M.and Topel, R. (eds)., Labor Statistics Measurement Issues, (Chicago University Press: NBER).

DYNAMICS OF ITALIAN INDUSTRIAL FIRMS: MICROECONOMIC ANALYSIS OF PERFORMANCE AND LABOUR DEMAND FROM 1989 TO 1994

Giancarlo Bruno[1], Veronica Corsini[2] and Roberto Monducci[3]

[1,2,3]*Istituto Nazionale di Statistica, Italy*

1 Introduction [*]

The need to develop microeconomic analyses of industrial systems arises from the necessity of a close examination of structural aspects (efficiency differentials between firms; firm typology identification; analysis of wage dispersion level etc.) (Corsini, Monducci, Vicari, 1997) and also from the recognition of a high heterogeneity in industrial behaviour as far as dynamic aspects, in particular with reference to firm size behaviour.

The main aspect which this paper wants to analyse is the connection between the industrial sector characteristics, firm size and performance and work use intensity condition in terms of employment levels, job composition, actual working time and wage levels. As regards segments of small-sized firms (30-99 employees) and medium-sized firms (100-499 employees) particular attention is given to dynamics of employment, i.e. growth and decrease, with reference to different behaviours (depending on size, sectors, geographical areas) during business cycle, as well as to the connection between employment dynamics and individual firm profitability level, mainly in terms of persistence. This connection is analysed through a wide set of indicators.

[*] This paper is the result of the authors' common work, who share the responsibility for it. However Giancarlo Bruno wrote paragraph 5, Veronica Corsini paragraph 6 and Annex A and Roberto Monducci paragraphs 2, 3 and 4. Veronica Corsini also set up the database. Particular acknowledgment to Tiziana Di Francescantonio and to Umberto Sansone for computing support in database building and to Cristina Di Mei for her collaboration in editing the paper.

2 Business size and growth of the Italian industry: debate

From the post-war period to today, the analyses carried out about the Italian economic system have pointed out an economic structure specificity of our country in comparison with the main developed western countries. This specificity means a very considerable and widespread presence of small and medium firms for most part of the country sectors and areas. A business system division in very small units[1] is recorded for market services; as far as industry, the configuration in a great number of sectors is characterised by an important presence of small and medium firms in remarkable integration processes (Rey, 1988).

Literature about factors determining a wide range of firm sizing coexistence in industry has fully studied the Italian specificity; particularly, small firms in the north of our country would represent a new industrial pattern based on flexible specialisation, with positive influences on the system efficiency as well as on social implications of industry development (You, 1995: 441).

As regards manufacturing firms, at least until the early '70s, this favourable situation was evaluated as a negative condition, as a sign of the Italian economic structure inadequacy and of the incapacity for a trend towards greater size, resulting in an inability to exploit at best scale economies, to use more advanced technologies mainly peculiar in medium-large firms and to obtain stable market shares in foreign markets.

After, evidences relating to small and medium firms performance and relating to the crisis of large industrial size have caused a wide debate related to some main explanatory trends underlining different aspects, not always in opposition, about Italian industrial size and sector evolution (Brusco and Sabel, 1981; Barca, 1985; Vaccà, 1985; Contini and Revelli, 1986).

Lately the debate (Signorini, 1991a and 1991b, 1993 and 1996; Contini, Pacelli, Rapiti, 1993; Traù, 1996; Meldolesi, 1996) has dealt with the performance of small firms, with their role in the job-creation process; with the coherence between the remarkable existence of small-sized units in the Italian industrial system and the image, remembered by many people, of a "frozen" labour market; with factors of success for the small firm system in specific country areas; with measurement problems about true dynamics of the industrial system (micro and macro).

The analyses below, arising from debate, allow to outline some connections between the different size segments of Italian industry, in this case small and medium firms. In the first early '90s this outline is characterised on the one hand by a considerable heterogeneity, on the other by a significant "regularity". In particular, the question is first if size factor is a basic segmentation of the

---

[1] Different interpretations of causes and effects of this phenomenon are in Barca and Visco (1991), Rey (1992), Monducci and Pisani (1993).

industrial system in terms of efficiency, productivity, profitability and employment growth tendency, or if sectorial, territorial and market factors predominate besides economic-financial arrangement peculiar to every firm. In fact the wealth of information used allows to understand the complexity of development pattern for small and medium manufacturing firms in view of the "effects" that can be associated with a wide set of indicators, both internal and external to each firm.

3 The database

3.1 Integration of micro sources and building of structural indicators of the sectors

Analyses based on a panel of 5,900 firms with employment between 30 and 499 employees in 1989 have been performed to analyse the cyclic dynamics of manufacturing firms during 1989-94 period, taken from the System of the Enterprises Accounts annual (SCI)[2] surveys for the years from 1989 to 1994[3]. As regards the macro level, this period was characterised by a progressive decline of activity levels, a clear recessive slump and a following resumption of development dynamics.

The integration between these data and other external sources has been required to organise micro dynamics in a more complex information context; in particular, a sectorial indicator set, sector classifying methods and micro data related to the panel[4] have been required.

Also, structural information from VII general Census of Industry and Services of 1991 have been used. Particularly, data processing of firms surveyed in 1991 have been performed in order to calculate different indices relating to firm size structure in every economic sector. In this paper, data relating to entropic average of firm employees for 3 digit Ateco 1991[5] sectors are used. The obtained

---

[2] This is a survey yearly performed by Istat of industrial and service firms with 20 or more employees, for which economic-financial data consistent with IV EEC Directive are available.

[3] Since our strategy is to analyse the dynamic behaviour of the each firm, the panel building criterion is solely referred to firm permanence in terms of identification code, without considering any society transformation which could alter company configuration.

[4] For problems about the integration among statistical sources see Monducci (1994) and Corsini, Monducci, Vicari (1997).

[5] As it is known, entropic average is used only for highly asymmetrical distributions, like that of firms by employee number, because it is less influenced by smaller firm weights,

classification has been used to define economic sectors in terms of prevailing "market size": therefore it deals with sectors in which small, medium, medium-large and large firm size are prevailing.

Other sectorial classifications used have been based on traditional product scheme and on approaches connected to the prevailing technological aspect of production or to economic destination of products. Moreover, the importance of firm outlet to the international market as discriminant factor with regard to efficiency, employment, profitability has suggested the need of an integration between SCI survey data and data relating to firm foreign trade statistics, at micro level. In this way a considerable microeconomic indicator set about export geographic penetration and product diversification for export sales have been available, anyway with regard only to the biennium 1993-94.

3.2 Main structural and dynamic features of the panel

The structural and dynamic features of the closed panel we selected are the following:

- the 5,901 selected industrial firms give an overall employment equal to 546,000 employees in 1989 and 544,850 employees in 1994;
- the division in two main size classes with reference to the employment in 1989 shows a number of firms with 30-99 employees (small firms) equal to 4,296 firms, whereas 100-499 employee firms (medium firms) are 1,605;
- firm distribution in economic sectors[6] shows that the small firm segment is divided in percentages equal to 17.5%, 32.8% and 49.7% respectively for branch 2 (iron metallurgy, chemical industry), branch 3 (mechanical industry) and branch 4 (food, textile and clothing industry, wood etc.); the medium firm percentages are respectively 19.3%, 37.1% and 43.5%;
- the firm territorial distribution[7] shows small firms percentages equal to 47.2%, 32.7%, 14.1% and 6% respectively for north-west, north-east, central and

---

in comparison with arithmetic average and median. On the basis of this indicator value each economic sector is classified in entropic average ranges (less than 20 employees; 20-49 employees; 50-99 employees; 100-499 employees; 500 employees and over). The 106 sectors of 3 digit Ateco 1991 have the following distribution by entropic average class: 24.5% of sectors has less than 20 employees; 39.6% has an entropic average value between 20 and 99 employees; 24.5% between 100 and 499 employees and 11.3% more than 499 employees.

[6] Economic sectors of 1991 Ateco classification were reduced to the three main branches of 1981 Ateco classification.

[7] We refer to legal head-office. For firms with offices in different geographical areas, classification uses the whole of segments in the geographical area where the legal head-office is located.

south of Italy; medium firms territorial structure shows percentages respectively equal to 51%, 31.5%, 11.7% and 5.8% for the four areas;
- according to four employee classes related to the first year (30-49; 50-99; 100-199; 200-499), the permanence percentages for the same class are respectively 66%; 70.2%; 70.6%; 76% in a comparison between 1989 and 1994.

4 Labour demand and Italian manufacturing firms performance: a general view of macro and microeconomic dynamics between 1989 and 1994

4.1 Manufacturing sector aggregate trends

As regards the macro level[8], at the end of '80s and in the first half of '90s, Italian industrial firms trends showed a clear downsizing of the real output growth rates in 1990, after a long development phase began in 1983 (Table 1). Between the end of '80s and the beginning of the 1994-95 development cycle, the firm system experienced a great number of shocks (of demand and supply) which remarkably conditioned company policies and firm demography.

As regards the macro level, the performed microeconomic analyses below (1989-94) concern a period marked out at least in three different cyclic phases: even if the real output growth rates are positive yet, the first phase (1989-90) foreshadowed the 1991-93 economic downswing; these years represented a phase for the Italian industry with the greatest competitiveness pressure and crisis (at least up to 1992). The "jump" in 1994 represented the first development wave which will continue until the end of 1995.

The employment adjustment began in 1991 and went on with a growing intensity until 1993. During the considered triennium, manufacturing firms lost almost 530,000 employees, with a following stabilisation which pointed out in any case negative rates in employment variation even if during the considerable recovery in 1994-95.

Profit dynamics, growing in the period of 1984-1988, points out a first decline in 1989 and a further aggravation of negative trend up to 1992. In 1993 margin recovery, supported by exchange adjustment and by the consequent export profitability recovery, occurred even if in the presence of a remarkable slump of real output, thus it showed anticyclical dynamics. Later on, profit boom seems to be produced by an extraordinary series of positive factors (wage control, productivity resumption, increase of competitiveness in home and foreign market

---

[8] In this case, data used are those given by National Accounts.

etc.) with an increase of profit margins; during 1995 this increase reached levels comparable with 1988-89 levels.

After a quadriennium of negative variations (1989-92), with regard to this outline, the mark-up course has to be underlined as it systematically increases from 1993, supporting in this way a gross profitability recovery. This "inflationary" trend of margins occurred both in the quite moderate input price dynamics (1993-94) despite the potentially destabilising influence of exchange adjustment, and in 1995, a period of maximum strength of inflationary pressures, particularly of foreign origin. Mark-up increased persistence in the different cyclic phases following the exchange adjustment in 1992 seems to underline competitiveness strengthening in home and foreign market only in part damaged by the exchange revaluation recorded in 1996. In parallel, from 1993 employment weakness is associated with the persistent loss of purchasing power of industrial wages.

4.2 Levels and dynamics of main economic indicators from the panel

The division of the panel in two main segments (units with 30-99 and 100-499 employees in 1989) allows to outline a comparative evolution of firms initially "small" or "medium". Through this particular explanation, the analysis of size differentials concerning the main economic indicators (Table 2), has to be interpreted not so much for its structural meaning as for its evaluation function of convergence and divergence processes between firm groups[9].

From 1989 to 1994 as regards the main economic indicators, cyclic dynamics seem to cause on the one hand a tendential change of relationship between small and medium industrial firms attributable to trends of labour productivity and of gross profitability, on the other hand a great stability of the differentials between the two size segments especially relating to labour cost indicators.

Comparison between data relating to 1989 and to 1994 points out a great stability of the differentials for labour cost and hourly wages: in the first case small firm labour cost is 12% lower than the medium firms both in 1989 and in 1994; hourly wages have more gap, the differential being approximately equal to 15%. In correspondence with this great wage dynamic homogeneity, concerning qualification data and economic activity branch too, a progressive gap of labour productivity unfavourable for small firms comes out particularly evident in the traditional sectors of branch 4 (food, textile industry etc.). Labour productivity for

---

[9] A comparison among distribution according to firm size classes in the panel, between 1989 and 1994, shows that 207 firms out of 4296 firms with 30-99 employees have moved to a superior size class; change is even greater if medium size firms are examined: in this case 202 out of 1605 firms with a number of employees from 100 to 499 moved to the lower class in 1994.

small business is 10.6% lower than the medium-sized firms in 1989, during the following years it tends downward and it reaches a level 14% lower than the greater size unit level in 1994.

This trend is associated with an average working time increase of small firms with reference to medium firms, attributable especially to branch 4 firms. A clearer gap is found for the average blue collars time differential between small and medium firms: in 1989 it was 3.7% and it systematically tends upward, except for a slight decrease in 1993, reaching up to 5% in 1994[10]. In order to examine the analysis of firm average working time, Annex A presents the results of a subdivision exercise of per capita hours variability according to some industrial classifications and different employment typologies.

Stability factors concern the structure of variable costs, too. In this case, small firms persistently present on the one hand a higher incidence of costs of raw material and semi-manufactured goods especially for branch 4, on the other less costs particularly for service purchases and for personnel costs marginally. In the examined period, the tendential "tertiarization" of prime costs, that is the increase of external service cost incidence, has equally concerned small and medium firms.

As far as output dynamics, small firms are less lively as regards nominal increase of turnover per employee whereas propensity to export, systematically lower for small firms, shows a very specific cyclic course and above all an interesting evolution of export structure (export to EEC countries and non-European countries). In 1989 the amount of export turnover is 21% and 25.4% of sales volume for small and medium firms respectively; in 1994 they are 26.8% and 32.2%. Data relating to the beginning and to the end of the period confirm the considerable acceleration of the firm outlet to international market at the beginning of '90s.

However, a different trend for the two phases 1989-91 and 1992-94 is one of the first differentiation factor. If compared with the medium firms, during the first phase small firms seem to increase propensity to export although competitiveness problems due to the trend of nominal exchange and of home and international prices. During the second phase, the medium firms capability to take the opportunities coming from change adjustment allow an extraordinary performance occurred not only in 1992-93 but also in 1994.

A further discriminant aspect is the different nature of export turnover according to the geographical area of destination: in 1989 the export share to non-European countries is 34.2% of the export volume for small firms and 34.3% for medium firms; in 1994 the incidences are respectively 44.1% and 41.7%. Small firms have showed a stronger increase of foreign turnover in non-European countries if compared with medium firms, especially in 1994.

---

[10] This evidence is confirmed even when a correction of every firm employment stock is performed to take into account the different use of wage supplementation funds.

4.3 Structural and performance indicators in balance-sheets data

Availability of balance-sheet data allows to consider some important structural and dynamic aspects, in particular on the one hand the firm capability to get a balanced ratio between available financial resources and their use, on the other a more exact evaluation of industrial profitability levels.

As far as property indices and in particular investment structure flexibility, small firms seem to have a greater capability to convert investments into liquidity, with a relative growing trend during the considered period. In fact in particular in 1993-94, they have less medium and long-term debts, whereas particular differentiation do not result from the share of total investments not funded by venture capital.

Moreover, as far as small firms, the analysis of some financial indices points out a greater immobilisation covering through internal funds with a clear relative growing trend if compared with medium-sized firms, during the considered period. Liquidity and solvency indices of small businesses allow to remark a lower cover rating of current liabilities by immediate and long-term available funds; the period trend represents an improvement in relation to medium firms. The capability to guarantee a satisfactory degree of coverage for current liabilities with instant liquidity appears clearly superior. Analysis of cover rating of the investments volume through net assets alone (leverage) points out a general situation of industrial undercapitalization not much stronger for small businesses.

As regards the outline from main structural and profitability indicators (Table 3), differential between small and medium-sized firms in relation to fixed capital intensity (and total capital) tends to be constant during the considered period. A capital intensity increase is a common trend of the two size classes particularly during the decline phase (1991-93), a strong decrease follows in 1994.

Debt indices, too, underline a remarkable cyclic trend: ratio between financial debts and output grows until 1993; in 1994 it experiences a decrease more remarkable for medium-sized firms. Differential between small and medium-sized firms, about 7%, anyway seems to be stable during all the firmed period. Financial debt cost remarks a considerable difference between the two size classes: in 1989 average debt cost is less than 6.5% for medium firms, it is 4.8% in 1994. From a dynamic point of view, indicator downturn occurs in 1993; in this case indicator slump is particularly relevant for small businesses (from 23.8% to 20.6%) if compared with medium-sized firms (from 17.7% to 15.6%). From 1992 to 1994, ratio between financial charges and financial debts decreases 7% in small firms and 5.7% in medium-sized firms.

Comparison between the two size classes return on investment (ROI) trend shows a positive differential more or less stable up to 1993 as regards small firms: in 1994 medium-sized firms good performance allow a partial recovery, differential decrease is 1.4% instead of 2.1%. On the whole, difference between debt cost and industrial profitability is remarkable especially in the small business segment. Return on equity (ROE), including the handling of finances, is higher than the return on total capital particularly as regards small firms; while indices tend to converge during the recessive phase of 1992-93 and to diverge again in 1994 as regards medium-sized firms.

As shown, in 1994 the handling of finances is fundamental to explain the small firm profitability increase, whereas medium-sized enterprises benefit from an improvement of industrial management results.

Return on sales (ROS) underlines a considerable collinearity between small and medium-sized firms, even if the structural outline points out a positive differential for small businesses, in any case less than 1%.

This outline confirms a small business performance higher than the medium-sized one in relation to industrial management profitability, a medium firm recovery occurs during 1994 go-phase.

At last, the ratio of gross profits over value added points out a profitability recovery of medium-sized firms in 1992, two years earlier if compared with small businesses data. Generally, from year to year, a more outlined cyclic pattern seems to come out from the analysis of data relating to firm rate with profitability increases and percent coefficient of variation of profitability indicator in medium-sized firms. In 1994 with respect to small businesses, they completely recover profitability losses of previous years if compared with 1990.

4.4 Labour demand

Labour demand analysis (Table 4) clearly points out the change as from 1991 for both size classes. After a good employment performance in 1990 (+2.8% in small businesses and +2.1% in medium firms), during the following triennium yearly variations of employment stock are systematically negative; in 1994 small firms recover (+0.7%) in correspondence with a further medium-sized firms slump (-0.4%) even if reduced if compared with previous dynamics. Between 1989 and 1994, firms initially small show an employment increase equal to 1.1% while 100-499 employees size class a 1.2% decrease in 1994.

The division of employment stock variation according to job destruction and creation[11] does not underline particular differences between small and medium-sized enterprises. In fact the order of magnitude of the two flows is not meaningfully different for the two size classes, even if a rate of employment creation is systematically higher in the growing small firms in correspondence with an essential homogeneity with medium firms during 1992-93 recessive

---

[11] Terms refer to an increase and decrease of every firm employment stock in the panel, except for demographic elements of aggregate employment variation because of database used.

phase. This is reflected in a Gross Job Turnover value slightly higher in the lower size class.

Table 5 allows to evaluate the sectorial classification of employment trends between 1989 and 1994 with regard to the size class of firms at the beginning of the period.

Generally, employment trend in small firms presents considerable sectorial uniformity clearer than in medium firms.

As regards the economic branch, a certain weakness of employment trend becomes apparent in the small firms of food, textile industry etc., particularly in the output segments of consumption goods. Sector re-aggregation, according to sector main technological aspects, confirms previous findings, with specific reference to traditional sector negative performance, whereas employment trend selection capability seems to be remarkable for sector classification according to prevailing size. In this case, small firms grow in sectors where the prevailing size is medium-large and large[12]. On the other hand, for both size classes, territorial segmentation confirms the leading role of the north-east area, whereas a firm classification according to profitability ranking referred to 1989 shows a remarkable employment performance for small and medium firms of high profitability enterprises.

These evidences, widely based on aggregate indicators, suggest a quite complex outline of relations among performance, reference markets, specific sectors and labour demand. However this outline is rather clear about the influence of some factors on several variables, first of all on employment variables.

The complexity of interaction inside the processes leading to firm size choices and of interactions about production factors mix makes it necessary a research strategy based on models adequate to unsderstand the different effects. On the other hand, the evidence of profitability as a discriminant element of firm employment dynamics suggest analysis based also on firm segmentation according to level and profit persistence.

5 A model for analysing changes in employment at the firm level

5.1 Foreword

The panel data set described above can be also analysed with the aid of econometric tools. In this work the construction of an econometric model was

---

[12] Similar evidences are presented by Monducci and Picozzi (1989) with reference to industrial firms dynamics in the 1983-87 period.

then attempted to obtain a synthetic representation of the main characteristics of the firms which showed an increase in employment in the 1989-94 period.

A classical approach to this problem is represented by the estimation of a labour demand function explicitly derived from a production function. In our case there are however some problems which make this solution a not very practicable one. First of all, available data would make it very difficult to build series of fixed capital stock evaluated at substitution price for the single firm, as well as the related use cost. The difficulties increase when one considers more than a single cross-section. In fact, in that case time dimension has to be taken into account. These problems could be overcome by using a labour demand function depending only on labour relative price, as that derived from a homogeneous linear CES (constant elasticity of substitution) production function (Giusti, 1994); however, this would require additional hypothesis about the output price, as there are no indications about this variable at the firm level.

In this paper an alternative approach has been carried out. We considered a binary dependent variable, which takes value one if the number of employees of the i-th firm has grown, if compared with the previous year. In all other cases the variable takes value zero. In this way a probability model can be built to explain the occurrences of the event "increase of the number of employees".

However, it is well known that the use of a qualitative dependent variable rises some problems in a classical linear regression framework; among these problems there is the fact that the predicted values are not necessarily bounded between zero and one, as it must be the case if they are to be interpreted as probabilities. Thus, a logit model has been used, which is adequate if the dependent variable is a binary one, allowing for the above constraints to be respected (Greene, 1993).

5.2 The model

As we have said above, in this model the dependent variable takes the value one if the number of employees in the i-th firm increases when compared with the previous year. The explanatory variables being used are: a scale variable, represented by the previous year firm size class (based on the number of employees); per capita labour cost; the export share of total turnover; the ratio of gross fixed capital formation to value added. In addition, a variable representing the "pressure" in labour force use was introduced, namely the hours worked per employee in the previous year; nevertheless, the coefficient estimate associated to this variable may be biased, due to the presence of the wage supplementation fund: in fact the number of employees includes those who benefited from these funds. Another variable has then been introduced to correct to some extent such a bias, namely the ratio of supplemented hours to the worked ones.

Moreover, given that the database is made up of balance sheet data, financial variables may be introduced into the model: in particular ROI, as well as the ratio of total financial debts to production have been used as regressors.

In the end, some dummy variables have been included to allow the model to pick up the effects linked to different classification schemes of the firms: i.e. the technology (high intensity of research and development, prevalence of scale economies, specialised supply, traditional sectors); the year of reference; the prevalent size class in the activity sector considered; the geographical location; the profitability class (according to yearly firm ranking in its economic sector and size segment on the basis of profit ratio[13]); the economic sector according to two digit Ateco 1991 classification.

The model has been estimated on the whole 1990-94 period, without taking explicitly into account the longitudinal structure of the observed data; moreover, and for the same period, two other models have been estimated, respectively for firms having less than 100 employees in 1989 (thereinafter small firms) and for those with 100 employees and over (thereinafter medium firms). In the last two models the dummy representing the size class has been replaced by the number of employees in the previous year. The three relationships have been estimated also for the single years 1990 and 1994. For the latter instance, the i-th firm has been classified as being small or medium on the basis of the number of employees in 1993.

The fit of the logit model can be evaluated by comparing the log-likelihood of the estimated model (lnL) with that of a model computed with only a constant term ($\ln L_0$):

$$\text{Pseudo} - R^2 = 1 - \frac{\ln L}{\ln L_0} \qquad [1]$$

This index, bounded between zero and one, can be considered an equivalent to the R squared coefficient in a conventional linear regression model (Greene, 1993); in fact, if all the explanatory variables were not significant, the ratio coefficient would have zero value. In our case it takes values between 0.044 and 0.128.

The results of the estimated models are shown in Table 6. The marginal effects computed at the means of the regressors are shown in the table instead of the estimated parameters; the reason is that in the logit model the latter do not correspond to marginal effects of the explanatory variables. In fact, indicating the dependent variable with y, the independent variable vector with **x** and the parameter vector with β, we have that:

---

[13] For this variable, see Section 6.

$$\frac{\partial E[y]}{\partial \mathbf{x}} = \Lambda(\beta' \mathbf{x})\big[1 - \Lambda(\beta' \mathbf{x})\big]\beta \qquad [2]$$

where Λ indicates the logistic cumulative distribution function.

5.3 Main results

The model estimated pooling all the available cross-sections shows that coefficients linked to the size class are highly significant, with a positive effect connected to firm size. This result, which in some ways contradicts some other empirical findings on this subject, is partially confirmed by the models estimated separately for medium and small firms. In particular, it is true for the latter, whereas for firms with 100 employees and over the marginal effect is less important.

The influence of labour cost per capita is always significant and with the expected sign; its estimated marginal effect is higher for small firms in every year, even if the gap tends to decrease during the period considered.

Worked hours per employee have always a positive effect on the probability of a growth in employment to occur in the following year, thus showing the prevailing choice of firms to enlarge the employee stock only when there is a continuous increase in the use of labour force. This confirms some macroeconomic results obtained from the survey on industrial firms having more than 499 employees (Istat, Annual Report 1996). The behaviour is quite similar both for medium and small firms, as well as for different years. On the other hand, the effect of the previous year supplementation wage is negative, as expected, and stronger for medium firms, with the exception of 1994, when there are no marked differences between the two firm segments.

The export share on total turnover increases the probability of employment growth. In this case, it becomes particularly interesting an analysis of the evolution of this effect during the period 1990-94, that has featured an extraordinary depreciation of Italian lira: in 1994 the marginal effect of export share has been three time larger than in 1990; in particular it has increased more than four time for small firms and more than twice for medium ones.

The ratio of gross fixed capital formation to value added has also a strong and positive impact on the occurrence of employment growth, especially in medium firms. Such impact has increased three times during the period considered. This can be interpreted as the fact that firms capital accumulation during the period considered has not had, in general, labour saving characteristics.

Concerning the financial variables, ROI has a markedly positive effect on employee growth: this effect is significantly stronger in medium firms. Given that no lags were introduced for this variable, this result is not to be interpreted as a causal relationship between profitability and employment increase. In addition, the effect of this variable in the period examined is quite volatile: for example, in 1990 it did not seem to be significantly linked to employment increase with reference to small firms. The effect of the other financial variable (the ratio of financial debt to production) is overall negative in the examined period, and it is slightly higher for medium firms. Anyway, if we consider estimation carried out on single year, this variable is not significant.

Classification variables used are in general very significant. Let us look first at the year as the reference variable: in this case the effect is consistent with the cyclical behaviour observed at the macroeconomic level; however, considering the different size segments, after 1990 it can be noticed that negative signs are more persistent for medium firms; in fact, while in 1993 there has been a slight uptrend for small firms (if compared with previous year), for the medium ones the negative effect was still very marked. This result could be also explained by structural changes, rather than different cyclical patterns; anyway a better evaluation can be provided only when additional data for the following years will be available.

Geographical differentiations show marked heterogeneous characters depending on size; small firms have a positive marginal effect in all northern and central regions; in north-eastern regions the effect is even higher (by 50%) than that found in central and north-western ones. Medium firms show a substantially homogenous condition among the different geographical divisions, with the only exception of north-east in 1994. Considering the time dimension, the gap between north-east and south in the probability of an employment growth to occur has always been within 13% and 17% for small firms, becoming narrower during the recession of 1992-93 (Table 7).

Technological classification is seldom significant, with an overall positive effect for medium firms working in sectors with high intensity of research and development, and negative for those in sectors characterised by specialised supply. Anyway, the technology variable is seldom significant when estimation is carried out just for 1990 or 1994.

The influence of the prevalent size class in the sector is negligible for medium firms, whereas it is positive for small firms working in sectors where the prevalent size is between 100 and 499 employees. This is confirmed even by the results stemming from the whole sample, which pay for the greatest presence of small firms. Furthermore, these results are much more evident in 1994 than in 1990.

Lastly, belonging to a high profitability class is strongly significant. This variable has always a very marked effect which is rather stable in the examined time period: the difference between the average probability to increase employment in a medium firms of the fourth quartile is about 17 percentage points higher than the probability of a first quartile firm; similar results hold for small firms (Table 7).

6 Profit persistence and employment dynamics

In the previous paragraphs (4.3 and 5.3) the importance of firm profitability was noticed in establishing a more or less positive employment dynamics; on the other hand, the cycle of aggregate profitability seemed to be quite remarkable in 1989-94 period. This suggested to examine closely the firm profitability analysis from a dynamic point of view: first of all, in order to verify whether and in which measure the previously outlined macroeconomic pattern had influenced each individual firm in the panel, individual profits were considered and their distributions were analysed; moreover, it seemed to be pertinent to measure profit persistence, and in particular the relationship between the latter and changes in employment. In this context, the variable we analyse represents, when adequately codified, a possible classifying typology of our units.

A first evaluation of firm profit persistence[14] can be obtained from an analysis of firm transition and permanence matrix between quartiles related to two years: data about 1989 and 1994 are shown in Table 8; 1989 and 1994 are the initial and final year of observation of the panel. It can be seen that the percentages of permanence, which can be read in the table diagonal are rather high in the first (52.5%) and in the last (58.3%) quartile, while in the second and third quartile it is less, with percentages that are respectively 35.9% and 36.5%. Permanence percentages are then higher than upward and downward transitions. Transitions to a superior quartile have a decreasing trend when recipient quartile grows, whereas transition to the immediately lower quartile are about 25%. Firm behaviour according to their relative ranking seems to be quite homogenous. This trend is the same even for transitions and permanence for employees in 1989.

This first aspect shows then a certain persistence of firms when profit ratio is considered, at least between the first and last period we examined.

This evidence of persistence (or cycles) in relative profitability can be verified through the definition of persistence classes during the six years of the analysis period: we define low range firms those always in the first quartile of the distribution, that is firms with markedly lower profits; low-medium range has firms ranked every year between first quartile and median; medium range has firms with profit ratios between median and third quartile; high range has firms with profits remarkably higher than third quartile; lastly there is a residual class of non persistent firms, that is firms which changed reference quartile in the analysed period, from one year to the next. It is clear that, given such a limiting filter for classification, it should be expected that this residual segment should

---

[14] More exactly, to rank firms the indicator given by profit ratio was used, defined as the ratio of gross working margin to value added of each firm. Each unit was assigned to a certain quartile of profit ratio distribution for each year, in the same employee class and economic division. According to this classification, it is possible to determine firms that in the examined years are always ranked in the same quartile of related distribution, thus showing a high persistence of their profitability.

count a remarkably high number of firms. However, in this first part of the analysis, the interesting element is the existence and the evaluation of the order of magnitude of size segments with a high persistence level of relative profitability, in a period which has markedly different cyclical phases.

Range classification of individual profit ratios was first related with some firm structural characteristics referred to 1989, that is with employee class and geographical area of each firm. Employee class has four levels (30-49 employees, 50-99 employees, 100-199 employees, 200-499 employees), whereas the four areas are north-west, north-east, central and south.

The analysis[15] of the relationships between persistence classes for profit ratios and employee classes, with 100 as the unit total for each employee class, show that percentage of firms steadily ranked in the last quartile, i.e. those with constantly high profits, decreases when the number of employees increases, changing from a 10.9% percentage for 30-49 class to 7.6% for 200-499 employee class; percentages of the other ranges are rather homogeneous for employee classes, in particular for medium-low and medium range, even if firms with 200-499 employees are prevalent in the low persistence range. This evidence is confirmed even at geographical area level except for central regions, where low range firms are clearly prevailing.

This early synthesis of the results of firm classification according to their relative position on profitability scale shows that: a) the number of non persistent firms is high, to show a high influence of business cycle on firm frequency distribution by profitability level; b) number of firms in high profitability range is greater than those in low range; c) smaller firms (less than 100 employees) show a greater persistence of higher performance in the six examined years. Moreover northern regions feature a share of firms in the higher range greater than firms in the lower range, whereas in the central and southern areas trend is opposite.

Given this outline of industrial firm system modification for profitability margin distribution in the 1989-1994 period, one of the most interesting dynamic aspect is employment evolution in the different firms ranges, which is to be analysed according to firm re-classification. To this purpose firms were furtherly classified according to number of employee variation sign between 1989 and 1994, thus we have firms where employment increases, firms where employment is stable and firms where the number of employees decreases[16]. The most interesting firms are those where employment increased, and which are subsequently classified according to employee classes and geographical areas.

From a behaviour analysis of firms classified according to 1989 distribution quartile in terms of employee variation between 1989 and 1994 (Table 9), it can be seen that percentage of firms where employees increase is greater when profit

---

[15] Table is not given.

[16] In this first part employee variation was defined as a simple difference between 1994 and 1989 employees. Later on other classification typologies will be used to consider every year from 1989 to 1994.

ranking increases, if 100 is the total in each quartile. 57% of firms with greater profit ratios positively change the employee number, while only in 38.8% of firms employment decreases. Stability percentages are rather homogeneous among quartiles.

Firms distribution among the persistence range previously defined for the six years, and intersected with employee class and geographical area (Table 10) gives a rather clear outline[17]: for both classifications employment increase percentage increases as firm persistence typology grows, given the same employee class or the same geographical area; however given such uniformity, there are remarkable differentiations among employee classes or geographical areas for each range. A greater propensity to increase employment is pointed out by firms with number of employees between 100 and 199 and among firms in the north-east if compared with other classes (respectively 24.4% and 25.9%). The total percentage of firms increasing employment in the panel is 41.1%.

It could be said that the more stable profitable firms (high range) are those where the percentage of employee increase is clearly higher than percentage of employee decrease, percentages being always higher than 50%. Within each employee class and geographical area, the stable relation between firm ranking on profitability scale and employment growth propensity seems to provide an important explanation of events connected to employment in manufacturing firms for the 1989-94 period.

To give further support to this evidence other classification modes in terms of employees have been selected: in fact the variation between the last and the first year of the period gives a too static outline if compared with the actual cycle occurred in the intermediate years. Thus the sign of the variation from one year to the next has been considered, for each of the five bienniums between 1989 and 1994.

Apart from those firms where employment always increased or decreased, the most interesting firms were those with different increase dynamics or even decrease dynamics, but always consistently with business cycle. An intersection of this classification with persistence range points out that firms where employees decrease every year are more numerous in the lower range (24.5%), with 100 representing the total for each range; this percentage is 14.5% in the medium-low range, 11.4% in the medium range and 5.5% in the high range, while for non persistence the percentage is equal to 12.9%. Percentage of firms increasing employees in several ways in the low range is 2.5%, in the medium-low range is 7.2%, in the medium range is 12.7% and in the high range is 20.7%; in this case non persistent firms are 10.8%. Thus this classification typology confirms the previous evidence: more profitable firms have more remarkable employment dynamic increase in comparison with firms ranked in other ranges.

---

[17] Values represent percentages of firms which increase occupation in relation to the total in each cell.

7 Conclusions

The set of calculations show that employment dynamics for firms, in the 1989-94 period, cannot be explained only by the size variable, considered as number of employees. Aggregate findings hide dynamics which differ within the different size classes. Then size classes are to be analysed and evaluated as number of "occurrences" for the different development modes rather than according to average data. On the basis of this approach, there are some "uniformity" that allow to outline a specific development model that fits the Italian industrial system of the early nineties.

One of the most interesting aspect of industry development is the high "turbulence" of employment dynamics in the different size range. The order of magnitude of the two flows of job destruction and creation for small and medium-sized firms is not significantly different for the two size ranges, even if a rate of employment creation is systematically higher in the growing small firms in correspondence with an essential homogeneity with medium firms during 1992-93 recessive phase.

Anyway, with these analyses we could single out some "regularities" linked to the different sectorial characteristics.

The importance of technological elements is clearly given by the analysis of employment development of manufacturing firms. More technologically advanced sectors have employment results constantly higher than average. The ensuing pattern seems to show, during the recovery, the existence of a relation of employment dynamics and firm size range within sector: small firms grow more in sectors where their actual size is relatively smaller.

The effect of geographical factors is remarkable and it confirms a better occupational performance in north-eastern regions as compared to the others. This is particularly clear in the class of small firms and during slow down phases.

On the other hand, some significant relationships between performance indicators and occupation dynamics come out. The evidence seem to confirm a clear influence of profitability conditions, especially their operating component, on the dynamic of firm-level employment, particularly in medium-sized firms and during recovery phases. In general, high persistence of firms in the higher positions of profit distributions has an evident effect on employment levels. Moreover, a positive impact of propensity to export on employment dynamics is established, in particular as regards medium-sized firms. Finally, within a framework where some adjustment mechanisms of labour stock exist, a positive impact of average working hours on the probability of employment growth comes out.

Annex A - Contribution of different factors to variability of actually worked hours per capita

The meaningful relation of working hours to employment dynamics (see paragraph 5.3) has suggested an analysis of average hours variability, to evaluate the presence of sectorial uniformity, or connected to employment composition, to explain actual working time differentials among individual firms.

A typical subject of analysis for microeconomic approaches to firm system survey is the subdivision of phenomena variability according to unit classification typology. In this part of the paper, we focus on average worked hours in every year by the several employee categories of each firm, analysing in particular white collars average hours, blue collars average hours, and the total average number of hours.

What is more interesting for this paper is to verify the existence of some meaningful influence on per capita working hours of firm size, economic division, geographical area and profit share distribution at individual firm level, and if positive, this effect should be adequately quantified.

An analysis of variance with only main effects has not pointed out a meaningful influence of those factors for each year; generally the model explains a very low percentage of data variability, even if some factors as class of profit and geographical area have meaningful coefficients. This evidence is confirmed by computing coefficients of variation of average hours for the three categories: they are between 12% and 16% and this coefficient is 19% only for white collars in 1989.

Another interesting aspect is variability subdivision of total per capita hours according to employment typology (white and blue collars) within different size classes, within divisions and profit ratio quartiles. Attention was given to logarithm average hour variance as dispersion index (in particular for Italy see Casavola, Gavosto, Sestito, 1996). Then total variance was subdivided into a component within white collars, into one within blue collars and into one between white and blue collars, according to the following formula:

$$Total\ Variance = \sum_i \frac{n_i^{wh}}{N}\left(\overline{w}_i^{wh} - \overline{w}^{wh}\right)^2 + \sum_i \frac{n_i^{bl}}{N}\left(\overline{w}_i^{bl} - \overline{w}^{bl}\right)^2 +$$

$$+ \frac{\sum_i n_i^{wh}}{N}\left(\overline{w}^{wh} - \overline{w}\right)^2 + \frac{\sum_i n_i^{bl}}{N}\left(\overline{w}^{bl} - \overline{w}\right)^2 \qquad [A1]$$

where i is firms, N is the total number of white and blue collars, n_i^{wh} and n_i^{bl} are respectively the number of white collars and of blue collars of the i-th firm,

$\overline{W}_i^{wh}$ and $\overline{W}_i^{bl}$ are the logarithm average of white collars and blue collars hours of the i-th firm, $\overline{W}^{wh}$ and $\overline{W}^{bl}$ are the average hours (log) of the two groups and $\overline{W}$ is the general average (log). The first two addenda on the right of identity [A1] are, respectively, variances within white and blue collars, whereas the last two addenda are between variances.

Analysing the subdivision for each year and intersecting the employee class with division there is a between variance share which is a very low percentage of total variance for a great number of cases, with few exceptions. In general the percentage of variance within blue collars is very high if compared to that within white collars, both for different employee classes as well as for economic divisions.

Dispersion of total average hours, then, seems to be ascribed to worker category variance. This evidence is confirmed by an analysis performed only for employee classes, even if differences between white and blue collars are diminished by classification exclusion according to divisions, and by one using profit classification intersected with division.

Annex B: Statistical tables

Table 1 Main sectorial indicators - Manufacturing industry (Percentage changes)

Year	VAD	LUE	LUT	LPR	RWA	PCC	CLP	INPP	VARC	MKUP	OUTP	PRO (*)
1986	2.6	-0.5	-1.2	3.1	0.1	6.8	5.0	0.6	-5.2	1.4	2.5	36.4
1987	4.4	-1.0	-0.4	5.4	3.1	7.6	1.1	2.5	2.8	0.3	2.8	37.2
1988	7.1	1.6	1.6	5.4	1.2	7.5	-0.3	4.5	4.1	0.0	4.2	38.2
1989	4.0	0.9	0.9	3.1	0.0	9.7	4.5	6.3	6.6	-0.8	5.8	37.3
1990	1.8	0.4	0.5	1.4	1.3	8.5	7.4	1.7	3.0	-0.9	2.0	34.7
1991	-0.6	-1.9	-2.2	1.3	2.5	9.7	9.4	2.0	3.4	-1.0	2.4	31.5
1992	0.3	-3.7	-4.3	4.1	1.6	7.2	2.4	1.7	2.0	-0.2	1.8	30.9
1993	-3.4	-5.0	-5.7	1.6	-0.6	5.0	5.4	4.1	3.5	0.1	3.6	30.8
1994	5.4	-0.5	-0.2	6.0	-0.9	2.2	-5.2	4.9	2.9	0.8	3.7	34.1
1995	5.7	-0.4	-0.5	6.2	-1.9	5.6	-0.3	10.6	7.7	0.6	8.5	37.2
1996	-0.8	-0.7	-0.9	-0.1	-0.3	4.8	5.8	0.3	1.2	0.7	1.9	37.3

Note to Table 1

VAD	Value added at factor costs (1990 prices)	INPP	Input prices
LUE	Labour units (employed)	VARC	Variable costs
LUT	Labour units (total)	MKUP	1+mark-up
LPR	Labour productivity (constant prices)	OUTP	Output prices
RWA	Real wage (deflated by private consumption deflator)	PRO (*)	Gross profits (per cent of value added)
PCC	Per capita compensation		
CLP	Labour cost per unit of output		

Table 2 Key figures by economic sector and size classes. Firms panel data (Manufacturing industry - 1989-94)

Size classes (1989)	Economic sectors (1)	1989											
		EMP	CLW	HOU	EXP	TUR	LPR	COM	HOW	LCO	INT	SER	PRO
	Branch 2 (2)	39267	22,7	1745	15,8	233	70,2	39,1	14,7	18,3	67,4	14,3	43,1
	Branch 3 (3)	74342	25,0	1745	28,1	171	60,3	37,9	14.5	23,6	63,9	12,5	35,3
30 - 99	Branch 4 (4)	108908	17,5	1685	18,9	195	52,8	32,4	12,8	17,5	70,8	11,7	37,4
	Total	223517	20,9	1715	21,0	194	58,4	35,4	13,7	19,4	68,1	12,5	37,9
	Branch 2 (2)	66545	32,3	1699	21,7	253	80,7	45,0	17,4	19,6	66,2	14,2	43,8
	Branch 3 (3)	119573	31,0	1694	32,8	178	63,6	41,1	16,2	24,2	63,7	12,1	34,5
100-499	Branch 4 (4)	136357	23,7	1646	22,1	215	59,4	37,5	15,1	18,5	66,0	15,5	35,9
	Total	322475	28,2	1675	25,4	209	65,3	40,4	16,0	20,6	65,3	14,1	37,4

Size classes (1989)	Economic sectors (1)	1994											
		EMP	CLW	HOU	EXP	TUR	LPR	COM	HOW	LCO	INT	SER	PRO
	Branch 2 (2)	40455	25,3	1741	20,0	299	88,9	53,8	20.4	19,2	66,0	14,8	38,0
	Branch 3 (3)	76859	27,5	1744	37,2	223	77,8	51,7	19,7	24,3	62,1	13,6	31,5
30 - 99	Branch 4 (4)	108773	19,7	1723	23,7	276	72,5	44,9	17,5	16,9	70,3	12,8	36,1
	Total	226087	23,3	1733	26,8	262	77,2	48,8	18,8	19,5	67,1	13,4	34,9
	Branch 2 (2)	67599	35,3	1699	30,0	347	106,6	62,3	24,7	19,7	65,2	15,1	40,7
	Branch 3 (3)	118816	33,7	1676	41,4	237	85,0	55,6	22,1	25,2	62,1	12,7	33,5
100-499	Branch 4 (4)	132336	26,2	1677	27,2	311	86,3	52,8	21,1	18,1	65,9	16,0	37,7
	Total	318751	30,9	1675	32,2	291	90,0	55,9	22,2	20,6	64,6	14,8	37,0

Source: Istat, System of the Enterprises Accounts.

Note to Table 2:

1.Data have been grouped together in an aggregate common nomenclature comprising three sectors. This aggregation is based on the Ateco 1991 three digits.

1. Branch 2 (iron metallurgy, chemical industry)
2. Branch 3 (mechanical industry)
3. Branch 4 (food, textile and clothing industry, wood etc.)

EMP   Employment
CLW   White collars (percent of total employment)
HOU   Hours worked per employee
EXP   Export (percent of turnover)
TUR   Turnover (per capita - millions of lire)
LPR   Labour productivity (at current prices - millions of lire)
COM   Compensation per employee (millions of lire)
HWA   Hourly wages (thousands of lire)
LCO   Labour costs (per cent of variable costs)
INT   Intermediate goods (per cent of variable costs)
SER   Services (per cent of variable costs)
PRO   Gross operating profit ratio (per cent of value added)

Table 3 Structural and profitability indicators by firm size class. Firms panel data (Manufacturing industry - 1989-94)

	1990	1991	1992	1993	1994
30-99 employees (*)					
Fixed capital intensity	22,0	24,8	25,2	25,5	23,3
Total capital intensity	76,3	80,5	82,5	83,5	81,9
Financial debts/output	13,5	14,4	15,4	16,6	15,8
Financial debt cost	23,1	22,6	23,8	20,6	16,8
ROI	12,0	11,0	10,5	10,0	10,1
ROE (gross)	20,9	16,9	14,1	12,7	16,6
ROE (net)	11,6	8,5	5,3	4,5	8,1
ROS	9,4	9,0	8,8	8,5	8,4
PRO/VA (**)	36,4	34,0	33,8	33,9	34,9
Coefficient of variation (%)	51,2	54,7	58,4	59,3	58,7
% firms with profitability increases	43,6	38,0	49,6	46,5	53,7
100-499 employees (*)					
Fixed capital intensity	27,7	31,6	32,4	32,7	30,2
Total capital intensity	87,2	91,5	93,4	94,0	91,3
Financial debts/output	21,0	21,7	23,0	24,5	23,3
Financial debt cost	16,5	16,3	17,7	15,6	12,0
ROI	9,6	8,8	8,3	7,9	8,7
ROE (gross)	15,4	12,5	8,6	6,1	13,5
ROE (net)	7,4	5,4	1,4	-1,1	5,2
ROS	8,6	8,3	7,9	7,5	8,1
PRO/VA (**)	36,2	34,6	35,1	35,3	37,0
Coefficient of variation (%)	69,3	57,4	58,8	59,7	60,2
% firms with profitability increases	42,2	38,7	51,6	50,3	54,6

Source: Istat, System of the Enterprises Accounts.

Note to Table 3:

(*)   Size classes (1989)

(**)   Gross operating profit ratio (per cent of value added)

Table 4 Employment trend by firm size classes. Firms panel data (Manufacturing industry - 1989-94) (Percentage change)

	1990	1991	1992	1993	1994
30-99 employees (*)					
Job creation (1)	5,6	3,8	3,0	3,1	4,4
Job destruction (2)	2,8	3,9	4,2	4,1	3,7
Gross Job Turnover (1+2)	8,4	7,6	7,2	7,1	8,1
Total employment (1-2)	2,8	-0,1	-1,2	-1,0	0,7
% firms with employment increases	47,7	38,2	32,8	33,6	41,1
100-499 employees (*)					
Job creation (1)	5,1	3,2	2,8	2,9	3,6
Job destruction (2)	3,0	3,5	4,1	4,2	4,1
Gross Job Turnover (1+2)	8,1	6,7	6,8	7,1	7,7
Total employment (1-2)	2,1	-0,3	-1,3	-1,2	-0,4
% firms with employment increases	51,2	40,4	31,5	31,1	41,6

Source: Istat, System of the Enterprises Accounts.
Note to Table 4:
(*) Size classes (1989)

Table 5 Employment trends by firm size classes and sectors. Firms panel data (Manufacturing industry - 1989-94) (Percentage change between 1989 and 1994)

Classifications	30-99 employees(*)	100-499 employees (*)
Economic sectors:		
Branch 2 iron metallurgy, chemical industry	3,0	1,6
Branch 3: mechanical industry	3,4	-0,6
Branch 4: food, textile and clothing industry, wood etc.	-1,0	-2,9
Economic use:		
Final: investment	4,5	-1,5
Final: consumption	-2,3	-4,2
Intermediate	2,4	1,0
Technological aspects:		
High-tech	2,1	-0,6
Scale economies	2,6	1,2
Specialized suppliers	3,1	-3,7
Traditional industries	-0,6	-1,9
Prevailing sectoral size (entropic mean):		
< 20 employees	-0,2	7,6
20-99 employees	-0,6	-4,9
100-499 employees	5,6	-7,2
> 499 employees	13,0	7,6
Territorial areas:		
North-west	-0,2	-3,4
North-east	4,1	3,7
Center	0,0	-3,0
South and Islands	-1,5	-4,0
Profitability ranking:		
I quartile	-8,5	-14,1
II quartile	-3,0	-4,2
III quartile	4,0	1,4
IV quartile	12,5	13,8
Total	1,1	-1,2

Source: Istat, System of the Enterprises Accounts.

Note to Table 5:

(*) Size classes (1989)

Table 6 Results of the estimation of the logit model. Firms panel data (Manufacturing industry - 1989-94)

		Period: 1990-94			Period: 1990			Period: 1994		
		Total	Small firms	Medi. firms	Total	Small firms	Med. firms	Total	Small firms	Med. firms
Firm size (Benchmark. <50 empl.)	50-99 employees (t-1)	0.06280 **			0.06479 **			0.08622 **		
	100-199 employees (t-1)	0.09344 **			0.10013 **			0.13436 **		
	Over 200 employees (t-1)	0.10627 **			0.11198 **			0.14048 **		
	Employees (t-1)		0.00170 **	0.00011 **		0.00191 **	0.00000		0.00208 **	-0.00011
	Wage sup. funds / worked hours (t-1)	-0.38175 ***	-0.27496 ***	-0.68427 **	-0.31231 **	-0.16246	-1.24842 **	-0.39438 **	-0.37169 **	-0.33611 **
	Labour cost per capita	-0.00569 ***	-0.00653 ***	-0.00409 ***	-0.00699 **	-0.00884 ***	-0.00378 **	-0.00676 **	-0.00754 **	-0.00511 **
	Export / turnover	0.00088 ***	0.00088 ***	0.00087 ***	0.00055 **	0.00030	0.00092 *	0.00152 **	0.00127 **	0.00210 **
	Worked hours per capita (t-1)	0.00029 ***	0.00028 ***	0.00030 ***	0.00031 **	0.00030 **	0.00032 **	0.00034 **	0.00030 **	0.00051 **
	Investment / value added	0.19410 ***	0.18085 ***	0.23587 **	0.11869 **	0.10182 **	0.16241 **	0.35704 **	0.31455 **	0.54531 **
	ROI	0.30595 **	0.23857 **	0.52426 **	0.06153	-0.05158	0.46330 **	0.44800 **	0.38669 **	0.68810 **
	Financial debts / production	-0.04655 ***	-0.04239***	-0.05824**	-0.01198	-0.00573	0.00655	-0.03991	-0.04407	-0.00575
Technological aspects (Bench.: traditional ind.)	High tech.	0.06686 **	0.00036	0.13372 **	0.32726 **	0.08303 *	-0.00886	-0.06665 *	-0.05398	-0.08991
	Scale economies	-0.02346 **	-0.01106	-0.02333	0.01421	0.02600	-0.04318	0.02875	0.02402	0.04537
	Specialized suppliers	0.00320	0.02664 *	-0.04096**	0.02437	0.06196**	-0.03750	0.03494	0.03934	0.03058
Year (Bench. 1990)	1991	-0.08200 ***	-0.08141**	-0.08425**						
	1992	-0.12677 ***	-0.11627**	-0.15555**						
	1993	-0.10807 **	-0.09180 **	-0.15262**						
	1994	0.00672	0.01401	-0.01259						
Prevailing size in the sector (Bench.: <20)	20-99 employees	0.01280	0.01245	0.00755	0.00510	0.00436	0.00964	0.03413 *	0.04202 *	0.00365
	100-499 employees	0.03566 **	0.03468 **	0.03924 *	0.01221	0.00433	0.02825	0.09449 **	0.09828 **	0.08421
	Over 500 employees	0.02612	0.03606	0.04379	0.00694	-0.01986	0.14064 **	0.07020 *	0.12493 **	-0.01779
Territorial areas (Bench.: south)	North-west	0.07491 **	0.10353 **	0.00746	0.10255 **	0.14196**	-0.00131	0.12134 **	0.13958**	0.08579
	North-east	0.12987 **	0.15470 ***	0.06246 **	0.16859 ***	0.21995***	0.02037	0.16246**	0.18051 **	0.12386*
	Center	0.07757 **	0.10944 ***	-0.01160	0.08550***	0.11858***	0.02281	0.12275**	0.14906**	0.04230
Profitability ranking (Bench.: 1st quartile)	IInd quartile	0.07008 **	0.07533 ***	0.05454**	0.05376 ***	0.06214**	0.03480	0.09984**	0.10230**	0.08983***
	IIIrd quartile	0.12191 **	0.11664 ***	0.13180 **	0.11807 ***	0.11295***	0.12764 **	0.15231**	0.15796**	0.12474**
	IVth quartile	0.16818 **	0.16334 **	0.17458**	0.17819 **	0.18046**	0.15899 **	0.16744**	0.16260**	0.17102**
	Pseudo - R²	6.6%	6.1%	8.7%	4.7%	4.8%	6.2%	9.5%	8.5%	12.6%
	Observations	29475	21458	8017	5890	4289	1601	5896	4278	1618
	Correct cases	19222	13917	5306	3592	2613	988	3866	2799	1096

Source: Istat, System of the Enterprises Accounts.

The values represent marginal effects of each variable.

significant at 10% level; ** significant at 5% level.

Table 7 Probabilities of employment increase by year, profitability and territorial areas. Firms panel data (Manufacturing industry - 1989-94)

Small firms

	North-west	North-east	Center	South-Islands	Italy
1990	42.0%	47.4%	42.7%	31.8%	43.2%
1991	33.9%	38.9%	34.5%	24.8%	35.0%
1992	30.6%	35.5%	31.2%	22.1%	31.7%
1993	32.9%	37.9%	33.5%	24.0%	34.0%
1994	43.5%	48.9%	44.1%	33.1%	44.7%
1990-1994	36.4%	41.6%	37.0%	26.9%	37.6%

	Profitability: Ist quartile	IInd quartile	IIIrd quartile	IVth quartile	Total
1990	34.2%	41.8%	46.1%	51.1%	43.2%
1991	26.9%	33.6%	37.7%	42.4%	35.0%
1992	24.1%	30.4%	34.3%	38.9%	31.7%
1993	26.0%	32.7%	36.6%	41.4%	34.0%
1994	35.6%	43.2%	47.6%	52.6%	44.7%
1990-1994	29.1%	36.2%	40.3%	45.2%	37.6%

Medium firms

	North-west	North-east	Center	South-Islands	Italy
1990	44.5%	50.4%	42.5%	43.7%	46.1%
1991	35.9%	41.5%	34.1%	35.2%	37.4%
1992	29.3%	34.3%	27.6%	28.6%	30.6%
1993	29.5%	34.6%	27.9%	28.9%	30.9%
1994	43.2%	49.0%	41.2%	42.4%	44.8%
1990-1994	36.2%	41.8%	34.4%	35.5%	37.7%

	Profitability: Ist quartile	IInd quartile	IIIrd quartile	IVth quartile	Total
1990	37.3%	42.9%	51.0%	55.6%	46.1%
1991	29.3%	34.4%	42.1%	46.6%	37.4%
1992	23.5%	27.9%	35.0%	39.2%	30.6%
1993	23.7%	28.1%	35.2%	39.5%	30.9%
1994	36.0%	41.6%	49.7%	54.2%	44.8%
1990-1994	29.6%	34.7%	42.5%	47.0%	37.7%

Source: Istat, System of the Enterprises Accounts.

Table 8 Firm transition and permanence matrix between quartiles related to 1989 and 1994 (%). Firms panel data (Manufacturing industry - 1989-94)

1994 / 1989	Ist quartile	IInd quartile	IIIrd quartile	IVth quartile	Total
Ist quartile	52.5	28.4	13.8	5.3	100
IInd quartile	26.4	35.9	26.8	10.9	100
IIIrd quartile	15.7	24.0	36.5	23.8	100
IVth quartile	7.3	10.2	24.2	58.3	100

Source: Istat, System of the Enterprises Accounts.

Table 9 Firms by profitability ranking (1989) and employment trend between 1989 and 1994 (%). Firms panel data (Manufacturing industry - 1989-94)

Employment / Profitability ranking	Increase	Stability	Decrease	Total
Ist quartile	26.2	3.1	70.7	100
IInd quartile	36.1	3.9	60.0	100
IIIrd quartile	45.9	4.3	49.8	100
IVth quartile	57.0	4.2	38.8	100
Total	41.1	3.9	55.0	100

Source: Istat, System of the Enterprises Accounts.

Table 10 Firms with employment increases by persistence of profits, firms size classes and geographical area (%). Firms panel data (Manufacturing industry - 1989-94)

Profit persistence / Firm size, geographical area	Low	Medium -low	Medium	High	Non persistent	Total
30 - 49	20.7	39.1	50.0	57.9	40.3	40.7
50 - 99	16.6	34.8	44.0	65.2	42.6	42.4
100 - 199	24.4	38.5	72.2	74.1	39.1	41.4
200 - 499	14.9	30.3	50.0	65.8	38.2	38.1
North-west	13.7	35.1	53.7	63.1	37.6	38.6
North-east	25.9	36.4	54.2	69.1	45.9	46.3
Center	19.1	50.0	50.0	56.5	40.3	39.6
South-Islands	23.1	-	50.0	50.0	37.6	37.2
Total	19.4	36.2	53.2	63.5	40.6	41.1

Source: Istat, System of the Enterprises Accounts.

REFERENCES

Barca F., Visco (1991), *"L'economia italiana nella prospettiva europea: terziario protetto e dinamica dei redditi nominali"*, Temi di discussione del Servizio Studi, Banca d'Italia, n.175.

Brusco S., Sabel C.F. (1981), *"Artisan Production and Economic Growth"*, in: Wilkinson F. ed., The Dynamics of Labour Market Segmentation, Academy Press.

Casavola P., Gavosto A., Sestito P. (1996), *"Technical progress and wage dispersion in Italy: evidence from firms' data"*, Annales d'Economie et de Statistique, nn. 41-42.

Contini B. (1989), *"Organization, markets and persistence of profits in Italian industry"*, Journal of Economic Behaviour and Organization 12.

Contini B., Revelli R. (1991), *"Pattern di espansione e contrazione occupazionale delle imprese italiane"*, L'industria, n. 4.

Contini B., Pacelli L., Rapiti F. (1993), *"Struttura dimensionale e demografia di impresa nell'industria italiana"*, CSC ricerche, n. 73.

Contini B., Monducci R. (1996), *"Analisi microeconomica e indagini sulle imprese: bisogni informativi e proposte"*, XXXVIII Riunione Scientifica SIS, Rimini.

Corsini V., Monducci R., Vicari P. (1997), *"Analisi microeconomica del sistema delle imprese e integrazione tra fonti statistiche: grandi e piccole imprese nell'industria italiana"*, Atti della Riunione Scientifica SIS 1997, La Statistica per l'Impresa, Torino.

Cubbin J., Geroski P.A. (1987), *"The convergence of profits in the long run: inter-firm and inter-industry comparisons"*, The Journal of Industrial Economics vol. XXXV.

Geroski P.A., Jacquemin A. (1988), *"The persistence of profits: a european comparison"*, The Economic Journal 98.

Giusti F., (1994), *"Modelli neoclassici di produzione"*, Univ. di Roma "La Sapienza" - Dipartimento di teoria economica e metodi quantitativi per le scelte politiche.

Greene W. H., (1993), *"Econometric Analysis"*, Macmillan Publishing Company.

ISTAT (1997), *Rapporto annuale. La situazione del Paese nel 1996.*

Marelli E: (1996), *"L'occupazione in Italia: un'analisi della crescita nei principali settori produttivi"*, L'Industria a. XVII, n. 2, aprile-giugno.

Meldolesi L. (1996), *"L'elevata mobilità del lavoro nel Mezzogiorno della speranza"*, in Galli G. ed., La mobilità della società italiana, vol II, Editore SIPI, Roma.

Monducci R., Picozzi L. (1989), *"Struttura ed evoluzione dell'occupazione nelle imprese manifatturiere italiane"*, Quaderni di ricerca - Economia e Ambiente, Istat, novembre.

Monducci R., Pisani S. (1993), *"La crescita dei servizi di mercato nell'economia italiana: l'evidenza empirica"*, Quaderni di ricerca - Economia e Ambiente, Istat, n. 6.

Monducci R. (1994), *"L'informazione statistica sulle imprese: problematiche relative all'integrazione tra fonti"*, Atti della Seconda Conferenza Nazionale di Statistica, Roma.

Rey G.M (1988), *"Redditività e paradigma organizzativo della piccola e media impresa"*, Piccola impresa, n. 2.

Rey G.M (1992), *"I mutamenti della struttura economica: fattori produttivi, distribuzione del reddito, domanda"*, in L'Italia verso il 2000: le istituzioni, la società, l'economia, SIPI, Collana Studi e Ricerche.

Signorini L. F. (1991a), *"Scala, efficienza e redditività negli anni Ottanta: un'analisi dei bilanci delle imprese manifatturiere"*, L'Industria, n. 4.

Signorini L. F. (1991b), *"Grandi e piccole imprese negli anni '80: la ristrutturazione dell'industria in un'analisi di dati di bilancio"*, Temi di discussione del Servizio Studi, Banca d'Italia.

Signorini L. F. (1993), *"Sulla crescita delle piccole imprese nell'industria manifatturiera Italiana"*, Temi di discussione del Servizio Studi, Banca d'Italia.

Traù F. (1991), *"Crescita, efficienza e dimensioni d'impresa nell'industria italiana"*, Centro Studi Confindustria Ricerche.

Traù F. (1996), *"La mobilità dimensionale delle imprese nell'industria di trasformazione"*, in Galli G. ed., La mobilità della società italiana, vol II, Editore SIPI, Roma.

You J.I. (1995), *"Small firms in economic theory"*, Cambridge Journal of Economics, 19.

THE INFLUENCE OF ADJUSTMENT COSTS ON LABOUR ADJUSTMENT: AN ANALYSIS USING PANEL DATA FOR MANUFACTURING ESTABLISHMENTS IN LOWER SAXONY[1]

Michael Gold

University of Lueneburg

1 Introduction

In neoclassical theory labour demand responds to external shocks without delay by returning to the optimum (see Hamermesh 1993, 20-28), but in general, enterprises change their demand for labour more slowly than shocks warrant, because each firm incurs adjustment costs when it changes the amount of employees (see Hamermesh/Pfann 1996, 1264). During the last several years a number of studies have investigated the costs of adjustment, the structure of adjustment costs and the influence of these costs on labour demand. Most of these studies used aggregate data at the level of industries, while micro data based studies remain rare. One problem for empirical studies at the firm level is the lack of panel data with a large number of cases and high quality of data. The following analysis of the influence of adjustment costs on labour adjustment is based on the *Hannover Firm Panel*, a new data set that is a representative panel covering some 1000 manufacturing firms from Lower Saxony, one of the German Federal States. This data set has information, inter alia, for an investigation of internal factors which influence labour adjustment.

The paper is organised as follows. In section 2 I present information about the *Hannover Firm Panel*. In section 3 a description of the change in the number of employees per firm between 1993 and 1995 by firm size follows. After a theoretical discussion of adjustment costs with a focus on investments in human capital and the role of works councils, in section 4, I present results from an empirical analysis of labour adjustment and the role of internal factors of establishments which affect labour adjustment (works councils, investments in human capital, over time, short time, firm size, and profit situation) in section 5. Section 6 concludes.

[1] This paper uses data from the project *Das Hannoveraner Firmenpanel*, funded by the Volkswagen-Stiftung. I would like to thank Marie Oamek and Joachim Wagner for helpful comments and suggestions. I'm solely responsible for remaining errors.

2 Data issues

This study is based on the *Hannover Firm Panel*, a new data set that is a representative panel covering some 1000 manufacturing firms from Lower Saxony. This project covers a period of 4 years (1994-1997) and is supported by the Volkswagen Foundation. Infratest Sozialforschung (Munich), a leading German survey and opinion research institute, is responsible for collecting the data each year. The first three waves of the survey have been successfully completed and fieldwork for the fourth wave has been completed in November 1997. The survey covers establishments which had at least 5 employees (including the owner and members of his family) in 1994 and which, in addition, could be categorised as 'producing,' so e.g. service enterprises are excluded. Note that very small establishments are excluded too, because usually they have a completely different structure with regard to organisation, production process and management decision-making processes (see Brand et al. 1996).

The high quality of the data form the *Hannover Firm Panel* was achieved by using professional interviewers, who completed individual oral interviews. Furthermore, the target person in the establishment is always a member of the executive or personnel management. The sample is stratified according to establishment size and industry on a representative basis. The design of the survey allows both an establishment-proportional and an employment-proportional weighting. Thus it is possible to make statements about the establishments in the Panel, about all manufacturing establishments in Lower Saxony and about all the workers employed in these establishments. More information about data editing procedures, sampling frames, and interviews are presented in Infratest Sozialforschung (1995).

The survey contains approximately 90 questions. The survey is divided into different topics, e.g., general information about the establishments, structure and development of personnel, wages and salaries, determinants of employment, information about product and process innovation, determinants of imports and exports, and the establishment's environmental protection activities. Different priorities were set each wave. The first and third waves directed their attention to 'the labour market, employment and remuneration,' while the second and fourth waves focused on 'international co-operation, market and innovation dynamics, and environmental measures' (see table 1). English translations of the survey questionnaires for the first and second waves are published in Brand, et al. (1996).

Table 1 Summary of the questions of the *Hannover Firm Panel*

Category	1. Wave	2. Wave	3. Wave	4. Wave
Company Policy and Company Development [#]	x	x	x	x
General Information about the Establishment	x	x	x	x
Structure and Development of Personnel	x	x	x	x
Wages and Salaries	x	x	x	x
Working and Company Hours	x	x	x	x
Determinants of Employment	x	x	x	x
Enterprise and Environment	x	x	x	x
Company Success and Employee Participation	x	-	x	-
International Co-operation	-	x	-	x
Innovations	-	x	-	x
The most Important Product Group	-	x	-	x

[#]In the first wave this was called 'Location Factors and Objectives of the Firm';
'x' = occur in the survey and '-' = not occur in the survey.

Table 2 gives an overview of the sample of the first three waves according to firm size classes. As it turns out, there is a relatively small attrition rate (less than 20 percent) between the single waves. This success has different reasons. First, good public relations initiated by the Chambers of Commerce in Lower Saxony in co-operation with the Research Group 'Forschungsstelle Firmenpanel' was important, because the establishments needed to know the regional importance of the project for Lower Saxony and this was explicitly revealed to the establishments and the public. Second, each questionnaire was pre-tested with establishments in other federal states. This concept protected against a high attrition rate, because there were then no questions, which could cause not to complete the questionnaire. Another advantage is the existence of a fixed contact person, because the interviewer did not change, if possible, during the 4 years of the Panel (see Brand et al. 1996; Brand/Carstensen 1995).

Table 2 Size distribution of Establishments in the *Hannover Firm Panel*

Firm size classes	Absolute number of establishments (Percentage of establishments)		
Number of employees	1. wave	2. wave	3. wave
1-19	212	187	145
	(20.8%)	(22.1%)	(20.1%)
20-49	212	165	165
	(20.8%)	(19.5%)	(22.9%)
50-99	199	161	127
	(19.4%)	(19.0%)	(17.6%)
100-250	242	200	174
	(23.6%)	(23.6%)	(24.1%)
more than 250	160	135	110
	(15.6%)	(15.9)	(15.3%)
Total	1025	848	721

Source: *Hannover Firm Panel*, waves 1 to 3.

3 Changes in the number of employees between 1994 and 1995

If there is a shock in the product market, e.g. the demand for products goes up or down, establishments have to adjust their labour demand. There are different methods of adjusting the labour demand, such as hiring or firing workers or outsourcing parts of the production (see Gerlach/Hübler 1987, 306/307). In the short run this could be done with over time or short time work (see Franz 1996, 132/133). In this article the focus is on the adjustment of the number of workers, that is hiring, firing, and retirement of employees.

The *Hannover Firm Panel* provides information about the number of employees in the firm, including the owner, members of his family and trainees, at the end of the previous year in each wave. Here no difference is made between full-time and part-time workers. Using information for 1993 to 1995 it is possible to determine the rate of growth of the number of employees for the years 1994 and 1995 as follows:

$$GRL_{t,i} = \frac{L_{t,i} - L_{t-1,i}}{L_{t-1,i}} * 100 = \frac{\Delta L_{t,i}}{L_{t-1,i}} * 100 \qquad [1]$$

with L as number of employees, i as index of the firm and t as index of time.

There is no information about the gross flows between t and $t+1$. It is the result of the net adjustment for 1994 and 1995. To get comparable results over time, only data for establishments with information about the number of employees in all years are used. Therefore, data for 683 firms were used for the descriptive analysis. Due to oversampling of large firms in the *Hannover Firm Panel*, the descriptive analysis is based on establishment-proportional weighted data.

Table 3 shows that about 40.0% of manufacturing firms in Lower Saxony had a constant number of employees in 1994 and 1995, while in 1994 (1995) 29.4% (32.1%) of the firms reduced and 31.7% (26.3%) expanded their numbers of workers. Only firms with a change in labour demand are considered in the following investigation.

Table 3 Employee growth rates in manufacturing firms in Lower Saxony in 1994 and 1995

Employee growth rate		Establishments (in %)	
		1994	1995
Reduction	more than 20%	9.0	9.7
	10% to 20%	10.5	12.2
	less than 10%	9.9	10.2
No change		39.0	41.5
Expansion	less than 10%	9.3	9.1
	10% to 20%	11.6	9.1
	more than 20%	10.8	8.1
Total number of firms		12,824	

Source: *Hannover Firm Panel*; waves 1-3; weighted data.

It is problematic to look at all firms simultaneously, because typically the growth rates of small firms will be higher than the growth rates of large firms. While the growth rate of a firm with 10 workers with a net adjustment of plus 3 workers is 30%, the growth rate of a large firm with the same number of new employees is much lower. Another problem is that the probability of no change is much higher in small establishments than in large establishments. So the next step of the analysis will pay attention to this by creating categories of firm sizes. The firm size equals the number of workers employed by the firm. The categories are 1 to 19, 20 to 49, 50 to 99, 100 to 249 and more than 249 employees.

This may cause a problem, because firms can migrate between size categories from one year to the next. This may lead to wrong interpretations, because small firms will tend to increase and larger firms will tend to decrease. The result of this would be that a classification like this might favour small firms. The following example will demonstrate this: Consider two firms, 'A' and 'B'. Firm

'A' is a small establishment which belongs to the category 1 to 19 employees, while 'B' belongs to the category 20 to 49 employees. Suppose 'A' grows from 15 workers in 1993 to 22 worker in 1994, and 'B' shrinks from 24 workers in 1993 to 18 workers in 1994. That means that the small firm has a growth rate of 46.6 percent in 1994, while the large firm growth rate is -25.0 percent. Both firms cross the size class boundaries. Consider now that this employment movement was transitory and reversed in 1995. So 'A' shrinks back down to 15 workers, while 'B' grows to 24 workers. The small firms growth rate here is 33.3 percent (firm 'B'), while 'A,' the large firm, shrinks by approximately 31.8 percent. Altogether the small (large) firm growth rate between 1993 and 1995 according to this calculation was 39.4 (-28.3) percent, but each firm has the same number of employees in 1993 and 1995. To take this problem of transitory movements into account it is appropriate to use size classes based on average firm size (see Davis/Haltiwanger/Schuh 1996 or 1996a; Wagner 1995).

Table 4 confirms the assumptions about small and large firms. The larger the firm is, the smaller the share of firms with a constant number of employees. While the smallest category shows more than 45.0 percent of the establishments as having no change in 1994 and 1995, the share of firms with more than 250 employees is 8.3 percent in the maximum. Additionally, the share of small firms with large positive or negative growth rates is always larger than the share of larger firms with high growth rates.

Table 4 Employee growth rates in manufacturing firms in Lower Saxony in 1994 and 1995 by firm size[*]

Employee growth rate		1-19		20-49		50-99		100-249		≥250	
		1994	1995	1994	1995	1994	1995	1994	1995	1994	1995
Reduction	more than 20%	10.7	11.6	7.0	6.7	4.7	4.7	1.8	4.5	2.5	5.5
	10% to 20%	9.7	12.5	13.6	14.1	9.7	10.9	6.6	7.4	16.2	8.0
	less than 10%	3.6	4.1	19.2	18.1	22.9	21.4	30.0	30.0	35.2	43.5
No change		45.7	47.9	29.9	33.5	22.5	28.9	19.6	20.1	7.2	8.3
Expansion	less than 10%	3.6	4.8	16.9	14.9	26.0	20.0	28.2	22.7	27.9	27.1
	10% to 20%	12.9	9.3	10.2	9.2	7.4	8.7	7.3	8.8	5.3	6.4
	more than 20%	13.7	10.0	3.1	3.5	6.9	5.5	6.5	6.7	5.8	1.2

[+] average firm size (1993, 1994 and 1995).

Source: *Hannover Firm Panel*, waves 1-3; weighted data; n = 12,824.

4 Internal factors on the adjustment of labour demand

4.1 Theoretical remarks

Evidently adjustment of labour demand does not only depend on firm size. There are other factors, especially internal ones, that affect the amount of adjustment which take place. In reality firms don't hire and fire all of their workers every day. Normally working contracts are made for longer periods. The standard explanation for this is that firms incur adjustment costs by hiring and firing. These costs are responsible for firms' slow changes in labour demand, and cause a rigid process of adjustment.

Fundamental ideas for the explanation of this phenomena are provided by Oi (1962) and Becker (1962). Oi integrated fixed labour costs into the neoclassical theory of employment (see Hart/Robb 1980, 1). Labour is defined by Oi as a 'Quasi-Fixed' factor, having in partly variable and partly fixed costs. Variable costs are the wages with all their components, like salary, pay, extra pay, and bonuses as payment for output. The fixed costs of labour are independent from the hours of work. They arise from investments by firms in hiring and training activities (see Oi 1962, 539). Becker (1962) looked at the investment in human capital, especially specific training, for example on-the-job training. This investment in human capital creates costs, which play an important role in firms' decisions regarding adjustment, taking into consideration uncertainty and the labour costs. So the decision regarding labour input can no longer be based solely on the current relation between the value of the marginal product of labour and the wage, but must include other criteria (see Oi 1962, 539; Becker 1962, 11-18).

Adjustment costs are always dependent on the complete fluctuation of employment, including hiring, firing, death, dismissals, and retirement of employees. The firm invests in the workforce in every stage of it's working life. Before the employees are in the firm there are selection costs. These costs include expenditures for searches and screening techniques and advertising for vacant jobs. In the next phase the firm incurs improvement costs through training programs or on-the-job training. These investments raise future productivity. These costs include the value placed on the time and effort of trainees, the 'teaching' provided by others, and the equipment and materials (see Hart/Robb 1980, 1/2; Becker 1962, 11). In addition to the costs of hiring and on-the-job training there are firing and dismissals cost. On the one hand there are costs of losing the human capital, while on the other hand there are firing costs. These costs include payments in lieu of notice, compensations for breach of contract and any costs incurred because it is necessary to fulfil certain legal requirements (see Nickel 1986, 474-476.). In the *Hannover Firm Panel* there is some information about these costs. The focus is limited to the information about training in the form of 'financing further education' and the existence of a works council.

4.2 Internal factors

In this subsection I will explain a selection of variables which are related to adjustment costs. I will start with further education, followed by the works council, an organisation representing the employees of a firm. Another important internal factor for labour adjustment is the profit situation, which can be seen as an indicator for the demand for products. Finally, I will discuss the impact of over time and short time on labour adjustment.

Further education

A part of adjustment cost is the lost of investment in human capital. The *Hannover Firm Panel* includes information, as to whether the establishment finances further education which can be interpreted as a part of investments in human capital. In 1994 (1995) 32.4% (33.8%)[2] of the establishments of the manufactory industry in Lower Saxony financed internal/external education for their employees. Under the assumption of the loss of human capital, labour adjustment should be c.p. significantly lower in firms with investment in human capital than in establishments without this expenditure. That means there should be a negative impact of this variable on labour adjustment.

Works council

Adjustment costs arise as a result of a multitude of institutional rules. On the one hand there is protection against unlawful dismissal and the right of advance notice about dismissal. On the other hand there is the works council with it's right to information, right to a say, and right to participate in decisions. For example, the works council must be informed in advance on, essentially, all personnel decisions (see Müller-Jentsch 1986, 220-225). The result of this may be delays, which can be interpreted as adjustment costs. Furthermore the works council can be interpreted as the 'Voice' of the employees against the management. In this way it contributes to better communication in the firm. The insiders, being represented through the works councils, try to expand their utility, i.e. save their jobs. So if there is a bad profit situation, the insider's interest is to have few dismissals, and if there is a good profit situation they try to compensate the manpower shortage through over time, because in this way the insider can increase his/her wage. Based on the *Hannover Firm Panel* Addison/Schnabel/Wagner (1997) and Jirjahn/Klodt (1997) find positive ceteris paribus relationship between wages and the existence of a works council, which may confirm this assumption. From this assumption we can conclude that the existence of a works council should c.p. lower the adjustment of labour. Frick (1996) confirms in his analysis that the existence of a works council lowers significantly the negative adjustment rate (dismissal). Regarding positive

---

[2] Source: *Hannoveraner Firm Panel*, waves 1-3; weighted data.

adjustment, Frick/Sadowski (1995) could not show a negative impact of a works council, but the result pointed at a positive impact of a works council for hiring.

Profit situation

Firms have different possibilities for responding to the change of profit situation as an indicator of the demand for goods. For example there are different methods for a firm to react to a bad profit situation. Either it may reduce the working time or fire employees (see Medoff 1979, 380). Under the assumption that the firm will react with the number of employees, the following adjustment will be expected: a bad profit situation will decrease positive adjustment of labour demand, while negative adjustment will increase by this.

Over time and short time

In addition to adjustment through the number of employees the establishments also have the possibility to assign over time or short time. Now, the question is, how do these internal factors impact the adjustment of the number of employees. If there is over time in a firm, then it is possible, that positive adjustment will be forced by over time, because this instrument of short run adjustment will be replaced by new employees. On the other hand it is thinkable that over time, as a instrument of short term adjustment, will only be used in this way, and that there will not be any other kinds of adjustment of labour demand. For negative adjustment there are also two sides imaginable. First it seems to be possible, if a firm is using over time, that this over time will be reduced before they fire workers, but otherwise it is plausible that the firm may fire too many workers in one period, because it is cheaper to fire a large number and after that to just assign over time to compensate for this defect for a while until the necessary number of employees is achieved. So the effect of over time is doubtful, and can only be estimated empirically. The arguments for the impact of short time are the opposite.

5 Empirical findings

5.1 Personnel problems and adjustment costs

We will start with an investigation of the impact of the variables discussed above on two personnel problems that may or may not occur in a firm: 'costs for personnel reduction are too high' and 'too many employees.' In the first and third waves the establishments were asked about these personnel problems. Using a pooled probit-model it is tested whether there is a significant impact of these factors on the probability of the occurrence of these problems in a firm. In addition to the variables 'number of employees,' 'works council,' 'overtime,' 'short time,' 'finance further education,' and 'bad profit situation', 'number of employees squared' is controlled for to consider possible non-linearity. Additionally 'industry dummies' are included to consider specific effects. The estimation uses unweighted data, because the sampling weight is a function of independent variables, i.e. firm size and industry (see Winship/Radbill 1994).

Results are reported in table 5. The probability of 'costs for personnel reduction are too high' increases significantly with the existence of a works council, with short time, and with a bad profit situation. Similar results are found for 'too many employees': a works council, the existence of short time and a bad profit situation significantly increase the probability of this problem. Additionally, there is a weak positive impact of investment in human capital on the problem 'too many employees .' By and large, these results are in accordance with the theoretical consideration.

Table 5 Determinants of the personnel problems 'costs for personnel reduction are too high' and ' too many employees' (Dependent Variable: Dummy for Personnel problem: 'Costs for personnel reduction are too high' or ' Too many employees'; 1 = yes; Method: Probit)

Independent Variables	'Costs for personnel reduction are too high'	'Too many employees'
Number of employees	3.18e-4*	0.001***
	(1.94)	(4.72)
Number of employees squared	-1.89e-8	-7.05e-8**
	(1.27)	(2.52)
Works council	0.213**	0.369***
(Dummy: 1 = yes)	(2.02)	(3.38)
Short time	0.480***	0.492***
(Dummy: 1 = yes)	(4.13)	(4.21)
Over time	-0.049	-0.157
(Dummy: 1 = yes)	(0.47)	(1.52)
Finance further education	0.162	0.175*
(Dummy: 1 = yes)	(1.58)	(1.72)
Bad profit situation in pervious year	0.711***	0.288***
	(7.21)	(2.80)
(Dummy: 1 = bad or very bad)		
Constant	-1.213***	-1.377***
	(7.83)	(8.70)
Industry Dummies	yes	yes
n	1342	1342
χ^2(19)	154.32***	147.47***
Pseudo-R^2	0.129	0.121

Source: *Hannover Firm Panel*, waves 1 and 3; t-value in parentheses; */**/*** = significant at 0.10/0.05/0.01 percent level.

5.2 Labour adjustment and adjustment costs

The way internal factors impact labour adjustment will now be discussed. The dependent variable is labour adjustment, distinguishing here between positive and negative adjustment. This is necessary because some of the independent variables have different influence on positive and negative adjustments (see previous section). Firms with no change in the number of employees will be excluded.

To use the 'panel-character' of the data, the empirical model is specified in two ways. The first model is pooled and has the following specification:

$$log \ /GRL \ / = \alpha + \beta' x_{it} + \gamma' y_i + v_{it} \qquad [2]$$

with $v_{it} \sim N(0, \sigma_v^2)$, and where $log \ /GRL \ /$ is the dependent variable and x is a vector of independent and time variant variables, while y is a vector of independent and time invariant variables. α and the vectors β and γ are parameters, which will be estimated with ordinary least squares (OLS). i is the index of the firm and t is the index of time.

The second model is a random-effects-model with the following structure:

$$log \ /GRL \ / = \alpha + \beta' x_{it} + \gamma' y_i + u_i + \varepsilon_{it} \qquad [3]$$

with $\quad u_i \sim N(0, \sigma_u^2), \ \varepsilon_{it} \sim N(0, \sigma_\varepsilon^2), \ E(u_i u_j) = 0 \ \text{for} \ i \neq j, \ E(\varepsilon_{it}\varepsilon_{js}) = 0 \ \text{for} \ i \neq j \ \text{or} \ t \neq s,$
$E(\varepsilon_{it} u_j) = 0$ for all i, j and t.

u_i is the random disturbance characterising the ith observation and is constant through time (see Green 1993). With a Lagrange-Multiplicator (LM)-Test (Breusch/Pagan 1980) it is possible to test for the existence of firm specific effects. Here the random-effects-model is tested against a pooled model without firm specific effects. The hypothesis is H_0: $\sigma_u^2 = 0$, i.e. there are no individual effects. The test uses v_{it} of the pooled model. The test statistic has a chi-squared distribution with one degree of freedom if the hypothesis is correct. (Note that a fixed-effects-model is impossible to use, because of the inclusion of time invariant variables in the model.)

The independent variables are 'overtime,' 'short time,' 'finance further education,' 'bad profit situation,' 'number of employees,' and the squared 'number of employees'. The latter tests for non-linear effects of the firm size. All these variables can vary over time, while the 'industry dummies' and the 'works council' are invariant in time. On the one hand this is because there is only a small number of firms for which the works councils status changed over time (see

Addison/Schnabel/ Wagner 1997, 3), on the other hand, information about the works council status is not available in each wave of the *Hannover Firm Panel*. Again the 'industry dummies' are included to control for unobserved industry effects including capital intensity. (Note that in the *Hannover Firm Panel* there is no information about the capital stock employed in the firm.)

Furthermore I test for the impact of the structure of the employees by including the percentage of women, the percentage of part time employees, and the percentage of jobs requiring an university degree. Assuming that the share of jobs requiring university degree is positively correlated with high human capital, and the share of women is negatively correlated with it, one can expect that a high share of 'university degree' jobs and a lower percentage of women in the firm will decrease labour adjustment. The variables 'bad profit situation' and 'finance further education' are included with a one year lag, while 'short time' and 'overtime' are for year t. (Note that the latter information is available only for the first half of the year.)

Table 6 shows the results of the regressions. The LM-Test shows that the pooled OLS model is preferred for positive adjustment, while the random-effects-model is preferred for negative adjustment. (However, comparing the coefficients for the two models we find that most of them do not differ substantially). The results confirm the expectations for most of the variables. The existence of a works council lowers significantly c.p. the positive as well as the negative adjustment. Over time and financing further education lower negative labour adjustment, too. Positive adjustment declines significantly c.p., if there is 'short time' in the firm, while negative adjustment increase c.p.. The negative impact of 'over time' for negative adjustment confirms the assumption, that firms will first reduce over time before firing employees. The bad profit situation increase the negative adjustment significantly, as expected, while for positive adjustment there is no significant impact. For the variables of the structure of the employees there are no significant impacts, too.

Table 6 Impact of Internal factors on labour adjustment - (Dependent Variable: *log* /*GRL* /; Method: 'pooled' OLS / Random-effects-GLS regression (REM))

Independent Variables	Positive adjustment		Negative adjustment	
	'pooled' OLS	REM	'pooled' OLS	REM
Number of employees	-0.001[*]	-0.001[*]	-9.73e-5	-1.11e-4
	(1.91)	(1.81)	(0.57)	(0.61)
Number of employees squared	3.50e-8[*]	3.49e-8[*]	1.26e-8	1.37e-8
	(1.77)	(1.69)	(0.61)	(0.63)
Works council	-0.362[***]	-0.368[***]	-0.645[***]	-0.643[***]
(Dummy: 1 = yes)	(3.25)	(3.10)	(6.35)	(6.17)
Short time	-0.270[*]	-0.282[*]	0.267[**]	0.275[***]
(Dummy: 1 = yes)	(1.66)	(1.72)	(2.53)	(2.61)
Over time	-0.184	-0.197	-0.229[**]	-0.232[**]
(Dummy: 1 = yes)	(1.55)	(1.64)	(2.35)	(2.38)
Finance further education	-0.234[**]	-0.241[**]	-0.105	-0.091
(Dummy: 1 = yes)	(2.20)	(2.23)	(1.08)	(0.94)
Bad profit situation in pervious	-0.088	-0.097	0.389[***]	0.381[***]
year	(0.64)	(0.71)	(4.27)	(4.18)
(Dummy: 1 = bad or very bad)				
Percentage of women in 1994	0.005	0.005	0.002	0.002
	(1.62)	(1.64)	(0.72)	(0.62)
Percentage of part time	0.002	0.002	-0.004	-0.004
employees in 1994	(0.41)	(0.39)	(1.04)	(0.98)
Percentage of jobs with	0.004	0.003	-0.005	-0.004
university degree in 1994	(0.38)	(0.24)	(0.62)	(0.51)
Constant	1.872[**]	2.785[***]	2.562[***]	2.588[***]
	[*](2.63)	(4.26)	(10.77)	(10.48)
Industry Dummies	yes	yes	yes	yes
n	462	462	518	518
R²	0.144	0.143	0.225	0.225
LM-Test (Breusch/Pagan-Test)		0.39		5.10[**]
		(0.53)		(0.02)

Source: *Hannover Firm Panel*, waves 1-3; t-value in parentheses; [*]/[**]/[***] = significant at 0.10/0.05/0.01 percent level.

6 Conclusion

Smaller establishments have a higher probability of no change in the number of employees than larger firms, but if there is a change, then this adjustment will most of the time be higher. In the theoretical part I discussed the influence of internal factors, here in the from of adjustment costs, on labour adjustment. The focus was on investment in human capital and the works council. The empirical evidence presented in this paper shows that positive and negative adjustment will be lowered through the existence of a works council, while only the negative adjustment will be lowered through the investment in human capital. Furthermore it is shown that works councils, investments in human capital, short time, and a bad profit situation increase the probability that an establishment will have problems with 'too many employees,' or 'too high costs for personnel reductions'.

REFERENCES

Addison, J. T., Schnabel, C., Wagner, J. (1997), *"Betriebsräte in der deutschen Industrie: Verbreitung, Bestimmungsgründe und Effekte,"* Arbeitsbericht des Fachbereichs Wirtschafts- und Sozialwissenschaften, Universität Lüneburg, Nr. 183, Lüneburg.

Becker, G. S. (1962), *"Investment in Human Capital: A Theoretical Analysis,"* in: Journal of Political Economy, 70, pp. 9-49.

Brand, R., Carstensen, V. (1995*), "Das Hannoveraner Firmenpanel. Ein Betriebspanel in Niedersachsen,"* in: Schasse, U., Wagner, J. (Hrsg.), Erfolgreich Produzieren in Niedersachsen, NIW-Vortragsreihe, Band. 10, Hannover, pp. 1-36.

Brand, R., Carstensen, V., Gerlach, K., Klodt, T. (1996), *"The Hannover Panel,"* Discussion Paper, No. 2, Universität Hannover: Forschungsstelle Firmenpanel, Hannover.

Breusch, T., Pagan, A. (1980), *"The LM Test and Its Applications to Model Specification in Econometrics,"* in: Review of Economic Studies, 47, pp. 239-254.

Davis, S. J., Haltiwanger, J. C., Schuh, S. (1996), *Job Creation and Destruction,* Cambridge, London.

Davis, S. J., Haltiwanger, J. C., Schuh, S. (1996a), *"Small Business and Job Creation: Dissecting the Myth and Reassessing the Facts,"* in: Small Business Economics, 8, pp. 297-316.

Franz, W. (1996), *Arbeitsmarktökonomik*, 3. Auflage, Berlin et al..

Frick, B. (1996), *"Co-determination and Personnel Turnover: The German Experience,"* in: Labour (Review of Labour Economics and Industrial Relations), 10, pp. 407-430.

Frick, B., Sadowski, D. (1995), *"Works councils, Unions, and Firm Performance,"* in: Buttler, F. et al. (Ed.) Institutional Frameworks and Labor Market Performance, London, New York, pp. 285-315.

Gerlach, K., Wagner, J. (1993*), "Employment Dynamics, Firm Growth, and New Firm Formation,"* in: Buttler, F. et al. (Ed.) Institutional Frameworks and Labor Market Performance, London, New York, pp. 270-284.

Gerlach, K., Hübler, O. (1987), *"Personalnebenkosten, Beschäftigtenzahl und Arbeitsstunden aus neoklassischer und institutionalistischer Sicht"*, in: Buttler, F., K. Gerlach, R. Schmiede (Hrsg.), Arbeitsmarkt und Beschäftigung, Frankfurt, New York, pp. 291-331.

Green, W. H. (1993), *Econometric Analysis*, 2. Edition, London et al..

Hamermesh, D. S. (1993), *Labor Demand, Princeton,* New Jersey.

Hamermesh, D. S., Pfann, G. A. (1996), *"Adjustment Costs in Factor Demand,"* in: Journal of Economic Literature, 34, pp. 1264-1292.

Hart, R. A., Robb, A. L. (1980), *"Production and Labour Demand Functions with Endogenous Fixed Worker Costs,"* International Institute of Management, Wissenschaftszentrum Berlin, Paper Nr. IIM/80-11, Berlin.

Infratest Sozialforschung (1995), *Das Hannoveraner Firmenpanel - Methodenbericht -, Eine repräsentative Umfrage im Verarbeitenden Gewerbe* 1994, Infratest Sozialforschung GmbH, München.

Jirjahn, U., Klodt, T. (1997), *"Betriebliche Determinanten der Lohnhöhe"*, Discussion Paper, No. 8, Universität Hannover: Forschungsstelle Firmenpanel, Hannover.

Medoff, J. L. (1979), *"Layoffs and Alternatives under Trade Unions in U.S. Manufacturing,"* in: The American Economic Review, 69, pp. 380-395.

Müller-Jentsch, W. (1986), *Soziologie der industriellen Beziehungen*, Frankfurt, New York.

Nickell. S. J. (1986), *"Dynamic Models of Labour Demand,"* in: Ashenfelter, O., R. Layard (Ed.), Handbook of Labor Economics, I, pp. 473-522.

Oi, W. Y. (1962), *"Labor as a Quasi-fixed Factor,"* in: Journal of Political Economy, 70, pp. 538-555.

Wagner, J. (1995), *"Firm Size and Job Creation in Germany,"* in: Small Business Economics, 7, pp. 469-474.

Winship, C., Radbill, L. (1994), *Sampling Weights and Regression Analysis, in: Sociological Methods & Research*, 23, pp. 230-257.

COMPANIES AND LOCAL UNITS: THE EMPLOYMENT TRENDS IN FRANCE

Vincent Hecquet[1] and Danielle Roualdès[2]

[1,2]Direction des Statistiques d'Entreprises, INSEE

1 The longitudinal follow up of companies and local units by the French statistical system

A company's staff may be spread out over several, geographically distinct local units, or they may be grouped together in just one. In managing their staff, companies can adapt in two different ways: they can adjust employment in each of their local units; at the same time they can reorganise by changing the number of local units via purchase and sales activities involving creation or closure.

Thanks to the data produced by the French statistic system, we are able to link the local units to the compagny which manages them. The French statistical system manages a national register of legal units and local units. The SIRENE register records all the local units set up in France, and links them to the legal units. On the whole, the SIRENE register holds 3.7 millions of local legal units. The French statisticians follow up each unit, distinguishing its economic continuity and the chronicle of its legal forms. Nevertheless, it is impossible to achieve a very high quality information for all the units òf SIRENE. The data of SIRENE are indeed supplied by the declarations filled by legal units as part of their administrative obligations. As a consequence, the employees of INSEE carefully follow up the large local units, and record this information in a data base called BRIDGE (see the annex for further information).

This study was carried out on companies comprising at least 50 employees in 1985 and which were still in business in 1993 (See «Understanding the results»). To each of these companies, we allocated all the local units it controled in 1985 and 1993, merging the data of the SIRENE register and the BRIDGE data base. Thanks to these sources, we are able to follow up from a longitudinal point of view each local unit of the surviving companies.

Depending on the business sector, French companies have conducted very different employment policies. Of all companies employing more than 50 people in 1985, just over two thirds were still in business in 1993.. Amongst these, manufacturing companies shed 19% of their staff in eight years, whereas those involved in trade services increased their staff by 21%. Manufacturing companies eliminated proportionately more jobs than they lost plants. In an effort to increase productivity from work, French manufacturing industries invested at the same time as they massively eliminated jobs, without making any profound changes to their original set-up. By contrast, the rapid development of trade services was accompanied by more rapid growth in the number of local units.

2 Structure and dynamics of the units

2.1 Productive logic and sales outlet logic

In most manufacturing activity, the amount of equipment necessary to run the business and the search for economies of scale require staff to be concentrated in large production plants. By contrast, in the trade and service sectors, company development depends partly on the distribution of sales outlets in order to win new markets. So it is that amongst companies with more than fifty employees, 55% have only one local unit in the manufacturing sector compared to less than 40% for those in the commercial sector. Organisational differences are also evident with respect to the largest companies. Amongst commercial and service companies that have several local units, 40% have at least ten: this percentage is only 10% in the manufacturing sector.

2.2 Three methods of company organisation

Trends regarding local units are strongly linked to company structure. In all sectors, the smallest companies are the ones with only one productive site. Their set-up is extremely stable by nature: even when staff increase, a company with more than fifty employees that has only one site waits before opening another. By spreading out over several sites, the company has to make profound changes to its organisation so as to co-ordinate its activities between the varies units. Thus, three quarters of single-site companies that increased their staff retained their original set-up.

When a company comprises several local units, the foremost among them is, on average, at least as big as a single-site company in that sector. In order to be viable, a company should therefore have at least one sufficiently large local unit that attains a threshold level of efficiency for the sector. Half of the time more than two thirds of the jobs available in the company are concentrated in this local unit which supports only one or two considerably smaller units. This sort of organisational lay-out is particularly frequent in the manufacturing sector but is also found in service companies employing between 50 and 200 people.

Only a minority of the big companies departs from this set-up where one local unit dominates all the others. In each sector the threshold of ten local units has to be crossed before the main site accommodates less than half of the company's jobs. It is also from this stage onwards that the second site accommodates more than one third of the staff employed at the first site. Companies of this type are more frequently found in the tertiary sectors than in manufacturing industry.

After eight years, the companies organised around one dominant local unit, such as those that comprise several, evenly-balanced local units have, for the most part, retained the same structure. The main local unit is the backbone of the business and remains stable over time. In 80% of cases the largest local unit of a company which owned several in 1993, already belonged to it in 1985. In 15% of cases the local unit was created, and it was acquired from another company in only 5% of cases. By contrast, the other units are subject to numerous rotations, essentially due to opposing actions of creation and closure. In 30% of cases when a company comprised two local units in 1985 and 1993, the smaller of them did not exist at the beginning of the period. Rotation increases with the number of local units within the company. Almost all companies with more than five local units thus experienced contrasting flows with respect to the latter.

2.3 Transfers of local units are limited to groups

Whatever their size and business activity, companies create or eliminate far more local units than they buy or sell. Those companies that lasted during these eight years closed 38% of the establishments they possessed in 1985 whereas they sold 8% of them.

The local units they possessed in 1993 were respectively created and bought in similar proportions. The transfer of local units thus plays the weakest role in job development within stable companies. Above all, it takes place mainly within groups. During the 1980s more and more companies came under the control of groups of companies. The largest companies invested in the capital of smaller firms and thus acquired central decision-making power over the latter. Companies belonging to a group grow according to the same mechanisms as other companies and the creation and closure of local units amongst them still largely exceed transfers. Nonetheless the majority of such transfers take place within groups. In 1985 roughly a third of all local units belonged to groups but 75% of those exchanged over the period between two stable companies were transferred within a group. Groups control large companies and numerous local units, and this encourages transfers. Thanks to their size it is easier for groups to finance the acquisition of local units from external institutions. Finally, within the same group, exchanges of local units make it possible to create synergies thanks to a rationalisation of the companies concerned. Eight times out of ten the absorption of companies occurs within a group. The same occurs when local units are transferred in order to set up a new company.

3 Three differents trends according to business activity

3.1 Staff reductions and reorientation in manufacturing enterprises

Stable manufacturing enterprises shed 222,000 employees through a higher number of plant closures than openings and through a higher volume of sales than of purchases (Table 1). But above all they reduced personnel in the local units that they retained. These staff cutbacks led to the elimination of 272,000 jobs, bringing the total number of losses to 494,000. In fact, while achieving the weakest growth of the European countries, French manufacturing industries changed their production methods: they cut staff while simultaneously making heavy investments which increased staff productivity.

Table 1 Management of local units and their staff by the 7,290 manufacturing enterprises with 50 or more employees, which continued to operate between 1985 and 1993

				Balance
Local units that were transferred to a company other than that to which they belonged in 1985	1 362 *205 000* (1)	Derived from a company other than that to which they belonged in 1993	1 338 *133 200*	-24 (2) *- 72 800*
Local units that remained within the same companies between 1985 and 1993	14 040 *2 137 000*	Local units that remained within the same company between 1985 and 1993	14 040 *1 865 500*	0 *-271 500*
Local units that disappeared between 1985 and 1993	7 372 *267 500*	Local units created between 1985 and 1993	5 585 *117 700*	-1 787 *-149 800*
Total	22 774 *2 610 300*		20 963 *2 116 400*	-1 811 *-493 900*

Reading: Stable manufacturing enterprises (including 1AA) first shed 271,500 employees from their local units, then eliminated large units. They also reduced their staff following restructuring

(1) The figures in italics show the number of jobs in the local units concerned.

(2) The number of local units transferred by the sector's stable companies between 1985 and 1993 does not tally with the number of local units they acquired during the period since part of the transfers involved other local units (new local units, ones which did not last or those from other sectors)

Source: Bridge, and Sirene, Insee

Plant disappearances concerned a limited number of large local units within the largest enterprises. Firms with more than 2000 employees and which have several plants, employed an average of 26 people in each in 1993, compared to 30 in 1985. Sixteen manufacturing enterprises with more than 1000 employees in 1986 have totally disappeared – something which has not occurred in any other sector for units of this size. Amongst the former, some belong to a branch which has long been in decline in France, such as coalmines, or are undergoing a serious slump, such as the textile industry. However, several large firms: automobile manufacturers (Renault, Peugeot, Massey Ferguson, etc); the metallurgical industry (Vallourec), electronic components (Thomson) and IT (IBM) have also eliminated local units with more than a thousand employees during restructuring operations.

The fabric of which companies are composed has profoundly changed. Manufacturing job losses occur for the most part in companies with more than five hundred employees. By contrast, in the wake of groups, those small and medium-sized manufacturing industries that survived hired people over the period. The iron and steel industry was transformed by a pronounced surge of concentration: many participants regrouped to form the only French group of national stature: Usinor-Sacilor. At the time of the reshuffle six companies initially attached to Sacilor or to other groups disappeared and their manufacturing plants comprising 22,000 employees in 1985, were taken over by a holding company belonging to the Usinor group. These plants lost 40% of their staff in 8 years.

Over the period, the big manufacturing companies rationalised by reorienting towards their principal activity. In 1985, 16% of manufacturing plants conducted a different activity to that conducted by the company whereas no more than 9% did so in 1993. More often than for others, manufacturing plants that are created carry out the principal activity of the company. By contrast, plants whose activity is different are more frequently closed.

3.2 Retail outlets have reorganised

During the last ten years, food retail stores have continued to transform. Hypermarkets have multiplied in number whereas numerous small stores have disappeared.

This phenomenon is not only the result of competition but also of company reorganisation. Stable companies in the food distribution sector (which comprise notably the self-service chains) have closed the smallest of their local units in order to create new, considerably fewer but very much larger ones. They have, furthermore, hired 8% additional employees in the initially larger local units, which they kept (Table 2). In eight years these companies reduced the number of their sales outlets by half but these are larger in size. They employ on average twice as many employees as at the beginning of the period.

The reorganisation of the sales outlets was pushed to extremes by the larger networks of outlets. French groups have followed the same strategy for their traditional stores.

Since the beginning of the 1990s some of them have even created new distribution companies to take advantage of the vogue for hard discount. This type of store is much smaller than the traditional supermarkets. They are very successful since they are situated in the city centres and offer particularly low prices. However, in spite of strong growth, hard discount stores represented only one tenth of the total number of supermarkets in 1993.

Table 2 Management of local units and their staff by the 511 foods retail trade companies with 50 or more employees, which continued to operate between 1985 and 1993

				Balance
Local units that were transferred to a company other than that to which they belonged in 1985	1 489 *45 800*	Derived from a company other than that to which they belonged in 1993	908 *28 300*	-581 *- 17500*
Local units that remained within the same company between 1985 and 1993	2 942 *128 000*	Local units that remained within the same company between 1985 and 1993	2 942 *138 900*	0 *+10 100*
Local units that disappeared between 1985 and 1993	6 047 *33 800*	Local units created between 1985 and 1993	1 785 *28 700*	-4 262 *-5 100*
Total	10 478 *208 400*		5 635 *195 900*	-4 843 *-12 500*

Reading: The stable companies in the foods retail trade eliminated 6,000 local units with less than 6 employees on average, and opened 1,800 with more than 16 employees.
Source: Bridge, and Sirene, Insee

In the non-food retail sector, stable companies with more than 50 employees globally increased their staff by 11% and the number of their sales outlets by 9%. Here again the balance of jobs is explained by the creation and closure of local units.

Confronted with networks of specialised subsidiaries, the large stores gave up some ground. Large chain stores lost 20% of their staff in total and a quarter of their local units. Groups reorganised by transferring several stores belonging to one company to another company. These moves accounted for 9% of the employees in the sector in 1993. During the same period the large distributors specialised in sport, do-it-yourself, textiles and hygiene increased the number of their sales outlets by 23% and increased their staff by 39%, essentially through setting up in new premises. These new openings allow them to come closer to customers. The large specialised distributors have notably set up branch stores in very busy places such as shopping malls and around hypermarkets. Only household-goods stores have simply maintained their staff while reducing the number of their branch stores by 30%. Whatever their business, the large, specialised trading companies have increased the size of their sales outlets so as to offer customers a larger choice.

In the non-food distribution sector, the large branch outlets represent only one form of network organisation. Stores are, in fact, often grouped together around one purchasing centre, or belong to a network of franchisees. A company or group can thus control numerous sales outlets without the latter being legally attached to it. Even here, however, companies organised in chains of branch outlets have experienced greater expansion.

3.3 Services have developed via new business set-ups

Services to households, like services to companies, have experienced remarkably rapid development. Their expansion has occurred above all via the creation of new local units (Table 3). Of the net 104,200 jobs created in sales services, 76,700 come from the balance between creations and closures. There have been twice as many new set-ups as closures. In 1993 the local units in business for eight years accounted for 29% of employees working in services to business and 25% in services to individuals as opposed to 12% in construction and 5% in manufacturing industry. This renewal reflects a configuration in which local units are limited in size: less than half of them has more than ten employees.

Table 3 Management of local units and their staff by the 1116 companies offering services to companies, with 50 or more employees, which continued to operate between 1985 and 1993

				Balance
Local units that were transferred to a company other than that to which they belonged in 1985	163 9 000	Derived from a company other than that to which they belonged in 1993	420 30 800	+257 + 21 800
Local units that remained within the same company between 1985 and 1993	3 620 189 000	Local units that remained within the same company between 1985 and 1993	3 620 188 300	0 -700
Local units that disappeared between 1985 and 1993	2 419 46 800	Local units created between 1985 and 1993	4 591 87 900	+ 2 172 + 41 100
Total	6 202 244 800		8 631 307 000	+ 2 429 + 62 200

Reading: The stable companies in the services to companies sector created a net figure of 41,100 jobs by setting up 2,172 additional local units. These figures do not take into account temporary jobs in temporary employment agencies.
Source: Bridge, and Sirene, Insee

The expansion of the tertiary sector has particularly benefited the largest networks of local units. In the service sector as in the non-food retail sector, new business set-ups are above all the work of large, nation-wide companies which are, more often than not, at the head of a group.

Growth in services to companies has been all the stronger, the bigger the company. Temporary employment agencies have all experienced strong growth via an unparalleled extension of the total number of their local units. However, the three big companies in this field (Ecco, Bis and Manpower) have more than doubled the number of their branches whereas the 150 smaller companies increased theirs by 50%. The largest networks of hotels and restaurants, travel agencies and office-cleaning services have similarly expanded far more quickly than the smaller companies. Only the large auto-repair chains are losing ground. In this sector, where almost all companies have reduced their staff, one of the biggest companies has nonetheless expanded considerably.

Annex

Methodological note

This study was carried out on companies comprising at least 50 employees in 1985 and which were still in business in 1993. It concerns the total number of companies in metropolitan France identified using annual company surveys for 1985. The agricultural, financial and non-trade sectors were eliminated as well as large national companies.

Each company was allocated the total number of local units it owned in 1985 and in 1993. These local units were identified using INSEE's BRIDGE files and SIRENE register. In 1993 a company was deemed to have survived if it still possessed at least one local unit and had a staff that was not nil at that date. Temporary staff placed at companies' disposal by temporary employment agencies were not taken into account. Surviving companies numbered 14,471. In 1985 these companies accounted for 70,190 local units and 4.3 million employees; in 1993 the figure was 70,455 local units and 3.9 million employees.

Definitions

Company: a company is an institutional unit, having legal autonomy, which combines production factors (capital and labour) to produce goods and services which are sold on the market.

Local unit: an local unit is an unit in which a company's business is conducted.

Group: a group is a collection of companies linked by equity financing and within which one company has decision-making power over the others. French groups taken as a whole are monitored by Insee's 'financial liaisons' survey.

BRIDGE, the French data base on the large local units

The follow up of large local units

The data base BRIDGE has been specifically designed by the French statisticians, in order to follow up the large local units. It gathers the most significant data about the large local units. No data provided by BRIDGE comes from a specific survey. The data are provided by the surveys held by the French statistical system, and by the administrative sources. They are collated and checked by the regional teams of statisticians of the INSEE. BRIDGE records all the local units which have employed at least 50 people for at least one year, and reconstitutes their economic evolution. This data base may be used to consult one local unit, or to make up files for economic studies.

With a data base such as BRIDGE, the statisticians draw benefits from the utmost concentration of the productive system, in terms of the size of the units. If we consider the private economy excluding the agricultural sector, around 2.4 millions of local units are set up in France. Only 41 600 among them employ more than 49 workers. Nevertheless these large units employ around 7 750 000 workers, that is to say 60% of the total employment of these sectors. Indeed, the statisticians can observe a large share of the economy, with the information they get on a relatively small number of large local units. This explains the use of BRIDGE, which gathers a controlled information on these units. The national threshold of size for BRIDGE is 49 workers, but in some regions the statisticians record the local units as soon as they have exceeded 20 workers.

The access to many variables on accounts and on the work force

BRIDGE is the outcome of a long succession of bases, which have been improved for thirty years. In 1968 the economic authorities decided the creation of a file recording the local units of 100 employees or more. This file was called « Fichier des Grands Etablissements » (File of Large Locals units). It already provided the information on the economic activity and the number of workers.

From the seventies to the nineties, the statisticians added a great deal of information on the accounts and on the structure of the work force. The information about the accounts is collected by a survey «Enquête Annuelle d'Entreprise» (EAE), which is held each year by the French Statistical System. This survey is sent to the legal units, but some questions focus on the local units they control. The information about the structure of the qualification of the work force comes from several administrative sources, collected by the French administrations of Employment.With all these variables gathered in one file, one may have direct access to a great deal of information on the big local units, while the SIRENE register just contains a few economic classification data (main activity, number of employees).

In 1992, the computer system was changed, and the file became a real data base. Since this year, it may have providing a full information on the relationships between the units. Consulting the base, one may immediately identify the legal unit which controls the local unit, and get data about it. If this legal unit is controlled by a business group, one may also identify the group. The data base was renamed BRIDGE to show these improvements.

Two kinds of continuity for the local units

Among the pieces of information supplied by BRIDGE, one of the most significant is the chronicle of the local unit. The data base relates all the evolution of the unit, either since its creation, or during the 10 past years. A local unit which has been recorded in the base for one year remains followed, even if it passes under the threshold of size. On the other hand, when a local unit enters the base, all its chronicle is recorded. The data base contains 75 800 units. BRIDGE is indeed a key tool to study the units from a longitudinal point of view. These units may be observed not only in a static way, but also in their evolution.

In BRIDGE as in the SIRENE register, each unit is considered from two points of view.
− Each legal unit is identified by a number, called the SIREN number. This registration number is the official identification of the legal units set up in France. The local units controlled by the legal unit (local legal unit) are identified by a number called SIRET.
− The local unit is identified by a second number linked with the economic continuity. If the production factors do not change, in particular as regards employees and the production factors, this number remains unchanged. Nevertheless, there used to be until nowadays slight differences between SIRENE and BRIDGE in the methodology of the economic continuity. As a consequence, the number of economic local units is not exactly the same in the two sources. The BRIDGE number is called NOREG, and the SIRENE number is called ETEC.

This duality brings obviously difficulties to make up files merging the two sources. The INSEE is currently modifying the register system. In the next system, there will be the same definition of the economic continuity and the same number for each of the local units, in both data bases.

Thanks to the distinction between the economic continuity and the legal form, one may follow up the evolution of the unit in longitudinal studies. If a local unit is bought by a legal unit from another one, the SIRET number will change, but not the identifier of economic continuity (ETEC or NOREG). The previous study has shown, for example, that 75% of such transfers from a legal unit to another one which happened in France between 1985 and 1993 have been realized by business groups.

REFERENCES

Insee, *La France des entreprises, L'Entreprise, A pour Affaires*, 1992.

Insee, '*Les restructurations industrielles de 1979 à 1991* ', première n° 318, May 1994.

Insee,.'*En 10 ans un nouveau paysage commercial s'est dessiné* ', Première n°371,March 1995.

RANK, STOCK, ORDER AND EPIDEMIC EFFECTS IN THE DIFFUSION OF NEW TECHNOLOGIES IN ITALIAN MANUFACTURING INDUSTRIES

Eleonora Bartoloni[1] and Maurizio Baussola[2]

[1]*ISTAT, Statistiche Industriali, Roma.*
[2]*Università Cattolica di Piacenza, Istituto di Politica Economica.*

1 Introduction

The empirical analysis of technological diffusion has concentrated on general tests concerning the impact of different explanatory variables on the adoption decision of firms. The debate has emphasised the role of market structure and firm size following the seminal analysis by Schumpeter (1934). In addition, the economic analysis of technological change received new theoretical improvements from different analytical approaches, i.e., game theory, the economics of information and integrated models focusing on both demand and supply factors affecting the diffusion of new technologies.

However, these improvements on theoretical grounds did not bring about new empirical investigations trying to test the relevance and significance of all these heterogeneous approaches. There is therefore a need for empirical investigations which may encompass the different theoretical approaches to technology diffusion. The only empirical investigation which fills this gap is presented in Karshenas and Stoneman (1993) (hereafter KS) and refers to the investigation of the determinants of CAD-CAM adoption in the UK engineering industries. This analysis allows the testing of different theoretical approaches to the diffusion process, focusing on four effects: rank, stock, order and epidemic effects.

The rank effect may be explained on theoretical grounds referring to the so called probit models (Mansfield 1968, David (1969) and Davies (1979), Ireland and Stoneman (1986)) where firm characteristics (e.g. firm size) are crucial to explain the decision adoption of firms.

The stock and order effect refers to the so called game theoretical approach (Reinganum (1981), Fudenberg and Tirole (1985)) where firms compete to be first in the technological race, while the epidemic effect deals with the role of information in the diffusion process (Mansfield 1968).

KS find strong support for the rank and epidemic effects, whereas the stock and order effects do not have significant impact on CAD-CAM diffusion, suggesting, therefore, that the game theoretical models explain little of the diffusion process.

We extend KS analysis to the Italian manufacturing industries, focusing on a larger set of industries and explanatory variables. One distinctive aspect of our investigation is that we do not refer to a duration model of technological adoption as we do not have information on the adoption dates. We use sectoral information of the adoption of new technologies in a given period of time (i.e., 1990-92) referring to both process and/or product innovations for more than 13,000 manufacturing firms selected from the 1995 Community Innovation Survey set up by ISTAT (Istituto Nazionale di Statistica).

Our empirical model explains, therefore, the probability of adoption of new technologies as a function of variables which are proxies of the four mechanisms described above.

This investigation is important as it contributes a larger and more representative data set to the empirical and theoretical debate on the determinants of technological adoption, following the encompassing approach proposed in KS.

The paper is organised as follows. Section 2 summarises the main stylised facts of technological innovation in the Italian industries, recalling the results of the empirical literature. Section 3 describes the characteristics of the data set and the empirical model is analysed in sections 4 and 5. Section 6 concludes the paper.

2 Stylised facts of technological innovation in Italian manufacturing industries

The analysis of the innovative process in Italian manufacturing industries received new impetus from the Innovation Survey set up by ISTAT at the end of the '80s. The first Survey took place in 1987 involving almost 23,000 firms and covering the period 1980-85[1]. A more detailed investigation on a sub-sample of innovative firms has been carried out to underline the main factors associated with innovative activity[2].

The second survey took place in 1995 and regarded innovations introduced between 1990-92. These surveys have been widely analysed using different approaches focusing on different aspects of technological diffusion. In this section we briefly summarise the main stylised facts which emerge from the empirical literature based on the analysis of these surveys and on the analysis of the sub- sample of firms we have created to estimate the model described in section 4.

---

[1] See ISTAT (1987).
[2] See ISTAT (1990).

We can concentrate on three main aspects of innovative activity:

a) the sectoral structure of technological innovations;
b) the role of firm size;
c) the distribution of technological opportunities among firms.

Following Baussola (1994) and Bartoloni and Baussola (1995) and looking at Figures 1 and 2 one may argue that:

i. sectors with high technological opportunities show a higher propensity to innovate, as shown by the ratio of innovative firms to the total number of firms in that sector;

ii. in traditional sectors (e.g. Textile, Wood Products, Food, Beverages and Tobacco) process innovation alone prevails, whereas joint process-and-product-innovation prevails in science-based industries where R&D and fixed investment are crucial components of the innovative process. Process innovation alone prevails also in sectors (Paper Products, Printing and Publishing, Metal and Non Metallic Products) where technology is crucially linked to scale factors and labour saving strategies are a central issue of the reorganisation process;

iii. product innovation mainly concerns those industries which may be defined as specialised suppliers of innovative goods both for large and small users (Professional, Scientific, Photographic and Optical Goods, Machinery and Equipment, Other Transport Equipment).

We can analyse now the empirical evidence for one of the most controversial issue in the debate on the determinants of technological change: the relationship between market structure, firm size and innovation. In Schumpeter (1934) a certain degree of monopoly power allows firms to successfully develop innovation through high investment in innovative activity (i.e., R&D investment). Market power allows firms to reduce the uncertainty associated with innovative activity and to gain monopolistic profits from the use of the new technology.

The literature on the so-called Schumpeterian Hypotesis is, however, controversial. On empirical grounds Mansfield (1968) and Scherer (1965,1983), show that this hypothesis may be accepted only within a restricted number of industrial sectors and when:

– the investment required for the innovation is high compared with the size of potential adopters;
– the firm's minimum efficiency size required for a profitable use of the innovation is relatively large;
– the size of the four largest firms is bigger than the average size of the other potential adopters.

Fischer and Temin (1973) and Kohn and Scott (1982) proposed a different interpretation of the Schumpeterian Hypothesis, crucially based on the elasticity of R&D expenditure with respect to firm size. However, it is worth underlining that these tests are crucially affected by the measure of firm size adopted and by the characteristics of the industrial sectors taken into account. In addition, more recent studies have shown that many innovative activities are carried out by small firms which are not correctly considered, thus underestimating the innovative propensity of small firms (Kleinknecht (1987), Kleinknecht and Reijnien (1991), Archibugi et al. (1994)).

The sectoral analysis of the two innovation surveys of Italian industries suggests, as pointed out in Baussola (1994), Bartoloni and Baussola (1995) and Barbieri and Rapiti (1995), that there is a positive and sufficiently high correlation between firm size, sectoral innovative propensity and R&D activities. This evidence is also verified in the sample of firms we use for the econometric investigation proposed in Section 4.

Figure [3] shows the gap in innovative propensity [3] between medium and small firms on the one hand, and large firms on the other. The positive relationship between firm size and innovation, does not imply, however, that there is a strong correlation with market concentration. If we consider Figure [4] the relationship between market concentration (as measured by the *CR4* index) and the sectoral innovative propensity (as measured by the proportion of innovative firms) is positive, implying, however, a low correlation coefficient (0.17).

Another measure of the different attitudes of small and large firms is given by the distribution of innovative expenditures by firm size (Figure [5]).

R&D expenditure is highly concentrated, as almost 85% of R&D investment among innovative firms is by firms with more than 500 employees. This concentration, decreases if one takes into account other innovation expenditures such as marketing, royalties and training expenditures (Figures [6,7,8]). Marketing expenditure is less concentrated, as 51% of marketing expenditure is by firms with more than 500 employees. Royalties and training expenditures show a corresponding ratio of almost 65% and 71% respectively. This distribution is even less concentrated if one considers a per capita (per worker) measure of innovative expenditure. This is also argued in Archibugi et al. (1996) where it is shown that the distribution of innovative expenditures (using a broad definition) is less concentrated in large firms than the corresponding distribution of R&D expenditure.

These stylised facts of technological innovation in Italian industries describe the framework in which the econometric tests will be analysed and enable us to select the explanatory variables used in the logit estimates presented in Section 4.

---

[3] Innovative propensity is measured by the ratio of the number of innovative firms in each class to the total number of firms in that class.

Figure 1 Distribution of innovative firms by sector

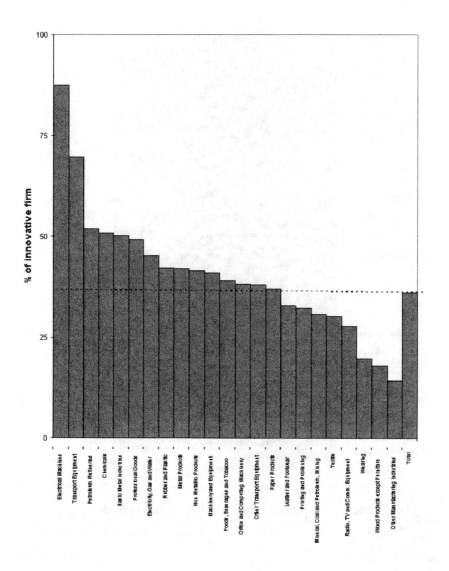

Source: Cis and Sci, sample of 13,1334 firms

Figure 2 Industries by Type of innovation introduced

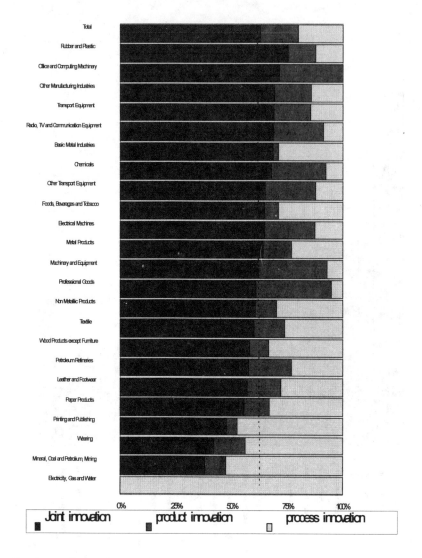

Source: see Figure 1

Figure 3 Gap in innovative propensity between large and small and medium firms

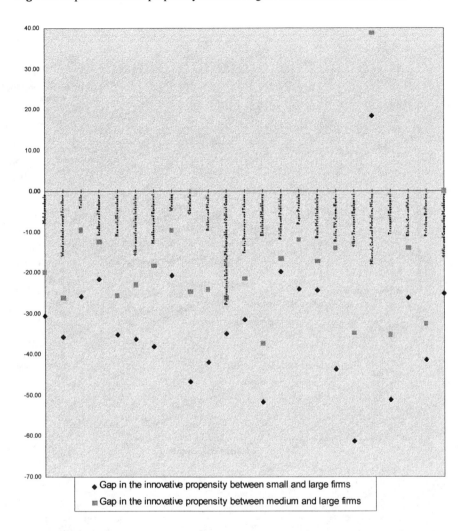

Source: see Figure 1

Figure 4 Sectoral innovative propensity and market concentration

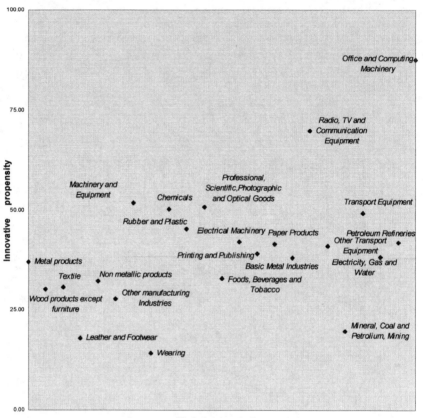

Source: see Figure 1

Figure 5 Distribution of R&D expenditure by firm size (innovative firms)

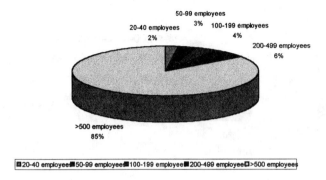

Source: see Fig. 1

Figure 6 Distribution of Making expenditure by firm size

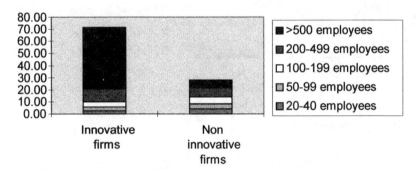

Source: Cis1 and Sci, sample of 13,334 firms

Figure 7 Distribution of royalties expenditure by firm size

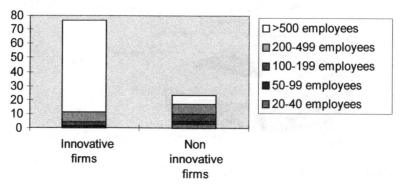

Source: see Figure 6

Figure 8 Distribution of training expenditure by firm size

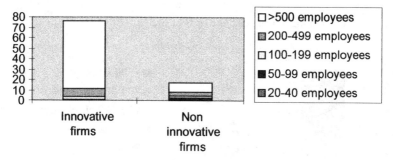

Source: see Figure 6

3 Data description

In this section we briefly describe the data used in the econometric analysis of Sections 4 and 5. The data originate from two different statistical surveys set up by ISTAT: the first is the Community Innovation Survey (CIS1) dealing with the analysis of product and process innovation in Italian manufacturing industries between 1990-92 and the second is the Firms ' Accounts System Survey (SCI, 1991, 1992).

Surveys' respondents are individual firms with more than 20 employees grouped in 23 industries according to ISIC standards.

There were 22,787 respondents to the CIS1 Survey of which 7,553 were innovative firms and 15,234 non innovative firms. On the other hand, the SCI Survey includes all the population of firms producing in both manufacturing and service industries.

In order to create and adequate set of explanatory variables describing technology adoption, we needed to link the two data sets. However, this procedure caused a reduction of the available number of firms because of two main problems:

a) the change in the classification of firms and sectors adopted in ISTAT Surveys;

b) the use of the growth rate variables $\Delta Y1$ and $\Delta Y2$ which reduced the number of firms in the sample between 1991 and 1992.

It is worth noting, however, that we have taken into account all the mergers and acquisitions which occured between 1991 and 1992.

The precise description of the variables used in the econometric estimates is presented in Appendix 1 together with summary statistics.

4 The empirical model

The model we consider differs from the KS investigation as we consider a probabilistic (logit) model and do not analyse technological diffusion in a duration framework.

The data set we use allows us to describe technology adoption as a discrete choice typical of qualitative-dependent variable models. In other words, we may model the probability of adoption of new technologies in a given time interval as a function of multiple explanatory variables reflecting mechanisms based on different theoretical approaches. The arguments we use follow from the KS empirical study of technological diffusion.

Four main mechanisms affecting the use of new technologies are considered:

a) rank effect;

b) stock effect;

c) order effect;

d) information or epidemic effect.

The first effect derives from the assumption that potential adopters have different and specific characteristics, and, therefore, gain different returns from the adoption of new technologies. The list of characteristics is heterogeneous and may include firm size, market structure, R&D expenditure, firm ownership and institutional factors.

The theoretical literature refers to both demand and integrated models of technological diffusion; among the first group it is worth recalling Mansfield (1968), David (1969) and Davies (1979). The second stream of analysis is mainly related to the studies by Stoneman and Ireland (1983), Ireland and Stoneman (1986).

The second effect is related to the so-called game theoretic approach (Reinganum 1981, Fudenberg and Tirole (1995)). The crucial assumption in this framework is that the benefit to the marginal adopter decreases as the stock of current adopters increases.

The third effect represents a generalisation of the stock effect and it may be rationalised, again using a game theoretic approach, in that firms moving first exhibit advantages compared with later movers. Therefore, there will be a race to be first in the order of adoption.

The last effect deals with technological information which is acquired either through formal external (or internal) sources or through informal contacts with earlier adopters (epidemic effect) (Jensen 1981, Stoneman 1981, Mansfield 1968).

The probability of adoption may be expressed as a function of a vector of variables reflecting the rank, stock, order and epidemic effect. We use a logit specification which allows us to analyse in more detail the impact of each variable on the adoption probability using marginal effects and odds ratio estimates.

Equation [1] summarises the empirical model:

$$y_i = \beta_0 + \sum_{j=1}^{k} \beta_j x_{ij} + \mu_i \qquad\qquad [1]$$

where y_i is a dummy variable taking the value of 0 if firm i has introduced an innovation [4] and 1 otherwise, β_0 is a constant, β_j is the coefficient of explanatory variable x_j and μ_i is the error term whose cumulative distribution is assumed to be logistic.

Thus the probability of innovation may be expressed as:

$$\text{Prob}(Y=0) \qquad 1 - F(\beta'x) \qquad\qquad [2]$$

where F is the cumulative logistic distribution function, x the vector of explanatory variables and β the vector of coefficients.

---

[4] Innovation may regard both processes and/or products.

We use the following variables as proxies of the four mechanism derived from the theoretical literature:

a) *rank effect:*

- firm size (*SIZE*), measured as the number of employees in each firm. The expected effect of this variable is positive following the standard probit models. It derives from the assumption that new technologies may have positive scale effects, implying that adoption is more profitable for larger firms and thus the probability of adoption increases as firm size increases;

- firm ownership (*STATUS*). This is a dummy variable reflecting whether the firm is a part of a corporate group. As suggested in KS the sign on the coefficient of this variable may be positive or negative depending on   which of the following effects prevails. On the one hand, one may expect a positive effect as independent firms may easily and quickly decide the adoption of the new technology. On the other hand, one can argue that within a corporate group information about the new technology is greater and uncertainty is reduced, thus positively affecting the adoption probability;

- output growth rate ($\Delta Y1$ and $\Delta Y2$). These are dummy variables which capture the effect of output growth on the probability of adoption. The expected sign on the coefficient of these variables is positive as an expanding (or at least steady) output allows the allocation of more resources to technology adoption;

- firm's labour force skills (*SKILL*). This variable is a proxy of firm's human capital level. The expected effect is positive as new technologies can more easily be introduced in firms with a more qualified labour force;

- marketing expenditure (*MARKET*). This dummy variable reflects the attitude of a firm to adapting its strategy to new market conditions. When firms invest in marketing they more likely adopt new technologies, in order to adjust their product/process to changes in demand.

b) *stock-order effects.* Both effects are related to the so-called game theoretic approach to technology diffusion. The stock effect may be proxied by the current number of adopters *(INNOV)*. However, our sample of firms is not longitudinal, implying that we just have the average number of sectoral adopters in a given period of time (i.e., 1990-92). We cannot observe the change in the number of adopters over time and, therefore, we cannot test the stock effect. In our model the number of sectoral adopters is used as a proxy of the epidemic effect.

The order effect may be proxied using those variables reflecting the strategic framework in which firms compete. We use sectoral R&D expenditure (*R&D*), sectoral marketing expenditure (*MARKSET*) and a sectoral skill proxy (SKILLSET) to test whether these variables may discourage potential adopters to innovate. Thus the expected sign on the coefficients of these variables is negative. In other words, a firm may   reveal a reduced probability of adoption if it produces in an R&D intensive sector or in sectors where high labour force skill or high marketing expenditure are required;

c) *information or epidemic effects*; we include two information variables reflecting the role of formal information sources acquired either internally or externally (*INFINT* and *INFEXT*). In both cases the expected sign on the coefficients is positive.

The epidemic effect is proxied by the number of adopters in each sector. The expected effect is positive as the probability of adoption may increase, as long as technological information is acquired through informal contacts with an increasing number of adopters (*INNOV*).

5 The estimates

Equation [1] has been estimated using a logit regression and estimates are shown in Table 1.

Table 1 Probability of innovation - Logistic regression

Variable	Coeff.	Estimate	p-value	Slope
Constant	β_0	-8.2682	0.0001	–
SIZE	β_1	0.5700	0.0001	0.2805
STATUS	β_2	0.0394	0.4727	0.0084
ΔY1	β_3	0.2462	0.0001	0.0672
ΔY2	β_4	0.1866	0.0951	0.0177
SKILL	β_5	0.2822	0.0001	0.0995
MARKET	β_6	0.1931	0.0001	0.0525
INNOV	β_7	1.4265	0.0001	0.2849
INFINT	β_8	-0.3044	0.1875	-0.0363
INFEXT	β_9	1.0540	0.1012	0.0218
MARKSET	β_{10}	0.0311	0.4843	0.0110
SKILLSET	β_{11}	-0.2441	0.0016	-0.0503
R&D	β_{12}	0.0137	0.6819	0.0075
AREA1	β_{13}	0.0796	0.1872	0.0218
AREA2	β_{14}	0.2289	0.0002	0.0591
AREA3	β_{15}	-0.4064	0.0001	-0.0613
-2LOGL	17461.576			

$$\chi^2_{15} = 1743.312 \text{ (1)}$$

Count $R^2 = 70.0\%$ (2)

$$\chi^2_{14} = 20.8 \text{ (3)}$$

$$\chi^2_{6} = 881.705 \text{ (4)}$$

$$\chi^2_{3} = 155.294 \text{ (5)}$$

$$\chi^2_{3} = 10.38 \text{ (6)}$$

$N = 13,334$

(1) Chi-Square test for the joint significance of the covariates.
(2) Ratio of the number of correct predictions to the total number of observations.
(3) Chi-Square test for the significance of the sectoral dummy variables.
(4) Chi-square test for the significance of the rank effect $(\beta_1 = \beta_2 = \beta_3 = \beta_4 = \beta_5 = \beta_6 = 0)$.
(5) Chi-Square test for the significance of the epidemic and information effects $(\beta_7 = \beta_8 = \beta_9 = 0)$.
(6) Chi-Square test for the significance of the order effect $(\beta_{10} = \beta_{11} = \beta_{12} = 0)$.

We can now compare the predictions suggested by the theoretical models of technological diffusion discussed in the previous section and the results shown in Table 1. The logistic regression we present does not include sectoral dummies, as the joint test for the significance of their coefficients allows us to specify a model with a unique intercept. This result is not surprising as we take into account sectoral characteristics using sectoral explanatory variables which reflect various adoption mechanisms. Among the variables which define the rank effect, firm size shows, as expected, a positive coefficient. The strong impact of this variable on the probability of adoption may be considered by looking at the slope coefficient. It shows the contribution on the adoption probability of the corresponding variable[5]. For the *SIZE* variable this value is 0.28.

The firm labour force skill variable has a positive and significant effect on the probability of adoption, with a marginal effect that is, however, less than half than that of the *SIZE* variable (0.099).

The *STATUS* dummy variable is not significant, implying that, given the selected specification, the probability of adoption is not affected by the inclusion into a larger corporate unit.

The dummy variable reflecting the use of marketing expenditure to capture market signals is significant, with a positive coefficient and a mild slope coefficient (0.05).

---

[5] The marginal effects we report refer to standardised estimate of the slope parameters as they take into account the standard deviation of the underlying distribution and the standard deviation of the explanatory variables.

Also the dummy variable reflecting the impact of output growth rate is significant with a positive coefficient and a higher marginal effect (0.07)[6].

We also test for the overall significance of the coefficients of the rank effect variables. As is clearly shown in Table 1 we can easily reject the homogeneous restriction $(\beta_1=\beta_2=\beta_3=\beta_4=\beta_5=\beta_6=0)$.

The epidemic effect is captured in our specification using the ratio of innovative firms to the total number of firms in each sector. The rationale behind the inclusion of this variable is that, following epidemic models, the probability of adoption is positively affected by the number of current adopters. Our estimate confirms this effect and shows that it has the highest impact on the adoption probability, according to the slope coefficient.

We also use two other information variables to test whether formal internal or external information sources play any role in the adoption of new technologies. Only external information sources play a significant and positive role in the adoption decision, thus increasing the adoption probability. It is worth noting, however, that this variable is significant only at the 0.10 significance level and that the impact on the adoption probability is small.

Internal sources are even less significant (almost 0.20 significance level) and enter the regression with a negative sign.

The joint test for the overall significance of the coefficients of the epidemic and information effects allows us to reject the null hypothesis of insignificant epidemic and information effects $(\beta_7=\beta_8=\beta_9=0)$ c) the order effect is proxied by variables reflecting the strategic behaviour of firms.

The sectoral R&D and marketing expenditures do not enter the regression equation significantly. The sectoral proxy of the labour force skill is significant and with the expected sign, showing, however, a weak effect on the probability of adoption. This evidence suggests that in sectors with high skill levels the skill of the labour force acts as a requisite for the introduction of innovation. The joint test on the significance of the order effect do not allow us to reject the null hypothesis of insignificant order effect $(\beta_{10}=\beta_{11}=\beta_{12}=0)$.

The analysis of the logistic regression gives a general idea of the significance of the different effects we have tested. However, we are also concerned with a more precise measure of the effect of each variable on the probability of adoption. In Table (2) we present estimates of the odds ratios which we now discuss.

The odds ratio (ω) for a qualitative dependent variable (x_j) is defined as the ratio of the odds for $x_j=1$ to the odds for $x_j=0$, i.e.:

---

[6] The dummy variable $\Delta Y2$ shows a positive effect on the probability of adoption. This variable is,however, less significant compared with $\Delta Y1$ and shows a milder impact according to the slope coefficient (0.02).

$$\omega = \frac{\Pr(Y=0|x_j=1)/\Pr(Y=1|x_j=1)}{\Pr(Y=0|x_j=0)/\Pr(Y=1|x_j=0)}$$

According to the logistic model ω is given by:

$$\omega = \frac{\exp(\beta_0 + \beta_j)}{\exp(\beta_0)} = \exp(\beta_j)$$

where β_0 and β_j are the intercept and the coefficient of x_j respectively. For a continuous independent variable the odds ratio shows the change in the odds for any increase in that variable. We have hypothesised one standard deviation increase in each continuous independent variable considered.

Table 2 Odds ratios

Variable	Odds ratio
Conditional odds ratios - One SD variation	
SIZE	1.663
SKILL	1.198
INNOV	1.677
INFINT	0.936
INFEXT	1.040
MARKSET	1.020
SKILLLSET	0.913
R&D	1.014
Odds ratio for the dummy variables	
MARKET	1.213
ΔY1	1.279
ΔY2	1.205
AREA1	1.083
AREA2	1.257
AREA3	0.666

In our regression we have seven dummy variables which reflect different mechanism affecting adoption propensity.

Within the rank effects we have four dummies, i.e., *STATUS*, *MARKET*, *ΔY1* and *ΔY2*. *STATUS* is not significant and therefore we do not take into account the implied odds ratio. *MARKET* has a positive impact on the probability of innovation and the corresponding odds ratio suggests that those firms which undertake marketing expenditures have an adoption probability which is 20%

higher than the corresponding probability of the other firms. In other words, these firms show an adoption probability which is 1.213 times higher than the corresponding probability of those firms which do not undertake any marketing expenditures.

The impact of output growth (variables $\Delta Y1$ and $\Delta Y2$) is of the same magnitude, implying that the adoption probability for those firms which show an increasing or at least constant real output growth, is more than 20% higher than the corresponding probability for those firms which experience decreasing real output growth rate.

It is worth underlining the values of the odds ratios for the geographical areas included as control variables. The reference area is Centre Italy. Firms in the North West area show almost the same probability of adoption of firms in Centre Italy, whereas firms in the North East have an adoption probability which is 25% higher. Firms in the South, on the other hand, have an adoption probability which is 34% less then the corresponding probability of the reference area. This result confirms previous empirical findings (Archibugi et al. 1996) particularly for the lower propensity to innovate in the South. The result of the other areas may be influenced by a small bias in our sub-sample, where the North East firms are over-represented.

As we have underlined above, the odds ratios for a continuous variable should be calculated conditional on a specified shock of the variable under observation. We use one standard deviation shock for each continuous variable to analyse the impact on the probability of adoption. The strongest impact is associated with changes in the *SIZE* and *INNOV* variables. In other words, a one standard deviation change (increase) in both variables determines a 60% increase in the probability of adoption. The *SKILL* variable shows a milder effect, implying that a one standard deviation variation increases the probability of adoption by almost 20%.

Among the information variables, the proxy for the external sources *(INFEXT)* implies a 4% increase in the innovation probability, whereas the internal sources *(INFINT)* which are, however, significant to a level of almost 0.20, reduce the innovation probability by almost 6%.

Within the order effect the only significant variable is SKILLSET, whose change decreases the innovation probability by 9%. The other two variables (R&D and MARKSET) show negligible effects as suggested their insignificant coefficients and marginal effects.

6 Conclusions

We have analysed the adoption of new technologies in Italian manufacturing industries using data on 13,334 firms involving the adoption of new process and/or product innovations in the period 1990-92.

The analysis follows the encompassing approach proposed in KS , which is a test of different theoretical approaches to technological diffusion. However, in our paper we consider all the manufacturing sectors and we model the adoption probability of firms as a discrete choice variable using a logit model. In addition we use a larger number of variables reflecting the rank, stock order and epidemic effects.

The results of the econometric tests suggest that technology adoption is significantly affected by the variables used to proxy the rank effect. The epidemic and information effects are significant too, whereas the variables used to test the order effect are not jointly significant. In other words, the effect suggested by the game theoretic approach does not significantly affect firms' adoption probability.

Among the variables which strongly affect the adoption probability it is worth underlining firm size and the number of adopters in each sector.

Our results are consistent with KS empirical findings for the UK engineering industries, suggesting that the rank and epidemic effects arise as the crucial and stylised mechanisms for the adoption of new technologies in a wider range of industries and in a different economic framework.

Appendix 1 Definition of variables, mean and standard deviation

Variable	All firms (N=13,334) Mean (Standard Deviation)	Innovative firms (N=4,832) Mean (S.D.)	Non innovative firms (N=8,502) Mean (S.D.)	Data source
SIZE Firm size: number of employees (1)	3.98 (0.8926)	4.29 (1.0742)	3.81 (0.7130)	$Sci_{(2)}$-1992
STATUS A dummy variable taking the value of zero for independent firms and one for firms being a part of a corporate group	-	-	-	Cis1 (3)
ΔY1 A dummy variable taking the value of one if firms shows a positive real growth rate of sales between 1991 an 1992 and zero otherwise	-	-	-	Sci -1991 and Sci-1992
ΔY2 A dummy variable taking the value of one if the firms' real growth rate of sales between 1991 an 1992 is zero and zero otherwise	-	-	-	Sci -1991 and Sci - 1992
SKILL A proxy of human capital. Ratio of the number of managers and entrepreneurs to the total number of employees in each firm	3.09 (0.6397)	3.25 (0.5713)	3.00 (0.6589)	Sci - 1992
MARKET Advertising and marketing expenditures. A dummy variable taking the value of one for positive expenditures and zero otherwise	-	-	-	Sci -1992
INNOV Sectoral number of innovative firms as the ratio to the sectoral number of firms			3.63 (0.4070)	Cis1

Variable		Data source
INFEXT A variable reflecting the importance of external sources of information. Ratio of the sectoral number of innovative firms who consider important external sources of information to the sectoral number of innovative firms	-0.20 (0.0564)	Cis1
MARKSET Ratio of sectoral advertising and marketing expenditures to sectoral sales	0.07 (0.7980)	Sci - 1992
SKILLSET A proxy of sectoral human capital. Ratio of the sectoral number of managers and entrepreneurs to the sectoral number of employees	1.50 (0.1856)	Sci - 1992
R&D Ratio of sectoral R&D expenditures to sectoral sales	-0.32 (1.5374)	Cis1 and Sci 1992
AREA1 A dummy variable taking the value of one if the firm is localised in the North West and zero otherwise	-	Sci - 1992
AREA2 A dummy variable taking the value of one if the firm is localised in the North East and zero otherwise	-	Sci - 1992
AREA3 A dummy variable taking the value of one if the firm is localised in the South and zero otherwise	-	Sci - 1992

(1) All variables are in natutal logs.
(2) Community Innovation Survey.
(3) Firms' Accounts System Survey.

Appendix 2: Sectoral Classification

Sectoral description	ATECO Cod. (2 digit)
1. Mineral, Coal and Petroleum, Mining	10+11+12+13+14
2. Foods, Beverages and Tobacco	15+16
3. Textile	17
4. Wearing	18
5. Leather and Footwear	19
6. Wood Products exept Furnitures	20
7. Paper Products	21
8.Printing and Publishing	22
9. Petroleum Refineries	23
10. Chemicals	24
11. Rubber and Plastic	25
12. Non Metallic Products	26
13. Basic Metal Industries	27
14. Metal Products	28
15. Machinery and Equipment	29
16. Office and Computing Machinery	30
17. Electrical Machines	31
18. Radio, TV and Communication Equipment	32
19. Professional, Scientific, Photographic and Optical Goods	33
20. Transport Equipment	34
21. Other Transport Equipment	35
22. Other Manufactoring Industries	36+37
23. Electricity, Gas and Water	40+41

The sectoral distribution of firms in our sub-sample (13,334 firms) has been calculated, showing a distribution close to the distribution of the whole set of firms in the CIS1 Survey.

REFERENCES

Archibugi D., M. Pianta (1994), *"Aggregate convergence and sectoral specialization in innovation"*, Journal of Evolutionary Economics, 1.

Archibugi D. et al. (1996), *"L'innovazione nelle imprese italiane: un'analisi dai risultati dell'indagine ISTAT"*, Economia e Politica Industriale, 89, 147-185.

Barbieri G., Rapiti f. (1995), *"I Risultati dell'Indagine Istat sull'Innovazione tecnologica: aspetti strutturali e diffusione del fenomeno, con particolare riferimento alle dimensioni d'impresa"*, Atti del seminario CNR: Innovazione e Risorse Umane nell'Economia della Conoscenza, ottobre , Roma.

Bartoloni E., Baussola m. (1995), *"Innovation Firm Size and Industry Growth"*, IX Annual Conference of the European Council for Small Business, Piacenza, November.

Baussola M. (1994*), "La Diffusione dell'Innovazione nelle Piccole e Medie Imprese Italiane"*, Rivista Internazionale di Scienze Sociali, 3, 313-338.

David P. (1969), *A Contribution to the Theory of Diffusion, Stanford Centre for Research in Economic Growth*, Stanford University, Stanford.

Davies S. (1979), *The Diffusion Process of Innovation*, Cambridge University Press, Cambridge.

Fischer F., Tamin P. (1973), *"Returns to Scale in Research and Development: What Does the Schumpeterian Hypothesis Imply?"*, Journal of Political Economy, 81 (1), 56-70.

Fudenberg D., Tirole J. (1985), *"Pre-emption and Rent Equalization in the Adoption of New Technologies"*, Review of Economic Studies, 52, 383-401.

Ireland N., Stoneman p. (1986), *Technological Diffusion, Expectations and Welfare*, Oxford Economic Papers, 38, 283-304.

ISTAT (1987), *Indagine sulla diffusione dell'innovazione tecnologica nell'industria manifatturiera italiana*, Collana d'Informazione, 19, 1987.

ISTAT (1990), *Indagine statistica sulla diffusione tecnologica nell'industria italiana*, Collana d' Informazione, 14, 1990.

Jensen R.A. (1982*), "Adoption and the Diffusion of an Innovation of Uncertain Profitability"*, Journal of Economic Theory, 27.

Karshenas M. , Stoneman P. (1993), *"Rank, Stock, Order and Epidemic Effects in the Diffusion of New Process Technologies: an Empirical Model"*, Rand Journal of Econiomics, 24, 503-528.

Kleinknecht A. (1987), *"Measuring R&D in small firms: how much are we missing?"*, Journal of Industrial Economics, 2.

Kleinknecht A., Reijnienen J.O.N. (1991), *"More evidence on the undercounting of small firms R&D"*, Research Policy, 20.

Kohn M., Scott J. (1982), *"Scale Economies in Research and Development"*, Journal of Industrial Economics, 30, 3, 239-250.

Mansfield E. (1968), *Industrial Research and Technological Innovation*, Norton Company, New York.

Reinganum J. (1981), *"Market Structure and the Diffusion of New Technologies"*, Bell Journal of Economics, 12, 618-624.

Scherer F.M. (1965*), "Firm Size, Market Structure, Opportunity and the Output of Patent Inventions"*, American Economic Review, 55, 1097-1125.

Scherer F. M. (1983), *"The Propensity to Patent"*, International Journal of Industrial Organization, 1, 107-128.

Schumpeter J. (1934), *"The Theory of Economic Development"*, Oxford University Press, Oxford.

Stoneman P. (1981), *"Intra Firm Diffusion, Bayesan Learning and Profitability"*, Economic Journal, 91, 375-389.

Stoneman P., Ireland N.(1983*), "The Role of Supply Factors in the Diffusion of New Process Technology"*, Economic Journal, 93, 66-78.

PROBLEMS OF COMPETITIVENESS INDICATORS

Maria Letizia Giorgetti

Scholarship holder working at the DCII/A,ISTAT

1 Foreword

The purpose of this paper is to analyze market structure in order to build statistic indicators to measure the competitiveness degree of the related markets. The research plan requires an analysis of the several approaches to industrial economy as well as an analysis of the available or the developing statistic sources, the former analysis is useful to evaluate degree of consistency between theoretical assumptions and empirical analysis. The research plan tries to supply an information integration at micro and macroeconomic level.

This paper is structured as follows:
1. survey of the several industrial economic theories;
2. verification of statistic indicators useful for empirical measurement of market competitiveness degree;
3. consistency between indicators and actual availability of official statistic information.

2 Theoretical approaches to industrial economy

Industrial economy approaches have always shown an alternation between the "inter-industry" and "intra-industry" vision.

The former is based on a comparison between firms (more or less detailed economic sectors), whereas the latter refers to an individual firm internal analysis.

2.1 The 50s and the 60s

In the last fifty years there has been an evolution of different approaches: "case study", which was prevailing in the 50s, showed growing crisis marks; these studies, mainly commissioned by antitrust authorities, are slowly sided by cross-section analyses, until they are completely replaced by the latter in 60s.

Cross-section analyses are based on the Structure-Conduct-Performance theory (SCP) (Harvard school: Joe Bain[1] and Edward Mason) at theoretical level. This theory, which is still widely used, starts from an analysis of market structure to evaluate firms conduct and to analyze industry performance.

The theoretical reference model is one of perfect competition, which represents the most efficient industrial configuration: where all firms produce at minimum average cost, market price is equal to minimum average cost and social surplus is maximized. How close an industrial configuration is to perfect competition equilibrium depends on a number of factors: number of firms in the market and width of economies of scale. The perfect competition configuration is an unreal configuration, which is not easily found in reality, however it is a very good base of comparison.

The SCP school was successful with the "Cournotian" approach that explains performance and behaviour on the basis of structure.

The Cournotian approach comes from Cournot oligopoly theory: in a market where n firms supply the same goods at linear costs $C=cq_i$, market configuration is efficient when the number of working firms goes to infinite. According to Cournot oligopoly model[2], there is a close approximation to perfect competition model when all firms have a $-k^{th}$ market share inside industry and no firm affects the conduct of other firms.

In this kind of approach, exogenous variables are : structure and size of firms composing industry, the presence of entry and exit barriers, demand elasticity of industry market: the decisive explanatory element has been found to be industry concentration degree.

The SCP school was remarkably criticized because of limits shown in sectors with growing returns to scale (considerable criticism comes from contestable market theory[3]). The structuralist theory which, as the name suggests, goes back to industry structure, is opposed to a theory where the exogenous variable is firm conduct (Donsimoni M.P. et al. 1984)[4] that is the behaviour of firms and competition degree against competitors.

---

[1] Bain J. (1951).

[2] Cournot A (1838)

[3] Baumol W., Panzar J., Willig R. (1982)

[4] Donsimoni M.P., Geroski P., Jacquemin A. (1984)

2.2 The 70s and the 80s

The coming of the game theory[5] in the 70s marked a certain loss of trust in cross-section analysis because it is conditioned by a number of limitations about competition type and information in the markets; this implies a certain degree of difficulty in the identification of structural variables that could be examined.

Because of difficulties in deducing conducts which could be reasonably generalized, an approach by cases spread, which is based on statistics (intra-industry analysis). In particular it is the NEIO[6] approach (New Empirical Industrial Organization).

This type of analysis adopts a direct connection between theory and econometric models that can be used[7]. In particular, in comparison with SCP approach, the connection with oligopoly theory seems to be stronger. The basic NEIO references are:

a) price-cost margins cannot be observed;
b) comparative statistic analyses of variations among different industries or markets are pointless unless markets or industries are rather close to each other;
c) conduct of firms and of industry is considered a parameter to be estimated;
d) when inferences about market power are to be made, all alternative hypothesis to perfect competition model are clearly detailed.

NEIO comprises the SCP heritage and the heritage of study by cases of the 50s.

Supporters NEIO, in opposition to the point of view of SCP supporters, do not believe that performance can be obtained directly from account data and do not believe that cross-section analysis could be performed on different industry structures starting from a limited number of variables that could be observed. Lastly, according to NEIO school, the different empirical works should not aim at evaluating the relation between structure and performance.

Then, limits of cross-section analyses are pointed out inside NEIO. In fact cross-section analyses do not seem to be adequate to solve problems arising from structural variables not meeting exogeneity conditions and from disequilibrium conditions.

In fact cross-section analyses include limitations about:

1. disequilibrium conditions;
2. causality;
3. omitted variables.

The problem of disequilibrium is caused by the fact that often literature deals with long term equilibrium conditions; as often deviation from equilibrium

---

[5] Tirole applied game theory to industrial economy, Tirole J., (1988 and 1991)

[6] Sembenelli A. (1995); Sembenelli A., Rondi L. (1995).

[7] See Brenaham, T.F. (1989).

positions is correlated with independent variables, those relations can be represented in a distorted way.

As regards the second problem, in cross-section regressions there could be independent variables that are correlated, and this results in problems not being exactly specified. Such problems could solved in the following way: 1) if it is a problem of disequilibrium, macroeconomics models should be used (partial adjustment models, error correction, etc.); 2) as regards the problem of selecting exogenous variables to evaluate structural equations, the tools used are lagged variables[8]. Evaluations performed on panel-data can only partially remedy problems posed by cross-section[9] (Donowitz I, Hubbard, R.G. and Petersen, B.C., 1988).

Even with the intra-industry approach there are econometrics problems; because costs and revenue are not obtained from account data but from price and quantity series. Therefore the NEIO approach needs rather long time series, during a period of time in which modifications of the reference model may occur.

2.3 The 90s

The latest trend, with Sutton[10], shows a return to "intra-industry" approach, even if there are differences with the SCP approach, because of a closer link with modern industry economy and because more refined data are used.

In his book *Sunk Costs and market structure*, Sutton focuses attention on the inverse relation between market concentration and size, which had not been given enough attention in literature: greater is the market size and less is its concentration.

3 Indicators of market competitiveness degree

Some indicators of market competitiveness degree are given below:

1. Lerner index;
2. Concentration indicators;
3. Indicators of vertical integration degree.

---

[8] For instrumental variables see Green W. (1993), p. 284.

[9] Panel data allow an examination of cross-sectional elements and of time elements to study firm and industry dynamics.

For study of panel see: Matyas L., Sevestre P. (Ed) 1996.

[10] Sutton, J. (1990), (1991).

3.1 Lerner index

From the Cowling and Waterson (1976) model we have Lerner monopoly degree index at firm level:

$(p - c')/ p = (s_i/ \eta) (1+ \lambda_i)$

where p, is price; c' is marginal cost; s_i is the firm market share; η is demand elasticity; λ_i is conjectural variation.

Excluding references to conjectural variations the Lerner index at industry level is given as below:

$L = (p - \sum_i^n c_i)/p = H (1+ R)/ \varepsilon$

where H is Herfindhal index, that is the sum of market share squared and R is the sum of each firm conjecture about total industry output variation referred to unit variation of the individual examined firm output, ε is the absolute value of total demand elasticity as regards price[11].

Conjectural variations[12] play a role when profit maximization from an oligopolist in a condition of strategic interdependence is to be considered, that is when the kth firm wants to maximize profit, taking into account that any decision about quantity to produce would affect the decisions of the other firms.

The kth firm has then to consider the following profit function:

$$\pi\left[x_i, x_j\right] = x_i f\left[x_i, x_j\right] - c_i\left[x_i\right] \qquad [1]$$

where π is profit, x_i is output from k^{th} firm, x_j is output from firms other than k^{th} -firm, $p = f\left[x_i, x_j\right]$ is the inverse function of demand; $c_i\left[x_i\right]$ is the function of total cost.

Given a concave profit function, maximization is possible if and only if equality of first degree derivative is equal to zero, that is if and only if marginal revenue is equal to firm marginal cost.

Marginal revenue is obtained by calculating first derivative of first addendum of the right part of expression [1]:

---

[11] The previous formula, if opening to international market is to be considered, should be completed as follows:

$L = H / \varepsilon (1+R)(1- t_m)$

in order to consider competitive pressure exerted by import and export, where t_m is import rate. See de Ghellinck (1986).

[12] The most extensive expression of conjectural variations is by Bowley A. (1924).

$$\partial\left(px_{ii}\right)/\partial x_i = f\left[x_i, x_j\right] + x_i f'\left[x_{i,}x_j\right]\left(1 + \sum_{j\neq i} dx_j / dx_i\right)$$

The $\lambda_j^{\ i} = dx_j / dx_i$ represent conjectures that the i firm makes about the way in which its output affects the output of every other j firm, while the sum of conjecture of all competing firms gives the conjectural variation $\lambda = \sum_{j\neq i}\lambda_j^{\ i}$.

Conjectural variations "à la Cournot"[13] $\lambda_j^{\ i} = 0$ are widely used in economic literature; in this case variations of output from k^{th} firm do not result in variations in output of other firms.

Bertrand develops a different type of conjectural variations: $\lambda_j^i = \sum_{j\neq i}\partial x_j / \partial x_i = -1$; each firm believes that variations in the quantity of its supply would determine variations in the total quantity from other firms of same entity, but having opposite sign, so that industry total supply and equilibrium price are not changed.[14]

3.2 Concentration indices

If the concentration degree is measured then horizontal, conglomeral and vertical concentration should be distinguished. When a firm produces differentiated goods then we have horizontal concentration, when a firm produces diversificated goods we have conglomeral concentration, and lastly we have vertical concentration when all production phases are performed in the same firm.

There are two classes of concentration indices: indices which consider the number of firms and indices which consider size.

Regardless of reference theory, the most adequate indicator to measure concentration is market share or size of firms; in this case we have high concentration if a small number of firms controls a great part of a sector.

Concentration is determined by two factors: total number of firms and their distribution by size; thus there are problems in selecting concentration indicators when both aspects are to be considered. However entropy indices and Herfindhal index are able to include both aspects.[15]

---

[13] To have more information on Cournot model see Cournot (1838): assuming that conjectural variations are equal to zero, translates into this language hypothesis on which the Cournot oligopolistic model is based and in which each firm maximizes profits by assuming as given the output of other firms.

[14] In the Bertrand model the strategic variable used by firms is price and not quantity as in Cournot model. Among the oligopoly models we should not forget the Stackelberg model and collusion models.

[15] The Herfindhal index can be derived from Cowling and Waterson model, see: Cowling K., Waterson M. (1976).

Concentration indices giving importance to the number of firms.

These indices are obtained by using the concentration curve:

1. *Concentration ratio.* If *n* firms belonging to industry are considered, then the concentration ratio is the value on the y-axis of concentration curve: $CR = \sum_i s_i$, where s_i is the market share of *i* firm. This index gives a partial information because it only provides information about a certain point of the concentration curve, whereas to have complete information, each point on the concentration curve should be known. The concentration ratio gives then aleatory results as regards the concentration degree of a sector, depending on the number n of firms considered as belonging to industry. Nevertheless this index gets an important meaning in the evolutionistic studies about industry[16].

2. *Number of firms covering a specified market share.* This is a partial index as well, because it gives information only about one point on the concentration curve.

Indices giving importance to distribution of firms by size

3. *Gini index.* The Gini index is derived from the Lorenz curve. The Lorenz curve is obtained form a cartesian plane, where on the abscissa there is the amount of number of firms in decreasing order, while on the ordinate there is the corresponding market amount. When firm distribution is uniform, the Lorenz curve is the bisecting line of the square where one of its sides is 100% of firms decreasingly ordered (abscissa) and the other side is 100% of market shares (ordinate).

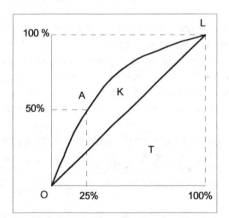

The Gini index is the ratio of the area between the Lorenz curve and the bisecting line, (K area) to the area of half the square (T area).

This ratio is equal to zero for uniform distribution, while it is equal to one when uniformity of distribution is totally absent. The problem connected with the

---

[16] Arrighetti A. (1989) applied the concentration ratio to manufacturing in Italy.

Gini index is that number of firms is not taken into account, in fact distribution can be uniform when there is a monopoly, or when there is a small number of oligopolist firms controlling the same amount of market share, or with a high number of firms, each with a kth market share.

Concentration indices considering total number of firms and their distribution by size[17]

1. *Entropy indices:* $R_e = -\sum_{i=1}^{n} \alpha_1 \ln \alpha_i$ (sum of shares multiplied by their logarithm). The entropy index has negative sign because being $\alpha_i < 1$ then logarithm is negative.; when the entropy index has high values then there is a lower concentration degree of firms.

2. *Herfindhal index:* $R_H = \sum_{i=1}^{n} \alpha_i^2$, sum of market share squared.

The Herfindhal index can be directly derived from the Cowling and Waterson model. It considers size distribution as well as number of firms. If firms are uniformly distributed (each has the same market share) the Herfindhal index is equal to the inverse of firm number, that is 1/N. The Herfindhal index grows when inequality among firms grows: if distribution is uniform, then the numerical equivalence index can be defined in connection with the Herfindhal index. The numerical equivalence index specifies the number of firms originating the Herfindhal index. For example, for uniform distribution, if the Herfindhal index value is 1/13, the numerical equivalence index is equal to 13 (there are 13 firms).

Concentration indices that can be used, according to the studies by Encaoua and Jacquemin (1980)[18], must have the following properties:

1. be symmetrical; they should not change if firms invert their market shares;
2. respect Lorenz criterion; a market share redistribution towards queue which preserves average values leads to an increase of index:
3. concentration with symmetrical firms is to decrease if the number of firms changes from n to n+1.

According to Encaoua and Jacquemin findings the family of indices respecting

this property is: $R(\alpha_1 \ldots \ldots \ldots \ldots \alpha_n) = \sum_{i=i}^{n} \alpha_i h(\alpha_i)$

---

[17] The building of sector indicators based on firm distribution by size (employees) characterizes a database at DCII/A office of Istat. (Research coordination and integrated system of economic statistics), where census data are aggregated by multiple keys (see: 1995 Particular Projects (Census data)). This database allows cross processing by sector/size/class/location indicators, for firms surveyed in 1991 short-form and long-form. Resulting variables concern firm and employee data by size class, and a rather complete set of structural indicators (size, concentration, variability etc).

[18] Encaoua D. and Jacquemin A. [1980].

h is a non decreasing arbitrary function so that $\alpha h(\alpha)$ is convex. Herfidhal and Entropy indices are included in this family.

3.3 Vertical integration indices

The vertical integration degree of firms in one sector has been interpreted in two contrasting ways by theory, in some cases it was considered an element adversing competition or an element favouring competition (Tirole)[19].

What follows is an example where it is believed that vertical integration may implie non competitive behaviours: if the monopolist producing intermediate goods cannot differentiate prices for sales to customers, it is downstream integrated with sectors characterized by high elasticity and thus it eliminates competitors that are in that market[20].

The term vertical integration means three types of vertical integration:
1. *"vertical formation"*[21]
2. *"vertical expansion"*
3. *"vertical merger"*

A firm may become vertically integrated through internal growth or through the acquisition of another firm.

We have vertical integration if the whole upstream output is used totally or in part as intermediate input by the downstream firm, or if the total amount of an intermediate input is obtained from a part or from the whole output of the upstream firm. Vertical integration means the control of the entire production or distribution process and not only the control of some particular input of that process.

In literature there are different interpretations as regards the definition of vertical integration: according to some of them (Grossman S.J., Hart. O.D., 1986)[22] there is vertical integration in a firm when assets are totally controlled or owned without any reference to work relations inside the firm; that is it is not relevant whether people working for the firm are employees or external assistants whereas for the others (Willliamson, O.E., 1975)[23] these work relations are fundamental to define a vertically integrated firm.

The reasons why a firm may decide to integrate vertically are basically three and are interconnected:
1. technological economies, that is saving costs at engineering level in following the whole manufacturing process instead of subdividing it into parts;

---

[19] Tirole (1991).

[20] Tirole (1991) pp 237-238.

[21] M.K. Perry (1989).

[22] See footnote n. 21.

[23] See footnote n. 21.

2. transaction economies, due to internalisation of markets;
3. market imperfection, among which the presence of information asymmetry has a remarkable importance.

The index mainly used to measure the vertical integration degree, obtained from account data, is given by the ratio of added value to sales revenue: IV= VA/ (VA+CA)=VA/ Sales Revenue, where IV=   Vertical Integration Index, VA= Added Value (obtained from output value deducted variable costs of raw materials, semi-finished products, etc.), CA= cost of purchases, Sales Revenue = sales.

When calculating the vertical integration index of a firm, attention should be given to all those forms of quasi-integration which cannot be identified as a single production unit but that are stable supply relationships, which are always useful to be detected for a correct statistical analysis.

3.4 Relevant markets to calculate indices

The calculation of concentration or vertical integration indices implies the definition of a relevant market for the analysis to be performed.

As regards the defining aspects, an analysis of tools used by the Autorità Garante della Concorrenza e del Mercato can be useful to specify the relevant markets[24].

The calculation of indices for markets defined as relevant can be performed for domestic market as well as for foreign markets. For example the Antitrust deals with domestic affairs. From this point of view, an evaluation of concentration degree implies a measurement of domestic market sales revenue.

The Autorità Garante della Concorrenza e del Mercato used the U.S. experience in choosing criteria to locate "relevant markets". According to the Antitrust, a relevant market is "... the smallest context, where, if monopolistic conditions should occur, the monopolist could profitably establish a price much higher than competitive price and keep it up for a long period of time".[25]

In the United States, there has been a shift in the definition of relevant markets: from giving attention to demand and to substitution degree of differentiated products[26] (purchaser substitutability), seen in terms of cross elasticity[27], to giving attention to a sort of analysis less economically grounded but

---

[24] The term "relevant market" was used for the first time by U.S. Supreme Court in 1948 (Columbia Steel).

[25] Definition of relevant market given by the Antitrust during Annual reports for 1992 and 1993.

[26] In the 50s, J. Bain supported the necessity of defining relevant markets in this way.

[27] Cross elasticity of demand is given by percentage variation of demanded quantity of product j when there is 1% increase of price of product i. Cross elasticity formulation is:

based on characteristics and use of products, this analysis developed in the 60s and 70s.

Problems in defining relevant markets arise (as pointed out by theoreticians of monopolistic competition[28]) from the presence of relations of imperfect substitutability among products. In defining relevant markets reference can also be made to substitutability of supply, that is the capability to provide products that other firms have as a reaction to a price reduction from a hypothetical monopolist. When evaluating competitive firms as regards supply, we are referring to firms which do not have to invest a lot in terms of manufacturing capacity to supply these products.

The EEC Commission, in the XXIII Report on Competition Policy, reserved the possibility to evaluate, by individual cases only, substitutability of supply when defining relevant markets; the Autorità Garante della Concorrenza e del Mercato[29] believes that substitutability of supply should intervene only if it is possible to specify a dominant position.

Reference is made to current price (before concentration) when evaluating market power degree, it is difficult to single out competitive price; since the Authority is mainly interested by market power increase and not so much by current market power, thus Antitrust goals often differ from Istat goals, as the Italian national Institute of Statistics wants to give a picture of the actual condition.

In order to single out relevant markets it is necessary to distinguish between horizontally differentiate products (products with different varieties) and vertically differentiate products (different qualities of the same product).

Relevant markets are defined on the basis of characteristics inherent to marketable goods and of geographical and time characteristics, because markets often change over a period of time. These problems are to be considered when calculating indices of market competitiveness degree.

$\eta_{ij} = \partial q_j / q_j / \partial p_i / p_i$

However cross elasticity is not immediately exactly determined, in fact to locate the relevant market it is necessary to:

1. calculate cross elesticity for all potential replacement of the examined product.

2. define the period of time during which cross elasticity is measured.

3. define a threshold level to discriminate when two or more goods belong to the same relevant market.

4. availability of a long sequence of data about prices and quantity of interesting products.

5. constant analysis of changes in the market (innovations) and which can make obsolete some calculations.

[28] Among theoreticians of monopolistic competition see: E.H. Chamberlin (1933) and J. Robinson (1971).

[29] See Bruzzone G. 1995.

4 Approach of official statistics to competition degree measurement

4.1 Report of international experiences

As far as international experiences, how to calculate competitiveness degree of two very advanced Countries in the field of Statistics: Canada and France and Eurostat too has been studied.

In Canada, an analysis of indicators used to define market competition degree has not been performed yet; as a result of NAFTA[30], North-America free trade agreement of 1989, studies about this subject were realized within the limits of foreign trade statistics where industrial firm performances were analysed.

Analyses, performed by Canada national statistics Institute for the work in footnote 30, want to point out if there are differences between Canada and North-America trades after the agreement signature; these analyses study firm performance.

One of the easiest way to evaluate firm performance, whether relative or absolute is to calculate share changes during a certain period of time, (S_t, S_0).

Among share changes, changes of import value in a particular industry in a market during a certain period of time are considered. These changes of import value are explained by Canada national statistics Institute in different ways: a) as market growth, b) as increase of good supplied from a industry, c) as increase of imported part for industry supply in the same period of time.

This last aspect is very useful for our analysis because Canadians identify it as indicator, even if raw, of market competition: analysis of competition degree is not based on the microeconomic analysis of market structure but on penetration degree of some Countries in national territory.

As far as French central statistics Institute, an analysis of market competition degree has not been performed yet, the Institute analyzes the concentration through Herfindhal index calculation; at present this kind of analyses is not included in a total analysis of market competition .

Analyses of concentration made by INSEE are in particular included in an horizontal structure analysis; vertical structure analysis is not performed. Competitiveness degree analysis is realized with regard to foreign trade: shares of market are evaluated through the ratio of a Country exports to exports of the nine more industrialized Countries: France, United-States, Japan, Germany, Italy, England, Benelux, Netherlands and Spain.

The French evaluate[31] market shares of France and its partners as concerns industrial products at current prices and 1980 prices. Other indicators of

---

[30] Trade Patterns: Canada-United States, (1993).

[31] Rapport sur les comptes de la Nation (1994).

competitiveness degree are export prices and industry wage costs with relation to France main partners.

Import competitiveness is calculated through the ratio of industrial product import prices to production prices of these products. Penetration rate, an index examined by French, is given by import volume at 1980 prices divided by domestic demand at 1980 prices.

As concerns competitiveness degree analysis of European Union, competition analysis is more and more a current question after the liberalization of European Union trade. The work "Una politica di competitività per l'Unione Europea" shows as the main problem is that an analysis through data often becomes a macroeconomics analysis leaving out others aspects: microeconomic characteristics, entrepreneurial attitude, firm trade trend and sectorial dynamics.

Tertiary sector, often neglected, should be taken into the necessary consideration to correctly analyze competition at European level; analyses including not only quantitative features (generally macroeconomics) but also qualitative features. A careful analysis of competitiveness indicators used in European Union indicates that they are connected to foreign Trade.

From 1995, as a result of the Commission White Book about "Growth competitiveness and employment", Eurostat prepared a database "Competitiveness Indicators Database" which gives an organic and complete outline of competition indicators in Union European countries, in USA, in Japan and in emergent Countries, on the basis of Nace 70 classification. Indicators calculated are:

1. Performance indicators
2. Cost and design indicators
3. Other indicators including infrastructure.

Among indicators, which are very numerous, there are:

a) shares of different Country export with regard to OECD (Organization for Economic Co-operation & Development) exports:
   $$X_{ij} / X_{oj}$$

b) shares of different Country import with regard to OECD (Organization for Economic Co-operation & Development) imports:
   $$M_{ij} / M_{oj}$$

c) total market share:
   $$Q_{ij} / \left(C_{ij} + X_{ij} \right)$$ where Q is the production value and C is the consumption

d) import penetration level:
   $$M_{ij} / C_{ij}$$

e) Return on net assets: (not available indicator)
   Profits before interest and taxes/fixed assets+net current assets

f) Sales to net assets ratio: (not available indicator)
   Sales/fixed assets+net current assets

g) other indicators of work utilization efficiency:
   1) Index of wage competitiveness on the domestic market (1990 = 100)
   2) Index of labour productivity relative to export competitors (1990 = 100)
   3) Index of labour productivity relative to import competitors (1990 = 100)
h) The ratio of stocks of finished and semi finished products manufactured by enterprises to production.
i) Share of R&D in total manufacturing industry as a percentage of total R&D spending
j) Percentage of capacity utilization (not available)
k) Total factor productivity (not available).

These indicators are a part of the great number of indicators calculated by Eurostat, they give an outline of the competition level; in this case too, it is possible to notice that a lot of these indicators concern foreign trade data and that only few indicators are calculated using firm accounting data, therefore Eurostat always privileges a macroeconomic approach rather than a microeconomic one. Indicators of concentration degree or vertical integration degree are not included among Eurostat competition indicators; they will be calculated by Istat, at a universal level when ASIA Register can be used.

Firm capacity utilization degree and expenses in R&D made by all manufacturing firms are Eurostat useful indicators to examine the potential competition level and so no longer actual.

4.2 Statistic sources available in Italy

As far as statistic sources available for firm competitiveness degree analysis, the main question to solve is the integration of different data sources: financial, fiscal and ad hoc surveys.

It is important to give full value to macroeconomic and microeconomic aspects to organize a system of integration for the different data sources.

The need for source integration is pressed by European Union Council Standard (1996) concerning structural statistics of firms.

Standard aims at giving rules to have data that can be compared among Member Countries of European Economic Community. The important element is to have data non "unidimensional" but that can be handled in aggregate way.

After an integrated system of firms is achieved, the following step is to obtain "integrated sub-systems" to allow different interpretations of the considered phenomenon: to this end building of an firm integrated file is very important.

Istat is now working to create ASIA (Statistic Register of Working Firms), an integrated file of statistic and administrative data included in a dynamic context[32].

---

[32] Garofalo G., Revelli R. (1996).

One of the main benefit that can be get from ASIA Register is to allow a finding of firms and local units with a high level of mobility or not very visible (by using different sources for cross controls); ASIA Register should help to consider, from a statistic point of view, realities such as groups of firms that are not yet surveyed.

As Asia is not available, Sirio-Nai is the register used at the moment,which doesn't allow a control about small firms demography.

Sources used for surveys of firms are two: SCI survey (general Survey of Account System of firms with 20 employees and over) and IPI (sample survey with less than 20 employees). These surveys are similar with regard to definition and classifications[33].

4.3 A partial empirical analysis of competition degree

Considering that at present ASIA data are not available, it is necessary to remember that ISTAT performed an analysis of concentration degree based on the individual firms and local units data of 1991 Census.

Census data, concerning firms as well as local units, allowed to calculate the following indicators, starting from market shares calculated on the basis of employee number.

1. entropic average:

$$\mu = \exp\left[\sum_{j=1}^{n}\left(N_{ij} \, / \, N_i\right) \times \log N_{ij}\right]$$

2. Theil index:

$$E_i = \sum_{j=1}^{n} P_{ij} \log\left(1/P_{ij}\right)$$

3. the variability:
   a) $X = 1 - m/\mu$
   b) the coefficient of variation: σ/m

4. arithmetic mean = firm average size
   $m = \Sigma j = 1n \, Nij \, / \, n$

where i=sector index, j=firm index, n=number of firms in the i sector, N_{ij}=employees in the j firm of i sector, $P_{ij} = N_{ij} / N_i$

Entropic average has the advantage, over arithmetic mean and median, of being less influenced by smaller firms weight; Theil index is used as concentration degree and it has a value between 0 (the highest concentration) and log n (the lowest concentration).

---

[33] Corsini V., Monducci R., Vicari P. (1997)

The two variability indices point out: the first one, the dispersion with respect to the entropic average (it has a value between 0 and 1 and it increases as gap between arithmetic mean and entropic average increases), the second one, the variability among sectors.

Below an exemplification is given for the analysis that can be performed for these indicators, four digits ATECO data are taken for some transport and trade subsectors.

Sector	Firms	Employees	Entropic average	Theil's Index	Variability	Variation coefficient	Average size
Vehicle maintenance and repair	113464	263718	3.2	11.2	0.3	453.7	2.3
Intermediaries food prod. Drinks tobacco	15852	23544	2.0	9.3	0.2	160.6	1.5
Meat charcuter. prod. Wholesale trade	3333	16991	9.9	7.4	0.5	11.1	5.1
Textile retail trade	14787	31209	3.0	9.2	0.3	171.2	2.1
Clothing retail trade	111800	240314	3.2	11.1	0.3	732.5	2.1
Rail transport	105	204667	99464.9	0.7	0.9	91.9	1949.3
Other passenger road transport	2315	113159	964.7	4.8	0.9	424.9	48.9
Taxi transport	12537	18376	3.0	8.7	0.5	412.9	1.5
Airliner transport	68	22877	5883.8	1.4	0.9	48.6	336.4

The first, the second, the fourth and the fifth row, respectively vehicle maintenance and repair, intermediaries of food products, drinks and tobacco, textile retail trade, clothing retail trade are sectors with an entropic average and arithmetic mean almost equal, that means a uniformity of firm size confirmed by a Theil's index high level. Whereas meat wholesale trade, rail transport, other passenger road public transports, taxi transport, airliner transport have a gap between entropic average and arithmetic mean which points out a greater weight of bigger firms; in this case Theil index has lower values showing a greater concentration.

The coefficient of variation allows to compare sectors where there is a smaller or greater variability with regard to average size. Among the chosen sectors, meat and charcuterie wholesale trade has the lowest coefficient of variation.

Vertical integration degree indicators, ASIA file and Foreign Trade data will complete these structure analyses to fully outline market competition degree.

5 Conclusive notes and some research lines to develop

Several problems caused by the difficulty of statistics to represent faithfully economic reality result from this brief analysis. As all the above different schools met with this kind of problems, industrial economists wondered which is the convenient relationship to have with data and empirical analyses.

Industrial economy has alternated inter-industry and intra-industry approaches; a bidirectional influence of theory concerning data requirement has occurred during this evolution: theoretical development has modified data requirement and at the same time theoretical analyses had to be adapted to data availability.

If attention is given to inter-industria trend, problems arise from available data to measure market power through the Lerner index.

The SCP school pointed out difficulties in observing data, as it can be seen in the Lerner index formula, in fact marginal costs, firm conduct, demand elasticity are considered as not observable variables.

Because of difficulties in examining those variables, account data are used, and a profitability account measure, π_{it} is used to replace the Lerner index.

If the "intra-industry" approach is considered, price and quantity dynamics are used, since interesting variables are not easily observable.

The two different approaches have different requirements as regards statistical data, in fact to have account data which can be compared in the interindustry approach, census sources or commercial databases are used; whereas in the intraindustry approach, the data used come from industry associations or from sector specialized reviews.

In cross-section surveys, data provided come from national statistics institutes, where sector classification is made according to their own criteria (often data are not disaggregate enough), in intra-industry analysis data not given by national statistics institutes are often more disaggregate.At a statistical level, problems posed by using account data are due to the fact that data are oversimplified and thus they are not ready to outline peculiarity of different firms; other problems arise from company drawing up of a balance-sheets, they are often not faithful to the real economic-patrimonial situation of the firm. Using data from trade database, another problem that can arise is the firm sample choice since these samples are not automatically a real description of general economic situation: sample estimations cannot be meaningful.The crisis of cross-section studies seems to involve also the national statistics institutes analyses, however an attempt to recover interindustry analyses can be made, as Sutton suggested (1991), trying in this way to get those general aspects which are not affected by non observable conduct variables.As regards the utilization of account data, problems are always posed by data reliability and by the possibility to obtain indicators and especially indicators of market competition degree. Among the different problems, there is the impossibility to examine marginal costs: this problem can be solved using unitary variable costs, even if an exact outline of variable and non variable factors is difficult to achieve for the profit and loss account.Problems of convergence between empiric and economic analyses can be solved if alternative account measures are found and if econometrics techniques are refined.

REFERENCES

Alchian A., Demsetz H.(1972), *'Production, Information Costs, and Economic Organizations'*, American Economic Review.

Arrigetti A. (1989), *'Forme di mercato e dinamica della concentrazione in Italia'* in Padoan P.C., Pezzoli A., Silva F., Concorrenza e concentrazione dell'industria italiana, Il Mulino, Bologna.

Autorità Garante Della Concorrenza e del Mercato (30 Aprile 1996), *Relazione annuale sull'attività svolta* , Presidenza del Consiglio dei Ministri, Roma.

Bain J.(1951), *'Relation of Profit Rate to Industry Concentration : American Manufacturing 1936-1940 '*, Quaterly Journal of Economics", 293,324.

Baumol W.J., Panzar J., Willig R.(1982), *Contestable Markets and the Theory of Industry Structure*, Harcourt Brace Jovanovich,Inc., New York.

Beretta S., Bianchi P.(1996),*'Cambiamento delle Istituzioni economiche e nuovo sviluppo in Italia ed in Europa'*, L'Industria,supplemento al numero 2/1996.

Bowley A. (1924) *Mathematical groundwork of economics* ,Oxford Economic Press.

Brensnahan T.F (1989), *'Empirical Studies of Industries with Market Power'*, Schmalenseer R., Willig R., Handbook of Industrial Organization, Vol. II, Elsevier Science Publishers B.V., Amsterdam, 1012,1055.

Bruzzone G.(1995), *'L'individuazione del mercato rilevante nella tutela della concorrenza"*, Autorità Garante Della Concorrenza e del Mercato, Temi e problemi, Presidenza del Consiglio dei Ministri, Roma.

Bruzzone G., Heimler A.(1997), *Le politiche per la concorrenza nell'esperienza italiana*, Ninni A., SILVA F., La politica industriale, Università Laterza Economia, Roma-Bari.

Chamberlin E.H.(1933), *The theory of Monopolistic Competition*, Cambridge, Harvard University Press.

Competitiveness Indicators Database 1996, *CD-ROM with CUB.X software,*Office for Official Pubblications of the European Communities, Luxembourg.

Corsini V., Monducci R., Vicari P.(1997),' *Analisi Microeconomica del Sistema delle Imprese ed Integrazione tra fonti statistiche : grandi e piccole imprese nell'industria italiana'*, Convegno SIS , La Statistica per le Imprese,Torino.

Cournot A.(1838), *Recherches sur les principles mathématiques de la théorie des richesses*, Hachette, Paris.

Cowling K., Waterson M. (1976), *'Price-Cost Margin and Market Structure'*, Economica, 43, 267,74.

De Ghellinck (1986*), "Effects de l'ouverture sur les structures et performances d'une petite économie"*, Ciaco, Louvain.

Denicolò V. (1994),' *La teoria dei giochi e l'economia industriale'*, L'industria, 15, 657,64.

Domowitz I.,Hubbard R.G., Petersen B.C.(1986), *'Business Cycles and the Relationship between Concentration and Price Cost Margins'*, The Rand Journal of Economics, 17, 1,17.

Domowitz I.,Hubbard R.G., Petersen B.C.(1987), *'Oligopoly Supergames: Some Empirical Evidence on Prices and Margins'*, Journal of Industrial Economics, 35, 379,398.

Domowitz I.,Hubbard R.G., Petersen B.C. (1988), *'Market Structure and Cyclical Fluctuations in U.S Manufacturing'* , Review of Economics and Statistics, 55-66.

Donsimoni M.P., Geroski P., Jacquemin A. (1984),*'Concentration Indices and Market Power :Two Views'*, Journal of Industrial Economics, 32, 419,34.

Encaoua D.,Jacquemin A. (1980), ' *Degree of Monopoly, Indices of Concentration and Threat of Entry'*, International Economic Review , 21, 87-105.

Feenstra R.C., Levinhson J.A. (1995), ' *Estimating Markups and Market Conduct with Multidimensional Product Attributes'*, Review of Economic Studies, 62, 19,52.

Ferrero M. - La Noce M. (Febbraio '96), *'Controllo delle concentrazioni fra imprese e criteri di valutazione'*, Autorità Garante della Concorrenza e del Mercato, Temi e problemi n.2, Presidenza del Consiglio dei Ministri, Roma.

Garofalo G., Revelli R. (1996), *'Le relazioni dinamiche tra le unità: definizioni , tecniche di rilevazione e implicazioni microeconomiche'*, XXXVIII Riunione Scientifica SIS, Rimini.

Greene W. H.(1993), *Econometric Analysis*, MacMillan Publishing Company, New York.

Grillo M., Silva F(1989), *Impresa, concorrenza e organizzazione,* La Nuova Italia Scientifica, Roma.

Grossman S.J., Hart O.D.(1986), *'The costs and benefits of ownership: A theory of vertical and lateral Integration'*, Journal of Political Economy , 691,719.

Jacquemin A., Buigues P., Ilzkovitz (1989),' *Concentrazione orizzontale,fusioni e politica della concorrenza nella Comunità Europea'*, Economia Europea.

Matyas L., Sevestre P. (1996), *The Econometrics of Panel Data,* Kluwer Academic Publishers, Dordrecht.

Ninni A. Silva F.(1997), *La politica industriale* , Università Laterza Economia, Bari-Roma.

Particular Projects (1995 Census data): *Costruzione di archivi di dati censuari (Cis 1991) per l'analisi strutturale del sistema delle imprese,* Final project report n. 1037, Project manager: R.Monducci, Istat 17th January, 1997

Perry M.K. (1989), *'Vertical Integration: determinants and effects'*,Schamalensee R., Willig R, Handbook of Industrial Organization, Vol. I, Elsevier Science Publishers, Amsterdam, 185,224.

Rapport sur le Comptes de le Nation 1994, *Economie Générale, Comptes et Indicateurs économiques*, Insée Resultats,Paris.

Robinson J. (1971),*The Economics of Imperfect Competition* , Mac Millan, Londra.

Rondi *L.(1997),* ' *Dati disaggregati e analisi della struttura industriale:* < *la matrice europea delle quote di mercato*' , L'Industria n.2.

Santarelli E. (1995),*'Pratici, teorici (dei giochi) e applicati. A cosa servono gli economisti industriali'* , *L'Industria,*n.1.

Sembenelli A. (1995), *'Dall'approccio SCP alla teoria dell'oligopolio. Il fabbisogno di dati dell'economista industriale applicato'*, Società italiana degli economisti, XXXVI Riunione Scientifica Annuale, 20-21 Ottobre 1995.

Sembenelli A. (1995),' *Price over marginal Cost and the Business Cycle: Evidence from Italian Firm Level Data'*, Mimeo, Ceris-CNR.

Sembenelli A. e Rondi L.(1995), *'Continua il dibattito: la ricerca applicata nell'economia industriale: alcune riflessioni sullo stato dell'arte'*, L'industria , 239,48.

Schmalensee R.(1989),*'Inter-industry studies of structure and performance'*, Schmalensee R., Willig R., Handbook of Industrial Organization,Vol.2, Elsevier Science Publishers B.V., Amsterdam, 952, 1001.

Sutton J. (1990),*'Explaining Everything, Explaining Nothing, Game Theoretic Models in Industrial Economics'*, European Economic Review, 34, 502-12.

Sutton. J. (1991), *Sunk Cost and Market Structure*, Mit Press, Cambridge (Mass.).

Tirole J.(1991), *Teoria dell'Organizzazione Industriale*, Hoepli, Milano.

Tirole J., (1988 and 1991) *The Theory of Industrial Organization*, Mit Press, Cambridge (Mass.)

Trade Patterns Canada-United States (1993), *The Manufacturing Industries* 1981-1991, Ministery of Industry, Science and Technology.

Vickers J. (1995), *'Competition and Regulation in Vertically Related Markets'*, Review of Economic Studies, 62, 1,17.
Williamson O.E., (1975), *Markets and Hierarchies: Analysis and Antitrust Implications*, New York,Free Press.

FINANCING CONSTRAINTS AND MARKUPS: FURTHER EVIDENCE FROM ITALIAN FIRM LEVEL DATA

Anna Bottasso[1], Marzio Galeotti[2] and Alessandro Sembenelli[3]

[1,3]*CERIS-CNR*
[2]*University of Bergamo and Fondazione ENI Enrico Mattei*

1 Introduction

How do capital market imperfections affect firms' markup policies? Do these imperfections tend to make markups pro-cyclical or counter-cyclical? These are the two main issues we address in this paper. The cyclical behaviour of markups has attracted the attention of economists trying to build models able to explain the empirical regularity of pro-cyclical factor prices: if markups are countercyclical, this would explain why the increase in output that follows a positive demand shock is generally accompanied by an increase in the real wage. A number of theoretical papers including Greenwald, Stiglitz, and Weiss (1984), Gottfries (1991) and Klemperer (1987) have shown that capital market imperfections can induce counter-cyclical markups. The basic economic intuition behind these contributions is that firms under the threat of liquidation are less likely to set low prices in product differentiated industries in order to gain market shares. Furthermore, since it is in recessionary periods that firms may find it more difficult to raise external funds because the value of collateral is low, they will have a greater incentive to raise price and increase current cash flow in order to meet their liabilities and to finance operations.

Despite the fact that there is now some empirical evidence supporting the importance of capital market imperfections in generating counter-cyclical markups in product markets with consumer switching costs (see among others Chevalier and Scharfstein, 1996), there is a number of both theoretical and empirical issues that are still unresolved. Firstly, as noted by Chevalier and Scharfstein (1996), it is difficult to draw macro-economic inferences from empirical papers where very specific models are applied to very specific industries. Secondly, there might be other, and perhaps more important, channels through which capital market imperfections affect firms' pricing decisions. For instance, Hendel (1996) presents a theoretical model where more financially constrained firms tend to reduce price in bad times in order to raise cash at the expense of inventories. His model predicts pro-cyclical markups for this type of firms. Thirdly, and more generally, the idea that financially constrained firms tend to raise prices in recession does not square with the common wisdom, widely accepted among business people, that troublesome firms cut prices in order to generate cash.

This paper makes a contribution to this literature from an empirical point of view. The empirical analysis is based on the model proposed by Bottasso, Galeotti, and Sembenelli (1997) which studies the optimal price decision of a firm operating in an industry with differentiated product and facing imperfect capital markets. That model provides an alternative channel through which imperfections in capital markets can affect firms' markup policies. The basic intuition is that firms might find it rational to cut price today in order to increase sales beyond the single period profit maximising level, if this allows them to face a relatively lower cost of debt tomorrow. This happens to be the case if the premium on external finance banks are expected to set tomorrow is inversely correlated with firms' today sales[1]. In this study we present fresh econometric evidence bearing on the effects of capital market imperfections on markup policies by estimating a dynamic markup equation for a large sample of Italian firms operating in industries with differentiated product. In particular, we present further empirical evidence relative to Bottasso, Galeotti, and Sembenelli (1997) in that we allow the parameters of interest to vary according to the form of ownership (affiliated versus independent firms).

The remainder of the paper is organized as follows. In Section 2, we summarize the basic assumptions of the estimated model and we discuss in details the implications that can be drawn concerning the impact of capital market imperfections on firms' markup policies. In Section 3, the characteristics of the data set used in the empirical exercise are highlighted and the relevant descriptive statistics are presented. Section 4 presents the econometric results which can be summarized as follows. Firstly, capital market imperfections exist in the sense that firms in our sample pay a premium on external finance which depends on the debt to sales ratio. Secondly, according to our estimates firms find it optimal to cut price compared to unconstrained firms. Thirdly, estimates show that the effects of financing constraints on markups are more severe for firms which are not affiliated to industrial groups or to multinational corporations. Finally, at least for independent firms, financing constraints are more severe during recessions, hence implying that financial market imperfections tend to make markups pro-cyclical. Section 5 concludes the paper.

2 The empirical model

The empirical analysis is based on the model proposed by Bottasso, Galeotti, and Sembenelli (1997). In that study the optimal price decision of a

---

[1] Obviously, this assumption is consistent with the empirical regularity which shows that the cost of debt is lower for large firms compared with smaller ones.

profit maximizing firm producing a differentiated good is modeled. The firm operates in an imperfectly competitive market for her product and price is used as strategic variable. Moreover, the firm faces imperfect capital markets for the funds needed to finance her operations. Because of this the cost of external finance is higher than that of internally generated funds and this aspect has been modeled through an increasing cost function of external debt (see, for instance, Bond, and Meghir, 1994). Debt is taken to be primarily given by bank credit, the major source of both short and long term financing for Italian firms; moreover the firm does not raise funds through equity issues, another assumption which is quite plausible for most Italian firms over our sample period.

The firm's demand for her product is represented as follows:

$$q_t = D(p_t, v_t) \tag{1}$$

where q is the quantity of output produced and p is the corresponding price. The model allows for strategic considerations in that the firm's price affects demand also via the impact upon the rivals' price.

The firm chooses price and debt policies in order to maximize the following objective:

$$E_t \sum_{s=t}^{\infty} \beta_{t,s} \left\{ (1-\tau_s) \left[p_s D(p_s, v_s) - c(w_s, D(p_s, v_s)) - h(D(p_s, v_s), D(p_{s-1}, v_{s-1})) \right. \right.$$
$$\left. \left. - i(b_{s-1}, p_{s-1} D(p_{s-1}, v_{s-1})) b_{s-1} \right] + (b_s - b_{s-1}) \right\} \tag{2}$$

where E_t is the expectation operator, $\beta_{t,s}$ is the discount factor between periods t and s, τ is the corporate income tax rate, $c(\cdot)$ is the firm's minimum variable cost function which depends, besides output, upon the price (vector) of variable inputs w, $h(\cdot)$ is the adjustment cost function for output, and $i(\cdot)$ is the cost of external debt function which depends upon the value of production and upon the (end of period) stock of outstanding debt b. Note that the product $i(\cdot)b$ is equal to the amount of interest payments due on external funds. Because of the existence of imperfect capital markets, the interest rate depends positively upon the end of period debt-to-sales ratio. In particular the agency cost function is defined as:

$$i(\cdot) = \alpha_2 + \alpha_3 \left(\frac{b_{t-1}}{p_{t-1} q_{t-1}} \right) \tag{3}$$

We will not explain the model in details, but we report the final equation which has been estimated.[2] Using [3] and assuming a quadratic specification for the adjustment cost function $h(\cdot)$, the optimality condition for the firm's output price results in the following Euler equation:

$$PCM_t = \gamma_1 + \gamma_2 \left[\frac{q_t - q_{t-1}}{p_t q_{t-1}} - 0.5 \rho_{t+1} \frac{q_{t+1}^2 - q_t^2}{p_t q_t^2} \right] +$$

$$+ \gamma_3 \rho_{t+1} \left(\frac{b_t}{p_t q_t} \right)^2 + v_{t+1} \qquad [4]$$

where ρ_{t+1} is the after tax discount rate between t and $t+1$ (based on β_t and τ_t) and PCM_t is the dependent variable given by the firm's price-cost margin and defined as follows:

$$PCM_t = (p_t q_t - \eta c_t) / p_t q_t,$$

This variable allows for the existence of variable returns to scale with η denoting the cost elasticity of output (the reciprocal of the scale elasticity): when returns to scale are decreasing ($\eta > 1$) marginal costs are higher than total average costs c_t, while the opposite occurs when returns to scale are increasing ($\eta < 1$). As for the parameters of [4] we have:

$$\gamma_1 = -\varepsilon / (1 + \lambda),$$

$$\gamma_2 = \alpha_1,$$

$$\gamma_3 = -\alpha_3 \left[1 + \varepsilon / (1 + \lambda) \right]$$

where α_1 is the parameter of the quadratic adjustment cost function $h(\cdot)$, α_3 is the parameter of the agency cost function defined in [3], ε is the inverse of the direct effect price elasticity, and λ is defined as follows:

$$\lambda = \left(\frac{\partial D(t)}{\partial v_t} \frac{\partial v_t}{\partial p_t} \right) \bigg/ \frac{\partial D(t)}{\partial p_t} \qquad [5]$$

---

[2] Model derivations can be found in Bottasso, Galeotti, and Sembenelli (1997).

Recalling that v_t represents the vector of the prices charged by the other firms in the industry, the variable λ summarizes the impact of a price change on the firm's production level and is given by the ratio of two terms: the strategic effect and the direct effect. While the direct effect is always negative, the strategic one is taken to be positive. This assumption implies that consumers view the products in the industry as substitutes (so that $\partial D(t) / \partial v_t > 0$) and that firms in the industry treat prices as strategic complements (so that $\partial v(t) / \partial p_t > 0$). Of course, in the case of a monopolistic firm $\lambda = 0$. More generally, the size of λ will depend on the size of the strategic effect compared to that of the direct effect, the former depending in turn on the degree of product differentiation, measured by $\partial D(t)/\partial v_t$, and on the tightness of price competition, measured by $\partial v_t /\partial p_t$. In equation [4] η, ε and λ are taken to be both time and firm invariant.

In estimating [4] we expect γ_1 to be negative and γ_2 to be positive. The last regressor of the equation measures the impact of imperfect capital markets on the firm's markup but the sign of γ_3 is not univocally defined as discussed hereafter. From equation [4] it appears that the impact of capital market imperfections on markup decisions depends crucially upon the sign of the following partial derivative:

$$\frac{\partial PCM_t}{\partial \alpha_3} = -\rho_{t+1}\left(\frac{b_t}{p_t q_t}\right)^2\left(\frac{\varepsilon}{1+\lambda}+1\right) \qquad [6]$$

In particular, following an increase in the premium on external finance parametrized here by α_3, firms will have an incentive to cut prices if:

$$\lambda > |\varepsilon| - 1 \qquad [7]$$

Obviously, if the inequality is reverse, firms will instead react to an increase in financial constraints by raising prices.

To make things simple, let us start from the benchmark case of a monopolisitc firm, where λ is equal to zero. Since ε is bounded between zero and one in absolute value, condition [7] always holds and consequently expression [6] is univocally signed and it is negative. This implies that monopolistic firms find it optimal to respond to an increase in the tightness of financing constraints by lowering the markup. Also, the more elastic market demand is, the bigger is the price cut, following a given increase in the premium on external finance, α_3. The intuition behind this result is simple: if financial market imperfections become more important, firms will cut prices to increase sales. The incentive to do so is higher when demand is elastic since in this case total sales are more sensitive to a price reduction.

Things become more complicated when we relax the assumption of a monopoly market structure and allow firms to compete in an oligopolistic setting. In fact, in this case the strategic effect of a price change is not zero and it depends both on the degree of product differentiation and the tightness of price competition. This can be easily understood if we rewrite condition [7] as follows:

$$\frac{1}{|\varepsilon|} - \omega \, \theta \, > 1 \qquad\qquad\qquad [8]$$

where ω denotes the cross-price elasticity of demand, $(\partial D_t / \partial v_t)(v_t / q_t)$ and θ denotes the conjectural elasticity, $(\partial v_t / \partial p_t)(p_t / v_t)$. Condition [8] has a straightforward economic interpretation: for given values of the parameters defining the demand conditions in the industry, ε e ω, the incentive to cut prices in order to increase sales becomes weaker the more aggressive price competition gets. Also, in some circumstances the negative strategic effect can more than offset the positive direct effect of a price cut on sales and consequently inequality [8] may not hold.[3] For instance, this happens to be the case if a price war follows the decision of financing constrained firms to cut prices.

Summarizing, the model suggests that firms facing imperfections in capital markets have a natural tendency to cut their output price in order to reduce the premium on the cost of external finance. This effect is stronger, the more elastic market demand is, the more products in the industry are differentiated, and the softer is rivals' behavior. However, if rivals react very aggressively to price reductions, overall conclusions may not hold and financially constrained firms might find it rational to raise their price. It is then an empirical matter to discriminate between these alternative hypotheses.

3 Data description

The dataset used in the econometric analysis below is based on an unbalanced panel constructed by CERIS-CNR by merging balance sheet data collected by Mediobanca, a large investment bank, with industry level data provided by ISTAT, the Italian Central Statistical Office. In its latest version, the panel includes 1,318 manufacturing firms with no less than five consecutive

---

[3] Formally inequality [8] holds only if : $\theta < (1 - |\varepsilon|)/(|\varepsilon| \omega)$.

observations over the 1977-1993 period. The total number of firm-year observations is equal to 11,127.[4]

For our empirical analysis we have extracted observations relative to privately-owned firms producing differentiated products, thus obtaining a smaller sample of 5,110 firm-year observations relative to 599 companies. Table 1 provides a description of the unbalanced structure of the sample. Even if the database covers the 1977-1993 period, the estimation period is 1981-1993, since four cross sections are lost in constructing lags and taking first differences.

In order to identify firms operating in industries with product differentiation, the methodology developed by Davies and Lyons (1996) has been adopted. In particular, firms are supposed to produce differentiated goods if the main industry in which they operate is advertising intensive or R&D intensive, or both. The term "intensive" refers here to advertising-to-sales or R&D-to-sales ratios higher than 1%. This definition is based on the observation that in most cases, (both horizontal and vertical) product differentiation is neither intrinsic to the product nor obtainable by simple design without any major investment. More often, product differentiation is a costly activity, requiring investments in R&D or advertising.[5]

Since our analysis also focuses on the impact of financing constraints on the behavior of the markups over the cycle, we have referred to the detrended industrial production series calculated by Schlitzer (1993) as the indicator of the general business cycle. Accordingly, 1977, 1980-1982, 1989-1993 are defined as recessionary years, while 1978-1979 and 1983-1988 are considered expansionary periods. This classification is rather robust to the use of alternative indicators of demand, like GDP or industry specific indicators.

In Table 2, we report descriptive statistics for the main variables used in the empirical analysis over both the full period (1977-1993) and the estimation period (1981-1993). The same statistics are also provided separately for recessionary and expansionary periods. In what follows we offer a few comments pertaining to the estimation period. However, very similar considerations hold for the statistics computed over the full sample.

The price-cost margin, PCM hereafter, has been calculated as the ratio of operating profits to sales, operating profits being given by the difference between

---

[4] The documentation concerning the characteristics of the dataset is contained in an appendix available from the authors upon request (see Margon, Sembenelli, and Vannoni, 1995). The industries with product differentiation are listed in that appendix and also in Davies and Lyons (1996). The after tax nominal discount rate used in estimation is based on the yield of 12 month Treasury Bills (BOT) plus a 3% constant risk premium and on the statutory rates of company income taxes at both regional (ILOR) and national (IRPEG) levels.

[5] This opens up the possibility that financially constrained firms in product differentiated industries cut on R&D and advertising activities in bad times. Unfortunately, at the present stage data limitations prevent us from pursuing this line of research.

value added and labour costs. This variable has been adopted as the accounting proxy for the ratio of price to marginal cost.[6] PCM is lower during recessions than during expansions and this fact provides support to the idea of procyclical behavior of markups. The same pattern is found for the average value of EMPLOYEES, whereas financial LEVERAGE, defined as the ratio of total financial debt to sales, is higher in recessions than in expansions. As can be seen from the statistics on SALES and DEBT, the countercyclical behavior of LEVERAGE depends more upon the procyclical behavior of SALES than upon the procyclical behavior of DEBT. Incidentally, this is what one would expect if capital market imperfections were likely to be more important in bad times.

4 Empirical results

Equation [4] has been estimated for the sample of 599 firms producing differentiated goods described in the previous section. The estimation technique used is the Generalized Method of Moments (GMM) discussed in Arellano and Bond (1991). Given the dynamic nature of our model and the endogenous nature of regressors, this estimation method allows to obtain consistent estimates of the coefficients by using appropriate lags of regressors as instruments. In all estimated equations, the error term is modeled as the sum of a firm specific effect and a white noise idiosyncratic shock. To deal with firm specific effects we estimate the model in first differences, thereby introducing first order autocorrelation in the error term. As the validity of instruments depends upon the absence of autocorrelation and differencing introduces first order correlation, valid instruments are dated t-2 or earlier. Appropriate tests for second order residual autocorrelation (m_2) are reported in the tables. Moreover, we also present the Sargan test on the correlation of instruments with the error term. Finally, Wald tests for the joint significance of regressors (W_1) are included.

In order to study the effects of capital markets imperfections on the behavior of markups, we have followed an approach which is very common in the literature on financing constraints. This approach consists in splitting the sample according to firm specific variables proxying for the extent of agency problems and testing the model on each sub-sample.[7]

---

[6] However, there exists a growing body of applied papers which obtain the markup over marginal cost as a parameter or a combination of parameters from the econometric estimation of structural models (see, among others, Galeotti and Schiantarelli, 1994; Sembenelli, 1996; and the references therein).

[7] In a previous paper (Bottasso, Galeotti, and Sembenelli, 1997) we found interesting results by using the firm's financial position at the beginning of each time period as sample splitting criterion.

The sample splitting criterion chosen has been the firm's association with business groups. In the literature on financing constraints business groups have been considered as organizational forms that help to cope with information and contract enforcement problems in the capital markets as financial intermediaries know that in case of financial distress individual firms may also rely on the financial resources of the group. For this reason a firm's affiliation to a business groups is likely to improve her access to external funds. Moreover, business groups allow the formation of an internal capital markets that supplement the capital allocation function of the external market. Finally, in the Italian case, dominant large business groups have special informal relationships with national financial institutions which play an important role in the financing of firms and this link represents a way to reduce agency costs.[8]

After splitting the sample on the basis of firms' affiliation to an industrial group or to multinational corporations, we have estimated equation [4] assuming constant returns to scale. Basic results are presented in the first column of Table 3.

The Sargan test does not point to any misspecification of the model. As expected, the m_2 statistic leads us to reject the hypothesis of second order autocorrelation, in line with the assumed stochastic structure of the disturbances. Moreover, all coefficients are significantly different from zero. In particular, the coefficient of the adjustment cost function $\alpha_1 = \gamma_2$ is positive as predicted by the theory.

By taking the ratio $\gamma_3 / (\gamma_1 - 1)$ we can recover point estimates of α_3 which is equal to 0.14 for independent firms and 1.3 for affiliated ones. The fact that these coefficients are positive and significant implies that firms are paying a positive premium on external funds due to the existence of imperfect capital markets. Moreover, the parameter of the agency cost function is significantly higher for the subsample of independent firms. The two coefficients are statistically different at conventional statistical levels and this result confirms the hypothesis that group membership relaxes financing constraints because of the existence of internal capital markets and of links between groups and banks which help to mitigate the effects of capital markets imperfections.

As it has already been discussed in Section 3, the impact of capital market imperfections on markup decisions depends upon the sign of the derivative in [6]: if it is negative, then capital market imperfections induce firms to lower markups (by cutting the output price) in order to mitigate agency problems. By replacing $\varepsilon/(1 + \lambda)$ with $-\gamma_1$ in [6] it can be easily seen that this is indeed the case: firms have an incentive to cut price in order to boost their sales and in turn to lessen financing constraints. In order to understand the relative importance of the

---

[8] This approach has been adopted in the literature on the impact of financing constraints on investment. See Hoshi, Kashyap, and Scharfstein (1991) for Japan, Schiantarelli and Sembenelli (1996) for Italy, and Chirinko and Schaller (1995) for Canada.

direct as opposed to the strategic price effect on output, we should be able to measure separately ε and λ. Unfortunately, since the model is underidentified, we cannot disentangle the two effects. What we can say is that, given demand conditions, firms are not competing too aggressively, so that it is rational for the firm to reduce her price, and hence the markup, as financing constraints become more severe.

One potential limitation of the results presented in the first column of Table 3 is that all parameters are assumed to be constant over time. Since the literature suggests that financing constraints may vary over the cycle, we have estimated equation [4] by allowing the parameters to differ across expansions and recessions (Bernanke, Gertler, and Gilchrist, 1996). To this end we have used a dummy variable taking on the value one in expansionary years and zero otherwise.[9]

In the second column of Table 3 we report estimates results. The implied point estimates of α_3 show that for independent firms the two parameters are significantly different over different stages of the business cycle (0.98 during recessions and 0.46 during expansions) whereas they are not different for affiliated firms (0.19 during recessions and 0.18 during expansions). These results suggest that, everything else equal, financial market imperfections are higher in bad times, since, at least for independent firms, α_3 is found to be lower when the economy is buoyant. This implies that the countercyclical behavior of financing constraints induces a procyclical behavior of markups. This finding is in line with the predictions of the theoretical model by Hendel (1996) and contrary to the countercyclical explanation put forth by Chevalier and Scharfstein (1995, 1996).

5 Conclusions

In this paper we have investigated from an empirical point of view the effects of capital markets imperfections on firms' markup policies and on their cyclical behavior. This is an important, yet still relatively unexplored area.

The empirical analysis is based on the model suggested by Bottasso, Galeotti and Sembenelli (1997) which results in an Euler equation describing the optimal intertemporal price strategy of a firm producing differentiated goods and facing imperfect capital markets and costs of changing output production levels. The wedge between the cost of external finance and internally generated funds driven by capital market imperfections has been modeled through an increasing cost function of external debt. In addition, the oligopolistic interaction among firms

---

[9] See Section 3 for the precise definition.

has been taken into account by considering both the direct and the strategic effects of price changes on output levels.

We have discussed the implications of the model as far as the impact of capital markets imperfections on markup policies is concerned: in particular, the model suggests that, for given demand conditions, the tightness of product competition is the crucial parameter. Whereas in monopoly the firm tends to cut her price (and to lower markup) in order to relax financing constraints, in an oligopolistic setting the direct effect of a price reduction by the firm must be compared with the strategic effect due to rivals' behavior, after taking into account the degree of product differentiation. If rivals do not react or react softly to a price reduction, then firms have a greater incentive to reduce markups when financing constraints become more severe; on the contrary, if firms react aggressively the previous conclusions may even be reversed and firms may find it rational to raise prices.

The empirical results suggest that capital market imperfections are present in the sense that firms in our sample pay a premium on external finance which significantly depends on the debt to sales ratio; moreover, according to our estimates, it is optimal for constrained firms to cut their price compared to unconstrained firms. Firms associated to business groups are found to be less sensitive to the effects of capital markets imperfections, thus confirming the hypothesis that group membership relaxes financing constraints. Furthermore, whereas the premium on external finance does not depend upon general macroeconomic conditions for affiliated firms, we find that independent firms pay an higher premium in recessions than in expansions. As a consequence our estimates show that independent firms are more likely to be financially constrained in recessions and this result implies that financial market imperfections tend to make markups procyclical, at least for firms which are particularly interested by the effects of capital markets imperfections.

Finally, to get a more complete picture of the determinants of observed markup behavior, it would be informative to disentangle the role played by demand conditions and by the nature of competition in explaining the relationship between capital markets imperfections and markups. More generally, additional evidence is needed, possibly stemming from modeling jointly the pricing, output and inventory decisions of firms. These issues are next in our future research agenda.

Table 1 Characteristics of the Sample

Years of observations	Number of firms
5	121
6	78
7	87
8	78
9	55
10	37
11	34
12	25
13	16
14	22
15	14
16	5
17	27
Total number of observations: 5110	Total number of firms: 599

Table 2 Sample Descriptive Statistics

(a) Full Sample:1977-1993

Variable	Total Period 5110 Observations	Recessions 2618 Observations	Expansions 2492 Observations
PCM	0.107	0.103	0.111
	(0.082)	(0.088)	(0.075)
EMPLOYEES	1134	1054	1217
	(4427)	(4613)	(4222)
SALES	169557	165388	173937
	(510716)	(416898)	(593571)
DEBT	34307	35191	33379
	(111620)	(103735)	(119357)
LEVERAGE	0.227	0.242	0.212
	(0.236)	(0.239)	(0.233)

(b)   Estimation Sample:1981-1993

Variable	Total Period	Recessions	Expansions
	2714 Observations	1549 Observations	1165 Observations
PCM	0.105	0.099	0.113
	(0.078)	(0.079)	(0.076)
EMPLOYEES	1076	866	1356
	(3299)	(1656.)	(4648)
SALES	207335	193054	226352
	(571820)	(381295)	(753982)
DEBT	37603	37767	37517
	(93647)	(63927)	(122535)
LEVERAGE	0.217	0.236	0.192
	(0.218)	(0.242)	(0.178)

Note to the table: Average values. Standard deviations in parenthesis.

Table 3 Estimates of the Markup Equation with Constant Returns to Scale and Cyclical Effects. - Independent and Affiliated Firms

Variable	Coefficient	Variable	Coefficient
$\gamma_1$aff	-0.0069	$\gamma_1$aff-rec	-0.0048
	(0.0002)		(0.0004)
$\gamma_1$ind	0.0106	$\gamma_1$ind -rec	0.0272
	(0.0028)		(0.006)
$\gamma_2$aff	0.0022	$\gamma_2$aff -rec	-0.0628
	(0.0018)		(0.0041)
$\gamma_2$ind	0.0697	$\gamma_2$ind -rec	0.1304
	(0.0323)		(0.0592)
$\gamma_3$aff	-0.1472	$\gamma_3$aff-rec	-0.1921
	(0.0026)		(0.0042)
$\gamma_3$ind	-1.3051	$\gamma_3$ind-rec	-0.9817
	(0.1857)		(0.2074)
		$\gamma_1$aff-exp	-0.0083
			(0.0006)
		$\gamma_1$ind-exp	-0.0198
			(0.0109)
		$\gamma_2$aff-exp	0.0652
			(0.0028)
		$\gamma_2$ind-exp	0.0546
			(0.0058)
		$\gamma_3$aff-exp	-0.1809
			(0.0053)
		$\gamma_3$ind-exp	-0.4603
			(0.2288)
W_1	4882.44 [6]	W_1	7409.07 [12]
Sargan	108.99 [98]	Sargan	103.62 [92]
m_2	0.135	m_2	0.321

Notes to the table:

Equation [4] in the main text. Dependent variable: PCM. (ii) Sample period: 1981-1993. Number of firms: 599. Number of observations: 2,714. (iii) Asymptotic robust standard errors in parenthesis and degrees of freedom in square brackets. (iv) W_1 is a Wald Test of joint significance of the regressors, asymptotically distributed as χ^2. (v) Sargan is a test of correlation among instruments and residuals, asymptotically distributed as χ^2. (vi) m_2 is a test for second order autocorrelation, asymptotically distributed as $N(0,1)$. (vii) Instruments used are a constant and the two regressors of equation [4] in the text, both dated (t-3)and earlier.

REFERENCES

Arellano M., Bond S.(1991), *"Some Tests of Specification for Panel Data: Monte Carlo Evidence and an Application to Employment Equations"*, Review of Economic Studies, 58, pp. 277-297.

Bernanke B., Gertler M., Gilchrist S. (1996), *"The Financial Accelerator and the Flight to Quality"*, Review of Economics and Statistics, LXXVIII, pp. 1-15.

Bils M. (1989), *"Pricing in a Customer Market"*, Quarterly Journal of Economics, 104, pp. 699-718.

Bond S., Meghir C. (1994*), "Dynamic Investment Models and the Firm's Financial Policy."*, The Review of Economic Studies, 61, pp. 197-222.

Bottasso A., Galeotti M., Sembenelli A. (1997) *"The Impact of Financing Constraints on Markups: Theory and Evidence form Italian Firm Level Data"*, Fondazione Eni Enrico Mattei, Nota di Lavoro N. 73.97.

Chevalier J.A. (1995), *"Do LBO Supermarket Charge More: An Empirical Analysis of the Effects of LBOs on Supermarket Pricing"*, Journal of Finance, 50, pp. 1095-1112.

Chevalier J.A., Scharfstein D.S. (1995), *"Liquidity Constraints and the Cyclical Behavior of Markups"*, American Economic Review Papers and Proceedings, 85, pp. 390-396.

Chevalier J.A., Scharfstein D.S (1996), *"Capital-Market Imperfections and Countercyclical Markups: Theory and Evidence"*, American Economic Review, 86, pp. 703-725.

Chirinko R., Schaller H. (1995), *"Why Does Liquidity Matter in Investment Equations?"*, Journal of Money Credit and Banking 27, pp. 527-548.

Davies S.W., Lyons B.R. (eds.) (1996*), Industrial Organization in the EU*, Oxford: Oxford University Press.

Galeotti M., Schiantarelli F. (1994), *"The Cyclicality of Markups in a Model with Adjustment Costs: Econometric Evidence for U.S. Industry"*, forthcoming Oxford Bulletin of Economics and Statistics.

Gottfries N. (1991), *"Customer Markets, Credit Market Imperfections and Real Price Rigidity."*, Economica, 58, pp. 317-323.

Greenwald B., Stiglitz J.E., Weiss A. (1984), *"Informational Imperfections in the Capital Markets and Macroeconomic Fluctuations."*, American Economic Review, 74, pp. 194-199.

Hendel I. (1996), *"Competition Under Financial Distress"*, Journal of Industrial Economics, 44, pp. 309-324.

Hoshi T., Kashyap A., Scharfstein D. (1991), *"Corporate Structure, Liquidity and Investment: Evidence From Japanese Industrial Groups."*, Quarterly Journal of Economics 106, pp. 33-60.

Klemperer P. (1987), *"Markets with Consumer Switching Costs"*, Quarterly Journal of Economics, 102, pp. 375-394.

Klemperer P. (1995), *"Competition when consumers Have Switching Costs: An Overview with Applications to Industrial Organization, Macroeconomics and International Trade"*, Review of Economic Studies, 62, pp. 515-539.

Margon D., Sembenelli A., Vannoni D. (1995), *"Panel Ceris su Dati di Impresa: Aspetti Metodologici e istruzioni per l'uso"*, CERIS-CNR, Working Paper.

Phillips G.M. (1996), *"Increased Debt and Industry Product Markets: An Empirical Analysis"*, Journal of Financial Economics, 37, pp. 189-238.

Schiantarelli F., Sembenelli A. (1996), *"Form of Ownership and Financial Constraints: Panel Data Evidence From Leverage and Investment Equations."*, Policy Research Working Paper, The World Bank, n. 1629.

Schlitzer G. (1993), *"Nuovi Strumenti per la Valutazione e la Previsione del Ciclo Economico in Italia"*, Banca d'Italia, Temi di discussione, N.200.

Sembenelli A. (1996), *"Price over Marginal Cost and the Business Cycle: Evidence from Italian Firm Level Data"*, Discussion Paper N.9603, University of East Anglia.

Sutton J. (1991), *Sunk Costs and Market Structure*, Cambridge: MIT Press.

MEASURING THE DURATION OF ITALIAN ENTERPRISES ON THE EUROPEAN MARKET (1997)

Luigi Pompeo Marasco

Istituto Nazionale di Statistica

1 Introduction[1]

Given the demand globalisation, market segmentation and international competition, enterprises must be better equipped to manage their own evolutionary process in the export sector which is itself constantly changing. In the specific case of the European market, it is no longer enough simply to know the values of dispatches (exports) for the time has now come to familiarize also with the seasonal behaviour patterns of market leaders in partner countries.

The integration and economic cohesion of the Italian production system within the European Union (EU) both require special capacities and commitment on the part of companies based in Italy and of national structures providing public support for internationalisation: the business world and public structures alike both orientated specifically to small-scale enterprise. Owing to fewer financial resources, this category is excluded from internationalisation which, as we know, incentivates innovation processes for a greater efficiency and competitiveness (Mariotti S., Mutinelli M., 1994, page 153).

From an analysis which was limited to real services promoting the structural competitiveness of businesses by boosting foreign sales and stabilising earnings through time, Italy has been found to present a scattering of foreign trade skills. But there are also numerous overlaps in the supply of services whose performance is never assessed. Moreover, export system services supplied by the Italian National Institute for Foreign Trade (Italian Trade Commission-Government Agency), are designed to foster the market stability of businesses which have already been exporting on a continuous basis for some time. The reason for this orientation is that the Institute's resources allow it to disburse services only when a return in development value is predictable or to defend existing export quotas (Norcio G., 1992, page 112). The result is that a statistic indicator is required to evaluate enterprise growth on foreign markets and in the Union market in particular.

---

[1] We wish to thank Francesca Nugnes (ISTAT) for assistance and for presenting the results of this study at CAED'97, "International Conference on Comparative Analysis of Enterprise (micro) Data" Bergamo, Italy, 15-17 December 1997.

This indicator is a measure of market duration and can be applied at a micro and macro level. At a micro level the indicator allows the enterprises to locate its position in the market with respect to other enterprises (in the same and in other countries or sectors). At a macro level the indicator allows to assess the effectiveness of public intervention in support of exporters.

The aim of this study is to measure the average permanence of Italian export enterprises of EU markets as well as their average earnings. The target is to establish a threshold both in terms of export earnings and market duration to distinguish between occasional business and companies with a more permanent position on the markets of their partner countries that may therefore be considered to be integrated within the single market. This threshold could also be an indicator of the effectiveness of public and/or private intervention in support of exports both at the general level of the national and sector economic system and at the level of single business.

2 Source of statistical information

The data used in this research derive from information on exchanges of goods among EU Member States collected by the INTRASTAT permanent system installed since the removal of customs barriers in Member States on January 1, 1993.

The new surveying system (INTRASTAT), common to all EU countries, envisages that the companies resident on Member territory and identifiable by their Value Added Tax (VAT) numbers, provide the statistical information on their inter-Union trade flows. As a source of information, this system replaces the data obtained from customs papers that accompanied goods from one Member State to another.

The new data collection system was incorporated within Italian legislation summarized with the proviso that VAT-liable operators present to the national customs offices periodical summarized lists of goods exchanged with other VAT subjects resident in other EU States. Specifically in the interests of establishing this indicator, the present study examines operators who totalled over Lit. 150 million in intra-Union dispatches (exports) in a solar year or who presume to do so in the current year. These operators are required to present their summary lists of exports on a monthly basis.

The study does not consider operators who have totalled or expect to total less than the above sum in exports since the lists they are required to present do not indicate the exact month of transaction.

The data refer to each month of 1996.

Each business with an annual export turnover of over Lit. 150 million was identified by its VAT number and, throughout 1996, its activity in relation to the

European single market was monitored. The resulting information was therefore an indication of its market duration.

3 The duration of businesses on the EU market

Italian exports flow mainly towards the 14 EU Members as opposed to other non-EU countries. In fact, 55.3 per cent of the overall 1996 Free On Board (FOB) value, equal to Lit. 386,947 billion, derives from the Union market. Specifically, exports to EU countries by companies resident in Italy and obliged to monthly trade declarations totalled Lit. 210,313 billion. This was the performance of a total of 51,987 businesses.

The values of monthly exports to EU countries reflect an intense flow of new businesses on to the market, countered by an equally intense process of elimination (Marasco L. P., 1996 a page 154).

If the market duration of each business is equal to the number of months in 1996 when it conducted at least one export operation, the resulting data are referred to a closed number of businesses; this, since other companies would be unable to penetrate in the course of that particular year and those already eliminated in a certain month would be unable to re-enter successively that same year.

Thus, the number of exporters - 51,987 businesses - may be analysed as a global unit in the same way as populations. The global unit remains valid as a point of reference until each of its elements stops exporting for any reason.

By monitoring each business-element from the month it started exporting until the end of the year and then summing up the number of months when it carried out export operations, we obtained the corporate distribution value, as shown in table 1, referred to duration on the Union market. This value is expressed in number of months for each company's market sector under study.

Table 1 Exporters by Sector and Duration on the EU Market (Year 1996)

Duration (months)	Agriculture, forestry and fishing products	Energy products	Ferrous, non-ferrous minerals	Minerals, non-metallic products	Chemical products	Engineering products	Transport facilities	Food, beverages, tobacco	Textiles, leather, clothing	Wood, paper, rubber, other manufactured products	Total
1	219	5	81	93	153	910	302	159	430	467	2,819
2	183	3	54	79	105	574	179	109	319	305	1,910
3	220	4	47	46	90	518	154	105	305	270	1,759
4	197	3	41	73	90	605	124	88	385	290	1,896
5	180	1	41	88	67	579	106	81	373	285	1,801
6	147	3	40	81	96	594	106	85	484	296	1,932
7	187	3	40	118	102	708	123	103	576	329	2,289
8	182	1	48	133	128	832	117	118	772	418	2,749
9	188	1	77	180	162	1,342	141	136	933	656	3,816
10	241	4	134	316	192	1,851	221	193	1,224	884	5,260
11	341	7	182	499	373	3,508	363	338	1,773	1,715	9,099
12	655	14	319	919	781	5,848	630	914	3,619	2,958	16,657
TOTAL	2,940	49	1,104	2,625	2,339	17,869	2,566	2,429	11,193	8,873	51,987

Source: ISTAT data analysis.

The table shows that just 5.4 per cent of export enterprises may be considered occasional in that they were present on the market for only one month of the year. Less than a quarter of the annual contingent of exports (23.3 per cent) exhausted their exports in the first six months. For this reason, they fell within the category of occasionals on the Union market and owing to the seasonal nature of the products they were trading. Lastly, 32 per cent of the entire contingent of businesses was present on the market on a stable basis having carried out an export operation every month of the year.

The average duration by sector, as per table 2, shows that the building materials sector, or minerals and non-metallic products, carried out export operations more often in the course of the year, for a mean duration of 9.4 months. These were followed by businesses in Italy's traditional export sectors: engineering products, textiles, leather and clothing, wood, paper, rubber and other unspecified manufactured products (9.1 months). Companies exporting products in the agriculture, forestry and fishing sector recorded a 7.5 month duration on the Union market, justified by the marked seasonal nature of its trade. In the same way, the average 7.6-month duration of transport facility producers could be attributed to the crisis in this sector in 1996.

Overall, the average EU market performance of companies resident in Italy can be satisfactory as it is protracted for three-quarters of the year, a wider period if compared with less than, six-month duration in non-EU markets (Marasco L.P., 1997 a).

Table 2 Average Duration of Businesses on the EU Market

Trade Sectors	Average number of months
01 – Agriculture, forestry and fishing products	7.5
02 – Energy products	7.7
03 – Ferrous, non-ferrous minerals	8.5
04 – Minerals, non-metallic products	9.4
05 – Chemical products	8.7
06 – Engineering products	9.1
07 – Transport facilities	7.6
08 – Food, beverages, tobacco	8.8
09 – Textiles, leather, clothing	9.1
10 – Wood, paper, rubber, other manufactured products	9.1
TOTAL	**8.9**

Considering the whole contingent of businesses at the beginning of the first month in 1996 and subtracting the companies which exhaust their exports, the progressive extinction of the contingent can be noted in the protraction of duration on the market until its exhaustion at the end of the 12th month.

The number of surviving businesses of increasing duration is shown in table 3, whose relative frequencies are but the empirical expressions of their probabilities of survival. The survival curve shows some irregularities owing to inevitable gaps between empirical frequencies and respective probabilities of survival.

Table 3 Surviving Exporters by Sector and Duration on the EU Market (Year 1996)

Duration (months)	Agriculture, forestry and fishing products	Energy products	Ferrous, non-ferrous minerals	Minerals, non-metallic products	Trade Sectors Chemical products	Engineering products	Transport facilities	Food, beverages, tobacco	Textiles, leather, clothing	Wood, paper, rubber, other manufactured products	Total
1	2,940	49	1,104	2,625	2,339	17,869	2,566	2,429	11,193	8,873	51,987
2	2,721	44	1,023	2,532	2,186	16,959	2,264	2,270	10,763	8,406	49,168
3	2,538	41	969	2,453	2,081	16,385	2,085	2,161	10,444	8,101	47,258
4	2,318	37	922	2,407	1,991	15,867	1,931	2,056	10,139	7,831	45,499
5	2,121	34	881	2,334	1,901	15,262	1,807	1,968	9,754	7,541	43,603
6	1,941	33	840	2,246	1,834	14,683	1,701	1,887	9,381	7,256	41,802
7	1,794	30	800	2,165	1,738	14,089	1,595	1,802	8,897	6,960	39,870
8	1,607	27	760	2,047	1,636	13,381	1,472	1,699	8,321	6,631	37,581
9	1,425	26	712	1,914	1,508	12,549	1,355	1,581	7,549	6,213	34,832
10	1,237	25	635	1,734	1,346	11,207	1,214	1,445	6,616	5,557	31,016
11	996	21	501	1,418	1,154	9,356	993	1,252	5,392	4,673	25,756
12	655	14	319	919	781	5,848	630	914	3,619	2,958	16,657

Source: ISTAT data analysis.

To eliminate these irregularities in frequencies, we interpolated the succession of observed duration with the following function of survival or market duration:

$$I_d = \frac{(12-d)k}{(12-d)k+d} \qquad \text{for } k > 0 \qquad\qquad [1]$$

which is a transformation of the proposal by de Moivre for the population, when $k=1$ (Pitacco E., 1989, page 35);

where:

d is the duration of the business on the market in the course   of the year which can vary from one to 12 months;

12 is the maximum duration on the market, beyond which the initial contingent is taken as extinguished;

k is the parameter to be estimated.

The function of the temporal-interval 0-12 is descending and assumes its maximum value at the start of the first month of duration for the entire contingent of exporters, while it is annulled when $d=12$, by the end of the company's 12th month of duration on the market.

In the hypothesis that elimination from the market comes about in a linear sequence in proportion to the company's market duration, the function of survival would be the diagonal *CA* in the graph. The function would diverge from the diagonal according to the higher or lower number of businesses exiting the market after a few months of duration.

The survival function in the first case will be convex *(0<k<1)*, and concave in the second case *(k>1)* towards the origin of the Cartesian axis (Graph 1).

If, on the other hand, the global contingent of businesses were all permanently on the market throughout the year, the function of survival would coincide with the CB segment parallel to the axis of duration and at a distance from it in proportion to the overall number of companies in the contingent, thus $k \rightarrow \infty$.

The values of the parameter k obtained, each for every trade sector to which the business belongs, through the interpolation (with the method of least squares) of the relative frequencies observed to the various periods of market duration, and the theoretical function of survival are reported in Table 4. This table also indicates the respective survival functions indices of conformity[2] with the frequencies observed (Giusti F., 1990, page 339).

---

[2] The calculated conformity index is that of Pizzetti-Pearson:

$$x^2 = \sum_{d=1}^{12} \frac{(I_d - F_d)^2}{I_d}$$

From the results obtained for the parameter k, emerges that it assumes value greater than 1 for all the trade sectors under study. Therefore, the respective market duration curves are concave. On non-EU markets for 1995, the respective curves are convex (Marasco L.P., 1997 a).

Table 4 Estimated Parameter k of Business Survival Function and the Corresponding Index of Conformity with Observed Data by Trade Sector

Trade Sectors	k	Conformity Index
01 – Agriculture, forestry and fishing products	1.6765	0.1152
02 – Energy products	1.7862	0.3442
03 – Ferrous, non-ferrous minerals	2.7150	0.1140
04 – Minerals, non-metallic products	4.7155	0.0213
05 – Chemical products	2.9977	0.1292
06 – Engineering products	3.8184	0.0540
07 – Transport facilities	1.6869	0.2434
08 – Food, beverages, tobacco	3.0706	0.1936
09 – Textiles, leather, clothing	3.8944	0.0218
10 – Wood, paper, rubber, other manufactured products	3.7500	0.0656
TOTAL	**3.3865**	**0.0681**

In the Cartestian quadrant, both the dotted survival curve and its corresponding theoretical survival curve in relation to the global unit of exporters is shown in Graph 1.

The theoretical values of market duration are shown in table 5 for each sector where the respective initial contingents were supposed equal to 1,000.

By the 12th month, agriculture, forestry and fishing, and energy products are the sectors where the initial contingent shows less probability of survival compared with other sectors. By contrast, the exporters of non-metallic products in the initial contingent record a 30 per cent duration rate by the beginning of the 12th month.

---

where I_d ed F_d are, respectively, the values of the functions of survival and frequencies at the companies' corresponding periods d of duration on the market.

From the values of the survival function in relation to the various periods of market duration, the most significant parameters of a table of elimination may be calculated, as follows:
- the probability that a business, on the market for d months, will prolong duration for another month;
- the probability that a business, with d months on the market, will not survive for another month;
- survival expectation, or the number of months that a business can hope to last on the market, after being present for d months.

Graph 1 Business Survival as Observed and in Theory Global Contingent of Exporters

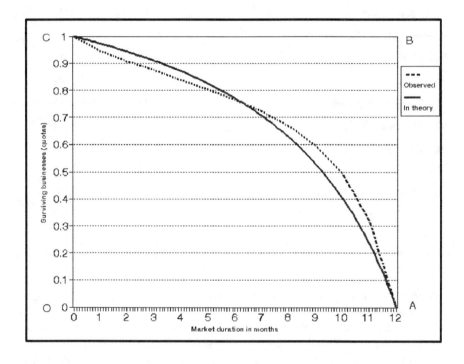

Table 5 Duration of Businesses in the EU Market by Trade Sector (Year 1996)

Trade Sectors	Market Duration (in months)											
	1	2	3	4	5	6	7	8	9	10	11	12
01 – Agriculture, forestry and fishing products	1,000	949	893	834	770	701	626	545	456	358	251	132
02 – Energy products	1,000	952	899	843	781	714	641	561	472	373	263	140
03 – Ferrous, non-ferrous minerals	1,000	968	931	891	844	792	731	660	576	475	352	198
04 – Minerals, non-metallic products	1,000	981	959	934	904	868	825	771	702	611	485	300
05 – Chemical products	1,000	971	937	900	857	808	750	682	600	500	375	214
06 – Engineering products	1,000	977	950	920	884	842	792	732	656	560	433	258
07 – Transport facilities	1,000	949	894	835	771	703	628	546	458	360	252	133
08 – Food, beverages, tobacco	1,000	971	939	902	860	811	754	687	606	506	380	218
09 – Textiles, leather, clothing	1,000	977	951	921	886	845	796	736	661	565	438	261
10 – Wood, paper, rubber, other manufactured products	1,000	976	949	918	882	840	789	728	652	556	429	254
TOTAL	1,000	974	944	910	871	826	772	708	629	530	404	235

4 The concentration of export values

The ratio between export values observed for businesses with a certain protracted duration on markets (table 6) and the corresponding number of companies (table 1) shows the distribution of average export values per business, according to their market duration (as shown in table 7).

This distribution may be considered to be representative of a transferable phenomenon, in the sense that it may be hypothesized that the monthly export values according to a company market duration are all attributable to one or just a few months and that this therefore constitutes a concentration of export values. It results that, if the average values of export earnings for each business were distributed in proportion to the company market duration, to any fraction of the year would correspond the same overall annual share of export value.

Otherwise, the following stands:

$$\frac{d}{12} \rangle V_d \qquad\qquad\qquad [2]$$

where d represents the duration of a business on the EU market (in months), and V_d the average export value per company, the latter having a d market duration.

As regards the global contingent of businesses, equal to 51,987 elements in 1996, the curve on the Cartesian quadrant of market duration and the corresponding average export values per company are shown in Graph 2.

Table 6 Export Values by Sector and Duration of Businesses in the EU Market (Year 1996) (in billions of lira)

Trade Sectors	Duration (months)												Total
	1	2	3	4	5	6	7	8	9	10	11	12	
01 – Agriculture, forestry and fishing products	41	53	131	164	168	186	275	399	373	498	1,229	,560	7,077
02 – Energy products	5	1	4	2	2	1	11	1	2	5	299	829	1,162
03 – Ferrous, non-ferrous minerals	37	48	29	17	97	133	109	330	363	1,797	1,135	,345	9,440
04 – Minerals, non-metallic products	7	9	8	18	32	98	149	114	412	729	1,446	,914	7,936
05 – Chemical products	34	19	62	40	157	190	87	556	411	1,046	2,251	12,378	17,231
06 – Engineering products	149	140	228	490	393	798	747	1,192	3,010	5,805	9,900	48,212	71,064
07 – Transport facilities	147	102	85	126	99	141	379	328	405	777	2,075	19,221	23,885
08 – Food, beverages, tobacco	16	24	54	60	65	79	161	191	305	459	1,230	7,467	10,111
09 – Textiles, leather, clothing	26	53	123	144	192	302	506	890	1,748	2,812	4,512	23,500	34,808
10 – Wood, paper, rubber, other manufactured products	32	64	64	182	192	170	321	465	1,005	1,900	3,814	19,390	27,599
TOTAL	494	513	788	1,243	1,397	2,098	2,745	4,466	8,034	15,828	27,891	144,816	210,313

Source: ISTAT data analysis.

Table 7 Average Export Values per Business by Sector and Duration in the EU Market (Year 1996) (in millions of lira)

Trade Sectors	Duration (months)												Total
	1	2	3	4	5	6	7	8	9	10	11	12	
01 – Agriculture, forestry and fishing products	187.2	289.6	595.5	832.5	933.3	1,265.3	1,470.6	2,192.3	1,984.0	2,066.4	3,604.1	5,435.1	2,407.1
02 – Energy products	1,000.0	333.3	1,000.0	666.7	2,000.0	333.3	3,666.7	1,000.0	2,000.0	1,250.0	42,714.3	59,214.3	23,714.3
03 – Ferrous, non-ferrous minerals	456.8	888.9	617.0	414.6	2,365.9	3,325.0	2,725.0	6,875.0	4,714.3	13,410.4	6,236.3	16,755.5	8,550.7
04 – Minerals, non-metallic products	75.3	113.9	173.9	246.6	363.6	1,209.9	1,262.7	857.1	2,288.9	2,307.0	2,897.8	5,347.1	3,023.2
05 – Chemical products	222.2	181.0	688.9	444.4	2,343.3	1,979.2	852.9	4,343.8	2,537.0	5,447.9	6,034.9	15,848.9	7,366.8
06 – Engineering products	163.7	243.9	440.2	809.9	678.8	1,343.4	1,055.1	1,432.7	2,242.9	3,136.1	2,822.1	8,244.2	3,976.9
07 – Transport facilities	486.8	569.8	551.9	1,016.1	934.0	1,330.2	3,081.3	2,803.4	2,872.3	3,515.8	5,716.3	30,509.5	9,308.3
08 – Food, beverages, tobacco	100.6	220.2	514.3	681.8	802.5	929.4	1,563.1	1,618.6	2,242.6	2,378.2	3,639.1	8,169.6	4,162.6
09 – Textiles, leather, clothing	60.5	166.1	403.3	374.0	514.7	624.0	878.5	1,152.8	1,873.5	2,297.4	2,544.8	6,493.5	3,109.8
10 – Wood, paper, rubber, other manufactured	68.5	209.8	237.0	627.6	673.7	574.3	975.7	1,112.4	1,532.0	2,149.3	2,223.9	6,555.1	3,110.4
TOTAL	175.2	268.6	448.0	655.6	775.7	1,085.9	1,199.2	1,624.6	2,105.3	3,009.1	3,065.3	8,694.0	4,045.5

Source: ISTAT data analysis.

Graph 2 Concentration as Observed and in Theory Global Exporters Contingent

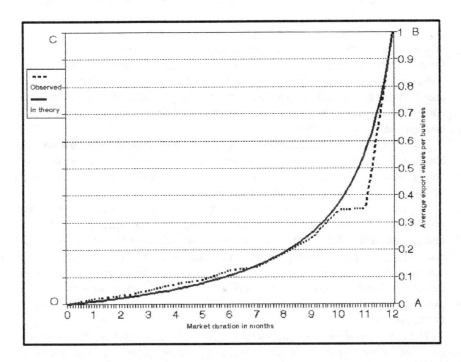

This shows both the dotted curve joining the ordinate points representing the average export values per company as observed depending on companies various periods of market duration, in abscissa axis , and the interjecting curve of concentration.

The interjecting curve is represented by the following equation:

$$V_d = \frac{hd}{hd+(12-d)}$$

[3]

where:

d is the market duration in months of businesses;

12   is the market duration ceiling of businesses throughout the year;

h is the parameter to be estimated.

The concentration function [3] varies from zero at the beginning of the year, that is when *d=0*, to one at the end of the 12th month, when *d=12*.

If export earnings per business were in linear proportion to market duration, function [3] would coincide with the OB diagonal; but if earnings per business were constant depending on the various market durations, the concentration curve would become the CB segment, parallel to the abscissa axis and at a distance in proportion to the average export value per company; this results from the overall annual export value and the overall number of exporters in the year.

The maximum concentration would be when the curve coincides with the horizontal OA and vertical line AB of triangle OAB, that is, when there have been no exports during 11 months of the year and the overall export value is concentrated in one month only.

Pratically, the concentration curve proves always to be convex towards the abscissa axis since successive equal increases of businesses market duration correspond to growing increases in average export value per company; this, because duration is a non-descending succession.

For each trade sector, table 8 shows the estimates of parameter h of the concentration curve obtained with the method of least squares and by the interjection of the dotted curve of average export values per company observed, according to various periods of market duration with the function [3] of concentration; this, after relating the average export values observed for each business, depending on the various periods of market duration, with the average export values of companies permanently in operation on the market throughout the whole year.

The table also shows the indices of proximity (note 1) between the theoretical data and those observed. In addition, these indices allow the conformity of equation [3] - formed out of theoretical considerations - with the data observed.

The estimates of parameter h show less concentration in agriculture, forestry and fishing though this is countered by a marked concentration in energy products followed by transport facilities.

Table 8 Estimated Parameter h of Business Concentration and the Corresponding Index of Conformity with Observed Data by Trade Sector

Trade Sectors	h	Conformity Index
01 – Agriculture, forestry and fishing products	0.2597	0.1266
02 – Energy products	0.0352	0.9818
03 – Ferrous, non-ferrous minerals	0.1971	0.4993
04 – Minerals, non-metallic products	0.1572	0.1823
05 – Chemical products	0.1061	0.2863
06 – Engineering products	0.1275	0.1655
07 – Transport facilities	0.0475	0.1788
08 – Food, beverages, tobacco	0.1295	0.0925
09 – Textiles, leather, clothing	0.1133	0.0727
10 – Wood, paper, rubber, other manufactured products	0.1114	0.1399
TOTAL	**0.1182**	**0.1115**

5 Estimate of the minimum market duration threshold

The most recent studies on the dynamics of small and medium-scale enterprise in the internal market point to a minimum survival threshold, expressed in terms of personnel on the basis of survival in years of the business.

In this study, by contrast, the companies under examination are exporters to the EU market in 1996 with reference both to their average export earnings and to their corresponding period of duration. These two elements were used to identify the demarcation threshold between businesses with occasional or periodical export activities and those operating in continuity.

All the businesses above this threshold may be considered to be solidly introduced to the common market.

For these businesses, market entry and elimination flows may be presumed to be less than those below the threshold.

In other words, the whole of Italian exporters may be said to fall into two corporate categories: core export businesses whose activities are an integral part of their corporate strategies and so they are above the threshold; businesses registering high birth and death rates on the common market denoting occasional export activity and, therefore, a position under the threshold.

To identify the demarcation threshold between occasional exports and stable exports to the EU markets, the survival function [1] and the concentration function [3] are both used for each trade sector. The point of intersection between the two functions shows the coordinates of the demarcation threshold on the orthogonal quadrant. This point may be defined OCSARAM'S point, following the name of the author.

In the event that the two functions (of survival and concentration) prove directly proportional to a company's period of market duration, they should become linear and would coincide with the two diagonals of the orthogonal quadrant in a graph. In this case, their point of intersection would be identified in correspondence with the sixth month of market duration, with an average export value per business of half that registered in the whole year for stable exports. This means that with a market duration of six months and a certain level of export earnings, the company has the same probability to remain on the market or to be excluded from it.

If average export earnings per company were in linear proportion to the company market duration, the threshold abscissa would lie before the six months, the curve of duration being convex while it becomes concave for those over six months. If the survival of businesses were in linear proportion to their market duration, the threshold abscissa would go beyond the six months in function of the degree of concentration of average export values.

But in general, the threshold abscissa represents the market duration of a business, that is the maximum protraction in months to realise the export earnings indicated by the ordinate, thus:

$$d = \frac{12\sqrt{\frac{k}{h}}}{1+\sqrt{\frac{k}{h}}} \qquad\qquad [4]$$

where:

k is the estimated parameter of a company survival on the market;

h is the estimated parameter of the function of concentration of average export values per companies.

The threshold ordinate, that is the average export value per business beyond which the company may consider itself a stable factor on the Union market, is given by:

$$V = \frac{1}{1+\sqrt{\frac{1}{kh}}} \qquad\qquad [5]$$

where k and h are the estimates of the parameters of the two analytical functions in question.

Since the ordinate of the point of intersection of the two curves is expressed in relative terms with reference to the observed value of the businesses operating in continuity on the market, it must be translated into an absolute value per business by multiplying it by the corresponding average value per business, observed to have a duration of 12 months on the market.

For the whole contingent of businesses - 51,987 - Graph 3 shows both their survival and concentration functions throughout the year. The result is that their point of intersection indicates average annual export earnings of Lit. 3,369 billion which may be realised in little over ten months of exporting that need not be continuous.

The businesses to the left of the demarcation threshold, and whose survival values are higher than corresponding concentration values, are presumably characterised by a more notable market mobility; those to the right of the threshold are more likely to occupy a permanent market position since they present higher concentration values than market survival rates.

Graph 3 Demarcation Threshold Global Exporters Contingent

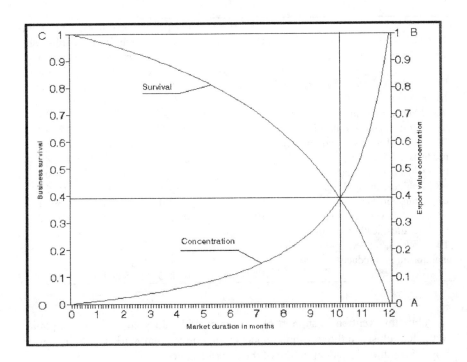

The ratio between concentration values, corrisponding to the various periods of market duration, and respective survival values may be assumed to be a measure of the risk of elimination from the Union market. It assumes a unitary value when the company's probability of survival is equal to that of elimination, and higher values than 1 when the business has surpassed the critical threshold point.

The results obtained for the threshold by sector shown in table 9 indicate that, in the course of 1996, the businesses present a very similar market duration, ranging from 8.6 to 10.5 months, independently of their trade sector. Therefore, the problems that the businesses must face are more dimensional in nature in terms of export earnings which differ according to the company's trade sector.

The sector of agriculture, forestry and fishing products present a lower export value (Lit. 216 million) than other sectors, one reason being the seasonal nature of its products and, therefore, its limited marketing period in the year. In order to out-do competition both at home and abroad, energy sector businesses should register a 10.5-month duration on the market with at least one export operation a month and with a total turnover of about Lit. 12 billion.

Table. 9 Market Duration and the Average Export Values of the Demarcation Threshold per Business

Trade Sectors	Duration (d)	% max	Average value per business (in millions of lira)	
			Observed values d=12	Estimated duration values d
01 – Agriculture, forestry and fishing products	8.6 10.5	0.3975 0.2006	5,435.1 59,214.3	2,160.5 11,878.4
02 – Energy products	9.5	0.4224	16,755.5	7,077.5
03 – Ferrous, non-ferrous minerals	10.1	0.4627	5,347.1	2,474.1
04 – Minerals, non-metallic products	10.1 10.1	0.3606 0.4110	15,848.9 8,244.2	5,715.1 3,388.4
05 – Chemical products	10.3	0.2206	30,509.5	6,730.4
06 – Engineering products	10.0	0.3867	8,169.6	3,159.2
07 – Transport facilities	10.3	0.3991	6,493.5	2,591.6
08 – Food, beverages, tobacco	10.2	0.3926	6,555.1	2,573.5
09 – Textiles, leather, clothing				
10 – Wood, paper, rubber, other manufactured products				
TOTAL	10.1	0.3875	8,694.0	3,368.9

Public intervention in support of exports could be directed to these companies to the left, closer to the threshold, so as to guarantee them market stability and to improve on the occasional nature of their performance.

It must also be said that the threshold established through time may be assumed to be a measure of the results of export support, both public and private, in the close framework of Union economic policy and its Member States' national industry policies.

The threshold, limited in this study to just one year with reference to EU Member States as a whole, may also be established for each single country.

It could be established for smaller national territories (regions and provinces) to measure each of these areas development through time in terms of EU market penetration. It may also be used in space analysis.

Moreover, the threshold could be calculated for partner countries if basic data are available; this, to measure the gap separating them from Italian exporters, with reference both to export activities as a whole, to sector and to individual product.

The threshold would thus become an additional means of diagnosis facilitating companies resident in Italy in their international marketing mixes.

6 Conclusions

By means of current statistics on intra-Union trade (INTRASTAT), this study has managed to construct an indicator, for the first time, to measure the degree of penetration of the Italian enterprises system on the European common market; this, on the basis of the coordinates of the demarcation threshold distinguishing the occasional and continuous natures of business performance, these coordinates having been obtained by considering the market duration of a business and its corresponding average export value.

The indicator could prove useful to businesses in order to allow them to:
– know their own position on the Union market with respect to other businesses at home in the same sector;
– know which are the parameters of reference in order to compete with businesses at home which are already well established in the market and which have achieved a position of continuity;
– orientate their international marketing strategies according to the positions both of Italian and foreign competitors.

Moreover, the threshold coordinates may be deployed by public and private bodies to select businesses eligible for export support services. This would optimise the use of financial resources available, and would represent a measure of the effectiveness of interventions.

Since the indicator was calculated for 1996 only, it remains to observe if the analytical functions interjecting with observed data stands the test of time.

Nevertheless OCSARAM'S point remains a notable point of reference for further studies and analyses of the Union market in a situation of:
– EU integration and economic cohesion;
– development of newly industrialised countries, which are our competitors and especially in so-called "traditional" or labour-intensive sectors;

– a potential apportioning of the world market between the United States and Japan.

REFERENCES

Biffignandi S., Martini M. (a cura di) (1995), *Il registro statistico europeo delle imprese. Esperienze e metodi per la sua costruzione in Italia*, Franco Angeli, Milano.

Carboni O.A. (1995), *"Le piccole e medie imprese di fronte al nuovo scenario economico mondiale: i problemi dell'internazionalizzazione"*, in Studi di Economia e Diritto, n. 1, Sassari, 129-151.

Contini B., Revelli R. (1986), *"Natalità e mortalità delle imprese italiane: risultati preliminari e nuove prospettive di ricerca"*, in L'industria, anno VII, n. 2, Bologna, 195-232.

Del Chiaro A. (1958), *Tavole di eliminazione*, Edizione Scientifiche Einaudi, Torino.

EUROSTAT (1981), *Sistema Europeo di Conti Economici Integrati SEC*, seconda edizione, Lussemburgo.

Gerbi Sethi M. (a cura di), (1992), *Internazionalizzazione incompiuta: la frequenza ad esportare, esportatrici occasionali, saltuarie, imprese che hanno smesso di esportare, imprese che hanno iniziato ad esportare*, Quaderni CERIS, CNR, n. 2, Torino.

Giusti F. (1990), *Introduzione alla statistica*, Loescher Editore, Torino.

ICE (1996), *Rapporto sul Commercio con l'estero 1995*, Roma.

ISTAT (1996 a), *Statistica del commercio con l'estero, gennaio-dicembre 1994*, anno 60, serie VI, n. 4, Roma.

ISTAT (1996 b), *Bollettino mensile di statistica*, giugno, Roma.

Garofoli G. (a cura di) (1994), *Formazione di nuove imprese: un'analisi comparata a livello internazionale*, Franco Angeli, Milano.

Marasco L. P. (1996 a), *"Struttura e dinamica delle imprese esportatrici nel mercato unico europeo"*, Quaderni di Ricerca, ISTAT, nuova serie, n. 4, 131-198.

Marasco L. P. (1996 b), *"Le imprese italiane nel Mercato Unico Europeo"*, Quintano C. (a cura di) Quaderni di discussione 11, Scritti di Statistica Economica 2, Istituto Universitario Navale, Napoli, 369-389.

Marasco L. P. (1996 c), *"Le esportazioni delle imprese italiane a livello territoriale: continuità e permanenza sull'estero".* Alcune considerazioni derivanti da una analisi statistica. Istituto Guglielmo Tagliacarne, Working Paper 10.97, Roma.

Marasco L. P. (1997 a), *"Mobilità delle imprese esportatrici italiane nei mercati esteri: un modello teorico e verifiche empiriche"*, Società Geografica Italiana, Roma.

Marasco L. P. (1997 b), *"L'integrazione e la penetrazione delle imprese italiane nel mercato unico europeo"*, in Economia & Lavoro Anno XXXI, Gennaio-Giugno 1997, 1-2, Roma, 97-110.

Mariotti S., Mutinelli M. (1994), *"Tecnologia ed internazionalizzazione produttiva. La posizione dell'Italia"*, in CNR, Atti del Convegno: I processi di internazionalizzazione dell'economia italiana, PF: Servizi e Strutture per l'internazionalizzazione delle imprese italiane e sviluppo delle esportazioni, (Roma, 24 marzo 1994), Roma, 153-185.

Norcio G. (1992), *"Intervento"* in CNR Atti del convegno I servizi informativi per l'internazionalizzazione delle imprese, PF: Servizi e Strutture per l'internazionalizzazione delle imprese italiane e sviluppo delle esportazioni, (Roma, 25 novembre 1992), Roma, 111-112.

Piergiovanni R., Santarelli E. (1993), *"Determinanti della formazione di imprese nei servizi alla produzione in Italia"*, in Moneta e Credito, n. 182, Roma, 259-280.

Piergiovanni R., Santarelli E. (1994), *"La demografia d'impresa nel comparto dei servizi alla produzione in Italia. Un'analisi territoriale"*, in Note Economiche Anno XXIV, n. 1, Siena, 110-136.

Pitacco E. (1989), *Lezioni di tecnica attuariale delle assicurazioni libere sulla vita*, LINT, Trieste.

Santarelli E., Sterlacchini A. (1993), *"Profili determinanti settoriali della formazione di nuove imprese nell'industria italiana"*, in Rivista di Politica Economica, Anno LXXXIII, Serie III, fascicolo V, Roma, 33-68.

Santarelli E. (1995), *"Sopravvivenza e crescita delle nuove imprese nei distretti industriali. Il settore turistico nel medio Adriatico"*, in L'industria, anno XVI, n. 2, Bologna, 349-362.

Solinas G. (1995), *"Mortalità e sopravvivenza delle piccole imprese"*, in Economia e Politica Industriale, nuova serie, n. 86 Franco Angeli, Milano, 147-178.

Vivarelli M. (1991*)*, *"Natalità e mortalità delle piccole imprese: un modello interpretativo"*, in L'Industria, anno XII, n. 3, Bologna, 467-481.

Vivarelli M. (1994), *La nascita delle imprese in Italia. Teorie e verifiche empiriche*, Egea-Università Bocconi, Milano.

TREND OF THE TOURIST FLOWS IN ITALIAN HOTELS: A MICROECONOMIC ANALYSIS DURING THE PERIOD 1990-95[1]

Roberto Gismondi[1] and Anna Pia Maria Mirto[2]

[1,2]ISTAT (Istituto Nazionale di Statistica) – Italy

1 A general overview about the tourist flows during the period 1990-95

The Italian Statistical Institute (ISTAT) carries on every month an exhaustive survey about the number of arrivals and nights spent in the receptive accommodations, distinguished by hotels and similar establishments and other collective accommodations. The main variables investigated refer to the nationality of the clients (breakdown by Italian and foreign tourists), the category of the hotels (number of stars from five to one), the typology of the other collective accommodations (holiday dwellings, tourist campsites) and the geographical area (data are referred to local bodies at provincial level with different juridical configuration: Apt: Board of Tourist Promotion, Ept: Provincial Body for Tourism, and others).

This kind of information has became very outstanding especially because of the great importance of tourism during these last years and, above all, for the Giubileo event in the year 2000, that is now behind the corner.

The aim of this paper is to contribute to the discussion about the lacking of information which must be accepted for what concerns tourist flows macrodata (at regional, macroregional or national level), instead of very heterogeneous microdata (at sub-provincial level) generally less used by researchers.

The specific problem consists in comparing the virtual trend about the tourist variables, based on the calculation of the macro-aggregates, with the real data derived from the individual series. A longitudinal study is proposed, referred to quarterly data crossing the period 1990-95, in which the units of analysis taken into account (Apt, Ept or whatever suitable body) are aggregations of elementary units (hotels only), provided by the monthly survey on the client movement.

The three main objectives of the present work are the following:

---

[1] This paper is the result of common reflections of the two authors. In particular, paragraphs 1 and 4 have been elaborated by A.P.M.Mirto, paragraphs 2 and 3 by R.Gismondi and paragraph 5 by A.P.M.Mirto and R.Gismondi.

a) to analyse the links between the nights spent in time t (time reference period) and those ones referred to the previous time period (t–1);
b) to study the variability of the previous measurement concerning control variables such as seasonality, trend, level of attraction of the considered locality and ratio between the quality and costs for the nights spent;
c) to individuate the differences among macroestimates and estimates at business level proposed in this contribution.

The first step of this process was the selection of the variables relevant for building up the work database. The Apt (from this point we will refer only to Apt as sub-provincial bodies) is the microarea that has been chosen to study the flows of tourists. Because of the quick change in number and composition of Apt themselves occurred during the selected reference years, especially in some North-Italian regions that have established new legislations, the actual number of Apt (about 520) has been reduced to the 317 without any relevant structural change during the period 1990-95.

Obviously, this choice could partially affect significance of results, especially if Apts with structural changes during the above mentioned period, not included in the panel of 317 considered hereafter, are characterized by trends and dynamic behaviours quite different from the steady units' ones, i.e. without any relevant structural change. Moreover, this choice led to the impossibility to take into account all the Italian regions, just because the main structural changes occurred just in 4 regions, located in the Centrum and in the North.

On the other hand, the recourse to the panel composed by the "steady" Apts only is a simple tool to manage a wide set of data, otherwise not fully suitable for our purposes unless a strong manipulation of basic data.

In this study the variable expressed by the number of nights spent by Italian guests in the hotels has been preferred respect to the other "flow" variables like Italian arrivals, foreign arrivals and nights spent, because of the greater importance both in terms of amount and political and economic influence. So the nights spent by Italians have been selected at an Apt level and with a quarterly frequency from 1990 to 1995.

The flow data have been matched with consistency information given by the number of hotels per category and per province and the number of bed places.

From the ISTAT price survey referred to the whole national collectivity, and concerning a single category, that is the price of a chamber in a 3-star hotel, price index numbers at provincial level and on a monthly basis have been selected in order to define a synthetic cost indicator.

Observing the general trend of the number of nights spent in hotels during the period from 1990 to 1995, the breakdown by quarters underlines the strong presence of a seasonal component. Moreover, it shows a peak between the second and the third quarter, in which the summer period falls and a strong decrease between the 3rd and the 4th quarter, corresponding to a sudden reduction until the arrive of the Christmas period (see Figure 1).

Looking at the yearly trend of the nights spent during the reference period, it's quite clear the real crisis occurred in the year 1993 and, later, a low recovery during the last two years (see Figure 2), still continuing during the current years. It is necessary to specify that the total figures are not comparable to the yearly data flow currently published, because of the differences in the number of Apt included in the analysis herein discussed.

Figure 1 Quarterly nights spent in hotels from 1990 to 1995

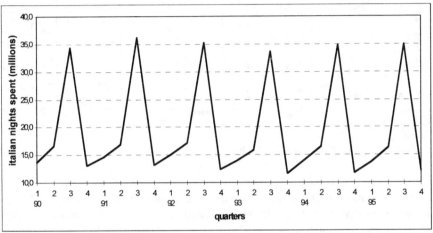

Source: elaborations on ISTAT data.

However, after the negative dynamics of the tourist flows registered in the country in 1993, the two following years present an inverse tendency. The increase of tourist flows coming from foreign countries, favoured by a positive evolution of the international economic situation, the lira depreciament regarding the other currencies and a general policy of price containment, matched with a recovery of the internal tourist demand because of the increasing of the private consumption.

The reference microdata shows a peculiar distribution in correspondence to the geographical stratification in the Italian territory (see Table 1). So it's natural that the greater concentration of Apt characterizes regions with an higher number of nights spent and bed places (especially Trentino Alto Adige and Lombardy).

Otherwise, in most of the regions the number of nights spent is proportional to the number of bed places, and only in Emilia Romagna the first figure is oversized comparing to the second one (14% respect to 9,4%). This result is also confirmed by the fact that Emilia Romagna is the region with the highest net bed places occupancy rate.

Figure 2 Yearly nights spent in hotels from 1990 to 1995

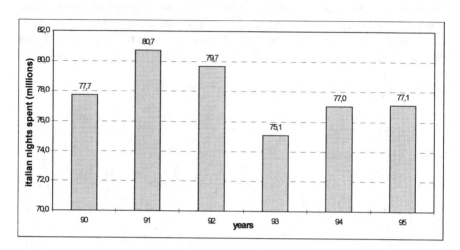

Source: elaborations on ISTAT data.

The monthly average number of bed places is over the national value (3.461) in some regions like Valle D'Aosta, Trentino Alto Adige, Veneto, Latium, Calabria and Sardinia, indicating a greater availability of bed places in the Northern Italy.

Referring to the distribution of average number of stars per region, it's evident the higher value in the Southern regions (respect to the national reference that is 2,69), that can be explained by the lower number of hotels and bed places, and consequently the higher weight of 4 and 5 star hotels located in these areas.

The paper will follow with the description of the model used to link the nights spent to the various independent variables (see § 2); then an analysis of the main results, obtained in the micro level framework and comparisons with the analogous results derived using a conventional macrolevel approach will be deeply presented and discussed (see §3 and 4); finally some concluding remarks will be pointed out.

Table 1 Some structural characters of Italian Apt by region (1)

Region	Number of APT	Number of APT %	Monthly average number of beds	Number of beds %	Number of nights spent %	Average number of stars
Piedmont	26	8,2	2.066	4,9	4,8	2,53
Valle D'Aosta	1	0,3	5.635	0,5	0,6	2,10
Lombardy	37	11,7	3.783	12,8	14,2	2,62
Trentino Alto Adige	44	13,9	5.390	21,6	17,9	2,41
Veneto	15	4,7	6.090	8,3	6,4	2,64
Emilia Romagna	29	9,1	3.571	9,4	14,0	2,63
Umbria	12	3,8	1.782	1,9	2,9	2,63
Latium	27	8,5	4.114	10,1	10,1	2,62
Abruzzo	25	7,9	1.689	3,8	3,8	2,70
Molise	5	1,6	889	0,4	0,4	3,04
Campania	28	8,8	3.419	8,7	7,9	2,97
Apulia	20	6,3	2.261	4,1	4,6	3,06
Basilicata	4	1,3	1.498	0,5	0,5	2,66
Calabria	3	0,9	5.833	1,6	1,1	2,75
Sicily	27	8,5	2.429	6,0	5,8	2,82
Sardinia	14	4,4	4.048	5,2	4,9	2,97
Italy average	317	100,0	3.461	100,0	100,0	2,69

(1) Apt = Aziende di Promozione Turistica (Boards of Tourist Promotion)
Source: elaborations on ISTAT data.

2 A "partial adjustment model" for tourist flows analysis

The problem consists in comparing the *virtual trend* about tourist flows, based on the calculation of the macroaggregates, with the *real trends* derived from the individual series.

The longitudinal study herein presented refers to the quarterly data crossing the period 1990-95, in which the units of analysis considered (Apt, Board of Tourist Promotion) are aggregations of elementary units (hotels) provided by the official monthly survey on the client movement in the Italian hotels. For a simpler exposition, in this context we'll consider as the variable of interest the nights spent by Italians only.

The basic idea, as proposed in other studies (for instance Carraro C., Costa P. and Manente M., 1994) is that the growth or the reduction of nights spent involve not only monetary costs, but also costs deriving from the adaptation action: for example management of good storage, adaptation of employment flows, fixed costs related to the location during the closing period for the hotels.

Regional aspects and seasonal dynamics play a fundamental role as well, and every attempt to analyse more in deep tourist flows, even in a short period like the one considered in this context, is deeply influenced by local and regional tourist trends, in which both supply and demand sides are condensed.

The proposed application seems the first on this topic at present available in the field of econometric studies on tourism. Given the previous considerations, in formal terms we can define the following variables:

P_{ti} nights spent at time t in the i-th APT

$SEAS_{ti}$ coefficient of seasonality referred to time t of the i-th Apt

$TREND_t$ trend variable referred to time t

Q_{ti} quality index referred to time t of the i-th Apt

C_{ti} cost index referred to time t of the i-th APT.

It must be remarked that the results of the following "microlevel" regressions will be discussed at a stratum level, where the strata composition is mostly derived by administrative breakdowns, like the regional or the "kind of locality" split, but three classes of bed places have been considered as well. In particular, because of the fact that we decided to consider the only 317 Apt, without any significant internal modification during the period 1990-1995, it wasn't possible to analyse every Italian region, so that the analysis has been carried out on Apt belonging to 16 regions instead of the global 20. In any case, the composition of strata is not relevant for implementing the estimation procedure, but it's useful to compare results obtained from the use of microdata with the ones derived from the common recourse to macrodata just referred to aggregates as regions or kinds of localities.

For every i-th Apt and every quarter t this model of "partial adjustment" has been estimated:

$$P_{ti} = \theta_i + \lambda_i P_{t-1,i} + \alpha_i SEAS_{ti} + \beta_i TREND_t + \eta_i Q_{ti} / C_{ti} + \varepsilon_{ti} \qquad [1]$$

and it has been iterated considering the nights spent by Italians.

For a better comprehension, the parameter θ represents the amount of nights spent, that can be considered as "fixed" and not dependent from other factors.

The nights spent delayed of three months represent the "persistence effect", so that the higher is λ, the higher is the degree of dependence of nights spent at time t from nights spent in the previous quarter, and viceversa.

The coefficient of seasonality is probably significant because of the strong dependence of tourist flows from the particular period of the year considered. Let's note that the missing of this seasonal effect, herein expressed in the form of a dummy variable, would have forced to a previous seasonal adjustment of every individual series, i.e. a more complicated situation, even if use of dummies cannot reproduce seasonal effects with the same precision.

The trend parameter was let into the main model just to verify if and in which cases it could be correctly estimated: generally speaking, and remembering Gavosto and Sestito (1994), it's an hard effort to succeed in such a scope, both for the simultaneous presence of a constant term and a delayed variable and for the shortness of the observed period.

The quality index has been estimated *at a regional level* by an arithmetic mean of the number of stars weighted by bed places available during the reference period t, and it can be considered as a rough approximation of the individual tourist supply quality level.

Finally, the cost index is available at a regional level and it is given by the index of the cost for a night spent in a "typical" hotel accommodation establishment, available by a special survey carried out by the Istat "prices service". Let's note that:

1. the recourse to a model in which nights spent at quarter t are explained by nights spent at the same quarter t, but referred to the previous year, could lead to R^2 indexes higher than 0,99, but this procedure is out of the real scope of the paper, in which we would like to emphasize the *conjunctural* dynamic at the "micro" level;

2. the choice to use a ratio between quality and prices instead of putting the two variables separately in the model [1] is due to a previous comparison among the 2 methods, of which the one based on the ratio revealed to be more significant in terms of Student's *t*.

All the variables have been expressed in their original form, because a preliminary attempt versus a logarithmic transformation remarked worst performances in terms of goodness of fit.

Moreover, it must be remarked that the regressions have been carried out with the "Enter" procedure, i.e. no "Stepwise", "Backward" or "Forward" procedure have been tried in advance, because the main scope is to apply *the same model* to a certain group of units (Wilson and Bennett, 1985).

The first step of the analysis consisted in a preliminary significance test for the variables included in model [1]. We carried out all the 317 individual regressions in order to estimate the 5 parameters in [1]. We obtained that the Student's *t* degree of significance for the constant θ and the trend parameter β was lower than 0,05 in less than the 5% of cases, so that these parameter were rejected from the model and a new, definitive and simpler model was defined as follows:

$$P_{ti} = \lambda_i P_{t-1,i} + \alpha_i SEAS_{ti} + \eta_i Q_{ti} / C_{ti} + \varepsilon_{ti}. \tag{2}$$

Therefore the second step of the analysis consisted in carrying out 317 new regressions, concerning the single Apt level, based on 23 quarterly data each (from the second 1990 quarter to the fourth 1995 quarter), from which 317 estimates for λ, α and η derived.

Before going to comment on the main results obtained, it's important to underline that in this framework the most relevant aim is not to discover the best forecast model for nights spent or to optimise goodness of fit in a strict sense, but to apply the same theoretical model to every Apt in order to:

1. analyse more in deep behaviour differences, in terms of parameters' variability, to verify the existence of a latent tourist model suitable for all the Apts, i.e. approximately for every hotel;

2. compare the *average values* for every parameter, obtained by an arithmetic mean of the parameter estimates of all the Apts belonging to a certain stratum s, and the *overall value* of the same parameter that could be obtained by a simple regression concerning the whole Apt values in a single solution.

Just to remind the main basic idea, the implementation of single regressions at an Apt level is needed if an overall macroregression on macrodata available, for instance, from data currently published, is strongly influenced by a few number of big Apt (in terms of tourist flows), which trends can seriously affects all the global results.

While the second aspect will be developed in §4, in the next paragraph the main regression results will be presented and commented.

3 Main results of the microlevel analysis

In Table 2 some main results of the micro-level analysis and the λ estimates distribution are available, with a breakdown in 11 λ classes.

First of all, goodness of fit is rather low, with an average R^2 equal to 0,40, and the sign that model [2] fits well just for a certain subset of Apt is given by the higher average R^2 levels for the Apt with λ lower than -0,75. These cases represent the 49,8% of the total, R^2 ranges from 0,50 to 0,64, decreasing when λ increases (i.e. when λ is less negative), and their average Fisher's F is highly significant[2]

Nevertheless, on the average F is not significant just for 4 λ classes on 11, mainly concentrated in classes where λ ranges from -0,74 to 0,25, and the

---

[2] The corresponding F value (with 2 and 23 degrees of freedom at a 5% probability level) is equal to 3,42.

average Durbin & Watson tests reveal signs of autocorrelation only for APT with λ lower than -1,50 (negative) and λ in the ranges (-0,99;-0,75) and (-0,49;-0,25).

Table 2 Main results of microlevel analysis by λ classes

λ classes	% comp.	Cum. % comp.	Average delay (λ)	Significance Delay	Season	Quality/ price	R^2	F test	D.W. test
until -1,50	11,0	11,0	-1,65	0,0001	0,0001	0,0812	0,64	13,52	2,93
-1,49 to -1,25	16,1	27,1	-1,36	0,0007	0,0006	0,2241	0,69	27,85	2,30
-1,24 to -1,00	14,2	41,3	-1,11	0,0021	0,0048	0,2391	0,57	15,20	2,07
-0,99 to -0,75	8,5	49,8	-0,86	0,0121	0,1502	0,1828	0,50	12,05	1,67
-0,74 to -0,50	8,5	58,4	-0,62	0,0746	0,0755	0,1213	0,28	3,14	2,05
-0,49 to -0,25	4,4	62,8	-0,35	0,2251	0,1717	0,0238	0,32	3,94	1,64
-0,24 to 0,00	6,9	69,7	-0,14	0,6493	0,3397	0,0203	0,10	1,37	1,90
0,01 to 0,25	9,1	78,9	0,15	0,5680	0,5181	0,0213	0,11	1,84	1,82
0,26 to 0,50	11,7	90,5	0,37	0,1362	0,4854	0,0421	0,14	2,38	2,01
0,51 to 0,75	7,6	98,1	0,62	0,0036	0,4509	0,0917	0,20	4,06	2,19
0,76 to 1,00	1,9	100,0	0,86	0,0003	0,3366	0,6369	0,33	7,40	2,11
Total	100,0		-0,59	0,1309	0,1957	0,1332	0,40	10,59	2,11

Source: elaborations on ISTAT data.

Resuming the previous considerations, as a first conclusion we can say that model [2] seems to be correctly specified, but more precise and detailed measures for the variables are needed in order to improve quality of estimates.

As a second step, we can observe the algebraic sign of the delay coefficient λ. It's negative in the 69,7% of cases, and in the 41,3% of cases is lower than -1,00. Generally speaking, the more negative is λ, the higher should be the inverse correlation existing from a quarter and the previous one, or in simpler words the higher should be the quarterly variability of nights spent. Moreover, this event should be strictly connected with a high significance of seasonality.

On the other hand, positive and high values for λ are the sign of a positive longitudinal correlation from quarter to quarter, and this evidence should happen when seasonality hasn't a strong relevance. In fact let's note that Apts with λ higher than 0,25 are characterised by high levels of significance for the "delay" parameter and low levels of significance for the "seasonal" parameter β; moreover, the average significance of the "quality/price" parameter isn't very high as well.

A third situation characterizes Apts with λ ranging from -0,49 to 0,25. In this case the longitudinal link between two following quarters shouldn't be very significant, and in fact in the 3 corresponding λ classes we can find the lowest levels of significance for the delay parameter, as well as low levels of significance for seasonality. The particular aspect that must be remarked is that this is the only situation in which the ratio quality/price reveals to be quite significant (significances range from 0,0203 to 0,0238).

Resuming, 3 main typologies have been identified by means of micro-level analysis. For a simpler comprehension, figure 4 can be observed too. Typologies are the following:

1. the first cluster, including almost the 60% of Apts. It's characterized by high significance of seasonality and delay, with a *negative* λ parameter lower than -0,50, and a very low significance of quality/price effect. This profile is typical of the most part of Italian tourist sites, for which the choice depends lightly from quality and prices and seasonality plays a fundamental role.

2. The second cluster, including about the 20% of Apts. It's characterised by high significance of delay, with a *positive* λ parameter ranging from 0,26 and 1,00, and low significances of seasonal and quality/price effects. This profile characterises not seasonal sites, rather homogeneous for what concerns quality and prices.

3. The third cluster, including about the 20% of Apts. It's characterised by a very low significance of delay, with a λ parameter ranging from -0,49 and 0,25, low significance of seasonal effect and high significance of quality/price effect. This profile is typical of not seasonal tourist sites with a strong heterogeneity of quality and/or prices.

Figure 3 Percentage APT composition by λ classes

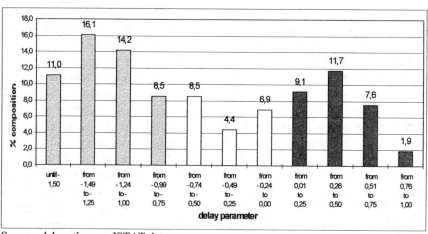

Source: elaborations on ISTAT data.

For what concerns the form of λ distribution, Figure 3 shows the existence of 3 curves, quite corresponding to the 3 clusters mentioned above: the first concerns Apts with λ lower than -0,75, the second the Apts with λ ranging from -0,74 and -0,24, and the third with λ higher than zero. It's evident the existence of a strong positive asymmetry both of the first and the third curve, higher in the first case. Moreover, these 2 curves are very similar, while the intermediate curve isn't very different from a uniform distribution.

Having seen how powerful can be an analysis carried out at a microlevel stage for identifying tourist behaviours and estimating causal parameters, it's worthwhile to examine more in deep the variability of results for some control characters as type of locality, region and average number of bed places per hotel. These comparisons have been included in Table 3.

Figure 4 Average significance levels by λ classes

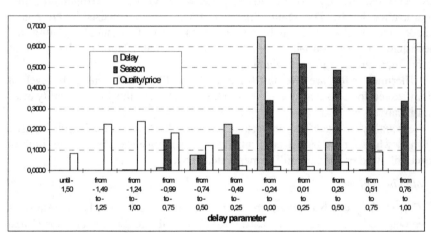

Source: elaborations on ISTAT data.

As a first remark, we note that the sign of delay effect is always negative, with the exception of chief towns and region Basilicata, and that in most cases its significance isn't high. This means that a certain degree of influence of seasonality is typical of each Italian region and each kind of locality except chief towns, but these administrative breakdowns don't permit to identify groups for which seasonality play a much more significant role than others.

The same conclusion can be drawn for bed places classes too, even if in this case it's clear that with the increase of the average number of bed places per hotel there is a decrease of the importance of seasonal effects.

More detailed considerations can be drawn from the analysis of Table 3, as follows.

It must be preliminarily underlined that the sign for the seasonal effect is always positive, as it could be imagined, just because higher values for the seasonal dummy, 3 and 4, correspond to the 3rd and the 4th quarters of the year, that are the more relevant in terms of nights spent for every kind of locality and every region.

On the other hand, we can note that the sign of the quality/price ratio isn't always positive, because in some circumstances, like for sea and thermal localities and some regions for which these localities are very important, a negative sign reveals the longitudinal tendency to prefer hotels with low quality levels and/or average prices increased more than quality itself.

Profile by type of locality

The localities "mountain" and "sea" represent the 37,3% of Apts and they are the ones for which we can find the highest R^2 values (0,70 and 0,48 respectively), as well as the highest F tests and the lowest average estimates for the delay parameter λ (-1,06 and -1,10 respectively), with corresponding high significance levels. The main difference among them consists in an higher importance of the ratio quality/price for the mountain sites, meaning the persistence of a sea tourism model mostly based on habits and "nearby" customs rather than quality and cost valuations.

"Thermal" sites are the third types of localities with an high level of significance for seasonality and delay effects, but with the lowest quality/price significance.

Seasonality is much less important for "Hills", "Chief towns" and "Artistic towns", while for these last ones quality/price significance raises to the highest level, followed by "Mountain" as mentioned above.

Profile by region

Considering as a benchmark the average R^2 value of 0,40, a better result has been obtained in 5 regions: Lombardy (R^2=0,41, with the second value for F, that is equal to 16,82), Sardinia (R^2=0,52), Calabria (0,55), Abruzzo (0,56) and Trentino Alto Adige (0,72, with the highest level for F, that is equal to 29,32).

Bad results characterise Umbria and Basilicata, with R^2 lower than 0,10, while in the remaining regions this coefficient varies from 0,20 to 0,40.

Generally speaking, regions with a high R^2 are the ones for which significances of delay and seasonality turn out to be more relevant: this is fully true for Trentino Alto Adige and, partially, for Sardinia and Abruzzo, while it isn't completely true for the other 2 regions mentioned above, because of a lower significance of seasonal effect. This fact is probably due to the particular Trentino, Sardinia and Abruzzo profiles, almost completely based on tourist sites, while in Calabria seasonal effects couldn't have been correctly estimated because of reliable and homogeneous time series, and Lombardy is characterised by very different kinds of localities (i.e., both chief towns and lakes or hills).

Table 3 Microlevel analysis main results by locality, region and bed places

Locality - region bed places	% comp.	Monthly average number of nights spent	Parameter Delay	Parameter Season	Parameter Quality/price	Significance Delay	Significance Season	Significance Quality/price	R^2	F test
ITALY	100.0	20.478	-0.59	33.777	725.766	0.1309	0.1957	0.1332	0.40	10.59
LOCALITY										
artistic towns	8.8	35.851	-0.04	14.216	2.841.076	0.2581	0.2776	0.0450	0.17	3.28
mountain	19.6	16.902	-1.06	18.977	2.840.176	0.0246	0.0855	0.0767	0.70	30.19
lake	5.7	13.491	-0.73	25.836	579.071	0.2668	0.1859	0.1270	0.27	3.85
sea	17.7	20.676	-1.10	84.919	-3.250.487	0.0686	0.1084	0.1377	0.48	8.41
thermal	6.3	18.404	-0.81	39.859	-247.800	0.0262	0.0569	0.3471	0.39	5.24
hill	10.7	5.825	-0.28	3.846	472.408	0.2430	0.3290	0.1853	0.25	3.06
chief towns	11.7	18.636	0.22	2.530	1.443.082	0.2277	0.3858	0.1151	0.21	4.09
other localities	19.6	28.772	-0.45	46.623	1.315.015	0.1117	0.2090	0.1405	0.35	7.95
REGION										
Piedmont	8.2	12.006	-0.26	2.705	1.558.949	0.1877	0.2639	0.0723	0.39	6.50
Valle D'Aosta	0.3	38.583	-0.53	4.300	11.903.884	0.0430	0.7505	0.0002	0.35	3.65
Lombardy	11.7	24.885	-0.62	16.679	2.634.896	0.1059	0.1373	0.0092	0.41	16.82
Trentino-Alto Adige	13.9	26.440	-1.13	44.304	2.865.791	0.0013	0.0689	0.1079	0.72	29.32
Veneto	4.7	27.828	-0.34	55.114	-829.744	0.2093	0.2216	0.1633	0.31	7.38
Emilia-Romagna	9.1	31.345	-0.33	85.371	-2.806.124	0.0875	0.1793	0.2141	0.31	6.50
Umbria	3.8	15.817	-0.18	8.754	1.642.234	0.2393	0.3794	0.0726	0.09	0.79
Latium	8.5	24.292	-0.34	17.694	1.277.583	0.1965	0.2023	0.1511	0.27	3.76
Abruzzo	7.9	9.915	-0.99	28.181	-258.427	0.0600	0.1054	0.1370	0.56	13.60
Molise	1.6	4.754	-0.28	3.559	462.406	0.3724	0.5665	0.0123	0.21	3.21
Campania	8.8	18.383	-0.70	30.269	661.828	0.2103	0.2196	0.1467	0.29	3.73
Apulia	6.3	14.808	-0.27	27.581	-238.618	0.1871	0.3285	0.1287	0.25	5.29
Basilicata	1.3	7.800	0.09	3.853	528.474	0.0698	0.2167	0.0288	0.08	1.56
Calabria	0.9	24.126	-0.75	71.785	-635.965	0.0051	0.2167	0.3101	0.55	11.97
Sicily	8.5	14.061	-0.42	23.585	593.380	0.1912	0.2450	0.2051	0.32	4.74
Sardinia	4.4	22.768	-1.16	85.134	-2.297.850	0.0223	0.1048	0.0855	0.52	8.88
BED PLACES (1)										
1-15	33.4	8.102	-0.64	9.925	883.327	0.1286	0.1725	0.1204	0.45	13.31
16-50	30.6	16.034	-0.62	27.538	893.789	0.1295	0.1934	0.1740	0.41	11.59
>50	36.0	35.767	-0.52	61.264	436.295	0.1343	0.2194	0.1104	0.34	7.20

(1) Average per hotel.

Source: elaborations on ISTAT data.

For what concerns the quality/price effect, it's very relevant in Valle D'Aosta (significance is equal to 0,0002), Molise and Basilicata, and quite important in Piedmont, Umbria and Sardinia, with levels of significances ranging from 0,007 and 0,008.

Trying to summarise, profiles by region seem less informative than the ones based on kinds of locality, except for regions, like Trentino Alto Adige and Sardinia, quite completely based on a holiday tourist supply structure.

The traditional conflict between Northern and Southern profiles isn't particularly evident, but this fact can be viewed as a good feature of the micro-level methodology, in the sense that it's able to identify similarities of behaviour independently from geographical location.

Notwithstanding these considerations, the model fits better in the Northern regions than in the Central and Southern ones[3], and this is the sign of a more developed tourist system in the North, in which different tourist sites exist at the same time and, especially in Piedmont, Valle D'Aosta, Lombardy and Trentino Alto Adige, valuations concerning quality and prices play a more relevant role.

Profile by classes of bed places

The breakdown in 3 bed places classes identifies groups weighting about one third of the total each. Clearly the monthly average number of nights spent increases with the increase of bed places: in particular, it doubles passing from one class to the following.

Seasonality loses importance as hotel size in terms of bed places increases, and this evidence is confirmed by observing that the delay and the seasonal affects significances decrease as size increases.

On the other hand, as partially imaginable, for biggest hotels the quality/price ratio holds a greater importance, even if a similar level of significance characterises hotels until 15 bed places as well.

Finally, let's note that the quality of regressions, in terms of goodness of fit and overall significance, is lower in the biggest hotels, because of the lower relevance of seasonal factors that in the general model [2] play a fundamental role.

4 Comparison between microlevel and macrolevel results

In this paragraph after a brief description of the main results derived by a macrolevel approach, a general comparison between the micro and macro patterns will be shortly developed. In fact, a model formally equivalent to model

---

[3] Northern regions range from Piedmont to Emilia Romagna; their average goodness of fit is equal to 0,43, against the 0,31 for the remaining Italian regions.

[2] has been estimated using macrodata, obtained by aggregation of microdata given by the single APT profiles.

The macro structure of the Apt can be considered under different points of view and precisely at level of "type of locality", at level of "geographical region" and, finally, at a national level (see Table 4). More in detail, the analysis of the general composition of the Italian territory per kind of locality shows a prevalence in terms of «seaside» (17,7%) and «mountainside» (19,6%) locality (naturally all these remarks are referred to the only Apt selected for this analysis and. Consequently, there could be some differences with the real overall Italian profile).

The results of macro regression show a great significance level of the *delay parameter* (λ) and of the *seasonality parameter* in most of all the localities and regions. In fact, at locality level only for «artistic towns», «hill» and «chief towns» locality not significative λ levels have been obtained (ranging by 0,47 to 0,87 significance values). At regional level only in Umbria, Latium and Basilicata not significative levels of the same parameter appear (ranging by 0,25 to 0,67 significance values).

Therefore the nights spent during the quarters before (delay effect) explain a good part of the variation of the actual level of nights spent; moreover the seasonal component (in most of the regions and localities) influences greatly the same level of nights spent.

The prevalent negative sign of the delay parameter (in all the localities excepting «artistic towns» and «chief towns» and in all the regions excepting Basilicata) indicates a negative correlation between the level of nights spent at time t and (t-1).

Referring to the ratio between quality and price, the highly significant values give evidence of a consistent influence in a lot of regions, indicating that also this variable is relevant for the general adapting model. More in detail if we look at the locality breakdown only in «lake» and «thermal sites» not significant level of the parameter quality/price have been obtained; if we observe the region classifications, only in Emilia Romagna, Abruzzo and Calabria the quality/price parameter is not significant.

Finally, in broad terms, the very high levels of significance of test F, could led to the conclusion that model [2] fits very well in every region and this is true, especially, for the regions Trentino Alto Adige, Emilia Romagna, Abruzzo, Calabria and Sardinia (ranging by F value over 12 to about 70)

Comparing the two models, referring respectively to micro and macro data, some existing discordances result among the estimates of the parameters obtained by the average of the available estimates at Apt level and the aggregated macrodata available by summed up figures currently diffused by ISTAT.

Table 4 - Macrolevel analysis main results by locality, region and bed places

Locality - region bed places	comp. %	Monthly average number of nights spent	Parameter Delay	Parameter Season	Parameter Quality/price	Significance Delay	Significance Season	Significance Quality/price	R²	F test
ITALY	100.0	20.478	-1.76	4.377	2.500.327	0.0000	0.0000	0.0000	0.78	24.26
LOCALITY										
artistic towns	8.8	35.851	0.19	3.923	3.257.910	0.4700	0.2520	0.0027	0.30	1.55
mountain	19.6	16.902	-1.21	18.708	3.382.593	0.0000	0.0000	0.0000	0.92	77.32
lake	5.7	13.461	-1.60	37.426	527.817	0.0005	0.0004	0.3093	0.48	6.16
sea	17.5	20.676	-1.83	97.358	2.942.998	0.0000	0.0000	0.0096	0.69	15.02
thermal	6.3	18.404	-1.12	47.895	-110.662	0.0006	0.0002	0.8940	0.51	7.04
hill	10.7	5.825	-0.25	2.895	680.214	0.4966	0.1806	0.8006	0.05	0.31
chieftowns	11.7	18.636	0.04	888	2.083.313	0.8692	0.3374	0.0024	0.31	2.96
other localities	19.6	28.772	-1.51	57.090	3.614.841	0.0000	0.0000	0.0000	0.74	18.89
REGION										
Piedmont	8.2	12.006	-0.89	4.377	2.790.803	0.0040	0.0185	0.0000	0.42	4.77
Valle D'Aosta	0.3	38.583	-0.53	4.300	11.903.884	0.0430	0.7505	0.0002	0.35	3.65
Lombardy	11.7	24.885	-1.30	15.042	6.282.317	0.0011	0.0019	0.0000	0.38	4.16
Trentino-Alto Adige	13.9	26.440	-1.33	46.255	3.605.172	0.0000	0.0000	0.0924	0.91	68.81
Veneto	4.7	27.828	-1.31	61.413	1.124.086	0.0033	0.0013	0.2657	0.35	3.53
Emilia-Romagna	9.1	31.345	-1.64	89.705	2.019.268	0.2472	0.1014	0.0004	0.65	12.64
Umbria	3.8	15.817	-0.48	10.737	3.265.616	0.3877	0.0252	0.0001	0.07	0.03
Latium	8.5	24.292	-0.24	8.154	707.036	0.0321	0.0355	0.0001	0.00	0.48
Abruzzo	7.6	9.915	-1.68	31.213	883.603	0.0011	0.0000	0.7639	0.79	24.36
Molise	1.6	4.754	-0.82	3.414	1.451.236	0.0000	0.0005	0.0035	0.09	0.64
Campania	8.8	18.383	-1.30	35.690	946.728	0.0000	0.0000	0.0018	0.45	5.37
Apulia	6.3	14.808	-1.54	1.905	781.908	0.6723	0.1429	0.0029	0.59	9.45
Basilicata	1.3	7.800	0.12	73.492	-518.242	0.0001	0.0000	0.5362	0.25	1.34
Calabria	0.9	24.126	-1.40	29.286	1.528.550	0.0001	0.0000	0.0002	0.73	18.11
Sicily	8.5	14.061	-1.51		1.528.550	0.0001	0.0000	0.0410	0.58	9.22
Sardinia	4.4	22.768	-1.60	91.578	-2.054.927	0.0000	0.0000		0.69	14.53
BED PLACES (1)										
1-15	33.4	8.102	-1.45	12.465	1.373.065	0.0000	0.0000	0.0000	0.91	68.32
16-50	36.0	16.034	-1.92	42.093	1.543.698	0.0000	0.0000	0.0000	0.90	60.57
>50	30.6	35.767	-1.64	71.658	4.612.507	0.0000	0.0000	0.0000	0.66	13.19

(1) Average per hotel. - Source: elaborations on ISTAT data.

At national level, for all classes of bed places, the delay parameter at macro level is always higher (in absolute value) than micro results, indicating a general tendency to overestimating the influence of the delayed variables (referred to the quarter before) on the flows of nights spent (see Figure 5).

Moving to the value of the seasonality significance the situation is almost parallel, indicating a weaker importance of the seasonal effect at microlevel, for whatever class of bed places.

The analysis per type of locality shows a situation non completely defined and interpretable, because the delay algebraical sign doesn't always agree with the delay significance one. Only for the other localities the pattern is identical to the general national scheme. Therefore it's better not to generalise the results referred to the type of locality.

The considerations expressed at national level can be observed in the regional breakdown, noting that the significance of the delay parameter referred to the macro analysis is confirmed in many regions, and particularly in Piedmont, Lombardy, Veneto, Emilia-Romagna, Abruzzo, Apulia and Sicily (see Figure 6). The seasonality is also less significant at micro level in most of all the regions showing a coherent tendency with the national case.

Also the variable quality/price plays a more significant role in the aggregated model at national level; referring to the regions breakdown, this pattern is repeated in all the areas and especially in Umbria, Molise and Apulia that are however the regions with the greater average number of stars.

Figure 5 Differences between microlevel and macrolevel results by bed places classes and type of locality

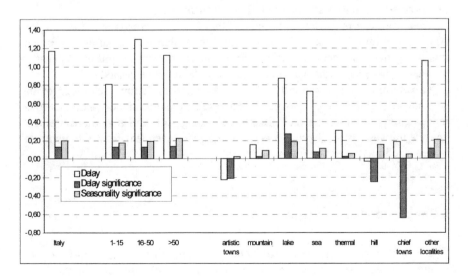

Source: elaborations on ISTAT data.

Figure 6 Differences between microlevel and macrolevel results by region

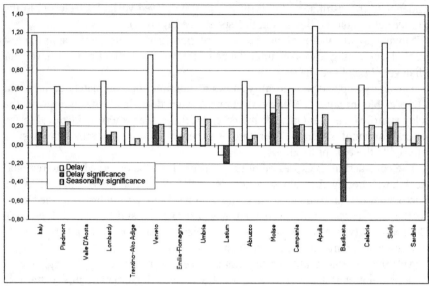

Source: elaborations on ISTAT data.

In conclusion, the application of the model [2] using aggregated data at regional or national level leads to a general overestimation of the effect of the seasonal variable, at least when this effect is expressed by the relation between nights spent at month t and month (t-1) of the same year.

This result can be attributed to the fact that in the macromodel a group of few Apt has a weight, in terms of nights spent, higher than the remaining ones, and this fact generates a general flatting of the pattern towards a significant negative correlation between nights spent in t respect to the previous period (t-1).

Therefore, even if apparently by the macromodel a strong relevance of the seasonal effect and of the delay parameter results, the micromodel turns out to be more representative of the real differences among Apt, and it is more useful to analyse the various local profiles because it's less dependent from the territorial bodies size in terms of bed places.

5 Conclusions and perspectives

In the light of the previous considerations it's quite difficult to identify a good dynamic model based on the analysis of all the available tourist microunits.

The results achieved by this adjustment model can be considered only a preliminary study and, therefore, the possibility to repeat a experimentation using the single hotels, and more precise quality and/or cost variables should be evaluated. More in detail, the regression analysis could be iterated considering the delay respect to the same quarter of the previous year; by this exercise, an higher R^2 value would be revealed, but additional problems concerning estimates of the seasonal component would raise up as well.

However, by the final model [2] good results have been achieved, similar behaviour typologies have been discovered, independently from their geographical localisation.

Among the three used control characters (region, type of locality and bed place classes), type of locality seems to discriminate better among different smoothing dynamics, followed by the bed places variable.

The final results have stressed the risk in using aggregations of elementary units not always coherent, from which an overestimate about the delay and the seasonal effect appears, and have confirmed the higher seasonal flexibility of economic small size units.

In conclusion, it is very dangerous to deduce easy results by too aggregated data, that usually do not allow the right evaluation on the individual heterogeneity, also because the last phenomenon is hardly observable with a macroeconomic approach.

REFERENCES

Arbia G. (1992), *Le relazioni degli aggregati economici nel tempo e nello spazio, in G.Alvaro*: "Contabilità Nazionale e Statistica Economica", Cacucci, Bari.

Carraro C., Costa P., Manente M. (1994), *Il modello STREP di previsione dei flussi turistici internazionali in Veneto*, quaderno Ciset n°8.2/94, Ciset, Oriago di Mira, Venezia.

ENIT, ISTAT, MERCURY (1997), *Settimo rapporto sul turismo italiano*, Mercury, Firenze.

Gavosto A., Sestito P. (1994), *"Costi di aggiustamento e flessibilità dell'occupazione: l'eterogeneità tra piccole e grandi imprese"*, Lavoro e relazioni industriali, aprile/giugno, 2, 71-106.

Gismondi R. (1998), *"La flessibilità dell'occupazione nelle piccole imprese commerciali al dettaglio: un'esplorazione per il periodo 1990-95"*, Commercio, gennaio/marzo, 1, 1-25.

ISTAT (anni vari), *Statistiche del turismo*, Istat, Roma.

Johnston J. (1983), *Econometrica*, Franco Angeli, Milano.

Lloyd P., Dicken P. (1979), *Spazio e localizzazione: una interpretazione geografica della economia,* Franco Angeli, Milano.

Piccolo D., Vitale C. (1984), *Metodi statistici per l'analisi economica,* Il Mulino, Bologna.

Wislon A.G., Bennett R.J. (1985), *Mathematical methods in human geography and planning,* John Wiley & Sons, Great Britain.

ASSESSING SLACKS THROUGH A NESTED RADIAL APPROACH IN AN FDH REFERENCE TECHNOLOGY

Antonio Pavone[1] and Sergio Destefanis[2]

[1]*Istituto Nazionale di Statistica, Rome, Italy*
[2]*Dipartimento di Scienze Economiche, Università degli Studi di Salerno, Italy*

1 Introduction

After having reiterated the point that the traditional Debreu-Farrell efficiency measure is not appropriate within an FDH technology, we show in this paper that for such a technology it is possible to obtain through a nested radial procedure various technical efficiency measures comprehensive of the existence of slacks. Considering for simplicity the case of input-oriented efficiency only,[1] we show that the input vector (of order m) of an inefficient observation can be decomposed in m radial projections on m subspaces. This decomposition procedure follows a hierarchically ordered (or nested) sequence from the space of dimension m (which allows the greatest possible radial reduction associated with the disappearance of slack in at least one input) to a space of dimension one. At every step of the procedure, Debreu-Farrell measures are obtained which correspond to the amount of slack in a given input that is cancelled by a radial contraction in the relevant subspace, or in other words to the ratio between the input quantity utilised by the efficient plan to that utilised by the inefficient plan. For all inputs we compute the product of these Debreu-Farrell measures, obtaining the total input contraction required to bring an inefficient observation in the efficient subset. This approach allows (a) to generate some nonradial measures proposed in the literature (asymmetric Färe, Färe-Lovell)[2] as the products of nested radial contractions; and (b) to show that the correct measure of technical efficiency always falls in an interval bounded by the asymmetric Färe and the radial Debreu-Farrell measures.

The paper has the following structure. In Section 2 we describe the FDH reference technology and we restate some desirable properties of efficiency

---

[1] No significant loss of generality is entailed by this assumption, as the concepts discussed below can be straightforwardly extended to the consideration of output-oriented efficiency.

[2] Recent accounts of the definitions and properties of these measures are given in Kerstens and Vanden Eeckaut (1995) and De Borger and Kerstens (1996).

measures, with emphasis on the axioms singled out in Russell (1988). As shall be seen, this strengthens the case for incorporating slacks in the computation of technical efficiency measures. Section 3 describes the nested radial procedure which is the crux of the approach here proposed. In Section 4 this approach is utilised to show how it is possible to generate some nonradial measures available in the literature (asymmetric Färe, Färe-Lovell) through the products of nested radial contractions, and that the correct measure of technical efficiency always falls in an interval bounded by the asymmetric Färe and the Debreu-Farrell measures. In Section 5 the analytical points of the preceding sections are illustrated by applying the procedure to a sample of Italian banking firms for 1995. This application indicates that the Färe-Lovell measure allows a better appraisal of the cost excess due to technical inefficiency than other measures available in the literature. Finally, Section 6 contains some concluding remarks.

2 Measuring technical efficiency within an FDH technology

2.1 The FDH reference technology

In order to give a sharper characterisation to the problems posited by slacks in the measurement of efficiency (unless otherwise specified, the term "efficiency" refers to technical efficiency), we assume in this paper a Free Disposal Hull (FDH) reference technology. This technology can be described as follows.[3] Consider a production set constituted by vector pairs (x, y) - the production plans - where $x = (x_1,...x_i,...,x_m)$ is an $m \times 1$ technically feasible non-negative input vector and $y = (y_1,...y_j,...,y_n)$ is an $n \times 1$ technically feasible non-negative output vector. The input correspondence $Y \rightarrow L\ (Y)$ assigns to each output vector y the subset of all input vectors x which produce y, and can be written as:

$$L(Y)^{FDH} = \left\{ x \middle| Y^{\tau} z \geq y, X^{\tau} z \leq x, I_k^{\tau} z = 1, z_i \in \{0, 1\} \right\}$$

where Y^{τ} is a $k \times n$ matrix of observed outputs, X^{τ} is a $k \times m$ matrix of observed inputs, z is a $k \times 1$ vector of intensity parameters and I_k^{τ} is a $k \times 1$ vector of ones. Note that no assumption is made about the convexity of the technology or about the existence of any given linear combination of the observed production plans. The only assumption made about the production set is, in the parlance of Shepard (1970), the strong free disposability of inputs and outputs. In other words, a higher amount of inputs is never associated to a lower amount of outputs, and a

---

[3] Further references on this technology can be found in Fried *et al.* (1993).

given amount of inputs always allows the production of a lower amount of outputs.

2.2 The measurement of technical efficiency. Some important properties

According to the classic definition given in Koopmans (1951), a production plan is technically efficient if increasing any output necessarily implies either reducing another output or increasing at least one input, and if reducing any input necessarily implies either increasing another input or reducing at least one output. Thus, a producer is technically inefficient if it can produce the same outputs after reducing at least one input, or if it can increase at least one output using the same inputs. Formally this is equivalent to define a subset of production plans (DO (x,y)) weakly dominating other plans (x^i, y^i) or in other words producing at least as much output with no greater amount of input:

$$DO(x,y) = \left\{ \left(x^i, y^i \right) \middle| x^i \underset{=}{<} x, y^i \underset{=}{>} y \right\}$$

According to this definition any feasible production plan is Koopmans-efficient if no other feasible plan exists that weakly dominates it. Hence, the dominant subset is equivalent to the efficient subset:

$$x \in EFF\ L(y) \iff DO(x,y) = \{(x,y)\}$$

Koopmans does not develop operationally his definition of efficiency. This is done on the other hand by Debreu (1951) and Farrell (1957), whose definition of efficiency is the maximum equiproportional reduction of the input vector that is compatible with the production of a given output vector y. Hence, a combination of inputs is technically efficient if and only if there is no $\mu \in (0, 1)$, such as $(\mu x) \in L(Y)$, and the Debreu-Farrell (DF) input-oriented measure of technical efficiency is the complement to one of the maximum equiproportional input contraction. As explained below, this measure is not without problems, not being able to satisfy Koopmans' definition in all circumstances. Indeed, consider the following four desirable properties (or axioms) of efficiency measures singled out by Färe and Lovell (1978) in their seminal contribution.

The first axiom, which could be labelled as indication of *Eff L (y)*, states that input vectors are efficient if and only if they belong to the efficient subset.

The second axiom, projection to *Eff L (y)*, requires that inefficient input vectors can be compared to vectors in the efficient subset.

The third axiom is the homogeneity of degree minus one of the efficiency measure in the inputs. That is, a (say) doubling of the input vector used by an inefficient plan halves the efficiency measure. A weaker version of this axiom (sub-homogeneity) implies that a scaling of the input vector by a factor greater than one brings about a reduction of the efficiency measure smaller than the inverse scaling of the efficiency measure by the same factor.

The fourth axiom, strict monotonicity, states that increasing at least one input while leaving all other inputs and outputs constant must reduce the efficiency measure. According to a less demanding version of this axiom, weak monotonicity, increasing at least one input while leaving all other inputs and outputs constant cannot increase the efficiency measure.

Russell (1985) demonstrates that projection to $Eff\ L\ (y)$ is in fact implied by the existence of indication of $Eff\ L\ (y)$, homogeneity of degree minus one in the inputs and strict monotonicity. Also, Russell (1988) adds to these properties the requirement, of paramount importance for empirical purposes, that the efficiency measure be invariant to changes in the units of measurement for inputs and outputs. It is well known that no existing efficiency measure satisfies all these properties simultaneously, at least in their strongest form.[4] However, the fact that the DF measure fails to satisfy the first axiom is surely the strongest argument against this widely adopted measure, and strengthens the case for allowing for slacks in the computation of efficiency measures.

Still, according to Cooper and Pastor (1996), a desirable efficiency measure should be a scalar (ranging from zero to one), comprehensive (that is, it should incorporate all the measurable inefficiencies of a production plan, including the slacks), readily interpretable in a managerial or economic sense and, finally, not excessively demanding from the computational standpoint. Now, it is clear that the wide empirical adoption of the DF measure can be easily justified on the two latter grounds. The available algorithms for the alternative measures (asymmetric Färe, Russell, Zieschang) are at any rate considerably more complex. Also, the radial measure has a straightforward interpretation in terms of cost efficiency, due to its independence from the vector of input prices. On the contrary, for nonradial measures relative costs depend on the vector of input prices and technical efficiency has no more a readily available interpretation in cost terms. An argument also often made in favour of the DF measure is that there is a dual relationship between this measure and the isoquant of $L\ (y)$, $Isoq\ L\ (y)$. Yet, note that *any* measure satisfying the first axiom singles out a functional representation of $Eff\ L\ (y)$, provided that $L\ (y)$ is a technology characterised by strong input disposability. As a consequence, if it is agreed that $Eff\ L\ (y)$ matters more than $Isoq\ L\ (y)$ from the standpoint of efficiency measurement, duality considerations might actually turn out to favour nonradial measures.[5]

---

[4] See on this Bol (1986), Russell (1985, 1988), Kerstens and Vanden Eeckaut (1995).

[5] This point is taken from Kerstens and Vanden Eeckaut (1995, pp. 21-22), where other relevant references can be found.

3 A nested radial approach to efficiency measurement

Let us suppose that output is given and that in the input requirement set there are only two production plans (a and b). We say that plan a dominates plan b since it is characterised by smaller input quantities for at least one input (in fact, for all inputs in the present case). Let us further suppose that the input requirement set only includes three inputs, x_1, x_2 and x_3, and can be represented by Figure 1.

Figure 1 Radial Contraction in the Three-input Case

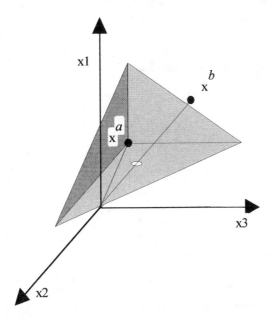

Finally, assume that technical efficiency in this input requirement set is measured radially, that is as the complement to one of the maximum equiproportional reduction of the input vector that is compatible with the production of a given output vector. However, this maximum equiproportional reduction, which is associated with the disappearance of slack in at least one input, is seen here only as the first step of a decomposition procedure following a hierarchically nested sequence from the input space of dimension m to an input space of dimension one. At every step of the procedure, the slack in a given input is cancelled by maximum equiproportional contraction in the relevant subspace.

To repeat, at Step 1 of the procedure, we apply to the $m \times 1$ input vector x^b the maximum equiproportional reduction compatible with the production of a given output vector. The new vector, which shall be denoted as x^{b*}, provides the projection coordinates on the frontier of the input requirement set and is characterised by the presence of slacks for inputs x_2 and x_3, but not for x_1. Then, we go to Step 2 of the procedure, where we carry out the maximum equiproportional reduction (compatible with the production of a given output) of the $(m-1) \times 1$ vector x^{b*}. In fact, input x_1 is no longer included in this projection of vector x^b, which is represented in Fig. 2, as this input cannot be further reduced through an equiproportional reduction. In the new projection point x^{b**} there is a slack only for input x_3 but no longer for x_2.

Figure 2 Radial Contraction in the Two-input Case

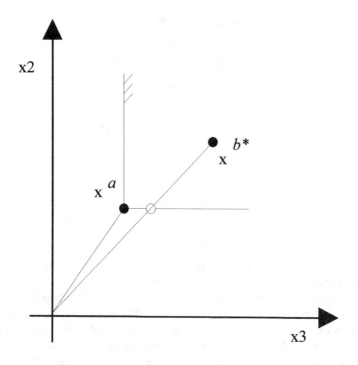

Similarly, in Step 3 of the procedure, we can take no longer into account x_2 and proceed to the maximum equiproportional reduction (compatible with the production of a given output) of the $(m-2)\times1$ projected input vector. Naturally, this corresponds to the elimination of the slack in x_3.

Note that since $x^{b*} = \lambda^b x^b$ and, analogously, $x^{b**} = \lambda^{b*} x^{b*}$, we have $x^{b***} = x^b \lambda^b \lambda^{b*} \lambda^{b**} = x^a$. Hence, an inefficient input vector (in this case, x^b) can be obtained as the product of m radial projections in m subspaces. Also note that the decomposition procedure follows a hierarchically nested sequence from the input space of dimension m to a subspace of dimension one. The scalar elements λ_{ij}, where subscripts i and j respectively apply to inputs and steps of the procedure, take values equal to the radial contraction undergone by input i at step j, and values equal to one otherwise. Each of them can be interpreted as the partial contribution, in a given subspace, to the total radial contraction applied to a given input. On the other hand, as is made clear by the numerical example given in table 1, the latter corresponds to the ratio between the input quantity utilised by the efficient plan to that utilised by the inefficient plan. This magnitude can also be defined as the proportional contraction to be applied in a given input dimension in order to obtain an efficient production plan.

Table 1 Radial Contractions and their Products

	x^a	x^b		λ^b	λ^{b*}	λ^{b**}	$\lambda^b_{i\bullet}$
x_1	38	40		.95	1.00	1.00	$\lambda^b_{1\bullet} = .95$
x_2	76	100		.95	.80	1.00	$\lambda^b_{2\bullet} = .76$
x_3	19	50		.95	.80	.50	$\lambda^b_{3\bullet} = .38$

4 Some features of the nested radial approach

4.1 Obtaining efficiency measures through the nested radial approach

It can be shown that the nested radial approach described in the preceding section can be used to generate as special cases some of the best known efficiency measures available in the literature. From table 1 it is clear that the highest ratio between the input quantity utilised by the efficient plan to that utilised by the inefficient plan (in the numerical example, the ratio relevant for x_1) is equal to the smallest radial contraction to be simultaneously applied to each input. Obviously, the latter is equivalent to the radial contraction carried out in Step 1 of the nested radial procedure or, in other words, to the traditional DF (input-oriented) measure, which is equal in the numerical example to 0.95. This manner of describing the DF measure turns out to have computional advantages in an FDH framework, not making it necessary any longer the calculation of the norm ratios of input vectors.

Alternatively, as it were at the other side of the spectrum, if we consider for the inefficient plan the product of the m radial contractions generated by the m projection vectors in the m input subspaces, we see that this product corresponds to the lowest ratio between the input quantity utilised by the efficient plan to that utilised by the inefficient plan. This ratio (which in the numerical example applies to x_3 and is equal to 0.38) corresponds to the Asymmetric Färe (AF) measure of technical efficiency. In fact, the latter is obtained by scaling down to the boundary of L (y) the single input for which the largest contraction obtains.

Yet other nonradial measures proposed in the literature can be conveniently obtained through the products of nested radial contractions. The well known Färe-Lovell (or Russell) input-oriented measure, usually defined as the arithmetic mean of the proportional contractions in each input dimension, is equal in the numerical example to

$$[\, 0.95 \; + \; 0.76 \; + \; 0.38 \,] \, / \, 3 = 0.70.$$

But clearly the above formula can also be obtained through the products of nested radial contractions:

$$[\, (0.95 \times 1.00 \times 1.00) + (0.95 \times 0.80 \times 1.00) + (0.95 \times 0.80 \times 0.50) \,] \, / \, 3 = 0.70.$$

Finally, note that in the present case, characterised by the presence of only one dominant observation (the efficient plan a) the FL measure is equivalent to another well-known nonradial measure, the Zieschang measure.[6] In the rest of the paper, however, we will not deal with this measure which is known to be non-monotonous within an FDH technology (Kerstens and Vanden Eeckaut, 1995, p. 13).

---

[6] In fact, this measure is obtained through a two-step procedure, whose first and second steps are respectively a radial contraction to reach the isoquant and a shrinkage of the input vector along Färe-Lovell lines in order to find an efficient subset. With only one dominant observation, one is bound to fall back to the same plan singled out by the FL measure.

4.2 Obtaining bounds for the correct measure of technical efficiency

As already said, the DF measure has a straightforward interpretation in terms of cost efficiency, due to its independence from the vector of input prices. Consider in fact the following formula which expresses, for an inefficient plan, the ratio of minimal (efficient) to actual costs:

$$\frac{\sum_{i=1}^{m} w_i \left(\prod_{j=1}^{m} \lambda_{ij} x_i^j \right)}{\sum_{i=1}^{m} w_i x_i^j} \qquad [1]$$

where w_i is the price of input i, and $\prod_{j=1}^{m} \lambda_{ij}$ is the product of the m radial contractions for each of the m inputs. Stopping at Step 1 of the nested radial procedure, one can characterise inefficiencies through the DF measure, yielding the following expression, which highlights the independence of this measure from relative factor prices:

$$\mathrm{DF}_{\mathrm{I}}\left(x^j, y^j\right) = \lambda = \frac{\sum_{i=1}^{m} w_i \left(\lambda x_i^j\right)}{\sum_{i=1}^{m} w_i x_i^j} \qquad [2]$$

However, it cannot be generally assumed that the DF measure satisfactorily sums up all inefficiencies, since it does not allow for input slacks. Alternative measures, allowing for slacks, are no longer independent from the vector of input prices, meaning that no simple relationship exists any longer between technical efficiency and the ratio of minimal to actual costs. However, even in this case expression (1) can be rearranged in order to give an empirically useful representation of the relationships between various measures of technical efficiency:

$$\frac{\sum_{i=1}^{m} \frac{w_i}{w_k} \left(\prod_{j=1}^{m} \lambda_{ij} x_i^j \right)}{\sum_{i=1}^{m} \frac{w_i}{w_k} x_i^j}$$

$$[3]$$

Quite obviously, w_k, taken as numeraire, denotes the price of input k. Now, the choice of a particular efficiency measure can be argued in terms of the values taken by the weights w_i/w_k.

Assuming that relative input prices are equal to the inverse of the ratio of input quantities available to the production plan $(x^i, y^i): w_i/w_k = x_k^j/x_i^j$, the ratio of minimal to actual costs can be obtained through the FL measure (see Kerstens and Vanden Eeckaut, 1995, pp. 22-23). If the ratio of minimal to actual costs is taken as the target of the measurement of technical efficiency, then in this case the FL measure is the correct measure of technical efficiency.

Reasoning along these lines, it is straightforward to find bounds for the correct measure of technical efficiency. Assume for instance $w_i/w_k \to 0$, $i \neq k$. In this case inputs $i \neq k$ are irrelevant and only input x_k matters for the cost valuation of technical efficiency. Now, if input x_k corresponds to input x_1 in the numerical example of table 1, the DF measure is the measure of technical efficiency to be preferred. At the other end of the spectrum, if input x_k corresponds to input x_3, it is the AF measure which is the correct measure. Hence, the nested radial approach yields a straightforward demonstration of the already known result (see Kerstens and Vanden Eeckaut, 1995) that the correct measure of technical efficiency has the DF measure for upper bound and the AF measure as lower bound. Also, in the presence of some a priori knowledge about the relative values of input prices, it can provide guidance as to which is the preferred measure of technical efficiency. As a matter of fact, from the above demonstration it can be surmised that the DF and AF measures will be limit cases not only in an analytical, but also in a practical sense because they rely on unlikely configurations of relative prices (one particular input price being much higher than the other ones and being at either end of the nested radial procedure). On the other hand, the assumption behind the FL measure (the existence of an inverse relationship between input prices and quantities) has much greater economic appeal.

5 An application

The data utilised in the application relate to a sample of 498 Italian rural banks and credit co-operatives taken from the Rating database for 1995.[7] Following a simple version of the value added approach, we will consider the following production set:

OUTPUTS: value of total loans, value of total deposits.

INPUTS: employees, equity.

Equity is taken as a proxy of capital inputs. Similar results were obtained using fixed assets (or the number of branches) and free capital. The version here adopted and illustrated was chosen mainly for its parsimony. Perhaps this is the point to make it clear that the present application only serves the purpose of illustrating the performance of the efficiency measures described above. A fuller analysis of efficiency for the DMU's here taken into account must be left for future research.

Positing an FDH technology for this production set and applying the nested radial procedure described in Section 3 yields results which are summed up in table 2.

Table 2 Main Results from the FDH Efficiency Analysis

N. DMU's:	498
N. EFFICIENT DMU's:	202
N. EFFICIENT BY DEFAULT DMU's:	54

SLACKS:
Contraction in output (%)
-14.81 (total loans)
-17.92 (total deposits)
Contraction in input (%)
 3.57 (employees)
11.45 (equity)

MEAN EFFICIENCY SCORE FOR THE 296 DOMINATED DMU's:

Debreu-Farrell	0.85
Färe-Lovell	0.75
Asymmetric Färe	0.62

---

[7] This dataset of this application is updated from Destefanis and Pavone (1996), while the format of the empirical analysis draws upon Destefanis (1996).

The main point that can be taken from table 2 is that a big gap shows up between the FL measure and the other two measures, standing at the opposite sides of the former one. It was noted above that the DF and AF measures might make economic sense only in the presence of pretty extreme assumptions about the structure of relative prices. This should imply that the DF and AF are poor measures of the cost gain due to technical efficiency, which is what is here meant by cost efficiency. In order to appraise this conjecture empirically, we built an empirical counterpart to expression (1), that is:

$$\frac{\sum_{i=1}^{m} w_i \left(\prod_{j=1}^{m} \lambda_{ij} x_i^j \right)}{\sum_{i=1}^{m} w_i x_i^j} \qquad [4]$$

A production set with inputs in value terms (that is, multiplied by their prices) was considered, and the λ_{ij}'s were found through the nested radial approach. Efficiency scores were calculated as the products of nested radial contractions, with input values being used as weights. These scores were subsequently compared to those obtained within the formerly considered production set.

More precisely, we started from the following production set:

OUTPUTS: value of total loans, value of total deposits.

INPUTS: labour costs, intermediation margins.

In other words, labour inputs were measured through labour costs and capital inputs were measured through intermediation margins. Clearly, assuming that the latter magnitude represents the remuneration of fixed assets and free capital is not as satisfactory as taking labour costs as the remuneration of labour. In fact, intermediation margins also include pure profits (that can be seen as the remuneration of the managerial input). Yet, as a first approximation, the efficiency scores obtained within this production set should provide a valuable empirical measure of the ratio of actual to minimal costs. The results obtained are shown in table 3.

The mean cost efficiency score is much closer to the mean score from the FL measure than to the other ones. Further comparison among the efficiency measures from the previous production set and the empirical cost efficiency measure was then carried out by means of coefficients of correlation. Beside the traditional Pearson measure, we considered here the Spearman and Kendall measures, which are particularly robust to the presence of outliers in the series considered. As customary,[8] we considered not only all DMU's, but also the subset of inefficient DMU's (in the present case, the *intersection* of inefficient DMU's

---

[8] See for instance De Borger and Kerstens (1996).

from the two production sets). In fact, the presence of efficient DMU's (all having scores equal to one) might bias the results of this exercise. Results are shown in table 4.

Table 3 Main Results for the Cost Efficiency Empirical Counterpart

N. DMU's :	498
N. EFFICIENT DMU's :	221
N. EFFICIENT BY DEFAULT DMU's:	57

SLACKS:
Contraction in output (%)
-12.20 (total loans)
-17.81 (total deposits)
Contraction in input (%)
  6.25 (labour costs)
  6.40 (intermediation margins)

MEAN C.Eff. SCORE FOR THE 277 DOMINATED DMU's = 0.77

Table 4 Coefficients of Correlation with $C.Eff._I$

N=498

KENDALL	PEARSON	SPEARMAN	
0.529	0.638	0.655	DF_I
0.524	0.639	0.658	FL_I
0.499	0.602	0.629	AF_I

N=212

KENDALL	PEARSON	SPEARMAN	
0.326	0.430	0.465	DF_I
0.349	0.486	0.503	FL_I
0.307	0.461	0.447	AF_I

Indeed, it can be seen that the presence of efficiency scores biases the results, putting the DF measure on a par with the FL one. On the contrary, when only inefficient observations are considered, the correlation between DF_I and $C.Eff._I$ falls considerably (even below AF_I in a circumstance).

As a check on these results, we carried out a slightly different empirical exercise. We considered the coefficients of correlation between the DF, FL and AF measures from the first production set (that is the one with employees and equity as inputs) and the ratios between minimum (efficient) and actual costs. In the previous exercise this ratio was calculated through expression (4). On the contrary, we now take for all observations the (inverse) ratio between actual costs and the costs of their dominant DMU, as singled out in the calculation of the DF, FL and AF measures from the first production set. Once again, we consider not only all DMU's, but also the subset of inefficient DMU's. Results are given in table 5.

Much the same considerations made about table 4 can be here repeated, although it should be noticed that the bias ensuing from considering all DMU's (including the efficient ones) seems to be less serious than before. FL_I has again an edge over the other two measures (including the still pervasively adopted DF_I).

All in all, both exercises suggest that slacks should be incorporated in the measure of technical efficiency in an FDH set-up, if obtaining a measure more representative of the cost gain associated to technical efficiency is a valuable target. Also, slacks seems to be much better accounted by the FL measure than by the AF one, which in many cases performs less well than the DF measure itself.

Table 5 Coefficients of Correlation with Cost Ratios

N=498

KENDALL	PEARSON	SPEARMAN	
0.458	0.533	0.584	DF_I
0.509	0.609	0.663	FL_I
0.458	0.553	0.604	AF_I

N=296

KENDALL	PEARSON	SPEARMAN	
0.317	0.419	0.451	DF_I
0.364	0.481	0.522	FL_I
0.281	0.397	0.410	AF_I

6 Concluding remarks

In this paper we propose a nested radial approach to the computation of technical efficiency in an FDH input-oriented framework. This approach follows a hierarchically nested sequence from the input space of dimension m to an input space of dimension one, obtaining at each step Debreu-Farrell measures which correspond to the amount of slack in a given input cancelled by a radial contraction in the relevant subspace. The products of these Debreu-Farrell measures yield the total input contraction required to bring an inefficient observation in the efficient subset.

Through this nested procedure it is possible (a) to reinterpret and to generate some nonradial measures proposed in the literature (asymmetric Färe, Färe-Lovell) in a computationally convenient manner; (b) to give a cost-efficiency interpretation of the result according to which the correct measure of technical efficiency always falls in an interval bounded by the asymmetric Färe and the radial Debreu-Farrell measures.

The procedure is then applied to a sample of Italian banking firms for 1995. This empirical exercise suggests that slacks should be incorporated in the measure of technical efficiency in an FDH set-up, if obtaining a measure more representative of the cost gain associated to technical efficiency is a valuable target. Also, slacks seems to be much better accounted by the FL measure than by the AF one.

REFERENCES

Bol G. (1986), *'On Technical Efficiency Measures: A Remark'*, Journal of Economic Theory, Vol. 38, pp. 380-385.

Cooper W.W., Pastoer J.T. (1996), *'Generalized Efficiency Measures (GEMS) and Model Relations for Use in DEA'*, mimeo, II Georgia Productivity Workshop.

De Borger B., Kersens K. (1996), *'Radial and Nonradial Measures of Technical Efficiency: An Empirical Illustration for Belgian Local Governments Using an FDH Reference Technology'*, Journal of Productivity Analysis, Vol. 7, pp. 41-62.

Debreu G. (1951), *'The Coefficient of Resource Utilisation'*, Econometrica, Vol. 19, pp. 273-292.

Destefanis S. (1996), *'Technical Efficiency in the Italian Banking Sector, A Nonparametric Approach'*, Rivista di Politica Economica, Vol. 86 serie III, nn. 11-12, pp. 385-414.

Destefanis S., Pavone A. (1996), '*Analisi dell'efficienza tecnica e Banche di Credito Cooperativo. Un'estensione e un'applicazione dell'approccio FDH*', Quaderni di Statistica e Matematica Applicata alle Scienze Economico-Sociali, Vol. 18, nn. 1-4, pp. 233-258.

Färe R., Lovell C.A.K. (1978), '*Measuring the Technical Efficiency of Production*', Journal of Economic Theory, Vol. 19, pp. 150-162.

Farrell M. J. (1957), '*The Measurement of Productive Efficiency*', Journal of the Royal Statistical Society, Series A, General, Vol. 120, pp. 253-281.

Fried O., Lovell C.A.K., Schmidt S. (eds.) (1993), *The Measurement of Productive Efficiency. Techniques and Applications*, Oxford University Press, London.

Kerstens K., Vanden Eeckaut P. (1995), '*Technical Efficiency Measures on DEA and FDH: A Reconsideration of the Axiomatic Literature*', CORE DP 9513, UCL, Louvain-la-Neuve.

Koopmans T.C. (1951), '*An Analysis of Production as an Efficient Combination of Activities*', in T.C. Koopmans (ed.), Activity Analysis of Production and Allocation, Wiley, New York.

Russell R.R. (1985), '*Measures of Technical Efficiency*', Journal of Economic Theory, Vol. 35, pp. 109-126.

Russell R.R. (1988), '*On the Axiomatic Approach to the Measurement of Technical Efficiency*', in W. Eichhorn (ed.), Measurement in Economics, Physica Verlag, Heidelberg.

Shepard R.W. (1970), *Theory of Cost and Production Functions*, Princeton University Press, Princeton.

UNOBSERVED REVENUES ESTIMATION FOR HOMOGENEOUS AGRICULTURAL FIRMS: AN ECONOMETRIC MODELLING APPROACH[1]

Marco Orsini[1] and Edoardo Pizzoli[2]

[1,2]*Italian National Institute of Statistic (ISTAT)*

1 Introduction

In recent years an increasing number of micro-data on some basic statistical units, as industrial and agricultural firms, or public and private institutions, are made available from administrative databases and national censuses. The main problems dealing with this kind of data are due to (i) measurement errors and partial observability of some characteristics, (ii) not correspondence of the observed population by alternative sources, and, finally, (iii) a relevant structural difference in at-first-sight homogeneous units. These problems are also met in the *ASIA* project carried on by the Italian National Institute of Statistic (*ISTAT*), in order to implement a new statistical database of active firms in Italy[2]. The *ASIA* database is mainly built up on information available from administrative sources, but in some practical cases these have to be completed or compared with estimations generated by statistical or econometric techniques[3].

This paper aims to bring a contribution in this direction, within the *ASIA*-Agriculture context. To find a solution to the mentioned problems we perform two main stages of research.

First, we classify agricultural firms in a number of clusters, making use of an *a-priori* information set about their structural characteristics. This preliminary classification is necessary as there is a wide dishomogeneity among families of firms. The assumption we make at this stage, is that structural homogeneity

---

[1] This paper is prepared for the *International Conference on Comparative Analysis of Enterprise (micro) Data*, held in Bergamo, Italy. This research is part of the *ASIA* project, promoted by *EUROSTAT* and financially supported by the Italian Government. The authors are very grateful to Roberto Filippini, responsible of the *ASIA*-Agriculture sub-project, for his scientific support and his encouragement. A particular thank goes to Loris Giusto who has constructed the sample data.
Chapters 1,5,6,7 by E. Pizzoli, Chapters 2,3,4 by M. Orsini.
[2] See the final reports of the two commissions *EUROSTAT* (1995) and *ISTAT* (1995).
[3] See Biffignandi and Martini (1995).

implies the existence of a common revenues function, that can be estimated on a sample of the firm's population.

Second, we estimate the cross-section revenues model for each cluster of firms and then we perform a point estimation of individual revenues for the population. In this way we are able to get an accurate measurement of this economic variable, that can be introduced in the *ASIA*-Agriculture database when the data is missing.

When the data on revenues is present for new firms to be included in the database, a test can be done to filter the observed data. If revenues are not significantly different from the corresponding theoretical level, coming from the model, then we accept its value and it is introduced in the database, otherwise it is replaced with the theoretical one.

At this stage of the analysis we are also able to test whether a firm is active from an economic view point and to exclude from the database the not-active ones, where a firm is said to be active if its revenues are greater than a minimum critical value.

The state of a firm is a main characteristic to be verified for the building of the *ASIA*-Agriculture database, as the data we use in our analysis are from the Agriculture Census, that is data collected on statistical units (farms) with a slightly different definition. The population of farms is for our purpose a wider one, since it includes a large subset of units that do not sell their output on the market but just perform farm consumption[4].

All the previous stages can be summarized with the following figure:

Figure 1 Modelling, data integration and filtering

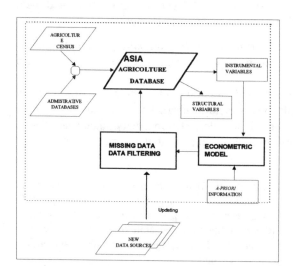

---

[4] See, for instance, Filippini (1996).

Finally, the model we estimate in our work can be used to study the relationship between the agricultural firms' structural characteristics and their economic performance.

Unfortunately empirical studies of this kind, involving individual revenues for agricultural firms, are not numerous especially for Italy, the main reason being the lack of micro-data sets available containing these individual data. The recent access to administrative data bank by the National Institute of Statistics, has opened a wide range of possibilities for micro-analysis and econometric modelling. In our research, in particular, the Ministry of Finance data bank has been an exceptional source, containing information on annual revenues declared by firms.

The rest of the paper is organized as follows: in the first two sections we discuss the data source and the statistical techniques we use in what follows. The Agriculture Census database contains detailed information on individual characteristics of firms. These data are described in detail in section 2.1. In section 2.2 we introduce the sample we use for our analysis and the firm's annual revenues received from a second source of data, that is the Ministry of Finance database. In section 3 we summarize the techniques we use in the analysis. In the following three sections we report the results of the two main stages of the analysis: section 4 is dedicated to the classification in clusters of agricultural firms, section 5 reports the model and finally three applications are given in section 6, to a better understanding of the results. Section 7 concludes the paper.

2 Data

2.1 Population

The data used in this paper come primarily from the 4° Agriculture Census, held in 1990[5]. The full population, Ψ, of $N(\Psi) = 2,940,546$ firms[6] has been observed and a large set of qualitative and quantitative characteristics has been measured on each of them.

In the analysis that follows we used only a subset H of $N(H) = m + k$ characteristics, that for our purpose has been divided into two subsets: (i) a set Z of m structural characteristics, and (ii) a set X of k instrumental ones. We used

---

[5] The selection of a 1990 data source has been a necessary one, as this is a complete database and other administrative data sources are delaying. For a methodological foundation of *ASIA*-Agriculture database and why this data source has been considered for its implementation see Filippini (1996), p. 29.

[6] From now on we shall simplify the terminology and we shall always call our statistical units *firms*.

the first set to cluster the population into *n* groups of homogeneous firms, while the second one as a vector of regressors in the revenues model.

The set *Z* includes main information about the geographical location of the firm, his economic activity, dimension and organisation.

Into set *X* we find, instead, measurements of the inputs used in the production process, that is land, labour, machinery and livestock.

The Selection of these characteristics and the subdivision into (Z, X) is the result of considerations based on an *a-priori* information set Ω, that includes the theory of agricultural economics and past experience. At this preliminary stage of the analysis has been fundamental Filippini's scientific support, for his long experience of work (about thirty years) at the National Institute of Statistics on censuses and microeconomics studies of agricultural firms.

2.1.1 Structural characteristics

Set *Z* is composed of 3 qualitative characteristics of the firms and 19 variables (*m* = 22). The qualitative characteristics are the legal form of the firm, its geographical location (macro-zone) and its prevailing economic activity (macro-activity). The other variables are the land available to the firm and several ratios introduced as indicators of the others inputs mix (labour, machinery and livestock), the organisation and the joint production processes implemented by the firm. The full list of this set of characteristics is reported in table 1.

An explanation is necessary for two main characteristics of the firm, the macro-zone and macro-activity, as they will play an important role in our classification[7].The subdivision of Italian territory in 36 macro-zones is the result of a bringing up to date of Rossi Doria (1969) subdivision in homogeneous agricultural areas. This subdivision is mainly based on the geographical characteristics of land (soil, altimetery, north-south latitude, climate, etc.), that is a fundamental factor in the production process of agricultural firms.

This territorial classification has been brought up to date and integrated to the present administrative subdivision of Italy in *Regioni*, *Province* and *Comuni*, by Filippini (1984, 1996). The list of macro-zones can be found in table 2 and a graphical representation is reported in figure 2.

---

[7] See section 4.

Table 1 Set Z of structural charateristics of the firms

Variables	Range	Definitions(*)
Z01	(1 - 32)	Macro-zones
Z02	(1 - 9)	Macro-activity (*OTE*)
Z03	(1 - 6)	Legal form
Z04	R^+	Total land
Z05	[0, 100]	Land not in use over total one
Z06	[0, 100]	Land in the same municipality (*comune*) over total one
Z07	[0, 100]	Secondary arable land over *SAU* land (i.e land in use)
Z08	[0, 100]	Joint cultivations over *SAU* land
Z09	[0, 100]	Irrigated land over *SAU* land
Z10	[0, 100]	Woodlands over *SAU* land
Z11	[0, 100]	Milk cows and buffalo cows over total one
Z12	R^+	Total labour over *SAU* land
Z13	[0, 100]	Family labour over *SAU* land
Z14	[0, 100]	Head family labour over *SAU* land
Z15	[0, 100]	Primary arable land over *SAU* land
Z16	[0, 100]	Arboriculture over *SAU* land
Z17	[0, 100]	Permanent meadows and pastures over *SAU* land
Z18	R^+	Big head of cattle over arable land and maedows
Z19	R^+	Units of economic dimension (*UDE*) over *SAU* land
Z20	R^+	Active minus passive agricultural contracting over *SAU* land
Z21	N	Tractors used in firms over *SAU* land
Z22	R^+	Milk transformation over *Z18*

(*) A deeper definition of these variables can be found in ISTAT (1991): "Caratteristiche tipologiche delle aziende agricole", 4° Agriculture census, fascicolo nazionale, pp. 137-47.

Table 2 Italian macro-zones

Id	Macro-zones
01	Western alpin mountain
02	Central alpin mountain
03	Eastern alpin mountain
04	*Liguria*'s appenninic mountain
05	*Tosco-emiliana*'s appenninic mountain
06	*Tosco-marchigiana*'s appenninic mountain
07	Appenninic mountain of *Lazio, Abbruzzo* and *Molise*
08	South appenninic mountain (escluded *Abbruzzo* and *Molise)*
09	Insular mountain
10	Prealpin hill
11	Central-northern preappenninic hill
12	Southern preappenninic hill
13	*Po, Monferrato, Langhe* and *Bormida* hills
14	*Liguria*'s coastal hill
15	Tyrrhenian's coastal hill
16	Adriatic's coastal hill
17	Plains and hills of southern Tyrrhenian, Ionian and southern Adriatic
18	Western partition of large estates in central internal hills
19	Eastern partition of large estates in central internal hills
20	Not partition of large estates in central internal hills
21	Southern internal extensive plains and hills
22	Southern promiscuous plains and hills
23	*Maremma tosco-laziale*
24	Southern arborical
25	Northern dry plain
26	Central internal plain
27	North-western intensive plain
28	North-central intensive plain
29	North-eastern intensive plain
30	Alta *Toscana*'s plain
31	*Agro pontino*
32	*Campania*'s coastal plain
33	Insular extensive areas
34	Insular promiscuous areas
35	Insular arboricultural areas
36	Insular intensive areas

Figure 2 Macro-zones subdivision of italian territory

The second classification of agricultural activity in macro groups has been done with the *OTE* subdivision (*ISTAT-INEA*) introduced for the agriculture census[8]. For each firm in our population we have the indication of his main activity, since, in general, a joint production is the normal case in agriculture. The list of 9 macro-activity is reported in table 3:

---

[8] See *ISTAT* (1990) for a definition of *OTE*.

Table 3 Macro-activity

Id	Macro-activity
1	Arable land
2	Horticulture and floriculture
3	Permanent cultivations
4	Herbivorous
5	Grainivorous
6	Polycultivation
7	Polybreeding
8	Cultivations and breedings
9	Others

2.1.2 Instrumental characteristics

The second set of characteristics, X, is equal to 2 qualitative characters, followed by a detailed list of variables on inputs employed in the production process, or proxy variables of them ($k = 39$). The list of this set is reported in table 4.

The two qualitative characters are the management systems of the firm (Table 5) and a flag (yes, no) to state if fish breeding is done.

The remaining variables measure the different types of labour, land and machinery employed in an annual production process (farm year).

A final variable of control, *UDE* (Unit of Economic Dimension), is introduced among the regressors to grasp the efficiency of the firm and his relationship with revenues. The *UDE* is used in agriculture as an administrative measure of the potential output of a firm, given his structural characteristics. We expect to find a strong correlation of this variable with revenues, but as we shall see in section 6 this is rarely the case. This point should be studied in depth in a further stage of the research, but an intuitive explanation is that it depends very likely on the special way revenues are measured[9] and on a wide technical inefficiency and not-market orientation of a subset of the firms (i.e. farms) used as our population.

---

[9] See section 2.2.1 for this point.

Table 4 Set X of instrumental charateristics of the firms

Variables	Range	Definitions
$X01$	$(1 - 6)$	Management system
$X02$	$[0, 100]$	Property land over total one
$X03$	R^+	*SAU* land (i.e. land in use)
$X04$	R^+	Primary arable land
$X05$	R^+	Primary dried cereals
$X06$	R^+	Industrial plants
$X07$	R^+	Potatoes
$X08$	R^+	Open air vegetables and fresh pulses
$X09$	R^+	Protected vegetables and fresh pulses
$X10$	R^+	Open air flowers and ornamental plants
$X11$	R^+	Protected flowers and ornamental plants
$X12$	R^+	Green fodder by rotation crop
$X13$	R^+	Arboriculture
$X14$	R^+	Vineyards
$X15$	R^+	Olive growing
$X16$	R^+	Citrus fruits
$X17$	R^+	Orchards
$X18$	R^+	Permanent meadows and pastures
$X19$	R^+	Grapes transformation over vineyards
$X20$	R^+	Olives transformation over olive growing
$X21$	R^+	Woodlands
$X22$	R^+	Cattle and buffaloes
$X23$	R^+	Sheeps and goats
$X24$	R^+	Pigs
$X25$	R^+	Rabbits
$X26$	R^+	Poultry
$X27$	$(0 - 1)$	Presence of fish breedings
$X28$	R^+	Big head of cattle
$X29$	$[1, 365]$	Family labour
$X30$	$[1, 365]$	Head family labour
$X31$	$[1, 365]$	Extra-family labour
$X32$	$[1, 365]$	Total labour
$X33$	R^+	Active agricultural contracting
$X34$	R^+	Passive agricultural contracting
$X35$	N	Total tractors
$X36$	N	Tractors used in firms
$X37$	N	Refrigeration sistema
$X38$	R^+	Milk transformation
$X39$	R^+	Units of economic dimension (UDE)

Table 5 Management systems of the agriculture firms

Id	Management systems
1	Direct farming with only family labour
2	Direct farming with prevailing family labour
3	Direct farming with prevailing extra-family labour
4	With wage-earners and/or share-croppers
5	Share-cropping
6	Other management system

2.2 Sample

The sample Φ, of $N(\Phi) = 156,642$ firms has been selected at time t from the population, based on revenues observability through an administrative database. In such a way, for each firm of the sample we got information on H, available from the 1990 Census, and on the variable y (revenues), from the Ministry of Finance databases.

The main problem we found to link individual data coming from two different database, has been to find a one-to-one link-key for each firm. To this purpose we used the fiscal code given to any individual and firm by the Ministry of Finance[10]. In theory a full linking of the databases would imply an observation of y for the whole population. In practice we could produce only a sample of firms of 5.19 % of the population with full (H, y) observed, that is, in spite of this, a large sample in absolute value.

This property of the sample has been very useful for the econometric analysis and the punctual inference we produced in our work, as we could rely on the law of large numbers and the asymptotic properties of the estimators[11].

2.2.1 Revenues information

The database of the Ministry of Finance contains information on total revenues and other characteristics annually declared by individuals and firms. This is an exceptional source of economic micro-data, but unfortunately the way the data are collected has several weakness that have to be considered in our analysis.

---

[10] See Giusto and Gianico (1996).
[11] See, for istance, Davidson and MacKinnon (1993), p. 99.

What is observed by the Ministry are the revenues annually declared by each firm for its direct taxation. In such a way, we expect to find a variable with two likely measurement errors.

First of all, some firms are not just agricultural ones, but they have a joint production that belongs to different sectors: agriculture and food-industry, or agriculture and distribution, or all of them. For this reason we need to identify the deviating or outliers firms in term of revenues, given the same structural characteristics of other firms in the cluster. In general, we found firms with a too high declared revenues; a difference that cannot be justified in term of just higher relative efficiency. Such firms outlier, have not to be considered for the estimation of the common revenues function of the cluster.

The second type of likely error is due to the purpose (taxation) and conditions (privately and individually) the revenues declaration is done. We expect in fact a systematic under-measurement of this economic variable.

In relation to this second problem it is impossible to find a solution, without a different data source, to get an estimate of the error's level and its behaviour at different revenues levels, or without to make a too narrow assumption on it.

3 Methods

3.1 Clustering Analysis

The techniques of clustering we apply in our research have been selected in relation to the purpose of the analysis; that is to get homogeneous clusters of firms that imply a common revenues function.

The algorithm used is the following: once a cluster is found, the function is estimated on a subset of the cluster and then it is applied to produce a point estimation of revenues. To reach this objective it is necessary to get an high fitting level of the function estimated. If we are not able to identify a good model for each cluster, than we can conclude that the cluster found is not homogeneous in the previous sense. Then a new round of search is started. The process can be stopped when a pre-fixed critical R^2 level is satisfied from any clusters of the population.

With this objective in mind we followed a general-to-specific approach, first making use of the full information set available, Z, and then looking for the subset of characteristics able to identify the clusters required.

The following methods are applied in our research:
1. The k-means method, to quantitative characteristics (variables) of the population;
2. The sample stratification, to just qualitative characters.

Both methods are appropriate to our analysis as we have a large set of observations and some qualitative characters in Z. In particular the k-means finds k disjoint clusters of coordinate data and is especially suitable for large data sets containing as many as 100,000 observations.

3.2 Model selection

As in the previous stage of the analysis, to select and estimate the revenues model for each cluster of firms, we followed a general-to-specific approach. This is suggested in the up to date econometric literature as the best searching procedure to find the "estimable" model of the data. This model is a particular form of the theoretical one (the "true" model) which is potentially estimable in view of the actual data generating process (DGP) and the observed data chosen[12].

Following this approach we specified a general model with a full information set X and then we reduced this model to reach a "correct" specification, in terms of the desirable properties of residuals and a good fitting level.

The final model estimated satisfies the following properties:
1. High fitting level (pre-fixed $R^2 \geq 0.8$);
2. Low collinearity of regressors;
3. Low heteroskedasticity of residuals.

The ordinarily least squares (OLS) estimator has been used for the parameters estimation. When we found heteroschedastic residuals and an estimation of the covariance matrix of the residual ($\hat{\Sigma}_\varepsilon$) can be found, we attempted an application of feasible generalised least squares (GLS). If we did not get a clear different estimation of the parameters, we preferred to leave the previous OLS estimations, as GLS become just a useless complication of the analysis.

We know from the theory that heteroskedasticity of the residuals create potentially serious problems to OLS estimator: (i) it is inefficient with respect to GLS estimator and (ii) OLS covariance matrix estimator (and so standard errors) is inconsistent. As a consequence all the diagnostic analysis based on t and F tests may no longer be appropriate[13].

The level of distortion depends on the divergence of Σ_ε from $\sigma^2 I$, that is the covariance matrix of residuals normally assumed for the regression model.

However, one can rarely be certain that the data are heteroscedastic and what form the heteroschedasticity takes. In practice, with a cross-section dataset, we can only assume a simple special type of heteroschedasticity.

In any case, a general conclusion is the following: "if heteroschedasticity is not correlated with the variables in the model, then, at least in large samples, the

---

[12] See Spanos (1986).
[13] See White (1980).

ordinary least squares computation, while not the optimal way to use the data, will not be misleading"[14].

Finally, at the end of this round of reseach, that is once we got a good estimated model, we checked its correct specification following the alternative step-wise procedure.

A final problem to solve is to find the outliers firms in term on revenues, as indicated in the previous section 2.2.1. As a diagnostic tool, we followed Belseley et al. (1980) suggestion to standardize the residuals by dividing them by the following appropriate standard error:

$$\widetilde{e}_i = e_i / \left(s^2 \left(1 - h_{ii} \right) \right)^{\frac{1}{2}}, \quad h_{ii} \in H \equiv \left[X \left(X' X \right)^{-1} X' \right] \qquad [1]$$

This standardized residual is approximately distributed as standard normal, and values in excess of 2 suggest observations that deserve closer scrutiny. The suggestion is to eliminate all of them as outliers, but in our work we prefered to start at an higher critical value (equal to 4) to minimize the eliminated firms.

4 Classification

We assume the existence of n clusters of homogeneous firms in terms of some structural characteristics, that implies, has we have already said in the previous sections, the existence of a common cross-section revenues function.

Given the set Z of structural characteristics, we attempted to identify the clusters through several stages of classification and estimation of the function, following the algorithm indicated in section 3.1.

4.1 First stage: m characteristics - equal weights

At the first stage of the analysis we applied the k-means technique to the set Φ, making use of all the variables in Z. After several attempts to find the right number of clusters and a grid-search to identify their central points, we found a pour distinction of the firms in just a main group and four marginal ones. The results are reported in the following table:

---

[14] See Greene (1991).

Table 6 Cluster analysis results

Cluster	Frequency
1	147.568
2	8.444
3	316
4	169
5	48

We got this result even if the k-means method tends to find clusters, with roughly the same number of observations in each cluster. The estimation of a model for the main group, revealed an unsatisfactory discrimination of firms inside this cluster. This result suggested us that too many information may produced a noisy-effect into the clustering procedure, reducing its discrimination power.

After that, we gradually reduced the number of characters considered into the analysis, weighting them on the basis of our *a-priori* information set Ω and accumulated experience.

4.2 Final stage: 2 characteristics - different weights

At the end of our search process we identify two main qualitative characteristics effective to distinguish the structural differences of agricultural firms: their geographical location (macro-zone) and their economic macro-activity. Both of them imply a substantial structural and behavioural difference among firms and so a different revenues function. This is because these characteristics are informative proxy of several others characteristics relative to soil, climate and social capability (human capital, culture, production organisation and so on) of the geographical area.

Making use of these two characteristics, we could identify the *234 clusters* of firms reported in table 7.

The positive result we found, has been confirmed from the very good fitting observed for all the estimated models and the wide variety of significant variables associated. Three clear examples are given in section 6, that illustrate very well the variety of situation we can find in the agricultural firm's population.

Table 7 Cluster analysis: final stage results

Cluster Id	Sample freq.	Cluster Id	Sample freq.	Cluster Id	Sample freq.	Cluster Id	Sample freq.
1	57	60	2242	119	158	178	1775
2	103	61	2510	120	157	179	2333
3	88	62	745	121	95	180	1840
4	66	63	347	122	189	181	631
5	978	64	682	123	1947	182	1985
6	915	65	210	124	311	183	264
7	86	66	283	125	230	184	725
8	81	67	693	126	263	185	155
9	136	68	137	127	99	186	69
10	52	69	217	128	337	187	118
11	117	70	194	129	1430	188	77
12	51	71	536	130	704	189	356
13	3029	72	96	131	395	190	747
14	4386	73	2984	132	442	191	731
15	103	74	572	133	230	192	929
16	92	75	844	134	283	193	199
17	302	76	352	135	1134	194	199
18	70	77	752	136	109	195	614
19	126	78	70	137	181	196	223
20	40	79	2176	138	429	197	667
21	100	80	89	139	361	198	264
22	44	81	114	140	132	199	169
23	102	82	37	141	304	200	120
24	48	83	256	142	92	201	349
25	389	84	164	143	64	202	959
26	1754	85	94	144	965	203	211
27	70	86	80	145	140	204	169
28	90	87	49	146	120	205	187
29	175	88	132	147	90	206	235
30	420	89	2523	148	144	207	365
31	93	90	167	149	1399	208	223
32	434	91	498	150	151	209	2068
33	156	92	117	151	1997	210	136
34	126	93	765	152	1497	211	281
35	359	94	100	153	483	212	56
36	151	95	253	154	323	213	287
37	688	96	646	155	1216	214	223
38	83	97	99	156	614	215	476
39	137	98	2630	157	72	216	869
40	314	99	411	158	60	217	194
41	641	100	415	159	74	218	153
42	310	101	101	160	98	219	55
43	568	102	242	161	3885	220	63
44	164	103	1225	162	165	221	650
45	202	104	128	163	373	222	325
46	639	105	975	164	2316	223	1262
47	92	106	754	165	339	224	881
48	122	107	570	166	157	225	43
49	539	108	259	167	1631	226	293
50	118	109	460	168	10978	227	171
51	899	110	1028	169	517	228	254
52	317	111	90	170	5911	229	129
53	1681	112	758	171	6608	230	50
54	2220	113	318	172	211	231	81
55	576	114	541	173	2837	232	120
56	530	115	215	174	474	233	45
57	1192	116	410	175	2174	234	232
58	1418	117	353	176	6478		
59	193	118	199	177	845	**Total**	**156642**

5 Revenues model

The general revenues model assumed in the analysis is the following:

$$y_i = X_i \beta_i + \varepsilon_i \qquad\qquad i = 1,...,n \qquad\qquad [2]$$

Where n is the number of clusters we found; y_i are revenues; X_i is the matrix of $(m-1)$ instrumental variables plus a constant and 5 dummies $(d2-d6)$ for a qualitative characteristics of the firm $(X01)$, times the number of observations for cluster i in the dataset (c_i); β_i is the vector of $(m+5)$ parameters to be estimated for the cluster.

We assume that model [2] is the true unknown model of the population and so that it exists and it is stable over the whole population at time t. This assumption allows us to estimate the unknown parameters of the model β_i, from our sample ϕ_i.

To get a clear exposition of the results of our analysis, it is very useful to illustrate the full results for three of the clusters selected.

6 Three applications

6.1 Cluster n. 6

This is a cluster of 23,093 firms that belongs to Central Mountain Alps macro-zone, in the North of Italy. The territorial distribution of the firms in the macro-zone can been easily seen with the following cartogram:

Figure 3 Firms of cluster 6 distribution in macro-zone 2 by *Comune*

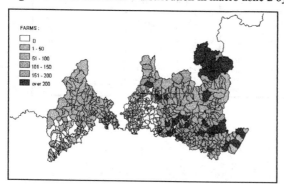

The geographical location of these firms imply a common structural characteristics in terms of soil, climate and social capability, as we have already said before.

The second common characteristic of these firms is their main macro-activity: herbivorous and grain-eating animal breeding.

This set of two qualitative variables is sufficient to get an homogeneous cluster of firms in term of the revenues function [2]. In fact, as we can immediately see, we got a well specified model with an high fitting of the function to the data:

MODEL 6:

$$y = 31.05 + 103.13X07 + 2.73X12 - 0.15X23 + 0.02X26 + 1.19X28 +$$
$$\text{S.E.} \quad (8.47) \quad (22.03) \quad\quad (1.1) \quad\quad (0.05) \quad\quad (0.0009) \quad\quad (0.07)$$

$$[3]$$

$$-0.07X30 + 1.42X31 - 6.24X36 - 179.79d2 + 435.91d3$$
$$(0.03) \quad\quad (0.02) \quad\quad (2.48) \quad\quad (9.23) \quad\quad (44.7)$$

$$R^2 = 0.9 \quad\quad\quad\quad \hat{\sigma} = 58.87$$

For the estimation of this model we used a set of $N(\Phi_6) = 915$ firms, that represent the 3.96 % of the population's cluster.

The coefficients of this equation were estimated with an *OLS* estimator.

6.1.1 Diagnostic analysis

The diagnostic analysis of the residuals revealed, as expected from a cross section model, heteroskedasticity of the residuals. The following tests reject the null hypothesis of homoskedasticity, at a 2 % significance level:

White's general test: $\chi^2 = 508.91 > \chi^2_{18,0.01} = 9.38$

As we said in section 3.2, this is a case where a re-estimation of the model with feasible *GLS* making a simple assumption on the form of heteroskedasticity, did not produce an elimination of the problem. For this reason, we preferred to use the estimated model [3] for inference analysis.

A graphical analysis of the residuals and of the model fitting, is reported in the following figure:

Figure 4 Grafical analysis for the model [3]

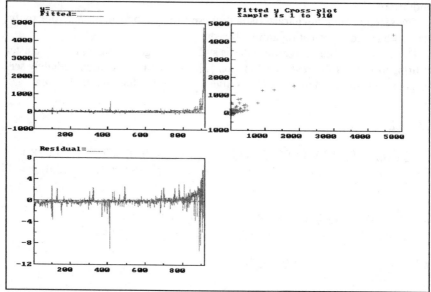

A comparison of the estimated revenues values and their observed levels, can be done in the top-left graph of figure 4, where firms are ordered by observed revenues levels.

Finally, once the model is estimated a punctual estimation of y is done when the data is missing for a firm. After that, the filtering on y and the test on the state of the firm are performed.

6.2 Cluster n. 173

The second cluster reported is that of firms in macro-zone 28, that is north-western intensive plain, and with macro-activity 6: polycultivations. The territorial distribution of these firms can be seen in figura 5:

This is a cluster of $c_{173} = 12,837$, while its size in the sample is $N(\Phi_{173}) = 2,837$, that is 23.45 % of the population.

In the estimation of model [2] for this cluster, we found a similar story to the previous example. We got the following well specified model with a very high fitting:

Figure 5 Firms of cluster 173 distribution in macro-zone 28 by *Comune*

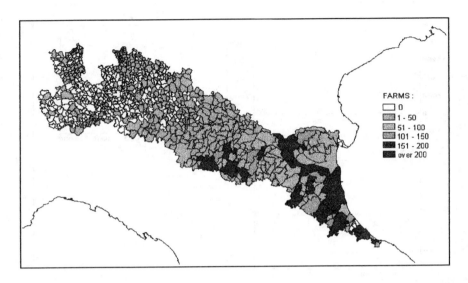

MODEL 173:

$$y = 22.78 + 31.13X10 + 24.02X11 + 174.97X12 + 1807X13 + 36.79X15 +$$
$$S.E. \;\; (14.97) \;\;\; (2.32) \;\;\;\;\;\; (11.01) \;\;\;\;\;\;\; (46.76) \;\;\;\;\;\;\; (184.42) \;\;\;\;\; (0.69)$$

$$-34.45X20 + 0.58X24 + 0.88X26 + 0.11X28 + 1966.5X29 +$$
$$(0.94) \;\;\;\;\; (0.22) \;\;\;\;\;\; (0.08) \;\;\;\;\;\;\; (0.001) \;\;\;\;\;\; (152.44)$$

[4]

$$-0.09X31 - 0.15X32 - 2.02X36 + 0.35X37 + 0.05X40 +$$
$$(0.03) \;\;\;\;\; (0.08) \;\;\;\;\;\;\; (0.5) \;\;\;\;\;\;\; (0.17) \;\;\;\;\; (0.01)$$

$$-46.17d2 - 167.91d3 - 219.01d4$$
$$(13.42) \;\;\;\;\; (29.64) \;\;\;\;\; (29.76)$$

$$R^2 = 0.88 \qquad\qquad \hat{\sigma} = 289.54$$

Figure 6 Grafical analysis for the model [4]

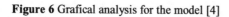
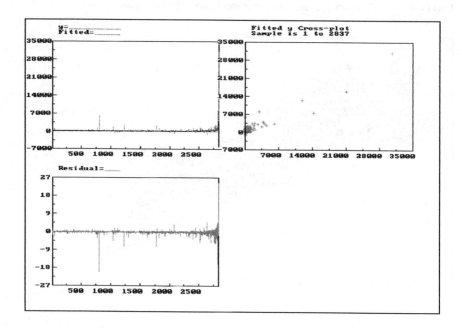

6.3 Cluster n. 190

The last example reported is the set of firms in macro-zone 31, that is a plain at the centre-east of Italy (*agro-pontino*), with macro-activity 2: horticulture and floriculture. The territorial distribution is shown in figure 7.

Figure 7 Firms of cluster 190 distribution in macro-zone 31 by *Comune*

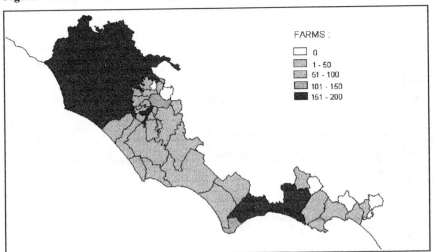

We have $c_{190} = 3,488$ firms in the population, while the set is of $N(\Phi_{190}) = 747$, that is the 21 % of the population.

The estimated model for this cluster is th following:

MODEL 190:

$$y = -21.09 + 48.40X03 - 77.34X05 - 82.17X14 - 106.75X15 + 14299X17 +$$
$$S.E. \quad (11.83) \quad (2.32) \quad\quad (10.67) \quad\quad (17.76) \quad\quad (37.22) \quad\quad (16.51)$$

$$[5]$$

$$-65.29X18 - 2.19X25 + 284.64d4$$
$$(7.11) \quad\quad (1.06) \quad\quad (120.7)$$

$$R^2 = 0.95 \quad\quad\quad \hat{\sigma} = 285.52$$

Figure 8 Grafical analysis for the model [5]

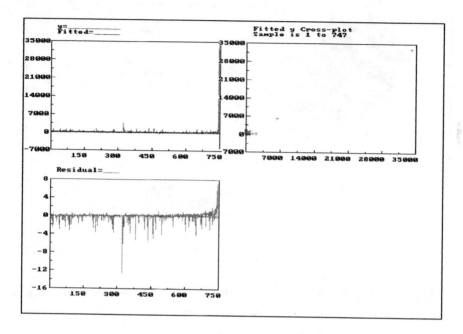

In relation to all the three models estimated, we can clearly see that most of the entered variables are different, and this is because of the structural differences we said before. Most of the significant variables are characteristic of the zone we considered; this explains why it has been necessary to use such a disaggregate estimation of model [2].

7 Conclusions

The results reported in this paper represent just a first attempt to find a solution to some of the problems we find dealing with several administrative data sources: that is (i) measurement errors and partial observability of some characteristics, (ii) not corrispondence of the observed population by alternative sources, and, finally, (iii) a relevant structural difference in at-first-sight homogeneous units.

The parametric approach we developed to estimate the firms' revenues not observed via administrative sources, and so to find a solution to one of the previous problems, has produced very encouraging results. What we expect is a further development of this econometric approach and an application to similar problems within the *ASIA* project.

An important check of the calculated estimations and so of the validity of the applied techniques, will be possible in the near future, as soon as other administrative data (*UNIONCAMERE, INEA,* etc.), already requested from *ISTAT*, will be made available.

REFERENCES

Belsley D., Kuh E., Welsch R. (1980), *Regression Diagnostics, Identifying Influential Data and Sources of Collinearity*, Wiley, New York.

Biffignandi S., Martini M. (1995), *Il Registro Statistico Europeo delle Imprese. Esperienze e Metodi per la sua Costruzione in Italia*, Franco Angeli, Milano.

Commission (1995), *'Repertori d'impresa: manuale di raccomandazioni repertori',* Report, n. 1-10, mimeo, *EUROSTAT*, Brussels.

Commission (1995), *'Archivio Statistico delle Imprese Attive (ASIA)'*, Final Report, mimeo, ISTAT, Rome.

Davidson, R. and MacKinnon, J. G. (1993*), Estimation and Inference in Econometrics*, Oxford University Press, Oxford.

Filippini R. (1984), *Il Part-Time in Agricoltura, CIPA.AT*, Rome.

Filippini R. (1996), *'Imprese agricole e registro delle imprese'*, ASIA-Agricolture Report, n. 3, mimeo, ISTAT, Rome.

Giusto L., Gianico G. (1996), *'Procedura per imporre sullo schedario delle aziende agricole il codice fiscale del conduttore rilevato da altre fonti amministrative'*, ASIA-Agricolture Report, n. 6, ISTAT, Rome.

Greene W. H. (1991), *Econometric Analysis*, Macmillan Publishing, New York.

ISTAT (1990), *'Categorie tipologiche delle aziende agricole'*, 4° Agriculture Census, Fascicolo Nazionale, ISTAT, Rome.

Rossi Doria M. (1969), *'Analisi zonale dell'agricoltura italiana'*, Collana di studi e ricerche, INEA-Ministry of Public Finance, Rome.

Spanos A. (1986), *Statistical Foundations of Econometric Modelling*, Cambridge University Press, Cambridge.

White, H. (1980), *'A Heteroskedasticity-Consistent Covariance Matrix Estimator and a Direct Test For Heteroskedasticity'*, Econometrica, May, Vol. 48, N. 4, pp. 817-838.

ISSUES IN FOLLOWING ENTERPRISES THROUGH TIME

Pierre Lavallée[1] and Peter Struijs[2]

[1] *Statistics Canada*
[2] *Eurostat*

1 Introduction

According to Kish (1965), a panel is a sample in which the same elements are measured on two or more occasions[1]. In the European Union, the statistical units[2] used for economic surveys by National Statistical Institutes (NSI) are usually either enterprises, local units, kind-of-activity units, or local kind-of-activity units (see Eurostat, 1997b). For business panels, any of these types of units can be followed through time. The followed units are called *longitudinal units*. The choice of the longitudinal unit depends on:

(1) the variables to be collected;
(2) the type of analysis envisaged;
(3) the requirements of the framework of which the panel may be part;
(4) the availability of data; and
(5) other practical aspects such as the stability of the units over time.

In the present paper, we will focus on the enterprise. Note that the discussion would be quite similar if any other type of unit was chosen[3]. The establishment as defined in ISIC Rev.3 is a unit often used outside the European Union. This paper focuses on the enterprise mainly because this unit is generally considered the central unit in the European system of business statistics.

Unfortunately, although the definition of the enterprise as a statistical unit is harmonized in the European Union (see Eurostat, 1996), there is no unique definition of a *longitudinal* enterprise. An enterprise is a dynamic entity whose composition can change through time. First, sameness through time should be

---

[1] This definition of panels is the one adopted for the paper. Some other definitions are sometimes however being used elsewhere.

[2] The statistical units are defined in Council Regulation (EEC) No. 696/93 of 15 March 1993 on the statistical units for the observation and analysis of the production system in the Community.

[3] Since concentration and deconcentration are rare events for local units and local kind-of-activity units, the discussion could be simplified if one of these units is chosen as the longitudinal unit.

defined; this determines whether any given enterprise can be observed on two occasions. In general this might depend on factors such as:
(1) the continuity of ownership or of the higher-level unit;
(2) the continuity of the lower-level units;
(3) the continuity of characteristics such as the economic activity and location;
(4) the continuity of utilization of production factors such as employees; and
(5) market continuity.

The time lapse between the two observations (for panels: the time lapse between the waves) also plays an important role. If one waits a very long time, it is improbable that sameness is preserved, whatever the specific criteria applied. For a detailed discussion of these factors, see Struijs and Willeboordse (1988 and 1995).

Second, what happens when enterprises concentrate or deconcentrate? According to Eurostat (1997a), a *concentration* is an event involving more than one enterprise before the event, and one enterprise after the event. *Mergers* and *take-overs* are the two possible types of concentrations. Similarly, a *deconcentration* is an event involving one enterprise before the event, and more than one enterprise after the event. *Break-ups* and *split-offs* are the two possible types of deconcentrations[4]. The issue is then: How to define the longitudinal enterprise? Or, how can we follow an enterprise through time? Note that this is a well-known problem in social surveys where the longitudinal household has to be defined (see Ernst, 1989).

This issue of defining the longitudinal enterprise is mainly of concern because concentrations and deconcentrations complicate longitudinal data analysis. Longitudinal analysis covers techniques such as survival analysis, time series analysis, regression, etc. The theory used for such analysis generally assumes that the *same* enterprises are followed through time, which implies that the longitudinal enterprises should be indivisible through time, and also cannot merge. To analyze data from a panel of enterprises, the longitudinal enterprise has to be defined in such a way that this requirement is met. Cases of concentration or deconcentration clearly pose a problem. A "good" solution would be one that reduces such cases to situations where one can *follow single entities* through time. As we will see later in the paper, there is no perfect solution to handle this problem. All solutions have advantages and disadvantages that need to be taken into account.

In the present paper, we will first discuss the important case where enterprises are followed through time by the use of their Business Register Identification (BRID). Secondly, we will see that following enterprises solely through their BRID might not be sufficient, which will bring us to discuss four solutions to handle concentrations and deconcentrations.

---

[4] It also happens that an event involves more than one enterprise before, and more than one enterprise after the event. These cases of so-called restructuring are treated in this paper by reducing them to combinations of concentrations and deconcentrations.

2 Following enterprises through their BRID

One common way to follow enterprises though time is to use the BRID. The BRID is a unique identifier that is assigned and managed through time by following rules associated to the Statistical Business Register. In the present section, the longitudinal enterprises are defined through their BRID. That is, an enterprise will remain the same through time as long as its keeps the same BRID. In particular, after a take-over or a split-off, the continuing enterprise is the one with the same BRID. In the case of a merger or a break-up, no enterprise is continued: there are only old enterprises that are discontinued and new enterprises created[5].

This definition of the longitudinal enterprise is often used mainly because it is easy to implement within the NSI, provided a Statistical Business Register is available. For example, the statistician willing to perform a longitudinal analysis based on annual data can simply merge the survey files for the years of interest by using the BRID as the merging key. As mentioned before, the longitudinal enterprises will be the ones keeping their BRID for the period of interest. On the other hand, enterprises for which the BRID will not match next year will be considered as leaving the population, while the new BRID appearing at a given year is considered to be a new enterprise. In particular, an enterprise that is taken over or which is split off is not a longitudinal enterprise. The same holds for enterprises involved in a merger or a break-up.

One important concern when following enterprises through time using the BRID is the fact that it is related with the management of the BRID by the NSI. If the rules for the assignment of the BRID change at a given moment, then the panel inflow and outflow as identified by matching the Statistical Business Registers of different years might not be comparable with the previous years. This phenomenon would not be related to any change in economic reality, but would simply occur because of changes in register management. In practice such changes in management are often induced by changes carried through in the administrative files that are used as information sources for the Statistical Business Register[6].

Another aspect is the management of BRID across countries. Again, if the rules as applied by the NSI are not the same between countries, the definition of the longitudinal enterprise is not same, even though the latter has been said to be

---

[5] There are no generally accepted definitions of take-over, splitt-off, merger and break-up; the definitions used here can be found in Eurostat (1997a).

[6] Note that the same is true for the application of the definition of the enterprise in the Statistical Business Register by the NSI. If an NSI changes its treatment of, say, partnerships, data would not be comparable over time, even if the factors used to determine sameness over time remain unchanged.

based on a common notion: the BRID. As a consequence, for example, the number of births and deaths identified within the countries concerned are not comparable[7].

In trying to overcome this problem of comparability of management of BRID across its member states, Eurostat has made up methodological recommendations for the Statistical Business Registers. In theory, the continuity of the enterprise would depend on the continuity of its production factors (employment, machines and equipment, land, buildings, management, and immaterial assets). Because this definition could be difficult to apply in practice, Eurostat has come up with practical rules. In practice, an enterprise is not to be continued if two or all of the following three factors change: (a) the controlling legal unit, (b) the principal economic activity based on the 4-digit NACE Rev. 1, and (c) the main location of the enterprise. There is one exception to this rule, which is related to one-person enterprises. If a one-person enterprise expands and moves to new premises, and changes its legal form, the enterprise is considered to retain its identity. Finally, it can be seen that for concentrations and deconcentrations, applying the above rules might lead to inconsistencies. In these cases, continuation of employment determines which enterprise keeps its identity. Further details are given in Eurostat (1997a).

3 Following enterprises through other factors than their BRID

As we have seen in Section 2, following enterprises through their BRID is relatively simple, provided a Statistical Business Register is available. However, it might not be the best for all applications. As mentioned in the introduction, sameness through time can be based on various criteria that might be different from the ones used to assign the BRID.

As an example, consider the Longitudinal Employment Analysis Program (LEAP) of Statistics Canada, where enterprises whose BRID do not match for two years are linked through their labour force. That is, using what is called the Labour Tracking Filter, no-longer identified enterprises can be reclassified as continuously identified enterprises. This happens if there is a tracking link to another enterprise and a "large" proportion of the employees of the no-longer identified enterprise is found in that other enterprise. For more details, see Baldwin, Dupuy and Penner (1992). This linkage of enterprises through time is motivated by LEAP's objectives, which are to assess job creations and losses by enterprises. Without the Labour Tracking Filter, the transfer of a large group of

---

[7] There is again a parallel with the definition of the enterprise as a statistical unit. It goes without saying that comparability of longitudinal enterprise data requires comparability of the way the enterprise is delineated in the Statistical Business Register.

employees from one enterprise to another would be counted both as job losses and job creations, whereas in reality, the jobs themselves never ceased to exist[8].

Three factors may affect the decision to not solely use the BRID to define the longitudinal enterprise. First, there is the application envisaged. For the LEAP, the objective of the panel can lead to the choice of a definition of the longitudinal enterprise that may be different to the BRID. Second, for practical reasons, the rules for assigning the BRID may have little economic meaning. If a country has poor administrative sources for updating the Statistical Business Register and cannot or does not want to spend resources on sophisticated and elaborate rules, it may make more sense to establish enterprise continuity on another basis than the BRID, for instance on the panel survey results themselves. The third factor is the requirement of data comparability between countries, which implies the use of a uniform definition of the longitudinal enterprise. Because of sometimes well-established country practices, the harmonized definition may have to take into account other considerations than what would be desirable from a more theoretical point of view.

It is important to note that the choice of not using the BRID, at least solely, might require some processing that can be difficult to implement in practice. For example, the LEAP identifies through the Labour Tracking Filter the percentage of employees that went from one enterprise to another, independently of the BRID. To perform this task, one needs to be able to identify the path followed by each employee of the enterprises contained in the Statistical Business Register. Clearly the Statistical Business Register does not usually contain enough information to perform this labour tracking. Hence, one needs to be careful in defining the longitudinal enterprise so that it *can* be implemented.

Checking the applicability of the definition chosen is particularly important in the case of concentrations and deconcentrations. For instance, it may not be easy to establish whether an observed enterprise that has no match with enterprises at a later date has really died or has been taken over by another enterprise. Moreover, in general, concentrations or deconcentrations may be difficult to distinguish from real enterprise births and deaths. If the BRID is not chosen to define the longitudinal enterprise, it might be useful to consult the managers of the Statistical Business Registers to be sure that the chosen definition can be implemented.

4 Some solutions to handle concentrations and deconcentrations

Whether or not sameness through time is determined solely on the basis of the BRID, we need some specifications for the treatment of concentrations and

---

[8] An extreme case would be if all employees of a large enterprise would turn out to work later for an enterprise with a different BRID, especially if that enterprise would not have other employees. In such a case the BRID would certainly not be useful for analysis of job creations and losses. But then there would also be reason for checking the rules applied that led to the change of BRID in the first place.

deconcentrations. This is especially true if the way the BRID is managed does not fit the chosen definition for the longitudinal enterprise. The specifications for the treatment of concentrations and deconcentrations depend on:

(1) the application envisaged;
(2) the requirements of the framework of which it may be part;
(3) the question whether the complete population is available, or only a subset (sample);
(4) the availability and timeliness of the data used in the criteria; and
(5) usual practices.

An example of the second factor is possible national accounts requirements, and LEAP provides an example of the third factor. The method applied to LEAP requires data from the complete population.

In this section, some solutions are presented to handle concentrations and deconcentrations. As mentioned earlier, a "good" solution would be one that reduces to *following single entities* through time. We will present four solutions that follow this desirable property. A list of advantages and disadvantages is provided for each.

Solution 1:   Choose a definition such that at most one longitudinal enterprise is recognized

This solution is based on the idea of predominance. For concentrations, if one of the concentrating enterprises is much "larger" than the other ones, then this one would be considered as the continuing enterprise. We would see this concentration as a take-over. If none of the concentrating enterprises is "larger", then no enterprise would be considered as continuing, and then all the concentrating enterprises would be considered as cessations and the new enterprise a creation. For deconcentration a similar pattern would apply. That is, the enterprise that is deconcentrating would be followed through only one of the remaining enterprises, provided that one can be considered as predominant.

This solution is motivated by reasoning that the growth of enterprises can be realized in two ways: (i) either by accumulating production factors (hiring more staff, buying more machines, etc.) or (ii) by absorbing other enterprises. Similarly, the shrinkage of enterprises may result of abandoning production factors or by splitting off an entire part into a new enterprise. Suppose that some enterprises concentrate at one given moment. If one is much larger than the other one(s), it might be reasonable to say that the large enterprise absorb the smaller one(s), leaving the surviving enterprise as simply the continuity of the preceding large one. If none of the concentrating enterprises are seen as absorbing the other ones, then it may be reasonable to consider the remaining enterprise as a new enterprise and the initial enterprises as cessations. Again, a similar reasoning can be applied to deconcentrations.

The terminology used is in line with the Eurostat recommendations for Statistical Business Registers (see Eurostat 1997a). This also suggests that a distinction is required between enterprise creations resulting from concentration and deconcentration, and real enterprise births. A similar distinction between cessations resulting from concentration and deconcentration, and real enterprise death is recommended. It is also suggested to link the enterprises involved in these cases by means of pointers from enterprises to their enterprise(s) of origin. This would facilitate quantification of each of the categories mentioned.

The main difficulty with this first solution is the definition of "large". This can be based on one or several quantitative variables at a time. For example, one can use the annual turnover, assets, number of employees, etc. It is important to note that "large" should normally be defined in relationship with the remaining enterprise after concentration (or the initial enterprise for a deconcentration). That is, the concentrating enterprises should be large or not compared to the remaining enterprise.

In addition to quantitative variables, one can also add some other criteria based on qualitative variables. For example, before looking if one of the concentrating enterprises can be considered to be "large" enough, one might exclude those that do not have the same economic activity as the remaining enterprise. These other criteria can also work in conjunction with the management of the BRID.

We illustrate this first proposed solution with an example that uses a criterion of size based on the number of employees.

Example:

For deconcentrations, the continuing enterprise is the one that keeps at least 70% of its employees. For concentrations, it is the one that contributes at least of 70%.

We first illustrate (see Figure 1) the above stated criteria for a deconcentration. Suppose that enterprise A has 100 employees at wave 1. Between waves 1 and 2, a deconcentration occurs and at wave 2, enterprise C now divides into enterprises A and B having 80 and 20 employees, respectively. Applying the above rule, since A has inherited more than 70% of the employees from C, A continues to exist via C and B can be considered as created from a split-off.

Another illustration of a deconcentration is the one given by Figure 2. An enterprise C divides into A and B, but now enterprise A has 60 employees while enterprise B has 40 employees. Applying the above rule, since neither A nor B has at least 70% of the employees from C, both A and B are considered creations from a break-up, and C as a cessation. This is because A nor B can be considered as sufficiently large compared to C to be considered as its continuity.

We now consider an illustration of a concentration. Suppose that enterprises A and B of wave 1 amalgamate to form enterprise C at wave 2. At wave 1, enterprises A and B have 80 and 20 employees, respectively. Then, applying the above rule, enterprise C is found to be the enterprise continuing from A, while enterprise B is considered as a cessation.

The more interesting cases are the complex ones, i.e., both concentrations and deconcentrations occur. Figure 4 illustrates a complex case where there are one concentration and one deconcentration. At wave 1, there are two enterprises A and

B having 100 and 10 employees, respectively. Between waves 1 and 2, a portion of enterprise A leaves and forms enterprise C. Also, the rest of enterprise A (80 employees) amalgamates with enterprise B to form enterprise D. This does not have to happen simultaneously, but it is assumed that the deconcentration and the concentration both occur between the two waves[9]. Enterprises C and D have 20 and 90 employees, respectively. We now apply the above rule. Looking at enterprise C, it is clear that it does not have the required 70% of the employees of A and therefore, C is not considered as continuing from A. Looking at enterprise D, we see that enterprise A provides 89% of the employees, while enterprise B provides only a small percentage. Thus enterprise D is considered as continuing from A, while B is a cessation and C a creation.

Another illustration of a complex case is the one given by Figure 5. This is the same complex case as in Figure 4, except that enterprise B now has 50 employees at wave 1. Looking at enterprise D, none of enterprises A nor B is providing 70% of its employees. Hence, A is not continuing through time. Enterprises C and D are considered as created while A and B are treated as cessations.

The choice of at most one longitudinal enterprise in cases of concentration and deconcentration has advantages and disadvantages.

Advantages:

1) It keeps the original enterprises, i.e., no aggregation of enterprises is performed. It will be seen that the three other proposed solutions to handle concentrations and deconcentrations propose to aggregate the data.

2) An estimation weight can be easily obtained for each enterprise of wave 2. This weight is simply the inverse of the selection probability of the corresponding enterprise of wave 1. Looking at Figure 4, suppose that enterprise A has been selected in the panel with selection probability π_A, while enterprise B has not been. Then, since enterprise D is continuing from A, it is considered as being part of the panel with the selection probability π_A. On the other hand, if, for example, enterprise D were continuing from B (instead of A), then enterprise D would not be considered to be part of the panel because B is not.

3) This solution is relatively easy to apply, even after several waves. The panel can also easily be linked with the Statistical Business Register if the BRID is applied to the enterprises.

4) It is possible to distinguish between mergers and take-overs, and also break-ups and split-offs. With the present solution, a merger corresponds in fact to a concentration where none of the enterprises of wave 2 can be considered as

---

[9] One could argue that two consecutive changes are not the same as two simultaneous changes, as that would constitute a different economic event, which therefore should be treated differently. More on this subject can be found in Struijs and Willeboordse (1995).

continuing through time (e.g., Figure 5). In a take-over situation, one main enterprise absorbs smaller other enterprises, and continues through time. This corresponds exactly to the case of a concentration where the enterprise of wave 2 can be considered as continuing from one enterprise of wave 1, as in Figure 3. For break-ups and split-offs, a similar discussion can be made. It is important to choose the definitions together with the subject matter experts for mergers, take-overs, break-ups and split-offs.

5) This solution allows for a proper treatment of cases where one of the original enterprises involved in a concentration comes from outside the scope of the panel, or where one of the enterprises emerging from a deconcentration leaves the scope of the panel. As we will see, this is not true for the other solutions.

Disadvantages:

1) In all concentration and deconcentration situations, the present solution results in creations and/or cessations of enterprises. One should be very careful in specifying that the cessations do not necessarily correspond to the disappearance of the production capacity represented by these enterprises from the population, and that creations do not imply the emergence of new production capacity. With this solution, the large amount of creations and cessations can be misleading if they are interpreted as real enterprise births and deaths, suggesting a very changing economy.

2) One needs to identify variable(s) for defining which (if any) enterprise can be considered as continuing. This might require a lot of work and consultation with subject matter experts. Different choices can lead to different sets of continuing enterprises. One has also to watch out for inconsistency of the rules. Clearly the chosen rules will depend on the factors to decide on sameness given in the introduction. For example, the LEAP needed some important studies to define what is the "large" proportion of the employees to reclassify some no-longer identified enterprise as continuously identified ones. For more details, see Baldwin, Dupuy and Penner (1992).

3) The chosen variable(s) discussed above must be available for all enterprises involved in the concentration or deconcentration situations. Returning to the above example, consider the case of a concentration involving several enterprises. If the number of employees is available only for a few of these enterprises, it might not be possible to identify if one of these enterprises contributes to at least 70% of the employees of the new enterprise, which makes the proposed solution difficult to implement. One situation where this problem can occur is when the variables needed are available only for enterprises that are part of the panel.

Solution 2:   Preserve the initial structure of the enterprises

This solution consists of the following rules. For deconcentrations, we sum for each variable the values of all new enterprises coming from the same initial enterprise, and we give the total to the initial enterprise. For concentrations, we divide for each variable the value of the new enterprise between its initial enterprises by prorating according to one or more auxiliary variables. When applied, this solution creates at wave 2, *synthetic enterprises* for which the structure corresponds to the one that existed at wave 1, i.e., before the concentration or the deconcentration. All original enterprises are considered longitudinal enterprises.

The idea behind this solution is to keep the initial structure of the enterprises of the population at the start of the panel, because this population is in fact the one for which the panel is representative (see Lavallée, 1997). Before the initial wave of a panel, a sampling frame is usually set up, and then a sample is selected. The panel is then created by simply keeping this sample through time. Because of this, the panel is then always representative of this initial population, even after several waves[10].

To illustrate the proposed solution, we can consider cases of concentration and deconcentration of enterprises similar to those used for solution 1. First consider the deconcentration situation where enterprise C divides itself into two enterprises A and B. See Figure 6. Applying the above rules, for each characteristic we sum the values of enterprises A and B to form a 'new' enterprise. This synthetic enterprise might be called A+B. With respect to the panel, enterprise A+B will then be considered as the continuation of enterprise C through time.

Now consider the case of a concentration (see Figure 7) similar to the one given by Figure 3. In order to apply the present solution in the case of a concentration, we need to choose one or more variables to prorate. Let us choose again the number of employees. At wave 1, enterprise A has 80 employees while enterprise B has 20. At wave 2, enterprises A and B have amalgamated to form enterprise C. With the present solution, each of the characteristics of enterprise C is divided by prorating according to the number of employees of enterprises A and B. For example, the revenue of enterprise C is divided into two parts according to the ratio 80 to 20. The same is done for the profits, assets, etc. Once this is done, we have created two synthetic enterprises that might be called C_A and C_B, where C_A is the new enterprise created for the portion of 80%. At the end, C_A is the synthetic enterprise considered to be the continuation from A, and C_B the synthetic enterprise continuing from B.

Complex cases are treated by directly applying the above rules. Consider, as an illustration, Figure 8. Enterprise C, which has 30 employees, is simply coming from enterprise A, and therefore no division is required for this one. On the other hand, enterprise D, which has, we assume, 120 employees, needs to be divided

---

[10] If the panel has a limited scope, for instance in terms of economic activities covered, the situation is slightly different. See the last disadvantage below.

into two synthetic enterprises D_A and D_B, according to the number of employees that come from enterprises A and B. For A this is 100 minus the number of employees of C, which is 30, and for B this is 50. The revenue of enterprise D is divided into two according to the ratio 70 (i.e., 100 minus 30) to 50 employees, and so on[11]. Once synthetic enterprises D_A and D_B are created, we need to sum the values of the enterprises C and D_A for each of their characteristics, because enterprise A is also subject to deconcentration. This results in the synthetic enterprise C+D_A. Finally, we obtain the synthetic enterprise C+D_A continuing from A, and the synthetic enterprise D_B continuing from B.

As was the case for solution 1, solution 2 also has advantages and disadvantages.

Advantages:

1) The first advantage of this solution is clearly its simplicity, especially in the case of deconcentration. When one needs to describe the proposed solution to users, it is often preferable to have something relatively easy to understand. Also, simplicity often allows for easier implementation.

2) There are fewer enterprise creations and cessations than in solution 1. With solution 1, a simple concentration case, such as the one of Figure 7, would lead to at least one cessation. With the present solution, we have created synthetic enterprises that continue from A and B, and there is no risk of overestimating birth and death figures. Note that the two synthetic enterprises created will have sizes relative to the initial enterprises A and B. Thus, if B is much smaller than A, then the enterprise D_B continuing from B will also be relatively small. Solution 1 is more radical in the sense that it would put the size of D_B to 0 and the size of D_A to the combined size of A and B.

Disadvantages:

1) An important disadvantage of the present solution is that it is easy to apply for only quantitative variables. In the situation of a deconcentration, it is not easy to "add" values of qualitative variables such as the economic activity or the region. If the values are the same, there is obviously no problem. For example, in Figure 6, if both enterprises A and B have the same economic activity, then the synthetic enterprise A+B will get the same one. If their economic activities are different, one solution is to keep the economic activity of the original enterprise C. Another solution would be to take the activity of the "largest" of the enterprises A and B, measured for instance in terms of employment.

---

[11] In the example we chose total employment to remain the same. In case this is not true, the method becomes slightly more complicated.

2) One needs to identify variable(s) to be used for prorating. This might require a great deal of research and consultation with subject matter experts. Essentially, we would like to have the synthetic enterprises C_A and C_B of Figure 7 to be as close as possible to what would have been enterprises A and B at wave 2, had they not concentrated.

3) The variable(s) chosen for prorating must be available for all initial enterprises involved in the concentration situations. Otherwise, the division of an enterprise can still be carried out, but no prorating can be applied. In that case, the division will have to be based on the assumption that the prorating variable(s) of the enterprise, for which all data are available, remain unchanged or follow a certain trend. For instance, with reference to Figure 7, if data are only available for the enterprises B and C, and enterprise C has 110 employees, the variables for enterprise C_B could be based on a ratio of 20 to 90, applied to the variables of enterprise C. If the panel shows an average employment increase of 5%, the ratio applied could be 21 (i.e., 20 plus 5% of 20) to 89.

4) The application of the rules for this solution can become cumbersome after some time. After several waves with concentrations and deconcentrations, simple or complex, it might be difficult to apply the present solution in such a way that the synthetic enterprises created still represent the initial enterprises of wave 1.

5) The synthetic enterprises may not represent the real economic reality if change has occurred. There are three reasons for this. First, economies of scale might play a role. In Figure 6 for example, we create the synthetic enterprise A+B from enterprises that have not really merged. If enterprises A and B had merged, then some expenses such as accounting would normally have been lower. Therefore, summing the values of the characteristics of enterprises A and B can overestimate values compared to a real merging situation. For further details on this subject, see Góis (1996). The second source of distortion is consolidation effects. For instance, if a book-printing business merges with its main client, a publishing business, the sales of the enterprise after the merger will be considerably less than the sum of the sales of the original enterprises. As a consequence, the two synthetic enterprises will show a significant decline in sales that does not reflect any real economic trend. In general, the distortion will be worst for cases of concentration and deconcentration where the participating enterprises have a relationship of vertical integration. The third way in which reality is misrepresented is in the distribution of the population of enterprises according to their size. This limits the use of the panel data for some types of analysis.

6) In contrast to solution 1, solution 2 does not distinguish between mergers and take-overs, nor break-ups and split-offs. In the case of a deconcentration, the values of the newly formed enterprises are added to form a synthetic

enterprise. This process is the same, whether we have a break-up or a split-off. In the case of a concentration, the enterprise of wave 2 is divided into the same enterprises that existed at wave 1. Again, the same procedure is done for mergers and take-overs. Note that in this case, however, the splitting to form synthetic enterprises will be done proportionally to the size of the initial enterprises. This would imply whether the concentration is a merger or a take-over.

7) If one of the enterprises involved in a deconcentration moves out of scope of the panel, it is incorrectly counted as belonging to the in-scope population of wave 2. However, it is part of the longitudinal enterprise[12]. This could happen, for instance, if the panel does not cover all economic activities. Similarly, if one of the enterprises involved in a concentration comes from outside the scope of the panel, it may remain as a synthetic enterprise with an activity that is still outside the panel scope. However, in reality it belongs to an enterprise within the panel scope. This can results in weighting problems.

Solution 3: Apply the final structure of the enterprises

This solution is inspired by retrospective surveys. In such surveys, we identify a population at a given point in time and select a sample from it. The selected enterprises are then asked questions that refer to events or characteristics concerning the past. For example, one can ask the revenue of enterprises for the last past five years. Retrospective surveys are in fact the opposite of panel surveys, in the sense that the first refers to past values while the second refers to values measured after the time of the identification of the population. With retrospective surveys, the structure of the enterprises that is considered is therefore the one of the population at the selection time of the sample, i.e., the final structure of the enterprises in the survey.

Solution 3 is the exact opposite of solution 2. For deconcentrations, for each variable we divide the value of the initial enterprise between the final enterprises by prorating according to one or more auxiliary variables. For concentrations, for each variable we sum the values of all initial enterprises that form the same final enterprise, and assign the total to the resulting final enterprise. The result is that at wave 2 synthetic enterprises are created for which the structure corresponds to the one that resulted from the concentration, or the deconcentration.

To illustrate this solution, we again consider cases of concentration and deconcentration of enterprises. We first consider the deconcentration case where enterprise C divides itself into two enterprises A and B. See Figure 9. To apply the present solution in the case of a deconcentration, we need to choose one or more

---

[12] Note that this would be less of a problem in a cohort analysis, where an initial population (cohort) is followed over time and where scope considerations do not lead to fall-out. On the contrary, cohort analysts are interested in what becomes of the population and why.

variables to prorate. We choose once more the number of employees. Each of the characteristics of enterprise C is then divided by prorating according to the number of employees of enterprises A and B. For example, the revenue of enterprise C is divided into two according to the ratio 80 to 20. Once this is done, we have created two new synthetic enterprises that might be called C_A and C_B. Finally, C_A is the "enterprise" of which A is considered the continuation, and C_B the "enterprise" of which B is the continuation.

Now consider the case of concentration. Between waves 1 and 2, enterprises A and B have amalgamated to form enterprise C. Applying the above rules, for each of the characteristics of enterprises A and B, we sum their values to form a new synthetic enterprise that might be called A+B. With respect to the panel, enterprise A+B will then be considered as continuing to enterprise C through time. See Figure 10.

Complex cases are treated by directly applying the above rules. As an illustration, consider Figure 11. Enterprise B, which had 60 employees, is simply continuing through enterprise D, and therefore no division is required for this one. On the other hand, enterprise A, with say, 90 employees, needs to be divided into two new synthetic enterprises A_C and A_D, according to the number of employees that end up in enterprises C and D. For C this is 20, and for D this is 130 minus the number of employees of B, which was 60. The revenue for example of enterprise A is divided into two according to the ratio 20 to 70 (i.e., 130 minus 60), and so on[13]. Once enterprises A_C and A_D are created, because enterprise D is also a case of concentration, we need to sum the values of the enterprises B and A_D, for each of their characteristics. This then creates enterprise B+A_D, say. At the end, we have enterprise B+A_D continuing through D, and enterprise A_C continuing through C.

Solution 3 has the following advantages and disadvantages. Because of the similarity between solution 2 and 3, several of the advantages and disadvantages are the same.

Advantages:

1) The first advantage of this solution is its simplicity, especially in the case of concentration.

2) There are fewer enterprise creations and cessations than in solution 1. With solution 1, a simple deconcentration situation such as the one of Figure 9 would lead to at least one creation. With the present solution, we have created synthetic enterprises to continue through A and B, and there is no risk of overestimating birth and death figures.

---

[13] In the example we chose total employment to remain the same. In case this is not true, the method becomes slightly more complicated.

Disadvantages:

1) It only works easily for quantitative variables. In the situation of a concentration, it is not easy to "add" values of qualitative variables such the economic activity or the region.

2) One needs to identify variable(s) that can be used for prorating. This might require a lot of prior research and consultation with subject matter experts.

3) The variable(s) chosen for prorating must be available for all final enterprises involved in the deconcentration situations. Otherwise, the division of an enterprise can still be done, but no prorating can be carried out.

4) The application of the rules for this solution can become cumbersome if applied to several waves. After a number of waves with concentrations and deconcentrations, simple or complex, it might be difficult to apply this solution so that the resulting synthetic enterprises still represent the enterprises that initially existed at the wave of reference.

5) The synthetic enterprises may not represent the real economic reality as if no change had occurred. This is because economies of scale play a role (see Góis, 1996), because there might be consolidation effects and because the population size distribution may be distorted.

6) Unlike solution 1, this solution does not distinguish between mergers and take-overs, nor break-ups and split-offs.

7) There are some problems associated with enterprises entering or leaving the scope of the panel as a result of concentration or deconcentration.

8) We need to have data for all initial enterprises involved in the concentration situations. This is a disadvantage because the data might not be available for all enterprises. This is the case when some enterprises involved in the concentration are not part of the panel. For example, consider Figure 10 and suppose that enterprise A is part of the panel and that B is not. Because enterprise B has not been selected in the panel, no data are available. In order to apply the present solution, we need to have data for both enterprises A and B to create the synthetic enterprise A+B, which might be difficult if we cannot get data retrospectively. Note that this disadvantage is not present for solutions 1 and 2.

9) The data only become available after the panel has terminated. This happens in this solution because the final structure of the enterprises is considered, unlike solutions 1 and 2 that are based on the initial structure. We need to wait until we have the enterprises of the last wave to apply the rules to create the synthetic enterprises of the preceding waves.

10) Some weighting problems might exist when sampled and non-sampled initial enterprises are mixed, in case the panel is not retrospective. The problem is to obtain an estimation weight for each enterprise of wave 2. The estimation weight of an enterprise of wave 2 is usually the inverse of the selection probabilities of the corresponding enterprises of wave 1. For example, return to Figure 10 and suppose that enterprises A and B were selected with selection probabilities π_A and π_B, respectively. Now, enterprise C will be selected if A and/or B is selected, and therefore the selection probability of enterprise C is given by $\pi_C \approx 1 - (1 - \pi_A)(1 - \pi_B)$. Suppose now that enterprise A has been selected in the panel and B has not. Then, the selection probability of enterprise B might not be known and then the preceding formula cannot be used. In that case, an estimation weight for enterprise C can still be computed by using a method called the Weight Share Method. See Ernst (1989), Lavallée (1995a) and Lavallée (1995b) for further details.

Solution 4:   Reduce the merging or split enterprises to a single enterprise

This solution uses the simplest rules of solutions 2 and 3. For deconcentrations, for each variable we sum the values of all new enterprises coming from the same initial enterprise, and we assign the resulting total to the initial enterprise. For concentrations, for each variable we sum the values of all initial enterprises that form the same final enterprise, and assign the total to the final enterprise. Whenever concentration or deconcentration situations occur, we always sum the value to obtain an *aggregated synthetic enterprise*.

This solution is motivated by simplicity. While solutions 2 and 3 used some prorating to divide enterprises into synthetic enterprises, the present solution does not require proration because no division is performed.

To illustrate the proposed solution, we once more consider cases of concentrations and deconcentrations. First consider the deconcentration situation where between waves 1 and 2 enterprise C divides itself into two enterprises A and B, as shown in Figure 12. Applying the above rules, for each characteristic of enterprises A and B, we sum their values to form a "new" enterprise called A+B. With respect to the panel, enterprise A+B will then be considered as the continuation of enterprise C through time.

Now consider the case of a concentration. Between waves 1 and 2, enterprises A and B have amalgamated to form enterprise C. See Figure 13. Applying the above rules, for each characteristic of enterprises A and B, we sum their values to form the new synthetic enterprise called A+B, which is considered as continuing to enterprise C.

Complex cases are treated exactly as concentrations and deconcentrations. Consider Figure 14 where the two enterprises A and B of wave 1 form the enterprises C and D after a restructuring. Applying the above rules, for each of the characteristics of enterprises A and B, we sum their values to form a "new" enterprise called A+B. Similarly, for each of the characteristics of enterprises C and D, we sum their values to form another "new" enterprise called C+D. With respect to the panel, the synthetic enterprise A+B will then be considered as continuing to the synthetic enterprise C+D through time.

We now look at advantages and disadvantages of the proposed solution for the treatment of concentrations and deconcentrations.

Advantages:

1) The proposed solution is very simple, for both concentrations and deconcentrations. It is very easy to explain to users and it is also straightforward to implement.

2) No prorating is required because no enterprises need to be divided. Therefore, there is no need to identify variable(s) to be used for prorating, which often requires a lot of work and consultation with subject matter experts.

3) There are no enterprise creations and cessations with this solution, because enterprises are always "added".

Disadvantages:

1) It works easily for quantitative variables only. In the situation of a concentration, it is not easy to "add" values of qualitative variables such as the economic activity or the region.

2) The application of the rules of this solution can become cumbersome if applied to several waves, although less so than is the case for solutions 2 and 3.

3) The synthetic enterprises may not represent the real economic reality if change has occurred. This is because economies of scale play a role (see Góis, 1996), because of consolidation effects and because the population size distribution is very likely to be distorted. In particular this solution can create very large synthetic enterprises, since it always suggests to "add" the enterprises for any restructuring situation. The distortion of economic reality of this solution tends to be bigger than for solutions 2 and 3, because the effects of synthetically aggregated enterprises are not compensated by the effects of synthetically split enterprises. The distortion severely limits the use of the panel data for certain types of analysis.

4) Unlike solution 1, the present solution does not distinguish between mergers and take-overs, nor break-ups and split-offs.

5) There are some problems associated with enterprises entering or leaving the scope of the panel as a result of concentration or deconcentration.

6)   We need to have data for all initial enterprises involved in the concentration situations. This is a disadvantage because the data may not be available for all enterprises. This is the case when some enterprises involved in the concentration are not part of the panel.

7)   The data only become available after the panel is over. This happens because we do not know until the end whether or not some enterprises will be "added" to form grouped synthetic enterprises.

8)   Some weighting problems might exist when sampled and non-sampled initial enterprises are mixed. The problem is to obtain an estimation weight for each enterprise of wave 2 and this estimation weight is normally obtained from the inverse of the selection probabilities of the corresponding enterprises of wave 1. However, in some cases these selection probabilities are not known and then obtaining an estimation weight for enterprises of wave 2 is more difficult. See the last disadvantage of solution 3 for more details.

5 Conclusion

We have seen that a very common way to define the longitudinal enterprise is through its BRID. This definition is however linked to the management of the BRID in the different countries. This management may differ amongst the countries, and for some countries it may not be possible to use the BRID. Also, in some applications, following enterprises through their BRID might not be sufficient.

After defining sameness through time, which may or may not be based solely on the BRID, the important question is: how to handle concentrations and deconcentrations? We have presented four possible solutions to solve this problem: (1) to recognize *at most one* longitudinal enterprise in cases of concentration and deconcentration; (2) to preserve the *initial* structure of the enterprises; (3) to apply the *final* structure of the enterprises; and (4) to reduce the merging or split enterprises to a single enterprise. These solutions are relatively simple and can be implemented in practice if some conditions are met. No solution is perfect, and each of the proposed solutions has advantages and disadvantages. It would be of interest to compare the four solutions using real data coming from different countries.

Choosing between the solutions is not easy. On the one hand, there are the applications envisaged, and on the other there are a large number of practical considerations. The use of the data for analysis is most hampered in solution 4, but solutions 2 and 3 also result in a distorted presentation of economic reality. This is not the case for solution 1, if enterprise creations and cessations are treated adequately by not confusing them with real enterprise births and deaths.

The most important practical consideration is probably data availability. The data requirements differs between the four solutions. Data availability does not solely depend on their collection in panel surveys, but also on what is available from other sources, and in particular the Statistical Business Register. The question of whether or not a system of prorating is to be developed has a number of practical implications (solutions 2 and 3), but not applying prorating as in solution 4 has its price as well. The practical problems of defining sameness through time are biggest for solution 1, because this is essential for the treatment of concentrations and deconcentrations. In all four proposed solutions sameness through time has to be defined for units that are not involved in concentration or deconcentration, in order to determine whether a single unit is continued or discontinued, resulting in a death followed by a birth. It seems that solution 1 can be sustained many waves, whereas the other solutions become cumbersome after a few waves.

Note that one could also consider different solutions for different parts of the panel population. For example, a different solution could be applied to large enterprises than to smaller enterprises. This would make complicate matters with respect to organization, interpretation of the panel data, explaining the panel to the users, and maintaining consistency. But it could still be considered if one thereby succeeds in combining the best elements of the different solutions and achieving an overall reduction of the disadvantages.

Assessing all considerations put forward above, on the whole it seems that solution 1 looks better than the others. However, we also have to consider the need for comparability between countries for multi-country panels such as may be held by member states of the European Union. In that case we need to define the longitudinal enterprise in a comparable way, and the present differences in the management of the BRID in the member states would make application of solution 1 problematic. In cooperation with the member states, Eurostat is currently trying to harmonize the management of the BRID across countries by means of recommendations (see Eurostat, 1997a), but it will still take many years before full harmonization is realized. If this is successful, it will be easier to produce comparable multi-country panel data.

Figures 1 and 2 Solution 1, Deconcentration situations

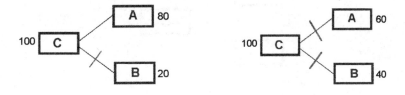

Figure 3 Solution 1, Concentration

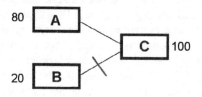

Figures 4 and 5 Solution 1, Complex Cases

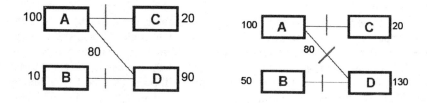

Figure 6 Solution 2, Deconcentration

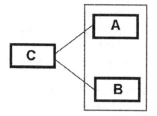

Figure 7 Solution 2, Concentration

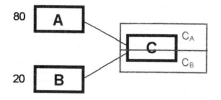

Figure 8 Solution 2, Complex Case

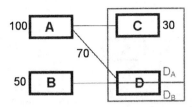

Figure 9 Solution 3, Deconcentration

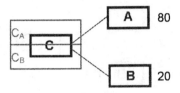

Figure 10 Solution 3, Concentration

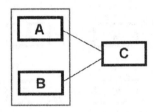

Figure 11 Solution 3, Complex Case

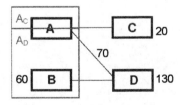

Figure 12 Solution 4, Deconcentration

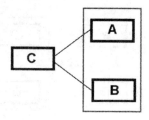

Figure 13 Solution 4, Concentration

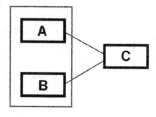

Figure 14 Solution 4, Complex Case

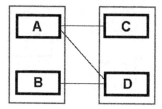

REFERENCES

Baldwin J., Dupuy R., Penner W. (1992), *"Development of longitudinal panel data from business registers: Canadian experience"*, Statistical Journal of the United Nations, ECE 9, pp. 289-303, 1992.

Ernst L. (1989), *"Weighting Issues for Longitudinal Household and Family Estimates"*, in Panels Surveys (Editors Kasprzyk, D., Duncan, G., Kalton, G., Singh, M.P.), John Wiley and Sons, New York.

Eurostat (1996), *Business Registers for Statistical Purposes: Methodological Recommendations*, volume 1, Office for Official Publications of the European Communities, 1996.

Eurostat (1997a), *Methodological Recommendations on Business Registers, Sections 11-18*, Working document S20/97/06, June 1997.

Eurostat (1997b), *Handbook on design and implementation of business surveys*, edited by Ad Willeboordse, October 1997

Góis M.E. (1996), *"Prise en compte des modifications de structure sur le panel d'entreprises portugais"*, Recueil des résumés des communications des XXVIIIème Journées de statistique, Association pour la Statistique et ses Utilisations, Québec, mai 1996.

Kish L. (1965), *Survey Sampling*, John Wiley and Sons, New York, 1965.

Lavallée P. (1995a), *"Business Panel Surveys: Following Enterprises versus Following Establishments"*, in Techniques and Uses of Enterprise Panels, Proceedings of the First Eurostat international workshop on techniques of enterprise panels, 21 to 23 February 1994, Eurostat, Luxembourg.

Lavallée P. (1995b), *"Cross-sectional Weighting of Longitudinal Surveys of Individuals and Households Using the Weight Share Method"*, Survey Methodology, Vol. 21, No. 1, pp. 25-32.

Lavallée P. (1997), *Theory and Application of Enterprise Panel Surveys*, Course notes sponsored by the TES Institute, Luxembourg.

Struijs P., Willerboordse A.J. (1988), *"Towards a Classification of Changes"*, paper prepared for the Third Round Table on Business Registers, Auckland, New Zealand.

Struijs P., Willerboordse A.J. (1995), *"Changes in Populations of Statistical Units"*, in Business Survey Methods (Edited by Cox, B.G., et al), John Wiley and Sons, New York.

AUTHORS LIST AND ADDRESSES

Arondel Philippe Planistat Luxembourg, 4 rue Alphonse Weicker, L-2721 Luxembourg, Phone: +352.422.244245, Fax: +352.422.244210, E-mail: philippe.arondel@planistat.lu

Bacchini Fabio ISTAT, via Tuscolana 1786, 00173 Roma, Italia, Phone: +39.06.72976275, E-mail: bacchini@istat.it

Badaloni Luigi Andersen Consulting, Phone: +39.06.59620252, Home: via Sangemini 42, 00135 Roma, Italia Phone: +39.06.3051850

Balk Bert M. Department of Statistical Methods, Statistics Netherlands, P.O. Box 4000, 2270 JM Voorburg, The Netherlands, Phone: +31.70.3374704, Fax: +31.70.3877429, E-mail:bblk@cbs.nl

Bartelsman Eric J. CPB Netherlands Bureau for Economic Policy Analysis, 14 van Stolkweg, P.O. Box 80510, 2508 GM The Hague, The Netherlands, Phone: +31.70.3383349, Fax: +31.70.338 3350, E-mail: ejb@cpb.nl

Bartoloni Eleonora ISTAT, Service of Structural Business Statistics on Industries and Services, via Tuscolana 1788, 00173 Roma, Italia, Phone 39.06.72976234, Fax: +39.06.7222457, E-mail: bartolon@istat.it

Baussola Maurizio Università Cattolica di Piacenza, Istituto di Politica Economica, via E. Parmense 84, 29100 Piacenza, Italia, Phone: +39.0523.599310, Fax: +39.0523.599303, E-mail: baussola@pc.unicatt.it

Bienvenue Jean-Yves World Systems ltd, c/o EUROSTAT, R&D, Methods and Data Analysis Unit, Batiment Jean Monnet, L-2920 Luxembourg, E-mail: bienvenue@wsel.lu

Biffignandi Silvia   Dipartimento di Matematica, Statistica, Informatica ed
                            Applicazioni, Università di Bergamo, Piazza Rosate 2,
                            24129 Bergamo, Italia,
                            Phone: +39.035.277516, Fax.: +39.035.249598,
                            E-mail: silvia@ibguniv.unibg.it

Blanchard Pierre   Université Paris Val de Marne, Faculté de Sciences
                            Economique et de Gestion, 58 Av. Didier, 94214 La
                            Varenne Saint Hilaire, France,
                            Fax: +33 1448852993,
                            E-mail: blanchard@univ-paris12.fr

Boccara Frédéric   INSEE, Timbre E220, 18 Bd A. Pinard, 75675 Paris
                            Cedex 14, France,
                            Phone: +33.1.41175896, Fax: +33.1.41176520,
                            E-mail: frederic.boccara@dg75-E220.insee.atlas.fr

Bonzani Sergio   AC Nielsen, via G. Di Vittorio 10, 20094 Corsico (MI),
                            Italia,
                            Phone: +39.02.45197808,
                            E-mail: sergio.bonzani@italy.acnielsen.com

Bottasso Anna   CERIS CNR, via Avogadro 8, 10121 Torino, Italia,
                            Phone: +39.011.5601225, Fax: +39.011.5626058,
                            E-mail: bottasso@ceristo.cnr.it

Bruno Giancarlo   ISTAT, via Cesare Balbo 16, 00184 Roma, Italia,
                            Phone: +39.6.46732469, Fax: +39.6.46732452,
                            E-mail: bruno@istat.it

Carone Andrea   ISTAT, via Tuscolana 1776, 00173 Roma, Italia,
                            Phone: +39.06.72976227, Fax: +39.06.7219021,
                            E-mail: carone@istat.it

Corsini Veronica   ISTAT,via C.Balbo 16, 00184 Roma, Italia,
                            Phone: +39.6.46732466, Fax: +39.6.46732452,
                            E-mail: corsini@istat.it

Destefanis Sergio   Dipartimento di Scienze Economiche, Università degli
                            Studi di Salerno, via Ponte Don Melillo, 84084
                            Fisciano (SA), Italia,
                            E-mail: destefa@ponza.dia.unisa.it

Depoutot Raoul   EUROSTAT, R&D, Methods and Data Analysis Unit, Batiment Jean Monnet, L-2920 Luxembourg, Grand Duché de Luxembourg, Phone: +352.4301.34926, Fax: +352.4301.34149, E-mail: raoul.depoutot@eurostat.cec.be

Dilling-Hansen Mogens Department of Management, University of Aarhus, 8000 Aarhus C, Denmark, Phone: +45.89421567, Fax: +45.86135132, E-mail: ecodilling@ecostat.aav.dk

Eriksson Tor   Dept. of Economics, Aarhus School of Business, Fuglesangs Allé 4, 8210 Aarhus V, Denmark, Phone: +45.89486404, Fax: +45.86.155175, E-mail: tor@hha.dk

Fabiani Silvia   Banca d'Italia, Servizio Studi, via Nazionale 91, 00184 Roma, Italia, Phone: +39.06.47923040, Fax: +39.06.47923720, E-mail: fabi.3713@interbusiness.it

Ferrari Guido   Dipartimento Statistico "Giuseppe Parenti", Università degli Studi di Firenze, viale Morgagni 59, 50134 Firenze, Italia, Phone: +39.055.4237221, Fax: +39.055.4223560, E-mail: ferrari@stat.ds.unifi.it

Galante Giuseppina   ISTAT, viale Liegi 13, 00198 Roma, Italia, Phone: +39.06.85227281

Galeotti Marzio   Dipartimento di Scienze Economiche, Università di Bergamo, Piazza Rosate 2, 24129 Bergamo, Italia, Phone: +39.035.277540, Fax: +39.035.249975, E-mail: galeotti@ibguniv.unibg.it

Gallo Baldessarri Francesca   Dip. Statistica, Probabilità e Statistiche Applicate, piazzale A. Moro 5, 00185 Roma, Italia, Phone: +39.06.49910473, E-mail: gallof@pow2.sta.uniroma1.it

Ganugi Piero Istituto di Statistica, Facoltà di Economia, Università degli Studi di Parma, via J.F: Kennedy 6, 43100 Parma, Italia,
Phone: +39.0521.902478, Fax: +39.0521.902375,
E-mail: statec@ipruniv.cce.unipr.it

Giorgetti Maria Letizia ISTAT, Direzione Centrale delle Statistiche su Istituzioni ed Imprese, via Cesare Balbo 16, 00184 Roma, Italia,
Phone: +39.06.46732466, Fax: +39.06.46732452,
E-mail: magiorge@istat.it (After 30th Jan. 1999 can be contacted at: via del Fagiano 56, 57125 Livorno, Italia)

Gismondi Roberto ISTAT, viale Liegi, 13, 00198 Roma, Italia,
Phone: +39.06. 85227306, Fax. +39.06.8415152,
E-mail: gismondi@istat.it

Gold Michael Institut für VWL, Empirische Wirtschaftsforschung, Universität Lüneburg, Scharnhorststraße 1, D-21332 Lüneburg , Deutschland,
Phone: +49.4131.782331, Fax: +49.4131.782026,
E-mail: Gold@uni-lueneburg.de

Gozzi Giorgio Istituto di Statistica, Facoltà di Economia, Università degli Studi di Parma, via J.F.Kennedy 6, 43100 Parma, Italia,
Phone: +39.0521.902466 Fax: +39.0521.902375,
E-mail: gozzi@ipruniv.cce.unipr.it

Hecquet Vincent INSEE, Timbre E220, 18 Bd A. Pinard, 75675 Paris Cedex 14, France,
Phone: +33.1.41175896, Fax: +33.1.41176520

Hildreth Andrew Department of Economics and Institute for Labour Research, University of Essex, Wivenhoe Park, Colchester, CO4 3SQ, UK,
Phone: +44.1206.873559, Fax: +44.1206.872724,
E-mail: andrh@essex.ac.uk

Jarmin Ronald S. Center for Economic Studies, U.S. Bureau of Census, 4700 Silver Hill Road, Stop 6300, Room 211/WPII, Washington, DC 20233-6300, Phone 1.301.4571858, Fax 1.301.4571235, E-mail: rjarmin@ces.census.gov

Laaksonen Seppo   Statistics Finland, P.O. Box 3A, 00022 Statistics
Finland, Helsinki, Finland,
Fax: +358.9.17342474,
E-mail: seppo.laaksonen@stat.fi

Lainé Frédéric   INSEE, Timbre H321, 18 Bd A. Pinard, 75675 Paris
Cedex 14, France,
Phone: +33.1.41175598, Fax: +33.1.41176907

Lavallée Pierre   Statistics Canada, Ottawa (Ontario), K1A 0T6
CANADA, Phone: 001.613.9512892
Fax: 001.613.9511462, E-mail: plavall@statcan.ca

Maliranta Mika   Statistics Finland, P.O. Box 3A, 00022 Statistics
Finland, Helsinki, Finland,
Fax: +358.9.17342474,
E-mail: mika.maliranta@stat.fi

Marasco Luigi Pompeo   ISTAT, via Cesare Balbo 16, 00184 Roma, Italia,
Phone: +39.06.46732561, Fax: +39.06.46732560,
E-mail: marasco@istat.it

McGuckin Robert H.   Director of Economic Research, The Conference Board,
845 Third Avenue, New York, NY 10022, U.S.A.,
Phone: +1.212.3390303, Fax: +1.212.9807014,
E-mail: mcguckin@conference-board.org

Mirto Anna Pia Maria   ISTAT, viale Liegi 13, 00198 Roma, Italia,
Phone: +39.06.85227269, Fax: +39.06.8415152,
E-mail: mirto@istat.it

Monducci Roberto   ISTAT, via Cesare Balbo 16, 00184 Roma, Italia,
Phone: +39.06.46732455, Fax: +39.06.46732452,
E-mail: monducci@istat.it

Motohashi Kazuyuki   Economic Analisys and Statistics Division, DSTI,
OECD, 2 rue André-Pascal, 75775 Paris Cedex 16,
France,
Phone: +33.1.45241788, Fax: +33.1.45241848,
E-mail: kazuyuki.motohashi@OECD.ORG

Nguyen Sang V.   Center for Economic Studies, U.S. Bureau of the Census, 4700 Silver Hill Road, Stop 6300, Washington, DC 20233, U.S.A., Phone: +1.301.4571882, Fax: +1.301.4571235, E-mail: snguyen@census.gov

Orsini Marco   ISTAT, via A. Ravà 150, 00142 Roma, Italia, Phone: +39.06.54900286, Fax: +39.06.70452162

Pavone Antonio   ISTAT, Servizio Amministrazione Pubblica, via Tuscolana 1788, 00173 Roma, Italia, E-mail: pavone@istat

Pellegrini Guido   Banca d'Italia, Servizio Studi, via Nazionale 91, 00184 Roma, Italia, Phone: +39.06.47924174, Fax: +39.06.47923720.

Pizzoli Edoardo   ISTAT, via A. Ravà 150, 00142 Roma, Italia, Phone: +39.06.54900286, Fax: +39.06.70452162, E-mail: Pizzoli@istat.it

Pudney Stephen   Public Sector Economics Research Centre, Department of Economics, University of Leicester, University Road, Leicester, England, LE1 7RH, Phone: +44.116.2522887, Fax: +44.116.2522887, E-mail: sep2@le.ac.uk

Radjabou Mohamed   World Systems ltd, 2 rue A. Borschette, L-1246 Luxembourg, Phone: +352.4231.13628, Fax: +352.424.608, E-mail: m.radjabou@wsel.lu

Rizzi Barbara   Dipartimento di Matematica, Statistica, Informatica ed Applicazioni, Università di Bergamo, Piazza Rosate 2, 24129 Bergamo, Italia, Phone: +39.035.277516, Fax: +39.035.249598, E-mail: barbara.rizzi@spm.it

Romagnano Ettore   Banca d'Italia, Servizio Studi, via Nazionale 91, 00184 Roma, Italia, Phone: +39.06.47923140, Fax: +39.06.47923720.

Roualdès Danielle   INSEE, Timbre E220, 18 Bd A. Pinard, 75675 Paris Cedex 14, France,
Phone: +33.1.41175898, Fax: +33.1.41176520

Sembenelli Alessandro   CERIS CNR, via Avogadro 8, 10121 Torino, Italia,
Phone: +039.011.5601225, Fax: +39.011.5626058,
E-mail: sembenel@ceris.to.cnr.it

Sevestre Patrick   E.R.U.D.I.T.E., Université Paris XII - Val de Marne, 58 avenue Didier, 94214 La Varenne Saint-Hilaire, France,
Phone: +33.1.49768150, Fax: +33.1.48852993,
E-mail: sevestre@univ-paris12.fr

Signorini L. Federico   Banca d'Italia, Servizio Studi, via Nazionale 91, 00184 Roma, Italia,
Phone: +39.06.47923713, Fax: +39.06.47923720.

Smith Valdemar   The Danish Institute for Studies in Research and Research Policy, Finlandsgade 4, 8000 Aarhus C, Denmark,
Phone: +45.89422397, Fax: +45.89422399,
E-mail: vsafsk.au.dk

Strøjer Madsen Erik   Department of Economics, Aarhus School of Business, Fuglesangs Allé 4, 8210 Aarhus V, Denmark,
Phone: +45.89486401, Fax: +45.86155175,
E-mail: ema@hha.dk

Struijs Peter   Eurostat, Bâtiment Jean Monnet, L-2920 Luxembourg,
E-mail: peter.struijs@eurostat.cec.be

Teikari Ismo   Statistics Finland, P.O. Box 6A, 00022 Statistics Finland, Helsinki, Finland,
Fax: +358.9.17343554, E-mail: ismo.teikari@stat.fi

Thollon-Pommerol Vincent   INSEE, Timbre E220, 18 Bd A. Pinard, 75675 Paris Cedex 14, France,
Phone: +33.1.41175896, Fax: +33.1.41176520, E-mail: vincent.thollon-pommerol@dg75-e220.insee.atlas.fr

Van Leeuwen George   Department of Statistical Methods, Statistics Netherlands, P.O. Box 4000, 2270 JM Voorburg, The Netherlands,
Phone: +31.70.3374925, Fax: +31.70.3877429.

Zeli Alessandro   ISTAT, via Tuscolana 1786, 00173 Roma, Italia, Phone: +39.06.729761/24, Fax: +39.06.7222457, E-mail: zeli@istat.it